OTHER PEOPLE'S MONEY

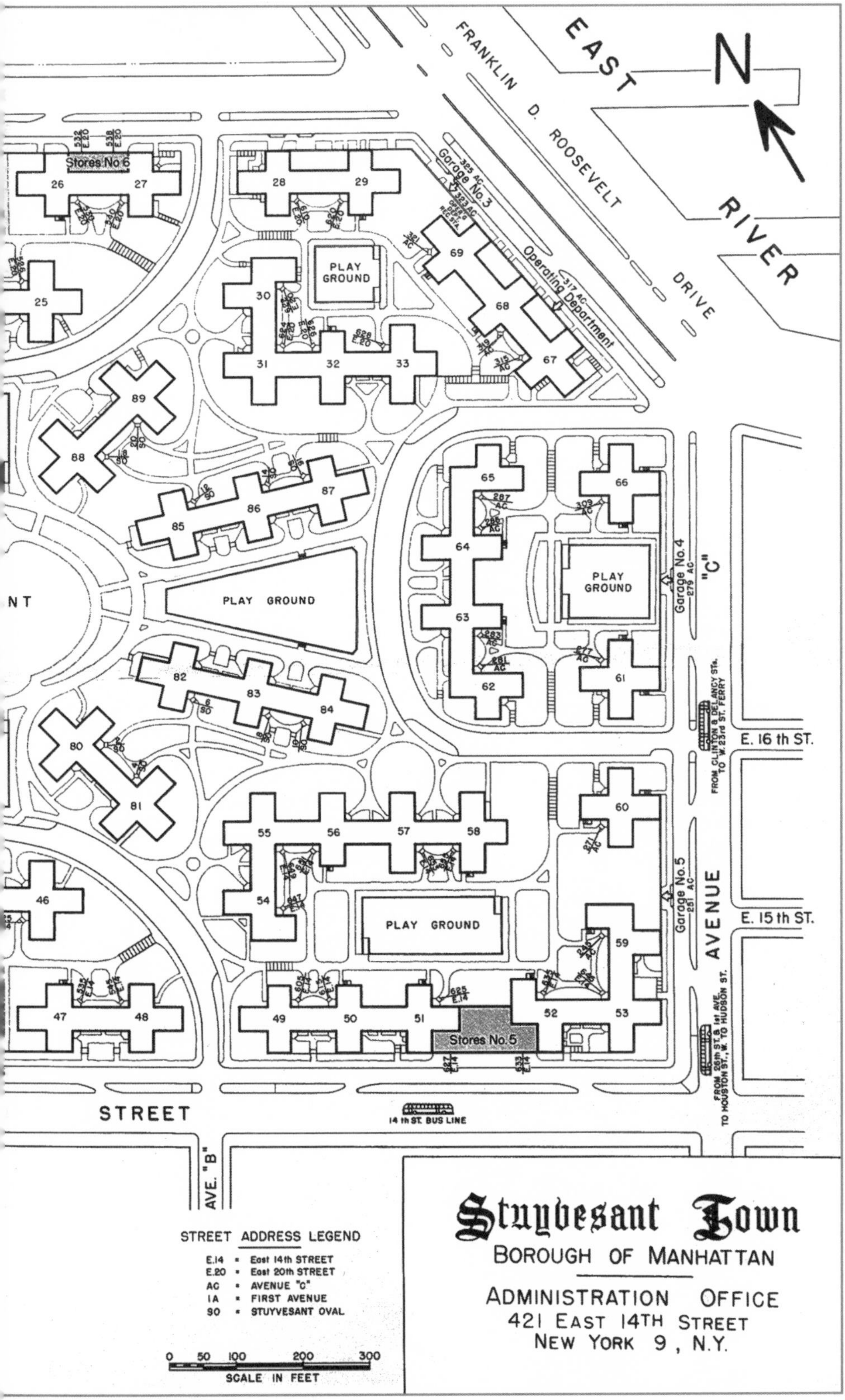
EAST RIVER
N
FRANKLIN D. ROOSEVELT DRIVE
Stores No. 6
Garage No. 3
Operating Department
PLAY GROUND
Garage No. 4
Garage No. 5
"C"
AVENUE
E. 16 th ST.
E. 15 th ST.
FROM CLINTON & DELANCY STS. TO W. 23rd ST. FERRY
FROM 26th ST. & 1st AVE. TO HOUSTON ST., W. TO HUDSON ST.
Stores No. 5
STREET
14 th ST. BUS LINE
AVE. "B"
STREET ADDRESS LEGEND
E.14 = East 14th STREET
E.20 = East 20th STREET
AC = AVENUE "C"
IA = FIRST AVENUE
SO = STUYVESANT OVAL
0 50 100 200 300
SCALE IN FEET
Stuyvesant Town
BOROUGH OF MANHATTAN
ADMINISTRATION OFFICE
421 EAST 14TH STREET
NEW YORK 9, N.Y.

OTHER PEOPLE'S MONEY

Inside the Housing Crisis and the Demise of the Greatest Real Estate Deal Ever Made

CHARLES V. BAGLI

DUTTON

DUTTON
Published by the Penguin Group
Penguin Group (USA) Inc., 375 Hudson Street,
New York, New York 10014, USA

USA | Canada | UK | Ireland | Australia | New Zealand | India | South Africa | China
Penguin Books Ltd, Registered Offices: 80 Strand, London WC2R 0RL, England
For more information about the Penguin Group visit penguin.com.

LIBRARY OF CONGRESS CATALOGING-IN-PUBLICATION DATA
has been applied for.

ISBN 978-0-525-95265-7

Printed in the United States of America
1 3 5 7 9 10 8 6 4 2

Endpaper art © Jay Seldin

Ellie, Nikki, and Katy,

you're my electricity.

Dad, you always said:

If you want it done right, do it yourself.

I did.

Contents

INTRODUCTION

The Poster Child of the Real Estate Bubble

October 16, 2006, 5:01 P.M.

Rob Speyer had spent hours pacing the small conference room near his office on the seventh floor of 50 Rockefeller Plaza, trading locker-room jibes and stories about real estate deals with Paul A. Galiano and Fred Lieblich, when the telephone finally rang.

Speyer, a thirty-seven-year-old with a marathoner's lanky build; sandy, close-cropped hair; and a machine-gun laugh, was the heir apparent to Tishman Speyer Properties, an international real estate company that operated on four continents and controlled some of New York City's most enduring icons, from Rockefeller Center to the Chrysler Building. For ten weeks, he and his colleagues had labored over a bid for a property whose size was almost unimaginable in densely packed Manhattan: Stuyvesant Town-Peter Cooper Village, a complex of 110 buildings with 11,232 apartments spread across 80 contiguous acres south of midtown, overlooking the East River.

Galiano, at forty-one years old, was Tishman Speyer's intensely focused co-chief of acquisitions. Lieblich was president of BlackRock Realty Advisors, forty-five years old and a partner in the prospective deal. They had formed a friendship with Speyer as they read the financial history of the rental complex and engineering assessments supplied by the seller, Metropolitan Life Insurance, or as it is known today, MetLife. By noon that day, they submitted their offer. They were up against an international who's who of real estate and finance that had gathered in New York for what promised to be the biggest real estate deal in history. Aside from New York's real estate royalty, like the Durst, Rudin and LeFrak families, there was the emir of Qatar; the Rothschilds and the Safras; the mysterious billionaire investor Simon Glick; the irascible Steve Roth of Vornado Realty Trust; Stephen Ross, a builder active in New York, Florida, Las Vegas and Los Angeles; the government of Singapore; and the Church of England, not to mention the many pension funds and private equity firms that had raised tens of billions of dollars to invest in real estate and other assets. Nearly a dozen rival bidders from around the globe were gathered in similar rooms high above Manhattan waiting to learn whether their multibillion-dollar offers had won the day and if they would spend the night negotiating contractual details of what would be the largest transaction in American real estate history.

The stark white walls of the Tishman Speyer conference room yielded nothing as the hours ticked by. One minute Speyer exuded the cocky confidence of a tycoon who prowled the world making deals, the next he wondered what might have gone wrong as a dark cloud of self-doubt descended over the conversation.

They had spent the afternoon of October 16, 2006, talking about anything but the call they desperately hoped would come. Adrian Fenty, who was running for mayor in Washington, DC, where the Speyers owned more than two dozen office buildings, popped into the room for a minute to say hello. He asked what was going on. Speyer explained it was "a fairly momentous day"; they were waiting to see who had won the bidding war. "I just came from Apollo's office," Fenty said with a chuckle, referring to Apollo Real Estate Advisors, Speyer's primary rival for the property. "They told me the same thing."

Then with the evening shadows gathering over Fifth Avenue, the phone rang a second and third time. Speyer snatched up the receiver and heard the voice of Darcy A. Stacom, the real estate broker conducting the multibillion-dollar auction of Stuyvesant Town-Peter Cooper Village.

Stacom, who was forty-six years old and a rare woman in the testosterone-fueled world of high-stakes real estate deals, quickly got to the point: "C'mon down to Two Hundred Park, now." But she warned, "Don't bring your whole team together. Come in ones and twos in case any reporters have staked out the lobby of the building." Two Hundred Park housed MetLife's law firm, Greenberg Traurig, and at the top, MetLife's ornate, old-world boardroom.

Stacom had not offered him congratulations, but Speyer knew what the call meant: If they could get through what promised to be hours of arguing over the final terms of the contract, Stuyvesant Town-Peter Cooper was his. He let out a yell as he put the phone down, almost simultaneously pumping his fist and hugging Galiano. Speyer turned and embraced Lieblich, who headed the real estate arm for one of the world's largest investment management firms for pension funds, institutions and high-net-wealth individuals.

Speyer and Galiano took the elevator to the ground floor and marched out the Fifth Avenue doors of the building, past the fifteen-foot bronze statue of a heavily muscled Atlas carrying the world on his shoulders. Speyer was under his own mythic strain and would remember little of the eight-block walk downtown.

Although not nearly as glamorous as Rockefeller Center, Stuyvesant Town held a pride of place in the minds of many New Yorkers. Stuyvesant Town, and its sister complex Peter Cooper Village, was unlike the real estate properties that seemed to trade like pork bellies on a daily basis in cities from Atlanta to Los Angeles, Boston to Dallas and Seattle during what was now a five-year-old real estate boom like no other in its intensity. Stuyvesant Town–Peter Cooper Village covered eighteen blocks of some of the most valuable real estate in the world.

The two complexes, which were erected by Metropolitan Life in what was once known as the Gas House District, were an urban version of Levittown, an inspiration for housing in the 1950s and 1960s that broke up the street grid rather than conformed to it, while keeping city life affordable to the middle class.

In the 1960s, Stuyvesant Town begat LeFrak City, a complex of ten eighteen-story buildings on forty acres in Corona, Queens, and Co-op City, a sprawling complex of 15,372 units in 35 high-rise towers and seven clusters of town houses spread across 320 acres in the Baychester section of the Bronx. Architecturally it was a failure. The red brick buildings were uniformly plain and looked more like the low-income housing projects nearby, the Jacob Riis, Lillian Wald and Alfred E. Smith Houses. But the buildings occupied neatly landscaped real estate on the East Side. In 2006, there were not eighty, or even twenty, contiguous acres available anywhere else on the thirteen-mile-long island of Manhattan, no matter what the price.

And Stuyvesant Town-Peter Cooper Village, despite its blandness, had been a safe, leafy oasis for thousands of middle-class firefighters, nurses, union construction workers, civil servants, writers, police officers, secretaries and even a few judges for nearly sixty years. For many New Yorkers, the complex had become a cherished landmark akin to the Empire State Building, the Statue of Liberty and Rockefeller Center. Early in their careers, Mayor John V. Lindsay, sportscaster Howard Cosell, reporter Gabe Pressman and presidential adviser David Axelrod had made their homes there. So had author Frank McCourt, mystery writer Mary Higgins Clark, actor Paul Reiser, operatic soprano Beverly Sills and Knicks basketball star Dick Barnett.

In 2006, hundreds of original tenants, many of whom had moved to Stuyvesant Town when it opened in 1947, were still living there. Thousands more had grown up in those twelve- and thirteen-story buildings and were now raising their own families in Stuyvesant Town-Peter Cooper Village.

"It's one of the most unique assets in the city," said Lieblich, who had himself lived in Stuyvesant Town when he was a MetLife executive in the 1990s. "A lot of people know of it. There's a lot of fond memories."

As Rob Speyer entered 200 Park Avenue, a fifty-eight-story skyscraper looming over Grand Central Terminal that had once been known as the Pan Am Building, he paused, noticing a handmade sign Scotch-taped to a storefront window promoting a sale. Tishman Speyer had bought the tower from MetLife eighteen months earlier for $1.72 billion, the highest price ever paid for an office building. The makeshift placard was just the kind of seedy thing that he had been trying to eliminate since taking control of the property. Shake it off, Rob said to himself, focus on the task at hand. He was up against eight other buyers who, in preparation for a bidding war, had collectively lined up a staggering $50 billion from money center banks, insurance companies, pension funds and private investors.

Every day seemed to bring another record real estate deal somewhere in the country and the prospect of windfall profits. The December 2004 sale of the 110-story Sears Tower in Chicago for $835 million had set a local record, despite the building's sizable vacancy. Maguire Properties, a publicly traded real estate investment trust, paid $1.5 billion for 10 office buildings in the Los Angeles area, thereby doubling the size of its portfolio and solidifying its position as the top landlord for first-class office space in Southern California. In the biggest retail deal of 2005, a joint venture of Regency Centers Corporation and Macquarie CountryWide Trust paid $2.7 billion for 101 shopping centers in 17 states and the District of Columbia.

Buyers jostled in line for bulk purchases of hotels, shopping malls, casinos, office buildings, apartment complexes and raw land. Prices accelerated far faster than rents, even as profit margins got thinner. Expectations were that prices would climb still higher. It was as if the markets had broken loose from their tether to the boom-and-bust nature of capitalism. At least that is the way the lenders acted, as well as the rating agencies whose job it was to judge the viability of the financial architecture underpinning the deals. And nowhere was the real estate market as hot as it was in New York.

That summer, Beacon Capital Partners, in partnership with Lehman Brothers, outbid thirty rivals when it paid $1.52 billion for 1211 Avenue of the Americas, a thirty-three-year-old, forty-four-story office tower whose prime tenant was News Corporation, the mass media conglomerate headed by Rupert Murdoch. At $800 per square foot, analysts expected Beacon to lose money, at least in the short term, because the mortgage payments were likely to exceed cash flow from the building. But Beacon, like many investors, was supremely optimistic about the future and it was determined not to lose out again. Previously, Beacon had been an also-ran in the bidding for twenty-three-story 522 Fifth Avenue, at Forty-Third Street, a prize captured by Broadway Partners with a bid of $420 million.

Speyer and Galiano settled into a small fifteenth-floor conference room off the main reception area at Greenberg Traurig, soon to be joined by Tishman Speyer's lawyer, Jonathan L. Mechanic, and two associates. Stacom, whose blond hair floated halfway down her back and who had a fondness for dangling costume jewelry and Technicolor clothing, was already present with her partner William M. Shanahan, the numbers specialist for the duo. In a conference room down the hall sat Robert R. Merck, a senior managing director and chief of MetLife's real estate investment unit; David V. Politano, who oversaw MetLife's real estate investments in the Northeast; and their coterie of lawyers. The insurer was selling the sister complexes as a single real estate asset.

Much of the contract had been marked up and completed in the course of the bidding, but now the lawyers would take over, hammering out language that would cover every possible contingency. The shuttling between the two rooms went on through the night, as lawyers for Tishman Speyer and MetLife inserted clauses to protect their clients against any possible trouble.

In between, Speyer, Lieblich, Galiano and other executives in the conference room debated the latest revisions. During the prolonged interludes, they played poker, five-card draw. One of the young associates from Mechanic's law firm cleaned up, even as the others teased him about how his skinny black suit and tie made him look like a member of the late-1970s New Wave group Devo.

Finally, at about nine thirty in the morning on October 17, they finished. Speyer had a $400 million nonrefundable deposit wired to MetLife for the biggest real estate deal of all time. He and his partners agreed to pay an astounding $5.4 billion—$70 million more than the number two bidder—for a single asset.

But that was not the total price tag. When all the acquisition costs were tallied, the sum would total $6.3 billion. Ultimately, the money would come from banks, foreign and domestic pension funds, a foreign government and the Church of England. A tiny fraction of the money would come out of the well-lined pockets of Tishman Speyer or BlackRock. Both firms traditionally bought property with what is known in the business as OPM (other people's money). They largely made their money on fees—asset fees, management fees, partnership fees, construction fees—while putting up only a sliver of equity, if that. Of course, no pension fund or wealthy family would invest with Tishman Speyer or BlackRock simply for the privilege of paying fees if the firms did not consistently generate annual returns on the order of 20 percent. Of the total cost of $6.3 billion, Tishman Speyer put up only $56 million of the firm's own money, less than 1 percent of the winning bid, with another $56 million coming from their longtime partner, the Crown family of Chicago.

The deal immediately created a media storm of headlines

around the world, generating editorial comment from the Agence France-Presse, the *International Herald Tribune*, National Public Radio and Bill Maher at HBO.

The *New York Post* put it succinctly: "$5.4 Bil Stuy Town Deal Shatters Record." Rob told the tabloid that "the opportunity to buy 11,000 units in Manhattan is what you live for."

Elated but tired, Rob called his father, the real estate magnate Jerry I. Speyer, to deliver the news in a voice scratchy with fatigue. The elder Speyer congratulated him, heaping praise on a son who had forsaken a career in journalism to join his empire a decade earlier. Now his son was debuting on a very public stage.

"It's a dream come true," confided the elder Speyer, whose powerful reach extended from his company to the Federal Reserve Bank of New York, the Council on Foreign Relations, the Museum of Modern Art and the New York Yankees. He helped Michael R. Bloomberg successfully clear the legal and political hurdles to run for a third term as mayor in 2009 and both he and his son were close to Andrew Cuomo, who would become governor in 2010. "I expect he'll be far more successful than I was," Jerry Speyer said of his son. "He has great vision, wonderful people skills, and above all, he loves what he does."

The two men quickly divided up a list of courtesy calls, with Jerry taking Mayor Michael R. Bloomberg and Rob reaching out to Daniel R. Garodnick, a lifelong resident of Stuyvesant Town-Peter Cooper Village and a newly elected city councilman. Rob assured Garodnick, "There will be no dramatic shifts in the community's makeup, character or charm."

But Garodnick did not greet the news with the same breathless enthusiasm as the *New York Post*, Wall Street, city hall and the Speyers' fellow private equity moguls, who never seemed to want for cash for the next deal. Sure, MetLife would make

$3 billion after taxes, fourth-quarter profits would soar and its stock would hit a fifty-two-week high. Mayor Bloomberg would endorse the Speyers' takeover and Robert White, founder of Real Capital Analytics, a research and consulting firm, would declare Stuyvesant Town an "irreplaceable property," saying, "It would be impossible today to get a property of that scale in an urban location."

Garodnick, a smart, handsome, dark-haired lawyer who had grown up in the complexes, was not concerned about corporate profits. For nearly sixty years, Stuyvesant Town-Peter Cooper Village represented a relatively affordable opportunity for construction workers, firefighters, designers, small-business owners and others to live in ultra-expensive Manhattan and raise their children. But all that seemed to be in jeopardy during this real estate boom in 2006. The "average" two-bedroom, one-thousand-square-foot condominium in many Manhattan neighborhoods was selling for more than $1.2 million. Residential life in the borough was drifting increasingly outside the grasp of middle-class families.

Garodnick worried that the extraordinary price paid by the Speyers would force them to oust longtime residents in favor of younger, more well-heeled tenants willing to pay rents that were 30, 40 or 50 percent higher. He was at his office at 250 Broadway, across from city hall, when Rob Speyer called. The two men had never spoken before.

Unlike the other bidders, Speyer had not contacted the tenant association or Garodnick prior to buying the complex. Speyer was both cordial and polite, telling the councilman that Tishman Speyer had no plans to make radical changes in the way Stuyvesant Town was run. He assured Garodnick that his intention was to be a proper steward of the property and to do right by the twenty-five thousand current residents.

Garodnick was encouraged. Tishman Speyer, after all, had a well-burnished reputation and might be a better landlord than some of the other bidders. But after an exchange of pleasantries, he asked about specific terms. He asked what his plans were for preserving the long-term affordability of the complexes. He felt Rob avoided the question other than to say he was open to any ideas.

"I thought, 'This is going to be a problem,'" Garodnick recalled. "I wanted to hear their plan for long-term affordability, and he didn't have one. Their plan was the opposite of long-term affordability. He said there wouldn't be any major changes, but when we saw him raining legal notices on tenants we realized we were in for a struggle."

Rob Speyer's relationship with Garodnick would be a source of endless frustration. The son of a lawyer and a public school teacher, Garodnick's life and career were inextricably bound to Stuyvesant Town, where legions of MetLife security guards shooed children off the carefully cropped grass, while the playgrounds offered seemingly endless rounds of kick ball, punch ball, basketball and baseball. As a teenager, one neighbor in his building taught him gin rummy and another tutored him in Spanish. He couldn't imagine a better place to grow up.

There was, however, an original sin in the creation of this idyllic community back in the 1940s. After razing an entire neighborhood of hundreds of tenements, factories and shops, MetLife by 1947 displaced more than ten thousand city residents, most of whom were forced to seek shelter in substandard housing elsewhere in Manhattan because they could not afford even the reasonable rent at the new complexes. Moreover, MetLife very publicly refused to rent apartments to African-American and Hispanic families. A remarkable group of tenants and their supporters battled MetLife's discriminatory policies in the late 1940s, disrupting the regimented environment established by the insurance company. But it would be more than twenty years before more than a handful of minorities could call it home.

The twenty-five thousand tenants ranged from the now-elderly residents who moved into the complexes on opening day in 1947, to second-generation families, workers from nearby hospitals and newcomers with tots in tow, as well as recent graduates of New York University. The vast majority of residents were protected by the city's rent regulations, which limited rent hikes in any one year. That was what made Stuyvesant Town affordable for a middle-class couple raising children in Manhattan. In 2006, rent regulations were the fiercely guarded salvation of the original residents, many of whom lived on fixed pension and social security benefits.

While many of his contemporaries were playing basketball at Playground 9 or rounding the bases during a Little League game, Garodnick had spent hours in the smoky rooms of the Jefferson Democratic Club on East Twenty-First Street, across First Avenue from Stuyvesant Town-Peter Cooper Village. His desire to run for public office was born in those rooms on open-house nights, when local residents would arrive desperate for help with problems large and small. He recognized that his political ambitions were tightly woven into the complex, whose residents voted in large numbers and almost always Democratic.

In the days after buying the complex, Rob Speyer also put in a call to Alvin D. Doyle, the tall, burly man with a salt-and-pepper brush mustache who headed the Stuyvesant Town-Peter Cooper Village Tenants Association. Like Garodnick, Doyle was a lifelong resident of the complexes. His mother and father, a newspaper reporter and a returning World War II veteran, were among the complex's original tenants.

Doyle's friends sometimes kiddingly called him "Fidel." He did not get the nickname because he delivered fiery, three-hour diatribes on the tenants' inevitable triumph over powerful landlords. It was simply a reference to his sixteen-year tenure as president of the tenants association, no easy task in a complex with 25,000 residents and perhaps 25,001 different opinions. But his calm, cautious and soft-spoken demeanor inspired trust and gave him the ability to bridge the gap between militant and more timid tenants.

He and Garodnick formed a Mutt and Jeff team on behalf of the tenants, with Doyle towering over the smaller Garodnick, who was nonetheless the more voluble character in this duo. On a brilliant fall afternoon a couple of years ago, Garodnick had stood next to a card table covered with leaflets on the grassy oval at the center of Stuyvesant Town, answering questions from dozens of tenants about the fate of the complex. As Garodnick patiently responded to every query, Doyle sat on a bench fifty feet away, consciously avoiding the spotlight. "I try to avoid it," Doyle explained. "I always thought you could get more done behind the scenes than you can get done in the spotlight."

Garodnick and the tenants association, its ranks ballooning with residents' fears of rent hikes and evictions, had enlisted support from New York's political establishment, including United States senators Charles Schumer and Hillary Clinton, Congresswoman Carolyn Maloney and city council speaker

Christine C. Quinn. Their political muscle helped the tenants association submit its own $4.5 billion bid for the property, despite MetLife's initial desire to lock them out of the sale process.

In a city of renters, the real estate boom in the early 2000s was prompting not only poor and working-class but also middle-class New Yorkers to wonder how much longer they could afford to make their home in one of the five boroughs. The real estate titans who had spent billions grabbing glamorous landmarks like the General Motors Building in New York and the Sears Tower in Chicago or building glassy condominium towers had turned their attention to brick, "meat-and-potatoes" tenements, unabashedly paying previously unheard of prices to unlock future profits as they accumulated thousands of apartments and boosted rents from New York to Chicago and San Francisco. In 2006, Mayor Michael R. Bloomberg would declare that MetLife had every right to sell Stuyvesant Town to the highest bidder, despite the very real public investment in the project by an earlier mayor, Fiorello H. La Guardia.

But many others decried the fact that easy credit and the real estate boom had turned a valuable urban resource, housing built with a sizable public investment for the middle class, into a commodity no different than corn futures. "Stuyvesant Town was a national model for middle-class people in an urban setting," said John H. Mollenkopf, director of the Center for Urban Research at the Graduate Center of the City University of New York. "It wouldn't have happened without eminent domain and favored tax treatment. It's disingenuous to say there's no public interest in what happens to housing."

Senator Charles Schumer sounded a similar theme when he addressed a tenant rally on the steps of city hall before the first bids were submitted. "When MetLife hung the 'for sale' sign on the doors of Peter Cooper Village and Stuyvesant Town, all New Yorkers, particularly those in the middle class, should have been troubled by the news," he said. "We need to do everything to preserve this vital stock of affordable housing."

The speculators and their Wall Street financiers, however, turned even their plain brick buildings into another commodity ripe for speculation. Perhaps the stage was set not long after MetLife converted in 2000 from a mutual company owned by policyholders to a corporation owned by stockholders with a keen eye on the bottom line. It was then that a plaque commemorating the vision of Frederick H. Ecker disappeared from the oval at the center of Stuyvesant Town. Ecker was the MetLife chairman who led the effort to build Stuyvesant Town and tens of thousands of other apartments in New York, Virginia and California for the middle class. The plaque's inscription harkened to a bygone era when Ecker and MetLife conceived of a project where "families of moderate means might live in health, comfort and dignity in park-like communities and that a pattern might be set of private enterprise productively devoted to public service."

So after a visit to see Rob Speyer at Tishman Speyer's impressive offices at Rockefeller Center, Doyle experienced as ominous a feeling as Garodnick had about the future of Stuyvesant Town and the tenants. Speyer asked Doyle and several other tenant leaders who were at the meeting to put aside their misgivings. "In another year, you guys will be happy how we turned things around," he said. "We pride ourselves on service."

Although Speyer exuded the confidence of a successful businessman, he did not allay their fears. "Other than saying he would turn the place around, he did not make any comments about searching for ways to keep the place affordable," Doyle recalled years later. "He really couldn't do that because he had to make the mortgage payments. We were cognizant of that fact."

From the beginning, Rob Speyer and the tenants were locked in a battle in which neither side ever spoke the same language as the greatest real estate deal of all time devolved over three years into one of the biggest business failures of all time. The tenants would file lawsuits, attack Rob Speyer for trying to evict what he claimed were unlawful tenants and even scorn his $19 million beautification program that introduced more trees, shrubs and perennials to the grounds.

At the same time, as tenants died or moved away, Speyer and his partners converted previously rent-regulated apartments to market rents, thus generating desperately needed revenue. They could not, however, convert enough apartments fast enough to cushion the crushing debt they had placed on the property. The legal battles, the landscaping and the conversions, which required more than $50,000 per apartment for installing granite countertops, stainless steel appliances and other renovations, all cost money, lots of it.

Instead of appreciating rapidly as his business plan predicted, the estimated value of Stuyvesant Town-Peter Cooper Village plummeted. In October 2006, Tishman Speyer and BlackRock valued the properties at $6.3 billion. Within two years, it was valued at $1.9 billion after the collapse on Wall Street in September 2008. The subsequent recession wiped out billions of investors' dollars. Rob Speyer and other moguls who bought and sold properties between 2005 and 2008 blame their gut-wrenching troubles on one of the most severe recessions in the country's history and a sharp 20 percent decline in the average rent in Manhattan.

After all, Tishman Speyer was in good company with other commercial and residential landlords who expanded rapidly in this period only to default on tens of billions of dollars in loans. Maguire Properties, once a dominant developer in Southern California, was crippled by the demise of the subprime mortgage industry in Orange County. In New York, the real estate mogul Harry B. Macklowe lost seven office towers he bought from Blackstone, along with the General Motors Building and much of his empire, after he was unable to refinance the $7 billion in short-term, high-interest debt he used to buy them. Well-regarded companies like the Extended Stay Hotels chain and the national shopping center developer General Growth Properties, which owned the South Street Seaport in New York, the Faneuil Hall Marketplace in Boston and Ala Moana Center in Honolulu, tumbled into bankruptcy under the weight of their recently accumulated debts.

But the Stuyvesant Town-Peter Cooper Village deal became the poster child for the first great economic bubble of the twenty-first century, a period in which tens of billions of dollars from insurance companies, pension funds and sovereign funds poured into real estate deals in every part of the country with the expectation that prices and values would soar forever, or at least until the property could be sold at a fat profit.

The collapse of the Stuyvesant Town-Peter Cooper Village deal and a legion of other celebrated deals from that era were brought on by far more than the vagaries of the real estate market.

Buyers were indiscriminate. They wanted trophy office buildings, see-through glass apartment towers designed by starchitects, shopping centers, golf courses and even a bunch of red brick tenement-like buildings at Stuyvesant Town.

The $6.3 billion acquisition, like so many at the time, required a financial leap of faith and a total disregard for worst-case scenarios by buyers, lenders and investors. Buyers once priced properties based on a multiple of existing cash flow. By that calculus, real estate experts said that the two Manhattan complexes would have generated a $3 billion or even $3.5 billion price. But buyers were operating in the Wall Street casino.

Buyers were looking to the future, building models of anticipated cash flow. Tishman Speyer and BlackRock's winning $5.4 billion bid, and even the tenant association's own $4.5 billion offer, reflected the new math. They did not expect a profit for years to come. The business plan projected that income would triple to $330.9 million by 2011, mainly by converting rent-regulated apartments to market rents. But almost every single assumption in their pro forma calculations proved wrong. Net income amounted to only $138 million in 2009, less than half the $284.4 million in annual loan payments on the $4.4 billion in debt ladled onto the property.

Wall Street was only too happy to fuel a speculative deal that required lenders and investors to believe that everything would go according to plan. Everyone was in on it. For a fee, the banks provided billions of dollars in mortgages for property with cash flow that did not even begin to cover the payments on interest-only loans. Instead of holding the loans on their balance sheets, Goldman Sachs, Lehman Brothers, Merrill Lynch, Wachovia and other banks bundled a set of individual mortgages and transferred them to a trust, which issued bonds or securities. The securities, in turn, got a seal of approval from Fitch Ratings, Moody's Investors Service and Standard & Poor's, bond rating agencies paid by the banks, and were sold to investors for still more fees. With no stake in the mortgage, the banks had little financial incentive to ensure that the deal made sense and the borrower could repay the debt. Instead of profits, the biggest real estate deal in history ended in default, which, if you were objectively looking at the deal at the time it was made, was the most likely outcome by far.

The apartment complexes, hotels, shopping centers and golf courses financed and refinanced during the boom ultimately changed hands after emerging from bankruptcy court. But deals like the one at Stuyvesant Town-Peter Cooper Village also tore at the social fabric of cities like New York, where working and even middle-class tenants increasingly found themselves priced out of a market as longtime affordable havens became targets of speculation. The pension funds that poured money into Stuyvesant Town-Peter Cooper Village essentially cooperated in displacing residents who were very much like their own pensioners: municipal clerks, teachers, police officers and small-business owners. The tenants in New York and investors from Florida to California, England and Singapore would feel the consequences from a roller-coaster ride in real estate values that would rival anything at a Coney Island amusement park. The losses by public employee pension funds would ripple into city budgets and the lives of retired teachers whose retirement funds faced life-altering shortfalls.

The story of New York City throughout the centuries is by and large the story of real estate. Even the epic social history of Stuyvesant Town-Peter Cooper Village and the extraordinary financial deal of 2006 fit into that story line. But, as we shall see, the Wall Street financiers and many deep-pocketed investors could be a forgiving bunch. Especially when the deals are done with other people's money. Even as Jerry and Rob Speyer wrote off their $56 million investment in Stuyvesant Town-Peter Cooper Village and walked away from the property in 2010, their company had already raised over $2 billion for a new real estate fund. A company spokesman was emphatic: the default had no effect on Tishman Speyer. Their partner also came out unscathed. By the last quarter of 2010, BlackRock, the world's largest asset manager, reported record earnings.

CHAPTER ONE

"Negroes and Whites Don't Mix"

On April 18, 1943, New York Mayor Fiorello H. La Guardia opened his regular Sunday-afternoon radio broadcast on WNYC with what he acknowledged was tough talk about speculators and food chiselers. He was unsparing in his vitriol for anyone who would overcharge for produce, potatoes, pork, eggs and butter in a city whose citizens were struggling to make ends meet while war raged in Europe, North Africa and the Pacific.

His own inspectors had found a half-smoked ham, shank end, bone-in, selling for fifty-nine cents a pound, seventeen cents a pound above the price ceiling set by wartime regulators. And to make matters worse, he said the ham was short-weighted. It was but one of three hundred and eighty-eight violations uncovered by the city's Department of Markets. Three hundred and seventy-eight violators had already paid their fines, the mayor assured his listeners.

"Anyone who willfully and intentionally and deliberately chisels or profiteers on foods is just a bad citizen," La Guardia warned. "He's a disloyal citizen and we won't have him in our midst and we don't want him in business."[1]

He also had a word of advice for frugal housewives looking to save every penny they could: save your egg box so you can bring it back with you to the store. The grocer was allowed to charge two cents for either the egg safety box or the regular square box.

Midway through the broadcast, La Guardia turned to the problem of housing, a topic of immense interest to the many New Yorkers desperate for a place to live. During the race to build the world's tallest building in the 1930s, New York saw the rise of skyscrapers, from the seventy-story office tower at 40 Wall Street downtown to the seventy-story 30 Rockefeller Plaza, the seventy-seven-story Chrysler Building, the one-hundred-and-two-story Empire State Building. Even by the 1920s, New York had nearly a thousand buildings eleven to twenty stories tall, ten times as many as Chicago, and fifty-one between twenty-one and sixty stories. They were clustered in midtown, especially around Grand Central Terminal, and downtown.

But they loomed far above the cramped, low-slung four-, six- and ten-story buildings in which most New Yorkers lived. The garment factories, warehouses and tenements that squatted on the West Side, from Hell's Kitchen to Chelsea, served the rail lines and the bustling piers along the waterfront. On the Lower East Side, tens of thousands of factory workers made their homes in cramped, old-style tenements where light and sanitary conditions were often hard to come by. And there never seemed to be enough housing for the steady stream of immigrants who made their way year after year to what was then a largely blue-collar city.

With vacant apartments a rarity throughout the city, couples across all class lines were forced to double up with their families and friends, some in substandard housing. La Guardia had a very personal and deeply held commitment to improve the city's housing stock that was rooted in the death by tuberculosis of his first wife, Thea, and their only child in 1921. By 1943, his administration had outlined a $110 million program to build modern apartments for low-income tenants as soon as the war ended.

But what he wanted to talk about that day was an unprecedented plan for a nicely landscaped, middle-class community in a dilapidated corner of the city known as the Gas House District, a drab, eighteen-block stretch from Fourteenth to Twentieth Streets, between First Avenue and Avenue C, filled with factories, bathhouses, flimsy tenements, small businesses and the gas tanks that lent the neighborhood its distinct and unpleasant odor. La Guardia and his building czar, Robert Moses, had spent several disappointing years trying to find a willing partner among the city's powerful financial institutions who could match his grand vision. Now he had one: Frederick H. Ecker, the seventy-five-year-old chairman of the world's largest insurance company, Metropolitan Life.

"Today I am very happy to announce a rehabilitation of a real blighted area in Lower Manhattan," La Guardia told his radio audience. "There will be a reconstruction of this area as a residential community."[2]

Metropolitan Life, the mayor said, would redevelop the seventy-two-acre site, building thousands of apartments for twenty-five thousand middle-class residents, nearly three times the number of people then living in the area. The mayor reassured existing residents that there would be "no dispossessing or no tearing down of existing buildings during the war." Construction would start afterward. The city would accommodate low-income tenants at municipal housing projects and assist higher-income residents in finding suitable apartments elsewhere.

Metropolitan, as it was then known, would soon christen the project Stuyvesant Town, a historical reference to old New York and the farm nearby that Peter Stuyvesant III, great-grandson of the Dutch governor, had carved out of the quiet woodlands in the late 1700s.

That same day, Ecker, a small, stocky man who wore wire-framed glasses and a precisely clipped mustache, told reporters that the plan was a step in the direction of a new Manhattan, "one in which wholesomeness of residential environment will combine with existing convenience to anchor families, especially those with children, to this borough."

At a cost of up to $50 million, the insurer planned to erect thirty-five thirteen-story buildings on lushly landscaped terrain with trees, playgrounds and paths, "such as many suburbs do not possess." Its proximity to midtown offered walk-to-work possibilities, added a press release from Metropolitan.

There is "an opportunity for private investment that will restore the residential values of the land," Ecker said. "Reconstruction can be accomplished on a sound, economic basis. It should have the effect of protecting Manhattan's position as a borough in which families with children can enjoyably and profitably live. It should promote the welfare of the city as a whole." [3]

La Guardia concluded his housing announcement by thanking Ecker and taking a jab at the city's other insurance companies, which had resisted his pleas to address the city's housing crisis. He thanked Metropolitan for providing "this very useful housing unit for our city. . . . It is not only a vision, it is prudence and good business and may I say in all kindliness to the New

York Life and Equitable Life and Mutual Life, that they should look into this housing proposition and the advantages it offers and they should also provide as much at least as the Metropolitan Life is doing in the area I have just described."[4]

The other insurers would never match Metropolitan's investment in urban housing. But now that La Guardia had finally found a willing partner he did not want to waste any time. Prior to the announcement, he and his aides drew up a schedule that set a record for municipal planning even by 1940s standards. It called for the planning commission to assess and approve the project in early May and the city's powerful Board of Estimate to give a final stamp of approval two days later, less than two months after Stuyvesant Town was first announced to the public.

Moses warned La Guardia in a memo that the development could be slowed by "some pretty mean critics on the outside—the real radical housing boys, who don't want private capital horning into their field."

The next day the mayor was unequivocal in his instructions to city officials. "I want no controversy on this subject," the mayor wrote in a terse note to city planning commissioner Edwin A. Salmon, five days after his radio show. "This is not Washington. This is New York. There will be no disagreement on this."[5]

But critics descended on La Guardia, Moses and Metropolitan and slowed their fast-paced schedule, albeit only by weeks. Urban planners and civic groups blasted the project for its unprecedented level of subsidies in the form of free public land and property tax breaks, its design as a "medieval walled city" and the lack of community facilities at a complex as large as Peekskill, New York, or Danbury, Connecticut. In order to gain maximum control over the property, Ecker did not want any public facilities—schools, churches or libraries—within its boundaries that might attract outsiders and the poor people who lived south of the complex, on the Lower East Side.

Ecker was not interested in flamboyant architecture. His architects designed buildings less for their aesthetic qualities than for practical economics. At twelve and thirteen stories, the buildings were more than twice the height of most tenements on the nearby Lower East Side. But the height allowed for more apartments, and a greater rent stream, to share the cost of creating the complex. The unrelenting uniformity of the buildings allowed construction to proceed swiftly and economically.

City officials agreed to provide what would become one-fifth of the land and to freeze property taxes for a quarter-century at relatively low pre-demolition levels, allowing MetLife to save millions of dollars a year. Most important, the city would use one of its most sweeping powers, eminent domain, to condemn land that MetLife could not purchase from private owners. Traditionally, cities and states used eminent domain to acquire property for schools, hospitals, highways and other public uses. Critics were alarmed that La Guardia had expanded the use of the power to benefit a wealthy corporation.

The debate exploded after Ecker publicly revealed exactly who would not be eligible for his company's grand version of suburban living within the urban grid. As he left a city planning commission hearing on May 19, 1943, he told a reporter for the *New York Post* that Negroes would be barred from Stuyvesant Town. "Negroes and whites don't mix," he told the reporter. "Perhaps they will in a hundred years but they don't now. If we brought them into this development, it would be to the detriment of the city, too, because it would depress all the surrounding property."[6]

Time and again, Ecker would say his position was a product of "business and economics, and not of racial prejudice."

By June, a young city councilman and minister from Harlem, Adam Clayton Powell, called for La Guardia's impeachment over Metropolitan's discriminatory policies at the city-backed Stuyvesant Town project before a roaring crowd of twenty thousand at the Freedom Rally in Madison Square Garden.

Ecker, like many employees at the Metropolitan, was a lifer who worked at the company for his entire career. Born in 1867 in Phoenicia, New York, a small village in the Catskills, he was the son of John Christian Ecker, a decorated Civil War veteran, and grandson of Jacob P. Ecker, a staff officer for one of Napoleon's generals. He graduated from public school in Brooklyn at fifteen and went to work for a law firm in the same downtown building at Park Place and Church Street that served as the home office for Metropolitan Life, a firm that had been founded in two rented rooms in a building on Broadway in Lower Manhattan the same year he was born.

Impressed by the prosperous appearance of the insurance executives, Ecker wrote a letter to Metropolitan asking for a job. "Knowing that you know of a situation for a boy," he wrote to an assistant to the president of the insurance company, "and being desirous of obtaining one, I will with your permission apply for it.

"I would like to get a position where I would have a good chance of advancement," he added.[7]

Ecker landed a job in the mailroom, paying $4 for a fifty-four-hour week, less than what he was getting at the law firm. But he was looking to the future. Metropolitan had grown swiftly since its early days insuring Civil War sailors and soldiers against disabilities due to wartime wounds and accidents and a searing recession that nearly crippled the company. But it soon focused on providing life insurance expressly for the middle class.

A tiny company, Metropolitan initially had to contend with the industry's Big Three: Equitable Life Assurance Society of the United States, New York Life Insurance and Mutual Life Insurance of New York. The company adopted a British program of selling "industrial" or "workingmen's" insurance policies, an area largely ignored in the United States because of the necessity and expense of sustaining an army of agents to sell policies door-to-door and to make the weekly rounds collecting five- and ten-cent premiums. Under Ecker's leadership, Metropolitan sold policies to both white and black families. Despite having more than one hundred thousand policyholders in Harlem alone, however, the company's workforce was entirely white.

The company imported English agents to train its workforce and was soon signing up seven hundred new policies a day. By the turn of the century, Metropolitan dominated industrial insurance, claiming 49 percent of the American market. By 1920 it had surged ahead of the "Big Three" in terms of assets under its control.

The methodical, soft-spoken Ecker rose rapidly within the Metropolitan. At twenty-five, Ecker ran the company's bond and mortgage department. Fourteen years later, in 1906, he was chief financial officer, overseeing all of the company's assets. He was elected vice president in 1919, president in 1924 and chairman in 1936.

Although Ecker could shoot a round of golf under 100, he was a man who lived to work. "I don't think anybody yet has invented a pastime that's as much fun, or keeps you as young, as a good job," he once told an interviewer.[8]

"Some people talk nowadays as if work is just something to be endured for the leisure it buys us," Ecker added. "I look at it just the opposite. I would be willing to endure quite a bit of leisure, if I had to, for the pleasure of working."

It was Ecker who led the giant insurer into real estate development. Like other insurance companies, Metropolitan invested in commercial and residential mortgages. But during the depression of 1893, Metropolitan got stuck with wide swaths of urban real estate, after it was forced to foreclose on scores of bad loans. Ecker, then in the real estate department, made a reputation for himself by rehabilitating and selling foreclosed properties. Over time, he was put in charge of the company's entire real estate portfolio and became an expert on building construction, market trends and real estate values.

In the early 1920s, Ecker and Metropolitan were ready to get involved in development. Their decision was spurred by the passage of new state laws designed to address a chronic housing shortage that had plagued the city since the end of World War I by encouraging insurers to invest a portion of their assets in housing production. Under the laws, new housing complexes were exempt from real estate taxes for ten years as long as the rents did not exceed $9 per month per room.

Metropolitan plunged in, spending $7.5 million to buy three

sites in Long Island City, Queens, to build 54 five-story walk-up apartment buildings with 2,125 apartments. A shrewd businessman, Ecker focused on locations easily accessible from Manhattan. Given the size of the project, Ecker also sought to achieve an economy of scale, while providing better housing for the middle class.

He imported brick from the Netherlands and Belgium at two-thirds the cost of local brick and purchased bathtubs at below-market prices. The buildings may not have been architecturally striking, but the apartments, though small, had a standard size and were designed to provide generous natural light and cross-ventilation, two things sorely missing in much of the city's older housing stock. Rents, at $9 per room, included two items not ordinarily found in mass housing: steam heat and hot water.

The apartments were an instant hit and filled quickly when they opened in 1924. During the Depression, Metropolitan was forced to drop the rent to $8.35 a room in order to maintain a high occupancy rate. In other words, tenants paid $36 a month for a two-bedroom apartment with a kitchen and bath. Still, the company noted, Ecker's Long Island City apartment buildings generated an impressive return of 8 to 9 percent, before depreciation, during the ten-year tax exemption.

Ecker's twin goals of public good and corporate profit were consistent with the company's long-standing philosophy. Dating back to its early years, Metropolitan saw the fortunes of the company as inextricably linked to the health and welfare of the middle class and the national economy. As a result, Metropolitan engaged in public health campaigns, including a seven-year demonstration project against tuberculosis in Framingham, Massachusetts, that enlisted every local club, church and civic organization in a successful effort to reduce the ravages of the country's number one killer.[9]

It encouraged healthy exercise among its employees, building one of the first gyms for office workers at its newly established headquarters on Madison Avenue and Twenty-Third Street. The company also issued a steady stream of pamphlets for its employees and policyholders covering everything from clean milk and personal hygiene to citizenship. Given that Metropolitan insured one out of three urban residents, *Business Week* concluded dryly that the "provision of better living conditions for city folks must accordingly improve the company's mortality experience and annual earnings."

During the Depression, Ecker negotiated two of the largest mortgages ever made, a $27.5 million loan to finance construction of the Empire State Building in 1929 and a $44.9 million mortgage for John D. Rockefeller Jr.'s vast office complex, Rockefeller Center, in 1931. The company went on to place 51 percent of its total assets in government bonds during World War II, making it the largest private contributor to the war effort.

But housing development held a special allure for Ecker. *Fortune* magazine described his approach this way in a 1946 article: "A great many years ago Mr. Ecker became intrigued with the idea that if life insurance funds could be made available for housing projects so planned as to eliminate the speculative element, Metropolitan might gain an advantageous new field for the investment of funds and at the same time be making an additional contribution to public welfare by supplying an existing need in housing—to say nothing of stimulating employment via the building industry."[10]

Fresh from his success building apartment buildings in Queens, Ecker and Metropolitan embarked in April 1938 on a more audacious plan to create the largest housing project ever built by the federal government or private enterprise, Parkchester. Ecker announced that Metropolitan had bought 129 acres in the East Bronx, most of it from the New York Catholic Protectory, in order to build 171 buildings, with 12,271 apartments.

"The area acquired is one of the largest single undeveloped properties within the greater city," Ecker said in describing his evolving vision of housing development. "Its size will permit the planning of a completely balanced community containing all facilities for family life, including necessary stores, schools, churches, parks, playgrounds and opportunities for recreational and social life. The development will be the largest integral housing project so far planned and built in this country. It will not only help in supplying the existing need for housing at moderate rents, but it will provide continuous employment to the building trades and construction industry for three years."[11]

Again, Metropolitan's venture was fueled with substantial government assistance, something rarely mentioned in modern accounts or when the company later moved to sell the properties. This was a joint effort by the private sector and government. The city granted Metropolitan substantial subsidies and incentives in order to get the company to build badly needed housing for the middle class, while the La Guardia administration and the federal government built housing projects for poor and working-class residents. The company, in turn, was able to make a tidy profit addressing a social problem. The legislature in 1938 amended state insurance statutes, permitting life insurance companies to invest up to 10 percent of their assets in housing construction. The insurers could create a limited-profit corporation to build the housing in return for special tax breaks.

In anticipation of the legislation, Metropolitan announced that it was willing to invest $100 million in housing.

Fortune estimated that Metropolitan earned a net return of 4 percent, after amortization, on its $62 million investment at Parkchester, better than the 3 percent generated by many of the company's bonds and other investments.[12]

"From the investment standpoint, Metropolitan's housing projects are attractive because they have enabled the company to put a small portion of its assets (3 percent presently, with a legal maximum of 10 percent) into properties that have been handsomely hedged against obsolescence and deterioration and afford excellent prospects of netting 4 percent for many years to come."[13]

It's no wonder that La Guardia and Moses would form what would become known decades later as a public-private partnership with Metropolitan. Ecker was at the helm of the country's largest private corporation and the world's largest life insurance company, with $6 billion in assets and 31 million policyholders. Under his leadership, Metropolitan was in the midst of its own residential building boom at a time when there was little new construction anywhere else in the country. Moses, the city's master builder, who did not tolerate critics or fools, once described Ecker as "exceedingly able, experienced, shrewd, hard-boiled and conservative."[14]

Not only had Ecker completed Parkchester, which had 30,000 residents, a larger population than Elkhart, Indiana; he announced plans for Parkmerced, 3,483 apartments on 206 acres near Lake Merced in San Francisco; Park La Brea, 4,253 apartments in a series of buildings stretching across 173 acres of what is now the Miracle Mile district in Los Angeles; and Parkfairfax, 1,684 town house units on 202 acres outside Washington, DC.

La Guardia also set a torrid pace when it came to building housing for the city's poorest citizens. He used city, state and federal funds to build 14 low-rent housing projects for 17,040 families at a cost of $90.4 million in the decade between 1934 and 1943. As the city evolved, he wanted to replace dangerous, substandard housing as well as the warehouses and factories that served the now-defunct piers on the East Side. He vowed that his postwar housing program, which included the Jacob Riis Houses, the Lillian Wald Houses on the Lower East Side and the Alfred E. Smith Houses in the shadow of the Brooklyn Bridge, would "put every city in this country to shame."

But his ambitions extended beyond that. What he had in mind was not simply erecting a housing development in a relatively remote part of the Bronx. La Guardia wanted to clear away broad swaths of the city's slums and anchor the middle class to the urban core. He was convinced that he needed the private sector to do it. The La Guardia administration had sponsored a series of state laws, including the Redevelopment Companies Law of 1942, that sought to encourage savings banks and insurance companies to get into the housing business. Moses spent three fruitless years wooing insurers, before lengthy negotiations with New York Life president George L. Harrison collapsed. The company's board voted against taking on the risk of housing development, despite the company's having lobbied for the Redevelopment Companies Law.[15]

La Guardia and Moses turned to Ecker at Metropolitan, who proved to be more receptive. But Ecker wanted certain economic assurances before he would agree to a deal. So Moses went to the state legislature in March 1943 with an amendment to the recently adopted Redevelopment Companies Law that was specifically tailored to assuage Ecker and guarantee a deal to build Stuyvesant Town.

Under the new legislation, the La Guardia administration granted Metropolitan a heavy platter of benefits. The city agreed to limit public oversight, to use the power of eminent domain on behalf of Metropolitan to acquire the land and to give Metropolitan unprecedented control over the selection of tenants. The amendment granted project oversight to the state superintendent of insurance and the city's Board of Estimate, leaving the City Planning Commission with only a minor role. The city also contributed nearly twelve publicly owned acres, or 19 percent of the total land, for the project.

It provided a twenty-five-year tax exemption worth an estimated $53 million. During the twenty-five-year exemption, which froze the tax assessment at pre-demolition levels, $13.5 million, Metropolitan agreed to limit its annual profit to 6 percent and to set monthly rents at $14 per room.

Critics like Charles Abrams, a housing reformer and a prominent civic leader, excoriated the mayor for his "lavish" gifts to Metropolitan.

"With all this expenditure," Abrams wrote in *The Nation*, "not a single slum dweller is actually to be rehoused. The present residents of the area are to be crowded into other slums, making them more profitable for the owners and stabilizing the mortgages of the very institutions which are most vociferous in acclaiming the Stuyvesant Town formula. All the city gets in return is a walled-in town . . ."[16]

At the time the legislation was approved, La Guardia confided that he had doubts about the provisions that ceded so much authority to Metropolitan. Moses convinced La Guardia that he needed the private sector for slum clearance, and after years of failed efforts to engage the city's powerful insurance companies in building middle-class housing, the mayor was unwilling to accept defeat. "The purpose of the bill, however, is of such great importance that I have resolved the doubt in favor of the bill," La Guardia continued. "The immediate practical problem is housing or no housing. The answer is in favor of housing."

La Guardia, Moses and Ecker set a speedy timetable for the project because the negotiations for the deal had already taken place in complete secrecy and La Guardia, who ran a powerful mayoralty, had lined up the votes with the help of Moses, the parks commissioner and the city's chief planner and construction coordinator, whom few councilmen dared to cross for fear of losing a favorite public project in their district.

Yet, after it was announced, Stuyvesant Town came under immediate attack. Some property owners filed a lawsuit in state supreme court claiming that the government's use of eminent domain to take private property on behalf of a private developer was unconstitutional. Few civic groups, unions or tenant organizations, however, challenged the notion of slum clearance, which required the demolition of five hundred buildings in the Gas House District and the displacement of hundreds of businesses and eleven thousand working-class tenants, in favor of a middle-class development. The project site stretched over eighteen city blocks, from Fourteenth Street to Twentieth Street, between First Avenue and Avenue C.

Abrams, an influential figure in New York's civic circles, continued to rail against the public-private partnership, which, he argued, amounted to a public subsidy for private profit, given the lavish concessions awarded to Metropolitan. Further, he said, the incentives were also a public subsidy for housing discrimination.[17] His argument against public-private partnerships, as well as the use of eminent domain on behalf of a private party, is as familiar today as it was in the 1940s.

Abrams highlighted the dangers of business that "assumes the function of a body politic without being responsible for the social obligations to which a body politic is subject" during Housing Week in May 1944.

The opposition, including the Citizens Housing Council, an advocacy group formed in 1937 that included housing experts, civic reformers, builders and landlords, listed a series of "undesirable elements," including the density of the project and the lack of a public school, as well as the extraordinary level of benefits—eminent domain and valuable, long-term tax exemptions—granted to a private company. The group, which later changed its name to the Citizens Housing and Planning Council, questioned why the La Guardia administration had expanded the city's list of redevelopment areas to include the land sought by Metropolitan north of Fourteenth Street. In a city where much of the housing consisted of four-to-six-story tenements, critics said Stuyvesant Town would be uncomfortably crowded, at 445 to 594 persons per acre, depending on how you counted, compared with the city's maximum allowance of 416 per acre.

The Housing Council and the American Civil Liberties Union, the Citizens Union, the American Labor Party, the American Jewish Congress, various unions and the NAACP also objected to Metropolitan's plans for a segregated complex. Ecker met privately with Harold S. Buttenheim and other members of the Housing Council on May 10, when he gave an inkling of the company's approach. Asked why Metropolitan had not included a school within the complex, Ecker stated, as Buttenheim later revealed, that "as one of the determining factors, that the Company desires to restrict the use of the entire area to its own tenants to the greatest extent practicable, and that if there were a public school in the project the City would allow some children, including Negroes, to attend from outside the area."[18]

Stanley M. Isaacs, the city council's sole Republican and a leading member of the City-Wide Committee on Harlem, testified at the hearing that the project would create a "medieval walled city privately owned, in the heart of New York," a phrase that was quickly adopted by the opposition and newspaper headline writers. Prentice Thomas of the NAACP declared at the hearing that unless a nondiscriminatory clause was written into the contract his organization would oppose the project.[19]

The next day, May 20, the Planning Commission voted five to one in favor of Stuyvesant Town, with the sole opponent, Lawrence M. Orton, saying he would have voted with the majority if Metropolitan had included a school.

Two weeks later, the city's Board of Estimate voted eleven-to-five in favor of Stuyvesant Town, after a raucous three-and-a-half-hour hearing in which twenty-four opponents argued that Metropolitan should be blocked from discriminating against Negroes because Stuyvesant Town was a public project by virtue of receiving a twenty-five-year tax exemption and the right of eminent domain. Assemblyman William T. Andrews read into the record a letter from George Gove, Metropolitan's director of housing, stating that "no provision has been made for Negro families" in the project.[20]

Henry Epstein, a former state solicitor general, predicted in

1943 that Stuyvesant Town would be "a new style ghetto" if it was permitted to exclude tenants based on race. "Today, with Stuyvesant Town, it will be the Negroes, the next day the Jews, the next day the Catholics and the next the undesirable aliens, whoever they wish to call them. This is what Hitler stands for, the superiority of one race against the other."[21]

For his part, Ecker rejected the notion that his policy was the result of racism. "Today, it is my personal opinion that an invitation to Negroes to apply for apartments in a neighborhood which is, and always has been, occupied by white people will result in depreciation of the property and neighborhood, serious differences between and among tenants and unfortunate incidents which would imperil the investment in the enterprise and its financial security."[22]

The battle galvanized residents of Harlem, which, like Detroit, Boston, Chicago and other cities, was in the midst of a great migration of African-Americans from the South to the North, where they hoped to find jobs and prosperity. The *Amsterdam News*, a black weekly based in Harlem, noted that Metropolitan had long scorned Negroes, well more than two million of whom held life insurance policies with the company. Yet, the insurer did not employ any Negro sales agents at its thirteen hundred offices, not even the one in Harlem where there were one hundred thousand policyholders.

Publicly, Moses was largely silent on the issue of racial discrimination, preferring to cast the battle as one between the pragmatists who sought to transform the slums versus the impractical or dishonest dreamers who opposed discrimination. "Those who would insist upon making projects of this kind a battleground for the vindication of social objectives, however desirable, and who persist in claiming that a private project is in fact a public project, obviously are looking for a political issue and not for results in the form of actual slum clearance.

"If the city were to insist upon ideal conditions, this project would be wholly unsound from the point of view of prudent investment."[23]

Throughout his career, Moses had at the very least accepted, if not promoted, racial discrimination in the building and operation of city and state parks. He had also blocked public works projects in Harlem. In the Stuyvesant Town fight, he privately advised the insurance company on how to defend itself against several lawsuits. At the same time, Moses blamed not Ecker but his advisers for Metropolitan's racial policy. He told New York lieutenant governor Frank C. Moore that his friend Ecker might be persuaded to relent on the "discrimination question" at Stuyvesant Town. He suggested that Ecker had "some very poor advisers," namely his son and heir apparent, Fred Ecker Jr., and George Gove, Metropolitan's executive vice president.[24] But there is no evidence that Moses himself ever pressed Ecker on the issue.

During the Board of Estimate meeting, only Ecker and Moses, who both dismissed their critics as demagogues and leftists, spoke in favor of the project. Moses downplayed the subsidies for Metropolitan, saying the concessions were "the minimum inducements necessary" to attract private capital to engage in slum clearance. He offered a take-it-or-leave-it proposition.

"If you don't want this contract," said the combative Moses, "I can assure you that it will be the last opportunity we'll have to attract private capital. It will mark the death knell of slum clearance by private enterprise."[25]

The *New York Times* and the *New York Herald-Tribune* concurred in subsequent editorials, without mentioning the color line imposed at the complexes. "Stuyvesant Town by now is presumably a closed subject, and closed the right way, too, in the opinion of a good many of us," the *Times* said. "The heart of the matter was expressed by Robert Moses, who has a habit of going to the heart of a good many things. Do we want to enlist private capital in behalf of slum removal and rehousing, or don't we."[26]

It certainly seemed as if the issue of racial discrimination was a closed subject. The state's highest court, the court of appeals, ruled in favor of Stuyvesant Town, rejecting a lawsuit brought by property owners claiming that the Redevelopment Companies Law was unconstitutional. A second lawsuit, brought by the Citizens Housing Council and other civic groups, including the United Tenants League of Greater New York, the ACLU and the Congress of Industrial Organizations, met a similar fate.

Many of La Guardia's supporters found his support for discrimination at Stuyvesant Town puzzling. La Guardia, who was well-known in civil rights circles locally and nationally, certainly did not fit the picture of a Southern segregationist. In June 1942, he had been instrumental in getting President Franklin D. Roosevelt to issue Executive Order 8802, the Fair Employment Act, which banned discriminatory employment practices by federal agencies and all unions and companies engaged in war-related work. And almost 15 percent of the tenants at the city housing projects built by La Guardia were black, although African-Americans comprised less than 7 percent of the population.

Even as Adam Clayton Powell very publicly condemned La Guardia as a hypocrite, Walter White of the NAACP sent a "personal and confidential" letter to La Guardia that desperately sought to understand the mayor's reasoning.

> Dear Mayor La Guardia:
>
> I wonder if you would let me know your reasons for approving the Stuyvesant Town project? I am sure they must be good ones and I know personally that they are honest ones.
>
> Deputy Mayor McGahen's casting of your three votes announcing your approval of the project, which, as you know proposes to exclude Negroes, puzzles me. Knowing of the long-time friendship which you and I have enjoyed, a number of people have asked me about your position on this project. I have refrained from expressing any opinion until I could first learn from you your reasons for approval. If you would rather I come in to talk with you, let me know and I will arrange my schedule accordingly.
>
> That was a swell party you and Mrs. La Guardia gave yesterday. I enjoyed it as did Gladys.[27]

There is no question that on the eve of signing a contract for Stuyvesant Town with Ecker, La Guardia was burning with the friction between his progressive personal beliefs and Ecker's discriminatory policies. The nation's simmering racial tensions were further brought into relief by a series of riots in 1943, culminating on June 20 in Detroit, where forty people were killed and seven hundred injured during a conflagration that lasted almost two days and saw $2 million worth of property destroyed. New York did not escape the unrest. A white police officer shot a black soldier in uniform on a Harlem street corner two months later, touching off a riot in which six people died, hundreds were injured and many white-owned stores were laid in ruin.

In a letter to La Guardia dated July 26, 1943, Ecker was unwavering in his position that Metropolitan must control tenant selection. His words were couched in the polite language of a prudent banker rather than a bigot's vitriol. "We shall rent to applicants solely on the basis of the standard which must govern a fiduciary's prudent investment in the particular neighborhood in which Stuyvesant Town, Inc. is located."[28]

La Guardia responded in a letter five days later.

> I deem it proper at this time also, because of the discussion, statements and even gossip during the course of the consideration of this project, and at hearings and even in judicial proceedings, to say that I consider this particular project as having a certain public obligation different from and greater than a like project financed entirely by private funds without any tax exemption or right of condemnation or other privileges. The standards or conditions or requirements for tenancy in a housing unit aided by the City through statutory authorization, as is the case in Stuyvesant Town, must be applicable to all. In other words, any person meeting all the requirements should not be barred because of belonging to any particular racial group. There can be no discrimination in tenant selection based on prejudice or contrary to any provisions of our state constitution or state law. If, after operating of the Stuyvesant Town is started, there should be any litigation or proceedings for

> judicial adjudication on the question of barring tenants who are otherwise qualified solely because of discrimination or solely because of racial prejudice, you should know now that I will take a position as above indicated.[29]

The handwritten notation "Not sent" is scrawled across the top of the letter. But there was a lively exchange of back-channel communications between Ecker and La Guardia that ran through Moses, who strongly urged Metropolitan's chairman to resist the mayor's last-minute attempt to ban discrimination. The exchange suggests that La Guardia had second thoughts about sending his letter because he feared that Ecker would scuttle the entire deal. Ecker's response to the mayor's unsent letter came in the form of a five-page "draft" letter that was marked "Not sent by Mr Ecker." Both letters made their way into Moses's files.

Ecker, who began by acknowledging the mayor's letter, was irate that La Guardia sought to completely "change the contract and to impose new conditions." La Guardia, Ecker pointed out, had drafted legislation and urged the governor to sign it giving Metropolitan full control over tenant selection at Stuyvesant Town despite strenuous objections from "persons who demanded that the law include a provision for public control over the selection of tenants, and a clause to prevent any possible discrimination."

Finally, he delivered a threat that La Guardia could not withstand.

> Under these circumstances I am compelled to state to you that I cannot sign the contract between

> the City and Stuyvesant Town Inc. since you have put a cloud on the contract by your interpretation of it . . . I believe I am not exaggerating when I say that your action in this matter ends all possibility of investments by fiduciaries in slum clearance projects in the City.[30]

Moses persuaded La Guardia not to renege on the contract. But La Guardia did not completely forsake his principles. At 12:30 P.M. on August 4, 1943, he and Ecker came face-to-face at a private ceremony at city hall to formally sign the contract for the Stuyvesant Town project. It was there that La Guardia delivered a verbal rendition of his letter, once again vowing that in the event of any litigation he would take the position that "there can be no discrimination in tenant selection based on prejudice."[31]

Ecker shot back days later, saying that Metropolitan's position was that "Stuyvesant Town management must have complete freedom in the matter of the selection of tenants and that the question was one of business economics, and not of racial politics." Ecker was incensed by what he called La Guardia's "change of attitude." Ecker went on to quote from a memorandum, submitted to Governor Dewey on La Guardia's behalf, specifically stating that if the amendment to the state's housing law contained a provision giving tenant selection to the city "no company would operate under it." Further, Ecker said, Metropolitan "would not have proceeded with the matter and certainly would not have invested large sums in the acquisition of real estate if [La Guardia] had not signed a memorandum indicating approval of the law" giving the company control over tenant selection.[32]

La Guardia remained especially sensitive about the issue and the mere mention of Stuyvesant Town could drive him to distraction, Councilman Benjamin Davis recalled more than twenty years later. "It was as though he realized he had made a political mistake, but couldn't turn back for fear of losing face."

But if La Guardia was content to let the courts sort it out, Moses was an advocate for the defense, sending a steady stream of memos to Ecker and his counsel, Judge Samuel Seabury, advising them on a legal strategy in defending the company against charges of discrimination and the improper use of the powers of eminent domain. Government did not have a uniform policy when it came to race and housing, Moses wrote to Ecker: "Even the federal public housing officials recognize the color line in the South and provide housing for negroes as such."[33]

Still, early in 1944, Moses told Ecker that the state supreme court and the appellate division had dismissed most of their opponents' arguments, save for one issue: "equal benefit under the law is not being afforded to negroes because no projects for negroes under this law are being undertaken contemporaneously with the Stuyvesant Town project." Moses said that was why he had been urging Metropolitan to undertake housing projects in Harlem and Bedford-Stuyvesant, largely black neighborhoods in Manhattan and Brooklyn.[34]

Ecker, however, was reluctant in light of the pending litigation. He was also worried about how the broader public might perceive such a concession. "I should not like to appear to have been driven into such a position and in that I feel quite sure you will agree. . . . It should not appear, even by inference, that either we or the City admitted that the Redevelopment Law or the Constitution of New York would require private capital to match each White project with a Colored project," Ecker said in a February 25, 1944, letter to Moses.

But Moses kept at it. He assured Ecker that his suggestion that Metropolitan undertake a project in Harlem or Bedford-Stuyvesant was based "on a much sounder theory that colored areas are entitled at least to an experiment in this direction."[35]

La Guardia added his own plea, telling Ecker he was eager to see a privately built housing project started in Harlem "where conditions are particularly bad." He said that the city had planned any number of postwar public housing projects using city, state and federal loans and grants. Despite government efforts, the projects were unlikely to clear even 10 percent of the city's slums.[36]

At the same time, La Guardia signed a bill in June 1944 sponsored by city council members Stanley M. Isaacs and Benjamin J. Davis Jr., a Communist from Manhattan, opposing housing discrimination by barring tax exemptions for any privately financed housing that practiced discrimination. The law was carefully written, however, so that it did not apply retroactively to Stuyvesant Town, only to prospective projects.

Two months later, in August 1944, there was a breakthrough. Metropolitan had acquired the land for Stuyvesant Town, from Fourteenth to Twentieth Streets, but the company was not stopping there. Metropolitan was quietly buying up several blocks to the north for an additional housing development, although it would not be built under the Redevelopment Companies Law, so the insurance company would be paying full taxes. The new development, which would eventually be known as Peter Cooper Village, would wipe out a set of noxious gas tanks owned by the Consolidated Edison Company.

Unlike Stuyvesant Town, Peter Cooper would be built without public subsidies on land from Twentieth to Twenty-Third Streets, from First Avenue to East River Drive. Rents for the 2,495 apartments there would be somewhat higher. The living rooms would be larger and the apartments would include a second bathroom.

Metropolitan was also actively buying a twelve-acre parcel in Harlem with nearly a dozen crumbling tenements, junk shops, and factories for a new residential community. On September 17, 1944, La Guardia announced on his weekly radio program that Metropolitan planned to build "Riverton" for an estimated 3,400 people at an average monthly rental of $12.50 per room.

Riverton, with 1,232 apartments in seven 13-story buildings arranged around a 700-foot-long grassy mall, would be one-tenth the size of Stuyvesant Town and Peter Cooper Village. But like the projects on the Lower East Side, Riverton's buildings would be arrayed around a leafy, parklike setting. In paying tribute to Ecker as a "young man past 70 years of age" with a vision, La Guardia zinged the five "blind" men representing five financial institutions who had failed to follow Metropolitan's lead.[37]

Ecker told reporters that the project, initiated by La Guardia and under consideration for a year, would turn an unattractive corner of the city—from 135th Street to 138th Street, between Fifth Avenue and the Harlem River—into a community with a suburban atmosphere. "The project is of great importance, forming part of the rehabilitation program so essential to the future of the city," Ecker said.

"Riverton and Stuyvesant Town represent the first use of private capital for the rebuilding of obsolete city areas under the

Redevelopment Companies Law which has been described by the Court of Appeals as 'an effort by the Legislature to promote cooperation between municipal government and private capital to the end that substandard insanitary areas in our community may be rehabilitated.'"[38]

The separate-but-equal approach adopted by Ecker, Moses and La Guardia, who retired in 1945, divided the opposition. At an informal meeting of civil rights and tenant activists at the Society for Ethical Culture on West Sixty-Fourth Street, Charles A. Collier of the NAACP flatly opposed Riverton, which he described as a "Jim Crow housing project that will not only keep the Negro walled in but will delay his fight to live in the community of his choice as a citizen."[39]

Goode Harney of the New York Urban League argued that it was proper to condemn Stuyvesant Town, but protesting Riverton would confuse the issue. "People are so badly in need of housing in the area that they would still apply over our protest," he said. It would be better to encourage white people to apply to Riverton, he added.[40]

For its part, Metropolitan, bound by the new city law prohibiting housing discrimination, said Riverton would be open to everyone. Stuyvesant Town remained closed to Negroes.

CHAPTER TWO

Thirty-Six Million Bricks

In the fall of 1945, bulldozers, pile drivers and steam shovels rumbled onto the Stuyvesant Town-Peter Cooper Village site to begin demolition of over five hundred tenements, factories, warehouses and storefronts. Carmela Garcea, who grew up nearby on East Tenth Street, used to play amid the rubble as Metropolitan knocked down block after block of buildings. "We used to walk through the neighborhood," said Garcea, seventy-seven and still marveling at the thought of it in 2011. "It looked like a war zone. It looked bombed out when they got through with it."[1]

Metropolitan had acquired the land over two years, sometimes using intermediaries to mask their shopping spree so that property owners would not suddenly hike their prices. With the war winding down in Europe, the insurer judged that the moment had arrived to start building. Some 765,000 veterans returned to New York City, exacerbating the existing housing shortage. The veterans were living in trailers, tourist camps and Quonset huts, or doubled up with friends and relatives. Most of them could not afford to buy a house, which the city's Veterans

Service Center said would require an income of $90 a week, $34 more than the average among veterans. Metropolitan announced that it would give veterans a preference at all its housing developments.

Moses and Ecker had portrayed the area as a blighted neighborhood, where the population had tumbled from twenty-three thousand in 1910 to about twelve thousand in 1940, as the old tenements crumbled, businesses failed and the garment industry migrated from the Lower East Side to the West Side of Manhattan. The Hungarian, Russian, Italian and Polish residents were largely poor, paying less than $30 a month for a two-room, cold-water flat. One out of four residents was looking for work and those who had a job earned less than $200 a month, mainly working in the shipyards and other defense industries.

The Gas House District had the city's greatest concentration of substandard housing. Three-fourths of the apartments in the aging buildings on the site lacked central steam heat. Hot and cold running water was a luxury. The area had devolved into "obsolescence," Ecker told the Annual Conference of Mayors, echoing the same description of blight used by planners and promoters in knocking down the slaughterhouses and breweries north of East Forty-Second Street to make way for the United Nations.

Although few critics challenged the necessity of wholesale demolition and the removal of the residents, the neighborhood was not exactly a burned-out husk. There were 200 active businesses and 150 industrial firms. A new Coca-Cola bottling plant sat near the East River and Dowd's Lumber Yard was on Avenue A. The Dairyman's League Cooperative Association called the Gas House District home, as did the Goodman noodle factory; Bull's Head Horse Auction Company; the Mecca Theater; one Lutheran and two Catholic churches, including the seventy-two-year-old St. Mary Magdalen; two schools; and scores of other businesses and factories. It marked the beginning of a growing consensus among the city's real estate interests, civic groups and planners that industrial neighborhoods no longer belonged in Manhattan. Over the next half century, the fur district, the flower district, the printing district and much of the garment district would disappear, much like the Gas House District. Still, most residents of the Gas House District were reluctant to leave their homes, despite the planners' intentions. "My husband died here," one resident, Concetta Tornabene, told a *Herald Tribune* reporter, "and I want to die here too."

Tenants, who organized the Stuyvesant Tenant's League, protested their expulsion with a succession of rallies, which distressed La Guardia. In January 1945, residents of one section of the Stuyvesant Town site were warned to decamp by the summer. Metropolitan hired James Felt, a real estate executive, to set up the Tenant Relocation Bureau, which would assist residents with the enormous task of finding new housing. Felt quickly assembled a list of six thousand vacant apartments and hired a team of multilingual female interviewers who escorted families "around in a station wagon without cost to examine new apartments."[2]

The Relocation Bureau could do little for tenants who could not afford more than $10 a month in rent. The City Housing Authority could absorb only a handful of the tenants. A few families made their way to the Parkchester complex in the Bronx, where there was a waiting list of two thousand veterans. Felt acknowledged that "only a small percentage of the former site residents could afford Stuyvesant Town, where rents per room were about $14 per room, $8 more than the average rent in the district." Most tenants moved to surrounding neighborhoods to the north and south, where the housing was equally bleak.

"By and large, families dislocated by slum clearance and not provided for in public housing or given some other form of assistance in securing decent housing must find shelter in other slum areas," a report by the Community Service Society concluded. "Thus slum living is not eliminated for these families."[3]

By November 1, 1945, all but seventy-seven of more than three thousand families had moved without a single eviction, according to a report by the Relocation Bureau, which was regarded as an inexpensive success and adopted by successive slum clearance projects. Meanwhile, Metropolitan worked with Richmond Shreve, Irwin Clavan and Andrew J. Eken to design the uniform L- or cross-shaped red brick buildings at Stuyvesant Town and Peter Cooper Village. It was the same team that had worked on Parkchester and the Empire State Building.

About 5,000 steelworkers, masons, carpenters, plumbers and electricians swarmed over the site, driving 42,000 steel piles into the ground and ultimately laying 36.5 million bricks for the buildings symmetrically arrayed around a grassy oval. They carved pathways and playgrounds out of the gently sloping land, which was ultimately planted with sweet gums, Oriental planes, pin oaks, azaleas, rose mallow, bush honeysuckle, rhododendrons and snowballs. Within a year, Metropolitan was showered with more than 110,000 applications for the apartments in yet another indication of the city's desperate housing crisis.

With Metropolitan nearing completion of the first buildings at Stuyvesant Town and Peter Cooper Village in 1947, three black veterans sued Metropolitan in June 1947, charging that its exclusionary policies violated their constitutional right to equal access under the Fourteenth Amendment. The lead plaintiff was Joseph R. Dorsey of Harlem, a former army captain who held a master's degree and worked as a social worker. Dorsey, joined by Monroe Dowling, another former army captain, and Calvin B. Harper, a disabled veteran from the Bronx, argued that their existing apartments were unfit for habitation and that they had tried unsuccessfully to find better housing closer to work. The suit was sponsored by the American Civil Liberties Union, the American Jewish Congress and the NAACP and argued by Abrams, joined by Will Maslow and Thurgood Marshall, who would later successfully argue the landmark *Brown v. Board of Education* case and become the first African-American justice of the Supreme Court.

They argued that Stuyvesant Town was a private complex built with extensive public support in the form of land, a generous tax exemption and the use of eminent domain, which conveyed a public purpose and a public use. Government limited the profits and imposed a rent ceiling. Therefore, Metropolitan was compelled to comply with the state and federal constitutions, which guaranteed equal access to all citizens.

"If the nation's neighborhoods are to be marked off into areas for the exclusive and the excluded, the involuntary ghetto will have become an unalterable American institution," the suit stated. "For, once the racial composition of the new neighborhoods is fixed, they cannot be easily changed, particularly if they are as rigidly controlled as Stuyvesant Town would be with all the freedom from public interference it asserts it has."

Metropolitan countered that the federal and state constitutions had no bearing on the matter. "Stuyvesant is not exercising any governmental power, nor is it acting as an agent or representative of the State or City," the company said. "It is exercising mere private rights in an undertaking which neither the State nor the City has the power to undertake."

Only days before the first tenants moved into Stuyvesant Town, Justice Felix C. Benvenga ruled in favor of Metropolitan, saying that designating the complex a public use did not make it a public project under state law. Benvenga wrote that the public use ended when the redevelopment project was completed. There was "no established civil right where the question of private housing accommodations were concerned," he said.[4]

"It may well be that from a sociological point of view a policy of exclusion and discrimination on account of race, color, creed or religion is not only undesirable but unwise," Benvenga continued. "But the wisdom of the policy is not for the courts."

The lawyers appealed to the state's highest court, which affirmed on July 19, 1949, that the state had no role in Stuyvesant Town. In a four-to-three decision, the court ruled that while the state played a role in helping Metropolitan clear the site, the state legislature had intentionally refrained from imposing any restrictions upon a redevelopment company in its choice of tenants, although the public housing law explicitly prohibited discrimination at state-constructed low-rent housing projects. The ruling noted repeated efforts by Moses and other city officials to fend off prohibitions against discrimination at the Board of Estimate.[5]

In his strongly worded dissent, Justice Stanley Fuld found that the city was wrong in approving the Stuyvesant Town contract in the first place, knowing that Metropolitan intended to bar Negroes. He referred to Stuyvesant Town as a "private barony" in the middle of Manhattan that should not be left free of constitutional safeguards. The Fourteenth Amendment proscribes discrimination in Stuyvesant Town and the state constitution also condemns it, he said.

"As an enterprise in urban redevelopment, Stuyvesant Town is a far cry from a privately built and privately run apartment house," Fuld concluded. "More, its peculiar features yield to those eligible as tenants tremendous advantages in modern housing and at rentals far below those charged in purely private developments. As citizens and residents of the City, Negroes as well as white people have contributed to the development. Those who have paid and will continue to pay should share in the benefits to be derived."

No sooner had the court of appeals issued its decision than a group of Stuyvesant Town tenants decided to take matters into their own hands with a direct challenge to Metropolitan on their home turf. A dozen Stuyvesant Town tenants, many of them veterans, had a year earlier formed the Town and Village Tenants Committee to End Discrimination at Stuyvesant Town, a group that would eventually swell to 1,800 members.

"It was a landmark in the struggle against segregation in this country," Lee Lorch, a vice chairman of the committee, recalled in 2011. An army veteran and a math professor, Lorch and his family would pay a high price for his role in this and other civil rights battles. "I thought then, and still do, that it was an important struggle worth any sacrifice in pursuing it."[6]

Lorch's fellow committee members included the chairman, Paul L. Ross, a former secretary to Mayor William O'Dwyer; Rabbi Daniel L. Davis, director of the New York Federation of Reform Synagogues; and Esther Smith, who wrote many of the group's letters and leaflets. The group also included Bill Mauldin, the cartoonist whose drawings of American GIs endeared him to a generation; Stefan Heym, author of the bestseller *The Crusaders;* and Lee Vines, the CBS radio announcer. It was a diverse group of liberals, civil rights advocates and Communist Party members, who played an energetic role among both New York City tenant and labor unions.

Edward A. Stanley, whose parents were original Stuyvesant Town tenants, recalls his father Stephen describing the picket lines and the chanting that enveloped the complex. "They had a song," said Stanley, who later was an NYPD detective in the elite bias unit, "that went: 'Stuyvesant Town is a grand old town; but you can't get in if your skin is brown.' "

Like many of his neighbors, Lorch had recently gotten out of the service, after serving as a corporal in the Army Air Corps in the Pacific. The only housing he and his wife, Grace, could find was half a Quonset hut at a veterans' housing project on Jamaica Bay in Brooklyn. It was a long subway ride from there to City College, where he taught mathematics. After getting a doctorate at the University of Cincinnati in 1941, Lorch had worked briefly for the National Advisory Committee for Aeronautics, a precursor of NASA, before resigning his draft-exempt job to join the army.

Lorch and his family were among the one hundred thousand applicants for apartments at Stuyvesant Town, which gave preference to veterans. They were happy to finally get an apartment, he said, but Metropolitan's racial policy was well-known. "There was no way of boycotting Metropolitan," recalled Lorch, who is white, "but going there carried an obligation to fight discrimination. That's the way a lot of people felt about it."

Not wanting to get too far ahead of their neighbors, the

committee drew up a survey designed to assess residents' views of Metropolitan's policy of barring black tenants at Stuyvesant Town. The activists were pleasantly surprised but a bit skeptical when their survey revealed that two-thirds of the twenty-five thousand residents opposed the segregated housing policy of the landlord. So they created a second poll, which produced the same results, and quickly gathered over three thousand signatures on a petition opposing the exclusion of Negroes and calling on Mayor William O'Dwyer to take all necessary steps to open apartments to Negro tenants who met the eligibility requirements.

The *Town & Village* newspaper, which has diligently reported the community news since Stuyvesant Town's inception, did a survey of its own with similar results. But the committee did come under attack from some readers of *Town & Village*, as well as Metropolitan executives, who insisted it was a Communist front group.

"If they want Negroes as neighbors we say let them move to Harlem," said one anonymous letter writer published in the *Town & Village*. "It is a shame we cannot keep them by themselves," wrote another. "When we signed our lease they did not say colored people would be accepted. Why don't they take a vote of all concerned."

Still other tenants were sympathetic to the activists but feared the repercussions if they were publicly associated with the antidiscrimination battle. "It was very unpleasant; they didn't want blacks to come in," recalled Elaine T. Haber, who moved into her Peter Cooper Village apartment in 1947 and still lives there today. "They wanted to keep it white." But she did not get involved out of a sense of self-preservation. Her first husband had died in 1950 and she was juggling two jobs to pay the rent. "We didn't want to risk being ousted. I think a lot of tenants felt as I did: There were people fighting the fight, let them continue."[7]

In a committee pamphlet entitled "What's wrong with this picture*," Leo Miller explained his reasoning. "In the Battle of the Bulge on December 18, 1944, the courage and sharp shooting of a Negro machine-gunner saved my life and a dozen other white GIs. Can anyone of us who live in T & V say he may not be my neighbor. . . . I can't."

In August 1949, Jesse Kessler, a committee member and a union organizer for Local 65 Wholesale and Warehouse Workers, offered his four-room apartment at 1 Stuyvesant Oval to Hardine Hendrix, a twenty-eight-year-old veteran and a fellow union member, while Kessler went away on vacation. An art student, Hendrix was living with his wife Raphael (Rae) and five-year-old son, Hardine Jr., in a cramped, rat-infested apartment in Harlem. They welcomed the move downtown, even temporarily.

The Hendrixes' appearance at Stuyvesant Town caused a sensation, but the insurance company was loath to risk a very public confrontation, especially since committee members, veterans and union activists often slept at the apartment to ensure that the Hendrix family would not be evicted without a fight. A *New York Times* reporter found that twelve of the Hendrixes' fifteen neighbors had no problem with African-Americans living in Stuyvesant Town. The Hendrixes, in turn, liked living in Stuyvesant Town even if they were the subject of occasional taunts from windows they passed or threatening phone calls.

"I can recall many nights my father left our apartment to stay at the Hendrixes', to protect them," said Karen Smith, whose father David was a jewelry worker. Her mother, Esther, a graphic designer who worked at home, was the committee's executive secretary and part of a core group of women who did the bulk of the organizing, Mr. Lorch said.[8]

Metropolitan kept a close eye on their critics, going so far as to send an employee undercover to an August 29, 1949 rally billed as "The East Side Welcomes First Negro Family to Stuyvesant." Daniel B. English, a Metropolitan executive in the company's publication division, wrote a six-page account of the affair, which he said was attended by about three hundred people and featured speeches from James E. Allen of the NAACP, Nathan M. Padgug of the American Jewish Congress, the Kesslers and Rae Hendrix, an organizer for the Domestic Workers Union. In his judgment, the meeting was designed to advance the cause of left-wing activists and the American Labor Party. Aside from a small number of Stuyvesant Town tenants and a sprinkling of Negroes, Mr. English reported, "Most of the audience seemed to me of Jewish appearance."[9]

Mr. English confided that he was forced to contribute money when a speaker called on the audience to stand and pledge a donation. "Your observer thought it politic to contribute $1 of Metropolitan money so he could sit down again!"

After Kessler returned from vacation at the end of August Dr. Lorch offered the Hendrixes his Stuyvesant Town apartment at 651 East Fourteenth Street. Metropolitan refused to accept Kessler's $76 rent check, which the activists suspected was a first step toward evicting him. Lorch, who figured he would face the same threat, was heading off to Pennsylvania State College, having lost his job at City College when the administration overruled his colleagues and refused to grant him tenure. Although City College denied that there were political reasons behind the action, Lorch's failure to get tenure was widely believed to be a reprisal for his Stuyvesant Town activism. More than twenty organizations called on City College to reconsider.

"It happens that he lives in Stuyvesant Town," Justice Hubert T. Delaney, one of the city's first black judges, said of Lorch. "It happens that he was vice president of a committee that got 3,500 signatures of tenants there who were opposed to the exclusion of Negroes. I get pretty sick and tired of having a man called a Communist just because he did a decent thing. I think we are giving Communists too much credit."[10]

Ross, chairman of the tenant committee, promised that their campaign would continue "until the Hendrixes and other Negro families live among us, not just as guests, but as permanent residents."

Rae Hendrix, who became active with the committee, insisted that Metropolitan should not issue any more leases at Stuyvesant Town until the complex was integrated. She told the *Amsterdam News* that "no more families should be housed until a certain number of Negro families are admitted." Metropolitan countered that that would be unfair to white families already on the waiting list. What was unfair, she responded, was "that Negroes have never been allowed the opportunity to apply."

Meanwhile, Lorch's career at Penn State came to a quick end the following spring, when, Lorch explained in a front-page article in the *New York Times*, a school official told him that Penn State would not renew his contract because his actions in permitting a Negro family to live as guests in his New York apartment were "extreme, illegal and immoral, and damaging to the public relations of the college." The school's decision sparked a protest from the American Association of University Professors over academic freedom, a campus rally of more than a thousand students and a letter of public support from a Princeton mathematician, Albert Einstein. Lorch, however, soon decamped to Nashville, for a teaching position at Fisk University.[11]

On the same day in June 1950 that the United States Supreme Court declined to review the Stuyvesant Town case, the court issued three decisions favorable to the civil rights movement. One prohibited the segregation of Negroes in railroad dining cars. The second barred the segregation of Negro students at the University of Oklahoma. The last case involved a student who was refusing to attend a new state law school for Negroes in Houston, Texas, demanding instead entrance to the University of Texas law school in Austin. The court ruled that the Negro school in Houston was not the equivalent of the university law school and therefore ordered his admission to the law school in Austin. The decisions, though narrowly drawn, marked what the *Amsterdam News* called the "beginning of the end of race segregation."

The color lines in America were beginning to break down in the years after World War II. Jackie Robinson signed a contract with the Brooklyn Dodgers in 1947, becoming the first black player in Major League Baseball. President Harry Truman desegregated the armed forces two years later, under pressure from A. Philip Randolph, the African-American labor leader and president of the League for Non-Violent Civil Disobedience Against Military Segregation. That same year, the Supreme Court barred restrictive covenants.

Back at Stuyvesant Town, Metropolitan finally made its move against the Town and Village Committee in June, notifying thirty-five tenant leaders, including Ross, Rabbi Davis, Lorch and the Hendrix family, that their leases would not be renewed. For nearly two years, the tenants fought the evictions in the streets, in the legislature and in the courts, where they were represented by Paul O'Dwyer, the brother of then-mayor William O'Dwyer. Allied with the New York State Committee on Discrimination in Housing, the activists mobilized public support to force Metropolitan to postpone any action.

The August doldrums broke with the news that Metropolitan would allow three "qualified" Negro families into Stuyvesant Town, although the company paradoxically denied any change in basic policy. The insurer simultaneously opposed a bill sponsored by Councilmen Earl Brown and Stanley M. Isaacs compelling Stuyvesant Town to accept Negro tenants by portraying the legislation and integration as Communist inspired. The charge was echoed in the *Daily News* and the *Daily Mirror.*

The Communist Party, which had thousands of members in New York City at the time, vehemently supported the bill and the fight at Stuyvesant Town, much to the embarrassment of some of its allies. Yet, the city council unanimously passed the Brown-Isaacs Law in March 1951, making discrimination a misdemeanor carrying a $500 fine. The Board of Estimate approved it and Mayor Vincent R. Impellitteri signed it into law.[12]

The battle at Stuyvesant Town culminated in a showdown at the complex. The city marshal had given the remaining tenants scheduled for eviction until 9:00 A.M. on January 17, 1952, to pack up and be gone. Instead, nineteen of the families refused to leave, barricading their doors after sending their twenty-six children to stay with relatives. Food was relayed from window to window by rope. That evening, tenants sent aloft a red meteorological balloon bearing a streamer emblazoned with the words "Stop the Evictions." The balloon was positioned so that it was even with the tenth-floor windows of Ecker's apartment at 660 Park Avenue.[13]

In a front-page editorial, *Town & Village* said, "These people are being forcibly ousted because they espoused a cause which the landlord found undesirable and embarrassing." Sixteen organizations, including the American Jewish Congress, American Veterans Committee, Citizens Housing and Planning Council, New York Society for Ethical Culture, Anti-Defamation League, New York Board of Rabbis, NAACP, New York City CIO Council, Commission on Christian Social Relations of the Episcopal Diocese of New York and Social Action Committee of the Community Church, urged Metropolitan to "reconsider its action."

Civic groups and labor unions set up picket lines with hundreds of people at Stuyvesant Town, at city hall and at Metropolitan's headquarters on Madison Avenue, where a nonstop vigil went on for three days. Hours before the deadline, Metropolitan backed down, agreeing to negotiate with the tenant leaders.

Three days of intense talks mediated by city council president Rudolph Halley ensued before a deal was struck. Metropolitan would drop the eviction proceedings on the condition that the Lorch, Kessler and Ross families would voluntarily leave Stuyvesant Town. Finally, the insurer agreed to provide the Hendrixes with an apartment. *Town & Village* reported that persons "close to the negotiations express no doubt that the insurance company felt, in the face of the violent public reaction, that it was in a 'tight spot' and was relieved when the negotiations offered a way out." Early in 1952, Metropolitan told officials that the company was processing the applications of a number of Negro families.

"We left without prejudice, according to the agreement," Lorch recalled fifty-eight years later in the living room of his apartment in Toronto. Lorch's storied career took him to Fisk University in Nashville and to Little Rock, Arkansas, where he and his wife, Grace, played a role in the desegregation of Central High School in 1957. Ultimately, he was blacklisted from teaching and moved to Toronto, where he became a distinguished professor at York University and continued to fight for justice and civil rights. "The Hendrixes were given an apartment in their own name, but they wouldn't let them stay in my apartment. The Stuyvesant Town fight mobilized public opinion against segregation. Because of its prominence, it was given enormous attention. I have no regret over what we did or what it cost us, although I would have much preferred living in my hometown."[14]

Many residents of Stuyvesant Town, and most New Yorkers today, know little of the fiercely waged struggle against discrimination during the birth of the complex. It was led by tenants, who wanted to define for themselves, outside the regimented strictures laid out by Metropolitan, how they would live and interpret the meaning of American ideals like justice and equality after the harrowing experiences of World War II.

The battle of Stuyvesant Town lasted from 1943 to 1952 and gave rise to the open housing movement in the United States, even if integration came very slowly to the sister complexes overlooking the East River. Seven years later, the 1960 census would show that only 47 Negroes lived among the 22,405 residents of Stuyvesant Town. Still, the heated struggle over Metropolitan's discrimination at Stuyvesant Town brought the issue into the public realm and inspired others to take up the cause. The groups involved in the effort to desegregate Stuyvesant

Town formed the New York State Committee on Discrimination in Housing in 1948, which in turn led to the establishment of the National Committee Against Discrimination in Housing in 1950, which campaigned for fair housing laws in cities across the country.

The New York committee helped win adoption of a 1950 law barring racial discrimination in any housing constructed with public funds and both groups supported a 1963 law barring discrimination in private housing. Their efforts culminated in passage of the Fair Housing Act in 1968, which prohibited discrimination in the sale, rental or financing of housing.

For some activists, the fight against discrimination at Stuyvesant Town was bound up with the way they viewed the complexes as a refuge for the middle class, where anyone could live and raise their family in an urban setting while struggling for a better life. Blacks and Latinos would never make up more than 5 percent of the residents. But that tradition of defending the middle class would wind its way through the residents' opposition to exorbitant rent hikes in the 1950s and 1960s. And it would find expression in their anguish over the sale of Stuyvesant Town-Peter Cooper Village during a real estate boom five decades later. If the working-class Gas House District was demolished to make way for a middle-class neighborhood, many of the residents were not going to let Stuyvesant Town be taken from them so that a wealthy elite could capture another corner of Manhattan.

CHAPTER THREE

The Golden Age

One of Al Doyle's fondest memories is Christmastime at Stuyvesant Town. The oaks and London plane trees were bare, having shed their leaves weeks earlier. As a young boy growing up in the 1950s, Doyle, with his brothers and their friends, would watch the maintenance men turn off the water and drain the fountains in Stuyvesant Oval, the geographic and social center of the sprawling complex. The workers would haul in a half-dozen newly cut pine and fir trees and install them in the basins of the fountains. Holiday music would waft through the limbs as workers decorated the towering trees and erected a manger and a menorah. Passing residents paused to watch.

"Stuyvesant Town was almost resortlike," said Doyle, the long-standing tenant union president who has never really lived anywhere else. "In the wintertime, you could sleigh down the embankments. Some kids would play roller hockey on the loop roads."

"MetLife was the best," he added. "They set all the standards and they never really wavered."[1]

Those are some of the memory loops that run through his head and are at the foundation of what he is willing to fight to preserve. The sense of community. Of commonality.

His father, Alvin D. Doyle, came back from the war in the Pacific, where he had served as a combat correspondent for the Third Marine Division. Like most veterans he did not talk much about the war. He got his old job back at the *Daily Mirror*, a newspaper owned by William Randolph Hearst. He and his wife, Therese, had just about given up finding their own apartment when they got a call from Stuyvesant Town, offering something very different from the tenement life they knew in Brooklyn.

"They thought it was wonderful," Doyle said.

Doyle can remember his father coming home for lunch, his big 1953 Chevrolet double-parked on the street outside. A quick hello to his wife and sons—Howard, Al Jr. and Kevin—and then his father was off to Room 9, the press room at city hall. Doyle played touch football and punchball on Playground 1. His mother served as den mother to his Cub Scout troop. He attended Epiphany Catholic School, and later Power Memorial High School, where Lew Alcindor was a star.

Moving day, August 1, 1947.

Martha Bernard and her husband, Peter, were shaking with anticipation as the moving men hauled their belongings into the newly built thirteen-story building at 605 East Fourteenth Street, the first of thirty-five buildings to open at the vast Stuyvesant Town complex on the Lower East Side. Like tens of thousands of other New Yorkers, they had been unable to find a vacant apartment anywhere in Manhattan. The young couple had lived doubled up, first with family and then with a friend in Greenwich Village. And waited, for a place of their own.

"We were the lucky ones," Bernard recalled sixty-four years later. "There were people dying to get in there. People came back from the war to live with relatives. The greatest thing was to be able to move out and find your own space."[2]

Admittedly conditions were rough. The blocks between Fourteenth and Twenty-Third Streets, east of First Avenue, were mostly a moonscape of half-demolished buildings sitting amid piles of brick and other debris while heavy trucks rumbled along rutted streets and gullies. Her building was surrounded by a fence, behind which the rest of Stuyvesant Town and its sister complex, Peter Cooper Village, would take shape over the next two years. That first year there was no phone service.

"It was a mud hole," she said. "There was nothing but mosquitoes, thousands of mosquitoes and no screens. All we did at night was take pillows and make blood marks on the walls."

But that one-bedroom apartment, with its parquet floors polished to a high sheen, spacious living room and a separate kitchen, was "heaven," said Bernard, eighty-eight, who now lives six blocks to the north in Peter Cooper Village. The difference between the two apartments was not insignificant. A one-bedroom unit in Peter Cooper is a spacious 947 square feet, compared with 755 square feet for the average one-bedroom in Stuyvesant Town.

Thousands of other tenants, 98 percent of them veterans, who followed Bernard in the 1940s and in the succeeding decades shared her sense of elation. For decades, Stuyvesant Town had a ten-year waiting list, making an apartment as hard to come by as the most cherished of New York treasures, season tickets for the Knicks, the Giants or the Yankees.

The Bernards' predicament was by no means unique; city officials estimated that 360,000 families in New York City were living doubled up.[3] Other veterans were living with their families in Quonset huts in Brooklyn. Josephine E. Springer, a captain in the Women's Army Corps, entered Columbia University on the GI Bill and applied for an apartment at Stuyvesant Town.

"The price was right," said Springer, ninety-two, one of the rare unmarried tenants at the time. "It was fresh, clean and had nice grounds. Beautifully maintained. It was like living in a small town. You spoke to everyone in the elevator, at least I did."[4]

Nearly half of the working residents at Stuyvesant Town were professionals, managers and entrepreneurs, according to the 1960 census, while most of the rest were police officers, construction workers, skilled tradesmen and sales workers. At the slightly more upscale Peter Cooper, professionals and managers accounted for two-thirds of the employed residents. Many of the women taught school, some were magazine writers, others worked in the home.

The population explosion that occurred shortly after Stuyvesant Town and Peter Cooper Village opened is the reason that some residents referred to the two complexes as Rabbit Town. By 1950, five years after the war ended, there were over 6,000 children under the age of five living in Stuyvesant Town or Peter Cooper Village, accounting for nearly one-fifth of the 31,173 residents.[5]

"Nine months after it opened, almost everybody had a baby," said Bernard.

Current and former residents say that Stuyvesant Town and Peter Cooper Village were places where you knew your neighbors. Their children often attended the same schools, or at least played on the same Little League teams and in the same playground basketball tournaments. Mothers gathered with their toddlers at other playgrounds with swings and jungle gyms. It was a level of intimacy unknown at most other New York apartment buildings. Many of the original Stuyvesant Town tenants eventually took the traditional middle-class path to a home in the suburbs of New Jersey or Long Island. But thousands stayed, and their children, now adults with their own families, comprise a sizable block of residents.

"I married someone from Long Island," said Stacy Mackey Pfeffer, who grew up in Stuyvesant Town, where her father ran the recreation department, and now lives there with her own family. "Everyone was geared up for us to buy a house on Long Island. I had no interest in moving out of the city, or out of Peter Cooper. I love city living. I wanted to pass it on to my children."[6]

Stuyvesant Town is easily the biggest apartment complex in Manhattan, with thirty-five nearly identical buildings arranged in a symmetrical pattern around the Stuyvesant Oval, a two-acre, tree-shrouded grass lawn at the center of the complex that features a gushing fountain. The red brick facades are relentless, save for the green framed casement windows, especially along the outer borders of the complex where they formed a fortress wall against the surrounding neighborhood. As Ecker planned it, there are no stores or schools inside the complex that might attract outsiders.

There were eight apartments to a floor, each with a similar layout, although the number of bedrooms varied. The standard colors were shades of tan: beige walls and beige-colored metal cabinets in the kitchen, sand-colored porcelain fixtures in the tiled bathrooms. Tenants had to pay extra for a different color scheme. Parquet floors in every room, including the twelve-by-eighteen-feet-seven-inch living room, which was larger than those of many Manhattan apartments and some suburban tract homes. There were two elevators in every building whose red, blue and green enamel interiors were shed during renovations in early 2000.

The twenty-one brick buildings at Peter Cooper Village, where rents were higher, were arranged in more of a herringbone pattern on the blocks between Twentieth and Twenty-Third Streets. But the lobbies were a little nicer and the apartments larger than in Stuyvesant Town. Most important to families was that the apartments had two bathrooms.

In the late 1940s, Hearn's and Gimbels department stores quickly grasped the significance of this new kind of urban middle-class complex and created furniture lines like the Dearborn with beds, dinettes, china cabinets and sofas designed to fit neatly into the apartments. Hearn's went so far as to build a four-room suite in its store at Fourteenth Street and Fifth Avenue to Stuyvesant Town specifications, including modern, postwar furniture and "warm beige for the walls and a deeper beige for the trim." Roving decorators were on hand to assist residents in making fabric choices.[7]

More than half the land at the complexes was given over to pathways, interior roadways, green lawns and fifteen playgrounds at Stuyvesant Town, three at Peter Cooper. Until the last decade, an eighteen-inch post-and-chain fence surrounded the grassy areas, which were off-limits to pedestrians. Metropolitan employed five to six hundred plumbers, painters, maintenance workers (brown uniforms) and security guards (blue uniforms), many of whom lived in Stuyvesant Town, to maintain the property.

The nature of Stuyvesant Town sparked a bitter debate among planners, newspaper columnists and housing experts. The *New York World-Telegram* hailed Stuyvesant Town in 1948 "as an example of private capital's capacity to lick the housing shortage." "Every bathroom and every kitchen are identical," gushed the newspaper. "By including the cost of electricity and gas in the rent, the insurer saved huge sums on metering, clerks and bookkeepers."[8]

But Lewis Mumford, the architecture critic, likened the complexes' rows of featureless brick buildings to "the architecture of the Police State" in a 1948 review published by *The New Yorker.* He deemed the buildings too tall, the apartment foyers too dark and the playgrounds slathered in asphalt, "a caricature of urban rebuilding . . . considering all the benefits it might have derived from beginning at scratch, on a site as large as this." It was a nightmare, he said, "of impersonal regimentation, apparently for people who have no other identity but the serial numbers of their Social Security cards."

Robert Moses, however, was having none of it. He called Mumford's musings "just plain tripe" and defended the vast housing complex as an outstanding accomplishment. He said Stuyvesant Town's buildings housed more tenants than the tenement "rookeries" they replaced, but the structures took up less than 25 percent of the land, leaving most of the property for tree-shaded lawns and playgrounds. As a practical matter, Moses said, neither Metropolitan nor the public housing officials could afford to build quaint two-story cottages housing a hundred people an acre on slum land that cost $8 to $10 a square foot.[9]

The raging debate was met with a shrug by most residents, who forged close bonds over their shared experiences within the uniform confines of Stuyvesant Town and Peter Cooper, be it in the hallways or on the playgrounds. The *New York Herald Tribune* seemed to capture the sentiment with its headline for a December 9, 1956, story about the complex: "We live in a 'barracks'—and like it."

Daniel Garodnick, whose mother moved into Stuyvesant Town in 1968, before he was born, can still recall the names of his neighbors. Seymour Altman, who lived in apartment 13A and worked in the nearby fur district, taught him how to play blackjack over Tetley tea at the kitchen table. Al Chappel, in 13F, spoke several languages and served as Garodnick's Spanish tutor when he was in high school. "I always had a close relationship with the neighbors in our hallway," he said.[10]

The playgrounds proved to be an important nexus for residents, at least the boys. Playgrounds 9 and 11 were where they played highly competitive basketball. A few Jewish residents also recall instances where Catholic boys on Playground 9 hurled anti-Semitic taunts, which led them to confine their basketball to Playground 11. There were also games of punchball and a quieter playground for mothers and their younger children. In the spring, there were Little League games on a field near the East River and the massive Con Edison power plant.

"For guys growing up, sports was very central," Steven Sanders, a former state assemblyman who grew up there, said. "There was always a football game. There were rivalries between the playgrounds. It took on a religious fervor."[11]

MetLife was very careful in its tenant selection, seeking the same uniformity in its residents as it had achieved in the design of the buildings. The company preferred married couples with steady jobs and sent employees to interview every prospective tenant. Elaine T. Haber and her husband Dr. Leonard D. Weinberg, a doctor and army veteran who died in 1950, were living with Haber's parents in a two-bedroom apartment on the Grand Concourse in the Bronx when MetLife came calling.

"They wanted to know if we paid our rent on time," recalled Haber, who lives in Peter Cooper Village. "They wanted to see our bank books, which were practically nil. I guess they felt we had potential, a doctor and a teacher making a pittance."[12]

After her first husband died, Haber remarried and moved from Stuyvesant Town to Peter Cooper, where she chose an apartment overlooking the basketball courts so she could watch her son Eric play ball.

Thirty years later, MetLife was still checking. "Somebody came over to make sure I didn't have any pets lurking around, that I seemed like a good upstanding citizen," said Susan Steinberg, who moved into Stuyvesant Town in 1980, after her Upper East Side apartment building was converted to a cooperative. "In those days you were shown a layout of the apartment but you couldn't go and view it."[13]

At one point, there was a twenty-year waiting list for Peter Cooper Village and a fourteen-year waiting list for Stuyvesant Town, said Mitch Ryan, a MetLife housing director.[14] Of course, there were always exceptions if you knew "someone" at MetLife or Stuyvesant Town. MetLife kept about a hundred apartments for its executives, including those rotating through the New York office. "It was a safe, conservative, employee-friendly institution," said Harry P. Kamen, a MetLife employee for thirty-nine years and chairman of the company from 1993 to 1997. "There was a good pension you could depend on. A lot of people who worked there also lived in Stuyvesant Town-Peter Cooper, so you could walk to work."[15]

Kamen himself lived in Peter Cooper for fifteen years, beginning in 1962.

It was not just MetLife executives who lived in the complexes. Carmela Garcea, seventy-eight, who is retired and living in Peter Cooper Village, worked for many years as a banquet coordinator at MetLife headquarters, only six blocks away on Madison Avenue, between Twenty-Third and Twenty-Fifth Streets. Headquarters was a small city complete with a medical clinic staffed with doctors and nurses, dental offices, a tailor, a commissary and twenty-one underground cafeterias that, Garcea said, "served nineteen thousand five hundred people every day for free."[16]

Mistresses tied to senior executives also shot to the top of the waiting list. It was also good politics to accommodate Police Commissioners Lee P. Brown and Howard Leary and the top FBI official in New York in the 1990s, James Fox. Police officers were given priority, as were FBI agents after MetLife hired a former FBI official to head its security force.

Martha Bernard, eighty-eight, kept the secret about her entry to Stuyvesant Town for more than six decades. Unlike most tenants, neither she nor her husband was a veteran. Her father, Isadore Binswanger, president of Thomson-Porcelite Paint Company in Philadelphia, put in a call to a senior officer at MetLife asking for help. His company supplied all the paint for Stuyvesant Town, Peter Cooper and Parkchester. "You had to be married to a veteran," she said with a giggle. "But we got in surreptitiously because of the pull I've never mentioned publicly before."[17]

It took Richard Toes, a former New York City narcotics detective, a while to find his connection. It turned out that a low-level bookie he knew had a relative working in the administration office. "It was really hard getting in here," said Toes, who has lived in Stuyvesant Town for thirty-three years. "Some people wondered if there really was a list, or was it just a way to keep some people out until they found someone they wanted."[18]

Once tenants got into Stuyvesant Town or Peter Cooper Village, they encountered MetLife's rules of engagement, which were in keeping with the regimented layout of the buildings: No pets. No walking on the grass. Carpets must cover the wood floors to muffle footsteps. No double parking. Bicycles were banned from the footpaths in the 1950s when kids started careening around the complex in packs of forty. And woe to anyone who broke the rules.

"If there was an infraction and security came to your apartment, the world stopped," said John Marsh, a tenant leader who lives in the same Peter Cooper Village apartment once occupied by his father. "There was a deep sense of law and order. Then, it felt oppressive, but now I think about it with a deep sense of melancholy."[19]

"It felt like a military camp at times," said Joseph Strasburg, who lived in Stuyvesant Town from 1977 to 1987, before buying a condominium on Staten Island. "When I moved in you couldn't have an air conditioner because the wiring wasn't up to standards. If you turned on the TV and plugged in a hair dryer at the same time, the electricity went out. They'd confiscate it if they found one."[20]

Denis Delaney, a second-generation resident, said the regulated environment seemed appropriate for a generation coming back from the war. His father, Raymond, he said, went from driving a milk wagon to the Civil Conservation Corps and then the army; he saw combat in Europe. After the war, he landed a job with the city's transit system, as a motorman. "My father's generation followed the rules," he said. "It didn't mean they liked them, but they liked living there."[21]

Delaney himself owned a bar for nearly twenty years in the 1980s and 1990s called First Avenue, across the street from Stuyvesant Town. He wanted to attract patrons interested in a short beer or Dom Perignon, but it was also marketed directly at Stuyvesant Town. First Avenue was known for its meat-locker temperature in the summertime, when the air-conditioner-less apartments were sweltering. He became a keen observer of the Stuyvesant Town culture.

"The identities were Jewish and Irish Catholic," Delaney said. "There were a lot of Protestants, but it divided up almost by schools. The Jewish kids went mainly to the public schools. Catholics almost exclusively to the parochial schools."

Many of the schools were within easy walking distance: Immaculate Conception on Thirteenth Street, just south of Stuyvesant Town; Epiphany, at Second Avenue and Twenty-Second Street; St. Emeric's, on East Twelfth Street at Avenue D; Public School 40 on Twentieth Street, between First and Second Avenues; and Public School 61, on Twelfth Street and Avenue B. If the lives of the Irish and Jewish youngsters revolved around their respective schools, they did mix on Little League teams, or in playground games of dodgeball.

Stuyvesant Town children were often warned not to venture south into the poorer, scrappier neighborhoods of the Lower East Side, where many Puerto Rican families lived. And MetLife's security guards kept a vigilant eye out for intruders. There were no gang wars. But on the rare occasion when Puerto Rican youths did venture onto Stuyvesant Town playgrounds in the 1960s and 1970s, local teenagers were very territorial. Word of the incursion leaped from playground to playground like lightning and suddenly the knots of teenagers were lined up on opposing sides like the Jets and the Sharks.

"The word would go out, 'There's a bunch of Spics on the playground,'" said Gerald O'Neil, fifty-six, a heavyset man with a reddish beard streaked with white, who described the scene sheepishly. His parents, Bill and Patricia, never swore, at least not in front of their four children, or uttered racial epithets. His friends referred to them as Ward and June Cleaver, for their straight-as-an-arrow, *Leave It to Beaver* style. "Kids would grab baseball bats, basketballs, whatever, and sometimes things got out of hand. But I don't recall anyone really getting hurt. It was more about teenage chest-thumping. We had a pretty limited exposure to blacks and Puerto Ricans, until later."[22]

As much as the residents praised Mother Met's paternalism and its management of the development, they went toe-to-toe with the giant insurer right from the beginning over rents, establishing the tenor of tenant-landlord relations that survives today. The often quiescent tenants of the 1950s and 1960s rose up in opposition to every rent hike proposed by Metropolitan, painting each request as a direct assault on the ability of not only Stuyvesant Town residents but also of the entire middle class to live and prosper in Manhattan. For many residents, salaries and wages rose only modestly even as families at Rabbit Town grew larger. Every rent increase put more pressure on the family budget.

Ecker set the rents for Stuyvesant Town in 1947, only months before tenants began moving into the first completed building. When La Guardia and Ecker announced the project in 1943 they said the apartments would rent for $14 a room per month. But the cost of building the development had gone way beyond the original estimate in 1943 of $40 million to $50 million.

Under the terms of the contract with the city and the state's Redevelopment Companies Law, Metropolitan had to get approval from the Board of Estimate, whose members included the mayor, the comptroller and the five borough presidents, for any rent increase needed to cover costs. The agreements also entitled Metropolitan to a 6 percent return on its investment.

With support from Moses, Metropolitan later got the approval and raised the rents to $17 a room per month, or $68 for a four-room apartment. Ecker said that the cost of the complex had doubled to an estimated $90 million, because of higher-than-anticipated construction costs. He got a similar rent increase for Riverton, the complex in Harlem, at the same time.

In 1952, Metropolitan went back to the city asking for an average rent hike of 46 percent to $24.87 a month per room, from $17, or nearly $100 a month for a four-room apartment. The company said the increase was necessary because the final price tag for Stuyvesant Town came to $112.2 million. "Even with the increase requested in our application," Metropolitan said in a letter to tenants, "the residential and commercial rents will yield a return substantially less than the return provided by the statute and the contract with the city."

This time there were tenants in place and they vehemently opposed the increase. Glenn C. Fowler, chairman of the Stuyvesant Town Joint Tenants' Organizations Committee, denounced Metropolitan and called on city officials to reject the request. One tenant, Lotte N. Doverman, framed the issue in a letter published in the *New York Times* as "a dilemma that is of most serious and immediate concern to a good many local members of our 'vanishing middle class.'"[23]

Metropolitan countered with a public relations campaign replete with full-page ads in *Town & Village* and *The Villager,* as well as a series of letters and leaflets placed under residents' doors, on the reasonableness of the company's request. "There Is No 'Profit' in Stuyvesant Town," one ad declared, adding, "At present there is not even a reasonable return on the investment."[24]

At the same time, the company said it was making a 4 percent return on its investment, less than the 6 percent profit that it was entitled to. Yet, Metropolitan argued, the company also had to put aside money for capital improvements, deal with 55,000 requests annually for repairs and stockpile 40,000 lightbulbs a year for upkeep and 20,000 pounds of salt for keeping walkways clear of ice.

Six hundred tenants, many in suits or dresses and cradling infants, packed the city hall hearing room on May 19, 1952, cheering on speaker after speaker who urged members of the Board of Estimate to vote down the rent increase or postpone action. Fowler, the tenant leader, spoke in favor of a bill that would prohibit rent increases at Stuyvesant Town altogether. The board voted fifteen to one to deny Metropolitan's application.[25]

Frank Reavis, counsel for Metropolitan, said afterward that the company would file suit in the state supreme court to reverse the board's action. Two months later, the court sided with Metropolitan, ruling that the company could increase rents by an average of $2.55 per room monthly each year for three years. In the fourth year, the company was permitted to raise the rent by another $3 per room.

The court said: "The correct and proper action by the Board of Estimate on the application presented required the grant to petitioners of the increase of the maximum average rental per room per month to an amount sufficient to provide a six percent return on the investment in accordance with the contract and the statute."[26]

But the pattern was established. MetLife's attempts to raise rents at the complex met with resistance from tenants and elected officials in 1961, 1963 and 1970, when the company wanted to set the average monthly rent at $56.48. Opponents argued that the rent would provide MetLife with a whopping 14 percent return. While MetLife insisted that the average annual family income at Stuyvesant Town was a comfortable $12,500, elected officials testified at one public hearing that 70 percent of the families surveyed at Stuyvesant Town had a take-home pay of less than $8,400 a year, and more than a quarter of the families relied primarily on their pension checks to pay the rent. Moving to cheaper quarters, they said, was not an option given the city's continuing housing shortage.

The insurer argued in turn that the rent hike was necessary to provide an adequate return and to make up for prior years when MetLife failed to make a 6 percent return. It claimed that it had fallen short during those years by $20.4 million and needed to make it up with the rent hike. The Board of Estimate routinely rejected the requests, while the courts ruled again and again in MetLife's favor, but not before the company took a battering in the court of public opinion.

Stuyvesant Town served as the quintessential illustration of the plight of the middle class in an article in the *New York Times*. A two-bedroom apartment rented for $62 to $87 a month when the complex opened in 1947. Seven increases later, in 1967, that same two-bedroom rented for $138 to $173.50 a month. Although some of the increase was offset by rising wages, the *Times* noted, "it costs more than twice as much to live in Stuyvesant Town today than 20 years ago."[27]

The picket lines, petitioning and raging debates at city hall in the battle to desegregate Stuyvesant Town subsided by the mid-1950s. But the issue and Stuyvesant Town's reputation as a no-go zone for African-Americans never went away. In May 1968, the city's Human Rights Commission launched a broadside against MetLife, charging that the company had engaged in "a deliberate, intentional and systemic" exclusion of Negroes and Hispanics from Stuyvesant Town-Peter Cooper Village and Parkchester, in the Bronx. The complaint followed two years of negotiations between the company and the commission, which had combed through MetLife's tenant records. The company routinely discouraged Negro and Puerto Rican tenants from applying to the three complexes, the commissioner said, referring them instead to MetLife's "black property," Riverton, in Harlem.

The commission said that minorities knew that applying to Stuyvesant Town-Peter Cooper Village and Parkchester would be "futile, embarrassing or degrading," because of the company's "open and notorious past exclusion of Negroes and Puerto Ricans from its 'white' properties."[28]

Only twenty-five Negroes and Puerto Ricans had ever rented apartments at Parkchester, the commission said, yet there were four hundred vacancies a year at the Bronx development. At Stuyvesant Town, where the top monthly rent was $213 a month for a three-bedroom apartment, fewer than fifty units were occupied by Negro or Puerto Rican families.

MetLife flatly denied that it discriminated against blacks and Latinos. Weeks later, however, the company held a joint press conference with the commission, promising to bypass its waiting lists and funnel qualified black applicants to the three complexes. The company was far more interested in burnishing its image on race relations in 1968, with the civil rights movement in high gear, than it was in 1947.

As the Human Rights Commission was making headlines, John "Butch" Purcell III, who had grown up in MetLife's Riverton complex, sought an apartment at Stuyvesant Town. A college graduate and newly married, Purcell called the recreation director at Stuyvesant Town, Edward W. Mackey. The two men knew each other well. Purcell, a standout basketball player at Rice High School, a Catholic prep school, had worked for Mackey at the recreation department for six months in 1965 and knew many of the young people there and their parents through the popular basketball league.

Mackey, a broad-shouldered man with red hair, green eyes and an abundance of charm, had been a minor league pitcher for the St. Louis Cardinals organization before going to work at Stuyvesant Town. A legendary figure at the complexes, Mackey, who died in 2004, had started many of the sports leagues, from punchball to basketball, as well as the arts-and-crafts programs.

His response to Purcell's request was immediate. "Where do you want to live?" he asked. "How much do you want to pay?"[29]

Purcell and his wife, Mary, director of human resources for the William Randolph Hearst Foundation, moved into a one-bedroom apartment renting for $129 a month, near Playground 9. "I wanted to be next to the playground with the best court, the best players," Purcell said.

His good fortune was connected to an accident of timing and the fact that he, like so many white tenants before him, had an "in" at MetLife. "I was the fifth black family," Purcell recounted over a beer at Quigley's, a tavern across First Avenue from Stuyvesant Town, where many customers stop by to say hello. "Once I got in, it was a piece of cake. I was close to a few of the Knickerbockers. I got an apartment for Dick Barnett and Dean Meminger. I must've been responsible for fifteen to twenty families in my years here."

Aside from a few uncomfortable encounters, Purcell, still a bull of a man at sixty-seven, said he has loved living in the complex. "My acceptance in Stuyvesant Town, they knew me already," he said. "But it had nothing to do with being black. I was a Catholic and an athlete. So I just went with it."

The color line did become more porous after 1968, although blacks never made up more than 5 percent of the residents. In 1970, Joseph and Lydia Brown, an interracial couple with two daughters at the time, had little trouble getting a two-bedroom apartment on Fourteenth Street. Lydia Brown, who is white, said it was a matter of timing. "Joe was the right color at the time," she said.[30]

They were drawn to the complex by the parklike setting and the affordable rents. But for Joseph Brown, who had grown up ten blocks to the south at the Lillian Wald Projects, there was a measure of irony. As a teenager, he and his friends frequently rode their bicycles up to Stuyvesant Town, only to be turned away by the complex's ever-vigilant security guards.

"It was like another world," said Brown, sixty-six, sitting at the kitchen table underneath the whirling fan of a first-floor apartment where few changes had been made since 1947. "It was literally across the tracks. People didn't even aspire to live here, it was so far removed."[31]

Rumors swept through Stuyvesant Town-Peter Cooper Village in the fall of 1972 that MetLife had signed a contract to sell the two complexes to Harry B. Helmsley, one of the city's biggest real estate tycoons. Residents feared that a new owner would jack up the rents to prohibitive levels, forcing them out of their homes.[32] MetLife seemed to be tiring of its role as landlord to thirty-four thousand families and Helmsley, who controlled the Empire State Building and Plaza Hotel as well as dozens of other properties, was an eager buyer.

Helmsley had bought MetLife's 12,271-unit Parkchester complex in 1968, for $90 million. Two year later, he picked up Parkmerced, the insurance company's sprawling complex of apartment towers and garden apartments near Lake Merced in San Francisco, for $40 million. Helmsley's plan was to convert the complexes to condominiums and make a fortune selling them off unit by unit. MetLife had also unloaded Parkfairfax, the 202-acre complex with a mix of town houses and apartments outside of Washington, DC, selling it for $9.8 million to Arlen Realty.

Stuyvesant Town's valuable property tax exemption was due to expire in 1974 and tenants feared their apartments were next on the hit list. The complex's assessment had been frozen at $13.5 million since 1949 under MetLife's original tax exemption from the city. By 1974, MetLife valued the property at $89.35 million. It had paid just under $1 million in taxes a year earlier, but would have had to pay over $6 million without the exemption.[33] Instead of watching the exemption expire, MetLife could reap a high sale price and get out of the landlord business, the thinking went. Nearly half a century later, the complexes would sell for $5.4 billion.

"Almost every year, especially in the seventies, there was talk about three things, none of which ever came to fruition," recalled Sanders, a lifelong resident of Stuyvesant Town and Peter Cooper Village. "MetLife would sell. Maybe there'd be a co-op or condominium conversion."[34]

The company itself seemed to be of two minds, denying rumors of sale, but at the same time acknowledging that the old place just didn't generate the returns it once did. "The bottom line is net profit," Charles T. Cunneen, MetLife's senior vice president for housing investments and real estate financing, said at one point. "In the beginning, the landlord role fit quite nicely into our image. It filled a social need and it was an opportunity for long-term investment with an adequate return."[35]

In May 1973, MetLife sent a letter to tenants announcing that it was considering a sale. But even if the development was not sold, the company warned, the end of the tax abatement in June 1974 would "require a substantial increase in Stuyvesant Town rentals." It anticipated that its property tax bill would jump by $5.2 million a year. By August, *Town & Village* reported that some residents did not want to wait for a new buyer to emerge. Instead, they were investigating a plan in which the tenants themselves would buy Stuyvesant Town and convert the complex to a cooperative.

"It dawned on people that when the tax abatement ended, Stuyvesant Town would become free market—rents at the whim of the owner," said Steven Sanders, a second-generation resident who was then vice president of the tenants' association. "The rents would immediately go up just because it would now include all these taxes."[36]

State senator Roy Goodman, who represented the East Side, including Stuyvesant Town and Peter Cooper, and Assemblyman

Andrew Stein worked closely with the tenant association exploring whether the tax abatement could be extended. They also sought to persuade MetLife to take the property off the auction block. But at least initially, the insurance company was unenthusiastic. The city, in its view, had reneged so many times on its agreement, forcing them to go to court to get rent increases. The company was tired of being portrayed as the evil landlord in the periodic scrums with elected officials and tenants.

Goodman and Stein, however, kept at it. They drummed up support in Albany, where the state legislature met, and continued talking to MetLife on behalf of the tenants. The residents of Stuyvesant Town and Peter Cooper Village always had an outsize political voice that elected officials keenly heeded. The reasoning was simple. There was the sheer number of people who lived there and their propensity to vote. Since the end of World War II, the district had been represented by a mix of Democratic and Republican politicians, several of whom went on to become mayor. They included Congressmen Edward I. Koch and John V. Lindsay, as well as Goodman and Stein, all of whom paid close attention to complaints and political trends at the complexes. By the late 1970s, the tenants elected one of their neighbors to office.

"I was the first public official representing Stuyvesant Town-Peter Cooper Village to actually live there," said Sanders, who was elected in 1978 to the state assembly, where he represented the district until 2005. "There was the sheer size of it. Stuyvesant Town-Peter Cooper Village comprised at least a quarter of my assembly district. If you calculated the voting population, it was thirty percent of the district."

For two years, the fate of Stuyvesant Town and Peter Cooper seemed to hang on the diplomacy of the elected officials and the conflicting views of the upper echelons at MetLife. Despite the prior rent battles, the tenants were ready to stick with the devil they knew.

"Since Metropolitan Life will have recovered their initial capital investment and will own the property free and clear, it seems to us that their continued ownership, with or without a tax abatement, would be a profitable investment for them, while maintaining moderate income residences for families," Charles Lyman, president of the tenants association said at the time. "We hope that they will reconsider and decide to continue ownership of the property. Aside from questions and disputes regarding rent increases, we can only commend Metropolitan Life for their general excellence as landlords."[37]

"The tenants of Stuyvesant Town do not want any outside investors taking over Stuyvesant Town," he added. "Since we are all captives of the housing market, we know that these investors will exploit tenants unmercifully."

Dismayed by the negative press surrounding the affair, MetLife president Richard R. Shinn met Goodman at an unprecedented "summit meeting" where he denied that the company was involved in any sale negotiations. He acknowledged the importance of retaining lower-middle and middle-class people in New York and assured the state senator that "Met does care about the tenants and is genuinely desirous of being cooperative." But, he cautioned, the company was still trying to determine whether it could, or even wanted to, retain ownership of the development.

"Metropolitan has 48 million policyholders," Shinn said, "and the company must get an adequate return on its investments for them."[38]

Shinn said that the company had fallen $23 million short of

recouping a 6 percent return in 1972 and still needed to invest another $25 million to upgrade the electrical wiring at Stuyvesant Town so that tenants could use air conditioners without causing a blackout.

Still, in December 1973, the tenants and their elected officials seemed to be suffering whiplash. Shinn told Stein and Goodman that "Met now has a policy not to continue to own Stuyvesant Town," and he revealed that Peter Cooper was also on the block. Nevertheless, Shinn, who acknowledged that many Stuyvesant Town tenants were Met employees, said that the company realized that it was important to keep lower-middle and middle-income residents in the city. A shocked Stein, besieged by calls from panicky tenants, said, MetLife is throwing Stuyvesant Town to the "real estate wolves of the city."[39]

But the following month, Frank M. Lieher, the resident manager at Stuyvesant Town, seemed to take a step backward in a letter to tenants. He said that the company was not in negotiations to sell the property to a private investor or the tenants. "It is our intention," he said, "to offer Stuyvesant Town for sale at an appropriate time." He also stated a willingness to at least consider some form of tax abatement.[40]

MetLife also let it be known that the expiration of the twenty-five-year tax abatement in 1974 would be followed by rent hikes of as much as 50 percent to cover the increased taxes, operating expenses and new capital investments.

The tenants' association ultimately decided against pursuing a plan to convert the property to a cooperative, in which existing tenants would be able to essentially buy their apartment at a discount from market prices. There were residents who favored the idea, mainly the Ad Hoc Committee for Self-

Ownership of Stuyvesant Town. "MetLife wants to sell," explained Rubin Singer, a member of the ad hoc committee who rented his first apartment in 1948. "We residents want to be prepared with a plan to buy. Why should we let some outside speculator take over?"[41]

But many older tenants, now living on small pensions and social security, wanted to remain as rent-regulated tenants. Four out of every ten residents of Rabbit Town were now fifty-five and older; the baby boom had petered out. Goodman's proposal to convert Stuyvesant Town into a nonprofit rental housing development also failed to gain any traction.

At Parkchester, Harry Helmsley had met with stiff resistance from tenants as he converted the rental complex to condominiums. The drama at Stuyvesant Town was also playing out as the city teetered at the edge of bankruptcy amid the worst economic and fiscal crisis in New York history. Manufacturers were heading south and many of the city's corporate headquarters were relocating to the suburbs.

"Does N.Y. realize it will lose a large percent of its middle class—which it can ill afford to lose," asked one tenant responding to a poll by *Town & Village*. "This is the only plan that would keep us in Stuyvesant Town," said another, C. Anzel. "I am one of the original tenants."[42]

"Our toughest fight is ahead," Lyman, the tenant association president, told a meeting of a thousand tenants and a long list of elected officials, including Stein, Koch, Goodman and council members Miriam Friedlander and Henry Stern, at Stuyvesant High School. "We must convince the city of New York to take a tax abatement, even though there is a huge city budget deficit.

"We must also convince Met. Met has gotten back all of the

money they invested in Stuyvesant Town to build it, and more than 50 percent of the annual rent is pure profit. And that's plenty of profit."[43]

Convince they did. Only days before the tax exemption was due to expire in June 1974, the state legislature approved a bill sponsored by Goodman that provided a ten-year extension of the tax abatement at Stuyvesant Town, Riverton and fourteen other complexes built by redevelopment companies, included under the state's moderate-and-middle-income housing program, known as Mitchell-Lama. The abatement would decrease by 10 percent a year until it was entirely phased out. The apartments would also come under the rent stabilization laws, which regulate the percent increase a landlord can raise the rent.

The legislation cited the "undue hardship and dislocation" if the tax exemption was allowed to expire. "Stuyvesant Town has a wealthy image because of some judges and commissioners who live there," said Assemblyman Stein. "In fact, a large percentage of the tenants are elderly people on fixed incomes."

A spokesman for MetLife seemed resigned. "Some tenants think that because we are a large company, we need not be too concerned about yields," he told the *New York Times*. "They expect more from us than other landlords. We are more susceptible to public relations problems than private landlords . . . However, we recognize that you can't please everybody."[44]

To this day, Sanders said, he was puzzled by MetLife's decision to accept the tenant-supported deal in Albany. The company was "reasonably acquiescent" to the proposal, which might have fallen apart, he said, if MetLife had opposed the extension vociferously. Ironically, the legislation brought the development under the rent stabilization laws and the Rent Guidelines Board, which restricted rent increases, usually, to 3 or 4 percent a year. For most landlords, rent stabilization is the bane of their existence.

"I'm not sure I fully understand it," Sanders said, "in the context of tenant-landlord relations today. Years later, MetLife may have come to rue what they did."[45]

Stuyvesant Town-Peter Cooper Village regained its footing in the 1980s, after suffering through a recession, the city's fiscal crisis and the loss of both manufacturing and headquarters jobs during the prior decade. State and city government eliminated one hundred thousand jobs. Crime and drugs had become a preoccupation in the 1960s and early 1970s in these once-impregnable complexes, much as they had in the rest of the city. Tenants complained of drug sales on the periphery of the playgrounds and called on MetLife to hire doormen for each building after a twenty-nine-year-old woman was raped and robbed in the lobby of her building. The company initially rebuffed the demands, but in 1967 it did install locks on the front doors of Peter Cooper Village buildings and a lobby-to-apartment intercom system. Stuyvesant Town's turn came three years later.

In response to a sharp rise in crime in 1972, state senator Roy Goodman called on MetLife to increase the size of its security force by 20 percent. He told a meeting of MetLife executives and the Town and Village Civic Association that serious violent crimes had climbed 327 percent over the past three years with no increase in either security guards or patrol officers. Raymond Ringler, the vice president of housing, told the group that the complexes were not immune to what was happening throughout the city. "However," he added, "it is the government's responsibility to provide adequate protection and safeguards for its citizens and not primarily ours." Goodman marched over to the Thirteenth Precinct house and within hours, "11 tough members of the Tactical Police Force were assigned exclusively to the community," *Town & Village* reported.[46]

By 1981, Stuyvesant Town was rated the safest neighborhood in New York, followed by Roosevelt Island, TriBeCa and Little Italy, according to a survey by *New York* magazine. "Manhattan's Stuyvesant Town-Peter Cooper Village, for one, recorded less crime last year than many upstate hamlets—less than one burglary and one robbery per thousand residents." That record stood in stark contrast to New York City as a whole, which averaged thirty burglaries and fourteen robberies per thousand.[47]

The kudos kept coming. A year later, the *Daily News* Sunday magazine ranked MetLife among the city's best landlords. It was quite a coup in a city where citizens generally regard landlords like the archvillain Snidely Whiplash. "A leaky pipe at midnight on a weekend is no problem in Peter Cooper," Mary T. Donahue told the magazine. "Efficient, courteous help is on the way in 10 minutes."[48]

The long-suffering tenants of Stuyvesant Town finally got air-conditioning in 1991, when MetLife invested $100 million in rewiring the thirty-five buildings and replacing fifty-seven thousand leaky, steel-framed windows. Peter Cooper had had air-conditioning since the 1960s. But this being Stuyvesant Town, change did not come easily. The $70 million rewiring effort took a series of delicate negotiations between Mitchell E. Ryan, then MetLife's director of housing investments; Assemblyman Steve Sanders; the state housing agency; the tenants' association; and Con Edison.

Even MetLife executives seemed to be in a more optimistic frame of mind when it came to their Stuyvesant Town asset, compared with their approach during the tax-exemption battle in 1974, when the company expressed a desire to unload the cash-strapped property. They clearly did not like being hampered by the city's rent-stabilization law, which limited the size of rent increases for one- and two-year leases.

"We have never offered the property for sale," Charles T. Cunneen, a MetLife senior vice president said in 1984. "There may come a day when the bottom line forces us to do it. But while stabilization is a bad thing for housing stock, we are making a profit."

CHAPTER FOUR

Who Would Drive the Last Dollar?

Eleven minutes after the closing bell at the New York Stock Exchange on July 18, 2006, MetLife issued a brief, five-paragraph press release announcing that it was considering the sale of Stuyvesant Town-Peter Cooper Village. "We believe current market conditions are very favorable, and we have decided to test the market to gauge buyer interest in these properties," said the release, quoting Robert R. Merck, the company's head of real estate investments. "MetLife believes there is a lot of capital seeking high-quality real estate of this caliber and anticipates that it will see excellent market pricing for these properties."

But Merck, who labored in MetLife's real estate office in Morristown, New Jersey, thirty-two miles west of Manhattan, sounded one note of caution: "Should market pricing not reflect our expectations, we will not sell the properties at this time."

He needn't have bothered. The real estate market was in a frenzy with billions upon billions of dollars from sovereign funds, foreign and domestic pension funds and private investors chasing real estate deals across the country. It was also easy to obtain loans from the Wall Street banks, no matter what the size of the mortgage. The volume of deals in excess of $5 million for real estate—be it residential complexes, office buildings, hotels, malls or industrial property—more than tripled to $314.9 billion by the end of 2005, from $82.7 billion in 2001, according to Real Capital Analytics. And it showed no signs of abating.

The MetLife announcement was a lot like a silent alarm going off at a bank for real estate investors. They scrambled like the police for a possible siege, while the public went about its business oblivious to the unfolding drama. In this case, Merck's pronouncement dominated discussions in the offices of real estate tycoons, speculators and bankers, who immediately started thumbing through their mental Rolodexes for bankers and investment partners for what was surely going to be a heated auction.

"This was the mama of all residential offerings and you knew it was selling into a piping-hot climate for large deals," said Doug Harmon, a top national sales broker based in New York.[1] With debt and equity in plentiful supply, the number of multifamily property sales nationally soared in 2005 to 4,317, worth $89.8 billion, from 1,397 transactions in 2002 worth $23.7 billion. In Manhattan alone, 292 apartment complexes changed hands in 2005 for a total of $8.23 billion, up from 36 deals in 2002 worth $1 billion.[2]

In 2005, Harmon had overseen the sale of Parkmerced in San Francisco, a 3,483-unit complex on 150 acres that MetLife had sold off in 1968. He sold Parkmerced to Stellar Management and the Rockpoint Group for almost $700 million in one of the largest apartment deals ever done on the West Coast.

With prices skyrocketing, these were heady days for brokers.

A sales commission for prime commercial property might be half a percentage point of the sale price, or $4.5 million on a $900 million transaction. But for the biggest deals, the commission was just another negotiating point. Sellers were loath to hand over so much money to the broker. Instead, they offered a smaller percentage of the price, assuring the broker that a rival company would accept the sum. Still, the broker was confident of making millions of dollars upon closing. Rarely, however, would a broker discuss a commission with anyone outside of the industry.

Over the July 4 holiday weekend, Harmon had completed the sale of 1211 Avenue of the Americas, a forty-five-story modernist office tower in Manhattan that had drawn a raft of bidders for a relatively nondescript building between Forty-Seventh and Forty-Eighth Streets. It was where Rupert Murdoch and News America made their home. But in yet another sign of an overheated market, a half dozen bidders, including Rob Speyer of Tishman Speyer, offered $1.5 billion for the property. That was more than double the $600 million that the owner, the German investment group Jamestown, had paid for the building only six years earlier. Beacon Capital edged out the competition with an offer of $1.52 billion. The sale came in second only to the $1.72 billion sale of the MetLife Building as the highest price paid for an American office building.

Hours before the announcement on July 18, C. Robert Henrikson, MetLife's new chairman and chief executive, introduced himself to Mayor Michael R. Bloomberg at city hall. Not wanting the city's top official to be caught unaware, Henrikson told Bloomberg that the company was putting Stuyvesant Town-Peter Cooper Village on the auction block.

Meanwhile, the Stuyvesant Town-Peter Cooper Village

tenants remained largely oblivious to the behind-the-scenes maneuvering over the fate of their homes for nearly two months.

Just prior to the announcement, Merck telephoned the top real estate brokers at four firms—CB Richard Ellis, Cushman & Wakefield, Eastdil Secured and Goldman Sachs—inviting them to compete in what is known in the business as a "beauty contest" to run the sale of Stuyvesant Town-Peter Cooper Village. He did not have to explain the enormity of what was at stake: 110 buildings, 11,232 apartments on 80 acres in one of the most lucrative real estate markets in the country. It would almost certainly fetch the highest price ever for a single asset at a time when the appetite for real estate, especially New York real estate, appeared insatiable. The fees could be substantial, but more important, a deal this big could be a career maker, one that generated fame and a roster of new clients.

Merck, a twenty-four-year veteran of MetLife, was all business when he reached Darcy Stacom, the top sales broker at CB Richard Ellis, who was outside Grand Central Terminal on Forty-Second Street. "We're announcing the sale of Stuyvesant Town and Peter Cooper Village," Merck said. "We're issuing an RFP [request for proposals] to four firms. You've got a week to prepare a presentation and we expect full underwriting."[3]

Around the same time, Harry E. Giannoulis, president of the Parkside Group and a longtime lobbyist for MetLife, placed a courtesy call to Daniel Garodnick, the city councilman who represented Stuyvesant Town and a lifelong resident of the complexes. "I just want to let you know," Giannoulis said, "MetLife is putting Stuyvesant Town and Peter Cooper Village up for sale."[4]

Garodnick, who had been elected to the council in November, dropped back into a chair in his council office at 250

Broadway, across the street from city hall. He brought the staff meeting he was holding to an abrupt end. Now what? he asked his aides.

"It's not every day that twenty percent of your district goes up for sale," he thought. "This is going to be a mess. People are going to be very scared about the future."[5] A new owner paying top dollar for the complexes would almost certainly seek to eject longtime residents from their homes to make way for tenants willing to pay far higher rents. The thirty-seven-year-old lawyer and councilman spent hours sitting by himself trying to puzzle out what to do next. Could he try to block the sale through some regulatory mechanism, providing that one even existed? Or could the tenants themselves try to compete for the complexes in the rarified world of billion-dollar real estate deals?

But even as Garodnick struggled to digest the shocking news, many real estate moguls took the announcement in stride, jotting down back-of-the-envelope calculations of the property's potential worth. Clearly, it was worth billions and a competitive auction would drive the number higher.

Several companies had approached MetLife over the years to talk about buying Stuyvesant Town and Peter Cooper Village. After all, MetLife had sold off every other major residential property—Riverton and Parkchester in New York; Parkfairfax in Alexandria, Virginia; Parkmerced in San Francisco; and Park La Brea in Los Angeles—decades earlier.

As far back as 1994, Richard Ravitch, a former developer who had turned around the city's subway system in the 1980s while serving as chairman of the Metropolitan Transportation Authority, had put a proposal before MetLife's chairman at the time, Harry P. Kamen. Ravitch and Harold S. Jensen, a successful Chicago developer who had ties to MetLife, wanted to convert Peter Cooper Village, the more upscale of the two East Side complexes, into condominiums. But Mitchell E. Ryan, the MetLife housing director at the time, persuaded Kamen and the MetLife board to oppose the idea. "We were kind of Mother Met, a benevolent mother," said Ryan, who left the company in 2004. "We were really about trying to do the best for tenants and keep it an affordable place to live. We weren't trying to squeeze every last nickel out of the place. We certainly weren't trying to work the rent roll."[6]

Ravitch was puzzled by their lack of interest. "We met with MetLife," Ravitch recalled. "They were never really interested. I always had the impression it was because half their executive officers lived there."[7]

MetLife executives also did not have the pressure of shareholders and quarterly earnings reports; it was a mutual company run for the benefit of policyholders.

In 2001, Lloyd Goldman, a billionaire and second-generation developer, had determined that MetLife's real estate assets in New York and elsewhere were worth more than the company itself, at least according to the company's share price at the time. Goldman and his partners, Jeff Feil and Stanley Chera, discovered that MetLife's then-chairman, Robert H. Benmosche, liked to eat at Prime, a kosher restaurant in Manhattan. Goldman and Chera arranged to get a table near Benmosche and then struck up a conversation. Gradually, Goldman proposed buying a stake in the insurer's entire real estate portfolio, including Stuyvesant Town and the MetLife Building in New York and the Sears Tower in Chicago. Benmosche was friendly but noncommittal.

"Bob was very guarded," said Goldman. "But Stanley convinced him I knew a little bit about real estate. I said, 'I'd like to buy a forty-nine percent interest and manage your real estate.' "[8]

Ultimately, MetLife declined Goldman's offer. But a year later, Goldman, Chera and several other partners did buy two of sixteen buildings the insurer put on the market, paying $259.4 million for the Fred French Building at 551 Fifth Avenue in New York and the Otis Building at 10 South LaSalle in Chicago.

Goldman was far from the only real estate executive chasing MetLife's real estate assets. Four months prior to the Stuyvesant Town-Peter Cooper Village announcement in 2006, William P. Dickey, the founder of the Dermot Company, a residential real estate company that owned property in New York and Colorado, took a run at buying the two adjoining complexes. Dickey and other real estate operators had started buying residential buildings in working- and middle-class neighborhoods with the expectation that rents would continue marching upward. Better management and renovations could bring higher profits, they gambled.

Stuyvesant Town-Peter Cooper Village was the biggest prize of all, with 11,232 apartments, many of them renting for below-market levels to longtime residents. Dickey and his then-son-in-law, Andrew MacArthur, calculated the property was worth $4 billion, or roughly 11 percent of MetLife's $35 billion market capitalization. "It dawned on me that this property was going to get sold," Dickey said during an interview in his office fifteen floors above Times Square. "It was going to be the biggest residential sale of its kind."

Dickey decided his company was too "small potatoes" to do the deal alone so he started talking about a partnership with Richard J. Mack, chief executive officer of what was then known as Apollo Real Estate Advisors, a global real estate investment and management firm. In the past, private equity firms had had little interest in anything other than trophy office buildings in Manhattan and other major business districts, glass condominiums, hotels and high-end retail. But with rents for housing sailing northward, Apollo and others saw an as-yet-underappreciated opportunity. Earlier in the year, Apollo, in partnership with Neil Rubler of Vantage Properties, had begun buying rent-regulated complexes such as Delano Village in Harlem, where they believed rents were 20 to 30 percent below market.

As the alliance with Apollo gelled, Dickey and MacArthur worked up a proposal and an "investment memorandum" for Stuyvesant Town and Peter Cooper Village entitled "Project X." The two men culled data about the two complexes from MetLife's website, public documents and newspaper articles and combined it with a market analysis of what the property was worth under "aggressive management." "Aggressive management" meant a thoroughgoing effort to weed out what they thought were hundreds of tenants who did not qualify for rent-regulated apartments. The rent for those apartments, in turn, could be raised by $1,000 or more after a significant renovation.

Their analysis projected a 13.1 percent internal rate of return over a fifteen-year investment horizon. They proposed a hybrid model in which Stuyvesant Town-Peter Cooper Village would be run as a rental property, but the owners would convert and sell one hundred units a year as condominiums. MetLife, which would retain a 25 percent equity interest valued at $500 million, would get $3.5 billion at closing and $1.5 billion over the next fifteen years under the proposal.

"We were prepared to offer them $4 billion for the property," recalled Dickey, who was hoping to preempt a possible auction by MetLife. His price was "aggressive," but, he thought, doable.

In March 2006, Dickey and MacArthur followed what was becoming a well-worn path to Robert Merck and MetLife's real estate offices in Morristown, New Jersey. Dickey and MacArthur spent ninety minutes laying out their presentation and the financial analysis for Merck and a group of MetLife executives. Merck, forty-seven, had joined MetLife in 1982, not long after getting his master's in business administration from Georgia State University. Smart and loyal, he rose steadily up the ranks. Polite as he is, no one mistook him for a pushover. His customary stance was to get the maximum possible price for MetLife, whether he was negotiating with buyers or brokers.

By 2006, he was a senior managing director and head of real estate and agricultural investments, overseeing a staff of 250, in the U.S. and overseas. Courteous but never gregarious, he was not about to disclose the internal deliberations of Mother Met.

"It's not for sale," Merck said after they'd finished their spiel. "We have no intention of selling, and if we do sell, we think we can get more."[9]

Afterward, Dickey said he left the meeting with a "sick feeling." He suspected that MetLife would hire a broker and put the property out to bid, which would push pricing to the way beyond. "Merck was all eyes and ears," Dickey said. "Why not? I was giving him all this information. Maybe he knew all this, but he did not indicate he knew it. I don't think they had a clue as to what it was worth."[10]

Unbeknownst to Dickey, MetLife had secretly engaged Stephen Jones, Scott Latham and John Feeney, top executives at Cushman & Wakefield, in 2005 to advise them on the fate of Stuyvesant Town-Peter Cooper Village, strategies for boosting revenues and alternatively, the value of the property if it was sold in the current market and the potential political fallout from such a move. They would eventually estimate the property's value at $4.8 billion to $5.1 billion. Like Dickey and others, their estimate was based in part on a rollicking market and the belief that big lumbering MetLife had been a soft landlord, often missing opportunities to evict "illegal tenants" and push rents closer to market levels.

By July 2006, real estate executives were buzzing with talk of a sale and MetLife's beauty contest for a broker to handle the auction.

Metropolitan Life was a far different company by 2006 than it had been in the days when employees and tenants referred to the insurer as Mother Met. The company changed its corporate signature to MetLife in 1990 and spent much of the decade refocusing on its life insurance business amid growing competition from other financial institutions and health maintenance organizations. In 1995, it acquired New England Mutual in the largest merger in the history of United States life insurers, providing access to higher-income clients and a better data-processing system. During the same period, MetLife shed its health care and health insurance businesses and sold its home mortgage division and the Century 21 real estate brokerage.

MetLife itself was a shrinking presence in New York, where it once had a payroll of over 20,000 employees. The widespread use of computers reduced the need for thousands of clerks to input policy data at the home office. Over three years, the company cut its staff by 15 percent, from 28,000 to 23,700. That enabled MetLife to clear out its landmark limestone building at

11 Madison Avenue and lease much of the space to an investment bank, Credit Suisse First Boston.

These actions set the stage for MetLife's decision to convert to a stock company after eighty-five years of being owned by policyholders. Mutual companies were designed to provide insurance to people at the lowest possible price. And MetLife had grown to be the largest issuer of life insurance policies by selling coverage to low- and middle-income families ignored by other companies. But with the industry rattled by rapid consolidation, MetLife and other mutuals, like Prudential Insurance Company of America in Newark, New Jersey, and John Hancock Mutual Life Insurance in Boston, sought to tap into capital markets for cash to acquire competitors, banks and other financial services in order to compete in the global markets. Under the conversion, which required approval by policyholders and the New York State Insurance Department, the company's stock would be distributed to more than nine million policyholders and sold to the public.

The conversion plan was led by MetLife's chairman, Robert H. Benmosche, who had not come up through the company ranks. He had been brought in by the board from Wall Street, via Paine Webber. On April 5, 2000, MetLife held its initial stock offering, raising $2.88 billion. A huge MetLife banner was stretched across the front of the New York Stock Exchange, while a thirty-five-foot version of the MetLife blimp floated nearby proclaiming that MetLife had "landed" on Wall Street.

The conversion also marked a distinct shift in the corporate culture that reverberated from MetLife's boardroom on Madison Avenue to Stuyvesant Town and Peter Cooper Village. The dining rooms, where the company served free meals to nineteen thousand employees on white china, were gone. The company offered policies through third-party distributors, reducing the need for a large sales staff. It also started selling its most valuable real estate and boosting income at its remaining housing complex. Executives now had a keen interest in containing costs and increasing profits.

"Certain changes occur with demutualization," said Suneet Kamath, a senior analyst at Sanford C. Bernstein & Co. who follows the insurance industry. "There is a lot more focus on earnings and a return on equity, because those are the drivers of share price. They're much more focused on bottom-line profitability. When you're a mutual company, you don't have that daily report card, the stock price."

The resulting changes came swiftly at Stuyvesant Town-Peter Cooper Village. MetLife tore up the reputed ten-year waiting lists for rent-regulated apartments and, for the first time in fifty-four years, brought in an outside firm—Douglas Elliman—to manage the two complexes. Instead of simply re-leasing the rent-regulated apartments, the company renovated the units and raised the rent by hundreds of dollars to free-market levels.

"You can date the day things changed to the day MetLife went public," said Soni Fink, whose living room window at Peter Cooper offers a mesmerizing view of the East River, Brooklyn and Queens. "They went from an altruistic approach to a profit center."[11]

As always, MetLife was extremely sensitive as to how the company was perceived by the public. It did not want any negative publicity that would hurt the company's ability to sell policies to working- and middle-class families. But MetLife's decision to cut services and hike rents at a complex built for the middle class put them on a collision course with the tenant association, which battled the company at every turn.

"They wanted to convert a lot of apartments to free-market rents," said Steve Stadmeyer, who was brought in as the first outsider to manage the complex in 2001. "And they wanted a political buffer, to have a management company take the brunt of the negative publicity that they might get."[12]

MetLife told its managers it wanted an improvement in revenues from Stuyvesant Town-Peter Cooper Village, where the average monthly rent was less than $1,000. Ordinarily, a landlord can only raise rent-regulated rents by a percentage mandated by the Rent Guidelines Board, usually 2 to 4 percent a year.

But under rent regulations in effect since 1997 an apartment can be decontrolled after it becomes vacant, or if the legal rent reaches $2,000 a month and the existing tenant's household income rises above $175,000 for two consecutive years. Owners can also pass on to tenants part of the cost of capital improvements, which can help push rents toward the $2,000 level.

At the time, MetLife said it was spending $30,000 to $40,000 per vacant apartment on upgrades, including new wood cabinets, stone countertops and fixtures in the kitchen, remodeled bathrooms and new lighting fixtures. The landlord could then increase the rent by one-fortieth of the cost of the improvements, or $1,000 a month for a $40,000 renovation. So the rent on an apartment that previously rented for, say, $1,500 could jump to $2,500. Once an apartment was deregulated, the owner could charge whatever the market would bear.[13]

There were fewer than one hundred market-rate apartments at Stuyvesant Town-Peter Cooper Village in 2001, but the rents were substantially higher, ranging between $2,100 and $2,500 a month for one-bedrooms and $2,600 to $3,200 a month for two-bedrooms, the company said at the time. At Peter Cooper Village, the comparable rents were $2,800 to $3,200 for one-bedrooms and $3,600 to $4,200 for two-bedrooms.

To increase vacancies, MetLife ousted tenants who illegally subletted an apartment without company approval and residents whose apartments were not their primary residence, although, at least in the beginning, an exception was carved out for MetLife executives who had a pied-à-terre at Stuyvesant Town. "A lot of senior MetLife executives had apartments there," Stadmeyer said. In a move that shocked many longtime tenants, Stadmeyer also took down the post-and-chain fences that surrounded every patch of grass and invited tenants to enjoy lounging on the lawn.[14]

Tenants, however, complained about cutbacks at the complexes and MetLife's lack of commitment to preserving Stuyvesant Town as a middle-class sanctuary. Tenants who could recount stories of a maintenance worker knocking on their door on Christmas Day only an hour after they'd called the administration office now had to wait days for a response. "On a New Year's Day my toilet flooded and within half an hour someone came to fix it," said Elaine Haber, who raised two boys in Peter Cooper, where she still lives today. "That doesn't happen now."[15]

Al Doyle said that when he first got involved with the tenants association in 1997 residents were reluctant to bother MetLife, which they viewed as a benign landlord despite the constant rounds of rent increases. "That feeling disappeared," Doyle said. "They seemed to cut back on maintenance and security. They didn't seem to be as helpful and, I guess, benevolent."

Like any volunteer organization, there was an ebb and flow

to the life of the tenants association in relation to the severity of the issues—straight rent hikes or the installation of new electric lines, air-conditioning and other capital improvements that also triggered rent increases—at any one time. When Doyle first got involved, the dedicated core group was down to less than a dozen. But their numbers started to swell with the flow of complaints about MetLife's cutbacks at the complexes.

Retirees living on a small pension and social security, who accounted for a substantial number of tenants, were acutely sensitive to any increase in housing costs. Many of them were union members, particularly teachers, who were accustomed to group action. Elected officials also paid attention, because Stuyvesant Town-Peter Cooper Village's twenty-five thousand residents represented a concentrated block of voters.

State senator Roy Goodman, a longtime advocate for the tenants, was also taken aback by MetLife's approach. "I consider MetLife to be one of the best landlords I know of," Goodman said, "but lately with the demand for more revenue they seem to have changed their emphasis."[16]

But Doyle was also upset about the broader trends as landlords like MetLife converted onetime bastions of the working and middle classes into luxury rentals. "It's a shame," Doyle said. "The same opportunities I had and my mother and father had are not available to people today. My father was an original tenant, a marine who came back from the war. When we grew up, my friends had fathers who were police officers and firemen. They made the city work and made this neighborhood desirable."[17]

There was one other change that some longtime residents noticed. MetLife removed the stone marker from the Stuyvesant Oval that had been erected in 1947 to commemorate

Ecker's eightieth birthday. The inscription on the bronze plate reminded all who read it of Ecker's vision for the Stuyvesant project, which had been created so "that families of moderate means might live in health, comfort and dignity in parklike communities, and that a pattern might be set of private enterprise productively devoted to public service." Stadmeyer, the general manager at the time, said the marker floated around the property for a while as first one area and then another was renovated. "Then they decided not to put it back."[18]

Although many analysts and tenants believe that MetLife's decision to sell can be traced back to demutualization in 2000, the company initially made no overt moves in that direction. In late 2003, the insurer did sell its historic twenty-nine-story headquarters on Madison Avenue for $675 million. The following year, it auctioned the Sears Tower for $840 million. In a sign of the times, the new owners, a group led by New York investors Joseph Chetrit and Joseph Moinian, slapped an $825 million mortgage on the property, 98 percent of the sale price.

Merck, the MetLife real estate executive, said in 2006 that the company had made a decision to diversify its real estate portfolio, which was concentrated in several large-scale office buildings in a handful of cities. "Diversification and high property values were the two driving forces behind our selling some of these really large assets," he said.[19]

In January 2005, MetLife announced that it was buying Citigroup's Travelers Life and Annuity and substantially all of Citigroup's international insurance business, a deal that made MetLife the largest individual life insurer in North America.

The $11.8 billion price tag prompted MetLife to tap into unrealized gains in the value of its trophy real estate assets in order to pay for the transaction. The company put 11 Madison Avenue, the forty-one-story building and clock tower at Twenty-Third Street, and the fifty-eight-story MetLife Building that sat astride Park Avenue up for sale.

The timing was propitious. Commercial property sales in the United States, and Manhattan in particular, had been climbing steadily since the slump after the 2001 terrorist attack on the World Trade Center in New York. In 2004, 2,745 U.S. office buildings sold for a total of $75.4 billion, more than twice the 1,237 properties that sold in 2001 for a combined $32.4 billion, according to Real Capital Analytics, a real estate research firm. The demand by investors for office towers was evident in the sale of the Bank of America Center, San Francisco's premier financial-district skyscraper. An investment group led by Mark Karasick and David Werner bought the fifty-two-story complex in 2004 for $870 million and then put it back on the market in 2005, eventually selling it to a Hong Kong consortium for a record $1.05 billion and a quick 21 percent profit.

Prices were the highest in New York, which attracted not only pension funds and insurance companies, but also foreign investors and sovereign funds who viewed it as one of the safest and most stable real estate markets in the world. The commercial vacancy rate was down throughout Manhattan and rents were up, with the best space leasing for more than $100 a square foot.

One hundred and twenty-five office buildings in Manhattan changed hands in 2004 for a collective $11.2 billion, an average of $291 per square foot. That compares with a national average of $165, or $126 less than New York City. As prices soared, buyers were willing to accept initial returns of 5 percent or less, primarily because there were few investment alternatives.

"It's probably the most competitive environment we've seen in a long time," Dan Fasulo, director of market analysis at Real Capital Analytics, said in the spring of 2006. "Whereas in the past you might have had two to four bids on a property, now it's not uncommon to have double-digit bids for the most desirable properties. For some unique assets here in Manhattan, I've actually heard of up to 30 bids, which blows my mind."

The broker's job is to sell the property. With both the volume and the size of deals escalating, there were numerous six-figure and even seven-figure commissions for the victor. Brokers' memories only go back as far as the last deal. They don't spend a lot of time worrying about real estate busts that happened years ago. Despite the euphoria surrounding the boom, a few brokers were worried, although they kept their misgivings to themselves. "Every deal exceeded expectations because the buyer knew they could get more debt," said one broker who competed to sell Stuyvesant Town. "Every new transaction was a record. We kept scratching our heads. It was this whole concept of negative leverage."

MetLife's property sales generated more than a dozen offers. Stacom, the broker from CB Richard Ellis, sold 1 Madison Avenue, whose relatively small floors with numerous columns were not well suited for modern office tenants, on behalf of MetLife for $918 million to SL Green, a publicly traded real estate investment trust that planned to convert the stately tower to condominiums.

The sale of 200 Park was handled by a separate group from Cushman & Wakefield, Stephen Jones, Richard Baxter, Scott

Latham, Jon Caplan and Ron Cohen. Rob Speyer of Tishman Speyer Properties emerged from a hotly contested auction as the winning bidder for the MetLife Building at 200 Park Avenue, with a record offer of $1.72 billion, the most money ever paid for an office building. The 2.8-million-square-foot tower was an enormous prize, offering more rentable office space than the Empire State Building.

Speyer was giddy as he drove out to MetLife's Morristown offices with a group of executives for his first all-night negotiating session on the evening of March 31, 2005, to hammer out the details of the contract. His partners, the New York City Employees' Retirement System and the Teachers' Retirement System of the City of New York, were putting up most of the money for the 2.8-million-square-foot tower. Lehman Brothers provided the financing.

Knowing that there was little or no food available at Met Life's offices, Speyer pulled up to the take-out window of a nearby Friendly's for dinner. As they waited for their food, a departing patron passed their car with his daughter in tow. "See, honey," the man said to the little girl as he eyed the five executives in their business suits crammed into the car, "that's why you never want to be a lawyer."[20]

Ultimately, Speyer made it through a night of relatively easygoing discussions fueled by cans of Red Bull. MetLife insisted that its corporate logo remain atop the skyscraper. The insurer also leased the penthouse floor at the top of the tower for its 112-year-old boardroom, which oozed old-world money. The forty-five-foot-long room featured hand-tooled leather walls, custom carved woodwork, a ceiling of ornamental plaster covered in three shades of gold leaf and a massive fireplace modeled after one in the Château de Villeroi in France. At the center of the room was a twenty-five-foot-long mahogany table surrounded by the directors' hand-carved chairs with green leather saddle seats. [21]

Built in 1893 for the company's home office on Madison Avenue, it was dismantled and reassembled in 1958 when MetLife renovated 1 Madison Avenue. The company painstakingly dismantled the boardroom again in 2005 and moved it to the fifty-seventh floor of the MetLife Building. The costly decision to move the ornate boardroom contrasted with Benmosche's simultaneous decision to send most of MetLife's executives into exile, at a converted factory in Long Island City, far from the company's historic home on Madison Avenue.

"Think about it," Speyer said the next day. "It's the opportunity of a lifetime. To buy one of New York City's iconic properties is an opportunity we just leapt at."

With the sale of the MetLife Building behind him, Merck and Steven A. Kandarian, the company's new chief investment officer, turned their attention to Stuyvesant Town-Peter Cooper Village. Prior to joining MetLife in 2005, Kandarian was executive director of the federally sponsored Pension Benefit Guaranty Corporation, which oversees retirement income for forty-four million American workers. He did not have the same sentimentality about the complexes as perhaps the MetLifers. "I didn't predict the day the bubble would burst, but I knew things had gotten overheated," Kandarian said during an interview in 2011. "The market was frothy. We were having a hard time finding things to buy in New York and elsewhere. We had a difficult time making the numbers work. It made sense to sell."

Kandarian and Merck concluded that the value of Stuyvesant Town-Peter Cooper had soared during the boom to the point where the complexes accounted for half the value of the company's entire worldwide real estate portfolio, up from 12 percent in 2001. There was little affection left in the executive suite for MetLife's greatest housing complex. The company needed to diversify; its portfolio was overly concentrated in New York and in a select group of trophy properties. Their recommendation to sell was endorsed first by Henrikson, then MetLife's chief executive, and later the company's senior management team.

"It was the last remaining extremely large asset," Merck said. "From a diversification standpoint it made sense. It also made sense to unlock the capital value in the property. Another reason was that the market was so strong, not only in real estate generally, but in Manhattan especially. We were also concerned that those market conditions would change."[22]

Darcy Stacom, her partner William M. Shanahan, and other members of her team, Eric Negrin, Paul Liebowitz and Robert Garrish, drove out to 10 Park Avenue in Morristown, New Jersey, on July 27, 2005, from their offices in the MetLife Building at 200 Park Avenue. They were early for the appointment with Merck at MetLife's real estate offices. Every broker competing for the job knew it would be a career-making or career-changing assignment.

"I knew it was likely to be a record-setting deal in New York," Stacom recalled. "I had a sense there was nothing bigger anywhere else. This was one assignment we wanted to win. It was so unique, so different than anything we'd done."

The team from Goldman Sachs had been out a day earlier. Unlike the other firms in the competition, Goldman had never sold a property for MetLife and the bank was not a major force when it came to investment sales. More important, the Goldman executives did not share MetLife's optimism about the price. As far as Merck and Kandarian were concerned, the Goldman executives were a scratch before their car hit the highway back to Manhattan.

Eastdil, which two years earlier had sold the Sears Tower in Chicago for $835 million, had made their presentation that morning. Merck, a straightforward executive whose soft Southern accent betrayed his roots in Georgia, had made it clear to the four broker teams that any one of them could do a good job. Merck liked to spread the work between the major firms, rather than favor one broker who might become complacent. The question in his mind was, Who would drive the last dollar? He made it clear that MetLife wanted the highest possible price for the asset, somewhere in the neighborhood of $5 billion.

Doug Harmon and John Celestin, who were part of the Eastdil team, had been involved in converting rental properties to cooperatives in the 1980s. Increasingly prices were predicated on a rapid conversion of rent-regulated apartments to market rents, which could be 20 to 30 percent higher. But a landlord could not simply evict rent-regulated tenants in New York, where tenant rights were still pretty strong and housing court was a nightmare for landlords. The conversion process had to balance the push to increase revenues against the possibility of antagonizing existing tenants and elected officials, creating a political quagmire that could make conversion nearly impossible.

They also evaluated some of the environmental issues associated with the site, where the long-demolished manufactured gas plants that gave the Gas House District its name had contaminated the underground soil. Con Edison, which owned the gas plants, had taken responsibility for the cleanup, but every property owner had a potential liability. Given the size of the property, they also outlined the possible difficulties in financing a sale that would presumably require the biggest mortgage of all time.

The Eastdil executives set a baseline value for the property at about $3.5 billion, with a series of steps and assumptions that, if met, would bring the number higher, but nowhere close to $5 billion. Investors had to buy into the idea that residential rents would continue to rise in the coming years and that rent-regulated apartments could be converted to market rents at a more rapid pace than customarily happened in New York. Privately, Harmon and Celestin were skeptical. From their own experience they knew how hard it was to dislodge rent-regulated tenants. But they wanted MetLife's business, so they offered a wide range of values. If everything went right, they said, the bids might come in at more than $4.5 billion.

But as they got up to leave, Celestin and Harmon, a street dragster of a real estate executive who jealously vied with Stacom for the crown of top sales broker in the country, could tell that their cautious approach did not match the expectations of the MetLife executives sitting across the table.

"We were very aware of the growing political storm in New York and the desire to keep housing more affordable," Harmon told me. "We reflected that in our pro forma and in our thought process to a higher degree than others."[23]

The Cushman & Wakefield group was just pulling into the parking lot when the brokers from Eastdil were leaving the building. They felt outnumbered by Eastdil's twelve-man coterie. Stephen Jones, who managed the company's relationship with MetLife, had brought along three brokers, Richard Baxter, Scott Latham and Ron Cohen, and a top appraiser of multifamily properties, John Feeney.

Jones had developed a close working relationship with Merck and other MetLife executives dating to 2002, when he and a colleague, Arthur Mirante, had sold a package of sixteen office buildings in New York, Houston, Boston, Chicago and Denver for about $1.75 billion.

It was not unusual for these brokers to bump into each other while they competed for a top assignment. They had been in the business for more than a decade and were arguably the most successful brokers in New York. Despite the friendly greetings, it was hard to tell who wanted the deal more.

As they started their presentation, Baxter, Latham and the others handicapped their chances. They had an advantage over the other firms in that they had been secretly evaluating Stuyvesant Town-Peter Cooper Village on MetLife's behalf for nearly a year. But hiring an adviser could also be perceived as a conflict of interest. And Jones and Latham had sold the MetLife Building at 200 Park Avenue for a record-setting price, so maybe it was another firm's turn. All in all, the Cushman guys felt like the underdogs in this fight.

Like the other teams, the Cushman executives ticked off the price-driving options for a new buyer, including the possibility of building new senior housing on all that green space at Stuyvesant Town. But over the course of the allotted hour, they focused on illegal tenants and the yawning delta between the rents for regulated apartments versus those for deregulated units. The Cushman team confidently predicted that a sale could yield as much as $5.1 billion.

As Stacom and her team sat in an anteroom, they could hear

the murmurs from the boardroom where the team from Cushman & Wakefield were making their presentation. A burst of loud laughter from inside the boardroom made Stacom's heart sink. Jones was scoring points. The door to the boardroom suddenly opened and out strode Jones, Latham and the others. There were friendly nods all around, but it was clear that Jones felt confident about whatever had happened inside.

Stacom led her team into the boardroom, where Merck; Steven A. Kandarian, then MetLife's chief investment officer; David V. Politano, a regional director in the real estate investment group; and Kevin Wenzel, the complex's manager, waited. She made a quick and calculated decision to start the presentation with a video instead of a long presentation about the underwriting for the property sale. They had spent $15,000 of their own money preparing the presentation. They rented a helicopter and flew north from the Battery to midtown, as a video camera recorded the vastness of Stuyvesant Town in the midst of Manhattan, an establishing sequence for any foreign investors who might not be familiar with the complex. There were also stills of the apartments and the grounds at Stuyvesant Town-Peter Cooper Village. As the video finished, the sound of Billy Joel's hit song "New York State of Mind" filled the room.

Merck looked quickly over at Kandarian and smiled. "Yes," Stacom thought to herself, "Billy Joel fans." Merck was actually more partial to a Southern blues band from his hometown of Macon, Georgia—the Allman Brothers. But the aerial shots, the music and the video were indicative, he thought, of a competitive spirit that could serve them well.

After that, the presentation flew by. The brokers laid out the cash-flow projections for the 12.7-million-square-foot complex, and the kind of revenue generation a buyer could expect by converting rent-stabilized apartments to higher, market rents, and the price it could sell for. Based on a vigorous conversion program and a steady increase in market rents, the annual rent stream at Peter Cooper Village could top $100 million by 2011, up from $67 million in 2007. Rental income at Stuyvesant Town could jump to over $320 million in 2011 from almost $208 million four years earlier, under the same conditions. Times were good; no sense figuring out what might happen in a recession.

There was a zoning study and data on the tightening rental market and comparisons with similar apartment buildings. The presentation also looked at other sources of income, including the six parking garages on the property, 100,000 square feet of storefronts, the laundry rooms and unused development rights. An estimated $1 million could be generated by offering 275 special parking permits for spaces along the inner roadways of the complexes, where parking had not previously been permitted. Electricity was currently included in the rent, but the brokers suggested that a buyer could reap substantial cost-savings from the installation of electric meters for individual apartments.

The brokers described the complex as Manhattan's only city within a city, combining serene pastoral living with convenient urban access. They predicted that the property could bring offers of well over $4.5 billion, a stunningly large number. But this was eighty acres on one of the most valuable islands in the world. If there was a selling theme it was simple: "We believe ongoing deregulation will continue to allow new ownership to fully leverage the unparalleled competitive advantages of the complex and take advantage of the soaring rental market."

As she was leaving, Merck asked whether she had plans for a

summer vacation. Yes, she replied. "My husband plans to swim the English Channel and we're going to spend some time in Wales. But I know I may have to cancel."

"Good answer," Merck said.

Stacom and the CB Richard Ellis team left the meeting in high spirits. But as she got back to Manhattan and the car pulled onto the East River Drive, her cell phone rang. It was an executive from TMW, a German investment firm that owned 666 Fifth Avenue and the Chrysler Building in a joint venture with Tishman Speyer Properties, with unexpected news. Stacom had been working with TMW to value 666 Fifth, a forty-one-story office tower clad in embossed aluminum panels between Fifty-Second and Fifty-Third Streets, in preparation for a sale. The tower, with the numerals 666 at the top, was a recognizable part of the Manhattan skyline, even if the elite Top of the Sixes club had been replaced by a cigar bar, the Grand Havana Room.

Now TMW told her that a different firm, Cushman & Wakefield, would be handling the assignment. The news hit hard. "I felt drop-kicked to the center of the earth," she said. "Based on the size of the building and the retail component, I knew it would be a record-setting sale." Brokers, particularly those operating at the stratospheric levels that Stacom did, want a piece of every deal that comes along. Stacom and her team had sold $7.1 billion worth of commercial property in 2005 alone. She wanted to top that number in 2006.

She and her sister, Tara, a vice chairman at Cushman & Wakefield who is currently overseeing the leasing at One World Trade Center in Lower Manhattan, are second-generation real estate executives. Their father, Matthew J. Stacom, was a top broker at Cushman & Wakefield who was involved in developing the Sears Tower. Even their late mother, Claire, was a broker.

Her father encouraged Darcy and her siblings to get a real estate license while they were still in high school. Stacom, whose corner office is crowded with pictures of her two daughters, established her career at Cushman & Wakefield, but later jumped to CB Richard Ellis.

After losing the 666 Fifth Avenue deal, Stacom would have to wait five days before Politano at MetLife called with the verdict on the Stuyvesant Town-Peter Cooper Village beauty contest. The deal was hers, he said. But the elation over her victory was tempered by a piece of business.

Merck set a hard line on the commission. Just because the deal was going to involve a record-busting price, it did not mean that the broker should get a windfall. Brokers at Darcy's firm had rarely if ever seen a commission fall below 35 basis points, or 0.0035 percent of the sale price. That amounts to $3.5 million on a billion-dollar sale. But a $5 billion sale was beyond anyone's experience.

Merck named an unusually low, but not insubstantial, number for a property whose price tag was so enormous. Stacom could have refused, but the deal would almost certainly have gone to Cushman & Wakefield. The tradeoff, of course, was that the sale would bring her team the biggest trophy of all, bragging rights, lots of publicity and a new round of clients.

Over the years, Stacom and Merck steadfastly refused to disclose the number to reporters. But it was known by many within her firm, and even outside the firm, to be $5 million. It is more money than many New Yorkers see in a lifetime.

Stacom and her team began to obsessively craft their approach to selling this deal. They took three-quarters of their winning presentation to MetLife and incorporated it into a full-color sales book for prospective bidders. They also designed a website that registered bidders could access with a special password that would provide even more detailed financial information about the complex and its history. The timeline was extremely tight: marketing was set to begin after Labor Day, with first bids due on October 5, and a second and final round set for October 16.

CHAPTER FIVE

Let's Make a Deal

In late July 2006, Rob Speyer and his father, Jerry I. Speyer, were sitting in a meeting with top executives from Black-Rock, one of the world's largest investment management firms, at its headquarters in a forty-four-story glass tower on Fifty-Third Street between Madison and Park Avenues in Manhattan. As the meeting ended, the conversation around the conference table turned to the pending sale of Stuyvesant Town-Peter Cooper Village. The temperature in the room went up as they debated the potential price for what everyone described as a unique asset, an eighty-acre complex on the East Side of Manhattan, overlooking the East River.

"This is going to be a rather large transaction," Laurence D. Fink, BlackRock's chairman and chief executive officer, said as he turned to Rob Speyer. "Why don't we do it together?"[1]

Speyer responded enthusiastically. Tishman Speyer and BlackRock were comfortable as partners. In January of 2006 the two companies had joined forces to buy a partial stake in a pair of suburban Chicago office buildings, paying $106.6 million.

A year earlier, Tishman Speyer and BlackRock Realty bought the Mellon Bank Center in Los Angeles for $245.6 million, while Tishman Speyer sold BlackRock a thirty-two-story office building in Burbank for $167 million. In a bit of serendipity, Fred Lieblich, the head of BlackRock Realty Advisors, was a former MetLife executive who had actually lived in Peter Cooper Village at one point. He and Rob Speyer started working on the project that afternoon.

"We at BlackRock have always preferred to be less visible," Fink said in 2006. "Tishman Speyer had a wonderful relationship with New York City, great visibility. It was obvious to me, with our desire to keep a lower profile, and our ability to raise equity, and our history of dealing with each other, that we should do it together."

BlackRock, which managed about $20 billion in real estate equity assets for public and private pension funds, endowments and private investors, and Tishman Speyer had similar reasons for chasing the deal, much of it resting on their belief that income from rental apartments would grow quickly, while the complexes themselves required far less capital for periodic modernization than office buildings, hotels and shopping malls. The demand for rental apartments would continue to grow, especially in New York City, where fewer and fewer buyers could afford the sky-high prices. But those frustrated buyers still needed somewhere to live and the only alternative was the rental market.

Dale Gruen, a managing director at BlackRock Realty who was heavily involved in the Stuyvesant Town bid, described the market at the time in a couple of breathless, jam-packed sentences.

> New York City's housing market has yet to experience a significant slowdown. Prices are high and continue to rise, which is depressing affordability. In fact, housing affordability, which takes into account home prices, incomes and mortgage rates, recently dropped to a record low. Above average job growth, favorable demographics and a record-low for-own housing affordability are driving strong demand for rental units. Against the backdrop of limited supply of new rental units, vacancy rates are extremely low and rent growth is strong. These strong trends are expected to persist, and we currently rank New York as one of the nation's best apartment markets for investors.[2]

Even before the property officially went on the auction block, dealmakers were building their teams and casting about for financing. Jeffrey A. Barclay, head of acquisitions for ING Clarion Partners, the real estate arm for a giant Dutch asset manager, was driving north on I-95 in late July 2006 to visit his kids at camp in Maine when Lee S. Neibart, a cofounder of Apollo Real Estate, called to tell him that MetLife had hired Darcy Stacom to sell Stuyvesant Town-Peter Cooper Village. Just as Dickey at Dermot had gone to Apollo with the Stuyvesant Town deal, Apollo, in turn, had brought Barclay and ING Clarion to the bidding partnership. The whole notion of a preemptive bid for the two complexes was dead, the two men concluded. "It's showtime," Barclay told Neibart.[3]

ING Clarion had just completed the $2.8 billion acquisition of the publicly traded Gables Residential Trust in partnership with Lehman Brothers. The sale included the assumption and refinancing of about $1.2 billion in debt and preferred shares. ING Clarion invested $400 million, with the remaining money coming from equity investors brought in through Lehman. The deal quintupled ING Clarion's multifamily real estate holdings. Gables, a publicly traded real estate company based in Florida, managed 41,750 units at 162 complexes in Atlanta; Houston; South Florida; Austin; Dallas; Washington, DC; and San Diego. ING already had 10,000 units in its vast real estate portfolio.[4]

Over at the Time Warner Center complex at Columbus Circle in Manhattan, Bruce A. Beal Jr., an executive vice president of the Related Companies whose internal motor always seemed to be revving at a higher RPM than anyone else's, called one of his closest friends, Michael Barr, then a senior vice president at Lehman Brothers, to see if the bank was interested in the Stuyvesant Town deal.

Beal joined Related in 1995, a couple of years out of Harvard University. As a teenager, he had immersed himself in the world of Jacques Cousteau, working during the summers in a fish market on Nantucket and at a dolphin laboratory in Hawaii. But his father was a prominent developer in Boston, chairman of the Beal Companies, so real estate held a certain allure.

His responsibilities grew as Related became one of the most prolific developers in New York. He eventually took over responsibility for Related's residential portfolio, as well as day-to-day oversight of development projects throughout the country. He was known to be amiable, blunt, facile with numbers and caustic. Occasionally, his booming voice could be heard rumbling down the hallway from his office at the Time Warner Center as he excoriated a colleague for some unimaginable offense.

Beal had gotten an early tip about the pending Stuyvesant Town sale from a real estate broker who had competed unsuccessfully to run the sale for MetLife. How many real estate companies had the experience and the ability to manage more than eleven thousand units, Beal wondered.

"I'm hearing about Stuyvesant Town," Beal said to Barr. "Why don't we work on it together?"[5]

"Funny," replied Barr. "I was going to ask you the same thing."

Related, which is based in New York and is also active in Miami, Boston, Chicago, Las Vegas and Los Angeles, as well as China and the Middle East, owns and operates $12 billion worth of real estate, including nineteen luxury apartment buildings, thirteen thousand subsidized housing units, office complexes and retail space. It also manages real estate investments for the State Teachers Retirement System of Ohio, the California Public Employees' Retirement System and others.

Related, which made a remarkable comeback after nearly capsizing during the recession in the early 1990s, is led by the tall, trim billionaire Stephen M. Ross, who also owns the Miami Dolphins football team. Intensely competitive, Ross, in partnership with the Mack family and Apollo Real Estate Advisors, built the first new commercial complex after the 2001 terrorist attack on the World Trade Center: the $1.7 billion Time Warner Center, a two-towered mixed-use complex at Columbus Circle that includes the headquarters for Time Warner, condominiums, high-end restaurants and shops, a Mandarin Oriental hotel, CNN Studios and Jazz at Lincoln Center. The glassy, fifty-five-story towers are a highly visible addition to the New York skyline.

The alliances were forming against a backdrop of unprecedented real estate deal making. Every day seemed to bring another record-breaker: the most money ever paid for any real estate asset; the most money paid for an office tower on a per-square-foot basis; or the most money paid per "key," or room, for a hotel. The volume of hotel deals alone jumped from $574.8 million in 2002 to a staggering $28.4 billion in 2005. Midway through 2006, multifamily and commercial property sales were headed for another record-setting year.[6] Very often, buyers and sellers were juggling multiple deals at the same time.

"It's probably the most competitive environment we've seen in a long time," Dan Fasulo, director of market analysis at Real Capital Analytics, said in the spring of 2006. "Whereas in the past you might have had two to four bids on a property, now it's not uncommon to have double digit bids for the most desirable properties. For some unique assets here in Manhattan, I've actually heard of 30 bids, which just blows my mind."[7]

The real estate boom had started amid the economic slump after the terrorist attack on the World Trade Center in September 2001. Alan Greenspan, the economist who served as the chairman of the Federal Reserve from 1987 to 2006, sought to reinvigorate the economy by initiating a series of interest-rate cuts that brought the federal funds rate—the rate banks charge each other for loans—down to one percent in 2004. The economy responded; employment numbers went up and credit was easily available.

The low cost of borrowing was a boon for both commercial and residential real estate, heating up an already boiling real estate market. With Treasury rates falling to record lows, real estate, which was offering 8 or 9 percent returns, suddenly became a more attractive option for pension funds, endowments, private equity firms and other investors. The California State Teachers' Retirement System, the nation's second-largest pension fund with $144 billion in assets, announced in the summer of 2006 that it would nearly double its target portfolio allocation for real estate assets to 11 percent from 6 percent.[8]

Pension funds were expanding their high-risk investments in real estate in order to make up for lower returns or losses elsewhere in their portfolios. With Treasury bonds providing a yield in the lower single digits, speculative real estate with its double-digit returns looked so much more attractive.

With more money pushing its way into the system, investment banks and real estate companies raised money from wealthy private investors, pension funds and foreign firms for funds designed to focus on office buildings in emerging international markets, or apartment complexes in major metropolitan cities, or hotels. Morgan Stanley Real Estate completed raising $1.75 billion for its fifth U.S. real estate fund and Shorenstein Properties, a well-regarded San Francisco–based real estate fund, closed its eighth private equity real estate fund, this one totaling $1.1 billion.[9]

There was just so much money chasing deals. So private equity firms, pension funds and other investors looked for new trends, new sectors in which to make their bets on the real estate market. In the spring of 2006, they suspected that the rental market would be the next hot real estate sector. Consumers, they figured, who could not afford to pay the escalating cost of buying a house or condominium would still need shelter, creating additional demand for multifamily housing. Blackstone, ING Clarion and other private equity firms also saw an opportunity in buying publicly traded real estate investment trusts, whose individual assets were thought to be worth far more than the company's share price would reflect.

But the continuing boom in the real estate market was also

fueled by a financing mechanism popular on Wall Street called commercial mortgage-backed securities, or CMBS. The idea with CMBS was to turn commercial mortgages into securities. Lenders had learned a lot from the collapse of the last big real estate boom in the 1980s, when commercial banks and savings-and-loan institutions stumbled—and in some cases died—under the weight of billions of dollars in bad real estate loans. For a good part of the 1990s, it was nearly impossible to get a commercial real estate mortgage from suddenly gun-shy commercial banks.

Lehman Brothers, Credit Suisse, Nomura Securities and other Wall Street firms stepped into the breach. The Wall Street banks provided the loans, but instead of letting them linger on their own balance sheets, they pooled the loans and divided the pools into classes with ratings from triple-A on down, just like municipal bonds, and then sold the loans to institutions, including pension funds, hedge funds and mutual funds. The bankers in turn made money underwriting the loans and by turning the loans into securities. The annual volume of CMBS loans surged 227 percent over five years, rising to $172.6 billion in 2006 from $52.8 billion in 2002, according to Trepp, a research firm that tracks securitized debt.

Scott J. Lawlor, chief executive of Broadway Partners and a relative newcomer to the real estate business, made news in 2006 when he paid $3.4 billion for ten office buildings in major cities across the United States, including the landmark John Hancock Tower, a sixty-two-story glass skyscraper in Boston's Back Bay. Lawlor was part of neither a multigenerational real estate family nor a publicly traded real estate investment trust.

He was not at all sentimental about the buildings he bought and sold like pork bellies. He was not interested in accumulating an empire. Lawlor was a trader, or flipper, who bought and sold heavily debt-laden property for quick profits for his investors and himself. In 2006, he boasted of delivering 38 percent returns for his investors, while he earned hefty fees as the general partner. By then, he had made it to the promised land, lavish offices in the Seagram Building on Park Avenue.

"We have a very strict discipline we try to bring to bear about sales," Lawlor said at the time. "Once the building's income has increased, the company's job is done. We never track assets under management as a measure of growth."

The high-flying Lawlor, son of a Queens, New York, cab driver, had worked for a couple years in the financial industry after earning an MBA at Columbia University in 1993. He opened his own company in the relative backwater of tony Greenwich, Connecticut, in 2000. His first deal was appropriately small, buying a former school building in Hartsdale, New York, for $4.8 million and converting it into an office building. He sold it three years later for $5.1 million and a modest 6 percent return. That same year he bought a retail and condominium complex in Washington, DC, for $185 million, a $30 million premium over what the seller had paid in 2001. Some analysts at the time said Lawlor had overpaid and predicted that he would soon be in trouble. But he quickly spruced up the retail space, signed new leases and sold the complex less than two years later for $220 million to Prudential Real Estate Investors.[10]

Lawlor's deals represented just a fraction of the commercial property deals nationally in excess of $5 million. According to Real Capital Analytics, 3,770 office complexes traded hands in

2006 for a combined $136.9 billion, up from 1,237 transactions in 2001 totaling $32.4 billion.

By the time Lawlor bought the John Hancock Tower, he was playing in real estate's major leagues. The skyscraper had been owned and operated by John Hancock Insurance until 2003 when the insurer sold the building and three related properties for $926.8 million to Alan M. Leventhal, the founder of Beacon Capital Partners. In a transaction typical of that period, Leventhal put up $304 million in cash, or roughly one-third of the purchase price, and took on a $623 million mortgage for all four buildings. Beacon valued the Hancock Tower and a nearby garage at about $639 million.

But by 2006, real estate financing had changed dramatically. The Wall Street banks were willing to provide a larger and larger chunk of credit toward the purchase price. Why not? The market was booming and the mortgages could be pooled, securitized and sold to investors. Once sacrosanct loan-to-value ratios went out the window. If Beacon's mortgage was a relatively safe 66 percent of the purchase price for Hancock Tower, Lawlor was upping the ante. His deal valued the Hancock Tower and the garage at $1.35 billion, more than double the price in 2003. And he loaded down the property with a mortgage and secondary loans totaling 82 percent of the purchase price.

The deal left little margin for error. Rents and property values had to continue to rise. He ran the risk of defaulting on his loan if he failed to replace a departing tenant with one paying a higher rent.

"This is a significant group of marquee properties in highly desirable markets that we are confident will deliver strong risk-adjusted returns to our investors," Lawlor said in 2006, three years before he lost the tower to lenders.[11]

No real estate sector was immune from the deal mania.

In March 2006, Blackstone Group, the giant asset management and financial services firm, announced its latest megadeal: it was buying CarrAmerica Realty, a publicly traded real estate company with a national portfolio containing 26.3 million square feet of office space, for $5.6 billion. But Blackstone, a standout in the takeover field, had not quenched its thirst for commercial real estate. The company, in partnership with Brookfield Properties, agreed in June to pay $4.8 billion for Trizec Properties, which owned 40 million square feet of office buildings in Canada and the United States, including 1 New York Plaza in Lower Manhattan and the swooping white Grace Building in midtown.

Although rents and prices for commercial buildings had been rising steadily for five years, Blackstone and other buyers of commercial real estate remained optimistic about the future. The economy was strong and commercial markets in major American cities were doing well, with employment up, vacancies declining and only a handful of new buildings under construction in any one central business district.

No real estate sector, however, was immune from the deal mania. That spring, Blackstone Group continued its high-stakes shopping spree, buying MeriStar Hospitality, a real estate investment trust based in Bethesda, Maryland, that owned 57 high-end hotels with a combined 14,404 rooms, including the Ritz-Carlton Pentagon City and the Hilton Washington Embassy Row Hotel. Blackstone, which already owned the La Quinta and Wyndham International chains, had its eye on the hotel sector's rising profit rate, up 13.1 percent in the first half of 2006 from a year earlier.

In both the CarrAmerica and MeriStar deals, Blackstone paid a 20 percent premium above the respective companies' closing stock price the day before the deals were announced on the presumption that the stock price undervalued the individual assets. Therefore, the parts were worth more than the whole.

Laurence Gluck, a founder of Stellar Management, acted with the same kind of exuberance in the residential market in New York when he paid $132 million in 2005 for the Riverton Houses in Harlem, the black middle-class complex of seven buildings that was built by MetLife in the late 1940s. "Getting into Riverton was a coup," Stephanie Tolbert, a retired library clerk who has lived in Riverton for more than forty years, explained. "At one time, you wouldn't dare go into the playground if you didn't live here. They didn't want outsiders sitting on the benches."[12]

But Riverton was a very different kind of deal than ING Clarion's acquisition of Gables Residential in that the Riverton apartments were rent regulated. Big-time landlords had rarely ventured above 125th Street in Manhattan or into scrappy neighborhoods in the Bronx or Brooklyn. But the demand for housing was cutting across all class and racial lines. New York is one of the few cities in the country with tens of thousands of apartments whose rents are regulated and kept below market levels by law.

Prospectors like Gluck realized that there was money to be made, even with pedestrian tenements. Under state law, there were a variety of ways to deregulate those apartments. Gluck had focused in recent years on buying sixteen rental complexes built under New York's middle-class Mitchell-Lama housing program. After twenty or twenty-five years, owners were allowed under certain conditions to buy their way out of the program and escape rent regulation.

Gluck and his financial partner, the Rockpoint Group, got a $105 million mortgage for Riverton from North Fork Bank to pay for the deal. A year later, the partners refinanced Riverton, more than doubling the debt on the property to $250 million, a $225 million CMBS mortgage from Deutsche Bank and a $25 million loan. The refinancing enabled them to take out about $60 million for themselves, after paying off the original loan, recouping their investment and establishing a $53 million reserve fund for renovations. Gluck, a shambling real estate investor who favors khakis rather than bespoke suits, renovated the lobbies, which dated to the 1940s; installed new elevators; and landscaped the seven-hundred-foot-long mall.[13]

But the rental income from the property covered less than half the debt service and turnover was slow. Mr. Gluck expected to refurbish vacant apartments and rapidly replace rent-regulated residents with market-rate tenants willing to pay a higher rent. It was a simple business plan that required lenders to buy into his projections for higher rental income in the years ahead. The lenders did require him to set up a separate reserve to cover the shortfall between the debt payments and income from the property, at least for a while.

In the end, the rating agencies, who are paid by the banks underwriting the loans, gave the mortgages an investment-grade rating. They bought into the speculative predictions of ever-rising demand and the upward march of rents. The rating agencies thought that the substantial reserve funds, established with borrowed money, would mitigate the risk. Critics would later say that the rating agencies were only too willing to go along rather than risk losing their fees.

In one of the largest multifamily real estate deals ever on the West Coast, Gluck and Rockpoint also bought another former MetLife project in San Francisco, Parkmerced, which had 1,683 middle-income rental apartments in 11 towers and 1,538 two-story town houses sprawled across 112 acres near Lake Merced. The partners paid about $700 million, with a $550 million CMBS mortgage and a $28 million secondary loan.[14] The secondary or junior loans are also called mezzanine loans, a cute catchphrase to denote that it is subordinate to the mortgage. In other words, the mezzanine lenders stand in line; their loan is paid each month with what is left over after the mortgage or senior loan is paid in full.

San Francisco, like New York, was one of the few cities that still had rent regulation. Annual rent increases for existing tenants at Parkmerced were governed by the San Francisco Rent Board. But leases for new tenants were subject to market conditions. Gluck's strategy at Parkmerced, however, was different than at Riverton. In San Francisco, he wanted to demolish nearly half the apartments at the rent-regulated, middle-class complex in order to erect a larger, high-density luxury complex. San Francisco State University and several neighborhoods had grown up around the once-remote complex in the southwest corner of San Francisco. Gluck and his partners pitched their project as an eco-friendly, transit-oriented development. Critics described the plan as a land grab designed to eliminate affordable housing, although the developer promised that the total number of rent-regulated units, 3,200, would remain the same.

Still, the partners' debt load accounted for roughly 83 percent of the purchase price. Parkmerced appeared to generate enough income to pay the debt service, but the partners were also spending money on architects, engineers, publicists and other consultants to develop a plan that they hoped would be approved by San Francisco.

Gluck, with his deals for Riverton and Parkmerced, triggered a new fashion trend. Another New York apartment operator, Neil L. Rubler, formed Vantage Properties in 2006 intent on following Gluck's lead in borrowing money to buy property while putting up very little of his own money. Rubler, who had married into the Olnick real estate family, rising to become chief executive of the Olnick Organization, went off on his own when the Olnicks declined to adopt his more aggressive approach to investing. He took note of Mr. Gluck's strategy of buying rent-regulated, working- and middle-class complexes with securitized debt and plans to upgrade the buildings and bring in market-rate tenants. Mr. Rubler's first purchase in what would become a $2 billion buying spree in 2006 and 2007 was Delano Village, a nest of seven buildings with 1,800 apartments sitting across Fifth Avenue from Riverton in Harlem. Rubler, backed by Apollo Real Estate Advisors and the Dutch ABP pension fund, paid $175 million, using a $128.7 million mortgage.[15]

A year later Rubler nearly tripled the debt on the property to $367.5 million with an interest-only CMBS mortgage. The new financing allowed him to recoup the original investment, repay the initial mortgage and establish $87 million in reserve funds, leaving the partners with a cool $100 million for themselves. The annual cash flow at the complex was only $4.3 million, yet the loans were underwritten for an ultimate cash flow of $19.1 million. But Rubler money was not at risk. The lenders bought Rubler's business plan: to rapidly replace rent-regulated residents with tenants paying higher rents.[16]

The hefty debt load also created enormous pressure to increase revenues swiftly. The lenders required Vantage to establish a $30 million interest reserve fund to cover the gap between the monthly mortgage payment and the income from the property. But the reserve would not last forever.

In regulatory filings, Vantage laid out its "recapturing" strategy, in which the company expected to convert 20 to 30 percent of the units in its properties from rent-regulated to market-rate rents during its first year of ownership. Vantage was setting a blistering pace considering that the average turnover at rent-regulated buildings in New York was less than 6 percent. In order to accelerate the departure of rent-regulated tenants, Rubler issued eviction notices to fully one-fifth of the residents, claiming that under state housing laws they were not entitled to a rent-regulated apartment since it was not their primary residence. Tenants had to vacate or hire lawyers to defend themselves against the charges. No doubt some rent-regulated tenants were there illegally. But the tenant association, and later the state attorney general's office, viewed the shower of eviction notices as a "systemic pattern of harassment" designed to prod illegal and legal tenants to move.

These deals emerged in a time when investors stopped looking at complexes like Riverton, Parkmerced and Delano Village "as housing and started looking at them as commodities," such as oil or tin, said Harold Schultz, a senior fellow at the Citizens Housing and Planning Council and a former city housing commissioner. Very often, he said, they did not make economic sense because the rents in those neighborhoods were already at or near market levels, regardless of whether the units were rent regulated.

As Rob and Jerry I. Speyer began working on a bid for Stuyvesant Town-Peter Cooper Village with Fred Lieblich of BlackRock, Rob and Lehman Brothers were bidding for CarrAmerica's Washington, DC, portfolio, more than two dozen office buildings totaling 6.3 million square feet. In effect, Blackstone bought CarrAmerica at a wholesale price, added a larger mortgage and was now unloading pieces of the portfolio at higher, retail prices to buyers in the local markets. Blackstone used the money it borrowed against the portfolio for its next deal and for executive bonuses. Whoever acquired the buildings would immediately become a major player in Washington.

The Speyers ultimately won the bidding with an offer of $2.8 billion. Their company invested $250 million for a 5 percent ownership stake and cobbled together a dozen investors, including Lehman and SITQ, a subsidiary of the Canadian pension fund manager Caisse de Dépôt et Placement du Québec, for an additional $350 million. That brought the equity total to $600 million. They also obtained $1.6 billion in senior loans and $570 million in mezzanine loans. The deal was put together by Rob Speyer, whose eleven-year apprenticeship would soon come to an end. Increasingly, Rob was speaking on behalf of the company, but his father was still the public face of Tishman Speyer. The plan, Jerry Speyer told the *Washington Post* at the time, was to renovate the building facades, refurbish the lobbies and install new elevator systems. "I'm thrilled our company was able to buy the portfolio," he said, "and we'll try to continue to do all the things the Carrs have done in the past and establish the name of Tishman Speyer as a first-rate landlord."[17]

But Rob Speyer, thirty-seven, was not just an eager buyer in 2006. He and his partner, the German investment firm TMW, also sold the forty-one-story skyscraper at 666 Fifth Avenue for $1.8 billion, deciding to use Cushman & Wakefield for the sale instead of Darcy Stacom and CB Richard Ellis, setting a new record for the highest price paid for a North American office building. But 666 Fifth was not just another generic Manhattan skyscraper; it was deeply woven into the family history. His grandfather Robert V. Tishman had built the tower. Robert was part of the third generation of a real estate family whose New York roots trace to the 1890s. He led the publicly traded Tishman Realty and Construction in 1958 when the firm built the tower with the distinctive embossed aluminum-paneled skin at 666 Fifth.

Robert Tishman, who died at ninety-four in 2010, extended the firm's operations well beyond New York, building the one-hundred-story John Hancock Tower in Chicago, the Renaissance Center in Detroit and Alcoa's twin-tower Century City complex in Los Angeles. "We package everything," Robert Tishman told *Business Week* in 1968. "We locate land, design the building, select the architect, work out interim and permanent financing, do the leasing, build and manage the building."

Jerry Speyer, son of a family of German-Jewish builders who fled Hitler in the 1930s, married Robert's daughter Lynne Tishman shortly after graduating from Columbia Business School in 1964 and joining Tishman Realty. Lynne's great-grandfather Julius Tishman had founded the company in 1898. Jerry Speyer, who graduated from Columbia with an MBA, had worked briefly as an assistant to the vice president and treasurer of

Madison Square Garden. Speyer tells friends that he wanted to work on real estate deals but found himself consumed with the Rangers and the Knicks. Tishman, a kindred soul who, like Speyer, was soft-spoken, polite and very smart, offered him unparalleled resources. Jerry quickly established himself as the heir apparent. "I believe in nepotism," Robert Tishman once told reporters, "so long as the son-in-law you're bringing in is smart."

But the public company, the largest builder-owner of high-rise office buildings in the country, ran into financial problems during the recession in the mid-1970s and dissolved in 1976, when the skyscraper at 666 Fifth was sold for $80 million. Three firms emerged from the demise: Robert's cousin John formed a construction company (Tishman Realty and Construction) and his brother Alan became a major force in leasing and building management (Tishman Management and Leasing). Robert Tishman and Jerry Speyer formed Tishman Speyer Properties. The two men were a physical contrast—Robert was tall and slim compared with Jerry's compact physique—but great partners, quickly establishing themselves as a force to be reckoned with. They developed the Equitable Center in New York and the NBC Tower in Chicago and the one-million-square-foot building at 520 Madison Avenue and the Saatchi Building at 375 Hudson in Manhattan.[18]

Speyer and Lynne Tishman separated in 1987 and eventually divorced. The breakup, however, had no effect on the partnership between Jerry and Robert. "It was about the most decent divorce I've ever heard of," Bob Tishman told the *New York Times* in 1998. "There was no reason in the world to destroy what we built up over 20-something years."[19]

As the Manhattan real estate boom lost air in the late 1980s, Speyer made a key decision to move to Germany rather than wait for the market to recover. Speyer, who speaks fluent German, built the seventy-story Messeturm, then the tallest tower on the European continent. The success of that project led to a larger development, a two-million-square-foot complex in Berlin that became the European headquarters for Sony.

Over the next decade, Speyer transformed the company from a mom-and-pop operation, albeit a lucrative one, into an international player when he tied up with a real estate fund and acquired his biggest trophy of all, a New York icon and an international symbol of capitalism, Rockefeller Center. Tishman Speyer had long relied on a small coterie of investors for its projects, including one of the world's richest families, the Lester Crown family of Chicago. But in 1997, Speyer and the Travelers Group put together an $800 million investment fund that allowed him to get involved simultaneously with a broader range of development projects.

A year earlier, Speyer and Goldman Sachs had led a group that bought Rockefeller Center and its ten landmark buildings, which sit between Forty-Eighth and Fifty-First Streets, from Fifth Avenue to the Avenue of the Americas. The Rockefeller family had sold the twenty-two-acre complex in 1989 to a Japanese company, Mitsubishi Real Estate. But the center fell into receivership in 1995 when Mitsubishi failed to make its mortgage payments. Speyer, with David Rockefeller's blessing, saw an opportunity to revive the complex, which had lost some of its luster. Mitsubishi initially accepted his $200 million offer for the property but then pulled out, creating a financial crisis for the trust that held the mortgage. The trust was led by Goldman Sachs and included the Rockefeller family.

Goldman Sachs, whose co-chairman Hank Paulson was a friend of Speyer's, soon forged a partnership to buy the famed complex that linked the bank, David Rockefeller, Gianni Agnelli of Italy, Stavros Niarchos of Greece and Tishman Speyer, which took a 5 percent stake in what was a $900 million deal. "Every project has one big idea," an elated Speyer said at the time. "The one big idea here was to bring Rockefeller Center back to having the majesty it had when it was first built."

In short order, Tishman Speyer gave the limestone surfaces of Rockefeller Center a facelift and boosted revenues. The company replaced the candy stands and shoe stores in the underground mall with national retailers such as Banana Republic, Sephora and Dean & DeLuca and installed the prestigious Christie's auction house in a once dowdy space used for a parking garage. It leased Radio City Music Hall to Cablevision for about $13 million a year and the Rainbow Room at the top of 30 Rock to Cipriani International, pushing the annual rent up by 25 percent to $4 million a year.

In 2000, Speyer and the Crown family bought out their partners in a $1.85 billion deal for Rockefeller Center, once again outmaneuvering other bidders, including Mortimer B. Zuckerman, chairman of Boston Properties; Steven Roth, chairman of Vornado Realty Trust; and Sam Zell, then chairman of Equity Office Properties Trust.[20] Speyer acquired not only a famed office complex but also international cachet that would soon have him doing projects in Brazil, India and China.

Jerry Speyer, whose ever-present Mickey Mouse wristwatch lends a dash of whimsy to an otherwise sober, buttoned-down mien, travels in rarefied political, social and corporate circles even for a New York real estate mogul. He is chairman emeritus of Columbia University; a minority owner of the Yankees; a member of the Council on Foreign Relations, an influential, nonpartisan think tank; vice chairman of the Museum of

Modern Art; and the only real estate executive to have served on the board of the Federal Reserve Bank of New York, much of the time with his good friend Richard S. Fuld, the former chairman of Lehman Brothers.

Indeed, Speyer has carefully established an image for himself as someone who rises above the craven self-interest of your typical real estate developer. He has been chairman of both the Real Estate Board of New York, the industry's powerful lobbying arm, and the Partnership for New York City, a not-for-profit comprised of the top two hundred corporate leaders that was created by David Rockefeller in 1979, in part as a counterweight to the real estate industry. When the Real Estate Board opposed Mayor Michael R. Bloomberg's property tax increase to close the city's budget gaps in 2003, Speyer and the Partnership supported it. The following year Speyer and the Partnership favored the mayor's plan to give middle-class homeowners a $400 tax rebate, much to the chagrin of the Real Estate Board.

"He's the only real estate executive who the corporate CEOs think of as one of them," said Kathryn S. Wylde, president of the Partnership. "He's truly unique in the real estate world as somebody who is a man for all seasons, much the way David Rockefeller has been."[21]

To a degree, Speyer modeled himself after Rockefeller, the patriarch of the famous family and the only surviving grandchild of oil tycoon John D. Rockefeller. David Rockefeller, an influential figure in banking, foreign affairs and philanthropic circles, rose to become chairman of Chase Manhattan Bank and oversaw construction of One Chase Manhattan Plaza, an office tower that is credited with reviving New York's downtown business district. Rockefeller was close to presidents and foreign leaders; intimately involved in influential think tanks, from the

Council on Foreign Relations to the Trilateral Commission; and a generous patron of both Rockefeller University and the Museum of Modern Art.

"Jerry loves the image of being a very important man in New York without necessarily cultivating that the way a Donald Trump does," said Burt Lehman, a corporate lawyer and a friend of Speyer's since college. "There is a kind of exalted standing that comes of not being seen to seek any standing at all."[22]

Shortly after joining the Modern in 1982, Speyer, whose substantial collection of contemporary art adorns his Rockefeller Center offices as well as his home, sought out Rockefeller, a founder of the museum. "He made it clear that he wanted to be in the inner circle of the museum," Rockefeller recalled in 1998. Several years later, Speyer endeared himself to the museum's elite board when he haggled with the family that owned a property next door to the museum. Speyer knocked their sale price down by a third to $50 million, allowing the Modern to buy the land and expand. "I'm not sure anyone else could have done that," Rockefeller concluded.[23]

Although Speyer acknowledges to friends that he "doesn't do warm and cuddly well," he is painstaking in nurturing his relationships with prominent figures in business, social and political circles. He is always discreet, offering judicious advice or a brief note of congratulations on a birthday. "He understood the entire business, and better than anyone else," said Geoffrey P. Wharton, a top executive at Tishman Speyer who left the company in 2001. "He was a master at creating relationships and transmitting a tremendous confidence in what the company could do."[24]

Just as he drew on those connections in acquiring Rockefeller Center, Speyer pulled all the philanthropic and social levers he could manage during the hotly contested bidding for the Chrysler Building in 1997. The negotiations involved a tricky two-part process of buying the building from a bank and working out a new lease with the Cooper Union for the Advancement of Science and Art, which owned the land underneath the Art Deco landmark on Forty-Second Street. The school was emphatic that it would not accept less than $4.5 million.

Speyer outmaneuvered seven other bidders with a phone call to the chairman of Cooper Union, Robert A. Bernhard, a longtime friend of the Tishman family. The two men shared an interest in the arts and memberships at the Century Country Club in Purchase, New York. "Speyer called me up and said, 'If we guarantee you $5.5 million will you give us an exclusive for sixty days?' " Mr. Bernhard told me. "He did, and he now manages the building. Another bidder was very irritated with me. But Jerry took an aggressive point of view, and nobody else came forward with anything like that."[25]

Speyer married Katherine G. Farley, an architect by training and a top executive at Tishman Speyer, in 1991. The couple, who live in a mansion on the Upper East Side that Speyer built, have a daughter, as well as three children from Speyer's first marriage. She, too, is actively involved in New York's cultural institutions, currently the chairwoman of Lincoln Center for the Performing Arts and, until recently, a trustee at Brown University and a board member at the Alvin Ailey American Dance Theater.

In 2000, the Speyers repurchased 666 Fifth, the tower where Jerry Speyer had started his career with the Tishmans thirty-four years earlier, for $540 million. The company's partner in the deal was the Crown family from Chicago, the same billionaire family that had been a partner in building the tower. By then, Tishman Speyer controlled a $10 billion international portfolio of mainly office buildings totaling 36.4 million square feet.

Rob, who joined Tishman Speyer in 1995 at twenty-six, put his own stamp on the building in 2002. He recalls as a young boy spying the deep-red numerals "666" atop the building from the living room of his grandfather's apartment, 1.5 miles to the north at Eighty-Sixth and Madison Avenue. Twenty years later, he was looking for ways to enhance revenues from the building and he viewed the signage as "an untapped asset." In 2002, Rob struck a deal with Citibank to put the bank's name at the top of 666 Fifth and to lease Citibank space on the fifth floor that had been vacant for three years. Real estate executives said the sign alone was worth $1.5 million a year. "It was ironic," Rob said with a laugh. "It was our 666 sign. I was proud of that sign. On the other hand, it was this red 666, definitely an oddity given the symbolism."[26]

Rob had few qualms about putting 666 Fifth up for sale in 2006, when the company's partner, TMW, pushed to sell the property. Prices for prime commercial towers had jumped to unimaginable levels. The Kushner real estate family, eager to make a mark in New York after selling its vast residential holdings in New Jersey, won the auction with a breathtaking bid of $1.8 billion, more than three times what Tishman Speyer paid for the building six years earlier and the highest price ever paid for a single office building in the United States. The previous record had been set by Rob in 2005 when he bought the MetLife Building for $1.72 billion. The Kushners in turn arranged for a massive interest-only, $1.215 billion CMBS mortgage from a group of lenders led by Barclays Capital that would haunt them for years. The existing cash flow from the building covered only two-thirds of the debt service for the first mortgage, let alone the payments on a set of junior loans. There was a $100 million reserve fund to cover the $5-million-a-month shortfall, until, theoretically, a rising market yielded higher rents.

But by Labor Day of 2006, Rob Speyer and Fred Lieblich and Rob Friedberg from BlackRock Realty were focusing on what promised to be an even bigger, record-breaking deal, Stuyvesant Town-Peter Cooper Village. Their rivals at the Related Companies had already paired up with one of Tishman Speyer's favorite banking partners, Lehman Brothers. So Tishman Speyer turned to a banker at Wachovia, Robert A. Verrone, the number one underwriter of CMBS in the country. He only did deals of $50 million or more. Rob wanted him to work his magic. BlackRock brought in a second lender, Merrill Lynch, which owned just under 50 percent of the capital stock in BlackRock.

Verrone's meteoric rise in the rarefied world of high finance was something of a rags-to-riches story. He had grown up in the late 1970s in Paterson, New Jersey, a crumbling, working-class city west of Manhattan whose proud days as the Silk Capital of America were sixty years gone. His parents were Italian immigrants; his father labored in the cutting room of a garment factory. A brash, funny man with a shaved head and raspy voice, Verrone attended Don Bosco Prep and Moravian College before heading for Wall Street and an apprenticeship at Bear Stearns.

He moved in 1995 to First Union, which merged with Wachovia, an upstart bank based in Charlotte, North Carolina, with aspirations to be a major player. With a keen interest in deal financing he made his way up the ranks until in 2003, top executives at Wachovia finally gave in to his constant pleadings and dispatched him back to New York to build a large loan department from scratch. The bank had made a decision to challenge the venerable Lehman Brothers, which seemed to be financing most of the biggest, most important real estate deals in the country.

Verrone, his tie always a little askew, his shirttail habitually escaping his pants, offered slightly better interest rates and slightly better terms to outmaneuver the competition. He set up a lavish office in the Seagram Building on Park Avenue and wooed borrowers at the city's power spots, the Four Seasons and San Pietro restaurants. Everyone wanted an invitation to his parties on the rooftop of the Hudson Hotel. Soon, Verrone was financing Donald Trump's seventy-story office tower at 40 Wall Street, the former Metropolitan Life Building at 11 Madison Avenue, the Insurance Exchange Building in Chicago and the Ritz-Carlton in New Orleans.

On his watch, the value of Wachovia's loan originations soared from $3 billion in 2003 to $10 billion in 2005. It was quite a coup for Verrone and for a bank whose name many potential clients did not even know how to pronounce. He pulled it off by being the most aggressive bidder for the financing deals.

The following year, *Institutional Investor* magazine named him to its 2006 "20 Rising Stars of Real Estate" list. "The biggest challenge is to find creative ways to finance deals with a low debt service coverage or high [loan to value] ratios so that you can get to a loan amount and spread that works for the borrower, while creating a loan that can be sold to investors, and all the while making money for your institution," he told the magazine. "The biggest reward is the opportunity to work with the most sophisticated borrowers in the world while competing against the most creative lenders in the world to try and win business."

It was a high-wire act, juggling a buyer's demand for bigger, interest-only loans at lower costs, while fending off siren calls from rival lenders with possibly sweeter deals, all the while making hundreds of millions for the bank. With the Stuyvesant Town deal, he planned to beat Lehman Brothers at its own game.

Daniel R. Garodnick, the newly elected city councilman who lived in Peter Cooper Village, had none of the business connections to Wall Street enjoyed by the tycoons lining up to buy Stuyvesant Town-Peter Cooper Village. After learning of the pending sale, Garodnick spent days talking to former colleagues at his old law firm, Paul, Weiss, Rifkind, Wharton & Garrison; city council speaker Christine Quinn; and anyone else he could think of who might be able to advise him on how tenants could intervene in a sale that he sensed could be disastrous for residents. He also talked to Alvin D. Doyle, president of the Stuyvesant Town-Peter Cooper Village Tenants Association. "It was kind of jaw dropping," Doyle said of the sale. "We were concerned that an unscrupulous landlord would purchase Stuyvesant Town-Peter Cooper and try to kick everyone out."[27]

Garodnick quickly discovered that they had some allies who could also give him a short course in the intricacies of real estate finance. He got a call from Kevin Gallagher, a real estate financing veteran, who had been relaxing on a Long Island beach in July when a friend from the banking industry told him about the pending sale of Stuyvesant Town-Peter Cooper Village.

Gallagher's interest was immediately piqued, but not because he saw a way to make a quick buck. Four years earlier, Gallagher had decided that there was more to life than money. He signed on as the director of housing for the New York City Central Labor Council, a coalition of four hundred union organizations with 1.3 million members. Gallagher immediately created a low-cost mortgage program for union members using pension funds. But affordable housing was a nagging problem in a city where the "average" condominium cost over $1.2 million. Union members in increasing numbers were moving as far as the Pocono Mountains of Pennsylvania, one hundred miles west of Manhattan, to find a house they could afford.

Gallagher was confident they could devise a way for the tenants to make a credible bid for the property so that this bastion of affordable housing could be preserved. Perhaps some kind of cooperative in which longtime tenants could buy their apartments while other units would remain as rent-regulated rentals. He estimated that 40 percent of the Stuyvesant Town-Peter Cooper Village residents were union members, including nine hundred current or retired teachers. He made an appointment to see Garodnick and then rushed downtown to see Ed Ott, executive director of the Central Labor Council, who happened to have lived in Stuyvesant Town for a dozen years.

"He comes barreling into my office," Ott recalled, "saying, 'They're trying to sell Stuyvesant Town!'

"I said, 'Oh yeah; we should buy it.'

"I understood how important it was on the affordability side," Ott continued. "Our goal was to get the CLC behind fighting for affordable housing in the city. It was a no-brainer."[28]

When Gallagher met with Garodnick at the councilman's office near city hall, he brought along John A. Crotty, a lifelong

Stuyvesant Town resident and executive vice president of the Housing Development Corporation, the city agency that issued bonds on behalf of affordable housing projects in the five boroughs. Gallagher suggested that the AFL-CIO's $5 billion housing investment trust could back a tenant bid, while Crotty outlined various city housing programs and tax breaks that might be available. Gallagher told Garodnick that the trust had been used to finance twelve thousand units of low-price housing over the past four years in New York City alone.

"We're interested in coming up with a solution that works for tenants," Gallagher told Garodnick. "Raising the money won't be difficult. We'll use pension funds as the anchor investor and we'll go to the opportunity funds that would provide credibility with MetLife."[29]

Garodnick blinked. "What do you mean, 'Don't worry about the money,'" he demanded. "This is a multibillion-dollar bid."

The three men batted around various possibilities, including whether the city could provide property tax breaks and even cash for a tenant-led purchase. Gallagher recommended that Garodnick and the tenants talk to a lawyer by the name of Leonard Grunstein, a partner at Troutman Sanders who headed the firm's real estate investment and capitalization practice. They were far from putting together a formal offer, but Garodnick decided to take the concept to the upcoming meeting of the directors of the tenants association on August 2.

Garodnick, who saw himself as a "deputy for the tenant leadership," was very careful in handling his relationship with the tenants association. He spoke to Doyle before every meeting he had dealing with Stuyvesant Town-Peter Cooper Village. Early on, Garodnick, a high achiever, had learned the importance of grooming his political relationships. At Trinity, the private school he attended, students were required to do some kind of community work. It was his mother who first suggested that he try the nearby Jefferson Democratic Club, where he met elected officials and political operatives. When Garodnick ran for office in 2005 his opponent for the Democratic nomination was Jack Lester, a lawyer for the tenants association. But the fresh-faced Garodnick diligently knocked on every door at Stuyvesant and Peter Cooper Village, impressing residents and securing the election.

"He was a natural," his mother, Barbara Garodnick, said proudly. "He was president of his class from eighth grade at Trinity, all the way through Trinity High School and Dartmouth. At U Penn, he was editor in chief of the law review."[30]

A few days later, Garodnick met with a half dozen directors of the tenants association near his apartment in Peter Cooper Village. The association had come off a hard-fought but ultimately unsuccessful campaign opposing MetLife's decision to replace building keys with electronic key cards emblazoned with tenants' photographs. Doyle and other tenants viewed the cards as an invasion of privacy, a sneaky attempt to gather data on residents. Still, the tenant leaders felt energized. Garodnick was the second item on the agenda that evening. He told them that they could not afford to sit on the sidelines while the complex was sold out from under them. He said they should begin work immediately on mounting their own bid for the complexes; it was the only way to preserve the community they loved at Stuyvesant Town and Peter Cooper Village. His enthusiasm was infectious. But there was a nagging feeling that a multibillion-dollar auction was well beyond the ken of their little tenants association.

"What're we going to do, pass the hat?" cracked Helen

Thompson, a white-haired, seventy-seven-year-old widow with a keen sense of humor. "It was the most ridiculous thought, that we could ever buy something like this."[31]

John H. Marsh III, the third generation of his family to live in Peter Cooper Village, said little, but he was intrigued by the idea. He wondered to himself, "How do we get twenty-five thousand tenants to agree?"[32]

"We were astonished," said Susan Steinberg, then the association's executive vice president, "although we were beginning to think there was nothing that MetLife could do to surprise us. They'd gone from a paternalistic Mother Met to a more bottom-line-oriented company. It became very mercenary."[33]

Still, the group decided to explore a bid. Quinn, the city council's speaker and a likely mayoral candidate in the next election, promised help. "It required a leap of faith," Garodnick said, "that we could structure something with a partner that would deliver good results, without us having to collect spare change on the corner of Twentieth Street."

Five days later, Quinn attended a cocktail party for Andrew M. Cuomo, the Democratic candidate for state attorney general, in the Chrysler Building on Forty-Second Street, near Grand Central Terminal. The affair was sponsored by Troutman Sanders and held at the law firm's offices. Not long after she arrived at 5:45 P.M., Quinn was locked into a discussion with Cuomo about the pending sale of Stuyvesant Town-Peter Cooper Village. Cuomo pointed to a bearded, heavyset man in a three-piece suit as he told Quinn, "Well, you've got to talk to Len Grunstein."[34]

Cuomo, the eldest son of former governor Mario Cuomo, had served as secretary of the Department of Housing and Urban Development in the Clinton administration, and had met

Grunstein years earlier in the midst of another affordable-housing battle. In 2002, Cuomo worked for Island Capital, a real estate company that had announced plans to take the West Village Houses out of the state's Mitchell-Lama moderate-income housing program. The tenants fought the plan, fearing that Island Capital would triple the rent and force them from their homes.

The West Village Houses, 420 apartments in 42 low-rise buildings on the far west side of Greenwich Village in Manhattan, were built with a set of tax breaks and low-cost financing. But after 20 years, landlords could withdraw from the program by paying off their government mortgages, if they met certain conditions, and then raise rents to market levels. The acrimonious dispute dragged on for nearly two years before Cuomo was able to reach a settlement with the tenants association and city officials. Under the agreement, tenants were able to purchase their apartments at a 20 percent discount, while the city forgave $19 million in accumulated mortgage interest and extended an existing property tax exemption.

The tenants association hired Grunstein to help design a tenant-sponsored, noneviction conversion to a housing cooperative. Existing tenants who did not buy their apartments were allowed to remain in place. The conversion was completed in March 2006, with tenants buying 250 of the 420 units.

"We didn't know where we were going to live," said Kathryn Bordenaro, the former president of the West Village Houses Tenants Association, who also attended the cocktail party at Troutman Sanders. "Len was very reassuring. He could bring experience and resources to bear on our behalf."[35]

When Al Doyle subsequently called to inquire about Grunstein, Bordenaro was emphatic: "If you're going to buy

Stuyvesant Town and you want to figure out how to get people to buy their apartments, these are the people who know how to do it." It wasn't as if they had many choices. It was hard to find a high-level real estate lawyer in Manhattan whose firm did not have a conflict of interest or wasn't already engaged by another bidder. Despite his role at the West Village Houses, Grunstein did not typically represent tenant organizations. He was a bit of an operator, serving as counsel for some of his wheeler-dealer clients and taking an equity stake in the same deal. But no one disputed his credentials.

Grunstein met first with Garodnick and then Doyle and the tenants association. "I tried to explain that they had nothing to fear," Grunstein said. "There was going to be an opportunity for some tenants to buy their homes. But the rent-regulated tenants had nothing to fear.

"I believe," Grunstein continued, "that in order to have a strong economy in the city there has to be housing available for people who work in the city. You're undermining the economy if all your firemen, construction workers and nurses have to commute in from Bucks County [in Pennsylvania.]"[36]

Doyle, for one, was impressed. "He had quick and authoritative answers to every question we asked," Doyle said of Grunstein. "He exuded knowledge." The tenants association gave Grunstein a $10,000 retainer.

"We had our lawyer and our strategist," Garodnick said.

It is perhaps fitting that Stuyvesant Town-Peter Cooper Village, an oasis for the middle class in Manhattan, is the perfect place to play six degrees of separation, even for the high-powered players who wanted to own it. Robert V. Garrish, a young broker on Stacom's team at CB Richard Ellis, had grown up there. Fred Lieblich of BlackRock had lived there for a year when he was a rising executive at MetLife. John Crotty, then a city housing official, is a lifelong resident. Robert Wertheimer, a lawyer at Paul Hastings who worked on the deal for the Apollo–ING Clarion–Dermot group, is married to Lynn Schackman, who grew up in Stuyvesant Town. Garodnick is a lifelong resident. Ed Ott lived there for twelve years and Doug Eisenberg of Urban American dated a woman who lived there. Finally, Richard Mack's grandfather H. Bert Mack owned Wreckers and Excavators, the company MetLife hired to demolish the five hundred buildings in the Gas House District to make way for Stuyvesant Town-Peter Cooper Village.

Now they and others were each ready to take a chair at a high-stakes poker game for numbers that were out of sync with the safe, stable, middle-class ambiance of Stuyvesant Town. It was all about how much risk the participants were willing to take, because the betting was about to go beyond all reason.

CHAPTER SIX

For Sale

For many New Yorkers, the headline on the front page of the *New York Times* on August 30, 2006, was the first they heard that Manhattan's largest residential development was on the auction block: "Housing Complex of 110 Buildings for Sale in City." The target price was $5 billion and the article identified a long list of potential buyers, including privately owned real estate companies like Tishman Speyer Properties and the Related Companies; publicly traded investment trusts like Archstone-Smith and Vornado Realty Trust; the ruling family of Dubai; and New York's multigenerational real estate families the Rudins, LeFraks and Dursts. "This is the ego dream of the world," Darcy Stacom, the broker handling the sale, confided to a reporter.

Almost immediately, the telephone in Stacom's corner office at the MetLife Building next to Grand Central Terminal rang and rang with calls from high-powered investors, global pension funds, Middle Eastern sovereigns and storied banking families from Europe like the Rothschilds and the Safras. She told potential buyers they had to register and sign a confidentiality agreement in order to get the 117-page sales book and a special password enabling them to access a website with the complex's financial history and tenant data.

The article sent a shock wave through Stuyvesant Town-Peter Cooper Village, where residents had a starkly different reaction from the clamoring buyers. They feared that their beloved complex was about to be turned into a yuppie enclave. Marilyn Phillips, fifty-two, a nurse who had lived in Stuyvesant Town for fourteen years, was bereft. She and her husband, a social worker, were paying $1,700 a month for a rent-stabilized two-bedroom apartment. "It may mean we may no longer be able to live here," she told the *Times*. "The management is intent on making this luxury apartments and driving the working class out."[1]

An agitated Al Doyle called Garodnick, the city councilman, at six o'clock that morning to say that the sale had hit the papers. Garodnick had just gotten a news alert on his cell phone. "Al," Garodnick replied calmly, "we knew this."[2] Now it was time to go public, drumming up political support as well as unifying and activating the tenants. Consumed with worry about what the future would bring, Garodnick had not been able to sleep well for a week. The next day, a Thursday, Garodnick's aides and tenant activists slipped a letter underneath all 11,232 apartment doors at Stuyvesant Town-Peter Cooper Village.

"As a lifelong tenant, I am concerned that a new owner, motivated exclusively by profit, will make decisions that could be unfavorable to all of us. That is precisely why we need to actively involve ourselves in this sale, and not sit passively by.

"Accordingly," the letter continued, "I am exploring the possibility of assembling an investor group to assist tenants by purchasing the property on terms that are favorable to us. The purpose of doing this would be to protect the rights of all tenants—both rent stabilized and market rate—to stay in their homes as renters, to maintain the current layout of the property, and if tenants so desire, to purchase their apartments themselves."

The tenants association issued a "fact sheet" outlining the public benefits MetLife received to build Stuyvesant Town and why this public resource should be preserved for middle-class families. On its www.preservestuytown.org website, the association listed answers to frequently asked questions. Finally, on September 1, as Stacom's marketing plan went into effect, Garodnick wrote to MetLife's chairman, C. Robert Henrikson, saying that he was encouraging tenants to explore assembling an investor group to make a competitive bid for the property, consistent with the founding principles of the property—"namely, to be a sustainable community for middle-class residents."[3] Finally, he demanded that MetLife make available all the documents being given to other bidders, ranging from audited financial statements to information regarding pending litigation.

Neither Stacom nor Merck believed that the tenants association could mount a credible multibillion-dollar bid. The notion seemed laughable. Yet, the tenants did represent trouble, if they were able to drum up the kind of political support and garner headlines that might scare off credible bidders.

If MetLife or any bidder believed that the sale of Stuyvesant Town-Peter Cooper Village would be treated as just another in a long line of blockbuster transactions, they scrapped that notion on September 5, when Garodnick, the freshman councilman, held his first public rally and press conference, under a copse of oak trees at Stuyvesant Town. Not only did Christine

Quinn, the council speaker, and Ed Ott from the Central Labor Council show up, but so did U.S. senator Charles E. Schumer, Congresswoman Carolyn Maloney, City Comptroller William Thompson, Manhattan borough president Scott Stringer and state senators Tom Duane and Liz Krueger, all pledging to support a tenant bid.

Schumer characteristically issued his own press release highlighting his support for the tenants and six types of federal aid that might help the tenant bid. "When MetLife hung the 'For Sale' sign on the door of Peter Cooper Village and Stuyvesant Town last week, all New Yorkers, particularly those in the middle class, should have been troubled by the news," the senator told the crowd. "It is getting more and more difficult for firefighters, police officers, teachers, nurses and other working folks to call New York City home and that is why we need to do everything we can to preserve this vital stock of affordable housing."

A *Daily News* headline the next day questioned whether it was a "Pie-in-Stuy-Plan." That was pretty much the view of city hall and most executives in the real estate industry; a tenant bid seemed fanciful when you got into multiple billions. But no one doubted that politics might play a role in the outcome. Garodnick and Doyle were buoyed by their gathering support. "We knew the deck was going to be stacked against us," Garodnick said. "But it felt like we were onto something big and important."[4]

Immediately more than 140 prospective bidders, financiers and real estate executives registered for the sale. The password-protected website contained, in the words of one bidder, "everything you could possibly want to know about the property." The idea was that prospective buyers would be able to conduct their due diligence on the property well before the bidding started, so the winner would sign a contract in October and close in

November. The proposed sale had the kind of highly condensed timeline that had become de rigueur during the boom. No one wanted a winning bidder to bail out before the closing, because of a rise in interest rates or a change in market conditions.

Stacom then organized what turned out to be nearly sixty eighty-minute tours of the sprawling property that fall for bidders, bankers, engineers and management executives. A seven-story banner hung down the side of a Stuyvesant Town building on Fourteenth Street heralding, "Luxury rentals." Dealmakers who rarely spared the time for property tours showed up, including Stephen Ross of the Related Companies, Richard S. Fuld of Lehman Brothers and Steven L. Cantor, head of leveraged finance and real estate at Credit Suisse First Boston. Richard LeFrak, who unlike other bidders already owned thousands of rent-regulated apartments, asked specifically to see the boilers for the buildings. Ofer Yardeni, the Israeli investor who co-founded the real estate company Stonehenge Partners, visited several times, once bringing his wife and children. The billionaire Simon Glick, who paid a publicist to keep his name out of the papers, also took the tour, as did Rob Speyer, Fred Lieblich, Rob Friedberg and Dale Gruen of BlackRock Realty. Richard Mack, a third-generation developer and the chief operating officer for Apollo Real Estate Advisors, toured the complexes several times.

"I did a lot of explaining about the property," said Steve Stadmeyer, Stuyvesant Town's general manager, who accompanied Stacom on many of the tours. "The most common question was about how much it cost us to renovate apartments." Stadmeyer told them he was spending $40,000 to $50,000 renovating vacant apartments. "Depending on the people," he added, "they thought it was too high."[5]

Stacom was broker lucky. There was little rain that fall and the property looked spectacular underneath vivid blue skies and the changing colors of the pin oak, sycamore and London plane trees. The tours meandered from lobbies and apartments recently renovated by MetLife as part of a $320 million upgrade, to the playgrounds and Stuyvesant Oval, before ending at the storefronts along First Avenue, the western boundary of the complexes. "It's magnificent," Douglas Eisenberg, chief operating officer of Urban American Management Corporation, said to himself as he looked out the window of a renovated two-bedroom apartment during one tour. "You could walk through the gate at Twenty-Second Street and stroll down a private tree-lined street with no cars. Not bad for Manhattan living, although it did have an institutional feel. I could do wonderful things here."[6]

"It was eighty acres in midtown," said James Simmons, a partner at Apollo." You can't replace that. They're not building any new land on the isle of Manhattan."[7]

By the time C. Robert Henrikson, MetLife's chief executive, arrived in San Francisco on September 19 for a real estate conference, he was ebullient about how the sale was proceeding. "There's been a terrific amount of interest in the properties," Henrikson told investors at the conference sponsored by Bank of America. "We're very pleased at the reception."[8]

Douglas Durst and other members of New York's real estate aristocracy—families that had been building office towers and apartment buildings in New York for several generations—picked up a copy of the sales book but blanched at the price tag. Having been through the highs and lows of the real estate cycle over the decades, he and the other aristocrats tended to avoid inordinate risk and oversize mortgages, even if their caution prompted modern deal-makers to refer to them derisively as lumbering dinosaurs. Durst discussed a possible joint venture with Richard LeFrak, but he had a difficult time with the new math that seemed to govern real estate.

The real estate investment trusts, publicly traded companies like Vornado Realty Trust, were also wary of taking part in a deal that required blind faith in future projections and a potentially unhealthy amount of debt. But there were plenty of others who were willing to pick up an auction paddle enthusiastically.

Yet, Henrikson wasn't only getting calls from wealthy buyers eager to pay top dollar for his apartment complex. Senator Schumer, Congresswoman Maloney and city council speaker Christine Quinn had each called Henrikson's office demanding a meeting to discuss the sale. Maloney and fourteen other members of Congress—mostly New Yorkers, but also Representatives Barney Frank of Massachusetts and Maxine Waters of California—sent the chief executive a letter urging MetLife "to not only identify a purchaser committed to maintaining long-term affordability of the units but also to try to secure financing to facilitate the sale and acquisitions of the buildings."

"Government helped MetLife build Stuy Town and Peter Cooper and it can help keep the developments affordable in the years to come," Maloney said.

Quinn was sitting in the back of her black Suburban outside the Moonstruck diner at Twenty-Third Street and Ninth Avenue when she finally got Henrikson on her cell phone. "He could not have been ruder and less helpful," Quinn said, her voice rising with the memory. "He said, 'I don't have to talk to you; I barely have to talk to Chuck Schumer.' He was unwilling to have a dialogue, unwilling to slow down the process. A furious exchange ensued. I got off the phone and my driver asked, 'Who was that?' "[9]

Schumer did not have better luck, although he did meet with Henrikson on September 25 at the Crowne Plaza hotel in White Plains, thirty minutes north of Manhattan, and the conversation was more civil. "I begged him not to do it," Schumer said, "but it was clear that they were going to maximize profits. It was home to nurses, life insurance clerks, the middle class. There's plenty of profit to be made in putting up new buildings. There seemed to be no justification for converting Stuyvesant Town into a luxury complex."[10]

The cover of Stacom's 117-page sales book featured an aerial view of a forest of red brick Stuyvesant Town-Peter Cooper Village buildings across the broad middle of the island of Manhattan, with the Empire State Building in the background and the East River in the foreground.[11] Inside was a playbook for potential buyers seeking higher revenues to justify the highest price ever for a single real estate asset in the United States. It was, as the brochure stated, a "once in a lifetime opportunity." It was maybe a hundred pages thicker than the typical sales brochure from a longtime landlord, which tended to sketch out some vital statistics about the number of units in the building and the current rent roll. The pro forma is almost always rosy, but not so rosy that it would discourage the buyer from thinking that he or she could do better.

Stacom's starting point was the sheer size of the sister complexes: 12.7 million square feet—the equivalent of nearly five Empire State Buildings—with 11,232 apartments, 100,000 square feet of convenience-oriented shops, 17,000 square feet of professional office space, 15 playgrounds and a total of 2,260 parking spaces in six separate garages. The book suggested a new owner could pull a variety of levers to boost the income stream, ranging from combining apartments for larger families and creating "senior friendly" buildings to filling the retail space with deluxe stores paying higher rents. The parking garages could be opened to the public at higher rates than those currently charged to tenants. In addition, the loop roadways in the complexes could be reserved for monthly parkers "with revenue potential approaching $1 million."

Although the rather spartan apartments at Stuyvesant Town-Peter Cooper never had a "luxury" image in the minds of most New Yorkers, the book suggested that "importing doormen" and adding "health club amenities" and "an elite private school" would establish a compelling ambiance for "the discerning tastes of Manhattan's market-rate apartment community." Finally, there were potential "development rights" on the eighty-acre site that might enable a new owner to erect a more typical brass-and-glass high-rise condominium building.

"New ownership has infinite opportunities to personalize, improve and transform the complex into the city's most prominent market-rate master community," the book from CB Richard Ellis stated.

But the sales pitch indicated that the primary way to increase revenues and, presumably, profits was to deregulate apartments and hike rents. If all went according to plan, the book estimated that rents could more than double by 2018 to nearly $519 million at Stuyvesant Town and to $170 million at Peter Cooper. Approximately 72 percent of the complex's 11,232 apartments were rent stabilized under New York law, meaning rent increases were restricted by the city's Rent Guidelines Board, usually to 2, 3 or 4 percent per year.

The disparity in rent and income between regulated and

market-rate rents was striking. At Stuyvesant Town, where few apartments have more than one bathroom, residents of rent-regulated apartments paid an average of $1,351 for a two-bedroom unit, while the average rent for a deregulated apartment was 134 percent higher, at $3,167.

At Peter Cooper Village, where the apartments are somewhat larger, the average rent for regulated units was $1,178 for a one-bedroom to $1,581 for a three-bedroom. The average rent for deregulated apartments, which routinely underwent a $50,000 upgrade at Peter Cooper with new kitchen cabinets, stone counters and a refurbished bathroom, ranged from $2,662 to $5,842. The yawning gap between rent-stabilized rents and market rates is what made so many buyers willing to, essentially, overpay. The question in their minds was, how fast can we bring apartments to market rents?

A landlord cannot simply evict a tenant and start charging higher rents. The New York rent-stabilization laws protect more than one million apartments from steep rent increases. However, under a byzantine set of regulations, once an apartment becomes vacant, it can be deregulated under certain conditions. Landlords are permitted to pass on to tenants a portion of the cost of certain capital improvements, which helps them in getting above the $2,000-a-month threshold. So for instance, MetLife said it usually spent $40,000 renovating vacant apartments at Stuyvesant Town. Under the law in 2006, the landlord would be permitted to increase the rent by one-fortieth of the cost, or $1,000 per month. Therefore, a vacant apartment that had rented for $1,100 or more per month would automatically be deregulated.

At the same time, MetLife and its managing agent, Rose Associates, sought to weed out tenants who did not qualify for a stabilized unit, either because the tenant had illegally subleased the apartment, or because the apartment was not the tenant's primary residence. Between the eviction of so-called illegal tenants and the renovation of vacant apartments, known as "vacancy decontrol," MetLife had deregulated roughly three thousand apartments in Stuyvesant Town and Peter Cooper since 2000. In other words, the MetLife executive, or anyone else, who lived in New Jersey but kept an apartment in Stuyvesant Town for the occasional weekend visit to Manhattan was now out of luck.

The sales book suggested that a new owner could more quickly deregulate apartments by adopting a more aggressive approach to eliminating those "illegal" tenants. And the turnover rate, the number of apartments that could be brought to market rents in any given year, became critical to any buyer's calculations. According to the projections in the book, the number of market-rate apartments in Stuyvesant Town-Peter Cooper Village would rise to 6,307, or more than half the total units, by the end of 2011, from 3,247 in 2006. That kind of rapid turnover—an average of 612 apartments per year, and nearly 100 units more than what MetLife had done in the prior two years—would result in a tripling of the net operating income to $316.7 million in 2011, and $437.6 million in 2015. That upside potential was what had captivated so many bidders. Of course, it all depended on rents and demand continuing to rise at a steady clip. And it meant they would have to evict many people and raise rents by 25 percent or more.

But in the first couple of years, the new owner would have to plug the shortfall between the income from the property and the mortgage payments or debt service. The CB Richard Ellis sales book estimated that the net income in 2007 would be

$167.4 million, meaning the initial return for an investor paying the target price of more than $4 billion would be less than the roughly 5 percent return on a Treasury bill. In the feverish market for apartment buildings in New York City, buyers had been willing to accept smaller and smaller returns, in part because of the ready availability of credit from Wall Street and equity from investors. Bidders had their pick of banks and pension funds for the Stuyvesant Town-Peter Cooper sale.

"There's a lot of interest in this asset because of the fact it's a one-of-a-kind purchase," LeFrak said at the time. "On the other hand, however they try to cast it, it's not a trophy. It's meat and potatoes."[12]

"There was a lot of buzz," said Fred Lieblich of BlackRock, who was working with Rob Speyer. "Capital sources came out of the woodwork."[13]

"The lenders weren't exclusive," added James Simmons, a partner at Apollo. "Every single lending institution wanted to be aligned with what it thought were the leading bidders."[14]

As giddy as the bidders and their lenders were, tenants and housing activists were appalled by Stacom's book. For Garodnick, Doyle and their supporters it sounded like the death knell for Stuyvesant Town-Peter Cooper Village as Manhattan's unpretentious bastion for middle-class families. "Stuyvesant Town is a middle-class community, and we do not want to lose that identity to the highest bidder," said Garodnick. "The tenants are not going to sit by and watch it become a place of pieds-a-terre. This is a place where people live and work in New York City."

The tenants association and their lawyer-strategist Len Grunstein said Stacom and MetLife had initially refused to recognize them as a legitimate bidder and provide the sale book and other pertinent financial information. That prompted another rally at city hall with Garodnick, Quinn and other elected officials chastising MetLife's arrogant posture. MetLife insisted that it never tried to exclude the tenants. Stacom subsequently called Garodnick saying there must have been a misunderstanding and quickly relinquished the documents. If MetLife hesitated, they may have wanted to avoid conferring any legitimacy on the tenants by providing the book.

Inside Stuyvesant Town-Peter Cooper Village, Doyle; John H. Marsh III, a computer programmer; and other tenant leaders began circulating resolutions and petitions throughout the complex, as a way of informing both rent-regulated and market-rate residents about the issues and building a united front in favor of retaining their middle-class community. Marsh set up forums on the tenant union website and organized a network of volunteers in every building in Stuyvesant Town and Peter Cooper to relay the concerns of residents and to disburse literature. Often, Marsh said, the most diligent volunteers, easily identifiable in their official yellow T-shirts, were former MetLife employees and retired teachers living on their pensions.

"I saw it as a way of building a stronger, more self-sustaining tenant association," said Marsh, an intensely private man in his forties. "I kind of saw each building as its own village and the board as the unifying federal government."[15]

Senators Schumer and Hillary Clinton, Congresswoman Maloney, the city's public advocate Betsy Gotbaum and other elected officials publicly endorsed the tenant-led bid. By the end of September, the New York City Central Labor Council had also signed on. The council sent a September 29, 2006, letter to Mayor Bloomberg asking him to call for a meeting between MetLife and the tenants "in order to mediate a positive outcome for the residents of Stuyvesant Town-Peter Cooper Village."

"We have secured the sources of capital to join in purchasing this property," the letter also said. "We have an economically viable plan for MetLife to preserve their profit so we can save this working middle-class neighborhood."

Broadly speaking, Grunstein and Doyle wanted to create a condominium or cooperative in which at least 20 percent of the units would remain at affordable rents in perpetuity and another block of apartments would be sold to existing tenants at a discount to the market. There would be restrictions on the resale of those units so that they would remain affordable in the future. Another chunk of apartments would be sold to outsiders, with the proceeds used to pay down the debt and subsidize the rental units. "We're trying to maintain affordability and the same opportunities we and our parents had when they first moved here," Doyle said at the time.[16]

Stuyvesant Town-Peter Cooper Village was becoming a cause célèbre for housing activists in a city where even 750-square-foot, one-room studio apartments rent for more than $2,000 a month. "We have a housing crisis," said Rosie Mendez, city councilwoman for the Lower East Side, who submitted a bill designed to hobble MetLife's sale. "The city really needs to take a look at this. It alarmed me how much affordable housing we might be losing."[17]

The city's inventory of affordable housing for low- and moderate-income tenants had fallen sharply in recent years as private investors with deep pockets had purchased tens of thousands of tenement apartments in the poor and working-class neighborhoods of Harlem, Washington Heights, East New York,

Brooklyn and parts of Queens. Increasingly, not only poor people were finding it difficult to find housing that fit their budget, but now many middle-class New Yorkers saw prices and rents soar beyond their grasp. In 2005, Mayor Bloomberg announced an expanded $7.5 billion program to build 92,000 units of affordable housing and to preserve 73,000 units that were in state and city programs due to expire by 2013. But activists complained that the city was losing affordable housing units faster than new apartments were being built.

"This sale is the perfect illustration of the hole in the bottom of the bucket in the Bloomberg housing plan," Michael McKee, treasurer of the Tenants Political Action Committee, told the *New York Sun*, a weekly newspaper. "The plan deals only with production. They will never build as much as we're losing."

Grunstein and Gallagher, just like the other bidders, set up "war rooms" at their respective offices stocked with data about the two complexes and an elaborate financial model and tapped into New York's financial networks for partners capable of investing or financing the tenant bid. Gallagher talked to bankers at Deutsche Bank and JPMorgan Chase, as well as RREEF (Rosenberg Real Estate Equity Fund, named after founder Claude Rosenberg) and SL Green, a publicly traded real estate investment trust. He also talked to Colony Capital, a private real estate investment firm based in Los Angeles that controlled $36 billion worth of real estate around the globe, about becoming involved in the deal. It was an unusual transaction for Colony, a clear-eyed investor. But the company thought that the tenant group might emerge from the crowded field as a contender, if only because of the increasingly political atmosphere.

"It was not, when you think about who we are, the most natural fit for us," recalled Richard B. Saltzman, Colony's president, who was involved in the negotiations. "That's why we ended up playing it with a different angle, dealing directly with the tenants. We thought, 'Maybe there's an opportunity for us to buy on a much more cost-effective basis, versus any of the other groups.' It was going to be a fairly visible hot potato and there was a chance that the seller might bite and deal directly with the tenants."[18]

Grunstein approached Ziel Feldman and Kevin P. Maloney of the Property Markets Group, a New York real estate firm with $3 billion in assets. He also turned to a client and onetime friend who owned the landmark Woolworth Building near city hall in Lower Manhattan, Ruby Schron. A billionaire, Schron ran a real estate company with holdings in fourteen states that managed over thirty thousand apartments. Despite the size of his empire, he was not well-known because he rarely if ever talked to the press. But he did operate a complex similar to Stuyvesant Town, Fresh Meadows in Queens, which was originally built by another insurance company, New York Life. Schron considered investing as much as $300 million and managing the two complexes.

As the October 5 deadline for the first round of bids neared, Grunstein and Gallagher hopped from one meeting to another with bankers, investors, the tenants association and Garodnick in an effort to formalize the offer. With the help of Quinn's office, Garodnick also met with many of the other bidders, who were interested at least in hearing the concerns of the tenants and at most in forming a partnership. He also met with city officials, including Shaun Donovan, then the city's housing commissioner, about enhancing the value of the tenant bid. Would the city provide subsidies for the units that would be rent stabilized and, perhaps, provide tax-free financing? Could the city also provide a property tax exemption to keep the complex affordable in perpetuity? Grunstein was already talking about creating a nonprofit corporation to own the property.

Early on, city officials had seemed receptive. Emily A. Youssouf, president of the city's Housing Development Corporation, which encourages private investment in low- and moderately priced housing through low-interest mortgages and tax-free bonds, told reporters that her agency could use its reserves to make a loan to a buyer that would enable them to offer the apartments to current residents at a price they could afford. "Clearly, the potential sale of Stuyvesant Town-Peter Cooper Village is of significant concern to the administration and the mayor would very much want to work with any potential buyer to preserve affordable housing in these properties," said Donovan, the housing commissioner.[19]

But as the weeks wore on and it became clear that the sale price would be well above $4 billion, two opposing views surfaced within the Bloomberg administration. Shaun Donovan, the housing commissioner, and Rafael E. Cestero, a deputy commissioner, began analyzing the sale book and the potential cost of subsidizing the tenant bid. City hall had gotten a heads-up from Henrikson about the pending sale, so it was no surprise. Separately, Emily Youssouf at the Housing Development Corporation conducted a similar analysis. In August, Deputy Mayor Daniel L. Doctoroff, Donovan and Cestero met with Stacom at city hall to discuss the sale process, the real estate market and the underwriting for the sale. They knew it was "going to create a lot of noise."

Cestero set up what he referred to as a SWAT team at the Department of Housing. The officials recognized that the sale did not have to go through a regulatory review, which somewhat limited the city's ability to intervene. But Cestero also knew that the loss of rent-regulated housing at Stuyvesant Town-Peter Cooper Village could knock a big hole in the mayor's much-heralded housing plan. He and his team spent weeks digging through Stacom's sale book and analyzing different financial structures in which the city could use its standard tools for creating affordable housing—low-cost financing, a property tax break and cash subsidies—on a $5 billion deal.

Doctoroff met at city hall on September 7 with MetLife's general counsel James L. Lipscomb and its senior vice president in charge of government relations, Michael A. Zarcone, in an effort to gauge the insurance company's reaction if the city were to intervene on behalf of the tenants. Was there a way for the city to preserve a block of units as affordable housing that would not impair MetLife's ability to make a profit? For their part, the executives were absolute: The sale of the property was a private transaction. MetLife was furious that the Stuyvesant Town sale was being cast as a blow to "affordable housing." They had kept true to the bargain struck with Mayor La Guardia by keeping rents low for thirty-five years. Moreover, John Calagna, a MetLife vice president, said, "This is not a middle-class oasis. The median income at Peter Cooper is $80,000 and the average is $120,000."[20]

Whether or not they qualify as middle class by MetLife's definition, a two-income family earning $100,000 finds it hard to raise children in Manhattan given the high rents and sale prices. According to census figures, 15 percent of the Stuyvesant Town-Peter Cooper residents were sixty-five or older and presumably living on social security and pension payments. Cestero came up with a plan and presented it to Doctoroff, a former investment banker, who poked holes in the proposal, questioned some of the assumptions and asked him to run the numbers again. By the third week of September, Cestero had revised his analysis and was questioning the economic viability of a $5 billion price tag for the two complexes. His judgment was that the sales book assumed a turnover rate that was far too aggressive.

He surmised that the size of the mortgage would be prohibitive and the revenue assumptions, based on the rapid conversion of rent-regulated units to market rents, were unlikely to be achieved. Therefore he concluded that it would be a poor use of scarce city resources to intervene in such an overheated market on behalf of tenants, a move that could cost as much as $700 million in cash, incentives and tax breaks, the equivalent of the capital budget for the city's housing agency for two and a half years.[21] In any event, his report said that 20 percent of the apartments would remain rent regulated for twenty-five years under the current laws. Cestero said he sent his conclusions to Donovan, who passed it on to Doctoroff, who concurred.

"Even after making a number of aggressive assumptions about what would happen at the property in terms of turnover, we couldn't figure out how to get to more than $4.5 billion in value, and that was at the far end of our projections," said Donovan, who was later appointed U.S. secretary of housing and urban development by President Barack Obama. "And $4.5 billion would've been a very high price to pay for that amount of affordable housing."[22]

Doctoroff, Cestero and Donovan met privately at city hall with what they viewed as the leading contenders for the property, including Rob Speyer, Jim Simmons of Apollo, and William P. Dickey of Dermot. All three men said that while city officials mainly asked questions, they left the meeting with the clear sense that the city would remain on the sidelines. "They said," Dickey recalled, "'We haven't seen a reason to intervene and we don't know what we'd do if there was one.'"[23]

Stephen Ross and Bruce Beal of Related also met with Donovan, Youssouf and Doctoroff, who had a long-term friendship with Ross. Ross and Beal had been hoping that Donovan or Doctoroff would make a public statement urging MetLife to ensure that one-fifth of the apartments at Stuyvesant Town remained under rent stabilization forever. They owned and managed subsidized housing in the city, as well as luxury buildings. Beal told them he would bid for the property and he wanted the city to pledge to freeze property taxes and provide incentives for affordable housing. But his plea was met with silence.

"They wanted the city to put in a ridiculous amount of money," Youssouf scoffed.[24]

Meanwhile, Youssouf, who continued meeting with Garodnick, was more sympathetic to a tenant-led bid. She had told the *Times* early on that MetLife had "built the properties with the help of the city" and the tenant today could make a winning bid with a city-assisted deal. Youssouf and her deputy John Crotty, a lifelong resident of Stuyvesant Town, devised a non-eviction plan to turn Stuyvesant Town and Peter Cooper into a co-op with city bonds and a cap on property taxes for ten years. William Thompson, the city comptroller, said he was willing to invest pension funds in support of the tenant bid, and Quinn offered enthusiastic political support.

It was nowhere near as expensive as her colleagues from the housing agency indicated, Youssouf insisted. Renters could remain in place, while the proceeds from the sale of thousands of other apartments could be used to pay down the initial debt. She sent her own report to Doctoroff and lobbied for its adoption by phone while attending a housing conference in San Francisco on September 19.

But Mayor Bloomberg had already assured MetLife executives at their first meeting at city hall that he had no intention of interfering in a private transaction. He had made public statements to that effect. His deputies were well aware of Bloomberg's views.

For those who said the city should not intervene in a free-market deal, Youssouf countered that MetLife was given free land in the 1940s to build the complexes and had since made a fortune on the property. She argued that the city should act to preserve this middle-class enclave in Manhattan. "This was a way to create a large amount of affordable housing," Youssouf said. "We tried to counter every argument to make it the least costly alternative. I was frankly devastated they didn't do this."[25]

Her relationship with Donovan, an equally strong personality, was stormy and she was unable to convince Doctoroff, who subsequently ordered her to fall into line. "You're off the reservation," Doctoroff told her, according to housing officials. "You've got to get on the same team."

Publicly, Doctoroff would only say that the city "continued to monitor the situation," but he warned reporters privately that he did not want to leave the impression that intervention by the city was likely.

CHAPTER SEVEN

"The More You Spend, the More We Can Lend Against It"

On October 5, thirteen bidders submitted their offers to Stacom in what was essentially the qualifying round for the sale. All the bidders knew that the second round would be the showdown. Like elite runners in a marathon, the question for the bidders was whether to come out strong and try to scare off the competition, or draft behind the front-runner until the last mile, then spring to the finish line with a blockbuster number. All of the bidders signed confidentiality agreements prohibiting them from disclosing information about the bidding, the sales book and the finances of Stuyvesant Town-Peter Cooper Village. But there are few secrets in the clubby world of real estate.

Rob Speyer and BlackRock were the highest, with a $5.1 billion offer, according to key figures in the sales process. Simon Glick, who owned a major stake in the Canary Wharf office complex in London, was not far behind. His partner was the Morgan Stanley Real Estate Fund and he had a $5 billion line of credit from Barclays. The Apollo–ING Clarion–Dermot group was also ranked near the front.

Garodnick, Doyle and the tenant association submitted a surprisingly high offer, $4.5 billion, in partnership with Colony Capital, Ruby Schron and JPMorgan Chase. Yet, it was a very tenuous alliance that threatened to unravel at any moment. The tenant group wanted to stay in the game. Even if it was not the highest offer, they hoped that a respectable bid might prompt MetLife to strike a deal with them, if only to avoid the political fallout from ignoring the residents.

The Related Companies and Lehman Brothers were in the same neighborhood, as was Steve Roth of Vornado Realty Trust, who had picked up the royal family of Qatar as a partner. Ofer Yardeni, the Israeli cofounder of Stonehenge Partners, offered $4.6 billion. He was backed by Cadim, a division of the giant Canadian pension fund manager Caisse de Dépôt et Placement du Quebec. Yardeni planned to move his headquarters to Stuyvesant Town if he won so that he could oversee what he saw as a long-term project, providing high-end renovations and better amenity packages. He said he would dedicate several buildings for "elderly people," hoping to move long-term residents, whose children had gone, from two- and three-bedroom apartments to smaller units.

Many of the city's wealthy real estate families decided to stay on the sidelines. In their minds, the risks were too great. The Rudins never made an offer. Douglas Durst, the patriarch of the Durst real estate family, which owned ten skyscrapers in Manhattan, had been talking about joining Richard LeFrak, who also dropped out, saying, "It was just too expensive."[1]

Durst had taken a chance in the late 1990s when he started building the first speculative office tower in Times Square in more than a decade, the forty-eight-story tower at 4 Times Square, on Forty-Second Street. As it turned out, the building was fully leased by the time it opened in 2000 and helped lead the revival of Times Square. At Stuyvesant Town, he was interested in erecting new buildings on the green spaces while LeFrak ran the existing housing. But the bidding made it riskier than Times Square. "When it got north of four billion dollars, it was just too ridiculous," Durst said. "It was too much of a hope and a prayer that all these things would happen. We just stopped."[2]

Douglas Eisenberg of Urban American also went to the sidelines. Residential buildings were his business, he said, but in the last year, he had been outbid for the Riverton complex in Harlem in 2005 and the nearby Delano Village complex in early 2006. To him, the prices were based on highly speculative assumptions about where rents and revenues would be in the coming years. "We got up to about $4.4 billion," Eisenberg recalled. "Darcy said, 'Guys, this is going for a lot higher than that.' But there was no way you could promise a reasonable return to your investors and make it work. A week before the bids were due, we came to the conclusion that this was really silly."[3]

Stacom's job, at this point, was to keep as many players in the game as possible while coaxing each of them to sweeten their offer, sometimes substantially. Stacom, bidders said, was very effective at leaving each bidder with the impression that she was telling them, and them alone, some piece of vital information that would help them gauge the unfolding battle. Discreetly, she would signal the bidders that they had to raise their offer to stay in the game.

"Nobody manages a complex, intensely competitive bid process better than Darcy," said Marty Edelman, a shrewd real estate lawyer who was working for the Apollo–ING Clarion–Dermot group. "She is like the best auctioneer at Christie's:

Every deal is priceless and she will help you understand why you must move your bid to the winner's circle."[4]

Dan Neidich, a partner at Dune Capital who was working with LeFrak, was more blunt: "What Darcy did well was pit people against each other who all wanted the same thing."[5]

Garodnick, Doyle, Grunstein and the unions had been hoping that they could catapult ahead of the other bidders with the political and financial support of the city. But a day after the first bids were submitted, Mayor Bloomberg expressed no willingness to jump into the middle of what he called a private transaction during his regular Friday radio broadcast. He assured listeners that regardless of the sale, the city would continue to build low-, moderate- and middle-income housing.

"MetLife owns it and they have a right to sell it," Bloomberg said of Stuyvesant Town-Peter Cooper Village. Moreover, Bloomberg played down the consequences of the sale for the ability of the middle class to live in Manhattan. "A lot of people want to live there," he told listeners. "That's part of the problem. When people want to live somewhere prices go up. When they don't, prices go down. The character of this community will change, but it will change slowly, over time. And it would change whether this is sold or not."[6]

Bloomberg's insistence that he would not interfere with a private transaction was somewhat disingenuous. The Bloomberg administration had played a critical financial role in supporting a tenant-led cooperative conversion plan at the West Village Houses. And in the late 1990s, the city and state had provided tax abatements that enabled an organization called CPC Resources to take over Parkchester, the 12,200-unit complex built and once owned by MetLife in the Bronx, where a condominium conversion had failed and the property had begun to crumble. In a partnership with a private developer, CPC was able to rescue the complex, restructure its finances and ensure that the apartments remained affordable. But it is also true that the scale of a Stuyvesant Town-Peter Cooper Village intervention would have been well beyond the $19 million in interest payments the Bloomberg administration forgave the owner of the West Village Houses.

Garodnick, of course, saw the situation far differently than Mayor Bloomberg. Just as Mayor Fiorello La Guardia and Robert Moses had encouraged MetLife to build Stuyvesant Town as a way of anchoring the middle class to the urban center, Garodnick argued that it was important for the city to ensure that the middle class could live in Manhattan. "The city cannot survive and attract new businesses if teachers, firefighters, municipal clerks and nurses are priced out of the market," he said.

"It's very important for the city's economy to do so," Garodnick told the *New York Times*. "That's why it's generated so much interest, not just locally, but nationally. We expect to make a competitive bid here, one that will allow MetLife to make a profit and also honor the tradition of affordability."

Stephen M. Ross and Bruce Beal of Related made a similar argument, even if city officials deemed their subsidy demand to be ridiculously large.

More than three-fifths of the fifty-one-member city council signed a resolution backing the tenant bid. Community Board Six, a city-sponsored advisory group whose district included Stuyvesant Town-Peter Cooper Village, also voted to support the tenants. Playing defense, Garodnick and Councilwoman Rosie Mendez proposed legislation that, in light of the loss of thousands of rent-stabilized units every year, would require large residential property owners to provide 120-day notification of their intention to sell if more than half the units were rent regulated. Sponsors said the proposed law was not meant to restrict an owner's right to sell, but rather to give the city time to assess the potential impact of a transaction on the city's housing crisis.

Bloomberg seemed to stake out an ideological position that government should not interfere with private transactions, even if government routinely mediates between business interests and the public good through environmental regulations, zoning, licensing and the bully pulpit. But it also would have been fiscally irresponsible for the city to feed the speculative fires by subsidizing a bid that housing officials believed would collapse from unrealistic assumptions and oversize debts.

However, many critics suggested that Bloomberg could have mounted the bully pulpit, much as he has to advocate for gun control, green buildings, bike lanes and banning supersize sugary sodas. He could have urged MetLife and prospective bidders to preserve some percentage of the apartments as permanently rent-regulated housing, ensuring that middle-class families could make their homes at Stuyvesant Town. After all, Stuyvesant Town was built jointly by the private sector and the city, which provided tax breaks, land and zoning to ensure its success. That kind of stance by one of the nation's most prominent mayors might have achieved a public good and tamped down the extravagant bidding that ensued. But that is exactly what MetLife wanted to avoid when it made its case to Bloomberg at city hall.

The trajectory of Richard S. LeFrak's bid illuminates the seasoned approach of a real estate veteran and the effect of a casino-like atmosphere on Wall Street that was driving prices higher and higher. Unlike all but a handful of bidders, LeFrak actually owned rent-regulated apartments in New York, more than ten thousand of them. Rent-regulated, or -stabilized, apartments were a distinct subset of residential housing, with their own culture, laws and tenant history. They couldn't be confused with luxury, market-rate housing. A landlord who failed to grasp the difference could end up subsumed in bitter courtroom battles with tenants, regulatory sanctions and political attacks from elected officials.

LeFrak, a third-generation developer with deep pockets, jumped at the opportunity to buy Stuyvesant Town-Peter Cooper Village. He figured few companies would be willing to risk entering the sometimes-treacherous terrain of rent-regulated housing in New York City. The LeFrak empire, which was all about large scale, was founded by Harry LeFrak, a glazier who moved to New York in the early 1900s. Harry made enough money to buy a 120-acre farm in Brooklyn, which he subdivided and then built small houses and apartment buildings on the subdivisions.

But it was his son Sam, a blustery, oversize personality with unbridled ambition, who took great chances on large-scale real estate development. Everything about Sam was big, even his business card, which was embossed with honorary degrees and knighthoods. Although Sam consistently denied craving acceptance by the Manhattan elite, he donated $10 million to the Guggenheim Museum, but only after they agreed to inscribe his name prominently on the fifth-floor gallery of the Fifth Avenue building.

Starting in 1959, Sam built LeFrak City, a vast network of twenty eighteen-story towers, comprising five thousand apartments and fifteen thousand residents, as well as two million square feet of retail space, atop a former swamp in Queens. It was far larger than most projects built by private developers. He was focused on the expanding working and middle class who lived outside of Manhattan, rather than building glass and brass towers for the wealthy. In those days, Sam, whose empire included a stable of fifty-five horses and oil wells in Louisiana, was fond of saying, "We serve the mass, not the class."

But many observers thought Sam had lost his touch in the 1970s when he bought a six-hundred-acre defunct railroad yard on the Hudson River waterfront in Jersey City, a declining industrial city. For years, the land sat fallow. He and his son Richard, however, typically bought property for the long term, rather than a quick killing. Over thirty years, they were instrumental in creating a modern skyline with more than twenty-five residential and commercial towers in Jersey City, one mile across the Hudson River from downtown Manhattan. Richard and his sons, Harrison and Jamie, now preside over twenty-two million square feet of residential property, the equivalent of about twenty-five thousand apartments, and twelve million square feet of office space.

Richard has none of the noisy flamboyance of his father but all the family's work ethic and aversion to high-risk financing. The LeFraks are wealthy enough to finance their own projects. "Our normal modus operandi," he said, "is to use our own capital. But that approach wasn't applicable" at Stuyvesant Town. Unlike many developers, he usually says what he means, regardless of whether it offends mayors or community groups.

LeFrak envisioned putting up perhaps a billion dollars of his own money to buy Stuyvesant Town-Peter Cooper Village and getting a $2 billion mortgage. He was largely unfamiliar with the exotic financing methods that had come into vogue on Wall

Street, be it mezzanine loans or "bridge financing," which are short-term loans designed to give a buyer time to line up equity partners to fill in any gaps.

Stacom's sale book indicated that MetLife had converted 525 rent-regulated apartments annually to market rates, or 4.7 percent of the total number of units, in recent years. Her projections indicated that a new owner could push the conversion number to 600 units in 2007 and 1,000 units in 2008. This was important information for any bidder trying to understand future cash flows.

"I didn't pay much attention to Darcy's projections," said LeFrak, then sixty-one, "only because I had my own statistics." Based on the history of his own apartment buildings, he knew that tenants in rent-regulated apartments tend to stay in place far longer than market-rate tenants, a critical point for anyone trying to calculate the value of the property. "The longer they stay the more likely it is that they'll never leave," LeFrak said. "So the remaining stabilized tenants at Stuyvesant Town-Peter Cooper Village are going to be much stickier than the first twenty-eight percent."[7]

Based on his experience with 13,000 stabilized apartments between 1996 and 2005, the turnover rate was likely to be 2.9 percent to 3.6 percent, which would translate into a far more modest increase in net income in the coming years than Stacom or most other bidders projected. By contrast, a quarter of all market-rate tenants turn over every year. He figured that there might be some "illegal" tenants, although MetLife had been weeding them out for six years. So in September, LeFrak ran his numbers and estimated that Stuyvesant Town-Peter Cooper was worth about $3 billion as a rental complex. He did not think that a co-op conversion was feasible.

But he knew that $3 billion would not win the day. So he ran his numbers a second time, adjusted his return expectations and raised his projections for rents on the commercial space at the complex. But that only got him to $3.35 billion. LeFrak was working with Steven T. Mnuchin and Daniel Neidich of Dune Capital Management, which invests in entertainment and real estate projects. Coincidentally, Neidich, a former investment banker at Goldman Sachs, had overseen the investment bank's purchase of Rockefeller Center in partnership with the Speyers. LeFrak and Mnuchin were also working with the bankers at Credit Suisse First Boston, Citicorp and UBS. The bankers, however, did not share LeFrak's sense of caution. "They kept saying, 'Don't worry about the money,'" LeFrak said. "In those days, nobody worried about the money. We always did.

"Our colleagues were encouraged by Darcy and the unbridled optimism of the debt community," LeFrak continued. "We were told, 'The more you spend, the more we can lend against it.' Our good judgment was cast aside. We finally came up with a bid of $4.5 billion in the first round."[8]

At that price, LeFrak figured there'd be "no cash flow for the first three to five years. You had to capitalize the negative cash flow until you could turn over more apartments." But LeFrak, by his own description, was like a man teetering on the ledge of a high-rise building. He felt sweaty and disoriented by the yawning gap between his revenue estimates and the sale price. Then, Stacom called him about the second round of bidding, saying, "If you come up to $5 billion you can keep playing," LeFrak recalled. "I thought it was ridiculous when it got beyond $3 billion."[9] Instead, the billionaire stepped down off the ledge and quit playing.

After the initial flurry of activity leading up to the first round, there were still nearly ten groups scrambling to refine their bids, locate partners and lock down lenders. The second, and presumably final, round was only days away, on October 17. With so much money at stake, Tishman Speyer, the Apollo–ING Clarion–Dermot group, the Related Companies and the others were meeting on a daily basis. How much higher could they go? The real estate industry is notoriously incestuous in New York and the grapevine was rife with information, however inaccurate, about each bid. The industry rumors put the Apollo–ING Clarion–Dermot group among the front-runners, along with Related. But Steven Roth, the chairman of Vornado Realty Trust, which owned mainly commercial, industrial and retail property, was still in the game, along with Ofer Yardeni, the Israeli commando turned real estate investor, who had nicknamed his bid Project Snoopy, in reference to MetLife's mascot. And even if few people in the real estate industry knew who he was, Simon Glick had the wherewithal and assets to buy the prize. But Tishman Speyer and the gigantic BlackRock firm were the team to beat. They had the connections and they both usually got what they wanted.

After a decade of on-the-job training, Rob Speyer was in command. Sure, his father's imprint was on every Tishman Speyer project. Jerry also had the long-standing personal relationships with Richard S. Fuld, chairman of Lehman Brothers; Sandy Weill, who merged Travelers into Citicorp; and Lester Crown, patriarch of one of the country's most wealthy families and Tishman Speyer's largest, most consistent partner. The Crowns owned hefty stakes in General Dynamics, Maytag, Hilton Hotels, Alitel, Rockefeller Center and the Chicago Bulls basketball team. Like Jerry Speyer, Lester Crown was also a minority partner in the New York Yankees.

But Rob had been running deals for his father's company for several years now, even if it was largely outside the media spotlight. He had proven to be a fast, if impatient, learner during his apprenticeship. Rob had been a latecomer to real estate, not having shown the slightest interest in the field until he was well into his twenties. He grew up in Manhattan, attending Dalton, the elite private school on the Upper East Side, where he was a top student and competed on the wrestling team. He went to Harvard, where he was a research assistant for Graham T. Allison, dean of Harvard's John F. Kennedy School of Government and an expert in foreign policy and nuclear deterrence. But not long after arriving in Cambridge, Massachusetts, Rob realized "it was the wrong place for [him]."

He stuck it out at Harvard through his second year, before dropping out of school. He moved back to New York, where his parents were in the middle of a divorce. Feeling adrift, Rob went to work for Andrew Cuomo, Governor Mario Cuomo's son, at Housing Enterprise for the Less Privileged. Cuomo had started the organization in 1986 to build and operate low-income housing for the homeless, with an abundance of social services, from job training to drug counseling. The two men developed a continuing friendship.

"I was a lost soul," Speyer said. "I asked Andrew if I could open his mail. He took me in at a tough point in my life. He was there for me, an important older brother figure at a critical moment."

After a year away from school, Rob transferred to Columbia University, where his father had been chairman of the board of trustees. He was set on becoming a political science professor and planned on going to England after graduation on a prestigious Marshall scholarship to study at Oxford University. But one day that spring he ran into a tumultuous demonstration at Columbia in support of striking campus workers. On a whim, he telephoned the *New York Observer,* a feisty weekly known for its irreverent coverage of the rich and powerful. He provided a breathless account of the demonstration and an interview with a provost whose office had been overrun by demonstrators. As Rob recounted the action, reporter Terry Golway took it down. A day later it was on the newsstands. Suddenly, Rob was hooked on journalism. He graduated but turned down the Marshall scholarship and joined the staff of the *Observer.*

"It was the most exciting experience of my life," he told me. "In that moment, I decided there was no way I was staying in school. I never considered going into the family business."[10]

Speyer spent a year at the *Observer* before moving to one of the city's tabloids, the *Daily News.* He wrote about everything from boxer Mike Tyson's love child to a riot at a New Jersey immigration center and the U.S. invasion of Haiti. During a fire drill at the offices of the *Daily News* in 1995, he was caught unawares when a colleague asked him about his father's pending purchase of Rockefeller Center in partnership with the Rockefeller family and Goldman Sachs. His love affair with journalism was about to end.

"We didn't talk much about real estate," Rob said of his father.

"I asked my father, 'What's going on?'" Rob was captivated by his father's two-year quest to buy the complex and his vision for Rockefeller Center, which treated the iconic complex as a living organism. His father wanted to buff the landmark towers while enlivening the shop fronts and plazas. "My first lesson was my father's intense focus on the deal, day and night, for a year," Rob told me. "Nothing was going to stop Jerry from getting the deal done."[11]

Rob joined his father almost immediately after they bought Rockefeller Center, starting in the management and leasing department. Even his sister Valerie, an executive at Tishman Speyer, was surprised by the move and doubted whether he would stick it out. Jerry Speyer tapped Geoffrey P. Wharton, the senior partner in charge of Rockefeller Center, to oversee Rob's apprenticeship. Early on, Rob was an eager student and a quick learner, those who know him say, but he had a tendency to be bullheaded. He had a reputation inside the company for anger-management problems and rotated through a succession of secretaries, unlike his father, whose assistant has worked for him for decades. Over time, people who know him say that he settled down.

"Jerry made it clear to me that one of my responsibilities as a partner and a friend was to make sure that Rob was ready to take over the company at the right time," recalled Wharton, who left Tishman Speyer in 2001 to run the World Trade Center.[12] Wharton narrowly escaped death on September 11, 2001, when he left a breakfast meeting on the 106th floor of the North Tower moments before terrorists flew a passenger jet into the side of the building.

Rob's first deal brought the upscale Reebok Sports Club to

the complex, replacing the U.S. passport office, whose long lines contributed to the bland, service-oriented ambiance of Rockefeller Center. Years later, he headed a team that figured out how to reopen to the public the observatory at the seventieth floor of 30 Rockefeller Plaza, the 2.9-million-square-foot centerpiece of the complex. The key was reengineering the elevators to carry visitors swiftly to the "Top of the Rock" observation deck without interfering with their demanding office tenants, such as Lazard, the 150-year-old investment bank. It turned into a gold mine, attracting two million visitors a year and throwing off $25 million in annual profits.

But even before he had chalked up his own victories, Rob was accorded respect from the real estate fraternity, which recognized that he was the heir apparent to one of New York's most powerful and politically connected families. At a late-1990s real estate party that drew over a thousand top brokers, lawyers, bankers and developers, one executive after another, many of them older and more experienced, approached Rob with deference, as if they wanted to kiss his ring. A gregarious man with a slim figure who always looked good in a suit, Rob seemed largely oblivious to their fawning.

In 1998, Rob joined the company's acquisitions and development department, where he helped modernize the headquarters of the Colgate-Palmolive Company at 300 Park Avenue, which was considered one of the ugliest buildings in midtown. Sandy Lindenbaum, one of the best lawyers at navigating New York City's arcane zoning regulations, worked with Rob on that project. Normally, Lindenbaum, who was friendly with Rob's grandfather Robert Tishman, did not bring his clients to the often-tedious meetings with zoning and landmark officials. Rob had other ideas. "I really want to learn the business," he told Lindenbaum. "Even if you don't need me, I want to go with you."[13]

Rob's team at Tishman Speyer, which bought the twenty-five-story building for $180 million in partnership with Travelers, transformed the dowdy structure, installing a new $12 million facade of aluminum spandrels and transparent green glass. The property is fully leased and now worth an estimated $1 billion.

Rob was also instrumental in developing an office building on a rare midtown parking lot, where his partner, Travelers, owned the development rights. But the land itself was owned by a cantankerous real estate developer named Stanley Stahl, whom Rob had met as a boy. He worked out a lease for the land shortly before Stahl died and began erecting an office tower, without having a single tenant. Speculative office buildings are a rarity in Manhattan because of the extraordinary cost of land and construction and the difficulty in getting financing without a blue-chip tenant. But Speyer caught the market on an upswing and landed a prominent law firm and technology firm. He sold the building for $76 million shortly before it was completed, netting a hefty profit on a $6 million equity investment.

"It was made clear to me by my father when I was a kid that there were two kinds of people who were born to privilege," Rob said. "One kind lived off the fat of the land. My father called them consumers. The other kind is more motivated to succeed. I fell into the latter category. I always wanted to be successful."

By 2006, Rob was a senior managing director of Tishman Speyer and chairman of the management committee. He threw himself into the Stuyvesant Town deal with the same fervor with which his father had chased Rockefeller Center. That fall he visited the complexes a dozen times, he said, sometimes on a Saturday, dressed in shorts and a T-shirt, just to get a feel for the place. "It's the only place in Manhattan with a neighborhood feel," he told me in 2006. "I grew up on the Upper East Side and didn't even know my next-door neighbor."

He had a team of twenty executives at Tishman Speyer working on the deal in their own "war room," much like every other bidder, including the tenants. He worked with an equal number of executives at BlackRock, refining projections, looking for new ways to make money at the complexes with better retailers and health clubs and calculating exactly how much higher they could go, or needed to go, with their bid. About 71 percent of the apartments were rent regulated, with residents paying an average of $1,338 a month, while market-rate rents averaged three times that number, or more than $4,000 a month. They estimated that they could push the proportion of market-rate units to 63 percent over the next seven years and boost net operating income to $397 million from $105.6 million.

Rob Verrone, the thirty-eight-year-old Wachovia banker who was nicknamed "Large Loan Verrone" for his prodigious ability to make huge interest-only commercial loans to developers who put little money down, had been keen from the beginning to do a deal with Tishman Speyer and BlackRock, particularly if it meant beating out Lehman Brothers.

But before he made a commitment, Verrone had also talked with Jeff Barclay of ING Clarion on behalf of his bidding group, as well as several other rivals. Jeffrey Scott, a senior Wachovia banker based in Washington who specialized in raising equity investors for real estate deals, championed the Clarion folks, because he knew them well. Although many of the banks talked to multiple bidders, it was a tricky business.

Whichever group Wachovia ultimately selected, there were sure to be hard feelings among the losers, who would suspect that the bank was then using inside information against them in the bidding. Verrone ultimately won the battle inside Wachovia to go with Tishman Speyer and BlackRock. As predicted, the executives at ING Clarion and Apollo were not happy.

Rob Speyer and Verrone were both relatively young, almost exactly the same age and cocky. They had done several deals together in Los Angeles. Verrone expected Tishman Speyer to come out on top at Stuyvesant Town; it was a bonus that he had nabbed a traditional Lehman customer.

Verrone promised them not only a $3 billion mortgage and $1.4 billion in mezzanine, or secondary, loans but also what was known in the business as "bridge equity." This was critical to the bid because MetLife wanted to pick a winner in October and close the deal thirty days later. That did not leave enough time to prepare an offer, conduct the due diligence on the property and gather almost $2 billion from equity investors so they could write a check in November. Hence, they needed bridge equity.

It was a lucrative line of business at Lehman Brothers, but one fraught with risk. Verrone was eager to expand into bridge equity. He had been losing financing deals to Lehman Brothers in part, he figured, because they were offering bridge equity. Before Stuyvesant Town, Verrone had only included bridge equity in two far smaller deals. In essence, the bank was buying a piece of the asset, say for $2 billion, until the bank and the buyers could resell it to new investors at a 4 percent markup. But if the market turned sharply downward and the buyers were unable to complete the deal, the bank would be left holding a $2 billion bag, which was suddenly declining in value. It was a danger that ultimately contributed to the collapse of Lehman Brothers.

Rob Speyer and the top executives at BlackRock confidently predicted they would have little trouble signing up equity investors. Verrone agreed, although he split the financing and the risk with Merrill Lynch. Wachovia would provide two-thirds of the senior mortgage, the mezzanine loans and the bridge equity; Merrill would cover the rest.

The partners also brought in Jonathan Mechanic, who ran the real estate department at the Fried Frank law firm and worked on many Tishman Speyer deals, to examine the proposed purchase and sale contract distributed to the finalists by MetLife and recommend any changes, knowing that MetLife frowned on revisions. Not long after submitting the initial offer, Rob Speyer and his colleagues from BlackRock arrived at the number that they thought would win the deal. On October 16, they began printing a half dozen copies of their bid package. "About a weekend beforehand," Rob Speyer said. "We decided to put our best foot forward in the second round, hopefully grabbing the deal and short-circuiting other rounds. We took a chance."[14]

Similar meetings and calculations took place all over Manhattan, with the Related Companies, Simon Glick and others. Glick's plan was not that different from the other bidders' in seeking to convert regulated apartments to market rents. But the pricing was not about some multiple of cash flow, the way buyers traditionally derived the worth of a property. That kind of thinking was passé. Wall Street lenders were willing to lend 70, 80, even 90 percent of the property's value, making a bet that the real estate boom would continue. The change in approach on underwriting fueled a surge in prices. Why not? The mortgages quickly dropped off their balance sheets, after being combined with other loans into a security and sold to other investors. On the first day a new landlord took over Stuyvesant Town-Peter Cooper Village, the rental income wouldn't even cover the debt service. But buyers, lenders and investors imagined that revenues would increase quickly in an ever-rising market.

"The price was dictated by the amount of debt you could put on the property," Glick said. "The assets were worth as much as the banks were willing to lend."[15]

Five blocks to the south, a dozen senior members of the Apollo group sat around a long table in a conference room at ING Clarion's office in the landmark Beaux Arts–style tower at 230 Park Avenue at East Forty-Sixth Street. Richard Mack and Andrew MacArthur had spent weeks visiting with state pension fund executives in an attempt to raise almost $3 billion in equity capital, so they could limit the amount they would have to borrow. They knew they were locked into battle with Tishman Speyer, but they also worried that they were getting "brokered up," meaning the broker was urging them to raise their offer higher than necessary to win. The debate over whether to increase their bid incrementally or go for a knockout punch dragged on for hours. Before lining up with Tishman Speyer, Verrone, the banker from Wachovia, had asked them, "Why are you bidding so low?" But Stephen J. Furnary, the chairman of ING Clarion, wondered whether it was possible to make money on a $5 billion deal. To resolve the dispute, they each agreed to write down the number they thought it would take to win the deal and drop it into a hat. Their scribbling sounded loud in the suddenly hushed room.

Furnary unfolded the slips and read out the numbers. The

spread was $5.2 billion to $5.45 billion. Furnary and Neibart, the voices of "moderation," were on the low end. Andrew MacArthur of Dermot, and Richard Mack and James Simmons of Apollo, were in between. Dickey, chairman of Dermot, wanted to go all in. Most of the people in the room were surprised when Barden Gale, usually a conservative investor, agreed with Dickey, arguing that once you got above $5 billion, it hardly made a difference whether they offered $5.3 billion or $5.5 billion. Gale was chief investment officer for APG Investments, a subsidiary of the largest pension fund administrator in the Netherlands, and a financial partner in the deal.[16]

Still, it took several more hours to come to an agreement. The next morning, October 17, the Apollo group was printing six copies of the bid documents and the purchase and sale agreement when the machine suddenly jammed. Jeff Barclay of ING Clarion called Stacom in a panic, saying he'd had a technology breakdown and would not be able to meet the noon deadline. Stacom urged him to get it to her as soon as possible. "I personally walked it across Forty-Fifth Street myself, took it up to her office and handed it to the receptionist," Barclay said. "It was a surreal moment. I don't think I'd ever handed over a bid package with a $5.33 billion offer. I didn't trust anyone else to do it."[17]

Meanwhile, Grunstein and Gallagher were scrambling to keep the tenant bid from unraveling. Their offer was different from the others in that Garodnick and Doyle were committed to retaining what they viewed as the ideals of Stuyvesant Town by converting the rental property to a cooperative. Although they were lining up the same kind of jumbo loans as the conventional bidders, the tenant plan envisioned paying off a chunk of the debt quickly through the sale of apartments to existing tenants at a discount and to outsiders for full price. Rent-stabilized tenants who did not want to buy could remain in place. The AFL-CIO pension funds were lined up for about $250 million to $300 million in equity.

Maura Keaney, deputy chief of staff for council speaker Quinn, worked with Garodnick, helping to set up meetings and assess the political landscape. But as Grunstein rejiggered the bid again and again in an effort to compete with the other bidders, Keaney got nervous. It was a case of diminishing returns, she thought, if your goal was affordable housing for teachers, construction workers and firefighters. "Every time you added a zero," Keaney said, "you lost something that was the whole reason for doing this."[18]

All the bidders, with the sole exception of Tishman Speyer, had met with Garodnick or Grunstein or both. They wanted to establish a friendly relationship with the tenants association, if not a partnership. If they won, they also wanted to avoid a potential lawsuit. Both Related and the Apollo group had talked to them about preserving a block of rent-stabilized apartments. "It was agreed that, if we won, the tenants would have a voice," Simmons said vaguely.[19]

"We met with all of them but Tishman Speyer," Garodnick said. "Everybody wanted to partner with the tenants if they could. But Tishman Speyer did not."[20]

But the enthusiasm of the tenants' partners in the bidding, the billionaire Ruby Schron and Colony Capital, waned after Mayor Bloomberg made it clear that the city would not intervene on behalf of the tenants. JPMorgan Chase had provided a $4 billion financial proposal, but it was marked "preliminary," not the rock-solid commitment that MetLife wanted. At the last minute, another participant in the deal, SL Green, pulled out. In a flurry of last-minute phone calls, Gallagher plugged that hole with help from a Deutsche Bank real estate fund.

"I hope the tenants are able to swing this," said Soni Fink, a resident of Peter Cooper and a tenant activist. "We want to buy this thing. It looks very good if they give us any kind of break at all."[21]

CHAPTER EIGHT

What $5.4 Billion Gets You

On October 17, 2006, messengers dropped off six thick bid packages for Stuyvesant Town-Peter Cooper Village on the fifteenth floor of the fifty-nine-story MetLife Building. Darcy Stacom collected the documents for the biggest sale of her or any other broker's life and took the elevator up to the MetLife offices, where Robert R. Merck, David V. Politano and Kevin Wenzel sat waiting. With some trepidation, she slit open the first package, from Related and Lehman Brothers. A sharp intake of breath greeted the $4.7 billion offer that sat on the page like a rotten egg, spoiled and sulfurous. It was well south of what they expected. Could it be a harbinger of what was to come?

"The first one was really low, $4.7 billion, from someone I expected to be really high," Stacom confided to a friend. "I had a heart attack. My career flashed in front of my eyes."

Stacom passed it around as she reached for the next thick manila envelope, and the next, as the afternoon wore on. There was a $5.1 billion bid from the billionaire Simon Glick and the Morgan Stanley Real Estate Fund. Steven Roth of Vornado

Realty Trust, with backing from the Emir of Qatar, came in at $4.5 billion. The tenant bid remained at $4.5 billion, with a slight twist, in which Grunstein offered what he described as a significant tax savings for MetLife by leasing the property for ninety-nine years, instead of buying it. But without hard commitments from its partners, the tenants' offer appeared to MetLife to be held together with Scotch tape and chewing gum.

The offer from the Apollo–ING Clarion–Dermot group was $5.33 billion. That was more like it. But Tishman Speyer edged them with a bid of $5.4 billion. Theoretically at least, there was an extraordinary amount of capital on the table from the nine bidders and only a $70 million gap between the front-runners, just over 1 percent. But price was not the only issue that concerned MetLife. How solid was the financing? Could they close within a month? How big was the down payment? How much did the bidder alter, or "mark up," the sales contract proposed by MetLife? Equally important, did they provide the indemnification that the company wanted?

Stacom, Merck and Politano then took the two highest offers back down to the fifteenth floor and MetLife's lawyer Robert J. Ivanhoe, chairman of the two-hundred-member global real estate practice at Greenberg Traurig. They asked Ivanhoe to sift the offers for distinguishing features or potential problems in any contract changes requested by either bidder. They waited while the lawyer pored over the documents.

"We had a provision where the buyer wasn't just releasing MetLife from environmental liabilities, meaning the buyer couldn't sue MetLife. That's not unusual," Ivanhoe said. "We also had the buyer assuming all the obligations and indemnifying the seller from environmental liabilities. The Apollo bid crossed that out and Tishman Speyer did not."[1]

MetLife very much did not want anything from Stuyvesant Town-Peter Cooper Village coming back to haunt them. Consolidated Edison Company had already entered into a voluntary cleanup agreement with the state Department of Environmental Conservation concerning coal tar pollution from a manufactured gas plant and related storage facilities that were knocked down to make way for Peter Cooper Village and Stuyvesant Town. A by-product of gas production was a toxic oily liquid called coal tar that had seeped into the ground long ago. A Con Ed report, approved by the state, found that there was no risk to tenants from the historic groundwater and subsurface soil contamination. But any company in the chain of ownership of the properties was potentially liable if more serious problems were uncovered in the future.

Both the Related Companies and the Apollo–ING Clarion–Dermot group had balked on the indemnification. Bruce Beal, a partner at Related, said the company had spent $500,000 on its own environmental study and did not want to "read about 'Toxic Town' on the front page of the *New York Post*" at some point in the future. The Apollo group had also commissioned its own environmental study and talked to state officials. They concluded that the problem was "manageable" but they were worried investors might panic so they refused to provide indemnification. But if the environmental issue was not enough of a hurdle, MetLife also wanted indemnification against any legal claims brought by tenants for past actions by the owner over rents. Like Glick and Morgan Stanley, Related and Lehman Brothers, the Apollo group had made extensive revisions to MetLife's proposed contract, effectively cutting the value of their offer.

Tishman Speyer and BlackRock, which subsequently bought

a ten-year pollution insurance policy for $8 million, were undeterred by either risky issue and changed relatively little of the language in the purchase and sale agreement.[2] They figured that Con Edison had already agreed to cover the cost of any necessary decontamination effort and they were not planning to start digging deep holes that might disturb the coal tar.

For MetLife, Tishman Speyer had not only the highest bid but also one that complied with all its demands. So when Ivanhoe wrapped up his review, Kandarian and Merck took the elevator to the fifty-seventh floor, where MetLife's fourteen directors were holding a special session in the company's historic boardroom. Several directors participated via telephone.

Harry P. Kamen, a former MetLife chairman and a MetLife employee for thirty-nine years, felt compelled to disclose that he had received a telephone call the night before from Jerry I. Speyer, Rob's father. Although Jerry did not participate in any of the negotiations and deal making, he wanted to make last-minute contact with an old friend, just in case. The two men had met when Speyer served as chairman of the Partnership for New York City and Kamen was treasurer. Turning to the current chairman, C. Robert Henrikson, Kamen said, "Bob, Jerry called me last night to say that he was bidding. If there is a question about his integrity, he was hoping I could speak to it."[3]

Henrikson responded, "Don't worry about it. He's the high bidder anyway."

Kandarian and Merck recommended that the board accept the $5.4 billion offer from Tishman Speyer–BlackRock pending final negotiations on the contract. They did, and at about 5:00 P.M., Stacom called Rob Speyer at Rockefeller Center and asked him to discreetly bring his team to Greenberg Traurig's fifteenth-floor offices at 200 Park Avenue, the MetLife Building. Speyer's lawyer Jonathan Mechanic and several associates walked over from the nearby Seagram Building on Park Avenue. The lawyers shuttled between the Tishman Speyer conference room and the MetLife room as negotiations dragged on until early the next morning. Speyer and Merck, whose soft-spoken Southern accent contrasted with his counterpart's seventy-miles-per-hour New Yawkese, were only in the same conference room twice over a fifteen-hour span. After the lawyers on both sides had stopped haggling early the next morning, Stacom went out to Forty-Second Street for doughnuts and a jug of coffee from Dunkin' Donuts to revive the weary participants. Rob Speyer, then thirty-seven, signed the $5.4 billion contract, had a $400 million nonrefundable deposit wired to MetLife and shook hands with everyone in the room.

MetLife and Tishman Speyer each issued a press release announcing the sale and within an hour, media websites around the world were rumbling with headline news of the $5.4 billion deal, the most money ever paid for a single asset in the United States. The comic Bill Maher joked during an episode of HBO's *Real Time*, about the stunning price tag for the complex in which he was conceived, while Robert Siegel on National Public Radio's *All Things Considered* provided a sentimental look back at his "childhood home."

"It was an inner-city oasis with no rich people and no poor people," Siegel concluded. "It has been sold in an age that celebrates the virtues of markets. It was built in a simpler time, when the glaring failures of the market, like no affordable housing, were considered targets for public action."[4]

After donning a fresh shirt and holding a hoarse conversation with his father, who offered an affectionate congratulations, Speyer got back to business. He knew he had to deal with the tenants. He sent out a brief letter to the residents of Stuyvesant Town-Peter Cooper Village with what he hoped would be a comforting message: "We are committed to maintaining the unique character and environment that have made Peter Cooper Village and Stuyvesant Town such a wonderful place to live for so long."

He also called Garodnick, whom he did not know, saying he looked forward to sitting down with him now that he had signed the purchase contract. He assured the councilman that they did not intend any major changes; they wanted to be good stewards of the property. "We love Stuyvesant Town and we're very excited," Speyer told him. "We want to work with you."[5]

"I told him I appreciated the call," Garodnick said, "but I asked him his plans for preserving the long-term affordability of the place. He avoided the question. I thought, 'This is going to be a problem.' "[6]

A few days later, Speyer invited the tenant leaders to his office at Rockefeller Center for a get-acquainted meeting. Doyle brought along Susan Steinberg, the association's executive vice president, and Jim Roth, a retired FBI agent and staunch tenant advocate. They were impressed by the colorful, oversize pieces of contemporary art that seemed to leap from the stark white walls of Tishman Speyer as they trooped into a small conference room. There were more white walls and white marble in the conference room, where Rob Speyer sat with David Dishy, a residential real estate executive whom Speyer had hired away from a rival developer to head the company's housing division. "In another year," Rob told the tenant leaders as a smile spread across his face, "you guys will be happy how we turned things around. We pride ourselves on service."[7]

But Doyle wanted to know what Tishman Speyer was going

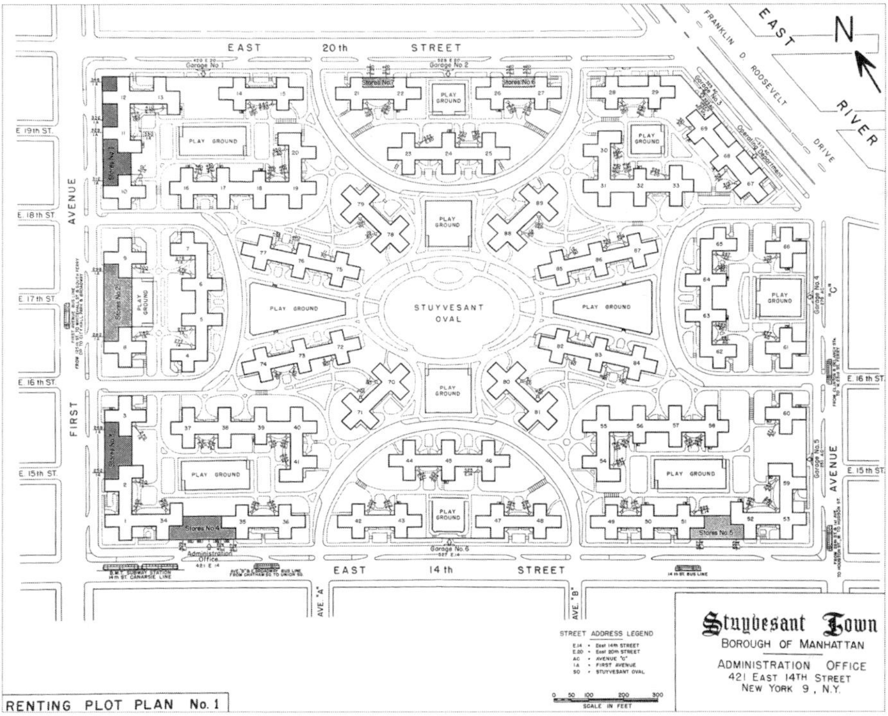

JAY SELDIN

The layout of Stuyvesant Town in Manhattan, overlooking the East River.

METROPOLITAN LIFE INSURANCE COMPANY

A cartoon from a MetLife magazine illustrating Frederick H. Ecker's career at Metropolitan Life Insurance, starting at sixteen in the mailroom and rising to become the company's longest-serving chairman.

METROPOLITAN LIFE INSURANCE COMPANY

Frederick H. Ecker, chairman of Metropolitan Life Insurance, conceived of Stuyvesant Town-Peter Cooper Village as a home for returning veterans of World War II. All told, he built more than thirty thousand apartments for the middle class in the 1940s in New York, Virginia, and California. He said, "Negroes and whites don't mix," when he imposed a strict policy barring black and Hispanic families from renting in the complexes.

THE NEW YORK TIMES PICTURES

Mayor Fiorello H. La Guardia swears in New York City Parks Commissioner Robert Moses as chairman of the Triborough Bridge Authority, November 14, 1936. Moses would become La Guardia's emissary to Metropolitan Life Insurance chairman Frederick Ecker for the Stuyvesant Town-Peter Cooper Village project.

METROPOLITAN LIFE INSURANCE COMPANY

One of the foul-smelling manufactured gas storage tanks that inspired the name for the neighborhood north of East Fourteenth Street, the Gas House District. The tanks and gas plants were among five hundred buildings demolished to make way for Stuyvesant Town-Peter Cooper Village.

METROPOLITAN LIFE INSURANCE COMPANY

The lunar landscape that remained in 1946 after the demolition of the Gas House District between Fourteenth and Twenty-Third Streets, east of First Avenue. The Empire State Building is in the background in the center, and the Chrysler Building is to the right.

METROPOLITAN LIFE INSURANCE COMPANY

The razing of five hundred tenements, churches, factories, and warehouses in the Gas House District started in 1945. The first buildings opened in 1947.

Stuyvesant Town's thirty-five cross-shaped buildings take shape, 1947.

METROPOLITAN LIFE INSURANCE COMPANY

For decades, MetLife provided prospective Stuyvesant Town tenants with a floor plan of a vacant apartment but not a tour of the unit.

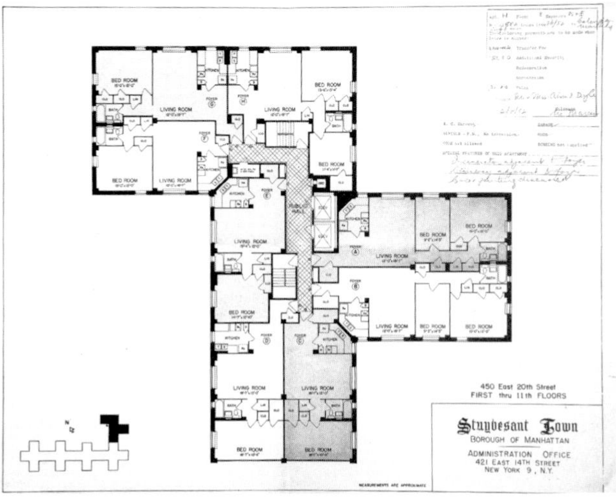

JAY SELDIN

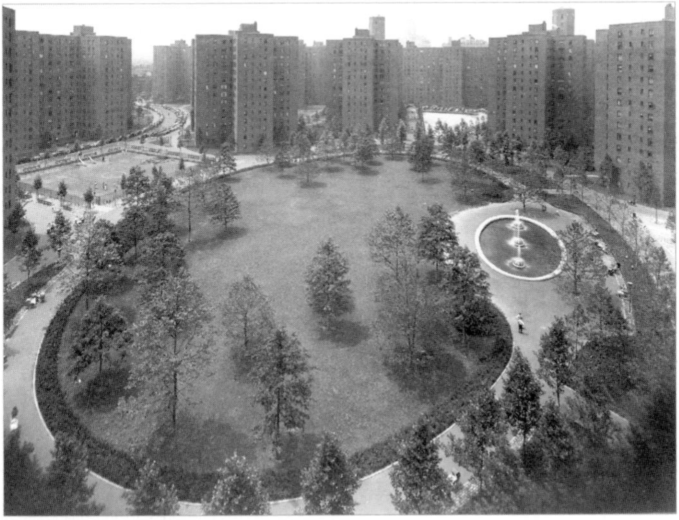

METROPOLITAN LIFE INSURANCE COMPANY

The apartment houses at Stuyvesant Town radiate out from Stuyvesant Circle at the center of the complex.

Stuyvesant Town-Peter Cooper Village covers a wide swath of Manhattan, between Fourteenth and Twenty-Third Streets, east of First Avenue, 1950s.

METROPOLITAN LIFE INSURANCE COMPANY

THE NEW YORK TIMES PICTURES

Lee Lorch, a mathematics professor and army veteran, helped to form the Town and Village Tenants Committee to End Discrimination in Stuyvesant Town, with his wife, Grace, who died in 1974, and five-year-old daughter, Alice, in 1949. Unable to get a teaching position in the United States because of his civil rights activism and left-wing views, Lorch and his family eventually emigrated to Canada.

STEVE PAYNE

Lee Lorch, professor emeritus of mathematics at York University, in his apartment in Toronto, 2010. Two of the schools that fired him, Fisk University and City University of New York, later awarded Lorch with honorary degrees.

THE DAILY COMPASS

A three-year-long battle with MetLife began in August 1949 when Jesse Kessler of the Town and Village Tenants Committee to End Discrimination in Stuyvesant Town invited a fellow union member, Hardine Hendrix; his wife, Raphael; and their six-year-old son, Hardine Jr. to stay in his apartment at Stuyvesant Town.

METROPOLITAN LIFE INSURANCE COMPANY

Robert R. Merck, MetLife's senior managing director in charge of real estate investments, ran the sale of the company's biggest asset: Stuyvesant Town-Peter Cooper Village.

METROPOLITAN LIFE INSURANCE COMPANY

Steven A. Kandarian, who joined MetLife in 2005 as chief investment officer, ordered the sale of Stuyvesant Town-Peter Cooper Village, which netted the company a $3 billion profit. Kandarian was subsequently promoted to chairman, president, and chief executive of MetLife.

JOE FORNABAIO

William M. Shanahan and his partner, Darcy A. Stacom, the top sales brokers at CB Richard Ellis, sold $9.4 billion worth of real estate in 2006, including Stuyvesant Town-Peter Cooper Village, the biggest deal of their lives.

PATRICK MCMULLAN, PATRICKMCMULLAN.COM

Robert J. Ivanhoe, MetLife's lawyer and the chairman of the global real estate practice at Greenberg Traurig, approved the $5.4 billion contract for sale to Tishman Speyer and BlackRock.

JAY SELDIN

Richard S. LeFrak, a billionaire real estate tycoon, raised his bid for Stuyvesant Town-Peter Cooper Village to $4.5 billion in 2006 after bankers told him, "The more you spend, the more we can lend against it." He ultimately pulled out of the auction rather than raise a bid that he already thought was outlandish.

LUX LIVING

Rob Speyer spent $21.8 million on landscaping, signage, and new storefronts to create a lush environment at Stuyvesant Town-Peter Cooper Village. The new shrubs and trees blocked the views of some security cameras, angering tenants, who dubbed the thickened landscaping Rape Forests.

LARS KLOVE

Rob Speyer and his father, Jerry I. Speyer, on a rooftop at Stuyvesant Town not long after buying the property for $5.4 billion, a record-setting price for a single real estate asset. The Speyers invested $112.5 million, or 2 percent of the purchase price.

The pension funds that were invested in the Stuyvesant Town deal lost more than $3 billion, but the subsequent financial debacle barely dented the reputation of Laurence D. Fink, chairman and chief executive officer of BlackRock, or his partners, the Speyers.

CHESTER HIGGINS JR./NEW YORK TIMES PICTURES

PATRICK MCMULLAN

Robert "Big Loan" Verrone, the Wachovia banker, erected the financial architecture for a deal that many analysts said was doomed from the start.

JAY SELDIN

The ten-pound crystal trophy that was given out at the closing dinner at Top of the Rock to top MetLife executives, brokers, lawyers, and buyers responsible for the record-setting $5.4 billion Stuyvesant Town sale.

WILLIAM ALATRISTE

Officials back a tenant-led bid to buy Stuyvesant Town-Peter Cooper Village at a rally in Stuyvesant Town on September 5, 2006, just as MetLife put the complexes on the auction block. (Left to right: Senator Charles E. Schumer, Assemblyman Jonathan Bing, resident Granville Leo Stevens, City Councilman Dan Garodnick, Manhattan Borough President Scott Stringer, State Senator Tom Duane, State Senator Liz Krueger, Assemblywoman Sylvia Friedman, Congressman Carolyn Maloney, and Central Labor Council President Edward Ott.)

JAY SELDIN

Al Doyle, president of the tenant association and a second-generation resident, and Dan Garodnick, a newly elected councilman and second-generation resident, were the Mutt and Jeff team that led the fight to preserve Stuyvesant Town-Peter Cooper Village as a rare haven for the middle class in high-priced Manhattan.

to do about preserving the complexes as an affordable oasis for the middle class. "Other than saying he would turn the place around, he did not make any comments about searching for ways to keep the place affordable," Doyle recalled. "He couldn't do that because he had to make his mortgage payments. We were cognizant of that fact."

But if Doyle was still willing to give Speyer a chance, Roth was not. "When Al Doyle asked what they were going to do for affordable housing, the temperature went down about forty degrees," Roth recalled. "Shortly afterward, we were invited to the Christmas tree-lighting ceremony at Rockefeller Center. I said to the others, 'If you go, I'm going to rat you out to the neighborhood and *Town & Village*. They're trying to buy you off.' "[8]

None of the tenant leaders attended the glittering tree-lighting that is viewed by millions of people every year.

For MetLife, the results of the Stuyvesant Town-Peter Cooper Village transaction could not have been better. The sale sent the company's share price to a fifty-two-week high of $58.60 and MetLife's end-of-the-year accounting revealed that it had reaped an incredible $3 billion gain, net of income tax, on the deal, or half the $6.16 billion in net income, or profit, for all of 2006. MetLife also reported that its net investment income from the two complexes was $73 million in 2006, up from $70 million in 2004.[9] So it had not been losing money on the property. But the gains from the sale were nothing short of spectacular.

Over the prior four years, MetLife had sold twenty properties for more than $10.5 billion. It only made $85 million on the $835 million sale of the Sears Tower, where it had foreclosed on a loan. But the other buildings had been built or purchased by the insurer decades ago, so most of the purchase price was profit. MetLife's former headquarters building at 1 Madison Avenue brought in $918 million. After buying the MetLife Building in Manhattan for $400 million in 1980, the company sold it twenty-five years later for $1.72 billion. The $3 billion gain on Stuyvesant Town-Peter Cooper Village was unparalleled.

No wonder MetLife, in preparing for the traditional "closing dinner" for the brokers, lawyers and company executives who worked on the deal, wanted something more substantial than the traditional Lucite block, known as a "tombstone," emblazoned with the names of buyer, seller and broker.

The insurer commissioned a crystal wedge that stood eight and a half inches high and weighed a full ten pounds. It was nestled in a velvet-lined black box. The company logos were affixed in their respective colors: blue for MetLife, green for CB Richard Ellis, silver for Tishman Speyer and black for BlackRock. Hovering inside the glass was a laser-etched schematic of the layout of the buildings at Stuyvesant Town-Peter Cooper Village. The inscription read: "Peter Cooper Village; Stuyvesant Town; Largest Real Estate Transaction in World History."

The tombstone was distributed to about 30 people at the closing party at Top of the Rock, the observatory atop 30 Rockefeller Plaza in midtown. From that perch 850 feet above the street, Rob Speyer and Steven A. Kandarian, MetLife's chief investment officer and soon-to-be chief executive officer, had unobstructed views of Stuyvesant Town-Peter Cooper Village, 1.5 miles to the south. Feeling expansive, Kandarian wished Speyer well, although he did not want to see him turn around and sell it for an even higher price tomorrow, a crazy possibility in the rollicking market. There was not a whisper of doubt among this gathering of some of the country's shrewdest real estate investors that the market would continue its upward march. "I sincerely hope you do well with this transaction," Kandarian said to Speyer, "just not too soon."[10]

Kandarian need not have worried that he had undersold Stuyvesant Town-Peter Cooper Village. Four years later, he looked uncannily prescient in selling the property at the peak of the market, before the boom collapsed in a devastating recession. The Stuyvesant Town deal, along with his decision to steer the company away from investments in automakers and subprime mortgages before the crisis, contributed to his being named in 2011 president and chief executive officer of MetLife.

Jerry I. Speyer was the doting father after his son won. Tishman Speyer was a family business even before Rob joined the company. Rob's sister, Valerie Peletier, was a managing director and his stepmother, Katherine G. Farley, was a senior managing director. In recent years, Rob had taken on increasing responsibility at the firm. But the $5.4 billion Stuyvesant Town deal marked his ascension to his father's side in a very public way.

"Obviously, Rob is on the deal side and has taken a leading role in the company as the heir apparent," Jerry told me shortly after they won the auction. "I expect he'll be far more successful than I was. He has great vision, wonderful people skills, and above all, he loves what he does."

The elder Speyer confided that he had received a "lovely note" from a fellow real estate magnate, Mortimer Zuckerman, the chairman of Boston Properties and the owner of the New York *Daily News* and editor in chief of *U.S. News and World Report*. Zuckerman, who had once hired Rob to work as a reporter at the *Daily News*, described him in glowing terms. Now Jerry and Rob were working in tandem, the hope of perhaps every father and son. "He said, 'You're a very lucky guy,'" Speyer said. "I was thrilled."

The deal not only confirmed Rob Speyer's ascension to the top ranks of real estate and goosed MetLife's earnings, but it also burnished the reputations of Verrone, Wachovia's big-deal banker, and Tishman Speyer's lawyer Jonathan L. Mechanic, who was named the Dealmaker of the Year by *The American Lawyer* for his role in the $5.4 billion sale. Darcy Stacom chalked up a personal best in 2006, selling $9.4 billion worth of commercial property. City and state government also scored, hauling in $262 million from the transaction: $162 million from MetLife in transfer taxes and $100 million from the buyer in mortgage recording taxes.

Richard and Bill Mack, William Dickey and Jeff Barclay from the Apollo–ING Clarion–Dermot Group were stunned by the news that Tishman Speyer and BlackRock had won. With information gleaned from the gossip-ridden real estate and banking industries, they figured their $5.33 billion offer had put them ahead of all rivals. Members of the group wondered aloud whether MetLife had given Tishman Speyer a "last look" and the opportunity to top the Apollo group's offer because of Jerry Speyer's ties to executives at MetLife. William P. Dickey, the founder of Dermot, called the real estate brokers, Darcy Stacom and her partner William Shanahan.

"I was concerned that Tishman Speyer and BlackRock had gotten a last look. Bill and Darcy told me point-blank that that was not the case," said Dickey. He paused and laughed before continuing. "But I also know that Tishman Speyer and BlackRock had better relationships with MetLife than we did."[11]

For many in the real estate industry, it seemed like déjà vu all over again. After MetLife's $1.72 billion sale of the MetLife Building at 200 Park Avenue to Tishman Speyer in 2005, a similar controversy arose. A rival bidder, Scott Rechler, then chairman of Reckson Associates Realty, had complained to many of his real estate brethren that he had actually won the auction, not Tishman Speyer.

Although MetLife executives attribute the story to "sour grapes," Rechler insisted that MetLife or their brokers initially called him to say that he was the high bidder and the winner, pending negotiations over a lease with the insurance company for the penthouse space at the top of the tower. He said his company had completed the due diligence, marked up the proposed contract and demonstrated an ability to finance the deal. The deal played out while Rechler was in Orlando, where he spent most of his time trailing ten steps behind his children at Disney World while tracking the progress of the deal on his cell phone.

At the last minute, Rechler said, he got a second call, from MetLife's broker, saying there had been a change in plans. Rechler said he was told that the chairman of MetLife had decided to sell the building to Tishman Speyer, which had offered $10 million less than Rechler. Top bankers at Lehman Brothers, which was working with Tishman Speyer, had called MetLife on behalf of their client. (In this internecine world, Fuld, Lehman's chairman, and Jerry Speyer were close friends, and both men served on the board of the Federal Reserve Bank of

New York.) MetLife, in turn, decided that the $10 million differential was less important than its relationship with Lehman Brothers.

"We thought we had jumped ahead of the pack with our final bid," Rechler said. "We got a call from MetLife saying, if we can resolve the lease terms, we're ready to go forward. Then they told us it was a Lehman play. I couldn't even look at the MetLife Building for a year."[12]

But MetLife executives and Stacom insist that the sale of Stuyvesant Town-Peter Cooper Village was a proper auction without any hint of favoritism. Merck told me afterward that the company was "not happy" about the rumors. "This was a very clean and detailed sales process and everyone was treated fairly," Merck said in 2006. "Any rumors to the contrary are totally false."[13]

A private owner can sell property to anyone at any price. The presumption is that it will go to the highest legitimate offer. Like most bidders, the Apollo group, which spent more than a million dollars preparing their offer, did not like being used as a stalking horse for a preordained winner. Still, in trying to sort out the claims and denials, it is also clear that the Apollo group was unwilling to comply with some of MetLife's contract stipulations concerning environmental indemnity, which would have reduced the value of their offer in MetLife's eyes.

In any event, the Apollo group was so incensed about the outcome that they took the highly unusual step of holding a "closing dinner" for thirty people at Café Gray, an upscale restaurant in the Time Warner Center. Traditionally, the winner of a real estate auction holds a "closing dinner," never the second-place finisher. Nevertheless, Richard and William Mack, Jim Simmons and Lee Neibart of Apollo; Bill Dickey and

Andrew MacArthur of Dermot; and Barclay from Clarion marked the occasion on October 30 with their bankers at Morgan Stanley, who distributed blank Lucite tombstones commemorating the occasion. "We felt we deserved a closing party," Richard Mack said in 2006. "We all worked hard."

Afterward Barclay of ING Clarion was more forgiving. "It's a great investment these guys have made," he told me in 2006. "We'll look back on this in ten or fifteen years as the one that got away."

Several years later, Barclay would point to the blank Lucite sitting on his desk and say to friends, "That was what was between my ears when we submitted our bid."

The political issues, however, did not subside. Michael McKee, treasurer of the Tenants Political Action Committee and a veteran of New York's tenant-landlord wars, called the Stuyvesant Town sale a "dark day for affordable housing." "I think it's deplorable that the mayor did not step up to the plate," McKee said at the time. "If he had, this might've turned out differently. Our rent-regulated housing is disappearing. It's not slow. In the last ten years, we've lost close to 300,000 units."[14]

Three days after the sale of Stuyvesant Town-Peter Cooper Village to Tishman Speyer and BlackRock, Mayor Bloomberg hurriedly announced his own plan for addressing the housing crisis for New York's middle class. He proposed building the largest middle-income housing complex in New York in more than thirty years on a twenty-four-acre parcel of crumbling industrial land on the waterfront in Queens, across the East River from midtown Manhattan. Under the proposal, the city would create a tree-shaded community with restaurants, shops and a mix of five thousand rent-regulated and market-rate apartments. He said the apartments would be for families of four earning between $60,000 and $145,000 a year. Residents would pay $1,200 to $2,500 in rent. "Not only will it give birth to a new community that's going to complement our efforts to revive the city's waterfront," the mayor said, "it will also provide much needed housing for the real backbone of our city, our teachers, nurses, police officers."[15]

It was a bold move cooked up by Deputy Mayor Doctoroff after he decided against intervening on behalf of the tenants at Stuyvesant Town. Doctoroff had planned to build an Olympic Village for athletes on the Queens site as part of the city's ill-fated bid for the 2012 Olympic Games. Doctoroff dusted off his Olympic Village proposal and put the administration's new venture in the context of affordable housing, more specifically workforce housing, for the middle class. He told reporters that the Queens project was a more efficient use of public subsidies: It would have cost the city about $107,000 per apartment to preserve Stuyvesant Town and Peter Cooper as an affordable complex, while the units in Queens would cost about $54,000 each to build. "So we can get two units here for every one there," Doctoroff told reporters at a press conference in Queens, "plus we get a major increase in the housing stock."

Tom Waters, a housing analyst with the Community Service Society, a nonprofit planning agency, did not buy it. He said that the construction of new housing would never keep pace with the loss of rental units rapidly moving from regulated to market-rate rents.[16] A 2006 study by the Community Service Society found that between 1990 and 2005, nearly a quarter of the roughly 121,000 apartments built under federal and state subsidy programs, dating from the 1960s and '70s, left those programs. In return for government aid, building owners were required to keep rents affordable to low- and moderate-income people for, usually, twenty years, before they could withdraw from the programs. A separate study by the city comptroller's office found that 25,000 units had been withdrawn from the state's Mitchell-Lama moderate-and-middle-income program since 2004 or had begun the process. That number was greater than the 24,000 units that left the program prior to 2004.

In 2006 alone, the CSS study said, New York City would lose more than 5,000 apartments for low- and moderate-income families. A third study, by the Brookings Institution, noted the sharp decline in middle-income neighborhoods since 1970 in cities from Baltimore and Philadelphia to Los Angeles–Long Beach.

Bloomberg's $7.5 billion housing program was far more ambitious than that of any other big-city mayor. But many analysts disputed Doctoroff's math when it came to Stuyvesant Town. It almost always costs more to build new apartments than it does to rehabilitate existing buildings, they said, even if the price for Stuyvesant Town-Peter Cooper Village was a record-setting number. Indeed, it subsequently cost the city $275 million just to buy the property in Queens, cleanse the land of toxic waste, create a ten-acre park and build roads and water and sewer lines. The project would need tens of millions more in subsidies and tax breaks. Although the city selected a developer for the first one thousand apartments, construction of the first building was not scheduled to start until December 2012.

Emily Youssouf, the former president of the city's Housing Development Corporation who had disagreed with the administration's position, said the implicit message was that the middle class should live in Queens; much like manufacturing, they don't belong in Manhattan anymore. "I was outraged," she said during an interview in 2011. "It was so elitist. I always thought that economically integrated buildings were the best way to go. Even if it had become a prime neighborhood, why can't middle-income people continue to live in housing built to be affordable to them twenty, forty, or even sixty years ago?"

Still, there was no disputing that Mayor Bloomberg's project in Queens would be the largest middle-class development built in New York since 1974 and the opening of Starrett City, a 140-acre complex of 46 high-rise towers on Jamaica Bay, at the far eastern end of Brooklyn, 12 miles from Manhattan. But subsequent events highlighted the city's rapidly dwindling supply of affordable housing, not Mayor Bloomberg's initiative in Queens. In December 2006, Starrett City went on the auction block in what promised to be another blockbuster sale that would reunite Stacom and Grunstein, the lawyer who had represented the tenants at Stuyvesant Town. The immediate and widespread opposition to the sale, however, signaled that the very public Stuyvesant Town-Peter Cooper Village battle had fed a backlash to the unbridled speculation over what many regarded as one of the city's most precious resources: its supply of affordable housing for impoverished New Yorkers as well as nurses, construction workers, firefighters, teachers and municipal clerks.

Starrett City, which had its own schools, churches, synagogues, shopping center, post office and power plant scattered among 5,881 apartments, had been a safe haven for poor and working-class New Yorkers for thirty years. Unlike the red brick buildings at Stuyvesant Town-Peter Cooper Village, Starrett City's eleven- and twenty-story towers have a modern appearance with light-colored brick, exterior balconies and neatly manicured lawns. "It has a blend of all kinds of races and religions, and maintenance is really good and security is really good," said Pasquale Santaniello, a retired carpet installer. "It's one of the safest neighborhoods in America."[17]

But the fifteen thousand residents of Starrett City, the nation's largest federally subsidized housing development, were less prosperous than those of Stuyvesant Town and Peter Cooper Village. Starrett City's longtime owners, seeking to take advantage of a red-hot real estate market, hired Darcy Stacom to market the property. She and the owner set the target price at more than $1 billion.

The original partnership group led by Disque D. Deane tried to mollify tenant fears by saying, "This is a sale of a nearly totally subsidized development where the tenants will continue to be subsidized, no matter who eventually buys it." But the Starrett City tenants association, low-income housing advocates, elected officials and even the Bloomberg administration expressed concern that anyone paying such an exorbitant price would be forced to cut services and raise rents substantially in order to meet the mortgage payments. "The big complexes are falling like dominoes," said Michael McKee, treasurer of the Tenants Political Action Committee. "Affordable housing is simply disappearing."[18]

Starrett City received nearly every available federal, state and city housing incentive, an estimated $75 million annually in rent subsidies and tax breaks. About 90 percent of the tenants received some type of government assistance for shelter. But even in far-off Brooklyn, the demand for housing continued to push rents higher. After David Bistricer emerged as the winning bidder with an offer of $1.3 billion in February 2007, he was nearly buried under an avalanche of criticism and scandal. Bistricer was represented by Leonard Grunstein, who desperately tried to curry favor with labor leaders and prominent African-American ministers. But Attorney General Andrew M. Cuomo, who had been silent during the sale of Stuyvesant Town-Peter Cooper Village, blasted Bistricer's "long and troubled history of tenant abuse" in New York City. He was referring to a court order forcing Bistricer to make $450,000 in restitution to tenants in two Brooklyn buildings and a 1998 court order obtained by the attorney general's office barring Bistricer for life from converting rental buildings in New York to condominiums.[19]

Mayor Bloomberg, who had taken a political hit over his decision to sit out the Stuyvesant Town-Peter Cooper Village fight, complained of Bistricer's "worrisome" history of building violations at Flatbush Gardens, a troubled housing project in Brooklyn where the entertainer Barbra Streisand had grown up.[20] He painted Bistricer as a bad landlord, in contrast with the Speyers. But unlike Stuyvesant Town-Peter Cooper Village, Starrett City offered a clear regulatory hook for public officials to derail the sale. Because of the extraordinary level of subsidies at Starrett City, state and federal officials had to approve the sale. The Bloomberg administration joined Senator Charles E. Schumer, community activists from the Association of Community Organizations for Reform Now (ACORN) and Cuomo, who would become New York's governor in 2009, in calling on U.S. secretary of housing and urban development Alphonso R. Jackson to reject Bistricer's application to buy Starrett City.

Aside from his checkered legal history, Bistricer, who lives in Brooklyn and is not a member of either the Real Estate Board of New York or the Partnership for New York City, did not have the social and political connections enjoyed by the Speyers. Federal officials scuttled Bistricer's attempt to buy the property on two separate occasions before he finally acknowledged defeat. But Bistricer's loss was rooted in the battle at Stuyvesant Town-Peter Cooper Village, which gave voice to average New Yorkers dismayed by the escalating cost of housing.

"I believe that the Stuyvesant Town battle in 2006 gave birth to the city's opposition to the sale of Starrett City," Garodnick said. "It's not a totally fair comparison because they had a much bigger hook. But people realized the failure at Stuyvesant Town and wanted to correct it at Starrett City."[21]

The month after the sale was a mad scramble for Tishman Speyer and BlackRock to finalize the financing for the deal with Wachovia and Merrill Lynch in order to close by November 17, MetLife's deadline. The Tishman Speyer–BlackRock joint venture had signed a contract to pay $5.4 billion for the property, but the total bill for the transaction came to an even more eye-popping number: $6.3 billion. Aside from the purchase price, there were $240 million in acquisition costs and $650 million in reserve funds required by the lenders.[22]

The whole deal was about OPM, other people's money. Robert Verrone, the banker who was instrumental in making Wachovia the number one underwriter of securitized commercial debt during the boom, orchestrated the financing. The superlatives surrounding the deal did not stop with the sale price. The $3 billion, ten-year, interest-only mortgage, which Wachovia and Merrill Lynch planned to combine with other loans into a commercial mortgage-backed security and sell to investors, was the largest ever for a single property. The second item in the debt stack was $1.4 billion in secondary loans, which were ultimately obtained from eleven different parties.

But in addition to borrowing $4.4 billion, the partners needed to raise another $1.89 billion from equity investors to cover the total cost. Tishman Speyer and BlackRock Realty kicked in a combined $225 million, or a mere 3.6 percent of the total capitalization. The buyers were able to pull off a record-breaking deal by putting only a relatively small amount of their own money at risk. And the interest-only mortgage itself was nonrecourse. If there was a default, the lenders could only come after the property, not either company's other assets. It's all part of what made this and other deals so enticing. Half of Tishman Speyer's $112.5 million share came from their most consistent partner and investor, the billionaire Lester Crown of Chicago. This was big-time deal making that the average home buyer could only imagine.

Few of the bankers involved in the deal actually understood the mechanics or the intricacies of the unique system of rent regulation in New York. The main question in their minds was: Can we sell the debt and equity so it's not on our books? "Outside of the real estate area, nobody really understood it," one banker confided. "It was all about, can we move the risk? That was the sole and only criteria. I think we all talked ourselves into believing the deal was going to work financially. We drank the Kool-Aid."

Larry Fink, Dale Gruen, Fred Lieblich and Rob Friedberg of BlackRock had expected to enlist $500 million each from the California Public Employees' Retirement System, or CalPERS, and the California State Teachers' Retirement System, or CalSTRS, by the date of the closing in November. Afterward, BlackRock, Tishman Speyer and the bankers would only need another $600 million or so to hit their goal of $1.89 billion of equity. But not everything went according to plan.

By the time the contract closed in November, CalPERS, the country's largest pension fund, was on the phone with

$500 million. It took a 26.5 percent stake in the property. The partners promised a 13.5 percent internal rate of return.[23] CalPERS itself had turned to higher-risk real estate investments for just those kinds of returns to fill their coffers and meet their obligations to pensioners. Any shortfalls could force communities to raise taxes to cover the gap—political anathema.

The closing itself—done in a conference room in the Seagram Building, at 345 Park Avenue, where Tishman Speyer's lawyer Jonathan Mechanic had his offices—was something of a nonevent, without any of the drama or headlines created by the auction. "We had the ability to write all the debt and provide bridge equity," said Verrone, who even four years after the event could not help bragging about the deal. "Ultimately, we brought in Merrill for 35 percent. We ran the deal. It was an aggressive underwriting, but it didn't feel outlandish. There were a lot of deals afterward that were considerably more outlandish."

CalSTRS, however, was not on board. The pension fund had been very receptive to BlackRock's offer. But a key adviser to CalSTRS, Nori Gerardo Lietz, was vehemently opposed. Lietz, a founder of the Pension Consulting Alliance, was a rigorous, blunt analyst who was ranked among the "30 most influential people in private equity real estate" by a business magazine in 2006.

Lietz advised not only CalSTRS, but also CalPERS and the Oregon Public Employees Retirement System. A positive recommendation from her could release a gush of investment dollars from the country's largest pension funds. A negative declaration could leave fund-raisers parched.

"It was a bad deal," Lietz said. "I advised CalPERS and CalSTRS against it. It was abundantly clear to anyone who looked at it that it would not work. It was overfinanced and based on aggressive assumptions. They grossly underestimated how difficult it would be to do the conversion."[24]

What did she see that the biggest names in real estate did not? "It had [a $400 million] interest reserve," she said. "That was a huge red flag. It was not cash-flowing on day one."

At the time, she said, she spoke to Ralph L. Schlosstein, the cofounder of BlackRock, who assured her that it was a great opportunity with a lot of upside potential as previously regulated apartments moved to market rents.

"He said, 'I'd put my mother's money in it,'" Lietz recalled.

"I said, 'You are putting my mother's money into it; she's a beneficiary of CalPERS.'"

"He said, 'You can take it to the bank.'"

"I hope so," Lietz responded, "but I don't believe so."

But Al Fernandez, the senior portfolio manager at CalPERS, liked the deal and had the authority to make the investment without her consent. The teachers' retirement fund was another matter. CalSTRS asked her what it should do. Once more, Lietz counseled against the investment. But, the CalSTRS executives said, they had already promised to put up $500 million. It would undermine their credibility if they went back on their word. Lietz suggested that they reduce their commitment to a minimum. So CalSTRS reconsidered and missed the closing.

"I remember getting a call from BlackRock saying CalSTRS was out," said one banker who worked on the deal. "That sent shivers down our spine. We now had a billion dollars in bridge equity to sell."

Like several people involved in the Stuyvesant Town purchase, the banker did not want to be identified by name because so many people had lost so much money on the deal. But most executives at BlackRock, Tishman Speyer, Wachovia and Merrill Lynch considered the AWOL CalSTRS to be a mere bump in the road.

The banks underwrote the property on the assumption that the two complexes would be worth an appraised value of $6.9 billion by 2011. Speyer and Lieblich from BlackRock told bankers, lenders, and later, bond-rating agencies that net income from the property would triple to $336.2 million in five years. Verrone and the partners described the property as the "Rockefeller Center of Manhattan residential real estate," as part of a forty-seven-page presentation to bond-rating agencies in December by Wachovia and Merrill Lynch, who paid the rating agencies to evaluate the creditworthiness of the loans and the level of risk to investors. The partners and the bankers wanted an investment-grade rating for the $3 billion mortgage so they could more easily sell it to investors without having to offer higher interest rates.

The presentation outlined many opportunities for boosting the net income, ranging from the parking garages, where rates were said to be 70 percent below market, to the retail spaces, where rents were roughly half the market rate. There was enough underdeveloped land, it said, that the new owners could also build seven hundred thousand square feet of valuable residential and retail space. But the big upside would come with the conversion of regulated apartments to market rates. New York had some of the highest rents in the country and the lowest vacancy rate. Demand was strong.

The new owners portrayed MetLife as a lumbering landlord that had failed to capitalize on its asset. Although the insurance company had deregulated more than three thousand apartments, the new owners could easily double MetLife's pace because the "previous owner did not aggressively pursue illegal sublets or tenants that did not meet rent regulation guidelines. The new owners anticipate that the percentage conversion to market will increase significantly as the sponsorship actively enforces subletting laws and market deregulation."[25] Tishman Speyer and BlackRock were eyeing as many as 1,600 apartments that were illegally sublet, or leased to tenants who did not qualify for rent regulation, and could easily be converted.[26]

Despite the fact that on day one income from the property covered only 40 percent of the debt service, Fitch Ratings, Standard & Poor's and Moody's Investors Service all believed that the shortfall would diminish over time as the new owners converted regulated apartments to market rates at a faster pace than either MetLife or most other landlords in New York had ever achieved. No small item, the gap between income and debt obligations was $172 million, based on 2006 financial results. So the loans did not get the highest, AAA rating, but they did manage a passing grade, one notch above a speculative or junk bond rating. The rating meant that there was a low to moderate risk of default, although market conditions could adversely affect the borrower's ability to make the mortgage payments.

The reports did not outline what might happen if any one of their assumptions about the strength of the rental market, the desirability of Stuyvesant Town apartments, the turnover rate and rent hikes did not pan out, let alone all of them.

"We convinced the rating agencies that a $3 billion mortgage was investment grade," Verrone said. "From a financing standpoint, everything went right for Wachovia and Merrill."

It sure did. By the time the deal closed six months later, after the $3 billion senior mortgage was sold to investors, after

$1.89 billion in bridge equity was sold to pension funds and others, and after $1.4 billion in junior loans were secured, one Wachovia banker who worked on the deal estimated that the bank had made $140 million. Merrill Lynch, in turn, pulled in about $70 million.

Rob Speyer finished 2006 by selling the skyscraper his grandfather built at 666 Fifth Avenue for a record $1.8 billion to another young scion, Jared Kushner. The Kushner family was selling its residential holdings in New Jersey and Pennsylvania and was willing to pay up for Manhattan real estate to make a splash. The price broke a record set by Speyer himself when he bought the MetLife Building at 200 Park Avenue for $1.72 billion. The market was still booming not only in New York but also nationally. There were twenty-two transactions for real estate investment trusts over the course of 2006 with a total value of $102.8 billion, including debt.

Early in January 2007, Verrone called Rob Speyer saying that senior executives at Wachovia's headquarters in Charlotte, North Carolina, wanted to meet him and talk to them about their progress in raising $1.165 billion in equity; Wachovia wanted the bridge equity off their books. Speyer, Galiano and Verrone boarded Wachovia's brand-new Challenger jet for a quick flight to Charlotte. The meeting went relatively smoothly as Rob spent the afternoon assuring a half dozen bankers from the commercial real estate group that his organization and BlackRock were already tapping into their network of institutional investors and sovereign funds.

The jolt came on the return flight. As the jet went into a landing pattern on the approach to Teterboro Airport, directly east of Manhattan in New Jersey, the pilot suddenly pushed the jet into a steep ascent, back into the sky, nearly taking out a passing helicopter. Apparently the landing gear had failed to release. The jet veered south and made a successful emergency landing at Newark Liberty International Airport, where emergency vehicles with whirling lights lined the runway.

It did take about six months for Tishman Speyer, BlackRock, Wachovia and Merrill Lynch to line up equity partners who shared their optimism. That was a little longer than they originally anticipated, because the headlines about tenant unrest and a lawsuit brought by current and former residents in January had unsettled some potential American investors. It was more evident than ever to the bankers and partners that they would need to go overseas as well to fill out the equity roster.

The much-admired CalPERS served as the flypaper for attracting the remaining $1.165 billion in equity because its successful investment strategies were scrutinized, admired and copied by pension funds from the United States to Europe and Asia. "CalPERS has the reputation of being the gold standard of pension investing, largely by virtue of its size," Edward Siedle of Benchmark Financial Services told HedgeWorld, a news service for the hedge fund industry.

The pitch from BlackRock, Tishman Speyer and the bankers was that even at $5.4 billion Stuyvesant Town-Peter Cooper Village was a bargain. It cost $498 a square foot, or an average of $480,810 per unit, less than half what it cost to buy the average condominium in that neighborhood. With rents at "leading rental properties in Manhattan" 15 to 30 percent higher than market-rent apartments in Stuyvesant Town-Peter Cooper Village, there was a lot of room for revenue enhancement. Their confidential investment memorandum cited a new rental building across First Avenue from Peter Cooper Village that commanded rents of $68 per square foot, the equivalent of $6,930 a month for a two-bedroom unit at Peter Cooper. But a newly built condominium tower with a doorman and various amenities was not a proper match-up for plain brick buildings without doormen, with sixty-year-old plumbing and with only one bathroom in the two- and three-bedroom apartments. Stuyvesant Town apartments were always going to rent at a discount to newly built residential towers.

Still, CalPERS, which had a 250-member investment staff, embraced the deal and others like it. The managers sought high-return real estate investments in order to meet their swelling obligations to retirees. As the real estate market surged in the early 2000s, the fund increasingly ceded decision making over property deals to outside advisers and moved from a focus on "core investments" that provided steady if unremarkable returns to riskier, highly leveraged joint-venture projects that theoretically offered better returns, like the 13.5 percent return projected in the Stuyvesant Town-Peter Cooper Village deal. In 2005, CalPERS and its real estate partner Rockpoint Group invested in the acquisition of another project built by MetLife, Riverton in Harlem.

After the closing Jerry Speyer set up a secret meeting with John E. Sexton, the president of New York University, whose seemingly insatiable appetite for dormitory space was creating tensions with residents of Greenwich Village. NYU had leased dozens of apartments at Stuyvesant Town in the past. But Speyer, who had served with Sexton as a director of the Federal Reserve Bank of New York, had something bigger in mind, an investment. Jerry Speyer's initiative illuminated the way in which father and son interacted. Rob was the heir apparent and a key decision maker, but it was still Jerry who had the relationships and set the table for the deals.

Of course, Larry Fink had his own connection to Sexton and NYU; he was a university trustee. Jerry Speyer attended the meeting at NYU, but Rob ran it, proposing that NYU become a partner in the Stuyvesant Town-Peter Cooper Village deal, investing more than $200 million and leasing a block of apartments for faculty housing. Rob Speyer suggested that over time the new owners would be able to assemble a contiguous block of apartments for NYU faculty for an academic community within a community. While that sounded intriguing, Sexton, according to two people who attended the meeting, was concerned whether NYU's investment would ignite a political firestorm. NYU never did put money into the project, but the university did lease about eighty apartments for use by undergraduates and another twenty-five for graduate students and faculty, according to Tishman Speyer.

BlackRock Realty continued to press the California teachers' pension fund to invest in the deal. BlackRock was already advising CalSTRS on multifamily housing projects. Christopher Ailman, CalSTRS's chief investment officer, and Michael DiRe, the real estate director, flew to New York to tour Stuyvesant Town-Peter Cooper Village and talk to tenants. The fund mulled over the investment for several months before finally giving it a green light in May, but for $100 million, not $500 million. CalSTRS's real estate portfolio was oriented toward "core" investments, properties that produced a positive cash flow from the first day. They determined that the Stuyvesant Town deal fell into a different category. "Staff concluded it should be classified as a tactical investment, with higher risk and potentially a higher return," said Ricardo Duran, a spokesman, "and lowered the allocation to $100 million."

At the same time, BlackRock contacted Florida's State Board of Administration, another pension fund that it advised, about a partnership stake in the deal. The board invested more than $100 million on behalf of one million current and future retirees. Early in January 2007, five BlackRock executives flew to Tallahassee to present the deal to Steve Spook, a senior acquisitions manager in the real estate unit; Doug Bennett, the senior investment officer; and Kevin SigRist, the board's deputy executive director. In March, Bennett and Spook recommended approval of a $250 million investment in the partnership. Spook's seventeen-page confidential analysis is remarkable for how closely it mirrors the investment memorandum, including notes on rent projections and apartment turnover, as well as the environmental and market risks associated with the deal and the unusually high cost of bridge financing. "Unless net operating income from the Property increases materially, the Partnership will not be able to meet its interest payment obligations, in which event it would default on the Ten-Year Debt," Spook's March 12, 2007, memo states.

But Bennett, like Spook and SigRist, enthusiastically endorsed the partners' strategy of replacing rent-regulated residents—who were very much like the pensioners represented by the fund—with tenants paying higher, market rents. They figured it was a potentially lucrative investment that over seven years would "add to [their] high return bucket." Curiously, Spook also said that "both venture partners have extensive experience in managing rent-regulated apartments," a claim that is not made in the Tishman Speyer–BlackRock investment memorandum.

Asked why Tishman Speyer, which was known for its portfolio of commercial buildings, was suddenly plunging into the multifamily residential market, Jerry Speyer told me the day that his son signed the contract that Tishman Speyer was not a newcomer to the housing field. He said he had built a five-hundred-unit residential tower in Manhattan in 2000, although the company sold it two years later for $209 million. "We were, at one point, one of the largest developers of residential properties in France. We've done residential in Germany. We have a significant residential business in Brazil and we're planning a large undertaking in India."

But while Tishman Speyer developed residential projects, it did not manage the properties and none of the buildings were rent-regulated housing. Indeed, the investment memorandum states that Tishman Speyer "has limited experience in managing multifamily rental properties." The memorandum did say that a BlackRock subsidiary managed apartment properties for the company's clients, but there was no mention of the very peculiar residential subset of rent-regulated units.

Nevertheless, investors from around the world found the arguments made by Tishman Speyer and BlackRock compelling. They also liked the idea of owning a piece of Manhattan. The projected internal rate of return, 13 percent, was a good deal better than many of their other investments. Tishman Speyer brought in the Church of England, which invested $75.7 million. The Wellcome Trust, a British trust for health-related research, took a $177.2 million limited partnership interest. KB Financial Group of Korea invested $155 million, after a meeting in a New York boardroom with twenty Korean investors and an equal complement of translators. The Ontario Municipal Employees Retirement System put in $75.7 million, as did PKA, a Danish pension fund. BlackRock was already a PKA adviser. "We thought it was a great opportunity to get into a core investment with a lot of potential," Nikolaj Stampe of PKA told one real estate magazine. "We didn't necessarily decide that we wanted to be in the US, but when the opportunity came along, it sounded interesting."[27]

Wachovia and Tishman Speyer, which is an active developer in India and China, landed the Government of Singapore Investment Corporation (GIC).

EQUITY INVESTORS[28]

Stuyvesant Town-Peter Cooper Village

CalPERS	$500 million
Florida State Board of Administration	$250 million
Government of Singapore Investment Corporation	$189.4 million
Wellcome Trust, England	$177.2 million
KB Financial Group, Korea	$155 million
Tishman Speyer Properties	$112.5 million
BlackRock	$112.5 million
CalSTRS	$94 million
Church of England	$75.7 million
Ontario Municipal Employees Retirement System, Canada	$75.7 million
PKA, Denmark	$75.7 million
Norinchukin Bank, Japan	$25 million
Credit Suisse First Boston	$15 million
Tishman family and friends	$12.9 million
Daiwa, Japan	$9.7 million
Gen Re	$9.3 million

THE DEBT STACK
Stuyvesant Town-Peter Cooper Village

Class	Class Size	Participants
Mortgage	$3 billion	Securitized Debt: WBCMT 2007-C30; WBMCT 2007-C31; Cobalt CMBS 2007-C2; MLCFC 2007-5; MLCFC 2007-6
Mezzanine 1–3	$300 million	Hartford Financial $100 million Deutsche Genossenschafts-Hypothekenbank AG $100 million Allied Irish Banks $50 million Winthrop Realty Trust $25 million Wachovia $25 million
Mezzanine 4–9	$600 million	GIC $575 million Brookfield Asset Mgmt. $25 million
Mezzanine 10	$300 million	CWCapital $90 million Fortress $50 million NY Credit $25 million JER $60 million Bracebridge Capital $75 million
Mezzanine 11	$200 million	SL Green $200 million

GIC was initially only interested in providing a $575 million secondary loan. But the partners convinced GIC that it should also buy a $100 million stake in the partnership. Rob Speyer was instrumental in 2004 in forming a strategic alliance with GIC, which managed a multibillion-dollar portfolio of direct and indirect property investments around the world. That year the two companies jointly purchased a dozen major office buildings in eight U.S. cities, including the Colgate-Palmolive Building on Park Avenue in Manhattan. Tishman Speyer handled management and leasing at the properties.[29]

One pension fund that did not heed the siren call from Tishman Speyer or BlackRock was the Washington State Investment

Board, which manages about $52 billion in state retirement and public trust funds. Joseph A. Dear, then the executive director of the Washington investment board, recalled getting a call from a senior executive at BlackRock asking whether he was interested in a limited-partnership stake in Stuyvesant Town-Peter Cooper Village. When BlackRock called, you listened. Dear, who grew up in MetLife's Parkfairfax complex outside Washington, DC, quickly sent off a note with BlackRock's investment memorandum to Gary Bruebaker, his chief investment officer in Olympia, Washington. He suggested to Bruebaker that it might be time to develop a closer relationship with BlackRock. But by the end of the day, Dear got his response and it was an emphatic no thanks.

"The price looked a little high," Bruebaker recalled. "The terms were not anything we would ever accept. The fees were kind of rich for the manager. But the biggest thing—the structure didn't work for us."[30]

The Washington investment board preferred to invest in real estate operating companies, where they were the principal owner and had a great deal of control, instead of making do with an impotent seat on an advisory committee for a limited partnership. Whatever the outcome of the investment, the Stuyvesant Town partnership structure entailed several ongoing revenue streams flowing to the operating partner. There was a 1.5 percent property-management fee based on gross residential revenues, which would amount to an estimated $3.2 million in 2007, plus reimbursable expenses and leasing commissions. That was typical in Manhattan. But then there was the 3.5 percent "supervisory fee" for a planned $100 million in future capital projects, total: $3.5 million. The asset management fee amounted to $10 million a year for a limited partner with a

$500 million investment and $2.5 million from a $100 million investor. The general partners received a 20 percent "promote," or percentage of profits, after the limited partners got a preferred 9 percent return on their investment.

The Washington analysts were concerned that the Stuyvesant Town-Peter Cooper Village acquisition was highly speculative, one in which the new owners did not take into account the fluctuating demand for market-rate apartments or the ebbs and flows of the real estate markets and the economy. "The plan was for perfection," Bruebaker said. "They never put together a contingency plan. That coupled with the controversy over affordable housing on day one was not a good combination."

CHAPTER NINE

"What Do They Have Against Trees?"

Tishman Speyer Properties, the large, well-regarded organization credited with rejuvenating signature commercial properties like Rockefeller Center, the Chrysler Building and the MetLife Building, turned its attention to the sprawling Stuyvesant Town-Peter Cooper Village complexes on the East Side of Manhattan. Although Tishman Speyer had never owned or operated a housing complex as large as the eighty-acre development, Rob Speyer and his company had big plans for transforming the sixty-year-old housing development into "an exciting, vibrant, desirable residential community."

The two complexes, their business plan said, suffered from a rather "modest" image in the Manhattan marketplace and a distinct lack of the amenities that would allow them to reposition Peter Cooper Village in particular as a "luxury product." They planned to spend $160 million to build an upscale health club, roof decks, children's playrooms and a concierge center, as well as remodel apartments with stone counters and high-end appliances, improve the outdoor lighting, refurbish the lobbies and establish a shuttle to transport residents to and from subway and bus stops.[1] Rob Speyer took a particular interest in turning the landscaped grounds into the kind of lush flower show you'd find at a botanic garden.

The new owners were going after a whole new demographic. The teachers, government workers and firefighters of yesteryear were out of fashion in Manhattan. If Stuyvesant Town-Peter Cooper Village had been created on the ruins of a demolished working-class neighborhood, Tishman Speyer now wanted to push the complexes farther up the economic ladder by appealing to younger, more well-heeled, upwardly mobile New Yorkers working in finance, advertising and communications. "When we first looked at the property, we thought there were quality of life issues that made it less desirable than other Manhattan properties," Rob Speyer told *New York* magazine. "Access to public transportation was a challenge, so we introduced a trolley. There were few entertainment options, so we created an event series. We tried to improve a stark living environment, so we planted trees and we invested in a health club."[2]

The first order of business, however, was to increase revenues by dislodging tenants who did not qualify for rent-regulated apartments and shifting previously rent-regulated units to market rents. The recovery of rent-regulated units was a preoccupation of the weekly staff meetings. Their obsession with the turnover rate was understandable given that the annual debt service on $4.4 billion in loans was $284.4 million, while annual net income in 2006 was just over $100 million. They had a $400 million reserve fund to make up the difference in the early years, but it would not last forever, unless they boosted rental income. But it soon became clear that Tishman Speyer had something to learn about managing rent-stabilized housing in New York, where every tenant complaint, no matter how specious, and every corporate misstep would find its way into the tabloids, the real estate trade papers and the often eviscerating blogs that sprang up to chronicle Rob's misadventures. It was unfamiliar terrain for a buttoned-down company that preferred to do business outside the public spotlight.

Early on, Adam Rose, the co-president of Rose Associates, who was managing the property at the time, caused a ruckus at one staff meeting in a boardroom at Rockefeller Center when he told the Tishman Speyer executives that they were unrealistic in assuming a double-digit recovery of rent-stabilized apartments in the first year. Their presentation to the bond-rating agencies in December estimated the conversion rate at "15 percent for the first year and 12 percent in the second year."[3]

"We've been screening the rent-stabilized tenants for years," Rose recalled telling them. "You'll get a four to five percent turnover. They said, 'Oh no. Our pro forma shows more than 10 percent.' "[4]

The exchange grew heated as a disembodied voice, presumably an investment partner from California who dialed into the meeting via telephone, demanded, "Where did those numbers come from?" And one young executive from Tishman Speyer became, in Rose's words, "apoplectic." Rose, scion of another prominent New York real estate family whose company managed thirty thousand apartments in New York, was steadfast. "This is my experience," he said. "This is what I believe."

Within two months, Rose was gone. Rose felt double-crossed. He said Rob Speyer had assured him that Rose Associates would continue to manage Stuyvesant Town-Peter Cooper Village. The complexes accounted for one-third of the thirty thousand apartments his company managed. He had gone to Yale University, working during the summers as an auxiliary policeman in

Provincetown, Massachusetts, before going into the family business. Usually a genial, talkative executive, he became a bitter critic of Speyer's tenure at the complexes. And years later he would get his revenge when he was brought back in to manage the complexes after Tishman Speyer left.

Tishman Speyer, which took over day-to-day management, had repeatedly told investors, lenders and the rating agencies that it would take a more aggressive approach to turnover than the "passive," or lackadaisical, strategy employed by MetLife. But after the dispute with Rose over the projected turnover rate, Tishman Speyer did adjust their numbers, somewhat. The investment memorandum that went out to pension funds in January and February 2007 indicated that the anticipated conversion rate was 7.5 percent in 2007 and 11 percent in both 2008 and 2009, on a declining number of rent-regulated apartments. By that time, net operating income was to have more than doubled to $253.2 million.

Tishman Speyer hired not one but three law firms to pursue cases against what it described as "illegal" tenants, mainly those residents who wrongfully sublet apartments without approval by the landlord, or tenants who did not qualify for a rent-stabilized apartment because their primary residence was outside Stuyvesant Town or Peter Cooper. Fred Knapp, a private detective once described by the *New York Times* as the "scourge of illegal tenants," was brought in to dig into the background of tenants whose leases were up for renewal. Knapp made a good living hunting through property records and other public documents for New York City tenants who had a home or employment elsewhere.

The first wave of lease-renewal notices from the new landlord sent a shock wave through Stuyvesant Town and Peter Cooper Village, as tenants saw their rents jump by anywhere from 15 to 33 percent. There was a great deal of hand-wringing during the sale over the fate of the elderly, rent-stabilized residents. The truth was that those tenants were locked in, protected by state law from eviction and hefty rent hikes. It was the market-rate tenants who were taking a beating. Dara Kane had grown quite fond of her spacious two-bedroom apartment in Peter Cooper Village, her friendly neighbors and the parklike setting of the complex where her seven-year-old played. Her renewal notice stated that the rent was going up $700 a month to $4,450 beginning February 28. MetLife was no piker when it came to rent hikes; her rent had gone up $500 a month a year earlier. But the jump to $4,450 was more than Kane and her family could afford.

"It's a really special place," said the departing Kane. "But they are not interested in retaining any stable tenancy. When people like us leave, you have to wonder. How are the public schools going to survive? How will the 14th Street Y sustain itself? All those things are going to suffer."[5]

Every weekend seemed to bring another convoy of moving trucks that deployed around Stuyvesant Oval, a rare sight in the past when tenants lucky enough to get an apartment would stay for years, even decades. Evan Horisk, a television producer for PR Newswire who had lived at Stuyvesant Town for four years, was forced to give up his newly renovated two-bedroom apartment in Stuyvesant Town when the rent jumped 26 percent to $3,350, from $2,660 a month. "It flipped my life upside down," Horisk said two weeks after he moved to a smaller apartment blocks away. "Living there was great. The renovations were superb. The maintenance was top-notch." But he continued, "I didn't get a big raise this year that can compensate for that kind of increase."[6]

The rent history for Horisk's apartment provides a glimpse of how the system worked. Prior to 2002, the rent for the two-bedroom unit had been a rent-regulated $888.87. But once it became vacant, MetLife and Rose Associates spent $42,204 renovating the apartment. To offset that expense, state housing laws allowed the landlord to bump the rent by $1,055.11 per month. The owner was also permitted "vacancy increases" of $309.33. So the total monthly rent for Horisk and his roommates came to $2,253.31 in January 2003, and since that was above the $2,000 threshold, the apartment was also deregulated. The rent rose to $2,495 in 2004, $2,550 in 2005 and $2,660 in 2006, before leaping to $3,350 in January 2007.[7]

Rob Speyer was unimpressed by the complaints from tenants like Horisk. After all, 80 percent of the tenants were renewing their leases, despite the increases. He figured he was only raising rents to market levels, a process begun by MetLife in 2001 when for the first time it hired an outside manager for the complexes and began deregulating apartments in earnest. The new owner pushed the rents hard. By Tishman Speyer's calculations, rents for deregulated apartments at Stuyvesant Town and Peter Cooper Village were running at least 12 percent below what was being charged at comparable buildings nearby, while rents for rent-stabilized apartments were 30 to 40 percent below market. "We're generating significant demand from existing residents as well as from the outside," Speyer countered. "Our rents are well within the market, and our renewal rates demonstrate that."[8]

The rumblings over the subprime mortgage crisis started to get louder by the spring of 2007. But whatever the problems with home mortgages, few developers, bankers or analysts expected the crisis to radically affect the booming commercial credit market for hotels, shopping centers, multifamily housing or office buildings. No one anticipated defaults on those loans.

Both trends emerged in an era of lax lending standards, high-risk mortgage products and heavy betting that property values would continue to rise.

Banks make high-interest subprime loans to buyers who lack the income or the strong credit history needed to qualify for traditional mortgages. Most banks in the past refused to grant mortgages in black, Latino and poor communities.

Under the Community Reinvestment Act the federal government encouraged institutions receiving Federal Deposit Insurance Corporation insurance to end discriminatory lending practices in low-income neighborhoods. Federal banking agencies assess a bank's performance in meeting credit needs in communities in which they operate before approving applications for new branches or for mergers and acquisitions.

Historically, subprime lending only accounted for a sliver of all home mortgages. But starting in the late 1990s subprime lending became big business.

Independent mortgage banks like Countrywide, Ameriquest and New Century, which operated outside of federal regulation, including the Community Reinvestment Act, began aggressively marketing subprime loans as their higher interest rates made them more profitable. The banks also tapped into the global capital markets, gaining access to seemingly unlimited amounts of capital.

The new private lenders typically offered easy initial terms—lower interest rates, called teaser rates—to encourage homeowners and buyers to take on difficult mortgages. After an initial period of time, say one year, the teaser rate was replaced by the regular, higher interest rate.

The effect on the homeowner was crushing. The monthly payment on a $500,000 mortgage at a 4 percent interest rate was about $2,400. But the same loan with a 10 percent rate would require a $4,220-a-month payment.

As home prices continued their rise, owners were encouraged to refinance again, at more favorable terms.

In many cases, mortgage brokers received bonuses for steering borrowers into high-interest loans larded with extra fees, even if they qualified for a traditional mortgage. The whole business was based on the assumption that house prices would never falter. But the securities were often so complex that it was difficult to assess the risk.

Wells Fargo, Bank of America, HSBC and other money center banks followed the lead of the independent banks, either acquiring subprime lenders or starting up their own operations.

These banks pooled the worst of their subprime loans with regular mortgages and sold these complex securities to investors around the world.

The percentage of lower-quality, subprime mortgages soared to 20 percent by late 2006, from 8 percent in 2003. In Florida, Southern California and Arizona it was even higher. By March 2007, the value of subprime mortgages had reached an estimated $1.3 trillion, with 7.5 million first-lien subprime mortgages outstanding.[9]

But once interest rates began to fall and housing prices slipped, modestly at first, homeowners could no longer refinance. Defaults and foreclosures escalated as the initial terms expired, higher interest rates kicked in and monthly payments jumped substantially. The securities packed with subprime loans suddenly turned toxic as investors fled, shaking the foundations of the world financial system.

"This is no longer a niche market that can be dismissed," said Keith Ernst, senior housing counsel at the Center for Responsible Lending. "It's a major component of the mortgage market and the growing rates of foreclosures should be a cause for alarm."[10]

The Center for Responsible Lending, a research group based in Durham, North Carolina, warned at the end of 2006 that 1.1 million homeowners who had taken out subprime loans in the prior two years would lose their houses by 2009. The foreclosures would cost those homeowners an estimated $74.6 billion, primarily in equity.

Still, the industry downplayed the growing crisis. Douglas Duncan, chief economist for the Mortgage Bankers Association, told the *New York Times* that the center's report was too pessimistic. "Every forecast models assumptions," he said, "but it seems they picked the worst-case scenario."[11]

The continuing fall in house prices meant that by one estimate nearly a quarter of all U.S. homes were worth less than their mortgage. The repercussions were felt in Florida and Arizona, where entire subdivisions looked like ghost towns as banks foreclosed on the properties.

The crisis had a particularly devastating effect on largely black and Latino communities, where even the middle class turned to subprime rather than traditional mortgages. In some neighborhoods in New York City, for instance, houses on block after block sat boarded up and vacant in once-thriving communities.

"This was not only a problem of regulation on the mortgage front, but also a targeted scourge on minority communities," Shaun Donovan, the secretary of housing and urban development, said in a speech at New York University. "Roughly 33 percent of the subprime mortgages given out in New York City in 2007 went to borrowers with credit scores that should have qualified them for conventional prevailing-rate loans."

Tishman Speyer had other problems to contend with. Only two months after the company took over, a group of nine current and former market-rate tenants at the complexes filed a class-action lawsuit in state supreme court on January 22, 2007, claiming that Tishman Speyer and MetLife had illegally charged market-rate rents for more than three thousand apartments after "wrongfully pocketing nearly $25 million in New York City tax benefits." The tenants said that MetLife had received $24.5 million in tax breaks since 1992 under the city's J-51 property tax program, which, they argued, prohibits a property owner from deregulating apartments. The J-51 program was designed to encourage residential property owners, particularly landlords with older buildings, to refurbish their properties and make capital improvements, be it new elevators, boilers or windows. The plaintiffs wanted the court to roll back rents at Stuyvesant and Peter Cooper Village and issue a formal declaration that all of the units at the complexes would remain rent stabilized until the J-51 tax breaks expired in 2020. The tenants also wanted hundreds of millions of dollars in rent rebates and damages.

"Even though this was the largest real estate transaction of all time, and MetLife certainly has a right to make as much profit as it could, the tenants who have rights under the law need to be protected," said Stuart M. Saft, a well-known real estate lawyer who filed what became known as the "Roberts case."[12] "Roberts" was a reference to the lead plaintiff, Amy L. Roberts, who remained in her sixth-floor apartment on Twentieth Street, on the north side of Stuyvesant Town.

The lawsuit brought a curt "No comment" from MetLife and a dismissive wave from Tishman Speyer, which declared that the lawsuit had "no merit." It had been common practice for years for landlords, primarily in Manhattan, to simultaneously take advantage of the city's J-51 program and deregulate apartments. The state housing agency sanctioned it, Speyer's lawyers said. Rents were substantially lower in the city's other four boroughs, Queens, Brooklyn, the Bronx and Staten Island, and therefore landlords were less likely to reach the $2,000-a-month threshold for deregulation. Tishman Speyer's lawyers argued that the plaintiffs had voluntarily signed leases agreeing to market-rate rents so nothing had been taken away from them. Although anything could happen in court, most real estate experts confidently predicted that the lawsuit had no chance of success, and even many tenant activists were skeptical.

The case, which began as a Hail Mary effort to stymie Tishman Speyer, had been hatched months earlier by Leonard Grunstein, the rotund, silver-tongued lawyer who represented the tenant bid for Stuyvesant Town-Peter Cooper Village.

Grunstein had actually learned about the J-51 issue during

a meeting with Michael Lappin and Kathleen Dunn of CPC Resources, an outfit with ties to ninety banks and insurance companies that finances affordable housing. Their lawyer, Stuart Saft, was also there. CPC had revived another MetLife project, the 12,271-unit Parkchester complex in the Bronx, and was considering a bid for Stuyvesant Town-Peter Cooper Village. They were discussing the history of the complex when Dunn, a former deputy housing commissioner for the city, paused. "It's clear to me that you can't deregulate while you're taking J-51 benefits," Dunn exclaimed.[13] At first Grunstein doubted her. But he subsequently had associates at his law firm dig into the history of the state housing laws.

Soni Holman Fink, the tiny, vivacious eighty-six-year-old woman who serves as the tenants association's co-director of communications, recalled the meeting when Grunstein first broached the idea of a J-51 lawsuit. As she often did, Fink played host to the association's monthly gathering at her Peter Cooper Village apartment, whose picture window offered a mesmerizing view of the East River. "I can still see the grin on his face," Fink said of Grunstein. " 'We're going to stick it to them.' "[14]

But John H. Marsh III, the treasurer, and James J. Roth, the retired FBI agent, were the only ones on the seven-member board who really wanted to pursue it. "Half the people were saying that the laws allowed for landlords to deregulate," Marsh said. "There wasn't enough legal footing. But Jim and I felt, why not? We had just been through a grueling time with the sale."[15]

Grunstein, however, had to turn the case over to Saft because Grunstein's firm, Troutman Sanders, had a conflict of interest: It did work for MetLife. Saft, in turn, went to Councilman Garodnick, who put him in touch with market-rate tenants like Roberts and Horisk who were willing to put their names on the lawsuit. "I thought all along it was promising, but never a gimme," Garodnick said. "The law was clear but with so many years of common practice it would be a tough battle."[16]

Six months later, State supreme court judge Richard B. Lowe dismissed the tenants' lawsuit, handing a victory to MetLife and Tishman Speyer, which was busily repositioning Stuyvesant Town-Peter Cooper Village. There was very little media coverage of the decision, an indication, perhaps, that it had been widely regarded as a futile fight. The tenants' appeal would not be decided for a year and a half. By then, everything would have changed in Stuyvesant Town, in New York and across the country.

Stuyvesant Town-Peter Cooper Village was not the only thing on Rob Speyer's mind in 2007. His company operated on four continents and the real estate markets were still booming, even if there were some faint rumblings about troubled subprime home mortgages that had been turned into securities and sold to banks, insurance companies and pension funds. His company bought ten office buildings in Frankfurt, Berlin, Hamburg, Dusseldorf, Munich and Stuttgart while he flew between development projects in India, China and Brazil.

In May 2007, Rob Speyer sold the former headquarters of the *New York Times* in Times Square to an Israeli billionaire for $525 million, three times the $175 million Tishman Speyer paid in November 2004. The *Times* was building a new headquarters three blocks to the south. Rents for office space were up, but not by 300 percent or even 30 percent in 31 months. Yet, buyers seemed willing to pay almost any price to get ahold of prime property. Rob Speyer had planned on turning the building into first-class office space, but the offer was too good to resist. The Israeli investor, Lev Leviev, had not even visited the fifteen-story building before signing the contract. Rob Speyer was in the airport in Dubai at midnight after meeting with an investor when he got a call from his broker, Darcy Stacom, saying she had a buyer at $525 million, "willing to go hard."

"Sign it up," Speyer replied, laughing, hardly believing the number. "What're we on the phone for?"[17]

Speyer also sold the famed Lipstick Building, an elliptical, thirty-four-story office tower on Third Avenue designed by Philip Johnson and John Burgee, for $648.5 million. It was yet another illustration of just how fast the market was moving. Speyer and his partner, the New York City Employees' Retirement System, had bought the building three years earlier for $235 million. Having sold 666 Fifth, the New York Times Building, the Lipstick Building and $2 billion worth of property in London, Tishman Speyer raked in spectacular profits for its partners and itself on $5 billion in sales.

But the Lipstick deal also emitted a warning bell. The new owner, a group led by two Israeli investors, had planned to pay $44.8 million cash and finance 90 percent of the purchase with a loan from none other than Robert Verrone at Wachovia. But with the market jittery over the gathering storm in the subprime mortgage market, Verrone suddenly demanded a higher interest rate and less leverage. The Israelis were forced to get alternative financing from Royal Bank of Canada before closing the deal, which was expected to provide a meager 3.6 percent rate of return. Many observers wondered whether the credit boom that had fueled the run-up in real estate prices was drawing to a close.

The Israeli investors, however, were betting that annual rents would rise further still, to $100 a square foot and beyond.

The Speyers were not just sellers in 2007, however. They had a role in the two mega-deals of 2007 that would mark the peak of the market, the $39 billion purchase of Equity Office Properties in February, and months later, the $22.2 billion takeover of Archstone-Smith Trust, a publicly traded company with 360 apartment complexes, mainly on the East and West Coasts. Those transactions checked in as the first- and second-largest privatizations ever of a public real estate company.

The bidding war for Equity Office Properties, the nation's largest office landlord, ignited in January 2007 when a group led by Steven Roth, the outspoken chairman of Vornado Realty Trust, offered $38 billion for the company, topping a $36 billion offer from the Blackstone Group. Sam Zell, the Chicago billionaire, had spent three decades assembling 590 buildings and over 105 million square feet of office space in virtually every major metropolitan market in the country. But the company's disappointing share price reflected that stock analysts never bought into Zell's strategy of creating a national brand for office space.

The Blackstone Group, the nation's largest private equity firm, had been on a shopping spree, buying one publicly traded real estate company after another and taking them private. Equity Office proved an irresistible target, and not just for Blackstone. The residential market showed signs of weakening, but office rents were expected to continue to rise. A gusher of capital from sovereign funds, domestic and foreign pension funds and wealthy individuals continued to pour into real estate. Roth, the sharp-tongued founder of Vornado Realty, a public company whose holdings include suburban strip malls, office buildings in Washington, DC, and New York and the retailer Toys"R"Us, wanted to create the largest commercial real estate company in the nation. But public real estate companies cannot assume a lot of debt without coming under fire from stock analysts. So Roth turned to two real estate titans for partners, Barry Sternlicht of Starwood Capital and Sternlicht's onetime mentor, Neil Bluhm, a Chicago real estate tycoon.

The parry-thrust between the rival bidders continued for weeks before Blackstone, headed by Stephen A. Schwarzman, won, with a $39 billion offer. Even as that drama came to a close, Blackstone was raising another $10 billion real estate fund. The company immediately flipped hundreds of EOP buildings for a premium to sixteen different buyers in record-breaking deals from Southern California to Austin, Texas; Chicago; and New York. Even as profit margins on the properties shrank, the buyers found lenders on Wall Street all too willing to finance as much as 90 percent of the price. Morgan Stanley, Wachovia, Goldman Sachs, Bear Stearns and Lehman Brothers, in turn, collected their fees as they packaged the loans and sold, or tried to sell, them to investors as commercial mortgage-backed securities.

In Los Angeles, Maguire Properties, one of the largest commercial landlords in Southern California, bought twenty-four Equity Office buildings. The developer Harry B. Macklowe took only ten days to buy seven EOP buildings in Manhattan for $7 billion with short-term high-interest debt. In one stroke,

Macklowe, a high-stakes gambler, doubled his real estate empire. Although rents in the buildings averaged less than $60 a square foot, the underwriting projected rents rising to $100 a square foot or more. Tishman Speyer paid $1.7 billion for six EOP buildings in downtown Chicago, solidifying its hold on that market. The company immediately put a "For Sale" sign on three of them, hoping to pay off some of the debt used to acquire the properties in the first place. "[It] taught everyone that no deal was too big," Scott Latham, then executive director of Cushman and Wakefield's capital markets group, told *Commercial Property News*, a trade paper.

Three months later, Tishman Speyer and Lehman Brothers did their own version of the EOP deal, announcing the $22.2 billion purchase of Archstone-Smith Trust and its 360 apartment complexes in cities from Phoenix to Fairfax, Virginia, and New York. The deal had an exotic financial structure and an interesting backstory. Top bankers at Lehman Brothers, one of the more aggressive real estate lenders, were upset at losing out on the $5.4 billion purchase of Stuyvesant Town-Peter Cooper Village. Lehman's ace commercial lender Mark A. Walsh had tied up with the Related Companies, the developer of the Time Warner Center in Manhattan, in that auction. But Jerry Speyer, a personal friend of Lehman's chairman, Richard S. Fuld, had won with financing from Wachovia. Taking a page from Blackstone's purchase of EOP, Walsh engineered a highly leveraged deal for Archstone in partnership with Tishman Speyer.

Tishman Speyer contributed $250 million, or about 5 percent of the $5.1 billion in equity in Archstone, with the potential to earn 13 percent of the profits. Archstone would survive as a corporate entity and key executives would remain in place. Walsh and Lehman Brothers matched them and led Bank of

America and Barclays in gathering $17.1 billion in debt plus $4.6 billion in bridge equity. Rob Speyer envisioned his company's investment as a hedge against the slowdown in the housing market. If people were not buying houses and condominiums, they would rent instead. But Speyer and Lehman Brothers also planned to retire some of the debt by unloading a block of Archstone's apartment complexes, starting with the sale of a 90 percent interest in sixteen properties in San Diego and Orange County, California, to Irvine Company for $1.4 billion. But by the time the deal closed in October 2007, Green Street Advisors estimated that the value of Archstone's assets had fallen by 8 percent as worries grew about subprime mortgages.

Rob Speyer seemed to be of two minds about the real estate market. He had sold a pile of trophy office buildings, making a fortune for his company and his partners. It was a signal, perhaps, that in his view real estate prices had topped out and would soon retreat. Yet, at the same time, he paid top dollar for a batch of Chicago office buildings and jumped into a highly leveraged acquisition of Archstone-Smith.

By the summer of 2007, the subprime mortgage industry that had flourished for years was threatening to pull down the national economy. The value of mortgage-backed securities held by banks, insurance companies, hedge funds and other investors was in free fall. They worried that they might not have sufficient capital to stay afloat. Many analysts and developers were still unsure whether the problem would ever swamp still-booming Manhattan. Still, advocates for low-income homeowners had been complaining for years that mortgage providers were issuing loans without regard to the borrower's ability to repay. But easy initial terms and rising housing prices had encouraged borrowers to assume oversize mortgages in the belief they would be able to quickly refinance at more favorable terms. Outright fraud by some lenders also contributed to the rise in the number of subprime mortgages. But once interest rates started to fall in 2006 and housing prices inched downward, refinancing became more difficult. Defaults by homeowners on subprime and adjustable-rate mortgages skyrocketed and subprime lenders in December 2006 started failing as more borrowers fell behind on their mortgage payments. Like a growing number of commercial loans, the subprime home loans had been combined with other mortgages, blessed by the rating agencies and sold to banks, insurance companies and other investors.

On February 8, 2007, HSBC, the large British bank, announced that it was setting aside an additional $1.76 billion because of expanding problems in its American subprime lending business. The bank indicated that the rate of subprime loan defaults was escalating faster than anticipated. HSBC said bad debt charges for the year would be about $10.56 billion, 20 percent higher than the average forecast by analysts. The bank's public statements triggered a sell-off of mortgage-linked securities.

On the same day, New Century Financial, the second-largest subprime mortgage lender, also warned of growing financial problems. Two months later, the publicly traded company filed in bankruptcy court for protection from creditors.

Over the following summer, the Federal Reserve cut the discount rate it charges banks to borrow money, a move that at least temporarily quelled fears in stock and credit markets and among investors and banks. The Fed reluctantly acknowledged that the credit crisis posed a threat to economic growth.

Bear Stearns later disclosed that two hedge funds it controlled were facing a wave of withdrawals by investors. In July,

Moody's and Standard & Poor's, which had given mortgage-backed bonds high ratings, suddenly downgraded more than $7 billion of them sold in late 2005 and 2006. The rating agencies also began cracking down on the lending practices in commercial real estate, where banks were issuing loans at generous terms while buyers put little or no equity into the deals. Office rents in New York and other major markets were still rising, but for the first time since 2004, the average vacancy rate for 58 metropolitan markets rose, albeit only slightly, to 12.6 percent from 12.5 percent, according to Torto Wheaton Research, a division of CB Richard Ellis. "Underwriting has gotten so frothy that we have to take a stand," Jim Duca, a group managing director at Moody's Investors Service told the *New York Times* in May 2007. "The industry was headed to Niagara Falls."[18]

At quitting time on Wednesday, May 23, 2007, an estimated seven thousand tenants and union members marched across Stuyvesant Town to highlight the need for new rent-stabilization laws to "preserve New York's dwindling stock of affordable housing." The "Hands Around Stuyvesant Town" march, which included more than fifty city and state elected officials and one hundred community organizations, marked the start of a campaign to overhaul the state's housing laws, which, organizers said, had swung in favor of landlords. "The price of housing in this city is effectively theft for working- and middle-class people," Ed Ott told the crowd. "Housing is hard to afford even with two incomes."

The median household income in Stuyvesant Town and Peter Cooper Village was close to $95,000. But the $5.4 billion sale of the complexes had served as a catalyst for both low-income and middle-class residents throughout the city who found it increasingly difficult to find housing they could afford. The housing crisis for poor and working-class New Yorkers was severe and more well-known, with many families paying more than half their income for shelter. Between 2002 and 2008, New York City lost more than two hundred thousand apartments affordable to tenants making less than $37,000, as median rents increased by almost 9 percent, according to the Furman Center for Real Estate and Urban Policy at New York University. At the same time, middle-income neighborhoods were disappearing. The problem was especially pronounced in Manhattan, where half the neighborhoods were identified in a study by the Brookings Institution as high income and 40 percent as low income.

City comptroller William Thompson focused on the continuing loss of apartments that were once in the state's middle-income Mitchell-Lama housing program. After twenty years in the program, developers were leaving in droves, paying off the government mortgages and pushing rents to market levels. "Forty thousand people are watching their homes change from affordable to no longer affordable," Thompson said at the rally. "We need to stand up to make sure all New Yorkers can stay."

It is hard to understand politics in New York without grasping the role of the real estate industry. Real estate is big business in a city whose economic health is often measured by the number of construction cranes swinging across the skyline. Property taxes account for the bulk of the city's operating budget. About 130,000 workers labored at construction jobs in the city in 2007. In this context, there is an intimate relationship between real estate tycoons and the city's 51 members of the city council. The council has little power relative to the mayor except in one area: land use. Most major projects and policies must get approval by the council. Therefore, real estate executives as a group are often the single biggest campaign contributors to council members, as well as state senators and assembly members from New York City whose votes could affect development policy.

But New York City is still primarily a city of renters, renters who vote, as elected officials well know. This dynamic can lend itself to peculiar maneuvers. City council president Christine Quinn, for instance, is a former tenant organizer who has fought to enlarge the city's affordable-housing program. She was an outspoken supporter of the tenant bid for Stuyvesant Town-Peter Cooper Village and a critic of the real estate speculators.

But few officials are willing to engage in a permanent state of war with the industry and risk losing its potential financial support. Nor are many developers willing to completely alienate a politician who can determine the fate of their next project. So, a few months after the sale of Stuyvesant Town, Rob Speyer emerged as one of the most generous supporters of Ms. Quinn's possible mayoral campaign, gathering up $22,275 in contributions from real estate executives.[19]

Still, the backlash against speculators who were buying tenements by the blockful in working-class neighborhoods was gathering steam. Activists had upended the sale of Starrett City, the sprawling Brooklyn complex, and were now pressuring state legislators to change the laws. "The large numbers being talked about drew people's attention," Neill Coleman, a spokesman for the city's housing agency, acknowledged to *The Real Deal*, a real estate magazine. "There's a renewed interest in what the city is doing from the press, from advocates and from elected officials."

Darcy Stacom, the broker who sold Stuyvesant Town-Peter Cooper Village, told executives at a real estate forum that she feared the "influence of politics on private transactions." Nevertheless, the speculative trend continued as Dawnay Day Group, a British real estate firm, bought a portfolio of 47 buildings in East Harlem for $225 million, and Stephen Siegel, a prominent commercial real estate broker, formed the SG2 group and acquired a large portfolio—1,137 apartments and 55 storefronts—in the Bronx for $300 million. In both cases, the buyers intended to exploit the gap between rent-stabilized and market rents.

At Stuyvesant Town-Peter Cooper Village, Tishman Speyer hiked the rents on deregulated apartments, renovated vacant units and ferreted out as many illegal tenants as they could find. Rob Speyer also sought to break down the institutional aura that surrounded the fifty-six (sometimes described as 110 buildings, because some structures have multiple addresses) nearly identical brick buildings. He established a green market inside the complexes on Thursdays and Fridays and, in a gesture of goodwill toward the tenants, brought former Mets star Keith Hernandez to Stuyvesant Town to toss out the first ball at a game sponsored by the Peter Stuyvesant Little League on Con Ed Field, near the East River. Rather than using pesticide, Tishman Speyer also released nearly 720,000 ladybugs in the fall of 2007 to eat the tiny mites and other insects destroying the extensive greenery. Some tenants welcomed the modern new health club that opened on Twentieth Street, the thoroughfare that separates Stuyvesant Town and Peter Cooper Village. But not the older residents, who were dependent on the supermarket that was ousted to make way for the health club, which they did not use.

Tishman Speyer's campaign to evict "illegal" tenants made a

far bigger impression on longtime residents of the two complexes than gyms and green markets. The company's lawyers and detectives identified tenants whose leases were up for renewal and who appeared to live elsewhere for at least 183 days a year. Ninety days before the leases expired, the law firms sent the so-called illegal tenants a "Golub notice," the equivalent of an eviction notice, because their Stuyvesant Town or Peter Cooper apartment did not appear to be their primary residence. "Tishman Speyer caused a lot of anxiety right from the beginning because we knew they wanted to get people out," said Richard Toes, a former narcotics detective who lived in Stuyvesant Town for more than thirty years.[20]

Under state law, a landlord can evict a tenant who is using a rent-regulated apartment as a pied-à-terre or subleasing the unit to another person at a higher rent. Tishman Speyer's lawyers and detectives culled information from property records and credit card databases. Hundreds of tenants were told that their lease would not be renewed unless they provided management with proof of employment and residency. Tishman Speyer discovered that one rent-stabilized tenant, Jeff Varner, actually lived in Kalamazoo, Michigan, where he worked as a news anchor for a local television station. He was not the only person who was unwilling to forgo a prized low-rent apartment after having moved away from New York City. "We want a community of people who actually live here," Rob Speyer said.

As word of the Golub notices coursed through the complexes, Al Doyle, the president of the tenants association, was inundated with calls from fearful rent-stabilized tenants who had received a notice or were afraid they would soon get a notice. The tenants association did not oppose evicting people who profited by subleasing rent-regulated apartments at a higher rent. But Tishman Speyer threw a much wider net, Doyle said. MetLife and Rose Associates had quietly issued nonrenewal notices to tenants who clearly were and were not entitled to a stabilized apartment. The widespread use of the notices generated a great deal of ill will among all residents, not just those who received the notices. Anxious residents were forced to produce pages and pages of documentation, and in some cases hire a lawyer, to prove their Stuyvesant Town apartment was their primary residence.

Agnes Lamy, a legal secretary who had lived in a one-bedroom apartment at Stuyvesant Town for a decade, initially ignored the nonrenewal notice she received in December 2007, thinking it was a mistake. But Tishman Speyer was intent on getting her out. The detectives had discovered that Lamy had signed a $60,000 loan for a studio apartment in Brooklyn. It was for her mother, she explained. Tishman Speyer demanded three years' worth of tax returns and bank statements to prove her residency. No sooner had she straightened out the matter, than she got another letter from the landlord wanting to know her connection to an apartment on East Thirty-Fourth Street, where she had lived with her now divorced husband fifteen years earlier. "They put me through the ringer, all the way," Lamy said of the four-month ordeal. "These were intimidation tactics."

Doyle asked the Urban Justice Center, which provides legal assistance to low- and moderate-income tenants, to hold an informational clinic for tenants at a junior high school near Stuyvesant Town. After more than a hundred residents showed up seeking advice, the Urban Justice Center turned it into a monthly event, consistently drawing fifty people per session.

Surfing through public records can also produce notoriously

unreliable or incomplete results. Dolores M. Shapiro, a sixty-two-year-old anthropologist and retired professor of nursing, was accused of living in Naperville, Illinois, a town, she said, that she had never even visited. She was forced to hire a lawyer, James B. Fishman, who discovered that a woman with the same name but a different middle initial appeared to be living in Naperville. Tishman Speyer dropped the case. "Their business model was fear," Fishman said. "It was all about scaring the crap out of people. Lots of tenants could not afford to fight back and hire a lawyer. Even when they won, it was a pyrrhic victory. It could cost thousands of dollars in legal fees."[21]

Suzanne Ryan was ordered to give up her Peter Cooper Village apartment after she got a notice claiming she and her husband lived in a beachfront home on Long Island. She too had to hire a lawyer to prove that Ryan's family used it as a summer beach house, while keeping their residence in the city, where her two children attended Catholic school. "It's a little Cape," Ryan explained. "We had fixed it up ourselves."

Jack Lester, a tenant lawyer, said he had represented dozens of tenants but lost only one case, a flight attendant who lived in Florida and used an apartment in Stuyvesant Town whenever she flew into New York.[22]

Rob Speyer vehemently denied accusations by residents and their lawyers that his company harassed tenants, saying Golub notices only went out when there was evidence of a second residence. Rob Speyer was bewildered by the tenant reaction. He had figured that legitimate tenants would feel no kinship with tenants who did not belong in a rent-regulated apartment. In the end, he said that one-third of the 1,099 tenants who received Golub notices in 2007, 2008 and 2009 left the complexes without a fight, a third proved that they were legitimate tenants and a third went to court. Ultimately, he said, half were illegal, although tenant advocates said that many tenants left rather than fight because they could not afford to hire a lawyer. "The numbers speak for themselves," Speyer concluded.[23]

But a climate of suspicion and distrust had set in, coloring much of what happened in the complexes, even efforts to beautify the grounds. In 2008, an army of workers armed with shovels, saws, tractors and backhoes swarmed across the eighty acres. Tishman Speyer expanded the lobbies of the buildings facing the grassy, tree-shaded oval at the center of Stuyvesant Town by knocking out some of the brick walls and adding glass boxes that housed new amenities, ranging from a day care center to a theater and a private event room. The transparent cubes contrasted nicely with the unrelenting brick of the complexes and lent a modern flair to the architecture. Although MetLife had spent $47 million refurbishing the complexes' fifteen playgrounds and installing new lighting and new landscaping throughout the grounds, Rob Speyer also brought in a new landscape architect, Peter Walker, and started all over again. He wanted a lush fantasia of colors and flowers worthy of the younger, wealthier tenants he was trying to attract. Eventually, he spent millions of dollars on an astounding array: 10,000 new dogwood, magnolia and cherry trees; 3,100 shrubs; 120,000 perennials; 40,000 annuals; and 100 hanging baskets. Every so often, the old plantings were yanked out and new ones put in their stead.

"We met with Rob every couple of weeks," said Walker, who is based in California. "It was his baby and he was interested in how it turned out. He wanted a show garden, something that would be spectacular, a transforming level of landscaping."[24]

Proud as he was, Rob Speyer could not help asking Doyle,

the tenant leader, what he thought of the results during a chance encounter at Stuyvesant Town. He was stunned when Doyle complained. Longtime tenants at apartment complexes are often wary of change, particularly one that turns the complexes into a construction site for extended periods. The new bushes at the base of the buildings offered some privacy for first-floor apartments, but Doyle said the older tenants complained that the plantings also obscured the views of the security cameras.

"What do they have against trees?" Rob Speyer said to me at the time. "I couldn't believe it. There's a group that will never be happy no matter what we do. That story sums it up."

Doyle acknowledged that "it sounds crazy." "But," he said, "the tenants were used to lush rolling green lawns. If you were a young mother, you could see your kids playing halfway across the property. The sight lines were blocked by the new trees."[25]

The landscaping and the glass cubes also proved to be rich fodder for a new blog, *Stuy Town Lux Living,* that premiered in April 2008. The blog dubbed the spots suddenly thick with bushes and young trees "Rape Forests," because of the impenetrable foliage. It got to the point that anything Tishman Speyer did at Stuyvesant Town was seen as a threat. Including the gardening.

The blogger behind *Lux Living* was a website designer and content provider living in a one-bedroom apartment, paying a rent-regulated $1,600 a month. A mix of *The Daily Show* and TMZ, *Lux Living*'s sharp-tongued parodies and fake news reports quickly found an audience, with thirty thousand unique visitors a month. The site linked to newspaper articles about the Stuyvesant Town deal and provided information concerning the latest doings. Faux reports highlighted the bare-breasted women at Tishman Speyer's Mardi Gras celebration and the high suicide rate among workers assigned to the nearly-always-empty Oval Lounge. The site was unsparing of Rob Speyer, who was described as a "real estate pirate," depicted in skimpy gym shorts and described as "reeking of alcohol and chain smoking." "It was a soap opera," the blogger told me. "The whole David-and-Goliath thing."[26]

The blogger of *Lux Living,* who was thirty when the blog started, also explored the tension between the recent college graduates and the established residents, be they originals who dated to the 1947 opening, their children now raising children themselves or young couples looking for a quiet corner of the city. Tishman Speyer's marketing aimed at a younger demographic to dispel the perception that Stuyvesant Town and Peter Cooper Village were more for the geriatric set. There were more than three hundred graduate students living in apartments rented by New York University, according to Tishman Speyer executives.

Many longtime tenants felt the students ignored their neighbors and played loud music when they got home at 3:00 A.M. on Saturday. Old-timers complained that the "kids" left garbage bags outside the garbage chute and neglected to sort their bottles and cans for the recycling bins.

"It changed from a stable community to a transient one," said Soni Fink, who has lived in her Peter Cooper apartment since 1961. "They were so eager to rent apartments at higher prices that the only people who could afford it were the kids, who put up dividing walls. Four or five of them would pile in. Young couples used to move in and settle down."[27]

In the late 1990s, MetLife removed the post-and-chain fences that protected every blade of grass inside the complexes. Appealing to young renters, Tishman Speyer took it a step farther, relaxing or even abandoning the pesky rules that once governed life in the complexes, including the prohibition on pets. Denis Delaney, whose parents moved to Stuyvesant Town in 1948, can still recall how the guards would chase after offenders who dared set foot on the lawns. So it was a shocking sight after Tishman Speyer took over to see young women lying out in the sun or people playing with their dogs on the grass. Soon there were footpaths crisscrossing Stuyvesant Oval's once-verboten lawn. "I used to jump over the chains and run on the grass because I was a kid," said Denis Delaney, fifty-eight. "But I liked it looking nice. Now there are cow paths."[28]

In 2007 and 2008, Tishman Speyer methodically went about renovating vacant apartments, raising rents and navigating the arcane system governing rent-regulated apartments in New York. The company spent more on apartment renovations than MetLife, about $53,000 per unit at Stuyvesant Town, installing maple cabinets, stone counters and higher-end appliances in the kitchens, refurbishing the bathrooms and laying down new parquet floors. At Peter Cooper Village, where the apartments were larger, the landlord spent $69,000, installing slightly better finishes.

Tishman Speyer diligently pushed the net effective rent for a one-bedroom at Stuyvesant Town to over $3,100 a month and over $4,000 for a two-bedroom. At Peter Cooper, one-bedroom apartments went for more than $3,200 and two-bedrooms for more than $4,700 a month.[29]

But a peculiar thing happened in the fall of 2007. Fewer and fewer people were renting apartments at Stuyvesant Town and Peter Cooper, where historically the vacancy rate was less than 2 percent. By the end of the year, Tishman Speyer had accumulated an inventory of 757 unrented apartments. The new owners discovered that they could in fact charge too much for an apartment in a sixty-year-old non-doorman building on the East Side. Renters found better deals elsewhere. Citi Habitats, a large rental broker, reported in 2007 that the average rent in the neighborhood west of Peter Cooper Village was $2,785 a month for a one-bedroom apartment and $3,846 for a two-bedroom unit.

Tishman Speyer was in a deep hole, considering that about 50 apartments a month turned over through normal attrition and now they had an additional backlog of 757 units, more than a year's worth of inventory. It was happening at complexes where traditionally there was a very low vacancy rate and a 10-year waiting list. Rob Speyer did everything to move product. The company dropped the rents and offered incentives to brokers who leased the most apartments: an all-inclusive trip to Cabo San Lucas for first prize; iPhones for the five runners-up. They offered tenants one month free rent and an American Express gift card loaded with $1,000. Rob Speyer later acknowledged that the company's effort to push rents to luxury levels had gone too far. "What happened, candidly, was we overstepped a bit," Rob Speyer told *New York* magazine. "In any business, you look at your inventory, you price your business to move your inventory."[30]

The rising vacancy rate was not just a concern of management. More than three hundred tenants showed up for an April 3, 2008, "town meeting" at the veterans' hospital on East Twenty-Third Street, sponsored by the tenants association and Manhattan borough president Scott Stringer. Speakers denounced the rising number of legal challenges launched against tenants, despite promises by Tishman Speyer that there would be "no radical changes." Garodnick, the councilman, told the crowd that Tishman Speyer had created a "landlord-versus-tenant culture" in which tenants lived in fear of getting an eviction notice. He also pointed out the suddenly high vacancy rate resulting from the new owners' relentless pursuit of higher rents. "Families moved to PCV/ST because it is renowned for its stability, its tranquil grounds and its sense of community," Garodnick wrote to Speyer. "Unfortunately, you are creating a culture of conflict that is having a negative impact. Everyone, from the original residents who moved into the complex in 1949 to the younger families who seek to settle down, is feeling the effects of these policies."

Tishman Speyer's financial model was also showing some signs of stress. Instead of net income rising as predicted, it had not really budged in a year. Expenses went up, what with three top law firms billing hundreds of hours to chase "illegal" tenants. Speyer's banker Rob Verrone of Wachovia called the trustee for the $3 billion first mortgage, suggesting that there was an inadvertent mistake, or what lawyers call a "scrivner's error," in the loan documents that prevented the new owners from shifting money from one reserve fund, say the one for repair and maintenance, to the interest reserve, which was used to plug the yawning $14-million-a-month gap between income and the actual loan payments. Their request to shift their reserve funds was denied. "They were looking to pull money from repair and maintenance to pay debt service," said Chuck Spetka, chief executive of CWCapital. "At that time, they weren't meeting projections so we could not and would not approve that. However, the magnitude of the problem was not yet evident."[31]

So early in 2008, Tishman Speyer elected to make a change in its payments for the $1.4 billion mezzanine loan, which was made up of eleven different segments. Under its loan documents, Tishman Speyer had the option to stop making payments and let the interest accrue for the tenth and eleventh segments, which totaled $500 million. That reduced the monthly debt service to $21 million from $23.7 million.[32] Speyer hoped that they had bought some time to reduce the inventory and boost revenues.

Whatever the issues at Stuyvesant Town, Rob Speyer was still in deal mode. They were not making more land in Manhattan, so the opportunity to snap up a rare undeveloped parcel was irresistible.

On March 21, 2008, Speyer vaulted to the head of a pack of prominent developers vying for the development rights to twenty-six acres of vacant land on Manhattan's west side, overlooking the Hudson River.[33] The competition for the billion-dollar deal had started months earlier when the economy was still on cruise control. But it now looked to be teetering at the edge of recession as lenders had all but shut the doors for large real estate deals because of the expanding credit crisis. Only a week earlier, Bear Stearns, a global Wall Street investment bank, had collapsed amid mounting losses on the huge amounts of mortgage-backed securities it had issued. The stock market tumbled as JPMorgan Chase bought Bear Stearns at a fire-sale price, ultimately, of $10 per share, a staggering loss as its stock had traded for $93 a share as late as February 2008. The deal was valued at about $1.2 billion, the worth of Bear Stearns' Madison Avenue headquarters.

Wachovia, the nation's fourth-largest bank and a leading lender for office buildings and multifamily properties, had announced in January that it would write down more than

$1 billion in commercial loans for the second half of 2007.[34] Morgan Stanley reported it was writing down $400 million in commercial loan losses. Unlike the borrowers for subprime residential mortgages, commercial landlords seemed unlikely to default. But investors suddenly refused to buy securities backed by commercial loans. That left banks like Wachovia, which packaged $24.2 billion worth of commercial loans as securities in 2007, stuck with loans that had dropped in value.

The shaky economic environment had already prompted one national developer, Brookfield Properties, to drop out of the competition for the twenty-six-acre parcel in Manhattan. But Rob Speyer and three rivals were not ready to give up the chase, at least not yet. After all, rents and occupancy rates remained fairly healthy. Maybe the markets would make a quick comeback from the credit crisis and the Bear Stearns debacle.

The billion-dollar deal offered an increasingly rare commodity: a large-scale development in Manhattan. The project was a political priority for Michael R. Bloomberg, whose administration had spent six years rezoning the once-industrial West Side for high-rise buildings, and a fiscal necessity for the Metropolitan Transportation Authority, which owned the land and hoped to reap a billion dollars from the sale. But while the deal presented a potentially lucrative opportunity, it came with enormous risks. A developer would have to spend an estimated $1.5 billion building platforms over active rail yards before starting the first tower in a roughly twelve-million-square-foot project that would take a decade to complete.

The Metropolitan Transportation Authority selected Tishman Speyer as the top bidder because of its blue-chip reputation and access to capital from around the world. The authority immediately entered into what turned out to be prolonged contract negotiations with Rob Speyer, whose company planned to erect four or five office towers and seven residential buildings with 3,053 apartments, a school and 13 acres of open space. Both Rob Speyer and his father, Jerry, saw a chance to do a project together that could have the same impact on New York as John D. Rockefeller Jr. had in the 1930s when he built Rockefeller Center.

Six weeks later, the negotiations foundered. Speyer insisted on delaying the closing and changing some of the economic terms. He did not want to start making payments for the development rights until the land was rezoned, a process that could drag on for eighteen months. In essence, Tishman Speyer wanted a free option on the development site. MTA officials did not want to wait that long for the first payment and risk Tishman Speyer's walking away from the project if the economy faltered or the zoning did not suit the developer's plans. Gary J. Dellaverson, the authority's chief financial officer, balked, telling Speyer in a series of tense phone calls that he had wasted the MTA's time and threatening to open talks with another bidder. Speyer, who was traveling in Europe, asked for more time. "Rob was just wracked with anxiety during that last week," Dellaverson said.[35]

On May 9, 2008, Mayor Bloomberg, desperate to salvage the project, invited the Speyers to his town house in London. Rob and his father flew in from Milan, where they had been meeting with investors. But the mayor had little leverage since he did not own the land. "The plan isn't dead by any means," Bloomberg declared in London. "Hudson Yards is the most exciting opportunity New York has." The Speyers issued a statement as well: "We still hope to complete this deal and reach an agreement that satisfies the needs of everyone."[36]

Back in New York on Monday, Rob Speyer met with Dellaverson and nearly signed the contract. But at the last moment, he asked to postpone and raced back to Tishman Speyer headquarters at Rockefeller Center to talk to his father. He seesawed between snatching up the headline-making deal and a paralyzing concern for the gathering financial storm. Sensing that the market had reached its peak, he and the company had started selling off some of their prime office buildings in January. As the sun set over Manhattan, Jerry and Rob went for a walk that stretched deep into the night before ending up at 3 Guys, an Upper East Side diner on Madison Avenue, between Seventy-Fifth and Seventy-Sixth Streets. Over tuna sandwiches, they weighed their desire to work together against the faltering economy and the potential risks in their portfolio. They had run the company with an explicit understanding: Either one of them had veto power over any major undertaking by Tishman Speyer. But Jerry told his son, "You're going to be living with this project a lot longer than I. It needs to be your decision."

Rob paused for a moment before responding. "We're not doing it," he said.

"It was a great opportunity to develop a game-changing project in our hometown, something that we'd both dreamed of doing," Rob recalled five years later. "But we both had an agonizing feeling that the timing was wrong."[37]

The markets were jittery and Rob had a full plate of projects. Tishman Speyer and Lehman Brothers had already announced the $22.2 billion purchase of Archstone-Smith and now Stuyvesant Town-Peter Cooper Village was demanding more and more attention. Investors like the California Public Employees' Retirement System, which had written a $500 million check, wanted to know why things were not going according to plan.

CHAPTER TEN

The Bubble Explodes

By the spring of 2008, Tishman Speyer had whittled down their huge inventory of unrented apartments to about four hundred units, by offering one month of free rent and other concessions to prospective tenants. Rob Speyer vowed once again that Tishman Speyer would be a longtime owner of Stuyvesant Town-Peter Cooper Village. Heckled by a tenant during a walk through Stuyvesant Town, he remained undaunted. Even if current residents did not always appreciate the lush landscaping, the health club and the amenities on Stuyvesant Oval, he said the new market-rate tenants did. "We've hit our stride," Speyer said at the time. "With all the positive changes at the property, interest is only going to grow from here."[1]

Yet, his business plan was even more out of whack with reality. Net effective rents—the rent after concessions, such as one month free rent—were slipping. The conversion of regulated apartments was moving even more slowly in 2008 than the year before. Moreover, Speyer and his partners had already burned through about two-thirds of their reserve funds.[2] On the political front, he was still getting angry letters from Councilman

Garodnick demanding that Tishman Speyer declare a moratorium on evictions and pay the legal expenses of residents who were able to prove that they were legal residents of Stuyvesant Town or Peter Cooper despite notices to the contrary.

"Tishman Speyer has launched a campaign against legal, legitimate tenants who have no business being pursued by their new landlord," Garodnick said. "This is a company that bills itself as a leader in New York and now they're using the cheapest of tactics against tenants who are clearly legitimate."

Beyond Stuyvesant Town, the Community Service Society, a nonprofit antipoverty group in New York, issued a study of the city's declining inventory of rent-regulated housing for poor, working-class and moderate-income New Yorkers. The group called for state and federal investigations of the loss of thousands of rent-regulated apartments that were once in a federal program for low-income tenants or the state's Mitchell-Lama program for moderate-income housing. "This was a combination of people trying to make fast bucks in a very overheated housing market and regulators taking the view 'anything goes,'" said David R. Jones, president of the society. "Someone should be held accountable for this kind of wrongdoing."

The mounting criticism of Tishman Speyer by tenants and housing activists, however, had no effect on the Speyers' reputation among New York's political, social and business elites. Jerry I. Speyer and Steven Rattner, a financier who managed the mayor's fortune, were instrumental in persuading Michael R. Bloomberg to run for a third term. But that required overturning the city's term-limits law, which would force Bloomberg to step down after eight years, on December 31, 2009. Speyer, Rattner and other business leaders appreciated the mayor's corporate approach to government and his friendliness to real estate development. Rattner served as an adviser to President Barack Obama on the auto industry and managed the mayor's personal fortune and philanthropic assets.

In their view, the middle of a financial crisis was the wrong time to replace the city's chief executive.[3] Bloomberg, who had previously been a staunch defender of term limits, agreed. Speyer and other business leaders aligned with Bloomberg then waged a campaign to convince the public that overturning term limits was a good idea, while running a bruising but ultimately successful lobbying effort to get the city council to extend term limits to twelve years. Bloomberg spent $105 million on his reelection campaign and won.

Still, Tishman Speyer had more than just Stuyvesant Town-Peter Cooper Village to contend with. Other highly leveraged assets purchased at the top of the market were showing signs of stress. Tishman Speyer and Lehman Brothers had planned to sell as many as half the 359 apartment complexes in the Archstone-Smith portfolio to reduce the debt on their $22.2 billion acquisition. The only problem was that prices were coming in a good deal lower than expected when they were even able to drum up bids for the properties. The partners sold the 948-unit Archstone San Jose complex in California for $192 million, $38 million, or 16.5 percent, less than the average price it paid per apartment. Another complex in Denver, Monterey Grove, sold for $56 million, $2 million below its allocated value. Despite those setbacks, Ian Lowitt, Lehman's chief financial officer, told analysts in June that Archstone was in serious discussions to unload $2 billion worth of property. Lehman and Tishman Speyer also wrote down their investment in Archstone by 25 percent.

Tishman Speyer was not alone. Record-breaking deals were suddenly unraveling from New York to California. The developer

Ian Bruce Eichner, who was building a high-end casino in Las Vegas called the Cosmopolitan, defaulted on a $768 million construction loan from Deutsche Bank, which took over the property. Centro Properties Group, an Australian mall operator, put itself up for sale after failing to refinance billions of dollars in short-term debt stemming from the acquisition of an American shopping center portfolio. In Los Angeles, Maguire Properties, one of the biggest commercial landlords in the region, was struggling with huge debts from buying a portfolio of buildings in Orange County whose tenants, it turned out, were imploding subprime mortgage companies.

Harry B. Macklowe, a prominent Manhattan developer with a willingness to double down as fierce as any riverboat gambler's, lost much of a vast real estate empire in May 2008 when he was unable to refinance $7 billion in high-interest, short-term loans. Macklowe, a ruthless, gravelly voiced negotiator, fended off his lenders for more than six months. But ultimately he was forced to sell his prized possession: the fifty-story General Motors Building on Fifth Avenue, and three other midtown towers, for a breathtaking $3.95 billion, to a group led by Mortimer B. Zuckerman, chief executive of Boston Properties.[4]

Only fifteen months earlier, Macklowe had been more successful than at any other point in his career. Son of a garment industry executive and a college dropout, Macklowe owned eight prime Manhattan office towers and a group of luxury apartment buildings. He also controlled two rare development sites in midtown. Macklowe wagered much of what he had to buy seven skyscrapers as part of the Equity Office Properties deal for $7 billion.

The market appeared to be booming and credit was easily available. He and his son put up only $50 million of their own money and borrowed $7 billion from Deutsche Bank and Fortress Investment Group to finance the rest of the purchase. The average annual rent from the seven midtown office buildings was $59 a square foot, William Macklowe, Harry's son, revealed during the crisis. But, he added, Deutsch Bank and Fortress underwrote the deal on the assumption that rents would soon soar to $100 a square foot. It was a remarkable illustration of the risks that Wall Street bankers and developers were willing to take. But William Macklowe also seemed to forget his symbiotic relationship with the bankers and the Macklowes' role in making the calculations on which the underwriting was based. Most of the loans were typical nonrecourse debt, meaning the lender could take the property in the event of default but not the borrower's other assets. Harry Macklowe, however, backed one loan with a $1 billion personal guarantee.

A year after the purchase, the senior Macklowe, seventy-one, found himself unable to refinance the debt and pay off the original loans. It was not the first time that Macklowe's back was to the wall. But in the midst of the crisis, he went sailing on his 112-foot racing yacht in the Caribbean, while his son stayed home to negotiate with the bankers. At least outwardly, Macklowe appeared to be stress free, oblivious to the possibility that his empire might once again slip through his fingers, much as it had in the early 1990s.

"Our lenders have supported us in the past to an extraordinary degree," Macklowe told me one evening in his office, shortly before he left for the Caribbean. "We're pretty confident that, going forward, we'll be able to achieve accommodations and extensions from our group of lenders."[5]

But after months of unsuccessful haggling and a journey to the Middle East in a fruitless search for partners, Macklowe was forced to relinquish not only the seven towers to his lenders but also the GM Building, across Fifth Avenue from the Plaza Hotel, where he'd bought a full-floor condominium.

The sale of the GM Building alone, for a record $2.8 billion, was an anomaly in this new era, made possible only in partnership with Zuckerman's partners—Goldman Sachs, Morgan Stanley and investment funds from Qatar and Kuwait. Otherwise, deal making was coming to a screeching halt as the bond market for mortgage-backed securities, the fuel for the rapid escalation of prices in 2005, 2006 and 2007, shut down amid concerns about defaults and delinquencies. The sales volume for office buildings plummeted by 74 percent nationally to $54.3 billion, from a $210.3 billion peak in 2007, according to Real Capital Analytics.

Multifamily housing was no different, with the volume of apartment properties dropping by 62 percent nationally and 64 percent in New York City. With office rents falling and vacancy rates hitting 10 percent in every metropolitan area in the country except New York, many of the buildings that had traded hands in recent years were in jeopardy as owners struggled to meet oversize debt payments with diminishing revenues. The underwriting for many of those loans was based on income projections rather than actual income. It didn't require a full-scale recession for the rickety financial architecture to collapse, only a slowdown in the rate of growth. Wachovia put the senior piece of the $3 billion mortgage on Stuyvesant Town-Peter Cooper Village on its watch list, because the net income from the property was so far below the debt service. Of course, that was also true the day that Wachovia closed on the loan.

Moody's Investors Services, the bond-rating agency, announced in the spring of 2007 that it planned to adjust how it rated commercial mortgage-backed securities (CMBS) to better reflect the risk. But the damage was done. Moody's, like Standard & Poor's and Fitch, had already stamped the loans with investment-grade ratings, based on what had quickly turned out to be fanciful projections. By then, Wall Street had repackaged hundreds of billions of dollars in loans as securities and sold them to investors.

"Loans with more aggressive terms that weren't available in '03 and '04 became the norm in '06, when suddenly lenders became very accommodating," said Mike Kirby, a principal at Green Street Advisors, a research company in Newport Beach, California, that tracks real estate investment trusts. "The attitude was, 'Gee, we're not going to own this stuff; we get terrific fees for underwriting these loans, and we can blow it out in a CMBS deal in three months."[6]

Analysts wondered if the credit crisis was about to swamp commercial real estate. Deutsche Bank had piled up $25.1 billion worth of commercial loans. Morgan Stanley had $22.1 billion and Citigroup held $19.1 billion. Lehman Brothers, the most aggressive of all, was actively trying to sell $40 billion worth of commercial real estate assets, a high-risk bridge equity loan for the Archstone-Smith acquisition. Lehman had not been as quick as others to package the loans as securities and get them off the company's balance sheet. More than half the assets were in the United States, with 26 percent in Europe and 17 percent in Asia.[7]

In August 2008, Laurence Gluck, a New York real estate investor, notified lenders that he was in imminent danger of defaulting on the mortgage for Riverton, the middle-class housing complex in Harlem that had been built by MetLife in 1947. Gluck had bought the property in 2005 for $132 million with a $105 million bank loan. A year later, Gluck and his partner, Rockpoint Group, refinanced the property with a $225 million senior loan from Deutsche Bank and a $25 million junior loan. Deutsche Bank combined the loan with other mortgages and sold it to investors. The refinancing enabled Gluck and Rockpoint to recoup their original investment, pay off the initial loan and set aside $53.3 million in reserves for renovating the complex and interest payments. They put the remaining $60 million in their pockets, without any legal obligation to give it back if the project went sour.[8]

Gluck planned, like Tishman Speyer and BlackRock at Stuyvesant Town-Peter Cooper Village, to dress up the sixty-year-old, middle-class complex and replace rent-regulated residents with tenants willing to pay market rents. The developer installed new elevators, upgraded the lobbies and landscaped a seven-hundred-foot interior courtyard at a complex whose residents once included jazz pianist Billy Taylor, former mayor David N. Dinkins and Clifford L. Alexander Jr., secretary of the army in the Carter administration. But Gluck's push to convert the apartments to market rents quickly fizzled. Rental income covered less than half his debt service. Less than two years after he refinanced the property, Gluck was on the verge of default. He ultimately walked away, turning the keys over to his lender.

Gluck, who has a Jimi Hendrix poster prominently displayed in his office, told me that the banks drank the "Kool-Aid" of the era by providing oversize loans based on "pro forma" underwriting. Asked if he hadn't had a sip of Kool-Aid himself and profited handsomely from the arrangement, he acknowledged that he had. In the meantime, the estimated value of Riverton had fallen to $170.3 million by October 2008, according to Realpoint, a research firm that assesses mortgage-backed securities.

Small wonder that some housing activists began describing Gluck and his bankers as "predatory equity."

Within a few weeks, Citigroup analysts issued a report in August entitled "Looking for Other Rivertons." They came up with a list of twenty-two properties—one in Chicago, two in San Francisco and nineteen in New York—in rent-regulated markets with CMBS loans based on projections of rapidly increasing revenues. In each example, the project revenues did not cover the debt service on day one of the deal. Stuyvesant Town-Peter Cooper Village figured prominently on the list, although Citi analysts were optimistic about its fate, given the complexes' desirable location and the fact that "cash flow [was] gradually improving."

In May 2008, Nori Gerardo Lietz, the adviser to the California Public Employees' Retirement System who had given the Stuyvesant Town investment a hearty thumbs-down, told her clients at CalPERS that they should demand a meeting with Tishman Speyer and BlackRock executives. She told them that the sponsors' rosy projections were not materializing. Revenues were not growing as quickly as predicted. Operating expenses were rising. The rental market in general was softening. Tenants were up in arms. As a result, Tishman Speyer was burning through the complexes' reserve funds at a faster rate than anyone anticipated. It might take a year or two, but eventually the reserves would fall to empty and the sponsors, Tishman Speyer and BlackRock, would be unable to make their mortgage payments.

"I kept harping," Lietz recalled, " 'This thing is going bankrupt.' "[9]

A meeting was finally set for May 22 at CalPERS's offices at

Lincoln Plaza in downtown Sacramento. Lietz drove out from her home in San Francisco. Rob Speyer flew out on a private jet with several other Tishman Speyer and BlackRock executives. Dale Gruen and Robert Lewis, the executive in charge of managing BlackRock Realty's relationship with CalPERS, also came in from the firm's San Francisco office. CalPERS and CalSTRS were major clients. Gruen had invested $2.75 billion in multifamily housing on behalf of CalPERS. In 2006, he declared that his firm viewed "New York as one of the nation's best apartment markets for investors." No more.

They were met at CalPERS by Judy Alexander, the soft-spoken real estate investment manager who was the primary contact at CalPERS for BlackRock, as well as her bosses, Ted Eliopoulos, CalPERS's newly installed senior investment officer, and Randy Pottle, a senior portfolio manager.

Given the enormity of CalPERS's investment, the pension fund had received periodic updates on the progress at Stuyvesant Town-Peter Cooper Village. But this was Speyer's first meeting with CalPERS and he quickly acknowledged that the property was "underperforming expectations."

He had e-mailed the group a mass of numbers. There was a detailed breakdown of how many one-, two- and three-bedroom apartments had been deregulated in Stuyvesant Town and Peter Cooper since they took over. The report showed how revenues had increased as a result. But operating costs were up too. The deregulation of units just was not happening fast enough. Speyer told them that the net operating income—the only number that really mattered to investors—was off by a stunning 33 percent from what they had projected.

It was no mere bump in the road. According to the private

placement memorandum that CalPERS and other investors had gotten eighteen months earlier, net income was supposed to top $211 million by the end of 2008. A $70 million shortfall was a big gap to fill.

Still, there were no fireworks. In the characteristic style of CalPERS's investment executives, Alexander and Pottle asked probing questions in a monotone that did not betray their concerns.

The BlackRock executives presented a thick overview of the residential market in New York, where rents still showed resiliency despite a slowing of condominium prices and the gathering wreckage from the subprime mortgage market. They conceded that the financial sector had become a drag on the economy. But Gruen did not foresee a severe slowdown.

Instead, Speyer offered hope to the CalPERS executives. Southern California was a mess. Entire subdivisions were defaulting on their mortgages. And the independent mortgage lenders who had popularized the sale of high-interest mortgages to buyers who could ill afford to pay them were tumbling into bankruptcy court, laying off thousands of employees and leaving their Orange County offices vacant. New York was different, or so it seemed.

"We had a plan for turning the situation around," Speyer recalled. "We had a capital program involving renovating units and upgrading the feel and look of the property."[10]

The CalPERS team expressed their disappointment, as well as their hope that a turnaround was in the offing. But Lietz, CalPERS's adviser, showed no such restraint. She snickered through much of the meeting, with an I-told-you-so tone that Speyer and Gruen found grating. Even the pessimistic Lietz, however, could not have imagined what would happen over the next couple months. Still, Lietz said, "They had a bunch of headaches. Everything was falling apart."

Many real estate investors in New York, the hottest market nationally throughout the boom, also held out hope that the credit crisis would pass quickly. The vacancy rate in midtown office buildings was still relatively healthy, even if deal making had slowed dramatically. Macklowe could be dismissed as an overeager gambler. The Stuyvesant Town-Peter Cooper Village deal had problems, but most analysts figured that Tishman Speyer would never let it slip into bankruptcy.

Then all hell broke loose in September as the crisis that began with the subprime mortgage market ballooned and the economy sank into a severe recession.

On September 15, 2008, Lehman Brothers, the fourth-largest investment bank in the United States, filed for bankruptcy protection, an event that shook the financial capitals of the world and led to a subsequent string of costly bailouts. It was the largest bankruptcy filing in U.S. history, and by the end of the day, the Dow Jones had fallen 504 points, the biggest drop in points since the 2001 terrorist attack on the World Trade Center.

Much like Bear Stearns four months earlier, Lehman's share price had been in a tailspin for weeks, but federal officials did not offer Lehman a lifeline. Lehman had borrowed heavily to fund its investments, principally in housing and mortgage-related assets. Lehman's ratio of assets to owners equity, an indicator of the bank's level of risk, jumped from about 24:1 in 2003 to 31:1 by 2007. The investment bank's bet generated handsome profits during the real estate boom. But once the housing market cooled and the subprime crisis unfolded, Lehman suffered unprecedented losses. Lehman also got stuck with huge positions in deals like Archstone-Smith and low-rated mortgage securities after the credit markets shut down. In the second quarter of 2008, Lehman reported losses of $2.8 billion and was forced to sell off $6 billion in assets, setting off fears that a fire sale would depress the value of commercial properties.

American International Group, the giant international insurance company, suffered a liquidity crisis on September 16, 2008, following the downgrade of its credit rating. At the opening bell of the stock market that morning, AIG's stock price plunged by 60 percent. Moody's and S & P downgraded AIG over continuing losses on mortgage-backed securities, which forced the company to deliver more than $10 billion in additional collateral to certain creditors. That evening the board of governors of the Federal Reserve Bank announced that the Federal Reserve Bank of New York had been authorized to create a twenty-four-month credit-liquidity facility from which AIG could draw up to $85 billion.

Merrill Lynch, fearing it was next to fall, agreed to a buyout by Bank of America. Panic spread. Investors lost confidence in financial institutions. Banks refused to lend to other banks. Hedge funds pulled out cash. Stocks fell by anywhere from 55 to 72 percent in once-booming Brazil, Russia, India and China. The International Monetary Fund estimated in October that banks and other investors would suffer $1.4 trillion in losses on loans and securities. The Bush administration devised a $700 billion bailout known as TARP, the Troubled Asset Relief Program, which was used to prop up banks and car companies. The Treasury pledged up to $200 billion to cover losses at Freddie Mac and Fannie Mae, the mortgage giants.

The crisis was not a natural disaster but the result of a poisonous stew of shoddy mortgage lending, the exorbitant pooling and sale of loans to investors who didn't know enough to ask the right questions about how risky they were and risky bets on securities backed by the loans, a federal inquiry led by the ten-member Financial Crisis Inquiry Commission concluded in its 2011 report.

The 633-page report highlighted the carelessness of the country's biggest banks, portraying Citigroup, AIG and Merrill Lynch as essentially asleep at the wheel. The report cited testimony showing how executives at AIG were oblivious to the company's $79 billion exposure to credit-default swaps, a quasi-insurance policy sold to investors seeking protection against a drop in value of securities backed by home loans. Merrill Lynch managers, in turn, were surprised when seemingly secure mortgage investments suddenly suffered huge losses, while Citigroup executives conceded that they paid little attention to mortgage-related risks. Both Citi and Merrill had portrayed mortgage-related investments to investors as safer than they really were. The commission noted that "Goldman Sachs has been criticized—and sued—for selling its subprime mortgage securities to clients while simultaneously betting against those securities."

"When the housing and mortgage markets cratered, the lack of transparency, the extraordinary debt loads, the short-term loans and the risky assets all came home to roost," the report found. "What resulted was panic. We had reaped what we had sown."

The same could be said of the commercial mortgage markets, where Tishman Speyer and BlackRock raised the debt and equity for the Stuyvesant Town deal. "The seeds of the default were present in the initial structure of the debt," said Sam

Chandan, president of Chandan Economics, an adviser to real estate investors and lenders, and an adjunct professor at the University of Pennsylvania. "We had a situation where three or four key assumptions were required to make the debt marketable. But those assumptions were made without any observable underpinnings."[11]

One key assumption at Stuyvesant Town was that the sponsors would be able to deregulate 12 to 15 percent of the apartments a year. "It was unprecedented," Chandan said. "There's no empirical basis for that projection in a project this size."

Further, the data presented to investors was often opaque, requiring someone with the diligence of a bloodhound to get to the bottom of it. In granting the Stuyvesant Town-Peter Cooper senior mortgage an investment-grade rating, Moody's stated that a critical indicator, the "actual" ratio of the complexes' cash flow to debt service, was a healthy 1.3. That meant that there was more than enough cash flowing from the property to make the debt payments. Deeper in the report, a reader could discover that the "actual" cash flow was based on estimates for 2011, not the actual cash flow from the property when the loan was written in November 2006. Moody's ultimately did raise a concern that the "current" cash flow only covered 40 percent of the debt payments.

Perhaps some of the fundamental shortcomings got overlooked by investors and lenders because the market was moving at top speed, leaving little time to scrutinize the numbers. There were only thirty days between the date Tishman Speyer signed the contract to buy the complexes and the day they closed on the deal, a process that customarily lasted three months. The bankers then raced to pool the mortgages in a security that could be rated investment grade and sold to investors. In 2007, for instance, there were $230 billion in commercial mortgage-backed securities, the equivalent of $4 billion to $5 billion in bonds being issued every week. "For some investors the speed of the market precluded the laborious analysis of any individual deal," Chandan said.

The commission found that the credit rating agencies—Standard & Poor's, Fitch and Moody's—were "cogs in the wheels of financial destruction." But the crisis could have been avoided, the report said, if not for widespread failures in government regulation, corporate mismanagement and heedless risks taken by Wall Street. The commission excoriated regulators—the Securities and Exchange Commission, the Office of the Comptroller of the Currency, the Office of Thrift Supervision—that "lacked the political will" to scrutinize and hold accountable the institutions they were supposed to oversee.

Low interest rates instituted by the Fed after the 2001 recession played a role in the crisis, along with the "aggressive home ownership goals" set by government and the government-controlled mortgage giants, Fannie Mae and Freddie Mac. It also pointed out how Fannie and Freddie, eager to stanch the loss of market share to Wall Street investment banks, had loosened underwriting standards, bought and guaranteed riskier loans and blithely increased their purchases of mortgage-backed securities. But Fannie and Freddie were not major factors in the crisis, the commission concluded.

A deep current of anger over Wall Street's heads-I-win, tails-you-lose culture poured into the public debate. Although Goldman Sachs denied it, newspaper columnists heaped vitriol on the investment bank for continuing to sell mortgage-backed securities while Goldman was purging them from its own accounts. E. Stanley O'Neal, chief executive of Merrill Lynch, left the firm in 2007 with a severance package worth $161.5 million, despite crippling losses from mortgage securities. In March 2009, AIG announced it was paying $165 million in executive bonuses. During a federal hearing, Representative Henry Waxman, Democrat from California, grilled Richard S. Fuld, the former Lehman chairman, over executive compensation. "Your company is now bankrupt, and our country is in a state of crisis, but you get to keep $480 million. I have a very basic question: Is this fair?"[12]

Fuld demurred, saying that he had in fact taken $300 million in pay and bonuses over eight years.

In November, the once-invincible Blackstone Group, one of the world's largest private equity firms, reported a third-quarter loss of $500 million.[13] The damage showed up in nearly every industry. Over the course of 2008, the S & P 500 stock index tumbled 39.5 percent, the steepest drop since the Depression. Blue-chip corporations from Bank of America to Citigroup and Alcoa lost more than 65 percent of their value.

Real Capital Analytics, a research firm, cataloged $106 billion in distressed and potentially troubled commercial properties by the end of 2008. The real estate market had deteriorated over the first nine months of the year, but foreclosures were still rare. The widening scope of the problem was startlingly evident, however, in the wave of defaults and foreclosures that followed Lehman's collapse. At least twenty metropolitan areas faced $1 billion or more in distressed or potentially troubled commercial property, Real Capital reported. New York and Los Angeles, ground zero for many highly levered transactions in 2006 and 2007, accounted for $23 billion in troubled or distressed properties. Phoenix, Houston and Atlanta had the most properties. Retail had the largest pipeline of potentially troubled properties, with shopping mall companies such as Centro and General Growth Properties struggling under enormous debts and a growing number of retail tenants filing for bankruptcy protection. The hotel sector was already seeing its fair share of distress.

The Urban Land Institute predicted that 2009 would be the worst year for commercial real estate "since the wrenching 1991–1992 industry recession." The downturn in the economy and the frozen state of the credit markets posed a danger even for property owners current on their loan payments but unable to refinance a maturing mortgage, especially when the value of commercial real estate dropped by 25 to 35 percent.

The much-celebrated 2007 deal for Equity Office Properties, with a portfolio of 573 commercial properties, had turned into a sterling example of the excesses of the real estate boom, with the wreckage strewn across the country, from Southern California to Austin, Texas; Chicago; New York; and Stamford, Connecticut. The Blackstone Group paid $39 billion for the portfolio and simultaneously flipped hundreds of buildings in it to sixteen different companies for $27 billion and a quick profit. The resale triggered record-breaking deals in Stamford, San Francisco, Portland, Chicago and Austin. Lenders provided lavish financing on the unrealistic expectation that rents and demand would continue to rise without pause. The mortgages were pooled and converted to commercial mortgage-backed securities.

Instead, the buyers were crippled financially by a recession, corporate layoffs and drops in both occupancy and rents. The new owners' inability to make their mortgage payments became a crisis for the pension funds, regional banks and insurance companies that held the asset-backed securities. Tishman

Speyer bought six EOP buildings in downtown Chicago and immediately tried to sell three in order to pay down its debt. But only one building brought an acceptable offer. So like many of the other buyers, Tishman Speyer teetered at the edge of default. Even Blackstone was hurt by the roughly one hundred EOP properties it held on to as their value skidded by 20 percent. "These were aggressive acquisitions under the best of circumstances," said Paul E. Adornato, a senior real estate analyst at BMO Capital Markets.

The New York office market's immunity to the downturn that was plaguing most American cities finally ended. "We have fallen further faster than any time in the last 20 years," Mitchell S. Steir, chief executive of Studley, a national real estate broker, told the *New York Times* in December 2008. "There has been more damage to real estate values in the last four months than in any other four-month period. The pace with which it has occurred is astonishing."

Long after the credit crisis began in 2007, many investors and real estate executives expected a "correction" to the rapid escalation in property values. The collapse of the bond market for mortgage-backed securities had served as a brake on deal making. But after the fall of Lehman Brothers, which was widely regarded as the "real estate ATM," it was clear that something more catastrophic was taking place. Tishman Speyer abruptly pulled out of a deal to buy the former Mobil Building, a 45-story, 1.6-million-square-foot tower on Forty-Second Street near Grand Central Terminal, for $400 million. Then Standard & Poor's dropped its rating on the bonds for the $5.4 billion purchase of Stuyvesant Town-Peter Cooper Village, citing an estimated 10 percent decline in the properties' value and the rapid depletion of $650 million in reserve funds.[14]

The rating cut had little impact financially on Stuyvesant Town tenants, Tishman Speyer or BlackRock. Bondholders, however, now held paper that was worth less than what they had paid for it. It would be difficult to resell the bonds except at a steep discount. But the announcement also generated yet another headline and a grim reminder to the public that Tishman Speyer's stewardship at Stuyvesant Town was not going well.

For Speyer, his relationship with Garodnick, the councilman who lived in a market-rate apartment in Peter Cooper Village, was a source of endless frustration as criticism of Tishman Speyer mounted in the city council, in the city's tabloids and on the blogs. The two men were about the same age, smart and well educated. They seemed to get along when they met at Tishman Speyer world headquarters. But it got to the point where Garodnick was calling Tishman Speyer every week or so to complain, about the landscaping, the high vacancy rate or the legal costs of tenants having to defend themselves against eviction. After reading the latest newspaper article in which Garodnick blasted Tishman Speyer for harassing tenants, Speyer would turn angrily to Martin J. McLaughlin, a longtime lobbyist and political fixer who worked for him, demanding, "Why can't we work together?"

"Rob," McLaughlin would explain as he outlined the Kabuki theater that accompanies tenant-landlord relations in New York, "he lives there. He gets up to go to work in the morning and five people complain to him. This tenant shit is normal. This is what happens when you're a landlord."[15]

McLaughlin would go on to say, "Rob couldn't quite wrap his

head around his role as a landlord and Dan's role as a tenant. Rob felt it had to do with his outbidding the tenants for the property. Rob took it personally. Dan did not."

In 2008, the lives of Garodnick and Speyer seemed to be on parallel tracks. On May 10, Garodnick, then thirty-six, married Zoe Segal-Reichlin, twenty-nine, a talented lawyer he had met on a blind date just as Stuyvesant Town-Peter Cooper Village was put in play by MetLife. She recalls little of their first encounter, at an East Village restaurant, which came only hours after she completed the bar exam. Their second date was the night before Garodnick's inaugural press conference, announcing a tenant bid for the complexes. She graduated magna cum laude from Brown University and received a law degree from Harvard Law. Their budding romance survived her move to Washington to work for the Lawyers' Committee for Civil Rights. After their marriage, she returned to New York and became associate general counsel for Planned Parenthood. The couple had a son in January 2011.

Rob Speyer, then thirty-nine, married Anne-Cecilie Engell six months later on November 12. They had met quite by accident at a friend's birthday party. For Speyer it was love at first sight, he said. For his wife, he added, "it wasn't."[16] Engell, a marketing director at Iconix Brand Group in New York, was from Denmark. She had graduated from Cornell and received an MBA from New York University. Marriage was a bit of a logistical problem. He is Jewish, while Engell is Lutheran. They resolved the dilemma by having Matthew A. Mitchell, her best friend from college and a Universal Life minister, preside over a small private ceremony at their apartment. Three days later, they flew to Copenhagen for another nondenominational ceremony in front of two dozen friends and family. His father was his best man. During the summer of 2010, the couple had twins.

Despite the similarities in their lives, there was no bridging the gap between Speyer's plan to displace tenants and transform Stuyvesant Town-Peter Cooper Village into a yuppie haven and Garodnick's effort to preserve the complexes as the last affordable harbor for middle-class tenants trying to raise families in an increasingly expensive Manhattan. "I would sit with Dan and I couldn't understand why there was such a gulf between our point of view and his point of view," Rob Speyer said. "He was a rational, decent guy. There was just a basic gulf between the way he saw things and the way I saw things."

Garodnick was equally puzzled by the real estate tycoon. "He never seemed to understand how I could criticize Tishman Speyer for how poorly they were treating the tenants at Stuyvesant Town," Garodnick said. "I was surprised how someone who seemed so nice was trying to push people out of their apartments."

Speyer and Engell spent their honeymoon in Copenhagen and later in the French Alps, hoping to get in some cross-country skiing. The rugged Alps are more known for downhill skiing. Mont Blanc, the highest mountain in Europe west of Russia, rises to 15,771 feet. Speyer retained his connection to high school wrestling with a secret passion for the soap opera matches of World Wrestling Entertainment. Other than that, he was not very interested in sports. Engell, the better athlete of the two, had grown up traversing the countryside in Denmark. As it turned out, Speyer spent less time on the slopes than on the telephone talking to bankers, investors and advisers about the deteriorating financial situation at Stuyvesant Town and Peter Cooper Village.

There were calls to lawyers and Morgan Stanley, the bank that Tishman Speyer and BlackRock hired to advise them on a restructuring plan, as well as the investors and the advisory committee comprised of equity partners. The complex was not meeting the numbers set out in their business plan. At the end of 2008, net income at the complexes was up almost 30 percent to $138 million from the prior year, but was still well shy of the $211.7 million projected in their business plan, and the $252 million in annual debt service.

There was no question that they needed an infusion of fresh capital and a restructuring of their debt stack if they wanted to salvage the asset. The property had lost as much as $2 billion in value in the downturn, if it was ever worth $5.4 billion. It appeared that the $3 billion first mortgage was safe. But Rob Speyer and his partners figured that the fourteen firms—ranging from Hartford Financial to the Government of Singapore's GIC, SL Green and Allied Irish Banks—that had lent the partners a total of $1.4 billion in junior loans would have to agree to major concessions. As for the hundreds of millions of dollars poured into the deal two years earlier by the Church of England, GIC, CalPERS, and the other pension funds, it was gone. All gone.

For CalPERS, Stuyvesant Town was one of a handful of speculative real estate deals into which the pension fund had plowed hundreds of millions of dollars. Instead of generating double-digit returns, the properties were losing value by the hour. "We took some very tough medicine in real estate," Clark McKinley of CalPERS would later say.[17]

Tishman Speyer and BlackRock, however, told their lenders that they would not inject additional capital into the asset unless their new money jumped ahead of the junior loans in priority. The question was whether the junior lenders would be accommodating or refuse to take a backseat to Tishman Speyer and BlackRock. Speyer figured that he still had twelve months to work out an arrangement with the junior lenders, since they did not expect to exhaust their reserve funds until January 2010. "She sat through a lot of conversations," Speyer said of his wife. "We were joined at the hip."[18]

The situation in New York had not improved for the complexes or the broader economy by the time they returned in January. Speyer's days were spent tending to Stuyvesant Town and other troubled assets, as well as their projects in Asia and South America, where the economy was still in relatively good shape. At night, Speyer and his wife went for long walks along the esplanade that skirts the Hudson River waterfront near their apartment in Greenwich Village. Huddled against the fierce winds blowing off the river, Speyer described the inner emotions that he rarely revealed in business meetings. "For some reason it hit me in that moment that all the equity that had been invested was likely lost," Speyer said. "We hoped to restructure, but the premise was that $1.9 billion in equity had been wiped out. I thought about the different investors who'd signed up for the deal. It really shook me. Cecile said to me, 'What's going to define you is how you react to this. It's not the failure. It's how you deal with the failure. You have decades to do other deals. You have to focus now on standing up to the failure.' "

But things were about to go from bad to worse.

Both sides in the Stuyvesant Town litigation, the so-called Roberts case, were expecting a decision from the appellate division of the state supreme court in the first quarter of 2009 on the tenants' appeal of the lower-court decision tossing out their case. They had made their arguments to the appellate division on September 28, 2008.

The choices were simple. The court could deny the appeal, handing a second victory to the complexes' owners, or rule in favor of the tenants by declaring that the owners had illegally deregulated more than four thousand apartments at Stuyvesant Town while taking tax breaks from the city. Either way, the case would almost certainly advance to the court of appeals for a final decision.

Tishman Speyer, BlackRock and MetLife still felt confident that they would prevail. But the stakes were high. If the decision went against them, the entire premise of Tishman Speyer's business plan—the rapid deregulation of apartments in order to charge higher, market-rate rents—would be gutted.

The plaintiffs, however, had a new litigator, if not a new law firm. Stuart Saft and Michael Fleiss, who had originally brought the tenants' challenge, left the law firm Wolf Haldenstein Adler Freeman & Herz after the case was dismissed in state supreme court on August 23, 2007. Wolf Haldenstein had taken the case on a contingency. After the case went up on appeal, the firm's senior class-action litigation partner, Daniel W. Krasner, turned it over to Alexander H. Schmidt, a jack-of-all-trades litigator whose résumé included contract disputes, antitrust litigation, derivative shareholder suits and real-estate-related litigation. But this was his first exposure to the wacky world of rent stabilization.

He had little time to waste in learning the thirty-year history and the mind-numbing nomenclature of rent-stabilization laws, and state and city housing codes. He also needed to familiarize himself with the periodic battles in Albany between landlords and tenants, Republicans and Democrats, that resulted in new and sometimes contradictory laws. "It was a steep learning curve," Schmidt conceded.

The Rent Stabilization Law was enacted by the city council in 1969 in response to a continuing housing shortage and the need to regulate rental buildings that were not covered by stricter rent-control laws. (Rent control covers apartments built prior to 1947 that have had no tenancy turnover since 1971.) Stabilization applied to apartment buildings completed after 1947 and before 1974, with the twin goals of allowing landlords to implement reasonable rent increases and to prevent profiteering and "unjust, unreasonable and oppressive rents," while ensuring that there was an adequate supply of stable and affordable housing in New York.

In 1993, there was a showdown in the state legislature over efforts to "reform" rent regulations. The real estate industry had long complained about the inequities of the rent-stabilization system, where rents for tenants were kept low regardless of their income. Republicans in the state senate who sought to eliminate regulation from apartments of higher-income New Yorkers were opposed by members of the Democratic-controlled assembly and tenant advocates, who cast the Republicans as advocates for the landlord class. The Republicans said it made no sense to regulate rents for the rich, but opponents feared that "luxury decontrol" was the first step toward the elimination of all rent regulation. The Republican-dominated senate threatened to let the rent law expire altogether unless it was revised.

Albany, the state capital, swarmed with tenant rallies, while lobbyists plied the halls of the legislature in what has become a ritual every time the stabilization law comes up for renewal.

In the end, the legislature compromised, with the Republicans getting a form of "luxury decontrol." Under the change, the owners of apartments that rent for $2,000 or more a month would be allowed to raise rents to market levels when the apartments were vacated. Rent protection would also be lifted from apartments with rents of $2,000 or more per month that were leased to tenants who made $250,000 a year or more. In exchange, the Republicans agreed to extend rent laws for four more years, twice as long as they had previously allowed.

Tenant advocates like Michael McKee, chairman of the New York State Tenant and Neighborhood Coalition, acknowledged that luxury decontrol would affect less than 2 percent of the one million rent-stabilized apartments. But the new law also contained provisions that would hurt all tenants with what they said were "hidden grabs for landlords."

The most important preserved the landlord's right to charge tenants each month a percentage, one-fortieth, of the cost of refurbishing an apartment. The increase did not expire at the end of forty months; it became a permanent addition to the legal rent for that unit. At the time, the state housing agency regarded the one-fortieth payback period as overly generous and had sought unsuccessfully to extend it to seventy-two months.

"So generous a rate of return provides a great incentive for owners to provide extensive and sometimes unnecessary renovations, especially on vacant apartments, when tenant consent is not necessary, thus reducing the supply of affordable housing," the agency said in a 1993 memorandum.

The legislature reduced the income threshold in 1997 for

so-called high-rent, or luxury, decontrol to $175,000 for two succeeding years. But the housing laws also established some exceptions to decontrol, and the exceptions were what was at the crux of the Stuyvesant Town lawsuit.

In December 1995, the state housing agency issued an operational bulletin stating that high-rent decontrol "shall not apply to housing accommodations which are subject to rent regulation by virtue of receiving tax benefits" from housing programs such as J-51, which was designed to encourage landlords of rent-stabilized or rent-controlled apartments to invest in their property in return for tax breaks. In other words, apartments whose rent was $2,000 a month or higher at a complex like Stuyvesant Town that was receiving J-51 tax benefits could not be decontrolled until after the benefits expired.

But Sherwin Belkin, a young landlord attorney at the time, and other lawyers from his firm wrote a series of letters to the housing agency in 1995 arguing that it had wrongly interpreted the law. Belkin focused on the three-word phrase "by virtue of." He argued that properties that were regulated "by virtue of" receiving J-51 tax benefits could not be decontrolled. But other properties, like Stuyvesant Town, which were subject to regulation prior to receiving the benefits, could be decontrolled.

The housing agency twice dismissed Belkin's interpretation. But in a January 16, 1996, letter, Assistant Commissioner Darryl J. Seavey of the state housing agency seemed to reconsider, telling Belkin he might have a point. Seavey said that Belkin offered a "feasible alternative" to the standard way of interpreting the statute. Since the sponsoring memorandum by the state senator who introduced the bill was "silent" on the meaning of "by virtue of," Seavey said he applied a lexicographical definition of the words to arrive at Belkin's interpretation. Seavey cautioned that if a landlord deregulated an apartment before the J-51 tax benefit period had expired, the tax abatement would be reduced proportionately.

Seavey concluded, however, by saying that his "opinion letter" was "not a substitute for a formal agency order issued upon prior notice to all parties and after having afforded all parties an opportunity to be heard." None of that happened. The letter was issued solely to Belkin.[19] The housing agency did not release an advisory opinion on the matter. But landlords throughout the city did use the letter as the starting point for what Tishman Speyer, the Real Estate Board and others from the real estate industry said was "15 years of practice" in which apartments were deregulated while receiving tax breaks.

In 2000, the housing agency did formally adopt the position embodied in Seavey's letter, in part by inserting the word "solely" before "by virtue of," thus reinforcing the real estate industry's interpretation. At the very least, it was odd that a housing policy reversal with enormous implications would take place based on a dizzying argument over the meaning of an ambiguous three-word phrase.

But it also amounted to a break in logic. Many landlords with rent-stabilized apartments complained that they did not make enough money to upgrade boilers, point the brick facades or replace roofs. The J-51 program was designed to entice those landlords to invest in their own aging properties by providing modest tax breaks. It is hard to imagine why legislators would then allow landlords receiving those benefits to bail out of the rent-stabilization system.

The net effect of the housing agency's adopting the landlords' "alternative" interpretation of the law is that it enabled New York City landlords to deregulate thousands of apartments in buildings that were receiving J-51 tax benefits. Just adding the single word "solely" to the statutory language led to the deregulation of over four thousand apartments at Stuyvesant Town-Peter Cooper Village and thousands of other apartments in an estimated nine thousand buildings in Manhattan and elsewhere over the span of fourteen years.

More than six years later, nine former and current tenants at Stuyvesant Town challenged the interpretation, contending that the complex had received J-51 tax benefits since 1992 worth $24.5 million, which precluded the owners from decontrolling so-called high-rent apartments. Belkin, now acting on behalf of Tishman Speyer, argued that the "plain language" of the statute had been applied by the state housing agency for fifteen years, permitting landlords to deregulate units.

"To me," Schmidt countered, "it seemed crystal-clear that the intent of the statute was to prevent deregulation so long as taxpayer funds were being accepted by the landlord. The housing agency in December 2000 violated all the rules by adding the word 'solely' to the statute in a way that completely changed the meaning of the statute. I thought landlords must've been laughing all the way to the bank."[20]

On March 6, 2009, Rob Speyer's car was just pulling up to the curb at Chhatrapati Shivaji International Airport in Mumbai, India, when his cell phone buzzed. He was exhausted. He had been in India for a week looking at what would become his company's first foray into the world's second-most-populated nation, behind China. The proposed project was a joint venture with one of India's largest banks to build a $100 million office complex in Hyderabad, a fast-growing technology center. It was

2:00 A.M. and the airport, South Asia's busiest in terms of international passenger traffic, was a mad whirl of private cars, black-and-mustard taxis and white buses funneling through a series of narrow, high-security checkpoints. There were seemingly thousands of people there in the middle of the night trying to make their flights at the international terminal.

George Hatzmann, Tishman Speyer's associate general counsel, was on the phone in New York, where it was still March 5. The New York State appellate division of the state supreme court had just handed down a stunning decision: The owners of Stuyvesant Town-Peter Cooper Village had wrongfully raised rents and deregulated thousands of apartments after receiving special tax breaks from the city's J-51 housing program. Tishman Speyer, and practically the entire real estate industry, had expected the appellate division to dismiss the case, upholding a lower-court decision in favor of the landlord. No one thought it was even possible that this would be reversed. The reversal could ultimately cost Tishman Speyer, BlackRock and MetLife hundreds of millions of dollars more, if they were required to repay residents of roughly 4,400 apartments for improper rent increases over the preceding four years.

"We lost the J-51 case," said Hatzmann, his voice clear and sharp despite the thousands of miles between them.

Speyer's response was a roar: "Shiiittttt!"[21]

Speyer felt like he had been punched in the stomach. His lawyers had assured him that the tenants' case was certain to be dismissed. They would appeal to the state's highest court, of course. But if this ruling was upheld, he knew not only that the partnership would be liable for rent rebates and damages, but it had also just gotten infinitely more difficult to restructure the financing and stave off bankruptcy. The starting point for a restructuring was determining the current value of the asset. He figured that the worth of the complexes had dropped to $3.2 billion since the meltdown on Wall Street and the resulting recession. But this ruling could take it down another billion because rents would be re-regulated, limiting their ability to exploit the gap between regulated and market rents. "It was not on the radar screen of possibilities," Speyer later recalled. "That ruling was a severe blow. It put the asset in free fall."

Judge Eugene Nardelli of the appellate division ruled on behalf of the tenants, saying that "the broader interpretation of the phrase 'by virtue of' urged by the plaintiffs was more consistent with the overall statutory scheme, which makes no distinction based on whether a J-51 property was already subject to regulation prior to the receipt of such benefit." The court customarily defers to the judgment of the appropriate state agency in applying the law. But Judge Nardelli declared that the state housing agency was not entitled to deference since a "legal interpretation" is the court's responsibility. Moreover, the court said, by inserting the word "solely," the housing agency had violated a legal principle. Citing precedents, Nardelli wrote that the "new language cannot be imported into a statute to give it meaning not otherwise found therein."[22]

On the same day, one of the law firms representing Tishman Speyer, Belkin Burden Wenig & Goldman, was set to celebrate its twentieth anniversary at its office on Madison Avenue near Fortieth Street when they learned of the decision. Sherwin Belkin, the name partner who played a historical role in the case, raised his glass of champagne before what turned out to be a somber group of partners and associates. "Here's to the worst decision in the history of the firm," Belkin said glumly.

Andrew Mathias, the president and chief investment officer of SL Green Realty, a real estate investment trust that had made a $200 million junior loan in the deal, told analysts during an earnings call a couple weeks later that the decision "had such negative implications for the property and the $2 billion of common equity that [sat] subordinate to [their] position" that they decided to write down 75 percent of the interest-only loan.

David Schonbraun, a senior executive at SL Green, told analysts that the company did not believe in 2006 that the Stuyvesant Town deal was "overly aggressive," particularly because it had "$2 billion in newly invested cash from a deep-pocketed sponsorship group," Tishman Speyer and BlackRock. "However," he continued, "the deal was doomed by a combination of the recession, poor execution by the sponsor, and most importantly, an adverse J-51 tax ruling, which is contrary to legal opinions we've received and the opinion by the DHCR. This ruling was a shock to the real estate industry and irreparably harmed the value of the asset and has generally wreaked havoc in that space."[23]

Many in the real estate industry, including the Rent Stabilization Association, a landlord lobbyist, predicted chaos, claiming that some eighty thousand deregulated apartments throughout the city were now subject to re-regulation. They said that building values would fall sharply, along with property tax revenues, which account for the bulk of the city's operating budget. "They've basically re-regulated tens of thousands of apartments overnight," said Joseph Strasburg, president of the RSA, who had once lived in Stuyvesant Town and helped revive the dormant tenants association. "Every single tenant living in a decontrolled apartment can file for overcharges. What's the incentive for landlords to do these kind of major renovations if at the end of the day the apartments will continue to be regulated?"

Contrary to Strasburg's hyperbolic "tens of thousands" estimate, the ruling mainly affected thousands of apartments in Manhattan, where rents were more likely to be over $2,000 a month and candidates for deregulation. Harold Shultz, a former city housing commissioner, put the number closer to thirty thousand. Tenants nonetheless were ecstatic.

The residents of Stuyvesant Town and Peter Cooper Village, where Tishman Speyer was deeply unpopular, cheered the ruling. It was vindication for those who believed that the landlord had conspired to purge the complexes of middle-class tenants. But no matter which side of the barricades you stood on, all the residents wondered when their rent would be rolled back and by how much. And that's good news any day of the week in Manhattan.

Privately, many tenant advocates and lawyers had been pessimistic about the lawsuit's chances of success. Now the appellate division had handed tenants a unanimous decision. "It's a good thing for the tenants and for affordable housing," said Al Doyle, president of the tenants association, who together with Councilman Garodnick, Manhattan borough president Scott Stringer, Congresswoman Carolyn Maloney, state senator Tom Duane, Assemblyman Brian Kavanagh, tenant advocate Michael McKee and Harvey Epstein of the Urban Justice Center held a celebratory press conference the day after the decision.

Stringer called on Tishman Speyer and BlackRock to surrender, rather than try to appeal the decision. "It is time for the owners of Stuyvesant Town and Peter Cooper Village to sit down with residents of the complex to resolve this dispute over rent overcharges in a fair and equitable manner," said Stringer, who had filed an amicus brief on behalf of the tenants.

Annemarie Hunter, a plaintiff in the case who attended the press conference, explained that she had not joined the lawsuit "to make a political stand for rent stabilization," although it was "a noble side effect." It was more a cry of survival for the middle class. She said she believed that MetLife and Tishman Speyer had acted improperly by deregulating apartments and collecting luxury rents to the point where she and her family could no longer live in Manhattan. She and her husband, David Hunter, and their two young boys moved to a market-rate, two-bedroom apartment in Stuyvesant Town in 2003. They enjoyed the Norman Rockwell ambiance of the complex; her sons were enrolled in local schools. Despite the perception among some residents that market-rate tenants are rich, she said, most are not.

"Rent and childcare quickly eat up two incomes in this city," she said. Expecting a 25 percent jump in her monthly rent of $2,995, Hunter and her family reluctantly packed up in 2007 and moved. The monthly mortgage and maintenance payments for the small apartment they bought in the Riverdale section of the Bronx came to $2,865, less than the rent at Stuy Town.[24]

The unanimous decision by the appellate division left Tishman Speyer little legal room, although their lawyers hoped that the state's highest court, the court of appeals, would overrule the more liberal appellate division of the state supreme court. But if the decision was upheld, it would have a devastating effect on the investors who put in $1.9 billion in equity and, at least, the junior lenders. The investment memorandum Tishman Speyer and BlackRock gave to potential equity partners listed the litigation as one of two dozen risk factors associated with the Stuyvesant Town-Peter Cooper Village deal. The memorandum stated that the plaintiff's claims were "without merit." But it warned that if the plaintiffs did prevail, "the Partnership would suffer an immediate and very substantial loss of revenues and would be unable to carry out a significant part of its plan to convert rent-stabilized units to market-rate units. The loss of revenues, as well as any money damages that the court might award against the Partnership, would have a material adverse effect on the Partnership's financial results and the Investor Limited Partners' investments."

CHAPTER ELEVEN

How to Lose $3.6 Billion in Two Years

In the six months after Rob Speyer's soul-searching walks along the Hudson River with his wife Anne-Cecile, the situation at Stuyvesant Town-Peter Cooper Village grew more bleak. No matter how many times Tishman Speyer revised its budget to account for changing market conditions, they could not keep up with the deteriorating financial performance. Revenues in the first six months of 2009 fell 6 percent, or $9.5 million, behind current budget projections, according to a quarterly internal analysis sent to lenders. At the same time, operating expenses ballooned by 16 percent, or $7.8 million over budget. Legal fees from the J-51 case, as well as bank consulting fees, gobbled up millions of dollars. The grim bottom line showed that the property lost $84.6 million after debt service in the first six months of the year and would top $174 million by the end of the year.[1] Tishman Speyer continued to "recapture" vacant apartments but the company had ceased renovating the units at the end of 2008 and waived its asset management fee starting in the fourth quarter of 2008, Speyer said, as part of a desperate effort to "preserve capital."[2]

No matter what happened with their appeal of the J-51, or Roberts, case, there were no signs of relief. The unemployment rate swelled to 8.5 percent nationally, the highest level in a quarter century. More than five million jobs had evaporated since the start of the recession in December 2007. Real estate values had fallen by as much as half since the CMBS-induced high of 2007. Even in once-robust New York City, corporations slashed payrolls and dumped suddenly unnecessary and expensive office space, sending vacancy rates upward and rents down. The price of apartments also retreated from an average of $1.3 million, but now even apartment rents in Manhattan were falling. The average monthly rent for a two-bedroom apartment slid 7.8 percent between 2008 and 2009 to $3,826, while the average for three bedrooms fell 8.2 percent, from $5,589 to $5,126, according to Citi Habitats, a residential real estate broker.

At the 2006 closing party for the Stuyvesant Town deal at Rockefeller Center, Rob Speyer and MetLife's Robert Merck had exchanged pleasantries over the relentless upward march of apartment rentals and sales. But it turned out that their deal marked the high point of the market. Now Rob Speyer was hoping that rents would not plunge any lower.

But the challenges faced by Tishman Speyer and its partner BlackRock at Stuyvesant Town were similar to those of other highly leveraged deals and companies from that era. On April 16, General Growth Properties, the country's second-largest mall operator, with two hundred shopping centers in forty-four states, filed for bankruptcy protection. Founded by the Bucksbaum family, General Growth had a reputation for innovation and a well-regarded portfolio, which included Ala Moana Center in Honolulu, the Glendale Galleria in Los Angeles and Water Tower Place in Chicago. But the company struggled during the recession because of an inability to refinance its debt, much of it piled up during a shopping spree at the peak of the market. In the largest retail real estate deal in history, General Growth paid $12.6 billion in 2004 to acquire the Rouse Company, another mall operator, which owned Faneuil Hall Marketplace in Boston and South Street Seaport in Manhattan. But when the credit markets shut down, the mall operator was caught with $27 billion in short-term debt and no ability to refinance. General Growth filed for bankruptcy after months of fruitless negotiations with its creditors.

Two months later, a national hotel operating company, Extended Stay, filed for bankruptcy protection with a story nearly identical to General Growth's. The hotel industry had been hammered by a drop in corporate and leisure travel during the recession, which cut property values in half. Extended Stay, which owned 680 properties in 44 states, also had to contend with a crushing load of debt. The filing came only two years after the Lightstone Group, a real estate firm based in New Jersey, bought the company at the market peak for $8 billion, including $7.4 billion in financing. The seller was Blackstone Group, the ubiquitous private equity firm that had acquired Extended Stay in 2004, when it had 425 properties, for $2 billion and the assumption of $1.1 billion in debt. Blackstone moved quickly to bulk up by adding to the company's stable of hotels using all manner of credit and then sold the company to Lighthouse in a leveraged buyout. Blackstone, and two partners, reacquired Extended Stay in 2010 for $3.9 billion as the company left bankruptcy protection. A group of creditors subsequently sued Blackstone in federal court claiming that it had grossly inflated the original $8 billion sale price and siphoned off $2.1 billion from the transaction.

A group led by Tishman Speyer defaulted on loans related to its $2.8 billion purchase in 2006 of twenty-eight office buildings in Washington, DC, once owned by CarrAmerica Realty. The other partners in the deal included Lehman Brothers and SITQ, the real estate subsidiary of a Canadian pension fund. It was a solid portfolio with a tenant list that included prominent lobbyists and prestigious corporations. In those heady days, buyers like Tishman Speyer were willing to pay a premium for office properties with vacant space on the assumption that new tenants would pay higher rents than existing tenants already locked into long leases. But empty space became a gaping problem in the recession as demand weakened and rents declined. Tishman Speyer and its partners were forced to suspend payments on junior loans totaling about $570 million. "It's great real estate," said Rob Speyer. "We're in discussions with our lenders to reach a compromise."[3]

The problems ran even deeper at Archstone-Smith, the national apartment complex operator purchased by Tishman Speyer and Lehman Brothers for $22.2 billion just after what turned out to be the peak of the market, in the fall of 2007. The value of the 88,000 apartments owned by Archstone stumbled badly with the recession. With the company in danger of default, Lehman Brothers and Bank of America put up another $500 million to keep Archstone afloat. But Tishman Speyer, which had invested $250 million in the initial deal expecting to get 13 percent of the profits, decided not to participate.

Despite the glaring problems at Archstone, Carr and Stuyvesant Town-Peter Cooper Village, Rob Speyer insisted that the sour deals represented only a fraction of the $35 billion in real estate assets that his company owned or managed around the world. Jerry Speyer sat next to him during an interview in Tishman Speyer's offices at Rockefeller Center. They insisted that the Tishman Speyer machine was still running full-throttle. The elder Speyer added that the company was still providing investors with "20 percent returns." "You show me anybody who measured up to that standard," he said. "None of us are good enough to have a 1,000 batting average. It doesn't exist."

Meanwhile, the backlash against predatory capital and speculative, debt-laden deals like the one at Stuyvesant Town, Delano Village or Riverton was in full swing in New York's state capital, where tenant advocates pressed legislators for a complete overhaul of the state's rent regulations. They argued that the new owners had defaulted on their loans after having overpaid for tens of thousands of apartments occupied by working- and middle-class New Yorkers. That housing, they said, was now in danger of falling into disrepair as the owners or lenders deferred maintenance on the buildings. Urban planners and housing experts like Harold Shultz of the Citizens Housing and Planning Council warned that the effect on surrounding neighborhoods, many of which were far more modest than Stuyvesant Town's, could be catastrophic.

The Democratic-controlled assembly passed and sent to the Senate for approval ten bills in the spring of 2009 that would severely undercut the ability of landlords, particularly those who paid extraordinarily high prices at the height of the real estate boom, to rapidly raise rents, re-regulate apartments and reap profits. For the first time in decades, Democrats controlled the Senate, albeit by a slim margin, prompting hopes of a quick coup. "The tenant movement has never been more united," said

Michael McKee, then treasurer of the Tenants Political Action Committee. "We're working hard to repeal vacancy decontrol and reform the rent laws."

The real estate industry launched a counterattack, lobbying Republicans and some select Democrats in the Senate to block the bills, saying that the measures would bring to a halt refurbishment and investment in older residential properties. "Everybody's worried," said Steven Spinola, president of the Real Estate Board of New York, the industry's powerful lobbying arm. "This is legislation that'll ruin housing and ruin investment."[4]

But tenant advocates and Democratic legislators countered that the new laws were aimed at speculators, whose financial plans were shaky to begin with. They said that the overhaul of state rent laws was necessary to curb abusive landlords and the loss of housing for working- and middle-class tenants on the Lower East Side and in Harlem, Queens, East New York and the South Bronx. Unscrupulous operators armed with "predatory equity" from the banks had saddled properties with unsustainable debts and showered tenants with eviction notices in an attempt to replace rent-regulated residents with market-rate tenants. Sheldon Silver, the assembly speaker, said, "We cannot sit back and allow the lifeblood of our communities—teachers, firefighters, police and everyday working people—to be priced out of where they live."

Edward Kalikow, a third-generation real estate operator whose company, Kaled Management Corporation, controls 6,500 apartments, mostly in Queens and Manhattan, blamed the Stuyvesant Town deal and others like it for igniting the tenant backlash in the legislature. He said new owners acquired properties with unrealistic plans for quick profits and debt amounting to 80 percent of the purchase price. "They were underwriting deals assuming that they'd relocate thousands of rent-stabilized tenants at a ferocious speed," Kalikow said. "Given the dynamics of the system, there was no way that could happen. Most of us understand that real estate is not a get-in, get-out business. Life has gotten a lot more difficult for us as a result of these abuses to the system. More tenants vote than landlords. I accept that."[5]

Kalikow said there were upward of sixty thousand rent-stabilized units in various stages of financial distress, most bought with easy money. "Now you have an overreaction in the legislature," lamented Kalikow, who opposed changes to the rent laws. In the past, the real estate industry had depended on the Republican leadership in the Senate—which Democrats then controlled, by thirty-two to thirty members—or a sympathetic Republican governor to block such bills. The top priority of the Real Estate Board and the Rent Stabilization Association was stopping the overhaul. The two groups implored members to send extra contributions and hired a Bronx political operative, Stanley Schlein, to make their case in Albany.

In the chaotic closing days of the legislative session, the real estate industry gained the upper hand, persuading a handful of Democrats in the Senate to join the Republicans in scuttling the pro-tenant bills. McKee and other tenant advocates vowed to continue the battle during the next legislative session.

But the Real Estate Board, the Rent Stabilization Association, the Community Housing Improvement Program and other real estate groups also moved to protect their interests in the courts, by backing Tishman Speyer's appeal of the J-51 decision. If the decision stands, said Joseph Strasburg of the RSA, chaos would ensue: landlords who took J-51 benefits would have great difficulty determining the legal rent for the re-regulated apartments since the court was silent on the issue. If the court decision stands, they said, apartments that had been improperly deregulated would again be subject to rent regulations and landlords would have to repay tenants for rent hikes that exceeded the annual increases set by the Rent Guidelines Board over the past four years. A landlord could be subject to triple damages if he was found to have knowingly exceeded the numbers set by the board.

Fearful owners, they said, would stop all renovations and improvements because of the uncertainty of recovering the costs. Strasburg appealed to contractors and construction unions who would, in turn, lose work. "All of a sudden, people who had dropped off the face of our earth have re-emerged and seen the seriousness of this," said Mr. Strasburg. "This would be disastrous."

Despite the appellate court ruling in March, Tishman Speyer was optimistic that the state's highest court, the court of appeals, would set the record straight. The firm sent a memo in October to lawyers who filed amicus briefs for the Real Estate Board of New York, the Rent Stabilization Association and other supporters suggesting that they keep a low profile in the event of a victory. "If we win, we don't want you to say anything in the press," the memo advised, said one lawyer. "We don't want to rub their noses in it."

But Tishman Speyer's equity partners were much less sanguine about the fate of their investment. As they waited for the court of appeals to issue its decision, Larry Fink, chairman of BlackRock, flew to California in July 2009 to personally apologize to the board of the California Public Employees' Retirement System for endorsing a $500 million investment in the

Stuyvesant Town-Peter Cooper Village deal, according to Bloomberg News. The value of the property had declined by more than half to $2.13 billion, according to the Realpoint credit rating agency. Now the junior lenders, along with CalPERS and all the other equity partners, were deeply underwater. CalPERS was also taking hits on a number of its more adventurous real estate deals, including LandSource Holding Company, which went bankrupt seventeen months after the pension fund invested $970 million. At the top of the bubble, the pension fund had poured billions into speculative, highly leveraged deals, hoping to recoup a return of 13 percent, rather than a customary 7 or 8 percent.

After topping out at $260 billion in October 2007, the value of CalPERS's assets, real estate included, plummeted by $100 billion over the following eighteen months. BlackRock, which wrote down its own $112.5 million investment in Stuyvesant Town-Peter Cooper Village, was among a network of real estate advisers for the pension fund that received $2.8 billion in fees between 2004 and 2009.

But CalPERS, which wrote off its $500 million investment in Stuyvesant Town, was now reconsidering its relationship with BlackRock. "We took our profits elsewhere and plowed them into these highly leveraged, in retrospect, too highly leveraged properties like this one in New York," said Clark McKinley of CalPERS. "When the market tanked, we got caught."[6]

The CalPERS board of administration and its staff held their annual weekend retreat July 27 through July 29, 2009, at the Lake Natoma Inn in Folsom, California, a suburb of Sacramento known for its famous Folsom State Prison. The point of the meeting was to make a strategic assessment of investment opportunities going forward for the nation's largest pool of investment capital. But the gloomy market and CalPERS's struggle to make up for its losses over the prior year was not far from anyone's mind. Nevertheless, someone had placed a cheerful quote from Albert Einstein atop the weekend agenda: "In the middle of difficulty lies opportunity."

CalPERS serves 1.6 million active and retired state workers, municipal employees, judges and school bus drivers. It is funded by billions of dollars in annual contributions from taxpayers and employees. But the level of contribution depends on how well CalPERS's investments perform. In the fiscal year that had just ended, CalPERS posted a record loss of $56 billion, or a 23.57 percent drop in the fund's performance, the greatest single-year decline in its seventy-seven-year history. The implications were enormous for municipalities that could be asked for larger annual contributions to make up the difference at a time when unemployment was climbing and property values falling.

Beginning in the late 1990s, the CalPERS board increasingly gave outside advisers like BlackRock more control over decision making on real estate investments. Like many pension funds, its liabilities were swelling as increasing numbers of members retired, while its assets shrank. In the hunt for better returns, the fund gradually shifted from conservative, income-oriented investments like malls and office buildings to more risky ventures, ranging from pinot noir vineyards in Oregon to LandSource Holding in Los Angeles and Stuyvesant Town-Peter Cooper Village. CalPERS often borrowed money to make the investments, a strategy that worked in a rising market but ended disastrously when the Great Recession set in.

The featured speaker on the first day was actually an outsider—Larry Fink, the chairman of BlackRock. In the course of an hour-long presentation, Fink acknowledged that the Stuyvesant Town investment had been unsuccessful and expressed his regret that CalPERS had lost so much money. Oddly, few in the audience focused on Fink's apology, recalled Joseph Dear, CalPERS's new chief investment officer.

What got everyone's attention was Fink's warning that the fund's newly established target for a return on investments was way too optimistic given the circumstances. The exuberant optimist had turned into a Cassandra. CalPERS figured it needed an annual return of 7.6 percent in order to be fully funded to meet its pension obligations in 2024.

"You're not going to get a seven point six percent return when the U.S. is seeing a subpar growth rate of two to three percent," Fink said. "You'll be lucky to get six percent . . . maybe five percent."

Fink's prediction found an echo in newspaper articles, which raised the possibility that taxpayers would have to bail out the fund. As it turned out, CalPERS's investments grew by 11 percent in 2010. But ultimately, all of the people responsible for the fund's crushing losses were pushed out or fired, including BlackRock.

Three thousand miles to the east, in Florida, executives at the State Board of Administration exchanged e-mails acknowledging that their entire investment had been "wiped out." On July 28, 2009, the SBA's senior investment officer, Doug Bennett, authorized the accounting department to write off the entire investment, $266,780,948, which included $16.8 million in fees associated with the deal. The board later blamed the loss on the recession, leverage and slow income growth. They did not share CalPERS's 20-20 hindsight that the Stuyvesant Town deal had been fatally flawed from the beginning.

The Government of Singapore Investment Corporation, which manages more than $100 billion of the city-state's reserves, recognized its losses on the deal, $100 million in equity and $575 million in junior loans backed by the property. The value of GIC's assets had fallen more than 20 percent following the collapse of the global financial markets.

Ben Thypin, an analyst at Real Capital Analytics, put the deal on a death watch, saying it was only a matter of months before the owners of Stuyvesant Town-Peter Cooper Village ran out of money and defaulted on their loans. The much-ballyhooed transaction was a metaphor for an era of easy credit, greed and highly speculative deals. "When we look back on this deal, it may be seen as the poster child for everything that was wrong and right with an era that we may never see again," Thypin predicted. "The assumptions used to underwrite the deal were fantastical at the time and now appear delusional, if not dishonest. Even the most seasoned apartment operator could not have turned these units to market rate fast enough to meet the assumptions, putting aside the risk of market rents decreasing."[7]

But if Rob Speyer held out any hope of salvaging Stuyvesant Town-Peter Cooper Village by forcing lenders to write down the debt, it was all but extinguished on October 22, 2009, when the New York court of appeals ruled in a four-to-two decision that MetLife and the Tishman Speyer–BlackRock partnership had improperly charged market rents for thousands of apartments at the adjoining complexes while taking special tax breaks from a city housing program. The ruling left the owners liable for an estimated $200 million in rent overcharges and damages owed to tenants of 4,400 apartments. Tishman Speyer might also have to roll back rents for the 4,400 apartments to some as-yet-undetermined level, further undermining the market value of the complex. More important, in its negotiations with lenders, Tishman Speyer could no longer hold out the promise of rising revenues as vacant apartments were converted to market rents. Tishman Speyer released a statement saying the decision was "an unfortunate outcome for New York."

Given the flip-flop by the state housing agency on the issue and the debate over the meaning of the statute, the court focused on the state legislature's "intent" in 1993 when it revised the rent laws and gave landlords the ability to deregulate apartments under certain circumstances. Lawyers for the owners said that Stuyvesant Town-Peter Cooper Village became subject to rent stabilization in 1974, eighteen years before receiving J-51 benefits. Therefore, under the "plain language" of the 1993 statute, the lawyers argued that the landlords were permitted to deregulate apartments while receiving J-51 benefits.

The judges, however, cited the legislative history of the law, including transcripts of the debate in the state senate before the statute was adopted. The judges wanted to understand the intent of the legislators in passing the bill, rather than the dictionary definition of a single word. The hard-to-find material had been excavated by Alexander H. Schmidt, the lead lawyer for the tenant-plaintiffs, and kept under wraps until he submitted his final brief to the court of appeals. The brief quoted remarks by state senator Kemp Hannon, the Republican sponsor of the bill, who in response to a question from another legislator said, "At no point do you have the decontrol provisions applying to the buildings which have received the tax exemptions." Asked for further clarification, Hannon reiterated his point: luxury decontrol was unavailable to building owners who "enjoy another system of general public assistance, such as J-51 benefits."

Schmidt believed that the legislative history, in particular the transcript of the debate in the legislature over the bill, was the proverbial smoking gun for the case. In federal court, it is easy to locate these kinds of materials, along with accounts of the congressional debates. But the New York courts were an entirely different matter. Indeed, he eventually located a private data service and paid "thousands of dollars" for the materials. Senator Hannon's statement was in response to a question from Senator Olga Mendez, who, he said, "was clearly concerned that public money should not go to the owners who want to deregulate."

"We believed we had the right interpretation of the law, the right arguments," Schmidt said. "But finding the legislative history was a real boon. The court of appeals cited the debate in its opinion."[8]

As it turned out, he added, "The real estate industry had the documents all along."

Schmidt was in the lobby of the Port Authority Bus Terminal on Eighth Avenue in midtown Manhattan on October 22 when he checked the court of appeals website on his BlackBerry to see whether a decision had been posted. The court normally posted decisions on Tuesdays and expectations were high that this was the day. At 9:05 A.M., the decision popped up on the tiny screen. Suddenly, he could feel and hear the blood rushing through his veins. They had won. He insisted that he had always expected this outcome. But his pulse was racing, just the same. He quickly e-mailed his office and the plaintiffs with the news. Everyone was elated. By 10:15, the *New York Times* was reporting the decision on its website.

Garodnick and Doyle pulled together an impromptu press conference underneath the oak tree at First Avenue and Sixteenth Street, just inside the boundaries of Stuyvesant Town. The small group of activists had goofy smiles stretched across their faces as they shook hands again and again.

"This is a huge win for tenants," Garodnick said. "The court made it clear that you cannot pocket millions in taxpayer dollars while pushing rent-stabilized tenants out of their homes."

But there were still a number of thorny and immensely complicated issues left undecided by the court. Were the owners required to refund any rent overcharges to current and former tenants of the 4,400 apartments in question? How many years do you go back in calculating the baseline for the legal rent of the apartments in light of the decision? Whatever that date is, what rent increases, if any, could the landlord impose if the apartment was renovated or became vacant during that period? Every one of the 4,400 apartments had its own rent history and required a separate calculation to determine the legal rent going forward.

The real estate industry warned of the dire consequences of the decision, which could affect tens of thousands of apartments in the city, and the likelihood of years of litigation over the issues. Strasburg, president of the Rent Stabilization Association, said the ruling had the "potential to force some buildings into bankruptcy or foreclosure if they're required to roll back rents, but it would also have a direct impact on the city budget."

There was no uncertainty that the decision was a coup de grace for Tishman Speyer and BlackRock at Stuyvesant Town.

"It's the final nail in the coffin," Daniel Alpert, managing partner of Westwood Capital, said on the day the court ruled. "It's been doomed for a while, but it's a spectacular way to go down."[9]

On November 6, 2009, CWCapital Asset Management, the country's second-largest "special servicer" of troubled mortgages, took control of the $3 billion first mortgage on Stuyvesant Town-Peter Cooper Village. With $650 million in reserve funds nearly exhausted, Rob Speyer and his partners at BlackRock asked the loan trustees for a forbearance agreement, to stave off foreclosure and allow time for a possible restructuring of the loan. CWCapital's job was to administer the loans on behalf of bondholders, oversee the property and determine whether to foreclose in the event of a default. The first mortgage initially provided by Wachovia and Merrill Lynch had been carved into five pieces. Each piece was pooled with other commercial loans in a securitized trust and sold on the bond market. Fannie Mae and Freddie Mac, the government-owned mortgage companies, bought the senior-most tranches, or segments, of the five bonds, but under the terms of the securitization, they had no right to intervene in a restructuring.

CWCapital came with several interesting connections. It was owned by Caisse de Dépôt et Placement du Québec, Canada's largest pension fund. A division of the pension fund had made a $90 million junior loan—part of the $1.4 billion in secondary loans—for the Tishman Speyer–BlackRock purchase of Stuyvesant Town and Peter Cooper Village. Later, it would rehire Adam Rose and Rose Associates to manage the complexes and put Andrew MacArthur, a key member of the second-place bidding team in the 2006 auction of Stuyvesant Town, in charge of the eighty-acre campus.

But no one was surprised by the turn of events at the two complexes. Monthly reports on the gloomy financial status of the property were public documents. The $190 million general reserve was exhausted, the $400 million interest reserve had dwindled to $6.75 million and there was a mere $3.74 million left in the $60 million replacement reserve fund. Fitch Ratings, a credit service, estimated that the worth of the property had plummeted to $1.8 billion, or one-third of the purchase price three years earlier. They had lost $3.6 billion on this one deal within two years of taking over the complexes. Astonishingly, rents were still falling along with property values. The drop in value meant that the senior loan could lose more than $1 billion, while $1.9 billion in equity and $1.4 billion in junior loans were essentially wiped out.

Investors in scores of other commercial mortgage-backed securities were also facing losses. Moody's Investor Services reported that 113 multifamily CMBS loans totaling $1.1 billion tipped into delinquency in December. The delinquency rate for all CMBS loans reached 4.9 percent, up 500 percent from a year earlier.

In the end, any one of the 2006 bidders for Stuyvesant Town-Peter Cooper Village would have run into a financial typhoon, whether it was the tenants or Richard LeFrak, who offered $4.5 billion, or Apollo–ING Clarion–Dermott, which put up $5.33 billion. For different reasons, perhaps, they all got caught up in what one Wachovia banker called "market momentum." In return for sizable fees that provided the banks with hundreds of millions of dollars and made the bankers themselves into swaggering millionaires, Wall Street provided the financing based on numbers and projections that never made sense.

CalPERS, CalSTRS, the government of Singapore, the Church of England and the other funds from around the world that threw billions of dollars at Stuyvesant Town saw their investment disappear in a puff of smoke. It is worth recalling that Wachovia and Merrill Lynch cleared an estimated $210 million on the Stuyvesant Town deal, although it did not enable either institution to survive the ensuing Great Recession.

Stuyvesant Town-Peter Cooper Village tenants and their supporters were not going to sit by quietly while CWCapital and Tishman Speyer negotiated the fate of the two complexes. By very publicly asserting themselves, Councilman Garodnick and Al Doyle, the longtime president of the tenant association, warned all parties, including, perhaps, a new buyer, that they were an unavoidable part of the solution. Four days after the appeals court ruling, Garodnick and other elected officials wrote to Fannie Mae and Freddie Mac urging them to protect the tenants' interest in any loan workout. Any new financing plan "must preserve" the property for middle-class residents and retain the two complexes as a single community, said the letter signed by Assemblyman Brian Kavanagh, state senator Thomas Duane, Congresswoman Carolyn B. Maloney, Manhattan borough president Scott M. Stringer and Garodnick. Some of them worried that a resolution might entail separating Peter Cooper Village from Stuyvesant Town so that it could be turned into a luxury condominium complex, with its larger apartments and renovated lobbies.

The two mortgage agencies, which had been placed in a conservatorship under the Federal Housing Finance Agency because of billions of dollars in bad loans, had their own problems and wanted no part of the political imbroglio in New York. In separate letters, Fannie and Freddie responded, telling the officials that they did not hold the mortgage, but rather a security that contained the senior portions of the Stuyvesant Town-Peter Cooper mortgage as well as debt from other properties. Therefore, they told the tenants, Fannie and Freddie had no "legal authority to dictate a restructuring of the mortgage." Typically, they advised, the investors in the most junior tranches of the security (those who get paid only after the investors in the senior certificates have been paid) are given the sole right to certain decisions with respect to management.[10]

Doyle was amazed at the sudden notoriety of the two complexes. He overheard people discussing the matter on a downtown bus and in his doctor's office. But he was primarily concerned about what a default meant for the twenty-five thousand residents of the complexes. "We're worried about what we may face going forward if Tishman defaults," Doyle said. "We're worried about maintenance, security and other things that might be affected by a lack of money coming into the complex."[11]

Rob Speyer sought to open talks with Charles Spetka, CWCapital's chief executive, to discuss some kind of workout that would involve retaining control of the complexes and investing fresh capital. Speyer asked Christopher A. Milner, a managing director at BlackRock who knew Spetka, to set up a meeting. Eventually, Speyer and Paul Galiano, co-director of acquisitions at Tishman Speyer, got together in New York with Spetka; Gregory A. Cross, CWCapital's lawyer; and Andrew J. Hundertmark, CWCapital's asset manager. Speyer described how the partners had been squeezed by the vagaries of the market and a devastating court decision. Later that afternoon, the group walked the grounds of Stuyvesant Town and Peter Cooper Village.

Speyer and his partners figured that they really had only three options. The first was a consensual restructuring in which each side put in something to make it work. Failing that, they could go for the nuclear option by taking the property into bankruptcy protection and trying to force the lenders to write down the mortgage. Finally, they could turn over the property to CWCapital and walk away.

In the meantime, Michael Ashner, a pugnacious and supremely self-confident investor, and a few of the other junior lenders were growing increasingly vocal about their unhappiness with Tishman Speyer. Ashner's company, Winthrop Realty Trust, had made a $25 million junior loan. It was most certainly underwater, but he did not want to walk away empty-handed. His demand for specific financial information about the property went largely unsatisfied by either Tishman Speyer or CWCapital. For his part, Rob Speyer concluded that there was little point to haggling with the junior, or mezzanine, lenders because they were so far out of the money.[12] If he could not reach an agreement with Spetka and CWCapital over the senior mortgage, there was no point in talking. "In our view," Speyer said, "the value fell within the senior loan. We were either going to make a deal with CW, or we were out. The mezz guys were not the critical path."

Ashner said he found Tishman Speyer's approach "arrogant." He said he also bluntly refused to sign a confidentiality agreement with the borrower.[13]

On January 8, 2009, the money essentially ran out, as everyone at that point knew it would. Tishman Speyer and BlackRock failed to make the required $16.3 million interest payment on the first mortgage and the $4.7 million due on the mezzanine loans. Their default triggered a blizzard of legal notices required under the loan documents, but Speyer was also hoping that the restructuring talks would finally begin in earnest.

CWCapital's lawyer Gregory A. Cross, chairman of the bankruptcy department at the Venable firm in Baltimore, sent a default notice to Tishman Speyer and BlackRock and notified Wachovia, Merrill Lynch and the lowest-ranked junior lender, Gramercy Capital Corporation, an affiliate of SL Green, that the default had occurred.

Three days later, on January 11, Wachovia and four of the twelve other mezzanine lenders notified Tishman Speyer that it had ten days to cure the default, or they would pursue their rights and remedies, including foreclosure.[14] The group—Wachovia, Allied Irish, Deutsche Genossenschafts-Hypothekenbank, Hartford Investment Management Company and Concord Capital—collectively accounted for $300 million in loans, the most senior tranche of the $1.4 billion in mezzanine financing. They were prodded, in part, by a very vocal Ashner, who urged a more aggressive approach with Tishman Speyer and BlackRock in a bid to recapture at least some of what they had put into the deal. Other junior lenders had signed a prenegotiation letter indicating their willingness to participate in a workout.

"I thought Stuyvesant Town had value, long term," Ashner said. "It was worth fighting over, as opposed to some one-hundred-thousand-square-foot building in Kansas."[15]

Ten days later, on January 21, Gramercy Capital announced its intention to replace Tishman Speyer with the Related Companies as the manager of the complexes, a move rejected by Spetka at CWCapital. Gramercy's executives, like Ashner, were still upset. Tishman Speyer refused to bargain with them or to provide the junior lenders with detailed financial information.

Speyer called Spetka the next day with a proposal. If CWCapital would agree to write down the mortgage to $1.8 billion, he and his partners would invest a quarter of a billion dollars in new money. But Speyer wanted a preferred return of, say, 12 percent. The ladder of payments under this scenario would begin with the monthly debt service for the newly reduced mortgage and then a payment on the fresh $250 million in capital. Everything after that would be split between the lenders and Tishman Speyer–BlackRock. Spetka, a taciturn man who rarely betrays his emotions, said he would consider it and get back to Speyer. But he saw little benefit to the arrangement. The upside for the bondholders he represented was reduced to zero, in Spetka's judgment, while he would have to pay an exorbitant 12 percent interest for the additional funding. He could get cheaper money elsewhere.

"The only thing that they [Tishman Speyer] brought to the table as a partner was a faster resolution than foreclosure and a continuity of management, which we didn't view as particularly valuable," Spetka said. "Their capital was expensive and not needed."[16]

The following day, Spetka called Speyer with his answer: No, thank you. But Spetka dangled what he thought was an inducement to let go of the property without a bruising battle in court. He offered Speyer a long-term contract to manage the two complexes. Speyer immediately rejected the offer. "Our investors had experienced a tremendous amount of pain," Speyer said. "It's not appropriate for Tishman Speyer Properties to create a new profit center out of their pain."[17]

Speyer and his company were juggling a number of sour real

estate deals at the same time, including Archstone-Smith, a $22 billion acquisition, and the CarrAmerica office buildings in Washington, DC, a $2.8 billion purchase. The Speyers were also in tough negotiations with a representative of the Federal Reserve Bank of New York to restructure their company's loans on five Chicago office buildings, including the Chicago Mercantile Exchange and the stately Civic Opera House, a pair of buildings purchased in 2007. Not long afterward, the vacancy rate in Chicago shot up to 15 percent and property values plunged.

The Fed inherited the debt in 2008 when JPMorgan Chase bought the original lender, Bear Stearns, and the government took on many of its troubled assets. Jerry Speyer had been a director of the New York Fed from 2001 through 2007. The Fed brought in his partner in the Stuyvesant Town-Peter Cooper Village deal, BlackRock, to handle negotiations over the Chicago buildings. They were being tougher, not easier, Jerry Speyer said ruefully. But none of Tishman Speyer's problems had generated as many headlines as Stuyvesant Town.

On Sunday, January 24, Speyer and Galiano gathered with a small group of lawyers and advisers at the offices of Fried Frank at 1 New York Plaza, a fifty-story tower at the south end of Manhattan, overlooking the ferry terminal and New York Harbor. Paintings of big sailing vessels lined the hallways, as at many downtown law firms. The mood was tense, solemn and resigned.

The chairman of the firm's real estate group, Jonathan L. Mechanic, handled a lot of work for Tishman Speyer, including the original purchase. He and Speyer debated the wisdom of filing for bankruptcy protection. But Tishman Speyer characteristically avoided legal slugfests that play out in open court. The economics of the deal were in shambles. CWCapital was uninterested in a restructuring. Unless they wanted to battle with the lenders over control of the property while the media recorded every move in tabloid headlines, there was little else to do but give the property back to the lenders and let their investors know that it was over.

"Those were tough calls," Speyer recalled in 2011. "It's always easy to call investors when you've generated a three-times or seven-times return for them. Try calling an investor when you've lost their capital and there's no more hope."[18]

It was already dark when Speyer left Fried Frank, jumped into a cab and headed home. He made one final call, to Spetka, who was home with his wife and daughter on the Upper East Side watching television. The conversation as the cab rolled toward Greenwich Village was brief and without rancor. "We want to give the property back to the lender," Speyer said. "A protracted legal fight is not good for us, the tenants, New York City or the bondholders."

Spetka exhaled slowly. He had dodged what could have been a very messy bankruptcy court battle conducted in the center of an international media spotlight. "It was exactly the right thing to do," Spetka said of Tishman Speyer. "When I hung up, I felt like I'd won the lottery.

"It was important to Tishman to maintain their reputation in the investment market and in the city," Spetka continued. "They could've put up a battle, but it wasn't worth the cost. The attorney bills would've been astronomical and the press would have been brutal. External factors, coupled with this asset being outside of their core competency, really doomed the investment."[19]

The next day the *New York Times* and the *Wall Street Journal* carried prominent stories about the demise of what MetLife had called "the largest real estate transaction in world history."[20] The ensuing deluge of wire service reports and radio and television coverage was comparable to the deal's announcement in October 2006. Tishman Speyer issued a brief statement: "It has become clear to us through this process that the only viable alternative to bankruptcy would be to transfer control and operation of the property, in an orderly manner, to the lenders and their representatives. We make this decision as we feel a battle over the property or a contested bankruptcy proceeding is not in the long-term interest of the property, its residents, our partnership or the city."

The Speyers simultaneously sent out a second message: Despite the recent setback, all was well with the Tishman Speyer empire, which spanned four continents and included a $33.5 billion portfolio of seventy-two million square feet of office space, the rough equivalent of all the office space in Los Angeles and Houston combined. They had sold $12 billion worth of property in 2006 and 2007 for enormous profits. "After writing off the equity in a handful of distressed deals," said Rob Speyer, "our annual returns on both a 10-year and a 30-year basis are over 20 percent on average." His father added, "We've done a lot of deals. We've had some fantastic results. We've also had some bad results. I'd argue that there's nobody that does what we do that has a better record."[21]

Asked about the events at Stuyvesant Town, Mayor Michael R. Bloomberg continued his cheerleading for Tishman Speyer. "It's not clear that the tenants of Stuyvesant Town are any worse off or better off," he said. "I can tell you, from what I know, Tishman Speyer's been a very reputable company. The way they manage buildings, the tenants are pretty happy in them."

The billionaire mayor then offered cold comfort to the

tenants. The deal, he said, had "generated a lot of tax revenues, which went to pay our cops and firefighters and teachers, and if you want to question that deal, go back and ask them would they like to give back part of their salaries which was paid by that."

Untangling Stuyvesant Town took the better part of 2010, as CWCapital worked through a thicket of legal issues. Until those matters could be settled, Tishman Speyer continued to manage the complexes, although it lowered its profile as much as possible and began reassigning senior executives. The fact that the mortgage was spread among five trusts rather than a single bank did not help either. But the two Manhattan complexes, with their plain brick facades, proved to be an enduring piece of catnip for hedge fund investors, old-line real estate families and other investors. Where else could you find 11,232 apartments and 80 acres of valuable land in Manhattan?

Two former bidders, Stephen Ross of the Related Companies and Richard LeFrak, the billionaire real estate developer, had already contacted CWCapital to talk about a possible sale. Douglas Durst of the Durst real estate family also called on CWCapital, as did Daniel Alpert of Westwood Capital. "Despite the turbulence surrounding this property in recent years," Ben Thypin, the senior analyst at Real Capital Analytics, said, "Stuyvesant Town remains an irreplaceable asset that many deep-pocketed players will be interested in."[22]

Spetka and his lawyers moved quickly to foreclose on the property. He hired Adam Rose, co-president of Rose Associates, the company that managed Stuyvesant Town-Peter Cooper Village for MetLife, as an adviser and ultimately as the property manager. Spetka also brought in Andrew MacArthur to oversee the complex, as well as other distressed properties. MacArthur was no stranger either. In 2006, he was part of a bidding group that narrowly lost out to Tishman Speyer in the Stuyvesant Town-Peter Cooper Village auction.

CWCapital met with Garodnick and the tenants association, promising to work closely with them and put the acrimony of the past behind them. But Doyle, Garodnick and their supporters had every intention of reviving their own effort to buy the adjoining complexes. They hired Moelis and Company, a real estate advisory firm, and Meredith Kane, a well-respected real estate attorney at Paul, Weiss, Rifkind, Wharton & Garrison. They also opened talks with city comptroller John Liu about a possible partnership with the big pension fund the New York City Employees' Retirement System. A March 13 forum sponsored by the tenant association drew an overflow crowd to the 1,100-seat auditorium at nearby Baruch College, where Doyle spoke of the necessity for tenants to speak with "a single voice." Volunteers from all 56 buildings at the two complexes circulated unity pledges, eventually signed by more than 7,100 residents. Soon, Related, LeFrak and others came calling on the tenants association as well.

Tacitly, all the suitors recognized that they could not execute a deal without, or in spite of, the tenants. The political opposition would be too fierce and no lender would want to step into the middle of that mess. "We don't think the politics are such that anybody can do a deal over the objections of the tenants," said Wilbur Ross, an investor specializing in distressed properties who had teamed up with Richard LeFrak after Tishman Speyer's default.[23]

Doyle listened patiently to their entreaties and promises. In a quiet voice, he delivered the same message to each and every one: "We would like the entire place to remain affordable, and we would like to own it."

In late February 2010, a billionaire hedge fund operator jumped into the fray, complicating the already byzantine political and financial picture at Stuyvesant Town and sending a nervous shudder through the tenants of the complexes. David Tepper, the founder of Appaloosa Management, a New Jersey hedge fund specializing in distressed properties, had quietly bought up nearly $800 million worth of bonds in the five trusts that held the $3 billion at Stuyvesant Town-Peter Cooper Village. He picked them up at a sometimes-steep discount, because of the property's well-publicized financial woes. Tepper filed a lawsuit in the U.S. district court in Manhattan seeking to block the Stuyvesant Town foreclosure, claiming that CWCapital had acted "irrationally and imprudently" in pursuing a course that could cost debt holders hundreds of millions of dollars. A foreclosure, the suit argued, could cost as much as $200 million in transfer taxes, which would cut into the amount of money bondholders ultimately received. Appaloosa said that CWCapital should have pushed the owners into bankruptcy, thereby avoiding the taxes and maximizing returns for investors.

Tepper asked the court to replace CWCapital, saying the company had "irreconcilable conflicts of interest" because it was both a "servicer" and a debt holder. "We're not trying to take control," Tepper told me at the time. "We're trying to prevent CW from acting in a reckless manner. We want a voice in the process." As for the tenants, he stressed that he was not an adversary. "We recognize that there needs to be some degree of rent-controlled apartments there," he said.

Tepper was a shrewd investor. His company had made $7 billion in 2009, including $2.5 billion for Tepper himself, by buying low-priced shares of Bank of America and Citigroup and betting that the Obama administration would not take over the financial system. But the tenants wanted no part of an opportunistic hedge fund. "The tenants are not in favor of prolonged legal wrangling," said Garodnick. "We don't think it will be helpful to extend the process here by fighting among the creditor parties."[24]

More broadly, housing advocates worried that meat-and-potatoes housing complexes that had been saddled with enormous mortgages during the real estate boom would fall into disrepair or be resold for an unsustainable price. "The fact that these investors so grossly overleveraged these buildings is a symptom of the larger economic crisis that we're dealing with now," Benjamin Dulchin, executive director of the nonprofit Association for Neighborhood and Housing Development, said at the time. "The fact that some of these players are trying to further maximize their profit, again at the expense of affordable housing in the city, is pretty horrifying."

At a hearing on April 29, CWCapital's lawyer Gregory Cross asked the court to dismiss Tepper's complaint, saying Appaloosa had no standing to intervene. Appaloosa owned certificates issued by five separate trusts that held the Stuyvesant Town mortgage and other commercial loans totaling $24 billion. The trusts typically selected a "special servicer" to maximize the recovery on behalf of all the certificate holders. Cross argued that there would be total chaos if every certificate holder was allowed to intervene, each pulling in a different direction. At the end of the hour-long hearing, Judge Alvin Hellerstein concluded, "Appaloosa's interests are not likely to be impaired or impeded," and dismissed the case.

Afterward, Judge Hellerstein's decision was cited again and

again in similar disputes that involved commercial mortgage-backed securities.

Councilman Garodnick and the tenants association were moving to revive their own plan for purchasing the complexes. They wanted to act quickly, before the lenders planted a new For Sale sign on First Avenue. There was a buzz about it on the blogs, in the tenant board meetings and at larger gatherings. "I think the people want stability," Garodnick said. "They want to get out of this model where the property is changing hands every three to five years, and where owners have a business plan designed to push people out."[25]

The tumult over Appaloosa had barely died down when two other creditors tried to seize control of Stuyvesant Town-Peter Cooper Village, before CWCapital could go through with its planned foreclosure in September of the Tishman Speyer–BlackRock partnership. Armed with a $45 million investment, Michael Ashner's Winthrop Realty Trust and Pershing Square Capital Management, a hedge fund, announced in August that they planned to foreclose on the property and convert the 11,232 rental apartments at the complexes into an "affordable cooperative" and reap a windfall.

Ashner, who was a junior lender in the Stuyvesant Town deal, took his long-standing interest in the complexes to Pershing's leader, William A. Ackman, who had much deeper pockets and a reputation as an activist investor. At one point, Ackman predicted there was a "$2 billion potential profit opportunity," which he eventually offered to split with tenants.[26]

By now, every potential buyer circling the property had concluded that the complexes were worth more than $1.8 billion.

The suitors also recognized that they needed the tenant association as an ally, given the broad public interest in the complexes from the public and from politicians ranging from Councilman Garodnick to U.S. senator Charles E. Schumer. It would be impossible to obtain a $3 billion mortgage in the still-frozen credit markets, but they would not need that much anyway if a large block of residents bought their apartments, at a discount to market. The profits would come with the sale of another block of units at market prices.

Ashner and Ackman had a plan that they said would please the tenants and the mortgage lenders, while making a tidy profit for themselves. "The unique circumstances of Stuyvesant Town today create the opportunity for us to make an attractive investment, for tenants to buy their apartments at below market prices and for the first mortgage lender to get back its money," said Ackman, the tall, trim chief executive of Pershing Square.

But CWCapital, which represented the bondholders who had a $3 billion first mortgage on the property, was not about to yield to an interloper with a relatively tiny $45 million investment. CWCapital had tried weeks earlier to buy out Ashner and a top swath of four junior lenders, who collectively had $300 million in secondary loans on the property. After initially offering $15 million, CW raised its offer to $45 million, hoping the lenders would take it, figuring something was better than nothing. But Ashner refused to go along with what had to be a unanimous decision. Instead, he bought the entire tranche for $45 million, or fifteen cents on the dollar, and enlisted Ackman in his quest to take over this iconic property. Ackman, whose company managed over $6 billion in capital, was a powerful partner.

"There was a lot of risk," Ackman explained during an interview in 2011, "but it was a relatively small amount of money for the opportunity to make multiples of our investment. I wouldn't have done it for $500 million, but for $45 million it was an interesting risk-reward."

Ackman, who at forty-five exuded boyish charm and intelligence, was in the midst of a $28 billion restructuring of General Growth Properties, the second-largest mall operator in the country. He had bought a 25 percent stake in the company during the financial crisis with the idea that the company was worth more than its flagging stock price. He lent the company $375 million after it fell into bankruptcy protection in 2009 so it could continue operating and then pushed the company to split into two, a move that ultimately generated enormous profits for himself and benefits for shareholders, lenders and employees.

The ever-brash Ashner trumpeted his own claim to fame. "I'm the reason Tishman Speyer threw in the towel in January," he told me. "They were so arrogant that they thought they'd tell everyone what to do. I got my group to send a default notice."

Although Speyer viewed Ashner as an obstructionist in the final weeks that he controlled the complexes, it is unlikely that Ashner's move figured prominently in the final decision to walk away from what had been a disastrous investment.

Many Stuyvesant Town-Peter Cooper Village residents viewed the Ashner-Ackman duo as Dracula preying on their embattled village. Certainly Doyle and Garodnick were wary. The most obvious question was, did Ackman and Ashner mean the same thing as the tenants when they used the word "affordable"? "These are profit-motivated investors," said James Sullivan, a managing director of Green Street Advisors. "That's their starting point. It's hard to envision any scenario in which they could accomplish that without alienating the residents of Stuyvesant Town."[27]

Garodnick, who met with Ackman and Carolyn B. Tiffany, Winthrop's president, said that he was disappointed but not surprised that the complexes were being treated as a "pawn in a financial chess game." He warned them in a letter that "tenants can only support a proposal that puts home ownership within reach" and allows existing, rent-regulated tenants to remain in place. Tenants would oppose a plan, he added, that involved an oversize mortgage that created financial pressure on the landlord to oust existing rent-regulated tenants. "It is of the utmost importance that this property remain accessible to New Yorkers of moderate means who aspire to live there in the future."[28]

There was also sniping from potential rivals for the complexes. Wilbur L. Ross, an investor in distressed assets who was working with the developer Richard LeFrak on a plan to buy Stuyvesant Town, was dismissive of the Ackman-Ashner gambit, as was Gerald Guterman, who also wanted to do a co-op conversion at the two complexes.

CWCapital went to court asking for a temporary injunction to block the Pershing-Winthrop auction scheduled for August 25. Its lawyer Gregory Cross argued that under the terms of the "inter-creditor agreement" that governed all lenders in the deal, Winthrop and Pershing had to pay off the first mortgage, which now totaled $3.7 billion with accumulated fees and penalties, before it could foreclose. CWCapital reckoned that Winthrop and Pershing would not be able to raise enough money to pay off the senior mortgage.

But CWCapital also paid homage to the tenant association and the concept of an affordable co-op, without spelling out any details. "We think that we have a plan that ultimately will be supported by tenants and will provide an affordable housing solution for this project," said Joseph R. Ryan, an attorney for CWCapital at an August 19 hearing before Judge Richard B. Lowe III. "That is a project now that is adrift without any new equity capital. What our people bring to the table is new equity capital and a plan to revitalize this project."

The battle was now swinging back and forth between the courtroom and the streets, for the hearts and minds of the residents. Ashner and Ackman fired off a letter to Doyle and the tenants association proposing an alliance in which the tenants would get a "substantial equity" stake in the 80-acre property, the ability to set apartment prices and the power to veto major decisions made in the course of converting the 11,232 apartments to a co-op. "Working together," the letter said, "we believe that we will be able to effectuate an affordable non-eviction conversion while protecting the long-term affordability of the property for current and future tenants and ensuring that those who wish to remain rent-stabilized renters can do so."

Subsequently, Ackman and Ashner offered the tenants "full veto rights with respect to all major decisions" and said the tenants association "will not be required to contribute any capital to obtain its ownership position."[29]

It was an extraordinary offer for a pair of financial swashbucklers and it got the tenants' attention. "We're intrigued," Doyle quipped. Garodnick added warily that he looked forward to digging deeper into the offer to see how it measured up against the tenant goals.

This maneuvering showed "that this time around people are paying attention to what the 25,000 people at Stuyvesant Town want," said former city housing commissioner Rafael E.

Cestero. "You have two big players reaching out to the tenants and saying, 'We want to work with you.'"[30]

In court, Ackman and Ashner's lawyers cited a different section of the intercreditor agreement than the one CWCapital relied on, saying that it gave them the right to foreclose and cure the default "following its acquisition of equity collateral." The two investors also conceded that they would put the complexes in bankruptcy protection if CWCapital refused to write down the senior loan, which would have almost certainly resulted in a forced write-down of the senior mortgage.

Ackman and Ashner's lawyers told the court that foreclosure would reduce the existing debt on the property by $1.4 billion, by formally wiping out the junior loans. They said nothing about the senior mortgage. CWCapital's foreclosure action would also have formally wiped out the junior lenders. Gregory Cross, CWCapital's lawyer, countered that Ackman and Ashner, as junior lenders, could have paid off the $3 billion senior loan and taken control of the property after the owners defaulted in January. But they lost the opportunity after CWCapital accelerated the loan three weeks later.

On September 16, Judge Lowe ruled against Ashner and Ackman, saying that the "intercreditor agreement prohibits junior lenders from acquiring ownership and control of the Equity Collateral unless they pay any outstanding indebtedness."

Moreover, he said, "the public interest is best served by maintaining stability in what [Pershing Square] concedes is 'the largest residential property in Manhattan and home to a significant portion of the city's moderate income housing.'"

Cross, whose law firm was based in Baltimore and was the subject of disparaging mutterings from his opponents about the quality of out-of-town lawyers, was elated. An angry Ashner vowed to appeal the decision and attempt to stop CWCapital's foreclosure sale.

But ultimately, Ashner and Ackman sold their interests in October to CWCapital for $45 million, their initial cost, and dropped the litigation. Ackman, who still insists that the judge got it wrong, likened the outcome to returning a lottery ticket to the store after you've lost for a full refund. "I have learned from prior experience," Ackman told his investors in a letter, "that sometimes the better part of valor in an investment situation is to move on. Onward."

CWCapital formally took control of Stuyvesant Town and Peter Cooper Village in October 2010, restoring Rose Associates as the manager of the complexes. It did not, however, foreclose on the loans, preferring to take over the entity that owned the complexes and avoid an estimated $100 million in transfer taxes. Technically, that meant that the junior lenders and the equity investors still had a stake in the property, but it was highly unlikely they would ever recover a dime.

One thing was sure: Tishman Speyer's forty-seven-month reign at Stuyvesant Town-Peter Cooper Village was now over.

CHAPTER TWELVE

Reckoning

The public can be forgiven if it expected Tishman Speyer and the BlackRock Group to suffer huge financial setbacks or tarnished reputations from the spectacular debacle at Stuyvesant Town and Peter Cooper Village. After all, an international array of investors, pension funds and lenders lost over $3 billion, which reverberated in state and city government budgets from California to Florida. Some twenty-five thousand tenants were left anxious and uncertain about the fate of their homes.

But the truth is that the well-oiled machine that is Tishman Speyer chugged along after the default, extending its development prowess to new markets. BlackRock, if anything, got bigger and more powerful. It is the nature of a business in which the principal players are using other people's money and the Wall Street casino supplied the markers for risky bets that investors or taxpayers would ultimately have to pay, while its croupiers collected enormous fees whether the players won or lost. The two companies came out of it relatively unscathed, belying industry lore that New York is one of the most unforgiving markets in the country. Indeed, those at the intersection of high finance and real estate are more often exonerated.

Tishman Speyer and BlackRock did lose a combined $225 million, the 4 percent of the $5.4 billion purchase price that they put into the deal. In the Speyers' case, the firm provided $56.25 million and their closest partner, the Crown family, put up an equal sum. But those losses were offset by a gusher of at least $48 million in acquisition, equity, asset and property management fees in 2007, 2008 and 2009 that flowed to Tishman Speyer, as the operating partner. Tishman Speyer and Black Rock also charged their equity partners multimillion-dollar fees to get into the Stuyvesant Town-Peter Cooper Village deal.

The Speyers received an additional fee based on the dollar volume of construction work at the property, which totaled $21.8 million for the landscaping, refurbished storefronts and new signage at the complex. But given the property's dismal financial performance, Rob Speyer elected to waive the asset management fee beginning in the fourth quarter of 2008 in a bid to "share the pain" and avoid antagonizing investors and lenders.

Before Rob Speyer formally turned over the keys to Stuyvesant Town-Peter Cooper Village in October 2010, he and his company moved rapidly to clean up a trove of troubled properties within their vast international portfolio, none of which were as deeply underwater as Stuyvesant Town-Peter Cooper Village.

Tishman Speyer raised $2 billion in equity to recapitalize the buildings in DC and to look for bargains among the office buildings and development deals now in trouble with their lenders. In June 2010, Tishman Speyer and a partner invested

$50 million each and restructured a $1.4 billion loan package covering the five Chicago office buildings it bought at the top of the market, including the Civic Opera House and 10 and 30 South Wacker Drive. Later in the year, the Speyers even added to their Chicago holdings, buying a newly erected forty-five-story office tower at 353 North Clark in Chicago for $385 million.

In Washington, DC, the Speyers and their partner SITQ paid off a $600 million junior loan, extended the term of the senior loan and invested $100 million in the twenty-eight Carr-America office buildings. SITQ, a real estate company with a $17 billion portfolio of office buildings, hotels and apartment buildings in Canada, the United States, France, Germany, the United Kingdom and India, was well acquainted with Tishman Speyer's debacle at Stuyvesant Town. SITQ then owned CW-Capital, the special servicer that took over the complexes after Tishman Speyer defaulted. But that did little to tarnish the firm's reputation.

In some cases, Tishman Speyer simply cut its losses. Rob Speyer had to stabilize a troubled office complex in Seattle that he bought at the top of the market in 2007 for $234 million. He put up $59 million in equity and financed the deal for the complex, known as Second and Seneca, with a $175 million mortgage from Bank of America. But the occupancy dropped to 60 percent during the recession. In 2010, he negotiated a loan modification and paid down a portion of the principal, reducing the debt to a $153.3 million senior loan and $16.7 million subordinate note, whose repayment was tied to the performance of the property. Finally in 2011, Speyer sold the building for $186 million, 20 percent less than he paid for it four years earlier.

But they were not licking their wounds. Rob Speyer was

particularly proud in August 2011 of selling a twenty-two-story office tower his company had just completed in Queens for $415.5 million, enabling Tishman Speyer to reap a $75 million profit on an initial investment of $28 million. Rob and his father were in constant motion. Their company completed 10 million square feet of new projects in the United States, Brazil, China and India, including the 2.2-million-square-foot WaveRock office complex in Hyderabad.

At the same time, the Speyers made $4 billion worth of new acquisitions and development deals in 2010 and 2011 in Los Angeles, San Francisco, Chicago, Paris, London, Brazil, India and China. As Stuyvesant Town faded from their corporate memory, Tishman Speyer had an impressive thirty-five million square feet of projects in their development pipeline, the largest being a sixty-six-acre mixed-use development in Shanghai called Jiang Wan (the Springs) New Town.

A long year after leaving Stuyvesant Town-Peter Cooper Village for good, Rob Speyer tried to describe what had gone wrong with their plans for the complexes. He was clearly tense and uncomfortable, as if the dentist had just told him he would need root canal work. He sat in a small conference room at Tishman Speyer headquarters with his friend and adviser Steven Rubenstein, president of Rubenstein Communications, a media-relations firm. Like Speyer, Rubenstein is an heir apparent, the son of Howard J. Rubenstein, a legendary figure who over the course of a fifty-year career advised mayors, governors, media titans and just about every real estate mogul in New York. Even if the clients hated each other, they all sought Howard's counsel.

Steven, who attended Dalton prep school with Speyer, has many of his father's qualities, including an ability to defuse a client's angry first reaction to a crisis and map out a strategic response that takes into account both the political and economic constraints in New York City. Tishman Speyer's decision to walk away from Stuyvesant Town-Peter Cooper Village, for instance, was described as stemming from the company's desire to do what was in the best interests of the tenants.

Speyer acknowledged the magnitude of the disaster, although both he and his father did not want the demise of the deal to become Tishman Speyer's epitaph. They expressed a conviction that this one deal would not affect the reputation of an honorable company that had year in and year out provided 20 and 30 percent returns for its investors. Indeed, the billionaire Lester Crown told friends that Stuyvesant Town-Peter Cooper Village was the only deal on which he lost money in five decades of investing with Tishman Speyer.

"We paid the ultimate penalty," Rob Speyer said. "We lost our investors' capital and our capital. [But] a company is not judged by a single transaction. A company is judged by the overall body of its work."[1]

Some of the Speyers' rivals gleefully put the blame for the outcome on Rob's shoulders. They depicted him as a privileged prince whose youthful arrogance blinded him to the obvious pitfalls. But this scenario only works if his father, Jerry Speyer, went into hibernation during the boom, like Rip Van Winkle, suddenly waking up years later to discover that his son had run the family business into the ground. The truth is that Jerry was the chairman of Tishman Speyer and had to approve every deal. "The two of us have a simple arrangement," Rob Speyer said. "Either of us can veto any decision the company makes. We work closely together. We both are invested in any decision the company makes anywhere."

The decisions they made were not that different from those made by other real estate tycoons who took advantage of fee-grabbing bankers and loose underwriting standards to borrow billions of dollars. Even if the deal did not work out, there were few downside consequences and little risk.

The potential upside was breathtaking. Jerry and Rob Speyer described Stuyvesant Town at the time of the sale as an asset they intended to hold on to for generations to come. At first glance, this might seem out of whack with the exit strategy outlined in the investor memorandum, which was to gentrify the complexes, more than double revenues, and then sell in seven years at a handy profit.

But at the time, the Speyers intended to be the ultimate buyer, following the same path they took with another landmark.

Jerry Speyer was a minority owner (he and billionaire Lester Crown owned a five percent stake) and the operating partner when he first bought Rockefeller Center in 1996 for $900 million, with partners David Rockefeller, the Agnelli of Italy, the Stavros Niarchos family of Greece, and Goldman Sachs. He carefully restored the landmark complex's luster as the real estate market soared. Speyer and Crown bought the complex for $1.85 billion five years later in 2001, when the partners put it on the auction block. But the strategy that worked so well at Rockefeller Center failed completely at Stuyvesant Town.

Rob Speyer, other real estate executives and even some pension fund executives who invested in these highly leveraged projects blamed their ultimate collapse on the vagaries of the market and the surprising J-51 court ruling that re-regulated thousands of apartments, cutting deeply into residential revenues. "The biggest driver in the underperformance of the investment was the deterioration of rents," Rob Speyer said. "We were a victim of our own bad timing. It couldn't have been worse timing."

But the catastrophic failure was not simply a matter of bad timing. The reality is that nearly every single assumption in their business plan for Stuyvesant Town-Peter Cooper Village was wrong, dead wrong. The company that seemed to have the golden touch when it came to overseas development or iconic commercial properties like Rockefeller Center or the Chrysler Building completely overestimated its ability to turn Stuyvesant Town-Peter Cooper Village into a luxury complex.

Their plan to deregulate and renovate apartments at a faster pace than most landlords have ever imagined was a failure. Within the first year, before the recession and the collapse of Lehman Brothers, Tishman Speyer discovered that its projections for market rents were higher than anyone was willing to pay for an apartment in a sixty-year-old complex without doormen and modern amenities. So they accumulated a backlog of hundreds of unrented, overpriced apartments. That set off a downward spiral as the company reduced the market rents to attract tenants, and reduced them again as the market softened and demand slackened.

They were no more prescient with their plan to evict 1,600 "illegal tenants" as a quick way to boost rents. They spent a fortune hiring investigators and three different law firms to ferret out illegals, only to discover that they had alienated virtually the entire population and come up far short of their goal. The bulk of the "illegals" had been culled by MetLife and Rose Associates prior to Tishman Speyer's purchase.

Their miscalculations could not withstand a slowdown in rent increases, let alone a full-blown recession. Small wonder that net income for the complexes in 2008 was $138 million, 35 percent less than the $211.7 million forecast in the "confidential private placement memorandum" given to investors two years earlier.

Between October of 2008 and August of 2009, Speyer said that net effective rents at Stuyvesant Town-Peter Cooper Village fell by 27 percent or more. There is no question that the market was getting soft, but the steep drop at Stuyvesant Town-Peter Cooper Village was one more example of just how badly Tishman Speyer miscalculated.

The average rent for a Manhattan apartment fell by only 8.7 percent to $3,399 between 2007 and 2009, according to one of Manhattan's largest rental brokers, Citi Habitats. But from the beginning of its tenure, Tishman Speyer pushed the rents for market-rate units so high that many potential renters sought better deals elsewhere. As a result, the vacancy rate climbed to more than 6 percent from 2 percent the year before Tishman Speyer took over. Small wonder then that the net effective rent plummeted from a peak of $4,250 a month at Peter Cooper to $3,050 in August 2009, and from $3,750 a month in Stuyvesant Town to $2,750 during the same period, according to Tishman Speyer's own figures.

Tishman Speyer had stopped renovating vacant apartments at Stuyvesant Town and Peter Cooper Village at the end of 2008, three months before the appellate division of the state supreme court ruled that Tishman Speyer and MetLife had wrongfully deregulated 4,400 apartments while taking special tax breaks from the city.

"The default at Stuyvesant Town really had nothing to do with the Roberts case," said Stuart M. Saft, the real estate lawyer who analyzed the deal for two potential bidders and for an investor after the collapse. "There was no economic basis in the first place," Saft said. "It's great middle-income housing. But people who pay top dollar won't rent there. It's never going to be considered luxury housing."

Saft had also devised the original tenant lawsuit challenging the deregulation of apartments at Stuyvesant Town and Peter Cooper Village. Having assessed the property from so many angles, he was hired by one investor after the default to determine whether there were grounds for a lawsuit against Tishman Speyer and BlackRock. There were not. But Saft concluded in a June 2010 report for the investor that the fundamental flaw in Tishman Speyer's analysis was that it ignored "the age, nature and reputation of the property and the determination of the residents and local elected officials to fight gentrification of the property or the fact that a newly constructed property would not have these disadvantages."

After he was no longer involved with the property, Speyer conceded that he had completely misunderstood the political complexity of buying and managing rent-regulated housing in New York, and the historical and cultural significance of Stuyvesant Town-Peter Cooper Village as a middle-class bastion in Manhattan. The hostility from residents, tenants in general and the elected officials took him by surprise.

"In retrospect," he said, "I realized I'd lived a bit of a charmed life, both professionally and otherwise. This was a failure and a failure on a pretty epic scale. I did not appreciate the political and social dynamics that came along with the real estate in this deal," he added. "I thought if we abided by the law and behaved honorably that everything would be okay on the civic front. It seems obvious now, but it didn't occur to me that people hated the law and therefore they hated us. We weren't used to being portrayed as the guys in the black hats.

"There was a connection between my single-minded focus on business and how I missed the bigger picture on this deal."[2]

At the urging of Rubenstein, Speyer hired Michele Adams, who ran a business and civic association founded by the Rudin real estate family, the Association for a Better New York, to keep him apprised of the political currents in the city and to build a portfolio of civic and philanthropic activities. In late 2010, Rob also took on a more high-profile role in the political sphere, establishing the Committee to Save New York to support the newly elected Democratic governor, his friend Andrew M. Cuomo. The group sponsored television and radio ads supporting the governor in his ultimately successful battles with public-sector unions over pensions, teacher tenure and government spending.

Speyer initially took responsibility for raising a treasure chest of more than $10 million for an ad campaign backing the governor's conservative approach to the state budget. He pledged to contribute $1 million on behalf of his firm. The campaign was designed to counterbalance the annual media offensive from state-employee unions during the legislative debate over the budget.

Some developers balked at turning over their checks to Speyer, as if he was the only executive who knew the governor. Not wanting to "feather Rob's nest," as one executive put it, they gave their money to the Real Estate Board or some other entity, rather than Speyer or Adams. As a result, there was friction with his cofounders, Kathy Wylde, president of the Partnership for New York City, and Steven Spinola, president of the Real Estate Board of New York. Still, in 2011, the group raised $17 million, according to public records, much of it from wealthy and powerful executives giving $250,000 or more. The group steadfastly declined to disclose the names of the donors and was not legally bound to do so.

But in keeping with Speyer's newfound sensitivity to city and state politics, Rob insisted that he sought to temper the animosity toward unions among some developers and business leaders, which could have undercut the we're-all-in-this-together message of the committee.

A full-on attack on unions, similar to Tea Party–inspired campaigns in Wisconsin or Ohio, could have provoked a backlash among liberals, Democrats and others in the most unionized state in the country. The committee included several private-sector union leaders from the construction industry, exacerbating tensions within the labor movement and providing political cover for a Democratic governor who did not want to be portrayed as antiunion. The group hewed closely to Cuomo's fiscal agenda: cutting state spending, capping local property taxes and cutting pension benefits for public employees.

In 2011, the committee was the single biggest spender in the state on lobbying, pouring nearly $12 million into ad campaigns in support of the governor. "All the messaging was positive, about bringing people together," Speyer said. "Many people had predicted that the committee would be much more divisive toward the other side."

Speyer also moved on another front, lobbying hard to follow in his father's footsteps at the real estate industry's powerful lobbying arm, the Real Estate Board of New York, or REBNY. In the summer of 2012, the group announced that Speyer would be its new chairman come January.

But the Speyers and others on the committee were the same people in 2008 who persuaded the billionaire Michael Bloomberg to jettison his support for term limits and overturn the city's election law so he could run for a third term as mayor. With the Committee to Save New York, some of the city's wealthiest citizens were seeking to exert more influence and control over a political process in which tenants and labor unions, in their view, had too much clout. The committee's members and agenda showed, as Bill Mahoney, research coordinator for the New York Public Interest Research Group, put it, "a small number of New Yorkers continue to play a disproportionate role in the state's political discourse."

The heads-I-win, tails-you-lose scenario played out in equal measure for BlackRock. The company's founder and chairman, Larry Fink, was depicted in an April 2010 *Vanity Fair* profile as possibly "the most powerful man in the post-bailout economy." His company, which controlled or managed a jaw-dropping $12 trillion in assets worldwide, emerged as the largest asset management firm in the world. His views were so highly valued that he served as a consigliere for Jamie Dimon at JPMorgan Chase, John Mack at Morgan Stanley, AIG's Robert Willumstad and even the U.S. Treasury. Fink, one of the highest-paid chief executives in the country, told *Vanity Fair* that the public's rage at Wall Street was misplaced. "I feel it was the culture of America that was guilty," he said. "We were living fat and happy and the whole system was one of excess speculation and leverage."

But few profited from that culture as handsomely as Fink. Certainly, the pensioners at BlackRock's clients might not feel the same way. CalPERS, CalSTRS and the Dutch PKA lost a combined $669.7 million on the deal, six times as much as BlackRock. Fink declined to be interviewed for this book, but in the *Vanity Fair* profile, he echoed Jerry Speyer's sentiment in saying that a money manager could not be "100 percent perfect." "Our real estate division is struggling because of bad performance, and we're making changes," he told the magazine. "I don't care if the whole industry blew up, our job is to do better than the industry, and we didn't in real estate. I am not making excuses. I lose sleep over these problems."

The Stuyvesant Town-Peter Cooper Village loss was "an embarrassment," he added. The reporter recounted that Fink's voice then dropped to a whisper. "I mean, my mother gets her pension from CalPERS."

In a rare public rebuke of Fink's company, CalPERS dumped BlackRock in October 2010 as manager of its $1 billion portfolio of apartment complexes. BlackRock had managed the portfolio since 1998. The value of the pension fund's total assets had plummeted 24.8 percent—while the real estate portfolio alone took a 48 percent hit—in the year ending June 30, 2009, the largest single-year decline in CalPERS's history. The investment losses could have triggered a substantial increase in annual payments from the municipalities and school districts that belonged to the fund to enable CalPERS to meet its projected obligations to retirees. But the pension fund adopted a "rate smoothing plan" that phased the losses over three years so as not to require one jolting increase at a time when many cities and towns were struggling to make ends meet in the face of a sharp recession and a steep drop in property values.

It wasn't all BlackRock's fault. Other outside managers were responsible for CalPERS's having to write off a $100 million equity investment in Page Mill Properties, a Palo Alto, California, complex where tenants had complained that rent hikes of as much as 33 percent had forced out residents who could no longer afford to live there. The fund also lost nearly $1 billion on LandSource Holding, which held fifteen thousand acres in Los Angeles County and would tumble into bankruptcy only seventeen months after the investment. But the debacle at Stuyvesant Town-Peter Cooper Village was a double whammy for what had been a renowned pension fund.

"It was a significant disappointment," Joseph A. Dear, chief investment officer of CalPERS, said of the $500 million investment in Stuyvesant Town. "We transferred about $7 billion from managers that let us down in the crash to others who performed better."

"The entire catastrophe with the CalPERS real estate portfolio was enormously painful," Dear added in an interview in 2011. "Stuyvesant Town was an acute source of that pain. I say that because it involved not only an enormous amount of capital, but it was also a source of embarrassment that appeared to be in contradiction of our good governance, responsible investor policies."

The pension fund purged many of the executives who promoted the Stuyvesant Town investment over the objections of CalPERS's adviser Nori Gerardo Lietz, who had warned that it was doomed from the start.

In 2011, CalPERS's board revamped its investment criteria, emphasizing income-producing core assets providing a 7 percent return, rather than devoting so much capital to chasing the ephemeral 13.5 percent return promised by more high-risk ventures like Stuyvesant Town. At the same time, the board pivoted away from raw land and residential properties to office buildings. After coming under intensive criticism for a deal that involved displacing rent-regulated tenants who were very much like the fund's pensioners, CalPERS also adopted a policy effectively prohibiting investments in deals that use excessive rent hikes to oust low- and moderate-income families from rent-regulated housing.

"This policy will help us ensure that external managers who deploy CalPERS capital won't inappropriately displace households in rent-regulated units as a result of their investment strategies," said Rob Feckner, CalPERS's board president, after announcing the policy change in April 2010. "Such strategies have exposed CalPERS to risks and have caused adverse impacts to renters that must not happen again."

BlackRock went through its own internal purge. Fink replaced BlackRock Realty's chief Fred Lieblich in 2008, although Lieblich remained at the firm until his retirement in March 2010. Lieblich turned to meditation and yoga to regain his bearings. Even so, Lieblich declined several times to discuss what he said was a still-painful period in his life.

However, Rob Friedberg, a former managing director of BlackRock Realty who worked on the Stuyvesant Town deal, was remarkably frank in his assessment of the winners and losers. Friedberg left BlackRock in 2008 amid the upheaval in the real estate department. "There are two winners: the borrowers who used this non-recourse, securitized debt [and] who cashed out are giant winners," said Friedberg, who now runs his own investment firm, Capstone Realty, in Englewood, New Jersey. "The property went down, they give the property back, no recourse to them personally. The other winners are all the investment bankers who made these loans. There are a lot of fees when you borrow $4.5 billion."[3]

In 2009, BlackRock paid $13.5 billion for Barclays Global Investors, the ailing British bank's investment management unit. Jittery banks and governments ranging from the Federal Reserve to the Bank of Ireland to Greece sought the company's advice. Whatever the smudges on BlackRock's reputation because of Stuyvesant Town and the dismissal by CalPERS, the world's largest asset manager regained its footing quickly, reporting in the spring of 2011 that its first-quarter profit soared 34 percent to $568 million over the same period a year earlier. BlackRock's assets under management, a key indicator of the company's financial health, rose 8 percent to $3.65 trillion, making it, by that measure, the largest financial institution in the world.

"We're very excited about the future of BlackRock," Fink told analysts in a conference call. "We believe this is principally over. We can look forward to growth now."

Rob Verrone, the banker who earned an estimated $140 million in fees for Wachovia by erecting the financial structure for the Stuyvesant Town-Peter Cooper Village deal, does not like to dwell on the past. Verrone, who once courted reporters, is now reluctant to do interviews, especially if they dredge up his Italian background and the *Godfather* movie poster that once decorated his office. But he couldn't help himself. He wanted to make clear that Wachovia and Merrill Lynch suffered no pain when it came to the largest real estate transaction in history. He and his colleagues got an investment-grade rating for the $3 billion mortgage and quickly pushed it off the banks' balance sheets.

"From a financial standpoint," he said, "everything went right for Wachovia and Merrill."[4]

He made no mention of the junior lenders he and his colleagues pulled into the deal, or the pension funds and other investors who ponied up over $1.8 billion and then lost it.

Besides, he added, far more "outlandish" deals were done after Stuyvesant Town-Peter Cooper Village, including Lehman Brothers and Tishman Speyer's $22.2 billion acquisition of Archstone-Smith's 359 apartment complexes in 2007 and Blackstone's $26 million all-cash buyout of Hilton Hotels Group. The value of the apartment complexes dropped swiftly before the deal even closed. And Hilton Hotels groaned under the weight of $20 billion in debt during the recession and the decline in business travel.

But any list of outlandish deals would have to include the Lightstone Group's $8 billion purchase of Extended Stay Hotels by Lighthouse, which put up only 7.5 percent of the purchase price. Verrone and Wachovia underwrote the financing along with Merrill Lynch, Bear Stearns and Bank of America. It wasn't long before Extended Stay tumbled into bankruptcy court. "We lost a lot of money on that one," Verrone conceded.

Verrone left Wachovia in 2008, before the bank was swallowed by Wells Fargo and before Bank of America absorbed what was left of Merrill Lynch. Verrone and his new firm, Iron Hound Management, now represent debtors in their negotiations with lenders for extensions, interest reductions and discounts for payoffs, sometimes for his old clients.

Manus Clancy, an analyst at Trepp, a credit rating agency that follows the market for commercial mortgage-backed securities, estimated that Stuyvesant Town-Peter Cooper Village was one among fifteen thousand "pro forma" mortgages for apartment complexes, office buildings, hotels and other real estate based on often wildly optimistic estimates of what the property would be in years to come, rather than actual income. The Kushner real estate family's $1.6 billion purchase of the skyscraper at 666 Fifth Avenue in 2006 from Tishman Speyer is a prime example of the phenomenon in commercial real estate, while the $8 billion sale of the Extended Stay chain stands in for the hotel industry.

The financial industry has resisted the reforms spelled out in the Dodd-Frank legislation that might inhibit indiscriminate lending by bankers who were only too willing to take the enormous fees and unload the loans and the risk on investors in the form of mortgage-backed securities. The legislation calls for institutions issuing those kinds of securities to retain a 5 percent stake in any offering, ensuring that the banks have skin in the game and an interest in prudent terms and the outcome of the deal.

"There's a real difference between what a conduit lender thinks and a bank executive who will hold the loan through maturity," said Sam Chandan, president and chief economist for Chandan Economics and a professor at the University of Pennsylvania.[5]

Otherwise, there have been few structural changes to the way the market for commercial mortgage-backed securities functions, whether it is the oversight of the rating agencies or the relationship of the different parties in the transaction to one another. The volume of lending today is simmering at only a fraction of the hundreds of billions of dollars issued during the real estate boom. But prices for multifamily housing in 2012 were once again on the rise, even as profit margins thinned as properties changed hands. That led some analysts to wonder whether another minibubble was in the offing.

"Participants in the market will point out that deals are of higher quality now and are more conservatively underwritten than a few years ago," Chandan said. "However, that's a cyclical feature of the market. We know from previous cycles that the loan quality deteriorates as the market picks up. The potential for problematic loans remains."

In the fall of 2011, Steven A. Kandarian assessed the winners and losers of the deal for Stuyvesant Town-Peter Cooper Village that he helped engineer as MetLife's chief investment officer. The complexes remain intact and most of the tenants, he said, "still have rent stabilization protecting them." The losers, he said, were the lenders and pension funds.

"The primary losers are the people involved in financing the transaction," said Kandarian, sitting in a boardroom on the forty-first floor of MetLife's corporate offices at Forty-Second Street and Avenue of the Americas, in Manhattan. "That's where the risk should be."

The outcome, however, could have easily gone the other way, he said. "The bubble could have kept on going." Rents could have continued to soar along with real estate prices. But they didn't.

It's unclear where the sponsors—Tishman Speyer and BlackRock—fit into Mr. Kandarian's evaluation.

MetLife, of course, came out a big winner. Kandarian, now chairman of the board, president and chief executive officer, is understandably proud that he picked the top of the market for the sale and got a record-setting price, $5.4 billion. It produced a one-time net gain of $3 billion for the insurance company and, he pointed out, generated $262 million in taxes for the city and the state.

But more than one long-term tenant at Stuyvesant Town-Peter Cooper Village said that MetLife's responsibility extended beyond the company's profit margins. John Marsh, the activist who succeeded Doyle as president of the tenant association in

2012, quoted a line from the commemorative plaque in Stuyvesant Oval that honored Frederick W. Ecker, the MetLife chairman. The plaque described Ecker as the man "who conceived and brought into being this project, and others like it, that families of moderate means might live in health, comfort and dignity in parklike communities, and that a pattern might be set of private enterprise productively devoted to public service."

In Marsh's judgment, the decision to sell the complexes set in motion the very forces that are destroying Ecker's noble intentions and devotion to public service, leaving aside for a moment his approach to racial discrimination. In the relentless pursuit of profit, Marsh said, Stuyvesant Town and Peter Cooper Village are becoming home to the well-heeled and a highly commercialized venture.

Kandarian dismissed the notion that he and the company have betrayed Ecker's vision. MetLife honored its promises and commitments well beyond the twenty-five years required by the deal with the city, he said. Ultimately, their obligation was to the company's financial well-being. And the company was now responsible to shareholders and Wall Street.

"We spent six decades owning and managing that property in a very responsible way," he said. "But the quote on the statue didn't say, 'in perpetuity.' Selling our interest to a high-quality New York real estate investor doesn't denigrate those words at all."

Even after Tishman Speyer's default and the continuing recession, Stuyvesant Town-Peter Cooper Village remained an alluring prize for the Related Companies, AREA Property Partners, the Durst real estate family in partnership with City University of New York, Gerald Guterman and Westwood Partners, and especially the tenants themselves.

One year after Tishman Speyer and BlackRock left Stuyvesant Town-Peter Cooper Village for good, Dan Garodnick, the councilman, and Al Doyle, the tenant leader, announced in November 2011 that they were once again seeking to buy the two complexes in order to preserve them as a leafy refuge for middle-class families in high-priced Manhattan. This time, however, they had a deep-pocketed partner.

They hoped that the lenders who controlled the property through CWCapital would sell it to them in a deal that would enable tenants to purchase their apartments or remain in rent-regulated units. The idea was to preempt another overheated auction that would put the property in the hands of a heavily leveraged owner who might try to oust residents in favor of higher-paying tenants.

"This is the beginning," Doyle told me in November 2011. "We're trying to take control of the destiny of Stuyvesant Town-Peter Cooper Village in order to keep it an affordable property."

They hoped that they could cobble together a financial deal that would not leave the tenants with the kind of outsize debts that drowned Tishman Speyer and BlackRock. It would almost certainly include some kind of city, state and federal subsidies, as well as property tax breaks.

Senators Charles E. Schumer and Kirsten Gillibrand, Congresswoman Carolyn Maloney, Assemblyman Brian Kavanagh, city council speaker Christine Quinn and other elected officials immediately endorsed the effort. "If tenants have an ownership piece of these complexes it will be good not only for them," Schumer said, "but will also help secure their affordability for future generations of middle-class New Yorkers."

The tenant association formed an alliance with Brookfield Asset Management, a real estate company that managed $150 billion worth of assets, including fifty thousand apartments. In 2006, Brookfield had made a relatively small junior loan, $25 million, to the Tishman Speyer–BlackRock joint venture. Like all the other junior lenders, they had written off their loan in 2009. Now the company wanted to get involved in the tenant buyout.

Barry S. Blattman, a senior managing director at Brookfield, said his company was eager to help the tenant association "take matters into their own hands." Brookfield was not interested in becoming the landlord. But given the difficulty in obtaining financing for large real estate deals, Blattman said a condominium structure, in which tenants buy their apartments, might be the best way for CWCapital to get the highest possible price for the property now.

At a standing-room-only community meeting at Baruch College a few days later, on Saturday, December 3, Blattman was described by tenant leaders and their advisers in glowing terms as a white knight for the beleaguered tenants. No one mentioned that Blattman's company, Brookfield, owned the private park downtown that had been taken over by the Occupy Wall Street movement. Brookfield and city officials had been trying for weeks to evict the group, whose daily forays against the banks and the wealthiest 1 percent of Americans were disrupting the city's financial district.

There were well over 1,200 Stuyvesant Town and Peter Cooper Village residents in attendance at the Baruch College auditorium, with 150 yellow-shirted volunteers from the tenant association circulating through the crowd with flyers and sign-up sheets. "The entire city is watching what you do here and they're cheering you on," said an ebullient Garodnick.

"This bid is not geared for quickly flipping apartments at a huge profit or any other actions that will undercut the character of our community," Garodnick told the crowd. "Our bid is motivated by a desire for stability and an affordable home-ownership option for those who want it with gradual appreciation over time."

You could have heard the pipes clanging in Stuyvesant Town, it was so quiet when Meredith Kane spoke. A real estate lawyer and an adviser to the tenant association, Kane described in general terms what a tenant-led condominium conversion would look like. She said the plan was to preserve the open space at the complexes from new development, improve the maintenance at the buildings and create permanently affordable rental units with government help. She was short on details, in part because there had been no negotiations yet over price or structure.

The idea was that the tenants would purchase Stuyvesant Town-Peter Cooper Village and convert the complexes to a single condominium, under a plan in which no tenant would be evicted. An unspecified number of units would be set aside for residents who wished to remain in a rent-regulated apartment. A second category would be comprised of tenants who believed in Stuyvesant Town-Peter Cooper Village as a middle-class enclave. They could purchase their units at a steep discount to market. But there would be restrictions on any subsequent sales so that the units would remain affordable to families earning the median income of those living in the complexes. Finally, tenants who wanted the relatively unfettered right to sell their apartment for the highest possible price could buy their units at a modest discount to market.

It was an attempt to provide something for everyone. Still, the auditorium rang with hundreds of questions that could not be answered at the time: What would the apartments cost? Would apartments on higher floors have a higher price tag? Could a resident swap for a larger or smaller apartment? Why a condominium rather than a cooperative?

Under a tenant-led conversion, Brookfield would provide a down payment on the purchase price and obtain a mortgage through either the lenders or an independent bank. This scenario presumed that a large block of tenants, perhaps 50 or 60 percent, would buy their units early on, allowing the condominium association to pay off a portion of the mortgage and lower their costs. Sales of apartments at market rates would subsidize the stabilized rental units.

Brookfield would earn a hefty fee for its role and arrange for individual apartment loans. Brookfield might also retain ownership of the complexes' garages and retail space.

Although Al Doyle declined to identify a potential price, most analysts figured that the tenants could afford to pay about $3 billion, or roughly $300 a square foot. It would be difficult to go higher. To make this complicated process work, the net monthly cost of owning an apartment had to be roughly equal to the current cost of renting one, otherwise there would be little incentive to purchase a unit. At the same time, the tenants were betting that a profit-driven real estate company would be unable to obtain the financing in tight credit markets that would allow them to pay a higher price for that eighty-acre set of complexes in Manhattan.

Eugene Costiglio, who has lived in the complexes for a

quarter century, found the prospect of ownership intriguing, but he was not ready to commit. Costiglio, who works at an investment bank, moved to Stuyvesant Town from Queens in 1987 after languishing for six years on the waiting list. Later, he moved to Peter Cooper Village. During the reign of Tishman-Speyer, he said he spent twenty-two months and $22,000 successfully fending off Tishman Speyer's attempt to evict him. They claimed that his small bungalow on Long Island was his actual home and sought to evict him, saying he was not entitled to a rent-stabilized unit by law. But he ultimately proved that his primary residence was in Peter Cooper Village.

For him, a condominium conversion came down to one issue: "I think it's a wonderful idea if the price is right."[6]

Linda Ayache, a semiretired tenant and an ardent tenant activist, said she probably could not afford to buy her apartment. Her parents were some of the first residents of Stuyvesant Town in 1947. She got her own apartment when she married in 1970. Now divorced, she is a self-confessed sports fanatic and the unofficial neighborhood watch commander on her floor. Her regulated rent is over $1,300 a month, up from $161.65 in 1970. She said she favored "anything that gets it under tenant rule, whether we buy or not."[7]

But CWCapital, the special servicer representing the bondholders who controlled the complexes, was not as eager to embrace the tenants as it had been during the wrestling match with Ackman and Ashner.

The official response to the proposal from the tenant association and Brookfield was simple: We cannot begin to discuss a sale before we resolve the Roberts litigation. Chuck Spetka and Andrew MacArthur from CWCapital argued that they could not calculate the value of the property without knowing the legal rents for the 4,400 apartments—nearly 40 percent of all the units—that had been improperly deregulated.

The court decision did not determine the legal rents going forward, nor the extent of the rent overcharges made to potentially thousands of tenants over an unspecified number of years. But Spetka and MacArthur, whose fiduciary responsibilities were to the lenders, not the tenants, estimated that the complexes were worth far more than the tenant group could pay.

Spetka and MacArthur suspected that Brookfield and the tenant association were trying to buy the complexes on the cheap. Privately, they dismissed Garodnick's press conferences as the tactics of a politician on the make. They knew that some of the city's largest real estate companies were still salivating over the prospect of owning the complexes, including the Related Companies, the Durst real estate family and others. Michael Ashner, who was now allied with Richard Mack from AREA Property Partners (formerly Apollo Real Estate), was still interested after having lost out to Brookfield in the competition to partner with the tenants. And Jerry Guterman directly challenged the tenant association with his own plan for a co-op conversion after they rebuffed his entreaties.

After all, the real estate market, especially the market for apartment rentals, was surging once again.

Spetka and MacArthur, the vice president who oversaw the two complexes, set out to purge the complexes of what they viewed as Tishman Speyer's legacy, establish at least a détente with Garodnick and the tenant association, and, like Tishman Speyer, renovate vacant apartments, push rents higher and enhance net income.

As the new landlord, CWCapital and Rose Associates tried to assure tenants that it was not on a wholesale campaign to oust longtime residents. But that does not mean that all twenty-five thousand tenants universally viewed them as a benevolent force. There were tenants who complained to their neighbors and in the blogs about Rose's decision to continue the weekly green market and allow noisy food trucks to pull up around Stuyvesant Oval, offering grilled meat, tacos, juice drinks and other items to residents.

Margaret Salacan and other tenants found what they called the commercialization of the complexes appalling. "The food trucks don't belong on the property," she said over coffee at a shop on Twentieth Street. "They bring noise, fumes and garbage. The original purpose of the oval was to create an oasis in the middle of the city."[8]

The opposition was by no means unanimous, as many residents liked the convenience. One of the biggest uproars came in the winter of 2011 when MacArthur, an amateur hockey player with children who skate, decided to install a temporary ice rink atop one of the playgrounds. A vocal group of tenants, though by no means all, rained criticism on the rink in the blogs and in letters to the tenant association and the local newspaper, saying it was an illegal, profit-making enterprise that drew nonresidents to the complexes. In a meeting with Garodnick, MacArthur told him, "You're caught between cranky tenants and gleeful kids. Anywhere else, this would be considered an amenity."

The rink opened anyway, attracting more than double the number of anticipated skaters on the first weekend.

In a telling move that had both symbolic and practical meaning, CWCapital tore out the extensive landscaping installed by Rob Speyer soon after he took over the complexes. Speyer had spent $21.8 million on new signs, a facelift for storefronts on

First Avenue and truckloads of trees, bushes, flowers. Workers planted ten thousand trees in two months, cramming thick copses of young ornamental trees beneath a canopy formed by mature London plane and pin oak trees. They stocked the flower beds with seasonal and ornamental flowers requiring periodic replacement and hung flowerpots from lampposts, which needed constant watering in the summer.

Early in 2011, Adam Rose, the property manager hired by CWCapital, gleefully yanked out five hundred trees, donating two hundred to city parks and disposing of the remaining three hundred. Rose, who never forgave Speyer for firing his firm when he took over, donated five thousand ornamental cabbages to the parks department. "They so overplanted," Rose said of the prior owners. "The landscaping didn't raise the rents one cent. Why? They're still non-doorman buildings with only one bath."[9]

Raising the rents to improve cash flow was foremost on the agenda of Rose and CWCapital. In that respect, CWCapital was no different from Tishman Speyer. They just did not have to carry as much debt or move as swiftly to try to make ends meet. After the 2009 court of appeals ruling, Tishman Speyer struck a deal with the tenant-plaintiffs in the court case, temporarily rolling back rents by hundreds of dollars for the 4,400 apartments covered by the decision. But that agreement expired in December 2010, and when CWCapital was unable to reach a permanent accord with the plaintiffs, the company took an aggressive position, unilaterally raising the rents as leases expired and throwing the issue back into the courts.

The rents for all 11,232 apartments at Stuyvesant Town and Peter Cooper Village were regulated, but over 2010, 2011 and 2012 two distinct classes of units emerged. Roughly 60 percent of the units were the traditional rent-stabilized apartments whose rents averaged about $1,500 a month. The rents for the other 40 percent, all of them renovated and modernized, were at or near market rates, although annual increases were restricted by the city's Rent Guidelines Board.

By the fall of 2012, rent for a two-bedroom apartment in Stuyvesant Town, for instance, was $4,385 a month, up from $3,850 a year earlier. One-bedroom units were going for $3,200 a month. A two-bedroom apartment at Peter Cooper Village cost even more, about $4,600 per month.

It is worth noting that CWCapital steadily increased the net income at the two complexes, but seven years after the original sale they still did not generate enough income to cover the debt service on the $3 billion mortgage. The property needed about $195.6 million in net income or cash flow to break even. But Manus Clancy, a senior managing director at the Trepp credit rating agency, estimated that the net cash flow for 2011 was only $130 million, up from $122.9 million in 2010. A $65 million shortfall.

But they are gaining ground. CWCapital has steadily increased the number of units renting at or near market rates from 4,300 to 5,331 by spending lavishly—$85,000 to $120,000 per unit—on the renovation of every vacant apartment. They installed wood cabinets, new wood floors, European bath fixtures, granite countertops and high-end appliances.

Under new rent regulations adopted by the state legislature in 2011, landlords can recover their investment by raising the rent by one-sixtieth of the renovation cost. In other words, the rent for an apartment that once went for $1,500 a month could be hiked by $2,000 after a $120,000 renovation, to $3,500. Plus, regulations permitted a 20 percent bump in rent for vacant apartments. It hardly mattered that the apartments were rent regulated.

The marketing of Stuyvesant Town-Peter Cooper Village today says a lot about the new tenants. The ads in 2012 are pitched to a younger, more well-heeled, and most likely, single tenant than the striving families typical in the past. The ads highlight a "sophisticated selection of services, amenities and events" and conclude with a tagline that many longtime residents find infuriating: "Stuyvesant Town. Live and Live It Up."

Judging from the young college students and recent college graduates who jammed into the leasing office on two separate days in July 2011, the incoming tenants are young, fashionable and single. Many were accompanied by their mothers. That month, 2,000 prospective renters visited the leasing office; 360 signed leases. Middle-class families can hardly afford the renovated units. Federal guidelines suggest that housing costs should not exceed 30 percent of the household income. With apartments renting for $4,000 or more a month, or $48,000 a year, a family would need to earn more than $160,000 a year.

Very often the young people crowding the leasing office are willing to double and triple up in order to pay the rent. Katie Schloer, a New York University student from Philadelphia, lived in a one-bedroom apartment with two friends, both students. Noah Nielsen moved to a two-bedroom apartment in Stuyvesant Town after graduating from the University of Vermont. He had two roommates. They built a wall in the center of the living room to make three bedrooms and split the rent, $3,500 a month.

But Nielsen, like Schloer, had no intention of setting down roots. He left after a year. "I didn't want to be surrounded by older people and families," Nielsen said. "I wanted to feel like I'm in Manhattan."[10]

The cultural differences between the newcomers and their dormitory lifestyle and the more established, family-oriented tenants created some tension. Complaints abounded about the young people who stayed up late, played their music loud at night or caroused drunkenly in the playgrounds. "They're filling apartments beyond their capacity, in many cases with people who have no regard for the community as a long-term home," Garodnick said.

But there is more at work here than simply the gulf between the twentysomethings and the families and retirees. People no longer work for the same company or institution for their entire lives, be it MetLife, the New York City public school system or Beth Israel hospital. Nor do they tend to live in the same apartment or house for decades at a time. We live in a more rootless era, where careers can change several times in the course of a lifetime, companies go in and out of business and personal addresses change periodically. The golden age of Stuyvesant Town-Peter Cooper Village as a stable redoubt where parents raise their children and retire may have passed.

"To me, this place was about family," said Margaret Salacan, who has lived in Stuyvesant Town since 1988. "Now it's about transients."[11]

At 5:00 P.M. on November 29, 2012, the tenant-plaintiffs and CWCapital, the company that controlled Stuyvesant Town-Peter Cooper Village, announced that they had reached a $68.75 million agreement to settle the class-action claims arising from the

Roberts case. The settlement, which had the preliminary approval of Justice Richard B. Lowe III, would put to rest all rent overcharge claims and set the legal rents for the 4,311 apartments that were illegally deregulated while the complex received city tax breaks. Judge Lowe set a hearing on final approval for April 9, 2013.

Thousands of current and former tenants would get anywhere from $150 to six figures, with the nine original plaintiffs receiving at least $25,000 each for the time and effort spent on the case since it was filed in 2007.

Rumors had swept across the complexes for more than a year that a settlement was near. But that was only after CWCapital's attempt to go around the plaintiffs by lobbying the state legislature for a "legislative solution" ended in total failure. They had persuaded a Republican state senator whose district was closer to Cleveland than Manhattan to submit a bill that would have allowed the owners of Stuyvesant Town-Peter Cooper Village to repay the $24 million in tax breaks it received at 9 percent interest, a total of at least $26.16 million. But the bondholders would not have to roll back rents or repay what tenant advocates once estimated were $200 million in rent overcharges. Although the bill had the support of the real estate industry, it had no chance of passage in the Democratic-controlled Assembly, so the bill died that summer without a vote by the legislature.

Months later, the two sides—three if you count MetLife—did get close to a deal. But what proved to be impossibly complicated was trying to cobble together a general agreement that covered the rent history for 4,311 separate apartments and, ultimately, a potential 21,250 tenants who at one time or another had lived in the affected units since January 2003. Some units had had multiple tenants over the seven years covered by the proposed settlement. The negotiations were covered by a strict confidentiality agreement, but one participant groused that MetLife had quibbled over a couple hundred thousands of dollars, delaying the announcement by several weeks.

The bondholders will pay $58.25 million toward the settlement, and MetLife, which had deregulated three-quarters of the 4,311 apartments and made a $3 billion profit on the sale, will pay the remaining $10.5 million.

In the immediate aftermath of the announcement, Garodnick was wary. He said he would withhold judgment as to the fairness of the agreement. "Tenants had overpaid for years as a result of illegal rent reregulation, and they have been waiting a long time for relief," he said. "I am concerned that a significant number of tenants may be subject to rent increases under this agreement."

He called on CWCapital to start meeting with the tenant association to discuss the conversion proposal.

Alexander Schmidt, the lead lawyer for the tenant-plaintiffs, provided a far more optimistic view of the settlement, saying that the agreement, combined with past rent rollbacks by Tishman Speyer, brought the total recover to $146.85 million. Just as important, he said, the settlement eliminated what CWCapital had described as an impediment to their sitting down with Garodnick and the tenant association to discuss a tenant-led purchase and condominium conversion.

Schmidt's firm, Wolf Haldenstein, and a second firm, Bernstein Liebhard—will receive 27.5 percent of the settlement, a total of $18.9 million.

CWCapital had expressed a willingness to discuss a tenant

conversion in 2010 when it was trying to fend off a takeover attempt by Ashner and Ackman. But two years later, the special servicer was in no hurry to sit down with the tenants or any other potential buyer. Andrew MacArthur from CWCapital said that it would take another year to sort through any potential legal challenges from disgruntled tenants. Besides, he said, the company would put the property up for sale only when it would enable bondholders to get maximum recovery.

"There's no change in our posture and we expect that will continue well into 2014," said Gregory Cross, the Venable lawyer who handled the case for CWCapital. "We have an appeal period and a lot of stuff to implement. We're not committing to any timeframe."

Since Tishman Speyer's default in 2010, the bondholders had made about $360 million in advances, for apartment renovations, legal fees, and other costs related to managing the property. Another $600 million in fees and penalties had also piled up. In other words, CWCapital would eventually be looking for about $4 billion so that bondholders "could be made whole."

In the meantime, the settlement also establishes the legal rents for the apartments under rent stabilization laws. A block of tenants in the affected apartments are facing the prospect of rent hikes. The "legal" rents for thousands of apartments are now above market, more than CWCapital could reasonably charge. Instead, management offers a lower, preferential rent.

The ultimate fate of Stuyvesant Town-Peter Cooper Village is not going to play out quickly, but there are clear trend lines that are working against its historic role as a middle-class bastion. This once stable and affordable refuge for firefighters, nurses, municipal workers and small business owners has increasingly become home to more well-heeled students and professionals who pay as much as $4,385 a month—or $52,620 a year—for a two-bedroom apartment with only one bathroom and no doorman.

At the time of the sale in 2006, less than 30 percent of the units were getting at or near market rents. Today, it is 48 percent, even if all those apartments are now regulated by rent stabilization laws. Every month, long-term residents vacate another 15 to 20 truly affordable apartments. The units are quickly renovated and re-rented at much higher rates.

Michael McKee, the long-time tenant activist, says that the reason this is happening in Stuyvesant Town-Peter Cooper Village and across the city is because of a "dramatic weakening of the rent laws" over the past 20 years. "A huge amount of damage has been done to affordability," he said.

As a result, the traditional middle-class families who live in Stuyvesant Town-Peter Cooper Village have become a shrinking minority, replaced by nomadic young professionals who have no intention of setting down roots.

Those tenants are unlikely to buy in to a tenant-led scheme whose goal is the preservation of Stuyvesant Town-Peter Cooper Village's legacy as a middle-class refuge.

In many respects the trend at the complexes reflects broader changes taking place in American society. The recession coupled with the housing bust has accelerated and cut deeply into the net wealth and income of the kind of families who typically lived in Peter Cooper Village or worked in Detroit's auto factories. "The middle class has shrunk in size, fallen backward in income and wealth, and shed some—by no means all—of its characteristic faith in the future" since 2000, according to a 2012 Pew Research Center study called "The Lost Decade of the Middle Class."

The Related Companies and other large real estate companies continue to argue that the complexes remain valuable as rental properties. To outbid them, Garodnick, Doyle and the other leaders of the tenants association will have the formidable, perhaps insurmountable, task of demonstrating that a significant block of tenants are ready, willing and able to purchase their units. A substantial number of tenants are also going to have to set aside their desire to cash in on any appreciation in favor of an ideal Stuyvesant Town-Peter Cooper Village that is forever home to the city's middle class. They would also need to obtain public subsidies and prove that it would be politically costly for CWCapital to pursue a sale to the highest bidder.

"We want to acquire the property and adhere to our principles of affordable housing with no changes to the configuration of the complexes," Doyle said shortly before stepping down as president of the tenants association. "We're trying to create an affordable condominium. It's not going to be where you buy an apartment and flip it for your own profit."

In the end, Tishman Speyer and BlackRock's ambitions for Stuyvesant Town-Peter Cooper Village blew up amid their hubris and greed. But the dynamic they set in motion is changing the historical, cultural and social significance of the complexes to New York City and the nation forever.

Acknowledgments

I have been locked on to Stuyvesant Town ever since I learned in August 2006 that Manhattan's largest complex was going up on the auction block. Like many New Yorkers, I knew *of* Stuyvesant Town. A friend and colleague, Terry Golway, had lived in that brickyard and described its special history and culture. Another friend, Dennis O'Neil, had even brought me over there to hear Black 47 in a bar on First Avenue. But I didn't *know* Stuyvesant Town. Nor did I realize that my first story for the *New York Times* in 2006 would lead to a string of stories that would extend for another six years.

When this project began, I thought I already knew all about the history of Stuyvesant Town, the intricacies of the sale and the subsequent collapse of the biggest deal in real estate history. Little did I know. Even after I completed the first draft, I continued to discover new and surprising information and anecdotes that left me wondering, "How did I miss that?"

I should start by thanking Brian Tart, the president and publisher of Dutton, who believed in this book and encouraged me all along the way. I also want to give a shout-out to the graphic artist who came up with the book jacket. Brilliant. Certainly a lot better than my idea.

I have a newfound admiration for the keepers of the records, letters, memos and photographs of the past—in short, the archivists, who often instantly put their hands on the perfect item in response to my endless queries. Douglas Di Carlo and his colleagues at the La Guardia and Wagner Archives at LaGuardia Community College dug up a favorite of mine: the transcript of La Guardia's announcement that Metropolitan would build Stuyvesant Town. The librarians at the New York Public Library were also quietly diligent on my behalf. Eric Wakin, the Lehman curator for American history in the Rare Book and Manuscript Library at Columbia University, was a big help early on. Daniel B. May, the company archivist at MetLife, was also helpful in guiding me through Metropolitan's voluminous files and photo library.

At the *New York Times*, Jeffrey P. Roth, a photo specialist, went above and beyond the call of duty in tracking down images at the *Times* and elsewhere.

John Crotty, a lifelong resident of Stuyvesant Town, served as a guide to the customs and folkways of Stuyvesant Town. He introduced me to one resident after another who shared their stories with me at Quigley's, a pub at First Avenue and Eighteenth Street. He also introduced me to the Stuyvesant Town Little League's annual spring parade. Maybe not so coincidentally, John was a city housing official in 2006 and played a role in the drama behind the sale of his beloved complex.

I also want to thank Lee Lorch, a math professor and a founder of the Town and Village Tenants Committee to End Discrimination in Stuyvesant Town, who plumbed his remarkable memory for me. He is an admirable man and his lifelong dedication to justice was rewarded with a reserved seat on the 1950s blacklist.

Karen Smith, a former judge and a serious student of city housing, generously shared memories of her parents' involvement in the tenants committee in the 1940s and 1950s and the involvement of the Hendrix family. She graciously provided me with some of the committee's original leaflets and pamphlets, many of which were written by her mother, Esther. Her father, Dave Smith, led a rent strike at Stuyvesant Town. He later became a tenant leader at Penn South, after MetLife refused to give his family a new lease at Stuyvesant Town.

Al Doyle also provided a small trove of artifacts, ranging from original MetLife maps and pamphlets about Stuyvesant Town to a 1967 Stuyvesant-Cooper telephone directory. Marie Beirne, coproducer of the Peter Cooper Village-Stuyvesant Town Oral History Project and an old friend, provided me many leads, helpful phone numbers and good-humored support, as did Annie, Richie, and Debbie.

Jerilyn Perine, executive director, and Harold Schultz, senior fellow, of the Citizens Housing and Planning Council, a nonpartisan research organization, shared their knowledge of housing, affordable and otherwise. They also unlocked the files of the organization, which played a critical role in the debate over the building of Stuyvesant Town and MetLife's racial policies, as well as the crisis in affordable housing during the recent real estate boom and its aftermath. Likewise, Benjamin Dolchin at the Association for Neighborhood and Housing Development was kind enough to share his wisdom and a chest of loan documents that shed light on what he vividly described as predatory lenders and their practices.

Sydney P. Freedberg, a talented reporter for the *Tampa Bay Times,* was very kind to share with me documents and insight relating to her own 2009 investigation into how the Florida Board of Administration, a state pension fund, bet $250 million in public money "on a huge Manhattan real estate deal and lost every penny of it."

I also want to thank Rob Speyer for sitting for hours of interview questioning knowing that there was no chance he would emerge as a hero in this story. We have known each other for more than twenty years, ever since he was a fact checker at the *New York Observer,* where I was a senior reporter. He certainly had more fortitude than Larry Fink or Michael Bloomberg, who both rebuffed my requests for an interview for the book.

John E. Zuccotti was a consistent source of encouragement, as was a certain banker who was not directly involved in the deal but was an endless spigot of key documents, names, and phone numbers. Thanks to Richie, Debbie, Jay, Joy, Ann, Cathy, Bruce, and Alan for their support.

Finally, I want to thank my editors at the *New York Times,* who encouraged the project and allowed me to take a four-month leave from the paper to complete the first draft of this manuscript.

To the tenants, real estate executives, brokers and bankers who shared their observations and then repeatedly asked, "Where's the book?," here it is.

Notes

Chapter 1: "Negroes and Whites Don't Mix"

1 Transcript, April 18, 1943, WNYC broadcast, La Guardia and Wagner Archives, LaGuardia Community College.
2 Ibid.
3 Metropolitan Life Insurance Press Release, April 18, 1943, company archives.
4 Transcript, April 18, 1943, WNYC broadcast, La Guardia and Wagner Archives, LaGuardia Community College.
5 La Guardia to Salmon, memo dated April 22, 1943, La Guardia and Wagner Archives, LaGuardia Community College.
6 "West Side Housing Project Will Bar Negro Tenants," *New York Post*, May 20, 1943.
7 "Frederick Ecker, Financier, 96, Dies," *New York Times*, March 21, 1964.
8 Ibid.
9 MetLife, "Underwriting America's Success: 125 Years of Metropolitan Life."
10 "Metropolitan Life Makes Housing Pay," *Fortune*, April 1946; Henry Reed, "The Investment Policy of the Metropolitan Life," *Task Magazine*, undated, Citizens Housing and Planning Council Archives; Simon Breines, "Stuyvesant Town," *Task Magazine*, undated, Citizens Housing and Planning Council Archives.
11 "120-Acre Housing Will Rise in Bronx as Private Project," *New York Times*, April 8, 1938.
12 "Metropolitan Life Makes Housing Pay," *Fortune*, April 1946.
13 Ibid.
14 Robert Moses, *Public Works: A Dangerous Trade* (McGraw-Hill, 1970), 432.

15 Dominic J. Capeci Jr., "Fiorello H. La Guardia and the Stuyvesant Town Controversy of 1943," *New-York Historical Society Quarterly*, October 1978.
16 Charles Abrams, "The Walls of Stuyvesant Town," *Nation*, March 24, 1945.
17 Joel Schwartz, *The New York Approach: Robert Moses, Urban Liberals, and Redevelopment of the Inner City* (Ohio State University Press, 1993), 103.
18 Arthur Simon, *Stuyvesant Town USA* (New York University Press, 1970), 36.
19 "Housing Plan Seen as a 'Walled City,'" *New York Times*, May 20, 1943.
20 "Stuyvesant Town Approved by Board," *New York Times*, June 4, 1943.
21 Ibid.
22 Simon, *Stuyvesant Town USA*, 37.
23 Robert Moses, letter to the editor, *New York Times*, June 3, 1943.
24 Robert Moses to Frank C. Moore, 1943.
25 "Stuyvesant Town Approved by Board," *New York Times*, June 4, 1943; "City Approves Metropolitan's Housing Plan," *New York Herald Tribune*, June 4, 1943.
26 "Topics of the Times," *New York Times*, June 5, 1943.
27 Walter White to Mayor La Guardia, June 16, 1943, Manuscripts and Archives Division, New York Public Library.
28 Ecker to La Guardia, July 26, 1943, La Guardia and Wagner Archives, LaGuardia Community College.
29 La Guardia to Ecker, July 31, 1943, Manuscripts and Archives Division, New York Public Library.
30 Ecker to La Guardia, August 1943, Manuscripts and Archives Division, New York Public Library.
31 "Memo Concerning Stuyvesant Town, Inc.," Office of the Mayor, August 9, 1943, La Guardia and Wagner Archives, LaGuardia Community College.
32 Ecker to La Guardia, August 16, 1943, La Guardia and Wagner Archives, LaGuardia Community College.
33 Moses to Samuel Seabury, September 3, 1943, Manuscripts and Archives Division, New York Public Library.
34 "Memorandum for Mr. Ecker," from Moses, Re: Pratt vs. LaGuardia, February 25, 1944, Manuscripts and Archives Division, New York Public Library.
35 Moses to Ecker, February 28, 1944, Manuscripts and Archives Division, New York Public Library.
36 La Guardia to Ecker, April 5, 1944, La Guardia and Wagner Archives.
37 "Housing Project to Rise in Harlem," *New York Times*, September 18, 1944.
38 Ibid.
39 Informal Meeting on Riverton Project, October 25, 1944, Citizens Housing and Planning Council Archives.
40 Ibid.

Chapter 2: Thirty-Six Million Bricks

1 Interview with author.
2 Rosamond G. Roberts, "3,000 Families Move to Make Way for Stuyvesant Town: A Story of Tenant Relocation Bureau," Metropolitan Life Archives.
3 "The Rehousing Needs of the Families of the Stuyvesant Town Site," June 14, 1945, Community Service Society.
4 "Race Housing Plea Quashed by Courts," *New York Times*, July 29, 1947.
5 "Stuyvesant Town Ban on Negroes Upheld, 4–3, by Court of Appeals," *New York Herald Tribune*, July 20, 1949.
6 Interview with author.
7 Interview with author.
8 Lorch and Smith, interviews with author.
9 Daniel B. English, file marked "confidential," memo concerning meeting sponsored by East Side Tenants Council, August 29, 1949, Metropolitan Life Archives.
10 "Protests Voiced on Faculty Action," *New York Times*, June 9, 1949.
11 "Teacher Fighting Bias in Housing Faces Loss of Second College Job," *New York Times*, April 10, 1950; "Professor's Ousting Hit," *New York Times*, June 7, 1950.
12 "Estimate Board Votes Anti-Bias Bill on Housing," *New York Herald Tribune*, March 2, 1951.
13 Simon, *Stuyvesant Town USA*, 95–100.
14 Interview with author.

Chapter 3: The Golden Age

1 Interview with author.
2 Interview with author.
3 "City Seen Stunted by Lack of Housing," *New York Times*, June 17, 1947; "No Apartments Finished in 1946," *New York Times*, December 14, 1946.
4 Interview with author.
5 1960 Census, courtesy Andrew A. Beveridge, sociology professor, Queens College.
6 Interview with author.
7 Mary Roche, "New Housing Suite Is Copied in Store," *New York Times*, June 9, 1947; Ann Pringle, "New Ideas Seen in Stuyvesant Town Dwelling," *New York Herald Tribune*, April 16, 1948.
8 Allan Keller, "Stuyvesant Town: Where Hard Heads Made Dream Come True," *New York World-Telegram*, June 11, 1948.
9 "New York: New Nightmares for Old?," *Time*, December 13, 1948.
10 Interview with author.
11 Interview with author.
12 Interview with author.

13 Interview with author.
14 Interview with author.
15 Interview with author.
16 Interview with author.
17 Interview with author.
18 Interview with author.
19 Interview with author.
20 Interview with author.
21 Interview with author.
22 Interview with author.
23 Lotte N. Doverman, letter to the editor, *New York Times*, May 29, 1952.
24 Metropolitan Life leaflets, company archives.
25 Blaine Littell, "Stuyvesant Town Rent Increase Rejected by City, Goes to Court," *New York Herald Tribune*, May 20, 1952.
26 "Court Authorizes Stuyvesant Town to Increase Rent by $2.55 a Room," *New York Times*, July 3, 1952.
27 Steven D. Roberts, "Spiraling Rents Worry Officials," *New York Times*, July 31, 1967.
28 Joseph P. Fried, "City Charges Bias at Three Projects," *New York Times*, May 28, 1968.
29 Purcell, interview with author.
30 Interview with author.
31 Interview with author.
32 "Metropolitan Denies S.T. Sale Rumor," *Town & Village*, October 19, 1972; "Met May Not Renew Stuy Town's Policy," *Town & Village*, August 16, 1973.
33 Wendy Schuman, "Stuyvesant Town, with Tax Reprieve Enters New Era," *New York Times*, June 16, 1974.
34 Interview with author.
35 Angela Taylor, "Stuyvesant Town: Residents Are Still Singing Its Praise," *New York Times*, May 9, 1973.
36 Interview with author.
37 "Met May Not Renew Stuy Town's Policy," *Town & Village*, August 16, 1973.
38 "Met's President Says ST Not For Sale—Yet," *Town & Village*, September 1973.
39 "Stuy Town-Cooper Are Up for Sale," *Town & Village*, December 1973.
40 Frank M. Leiher, letter to Stuyvesant Town residents, January 10, 1974, Metropolitan Life Archives.
41 Wendy Schuman, "Stuyvesant Town, with Tax Reprieve, Enters New Era," *New York Times*, June 16, 1974.
42 "Poll Results: 59.7% Vote for a Tax Abatement," *Town & Village*, April 11, 1974.
43 "1,000 Rally for Abatement," *Town & Village*, undated, 1974, Metropolitan Life Archives.

44 Wendy Schuman, "Stuyvesant Town, with Tax Reprieve, Enters New Era," *New York Times*, June 16, 1974.
45 Interview with author.
46 "Met Asked to Hike Number of Guards," *Town & Village*, February 3, 1972.
47 Randy Young, "The City's Safest Neighborhoods," *New York*, October 19, 1981.
48 Jonathan Mandell, "New York's Best Landlords," *New York Sunday News Magazine*, October 10, 1982.

Chapter 4: Who Would Drive the Last Dollar?

1 Interview with author.
2 Real Capital Analytics. Office and residential sales of properties and portfolios greater than $5 million.
3 Participant interviews with author.
4 Interview with author.
5 Interview with author.
6 Interview with author.
7 Interview with author.
8 Interview with author.
9 Interview with author.
10 Interview with author.
11 Interview with author.
12 Interview with author.
13 Alan S. Oser, "The Upscaling of Stuyvesant Town," *New York Times*, January 28, 2001.
14 Interview with author.
15 Interview with author.
16 Oser, "The Upscaling of Stuyvesant Town."
17 Bruce Lambert, "2 Big Projects Deregulating Vacant Units," *New York Times*, July 13, 2001.
18 Interview with author.
19 Interview with author.
20 Speyer, interview with author.
21 MetLife pamphlet.
22 Interview with author.
23 Interview with author.

Chapter 5: Let's Make a Deal

1 Interview with author, 2006.
2 Mike Sheridan, "Manhattan Transfer: BlackRock Realty Acquires Landmark New York City Apartments," *National Real Estate Investor*, April 2007.

3 Barclay, interview with author.
4 "Deals of the Year," *Real Estate Forum,* March 2006; Les Shaver, "2006 MFE 50: Private Choices; Apartment REITs say Goodbye to Wall Street in '05 in Search of Higher Valuations," *Multifamily Executive,* May 15, 2006.
5 Beal, interview with author.
6 Real Capital Analytics.
7 Maria Wood, "In the Acquisition Market, Anything Goes," Real Estate Forum, April 2006.
8 "Shifting Assets," Private Equity Real Estate, October 2006.
9 Ibid.
10 Terry Pristin, "Square Feet; Real Estate Deals to Flip Over," *New York Times,* August 30, 2006.
11 "Broadway Partner Purchases 10-Building Portfolio for $3.3 Billion," *Mortgage Banking,* February 1, 2007.
12 Charles V. Bagli, "Default Talk and Frayed Nerves," *New York Times,* August 25, 2008.
13 Ibid.
14 Charles V. Bagli, "They Bet the Rent, and Lost," *New York Times,* May 29, 2010.
15 Pristin, "Square Feet."
16 Charles V. Bagli, "In Harlem Buildings, Reminders of Easy Money and the Financial Crisis," *New York Times,* June 10, 2011.
17 "N.Y. Firm Closes on Purchase of CarrAmerica Portfolio," *New York Times,* January 8, 2007.
18 Tom Shachtman, *Skyscraper Dreams: The Great Real Estate Dynasties of New York* (Little, Brown, 1991).
19 James Traub, "The Anti-Trump," *New York Times Magazine,* December 20, 1998.
20 Charles V. Bagli, "Era Closes at Rockefeller Center with $1.85 Billion Deal on Sale," *New York Times,* December 22, 2000.
21 Interview with author.
22 Traub, "The Anti-Trump."
23 Ibid.
24 Interview with author.
25 Charles V. Bagli and Robin Pogrebin, "New York's Cultural Power Brokers: Mixing the Real Estate Business and Everyone's Pleasure," *New York Times,* June 2, 2004.
26 Interview with author.
27 Interview with author.
28 Interview with author.
29 Interview with author.
30 Interview with author.
31 Interview with author.
32 Interview with author.

33 Interview with author.
34 Quinn, interview with author.
35 Interview with author.
36 Interview with author.

Chapter 6: For Sale

1 Charles V. Bagli and Janny Scott, "Housing Complex of 110 Buildings for Sale in City," *New York Times,* August 30, 2006.
2 Interview with author.
3 Garodnick to Henrikson, September 1, 2006.
4 Interview with author.
5 Interview with author.
6 Interview with author.
7 Interview with author.
8 Alistair Barr, "MetLife Has Seen 'Terrific' Interest in NY Properties, CEO Says," MarketWatch from Dow Jones, September 18, 2006.
9 Interview with author.
10 Interview with author.
11 CB Richard Ellis, Peter Cooper Village-Stuyvesant Town sales book
12 Interview with author.
13 Interview with author.
14 Interview with author.
15 Interview with author.
16 Interview with author.
17 Charles V. Bagli, "Tenants' Bid Among a Dozen for Complexes," *New York Times,* October 6, 2006.
18 Interview with author.
19 Janny Scott, "Complications of a For Sale Sign," *New York Times,* August 31, 2006.
20 Interview with author.
21 Interview with author.
22 Interview with author.
23 Interview with author.
24 Interview with author.
25 Interview with author.

Chapter 7: "The More You Spend, the More We Can Lend Against It"

1 Interview with author.
2 Interview with author.
3 Interview with author.
4 Interview with author.
5 Interview with author.

6 Transcript.
7 Interview with author.
8 Interview with author.
9 Interview with author.
10 Interview with author.
11 Interview with author.
12 Interview with author.
13 Lindenbaum, interview with author.
14 Interview with author.
15 Interview with author.
16 Interviews with author by three different executives who attended the meeting, including Dickey.
17 Interview with author.
18 Interview with author.
19 Interview with author.
20 Interview with author.
21 Interview with author.

Chapter 8: What $5.4 Billion Gets You

1 Interview with author.
2 "Peter Cooper Village-Stuyvesant Town Partners L.P.; Confidential Private Placement Memorandum," 40.
3 Interview with author.
4 Robert Siegel, "From Gashouse to Stuyvesant to Luxe Condos," *All Things Considered,* National Public Radio, October 18, 2006.
5 Interview with author.
6 Interview with author.
7 Doyle and Speyer, interviews with author.
8 Interview with author.
9 MetLife 10-K filing for 2006, Securities and Exchange Commission, March 1, 2007.
10 Speyer and Kandarian, interviews with author.
11 Interview with author.
12 Interview with author.
13 Interview with author.
14 Charles V. Bagli, "$5.4 Billion Bid Wins Complexes in New York Deal," *New York Times,* October 18, 2006.
15 Damien Cave, "City Plans Middle-Income Project on Queens Waterfront," *New York Times,* October 20, 2006.
16 Ibid.
17 Charles V. Bagli, "Brooklyn Tract Goes on the Block; Home to 14,000," *New York Times,* December 1, 2006.
18 Ibid.
19 Charles V. Bagli, "Cuomo Says Investor's Past May Stop Starrett City Sale," *New York Times,* February 17, 2007.

20 Ibid.
21 Interview with author.
22 Wachovia and Merrill Lynch mortgage trust documents for Peter Cooper Village-Stuyvesant Town.
23 Term sheet for Stuyvesant Town-Peter Cooper Village investment, California Public Employees' Retirement System (CalPERS).
24 Interview with author.
25 "Rating Agency Presentation $3,000,000 First Mortgage on Peter Cooper Village/Stuyvesant Town Acquisition Financing," Wachovia Securities, Merrill Lynch, December 2006, 7.
26 Ibid.
27 Maha Khan Phillips, "Home Concerns from Abroad," *IPE Real Estate*, December 3, 2007.
28 Assembled from public sources and interviews with participants in the deal.
29 Erica Tay, "GIC Unit Seals $3b Property Deal with Tishman Speyer; Together, the Two Will Own Choice Real Estate in the US: 12 Buildings in 8 Cities," *Straits Times* (Singapore), December 3, 2004.
30 Interview with author.

Chapter 9: "What Do They Have Against Trees?"

1 "Peter Cooper Village-Stuyvesant Town Partners L.P.; Confidential Private Placement Memorandum," 2, 30.
2 Gabriel Sherman, "Clash of Utopias," *New York*, February 1, 2009.
3 "Rating Agency Presentation $3,000,000 First Mortgage on Peter Cooper Village/Stuyvesant Town Acquisition Financing," Wachovia Securities, Merrill Lynch, December 2006, 7.
4 Interview with author.
5 Charles V. Bagli, "After Sale, Rent Increases Give Some Sticker Shock," *New York Times*, January 16, 2007.
6 Ibid.
7 Housing documents provided by Horisk.
8 Bagli, "After Sale, Rent Increases Give Some Sticker Shock."
9 Nelson D. Schwartz and Vikas Bajaj, "Credit Time Bomb Ticked, but Few Heard," *New York Times*, August 19, 2007.
10 Ron Nixon, "Study Predicts Foreclosure for 1 in 5 Subprime Loans," *New York Times*, December 20, 2006.
11 Ibid.
12 Charles V. Bagli, "Suit Contests Rent Increases in Complexes MetLife Sold," *New York Times*, January 23, 2007.
13 Interview with author.
14 Interview with author.
15 Interview with author.
16 Interview with author.

17 Interview with author.
18 Terry Pristin, "Square Feet; A Warning on Risk in Commercial Mortgages," *New York Times,* May 2, 2007.
19 Mark Wellborn, "Stuy Town Is So Last Year Quinn, Speyers Make Nice," *New York Observer,* March 12, 2007.
20 Interview with author.
21 Interview with author.
22 Interview with author.
23 Interview with author.
24 Interview with author.
25 Interview with author.
26 Interview with author.
27 Interview with author.
28 Interview with author.
29 Tishman Speyer Properties.
30 Sherman, "Clash of Utopias."
31 Interview with author.
32 Author interviews with Tishman Speyer executives and lenders.
33 Charles V. Bagli, "At Eleventh Hour, Rivals Vie for Deal on West Side Railyards," *New York Times,* March 25, 2008.
34 Christine Haughney and Terry Pristin, "Wachovia's Big-City Splash Has a Sobering Aftermath," *New York Times,* January 23, 2008.
35 Interview with author.
36 Charles V. Bagli, "Deal to Build at Railyards on West Side Collapses," *New York Times,* May 9, 2008.
37 Interview with author.

Chapter 10: The Bubble Explodes

1 Interview with author.
2 Commercial Mortgage Alert, 2008.
3 Michael Barbaro, "As Bloomberg's Time Wanes, Titans Seek Mayor in His Mold," *New York Times,* July 7, 2008.
4 Charles V. Bagli, "Macklowes Sell G.M. Building for $2.9 Billion," *New York Times,* May 25, 2008.
5 Interview with author.
6 Interview with author.
7 Terry Pristin, "Risky Real Estate Deals Helped Doom Lehman," *New York Times,* September 17, 2008.
8 Mortgage documents and prospectus, Riverton Apartments, Ackman-Ziff Real Estate Group; *Wells Fargo v. RP Stellar Riverton,* New York State supreme court, 101491/2009; Charles V. Bagli, "Default Talk and Frayed Nerves," *New York Times,* August 25, 2008.
9 Interview with author.
10 Interview with author.

11 Interview with author.
12 Helen Kennedy, "You're the Villain, Pols Tell Fat Cat," *Daily News,* October 7, 2008.
13 Michael J. de la Merced, "Blackstone Group Reports $500 million 3rd-Quarter Loss," *New York Times,* November 7, 2008.
14 Standard & Poor's Stuyvesant Town release, September 26, 2008; Charles V. Bagli, "Failed Deals Replace Real Estate Boom," *New York Times,* October 1, 2008.
15 Interview with author.
16 Interview with author.
17 Interview with author.
18 Interview with author.
19 Seavey to Belkin, January 16, 1996; Martin J. Heistein of Belkin, Burden, Wenig & Goldman to Nathaniel Geller, Division of Housing and Community Renewal, June 22, 1995; Erik Strangeways of Division of Housing and Community Renewal to Heistein, September 28, 1995; Heistein to Marcia Hirsch, Division of Housing and Community Renewal, October 13, 1995; Geller to Heistein, October 19, 1995; Belkin to Geller, December 14, 1995.
20 Interview with author.
21 Interview with author.
22 J. Nardelli decision, *Roberts v. Tishman Speyer Props., LP,* March 5, 2009.
23 Transcript of SL Green, December 6, 2010.
24 Court filings in Roberts v. Tishman Speyer.

Chapter 11: How to Lose $3.6 Billion in Two Years

1 Monthly reports, Wachovia Bank Commercial Mortgage Trust Series 2007-C30 (Stuyvesant Town), Realpoint, a credit agency, 2009.
2 Interview with author.
3 Interview with author.
4 Charles V. Bagli, "With Rent Rollbacks and Refunds Looming, Landlords Fight Back," *New York Times,* March 15, 2009.
5 Interview with author.
6 Interview with author.
7 Interview with author.
8 Interview with author.
9 Interview with author.
10 Ann Segrest McCulloch, senior vice president, Fannie Mae, to Honorable Carolyn B. Maloney etc., November 12, 2009; Charles E. Haldeman Jr., chief executive officer, Freddie Mac, to Coalition of East Side Leaders etc., November 11, 2009.
11 Interview with author.
12 Interview with author.

Simon, Arthur. *Stuyvesant Town USA: Pattern for Two Americas.* New York University Press, 1970.
Sorkin, Andrew Ross. *Too Big to Fail,* Viking. 2009.
Zipp, Samuel. *Manhattan Projects: The Rise and Fall of Urban Renewal in Cold War New York.* Oxford University Press, 2010.

About the Author

Charles V. Bagli covers the intersection of politics and real estate. He has written about the sale of high-profile buildings, political contributions of the real estate industry, the battle to build a $2 billion stadium for the Jets, bid rigging in the construction industry, payoffs at the tax assessors office, and a Sutton Place co-op that turned public land into a private park. He has worked for the *New York Observer,* the *Daily Record* of Morristown, New Jersey, the *Tampa Tribune* and the *Brooklyn Phoenix.* He lives with his wife in New Jersey. They have two daughters.

SHADOW FLIGHTS

Other books by Curtis Peebles

Asteroids: A History Flying Without Wings
The Corona Project
High Frontiers
Dark Eagles
Watch the Skies!
The Moby Dick Project
Guardians
Battle for Space

SHADOW FLIGHTS

America's Secret Air War Against the Soviet Union

Curtis Peebles

★

PRESIDIO

Published by Presidio Press, Inc.
505 B San Marin Drive, Suite 160
Novato, CA 94945-1340

Library of Congress Cataloging-in-Publication Data

Peebles, Curtis.
Shadow flights : America's secret air war against the Soviet Union / Curtis Peebles.
p. cm.
Includes bibliographical references and index.
ISBN 0-89141-700-1
1. United States—Foreign relations—Soviet Union. 2. Soviet Union—Foreign relations—United States. 3. United States—Foreign relations—1945–1989. 4. United States—Military relations—Soviet Union. 5. Soviet Union—Military relations—United States. 6. Air warfare—History. 7. Espionage, American—Soviet Union—History. 8. Cold War. I. Title.

E183.8.S65 P44 2000
327'.73047—dc21

Printed in the United States of America

Contents

Acknowledgments

A special thanks to R. Cargill Hall, chief historian at the National Reconnaissance Office, for supplying most of the documents and photos used in this book. My thanks also go to the speakers at the U-2 seminar held in September 1998. Others who provided information and assistance include Hervey Stockman, Carmine Vito, Dino A. Brugioni, Donald E. Welzenbach, Chris Pocock, Keith Bryers, Peter W. Merlin, Robert J. Hanyok, C. B. Moore, Robert L. Burch, George Mathews, Paul M. Lovrencic, James A. Winker, Walter Levison, Leroy C. Stables, William S. Bissell, Dr. Raymond L. Puffer, Svein Tonning, R. W. Koch, Sue Henderson, Joel Carpenter, Joseph G. Majarowitz, Darryl Starks, the Center for the Study of Intelligence, the National Archives, the Dwight D. Eisenhower Library, the National Security Agency, the Edwards Air Force Base History Office, the NASA Dryden Flight Research Center Public Affairs Office, the National Security Archive, George Washington University, and the San Diego Aerospace Museum.

Introduction

At 10:04 A.M. Pacific standard time (PST) on December 20, 1996, the roar from the rocket engines of a Titan IV booster echoed across Vandenberg Air Force Base. The booster lifted off Satellite Launch Complex 4-East and climbed into the clear blue sky trailing a plume of white smoke and orange flame. A few seconds later, the wall of sound reached the press site. It was a loud, crackling noise that grew in volume and physical power until one's chest vibrated. The rocket climbed vertically, then turned south and headed toward polar orbit. The two solid-fuel boosters burned out, then fell away. Soon after, the first-stage engines shut down. The second stage then separated; its engine ignited and propelled the payload toward orbit. Within a few minutes, confirmation was received that the satellite was successfully placed into orbit.

Before the launch, each member of the small group of reporters was given a blue folder. Inside was a single-page press release stating that the payload aboard the rocket was "a satellite designed and built by the National Reconnaissance Office (NRO)." It continued: "This event is the first time the U.S. Government has acknowledged, in advance, the launch of a reconnaissance satellite." Also in the press kit was a small booklet explaining that "the NRO manages the research, development, acquisition and operation of U.S. spy satellites. . . . NRO-gathered intelligence is used to monitor arms control agreements, to support indications and warning requirements, and to help plan and conduct military operations." Some of the NRO's successes included providing accurate information on the Soviet Union's ICBM programs, exposing deception operations such as North Korea's attempts to mask a nuclear weapons facility, and detection of Iraqi violations of United Nations (UN) sanctions as the Iraqis massed troops along the Kuwaiti border.

But all of this did not spring into existence fully formed. The satellite and the NRO both trace their existence back fifty years.

In May 1945, as Nazi Germany surrendered to the Allies, another war was about to begin. The Union of Soviet Socialist Republics (USSR) now controlled occupation zones in the eastern half of Germany and part of Austria and was pressing for substantial reparations from those defeated nations. In Eastern Europe, the Soviets soon established effective control of Poland, Romania, Bulgaria, Czechoslovakia, and Hungary via coalition governments with communists in key positions. The amount of noncommunist participation varied in each country. Communist governments had also taken over in Yugoslavia and Albania.

Soviet dictator Josef Stalin was also attempting to extend his influence beyond these boundaries into Western Europe, the Near East, and Asia. In France and Italy, the local communist parties were part of coalition governments. Greek communists launched an uprising against the British-backed government. Stalin demanded the return of two districts in eastern Turkey that had been transferred from the USSR in 1921; he also demanded that Soviet bases be established in the Turkish Straits, which connected the Black Sea and the Mediterranean. The USSR was also trying to establish pro-Soviet separatist states in northern Iran. Finally, the USSR's brief war against Japan in August 1945 placed the Red Army in northern China and Korea. Stalin sought repeatedly to gain an occupation zone in Japan.

Within the USSR, Stalin sought to isolate the Soviet people from foreign ideas and contacts. The first sign of renewed repression came in early 1946, when a campaign was started to purify Soviet culture of Western or non-Soviet ideas. Stalin oversaw the demands for "socialist realism" in all forms of art; he closed down magazines and banned numerous artists, composers, and poets, many of whom were Jewish. He also considered efforts to gain more direct control of the foreign communist parties.

The uneasy wartime alliance began to break down under the pressures of conflicting policies and goals. An observer of communism and the USSR sensed the change in the air. His name was George Orwell, and in October 1945 he coined a phrase to describe this new postwar situation: "Cold War."

The Soviet actions were unacceptable to the United States and other Western nations. As part of this struggle, a secret air war was fought between the United States and the Soviet Union and its allies. For more

than a decade, U.S. and British pilots made covert overflights behind the iron curtain. They were the pathfinders who flew into the unknown, seeking information on Soviet military and industrial power and looking for any indications that the USSR might be preparing an attack on the West.

This is also the story of a small number of farsighted and courageous men: of a single individual who, in a 1946 speech, defined the role of aerial reconnaissance in the nuclear age; of the designer who created the aircraft—the U-2—that made that vision a reality; of the scientists and engineers who created the cameras and electronic equipment necessary for the missions; of the pilots who flew the tricky and demanding U-2 aircraft over the USSR; and of the president who understood the need, who approved the overflights, and who paid the political price when a U-2 was lost.

As this struggle began, the United States needed intelligence on all aspects of the USSR's military and industrial strengths and weaknesses. This posed difficulties for U.S. intelligence. It was disorganized and divided, with limited resources compared to those of the World War II era. The USSR, its opponent, was a huge land, a police state whose reach extended into every Soviet home and around the world.

The threat facing the United States had also been changed by technology. The A-bomb had altered the nature of warfare and the measure of a nation's military power. Just as once the number of battleships in a nation's navy was the yardstick by which its power was judged, now it was the possession of A-bombs. The United States had a monopoly on the A-bomb, but it was unknown what progress was being made by the USSR in developing its own nuclear capability. Even as relations between the United States and the USSR were breaking down, the first ideas about how to meet these emerging intelligence requirements were beginning to take shape.

Chapter 1
Early Covert Overflights

From Stettin in the Baltic to Trieste in the Adriatic, an Iron Curtain has descended across the continent.

—Winston S. Churchill, March 5, 1946

The beginnings of the early covert overflights of the USSR date to the period immediately following the end of World War II. Among many U.S. military leaders, there was a realization that the A-bomb had fundamentally changed the nature of warfare. These included the Army Air Forces (AAF) commander, General of the Army H. H. "Hap" Arnold. In November 1945, he warned Secretary of War Robert Patterson that in the future, U.S. leaders would require "continuous knowledge of potential enemies," including all aspects of their "political, social, industrial, scientific and military life," if the United States were to have advanced "warning of impending danger." General Arnold advised that this could not be acquired using traditional methods, such as air attachés. How this might be done, however, he did not say.

Richard S. Leghorn and the Birth of Cold War Reconnaissance

The first to articulate a vision of how the intelligence demands of this new postwar era might be met was Richard S. Leghorn. He had graduated from the Massachusetts Institute of Technology (MIT) in 1939 with a degree in physics and a reserve commission as an army second lieutenant. In late 1940, Leghorn accepted an active-duty assignment at the Aeronautical Photographic Laboratory at Wright Field. Arriving in March 1941, Leghorn began working with such optical scientists and engineers as James G. Baker, Amrom Katz, Richard Philbrick, and Duncan Macdonald. Leghorn remained at the Aeronautical Photographic Laboratory until late 1942, when he received orders to report for pilot training.

In April 1943, Leghorn was assigned as commander of the 30th Photographic Reconnaissance Squadron. He and the unit arrived in England in January 1944 and began flying missions over northern France, photographing German forces, transport networks, and communications facilities, in preparation for the D-day invasion. After the landings on June 6, 1944, Leghorn's unit flew in support of the U.S. First Army as it advanced through France, during the Battle of the Bulge at year's end, and finally for its drive into Germany during the spring of 1945.

In the fall of 1945, Leghorn, now a reserve lieutenant colonel, was offered the position of deputy commander of Task Unit 1.52, which was assigned to photograph the Crossroads A-bomb tests. Leghorn returned to active duty and was again working with his former colleagues from the Aeronautical Photographic Laboratory days. During the long trip from the staging base at Roswell Army Air Field to Kwajalein, Leghorn read a copy of the *United States Strategic Bombing Survey (Europe)*, which examined the results and lessons of the air campaign against Nazi Germany.

Leghorn was struck by the conclusions reached by the study's authors. They noted, for example, that "in the field of strategic intelligence, there was an important need for further and more accurate information, especially before and during the early phases of the war." The report's conclusions ended with a look to a dark future: "The combination of the atomic bomb with remote-control projectiles of ocean-spanning range stands as a possibility which is awesome and frightful to contemplate."

Leghorn continued to mull over the report, as well as his own experiences with photoreconnaissance, after reaching Kwajalein. The missions that he and his squadron had flown before D day had been able to monitor the activities of German forces, and Leghorn became convinced that high-altitude reconnaissance could detect in advance any threatening moves by a foreign power. Leghorn saw the power of the A-bomb during the Crossroads tests. Capital ships were sunk or were reduced to "radioactive ovens." Leghorn's ideas about what he now called "pre-D-day photography" were crystallized in conversations with the other optical scientists that lasted long into the evening.

What would be required was a whole new philosophy of reconnaissance that would look for warning indicators, force levels, and an enemy's capability to launch an attack rather than traditional targeting and damage assessment. In the nightly discussions in the makeshift officers' club, Leghorn argued that this was the only way to protect the United States against an atomic Pearl Harbor. One of the earliest converts to Leghorn's

ideas was Dr. Duncan Macdonald, who had been named head of the new Boston University Optical Research Laboratory (BUORL). It was also Macdonald who gave Leghorn the chance to present his ideas to an influential audience as keynote speaker at the December 13, 1946, dedication of BUORL.

Before representatives from the major film and camera companies, as well as senior AAF officers, Leghorn described his vision of pre-D-day photography. He began by saying that although efforts were under way to create an international political structure to ensure peace, "should an adequate political structure not be established, or if a suitable one is formed which should break down at any time in the future, then military intelligence becomes the most important guardian of our national security."

Having seen the Crossroads tests, Leghorn understood how the power of atomic weapons had changed the ways in which wars would be fought. He continued: "The nature of atomic warfare is such that once attacks are launched against us, it will be extremely difficult, if not impossible, to recover from them and counterattack successfully. Therefore, it obviously becomes essential that we have prior knowledge of the possibility of an attack, for defensive actions against it must be taken before it is launched. Military intelligence is the agency for providing this information, and our national security rests upon its effectiveness, next to a sound international political structure."

Leghorn then noted: "Aerial reconnaissance, as one of the principal information collecting agencies of military intelligence, can play an exceedingly important role in this period prior to the outbreak of hostilities. This situation is particularly true in the case of potential enemies of a totalitarian, police-state nature where the acquisition of information by the older means of military intelligence is more successfully blocked." These nations were unlikely to give permission for an overflight, however, and without this authorization such a flight "would be considered an act of military aggression." Leghorn found it unfortunate that although "peacetime spying is considered a normal function between nation-states, military aerial reconnaissance—which is simply another method of spying—is given more weight as an act of military aggression."

Because any peacetime overflights of police states would have to be done covertly, Leghorn added: "It is extraordinarily important that means of long-range aerial reconnaissance be devised which cannot be detected. . . . The accomplishment of this objective is not as technically

difficult as it might at first appear. Extremely long-range aircraft, capable of flying at very high altitudes, are currently on the drawing boards. . . . Effective means of camouflaging them at high altitudes against visual observations are well known. It is not inconceivable to think that means of preventing telltale reflections of other electro-magnetic wavelengths, particularly of radar frequency, can be developed. With such a tool at hand, information can be secured of a potential enemy's mining of radioactive materials and his plants—necessarily large—for the production of fissionable products, as well as a variety of other essential data. . . ."

In his one-hour speech, Leghorn outlined the future basis of Cold War reconnaissance: the regular monitoring of an adversary's military forces to detect any threat of attack. These missions were to be made as an act of national policy, by a specially designed, very-high-altitude aircraft able to escape detection. But his vision was ahead of its time.

As the Cold War was beginning, there was little time or money for Leghorn's vision of a new kind of reconnaissance. The most pressing intelligence requirement at the time was to assemble target lists for the Strategic Air Command (SAC). The primary source of this information was the Library of Congress. The Air Force Directorate of Intelligence realized that the library contained "open source material" on Soviet cities, industry, and terrain, and Project Treasure Island was begun in 1948 to make use of these resources. Western companies that had built industrial complexes in the USSR during the 1930s were another source of information on the precise locations, layout, and production capability for the original plants.

This open information was combined with captured Nazi intelligence reports and the archive of German aerial photos of the western USSR. Dubbed the "GX" photos, they provided coverage of Soviet cities, industrial areas, shipyards, and military bases. For Soviet Central Asia and Siberia, the air force and the Central Intelligence Agency (CIA) relied on maps prepared by Mil-Geo, the geographic section of the German Wehrmacht. These maps, which showed rail lines, cities, and natural features such as rivers, were the most accurate then available.

A window into postwar Soviet activities came from interviews of German ex–prisoners of war (POWs) who had been held in the USSR, then returned to occupied Germany. Captured German soldiers had been used as forced labor in the USSR for years after the end of the war. The POWs had worked on repairing damage and on new construction projects such as dams and factories. Despite Soviet security precautions,

some POWs were misassigned to work on sensitive projects. The Soviet atomic facilities, for example, were all built by forced labor. As the POWs were moved around the USSR to work on different projects, they picked up information on Soviet industry, power and communications, urban areas, military bases, and military activities such as missile and aircraft development. This material was combined to produce the Industrial Register, a listing of all known facilities in the Soviet Union.

The situation in Europe and the Far East was becoming increasingly dangerous during this period. The economic collapse of Western Europe in early 1947 caused the United States to propose the Marshall Plan. The Soviets saw this as posing the threat of a unified Western Europe and endangering what they saw as their fragile control of Eastern Europe. In early July 1947, the USSR rejected the Marshall Plan and, over the next few months, imposed one-party Stalinist police states on the nations of Eastern Europe. By the spring of 1948, the Soviets were deeply concerned about Western policy over occupied Germany. In an effort to prevent the Western powers from establishing a West German state, the Soviet cut off all road, rail, and canal traffic on June 23, 1948, between the Western occupation zones and the divided city of Berlin, which was deep inside the Soviet-controlled zone. In response to this Berlin Blockade, an airlift began into the city. With the threat of World War III now hanging over Berlin, the first U.S. covert overflights were begun.

Initial Postwar Covert Overflights

The U.S. Far East Air Forces (FEAF) was the first to undertake postwar covert overflights. They started in the spring of 1949, at the direction of the FEAF commander, in response to the Berlin Blockade. Two lieutenants with the 8th Tactical Reconnaissance Squadron stationed at Yokota, Japan, were selected to make "carefully controlled, highly classified reconnaissance flights" to monitor the Soviet Air Force in the Far East. One of the pilots was 1st Lt. Bryce Poe II. The RF-80As used for the flights were modified with special long-range tip tanks, which added weight and drag. The missions were initially flown against the Kurile Islands and Sakhalin, then later against the Soviet mainland.

Poe and the other pilot were instructed that if the coast was clear (literally), they would dart into Soviet airspace, cover their targets, then run for home. Poe made his first overflight on May 10, 1949, taking off from Misawa, Japan, and overflying the Kurile Islands. His first overflight of

the Soviet mainland was carried out on March 10, 1950, and covered Vladivostok.

Poe recalled later that "all Soviet target areas had many military airfields with numerous aircraft." A few of the airfields were covered with stored P-39s and P-63s—parked nose to tail—which had been supplied under Lend Lease during World War II. Poe noted, however, that there were still plenty of the later-model Soviet La-9 and La-11 fighters.

Although the RF-80As had the advantage of surprise, they were frequently chased by these Soviet fighters. Poe recalled: "Although piston-engined, the La-11 had more than enough performance to catch our attention when they attempted interception and we had clumsy extra long range tip tanks on our RF-80As." The results of the flights were sometimes unexpected. In one case, an intelligence source reported a missile standing vertically on a launch pad. An RF-80A mission was flown to photograph the suspected missile site. When the film was developed, the "missile" proved to be a large statue of Lenin.

These overflights were accomplished in the face of major technical and logistical shortcomings. The cameras, which were originally designed for use in piston-engine reconnaissance aircraft, could not provide the overlap needed for stereo images at the RF-80A's higher speeds. Spare parts were in short supply, so cannibalization of air and ground equipment was commonplace, as was "moonlight requisition" among units. Because of the shortages and disruptions, it was difficult to estimate unit readiness or make schedules. For military personnel and their families, strikes by U.S. longshoremen meant that food was in short supply. They had to get by on Australian bully beef, Japanese white fish, and "withered boxes of wartime rations."

During this period, U.S.-Soviet relations, as well as the political and military situation in Europe and the Far East, continued a downward spiral. The Soviet effort to force the West to accept its conditions for a settlement of German issues had failed. The Berlin Blockade was lifted on May 11, 1949, with the Soviet efforts ending in complete failure. The North Atlantic Treaty Organization (NATO) was established, and the Federal Republic of Germany was formally established. The Soviets responded by creating the German Democratic Republic in their occupation zone. The division of Berlin, of Germany, and of Europe itself was now formalized.

By this time, the military situation had also changed. On September 23, a brief statement was issued by the White House: "We have evidence

that within recent weeks an atomic explosion occurred in the USSR." The arms race was now joined. Fallout from the "Joe-1" test, which was collected by U.S. Air Force and British Royal Air Force (RAF) weather planes, indicated that the Soviet A-bomb was a copy of the U.S. design. The shock wave from the test was detected. This sonic data indicated that the test had taken place near Semipalatinsk, in Soviet Central Asia. On October 1, 1949, the People's Republic of China was proclaimed by Mao Tse-tung. Mainland China had fallen to the communists, and the remaining Nationalist Chinese forces under Chiang Kai-shek had fled to Taiwan. Stalin was now more confident of Soviet power and less fearful of any Western response to Soviet military actions. He decided to take action in Korea.

On June 25, 1950, the North Korean Army, backed by tanks provided by the USSR, attacked South Korea. The attack, which came as a complete surprise, drove the poorly equipped South Korean Army, as well as U.S. units sent from Japan, into a headlong retreat. Following the outbreak of the Korean War, U.S. reconnaissance pilots were warned to stay well clear of Soviet or Chinese airspace. Poe and the other pilot found themselves operating under two sets of rules. Coverage of the Yalu River bridges had to be flown at a right angle to the Chinese border. To photograph the Antung airfield, an RF-80A pilot had to raise the airplane's wing, fly at slow speed, and aim the camera at an oblique angle across the Chinese border.

In August 1950, Poe was recalled to Yokota for ten days to fly the special missions against Soviet airfields. He said that his orders "seemed diametrically opposed to the importance of what I was charged to do. I could go for broke on relatively benign non-combat intelligence gathering missions, but on combat sorties in war was forced to do things that reduced success and increased risk." Poe flew out of Misawa against targets in the Kuriles, Sakhalin, and the Vladivostok area. He recalled later: "With the exception of one new airfield, I found little change in either the numbers and types or dispersal of threat aircraft. Intercept attempts were a bit more aggressive, but not difficult to avoid." The missions completed, Poe returned to his squadron and "reverted to the more difficult efforts to stay legal and still get useful photographs."

The initial defeats suffered by the United States and South Korea sparked fears of a wider war. As a result, U.S. covert overflights were expanded. On July 28, 1950, a month after the North Korean attack began, the Joint Chiefs of Staff (JCS) sent a memo to Secretary of Defense Louis

Johnson requesting permission to cover areas of the Chinese coast. The memo noted: "It is considered vital that we obtain advance knowledge of Communist intentions to launch an amphibious assault against Taiwan. Existing sources of information do not ensure that we will obtain the advance knowledge required to defeat such an attack. . . . It is doubtful, however, that information of an imminent attack may be obtained except through photographic reconnaissance." The memo concluded: "It is recommended that the necessary political clearance be obtained and that the Joint Chiefs of Staff be authorized to direct the Commander in Chief, Far East, to conduct periodic photographic reconnaissance flights over the coastal areas of China south of the 32nd parallel of latitude . . ."

President Truman submitted the request to the National Security Council (NSC) for consideration. By August 2, representatives of the Defense and State Departments had reached agreement on the overflight proposal. Secretary of State Dean Acheson asked that the JCS require the Commander in Chief, Far East, to conduct the reconnaissance missions "to the maximum extent possible" outside Chinese territorial waters, even though Acheson said that he realized "that this limitation will be difficult to apply." He continued: "It is important, however, to avoid giving the authorities on the mainland any impression that the United States is making a serious attempt to penetrate the mainland by U.S. military aircraft."

To avoid this misimpression, Acheson recommended that the overflights be restricted to coastal areas and not include targets deep inland, "where there would be no doubt about a serious infringement." He noted that it would be "desirable" that the overflights be made "by fast single planes which, while authorized to defend themselves, would attempt to evade attack whenever possible." Reconnaissance by formations of aircraft over the mainland "would create most serious political problems" and subject the U.S. government "to charges which it would be exceedingly difficult to meet."

The NSC met to discuss the proposed missions on August 3, and its members gave their approval. The missions against China were flown within a matter of weeks. President Truman's August 25 intelligence briefing noted: "Aerial reconnaissance has not detected any significantly large concentrations of landing vessels in ports opposite Taiwan." This one sentence indicated that the Chinese were not planning a seaborne attack and showed the potential of covert aerial reconnaissance.

The air force was also looking toward future overflights. In the fall of 1950, Col. William A. Adams, director of intelligence at SAC headquarters, sent a draft study to Maj. Gen. C. P. Cabell, director of air force intelligence, on possible overflight routes of the USSR. The study envisioned four flights by RB-45C reconnaissance aircraft. The first three would be made from West Germany and cover the Murmansk area in the northwest USSR—which was the closest point to the U.S. East Coast—as well as the Leningrad-Moscow areas. The fourth overflight would take off from Japan and cover the Chukotski Peninsula, opposite Alaska.

A review of the study noted that there was no question about the need for the information, the availability of the means for undertaking the missions, or the value of the flights. The three missions out of West Germany would update the GX photos and provide new target information as well as data on Soviet air defenses. The fourth mission was considered even more valuable, because there was no existing coverage of this area. The review noted, however, that the missions could not be made without detection and risk of the loss of the aircraft and crew.

The review also noted the political problems that the flights would entail: "Because of the political implications that are bound to result, the Air Force is not in a position to authorize such missions without reference to the Secretaries of Defense and State. If our past experience with the Department of State on matters of this type still is a criterion, our chances of getting approval on this plan at this time are believed to be zero. It is therefore recommended that no action be taken on the attached proposal for RB-45 reconnaissance over the USSR until there is more favorable political thinking towards such proposals."

General Cabell made an informal reply to Colonel Adams's study on October 5, 1950: "My forecast is that it would not get by either the A.F. front office, the JCS, Defense, or State." Cabell did not feel like going on record as urging its accomplishment. He continued: "If SAC wants formally to request it anyhow, I would recommend against it, and unless SAC specifically requested otherwise, I would not forward it." He ended by noting: "All this is entirely aside from the desirability for SAC Recon to perfect the capability, [*sic*] looking forward to a day when it becomes either more essential or less objectionable."

Despite General Cabell's rejection of the RB-45 study, air force intelligence continued to look at ways of making deep overflights without the political entanglements that manned aircraft involved. This could be done using unmanned vehicles, but the problems then became techni-

cal and involved the time required to overcome them. The Snark cruise missile could be fitted with cameras and an inertial guidance system, but it would not be ready until 1953. A reconnaissance satellite was considered an even longer-term prospect. The only near-term possibility seemed to be camera-carrying balloons that could drift across the USSR, then be recovered once they reached friendly airspace.

Balloon reconnaissance had originally been considered in the fall of 1949 but was abandoned due to lack of funds and doubts about the idea's feasibility. In July 1950, however, C. B. Moore of General Mills had made four test flights of camera-carrying balloons; the flights had proven highly successful. By September, the concept gained the backing of both the Panel of Strategic Air Committee and the Air Force Scientific Advisory Board. They believed that the hardware was available, and only minor modifications were now required. The panels estimated that the reconnaissance balloons could be operational in late 1951.

On October 9, only four days after he had rejected the SAC study of RB-45C overflights of the USSR, General Cabell requested that Maj. Gen. Donald L. Putt, director of research and development, start a project to develop the necessary balloons and camera systems. The approval was given on November 6. The initial test program was given the code name Gopher, and fabrication of the test vehicles was given the highest possible national priority rating—1-A.

By late 1950, U.S. and South Korean forces had reversed the tide of war; they had destroyed the North Korean Army, driven north of the thirty-eighth parallel, which had been the dividing line, and were close to the Chinese border. Poe was once more ordered to Japan for special missions. The other pilot had been killed in action, and there was no one else who was cleared to know about the missions. Poe did all of the flight planning. He was told what information was needed, then he selected the targets and worked out the flight routes, the camera equipment used, and the altitudes and times. He flew the missions, going right down the Soviet runways. He found that, despite the continuing war in Korea, the only change was a further step-up in the reaction of Soviet air defenses. As a precaution, an F-80C fighter met the RF-80A about halfway home to "scrape off" any persistent La-11 that might try to follow the reconnaissance airplane. "The escort was never needed," Poe recalled, "but it was nice to have it appear on the horizon."

After the RF-80A landed, a warrant officer developed the film. Poe interpreted the photos, then hand-carried the photo materials to the three

other people authorized to know about the overflights: Gen. Douglas MacArthur, the FEAF commander, and his deputy for operations (DO). Until Poe briefed them, even they did not know what targets the special missions had covered. It was an extraordinary degree of responsibility for a junior officer. When Poe thanked the DO for giving him this latitude, the DO quoted Gen. George S. Patton: "Don't tell people what to do, tell them what you want done and let them amaze you with their ingenuity." As Poe's tour neared its end, his squadron commander began flying some of the USSR overflights. After Poe rotated home in January 1951, the commander and others continued the missions.

The RF-80A was short on both speed and range, but the more advanced RF-84F Thunderflash reconnaissance aircraft was still more than a year away from making its first test flight. To expand the covert overflights, a single F-84 Thunderjet was secretly modified. The aircraft, normally used for close air support in Korea, was fitted with a single K-39 camera and a 36-inch focal length lens. On February 11, 1951, the F-84 made an overflight of Vladivostok at 39,000 feet, without incident.

By this time, the political climate regarding a more extensive overflight effort had changed. Unwilling to accept U.S. forces on their doorstep, the Chinese had intervened in the Korean War. The massive attack had shattered the U.S. and South Korean forces, drove them south, and raised the possibility of an expanded war.

Spitfires over China

The atmosphere following the Chinese attack bordered on panic. The sudden collapse of U.S. and South Korean forces before the Chinese onslaught, combined with intelligence on the positions of Soviet forces in Eastern Europe, caused many U.S. political and military leaders to believe that a Soviet land attack in Western Europe and an air attack against the continental United States was a serious possibility.

President Truman responded by declaring a state of national emergency, reinstating wartime presidential powers, calling National Guard units to active service, and bringing Gen. Dwight D. Eisenhower out of retirement and naming him as Supreme Commander, Allied Forces in Europe, in charge of NATO forces. The JCS reviewed existing war plans and notified U.S. commanders of the possibility of global war. The JCS chairman, General of the Army Omar N. Bradley, directed that a study be made of how overflights might be used to detect preparations for an

attack by the Soviets. These would not be the quick dashes made previously but rather flights deep into the interior of the USSR.

In late December 1950, air force vice chief of staff Gen. Nathan Twining briefed President Truman on overflight plans. Two months before, daytime overflights of the USSR by manned aircraft were judged too risky. Now, the possibility of a nuclear attack on the United States made such flights critical. Twining recalled later that the JCS wanted to use the new B-47B, which was just entering production. The aircraft would be modified with a camera capsule in the bomb bay. Two overflight routes were proposed over the Soviet Far East: one to cover the northern shore of Siberia and the other taking the southern route, over the coastline nearer Japan. After reviewing the plans, Truman signed papers approving the two overflights.

On January 4, 1951, air force headquarters assigned the overflight mission to a B-47B scheduled for delivery in the spring of 1951. Although the original plan was for two aircraft, only the fourth-production B-47B was modified. Identified as Project WIRAC, the B-47B, serial number 49-2645, was to be delivered on April 25, 1951. In addition to the camera capsule, the B-47B was also fitted with special compass and autopilot equipment as well as a high-latitude directional gyro system. The pilot selected for the overflights was Col. Richard C. Neeley, a B-47 test pilot.

The British were also now involved with the U.S. overflight program. President Truman's remarks to a reporter on November 30 seemed to indicate that the United States was considering the use of A-bombs in Korea, at the discretion of Gen. Douglas MacArthur. In response, the British prime minister, Clement Attlee, flew to Washington, D.C. He arrived on December 4, having already been assured that Truman was not actively considering using nuclear weapons and that any decision would be in the president's hands, not MacArthur's. Prime Minister Attlee stressed that a limited war against China would leave Europe open to a Soviet attack.

It was at this time, or soon after, that Truman and Attlee secretly agreed to divide worldwide responsibility for overflight activities and to undertake a joint reconnaissance program against the western USSR. The United States would supply the RB-45Cs as well as train the RAF crews who would make the actual overflights. It is not known whether Truman gave further assurances about the use of nuclear weapons in Korea, but it is thought likely.

The Truman-Attlee agreement was soon put into effect, with great subtlety. Just before Christmas 1950, RAF flight lieutenant Edward C. Powles was told that he was to be the officer commanding the No. 81 (PR) Squadron Detachment at RAF Kai Tak, Hong Kong, which operated a pair of Spitfire PR Mk.19 photoreconnaissance aircraft. Two F-52 cameras were mounted in the Spitfire, each with a 36-inch lens.

For the first two weeks after Powles arrived, he had no orders or "terms of reference" as to what his duties were. Then in mid-January 1951, an RAF photointerpreter came into his office, laid a map on the desk, and asked if Powles could fly reconnaissance missions over several of the Chinese islands in the area. They discussed the scale of the photos needed, and Powles said he would be glad to oblige. He now knew what his job was. Powles wrote later: "No mention was made of authorization to carry out these flights over the Chinese islands, and I presumed that they had been approved by higher authority. Otherwise I would not be asked to do them, and there would be no need to have PR aircraft at Kai Tak."

Powles made his first overflight of China on January 16, 1951. By the end of the month, he had completed three more overflights, which were followed by another four in February. The flights had all been made at 30,000 feet. Powles was then asked if he could take low-level oblique photos of an airfield on the Chinese mainland. He made six such flights in March and April.

In mid-May, Powles was summoned to air headquarters on Hong Kong Island. There he was given a briefing by a Captain Black, chief of U.S. naval intelligence, a U.S. Navy admiral, two American civilians, and an RAF group captain. They asked Powles to cover Yulin Harbor, the dock areas, and the airfield on Hainan Island. They added that they had no authority to authorize Powles to make an overflight of China, and if he agreed he would be on his own. Under no circumstances was Powles to fly lower than 30,000 feet. If he did make the flight, Powles was told, a U.S. Navy destroyer would be positioned off Hainan Island and an RAF Sunderland flying boat would also be on hand.

Powles told the group that he would have to make careful plans for the mission, because it was close to the range limit of the Spitfire PR Mk.19, and he would have to calculate the number and length of the passes needed to cover the target area. He said he did not want to make a direct flight from Hong Kong to Yulin and back, and he wanted to change his call sign once clear of Hong Kong. The timing of the overflight would depend on the weather forecast, which was not reliable in the Hainan Is-

land area. Powles was told that the destroyer and the Sunderland would require twenty-four-hours' advance notice to be in position.

Powles worked out the basic flight plan, then discussed it with Captain Black. They agreed on the U.S. Navy call signs, procedures, and radio frequencies. All that was now required was good weather. On the morning of May 21, the forecast looked favorable, and Powles notified Captain Black that he would make the overflight the next morning.

At 10:00 A.M. on May 22, 1951, Powles took off from Kai Tak, then turned southeast for fifty miles. As he climbed to 30,000 feet, he could see two-tenths cloud cover to the west, over the Chinese mainland, but the sky was clear over the Pacific. He turned to the southwest and headed to a point fifty miles from Hainan Island, where the U.S. destroyer was waiting. As he flew, he could see clouds building up to the west, then a heavy layer of clouds at 20,000 feet over the northern end of Hainan Island. The weather was deteriorating.

Five minutes before reaching the next turning point, Powles, using an American accent and call sign, radioed for a weather check. This was the signal to the destroyer and Sunderland that he had reached the area and was about to head for the island. Powles then turned and flew forty miles to the west-northwest, where the Spitfire was to head north. Powles was about ten miles from Hainan Island when he saw a thin cloud deck over the coastline. The base of the clouds was at 28,000 feet. Although Powles knew that he should not, under any circumstances, fly as low as this, the weather and lighting conditions were otherwise good. He decided to make the overflight at 27,000 feet, just below the cloud base. The lower altitude would mean that three passes were needed rather than the two originally planned. Powles turned away from the island as he marked the three flight lines on his map and changed the interval setting on the camera control.

Powles then turned back toward Yulin Harbor, spotted the turning point to begin the first photo run, and rolled out on the proper heading. With the cameras turned on and the camera control lights flashing in the proper sequence, Powles kept watch for any Chinese aircraft, but he saw none. Reaching the end of the first flight track, Powles rolled the Spitfire on its port wing to check that he had covered the area, then set up for the second flight line. He lined up on a prominent landmark about one third of the way along his planned track. With the second flight line completed, Powles felt that he had completely covered the harbor and dock areas.

He spotted the airfield, which was farther from the harbor than he expected. He decided to make the last run directly across the field. About halfway through the third run, he saw sunlight glinting off two aircraft approaching from the north in a direct intercept course toward him. He completed the run, then pushed the prop pitch and throttle lever forward and climbed into the clouds. Now hidden from any Chinese aircraft, Powles turned off the cameras, leveled out, and turned toward a point about fifty miles from Hainan Island. When he reached the area, he radioed a fictional U.S. aircraft with weather data; this was the signal that he had completed the overflight and was heading back to Hong Kong. Both the destroyer and the Sunderland acknowledged the message.

Although Powles had completed the overflight, a greater challenge now presented itself. The original flight plan allowed a twenty-minute fuel reserve on arrival back at Hong Kong. Because of the time spent making the third photo run, even a direct route would leave only five minutes of fuel. As Powles flew back, he slowly descended to 22,000 feet, the Spitfire's best-range altitude. He soon entered the clouds that he had seen on the trip out and saw ice forming on the wing leading edges. He knew he did not have the fuel to climb above the icing, so he descended to 15,000 feet, cutting the fuel margin even thinner. The buildup of ice stopped, but it did not clear off until he left the clouds.

By the time Powles reached Hong Kong, he had less than five gallons of fuel left. He radioed the Kai Tak tower to ask for an emergency landing on runway 31. This was refused, because there were twelve- to seventeen-knot crosswinds. He was cleared to land on runway 07, which was short and whose buildings and mountains at its far end prevented an overrun. As Powles began his approach, the fuel gauge needle was bouncing on empty. He turned onto the runway heading and lowered the landing gear. Before he could extend the flaps, however, the engine quit for lack of fuel. The Spitfire touched down on the grass, then bounced onto the runway and came to a stop. Total flight time was three hours and thirty minutes.

By the end of 1951, Powles had completed sixty-three missions over China. He had been given only special briefings for four of the overflights. Each time, he was reminded that he had no authorization for the missions and was on his own. Most of the overflights were made at 30,000 feet. Whenever Powles saw aircraft or contrails heading toward his Spitfire, he would begin to climb and turn toward the coast. Once he was sure they were not trying to intercept him, he would return to the previous course.

Powles continued to make overflight missions in the spring of 1952, despite some disquieting rumors. He had heard that an air vice marshal newly assigned to Singapore had seen some of the photos of China and begun asking who had authorized the missions. Subsequent word on the grapevine was that he had convened a court of inquiry to identify the officer responsible.

Powles expected to be ordered to Singapore to face a possible court-martial. Every time his phone rang, he thought it would be the bad news. When he got a call in early June 1952 from air force chief marshal Bonham-Carter, he immediately thought that he was in trouble. But the caller said, "Congratulations! Her Majesty the Queen has graciously awarded you the Air Force Cross." Powles told him he must have the wrong number, but the caller assured Powles that he was being given the award. Powles was also invited to lunch and was sent on a week's leave with his wife and son.

Later in June, Powles went to Singapore to be congratulated by senior RAF and U.S. Navy officers and high-ranking civilians. Amid the praise heaped on him, he did not recall any of them mentioning the area he had photographed. Indeed, the Air Force Cross commendation read, "In addition to his photographic reconnaissance duties he has undertaken meteorological reconnaissance flights in weather unfit for photography and a number of special and, on occasion, long and arduous flights in connection with ferrying operations." The reconnaissance flights were mentioned almost in passing.

By September 1952, virtually all the important intelligence targets along the Chinese coast from about 400 miles southwest of Hong Kong to 160 miles to the northeast had been photographed. Also covered were specific areas up to 100 miles inside the mainland. Powles's final total was 107 reconnaissance missions. Additional overflights of the Chinese coastal islands were made by the other pilots attached to the unit. These were authorized by Powles, but he always preferred to make the long-range flights himself. These required that Powles fly the Spitfire beyond its design limits. Two overflights of Hainan Island ended with dead stick landings at Kai Tak, and on two other missions he did not have enough fuel to taxi back to the flight line after landing.

The RAF Special-Duty Flight: RB-45Cs over the USSR

Although Powles's overflights of China were the first fruits of the Truman-Attlee overflight agreement, these were only the start of a much larger effort. In early 1951, Gen. Hoyt S. Vandenberg, the air force chief

of staff, offered the loan of four RB-45Cs (three mission aircraft and one spare) to the RAF. They would make simultaneous night overflights of the western USSR to obtain radarscope photographs of target areas.

In the event of war, SAC and the RAF's Bomber Command would attack at night or in bad weather—using radar to navigate and hit their targets—to minimize losses. Aerial photos would be used to create "synthetic radar predictions" of how target areas would appear on the radarscopes. Because the GX photos were seven to eight years old, the predictions might not be valid. What was needed were up-to-date radarscope photos of long-range air force bases, industrial and military facilities, and Soviet cities.

Air chief marshal Sir Ralph Cochrane, the vice chief of air staff, was given operational responsibility for the overflights. In June 1951, he asked squadron leader H. B. "Micky" Martin, who had flown during World War II with the No. 617 Squadron (better known as the Dambusters), to set up and lead a "special duty flight." Martin was apparently told only that they would be doing some special flying. In turn, Martin saw Rex Sanders, then a flight lieutenant at the Air Ministry who was responsible for navigator training. Martin asked Sanders, who had flown thirty-three bombing missions over Europe in World War II, to recommend a good navigator. Sanders realized that whatever he would be doing, it would be interesting, so he said, "Well, I nominate myself." Martin accepted his offer.

On July 12, 1951, Martin and Sanders went to RAF Sculthorpe to look over the U.S. Air Force RB-45Cs that had been assigned to the base a few months before. These were brand-new aircraft. The first flight of an RB-45C had been made only in April 1950, and the first had been delivered to the air force in June 1950. In order for the aircraft and its reconnaissance capabilities to be tested under wartime conditions, three RB-45Cs were sent to Japan in late September 1950. With the introduction of MiG-15s two months later, the three RB-45Cs had to carry much of the reconnaissance burden, because the RB-29s were no longer able to operate with impunity.

One of the RB-45Cs was lost over North Korea on December 4, 1950. Aboard the aircraft were the pilot, Capt. Charles McDonough, two other crewmen, and Col. John R. Lovell, a senior air force intelligence officer. A cable sent on December 17, 1950, to Marshal Stepan Krasovsky, chief of the Soviet general staff, reported, "An aircraft shot down on 12-4-50 of the B-45 type fell in a region 70 km to the east of Antung. The aircraft

caught fire in the air and upon falling to the earth burned up completely. The crew bailed out on parachutes. The pilot Capt. Charles McDonough was taken prisoner. . . . The captive himself was burned and is in a critical condition." A follow-up cable the next day reported that Captain McDonough had died. None of the other crewmen returned.

By the spring of 1951, it was apparent that the RB-45C lacked the performance capability to compete with the MiG-15. On April 9, 1951, one of the RB-45Cs barely survived a series of fighter attacks. As a result, the FEAF required that RB-45Cs flying missions over northwestern Korea (better known as MiG Alley) have fighter escorts. At the same time, RB-45Cs were also making covert overflights of Manchuria and the Soviet Far East. In contrast to the rough handling the aircraft faced in North Korean skies, these overflights were without mishap.

One such RB-45C overflight, designated Project 51, was made on October 9, 1951. The plane took off from Yokota Air Base at 10:30 A.M. to cover the southern end of Sakhalin Island. The RB-45C flew at 18,000 feet and was able to cover all its targets using both the aircraft's cameras and the radarscope photography. No flak or fighters were encountered, and the aircraft landed without incident at Yokota at 2:40 P.M., after a flight of four hours and ten minutes.

Whereas the overflight operations went smoothly, the situation in northwestern Korea had deteriorated. On November 9, 1951, exactly a month after the Sakhalin Island overflight, another RB-45C was nearly shot down over MiG Alley. As a result, FEAF ordered a halt to daylight RB-45C flights over northwestern Korea.

The RB-45C overflights of mainland China, Sakhalin Island, the Kamchatka Peninsula, and Vladivostok, although few in number, eventually went to nighttime missions for radarscope photos. One of the two remaining RB-45Cs was painted all black so it would not be spotted by radar-guided searchlights. Threats to these overflights came from both sides. On two occasions, an RB-45C was detected by navy carriers operating off the west coast of Korea. It was identified as an Il-28, a Soviet-built jet bomber; U.S. Navy fighters chased after it, without success. The RB-45C overflights continued to be made until April 1953 without any further losses.

As these events were unfolding, the full complement for the RAF overflights was assembled. Each RB-45C required a crew of three: the pilot, copilot, and navigator. In addition to the nine crewmen, a doctor was assigned to the special-duty flight. They were not volunteers (other than

Sanders) but rather had been assigned to the unit. Because the crewmen would be flying the RB-45C at altitudes in excess of 40,000 feet, they underwent special medical exams. During the tests, squadron leader Martin was found to have a lung condition that prevented him from flying the mission. A new commander was needed.

In July 1951, squadron leader John Crampton was ordered by the commander in chief of Bomber Command to take charge of the special-duty flight and prepare to head for the United States for conversion training. Crampton had flown Whitley and Halifax bombers during World War II, then Meteor and Vampire jet fighters after the war. Crampton had a reputation for an upright manner and for the way he drove his Maserati.

Crampton and the other crewmen left RAF Sculthorpe aboard a C-97 Stratofreighter on August 3, 1951, heading for Barksdale Air Force Base. Here they spent ten days with a B-45 squadron to become familiar with the aircraft, then were flown to Langley Air Force Base, where they were introduced to the RB-45C version. On September 2, they went to Lockbourne Air Force Base, the home of the 91st Strategic Reconnaissance Squadron (SRS), and began a short but complete RB-45C conversion course. During the training, one of the RAF pilots made a heavy night landing, which damaged the RB-45C beyond repair. The pilot and other crewmen were not hurt, however.

As a result of the accident, the base commander, Crampton, and the RAF pilot were flown to SAC headquarters to be interviewed by Gen. Curtis LeMay. Crampton recalled later that General LeMay "did not like people who broke his aircraft, and left us in no doubt of the fact." General LeMay's anger was directed primarily at the RAF pilot, who was soon sent home. Crampton later learned that the pilot had a reputation at his previous unit of being a "pranger" (RAF slang for a pilot who made hard landings), and his assignment to the special-duty flight had been to get rid of him. His replacement was an RAF pilot who was already on an exchange tour with an air force B-45 squadron.

Although the members of the special-duty flight were undergoing training, senior RAF and U.S. Air Force officials were not sure of their future. A letter from air chief marshal Cochrane to Gen. Nathan L. Twining expressed concern that Attlee would not give his approval. Cochrane said, "We have not yet obtained the political agreement which will be necessary if the full project is to be undertaken." Within the air force, only Vandenberg, Twining, LeMay, and Gen. Thomas D. White knew about the plan. This caused some problems, however. Only thirty-three RB-45Cs

had been built, and they were in heavy demand. Major General Roger M. Ramey, air staff director of operations, objected to loaning the aircraft to the British. General Twining had to smooth things over. British participation in the joint overflight program was increasingly important, because the early American plans were running into trouble.

The B-47B selected for the Soviet Far East overflights had, by this time, been delivered and test flown. In late July 1951, Colonel Neeley and his crew flew to Eielson Air Force Base in Alaska. While the crew waited for clear weather over Siberia and the final authorization, Boeing technical representatives worked on the B-47B. On August 15, while the Boeing personnel were practicing a single-point refueling of the tanks over the airplane's bomb bay, a float valve stuck, causing the fuel to spill out an overflow vent and onto a wing. The fuel ran down onto a power cart and was ignited by an electrical spark. The B-47B burst into flames and was totally destroyed. Colonel Neeley was awakened from a nap in the barracks by a phone call saying that his airplane was burning on the ramp. He ran outside and saw a column of smoke and flames rising in the distance.

The charred wreckage of the airplane was still smoldering on the ramp when the orders to make the overflight finally arrived. Colonel Neeley responded by sending a message to SAC headquarters reporting the loss of the B-47B. The reply from SAC was quick in coming and to the point: "Fix responsibility and court-martial!" Because the airplane had been destroyed due to a mechanical failure, there was no court-martial. It would be another year, however, before another attempt could be made.

The ambitious plans for balloon reconnaissance had also run into problems. The relationship between the air force and General Mills was becoming increasingly strained. In a progress report, C. B. Moore wrote that the air force wished General Mills to deliver more than they thought they could, and more than they had proposed to undertake, and was planning military operations on that basis. Its requirements, Moore continued, had become unrealistic, such as the ability to launch the balloons in twenty-five-knot winds. Moore also complained that the air force did not trust General Mills's judgment and was providing no support. It had taken a month to get a statement of priority from the air force on Project Gopher, and a request for radio frequencies was still unanswered after nearly four months of letters, visits, and telephone calls. The original plan had envisioned operational flights being under way by the end of 1951. The reality was that little progress had been made on Project

Gopher. A conference was held by air force representatives to discuss the situation. In their view, the delay was due to several factors. The first was delivery of defective polyethylene to General Mills in early 1951. This caused the balloons to fail after launch, which required a prolonged investigation. Primary blame was put on the Air Research and Development Command (ARDC) for failing "to push vigorously and to coordinate properly the development of this project."

Development of Project Gopher on a crash basis still had air force support. A request was made for trial balloon flights across the United States, and it was suggested that work on the midair recovery system not be allowed to lag behind that of the vehicle itself. Despite the continued support, by late 1951 it was clear that balloon reconnaissance was not the near-term possibility that had been foreseen a year before.

At the same time, the fortunes of the special-duty flight were beginning to change. In October 1951, the British electorate gave a parliamentary majority to the Conservative Party, resulting in Winston S. Churchill becoming prime minister. As England's wartime leader, Churchill was deeply involved with intelligence operations. He understood their importance and their risks.

The special-duty flight completed the training by early December 1951 and was assigned to RAF Sculthorpe as an additional flight with the U.S. RB-45C squadron based there. The nine RAF crewmen, Crampton recalled, "raised eyebrows, which we were unable to lower." This eased when Lt. Col. Marion C. "Hak" Mixson was assigned as their liaison officer and handled many of the questions. The RAF crewmen still had no idea of what they were doing. Crampton recalled that he thought the project was to evaluate the air force "flying boom" refueling system against the RAF's probe and drogue. Flight sergeant Bob Anstee thought the project was an assessment of the RB-45C for possible RAF use. They were now flying practice missions over England and Western Europe with the RB-45Cs. These were both day and night missions, with mixed RAF and U.S. Air Force crews, and used cameras and the radarscopes.

Early in 1952, Crampton and Sanders were ordered to Bomber Command headquarters at High Wycombe for their briefing on the overflights. Crampton confessed to "some apprehension" when the charts were unrolled. The three separate routes went from Sculthorpe to the Baltic States, the Moscow area, and central southern USSR. The three missions would take off in rapid succession, then refuel from tankers to the north of Denmark. The RB-45Cs would climb at maximum contin-

uous power, at about Mach 0.68, to the highest altitude that the temperature of the night would permit. They would cover targets throughout the western USSR. Timing was critical, they were told, because ground signal intelligence (SIGINT) stations would be listening for the Soviet response to the deep penetrations, and there were certain diversionary exercises planned to keep the Soviets clear of the routes. If the RB-45Cs were attacked, the crews would use an emergency OMG (O My God) radio frequency to report the situation.

Crampton was relieved to finally know what they would be doing, but he was concerned about how to break the news to the other crewmen. His concerns were soon justified. Anstee was shocked when he learned of the mission. "Oh my God, what have they let us in for?" Anstee said. "Why? Why us? Why did we get lumbered with it?" One of the other pilots refused to fly the mission and returned to his original unit. Crampton was afraid that "he might well entertain his chums" with this "extraordinary tale," thus compromising the mission's security. As with the pilot who washed out of training, he was replaced with another RAF pilot who was flying an exchange tour with a B-45 squadron in the United States.

Before the deep overflights were made, a test mission was flown by Crampton's crew on the night of March 21, 1952. This was a half-hour flight through the Berlin corridor at high altitude, to determine the Soviet's reaction. The SIGINT ground stations monitored radio and radar activities, but nothing was noted, and final preparations were started for the overflights.

The three primary aircraft and the spare were to be stripped of all U.S. Air Force markings and repainted with RAF roundels. Crampton assumed that if one of the RB-45Cs was lost, the United States could point to the markings and disavow any knowledge of the airplane; the RAF could say that it did not have any RB-45Cs in service. Crampton's security worries were increased by the ploy, however. To get the airplanes ready in time, two had to be sent to nearby RAF West Raynham. A hangar was cleared out, and several mystified airmen used gallons of paint stripper to remove the markings.

The missions were scheduled for the night of April 17–18, 1952. As "cover," each of the three crews had to endure no less than three preflight briefings: the real one for the overflights, another for their Sculthorpe cover story, and a third that they would give to Soviet interrogators should they be shot down. If captured, the crews were to say that

they had been on a weather flight. For the southern route it was over the Black Sea; for the two northern routes it was the Gulf of Bothnia. Each plane had a complete set of false maps and plots to back up the cover story. Crampton later called the cover story "a gross professional insult to my crew and myself, but an acceptable one if dire need arose." Anstee wondered how well this would work if the Soviets found the equipment aboard the aircraft.

In late afternoon, the three RAF RB-45Cs took off and headed east toward their tankers. All three airplanes were successfully refueled, taking every pound that the tanks could carry. The three crews doused their airplanes' lights and, now hidden by the night, turned toward their courses over the USSR. Crampton had selected the longest route, across the southern USSR, for himself. As they flew along, everything was going well. Sanders reported that he was getting good radar plots, and he periodically requested course changes to the next target. The copilot, Sgt. Bill Lindsay, reported that the aircraft systems were working normally and, most important, they were on the right side of the fuel consumption curve. The middle route, near Moscow, was flown by the crew of flight lieutenant Gordon Cremer, flight sergeant Bob Anstee, and Sgt. Don Greenslade. The northern route, over the Baltic States, was flown by the crew of flight lieutenants Bill Blair and John Hill and flight sergeant Joe Acklam.

Crampton's most significant memory of the flight was the "apparent wilderness" over which they were flying. There were no lights on the ground or any signs of human habitation. Anstee recalled that there were many lights visible on the ground as they left Copenhagen after refueling, but over the USSR it was "one large black hole with odd lights here and there." This changed as they approached Moscow. Anstee continued: "When you do see lights they really stand out. . . . once we came up south of Moscow itself you could see all the lights. Moscow's a big place and lit up so you do get a good reference point from that."

Crampton and his crew continued their flight across the southern USSR. The RB-45C maintained a slow climb at about Mach 0.68 to 36,000 feet, following the briefed route and covering the targets. There was no visible reaction from Soviet air defenses. Crampton said later: "It was all so quiet as to be distinctly eerie." Finally, the three aircraft made the turn for home, covering more targets before reaching friendly airspace. Due to the length of their flight, Crampton had to refuel from a tanker a second time before flying back to Sculthorpe.

The only real problem with the overflights was the weather back in England. About twenty minutes before the first aircraft, flown by flight lieutenant Blair over the Baltic States, was due to arrive, clouds rolled in from the North Sea and the aircraft had to divert to RAF Marston. Crampton was able to land at Sculthorpe during a break in the fog, after ten hours and twenty minutes in the air. The third RB-45C, flown by flight lieutenant Cremer, had to make a precautionary landing in Copenhagen due to engine trouble caused by icing up of the fuel filters. The crew took off again and landed at Prestwick.

The Growth of Soviet Nuclear Forces

As these covert overflights were under way, Soviet nuclear forces were growing in capability and number. The Soviets had begun mass production of their Tu-4 bombers (NATO code name Bull) at the end of the 1940s. There were reverse engineered copies of U.S. B-29s, which had landed in the USSR after being damaged over Japan during World War II. As of mid-1951, the CIA estimated that the Soviets had six hundred to seven hundred Tu-4s in service. This number was expected to increase to roughly a thousand aircraft by mid-1952. These were divided between three long-range air armies, two of which were based in the western USSR and the other in the Soviet Far East.

As the Soviet Tu-4 force was increasing in size, so was the number of Soviet nuclear weapons they would carry. A CIA estimate of September 4, 1951, projected the Soviet stockpile to be forty-five atomic bombs in mid-1951; the estimate for mid-1952 was a hundred weapons. These A-bombs were expected to have a yield of thirty to seventy kilotons of TNT and weigh between two and five tons. Based on this, the CIA believed that the USSR already had the theoretical capability to inflict a damaging blow on the United States. According to military estimates, if the United States were hit with between ten and fifty Soviet A-bombs, the country would suffer up to a million casualties, and most major cities would be partially destroyed. Attacks on SAC bases and port facilities would reduce or delay a U.S. atomic counterattack and hamper the country's ability to supply its overseas forces.

The Soviets were also in the process of improving their nuclear weapons. In the fall of 1951, two years after the Joe-1 test, two more A-bombs were exploded. A report on the Joe-2 test to the acting Director of Central Intelligence (DCI), Allen W. Dulles, read: "An acoustic signal

of unusual intensity, apparently originating within the USSR, was picked up by stations of the Air Force's Atomic Energy Detection System on 24 September 1951. The source of the signal was tentatively located . . . about 100 miles south southeast of Semipalatinsk, USSR. . . . The time of origin of the signal was 1015Z [that is, Greenwich mean time, or GMT] 24 September (about 1515 local time). . . . Considering this signal as a possible atomic explosion, weather prognostications were made to determine when and where the air masses would come out beyond the border of the USSR." Weather aircraft were sent to pick up radioactive samples. The subsequent analysis of these samples indicated "fresh fission products of an age corresponding to 24 September, which could only have come from a high order atomic explosion."

The Joe-2 test was of an improved implosion bomb, with half the weight and twice the explosive yield of the copied U.S. A-bomb. It also used a new method of implosion, which reduced the diameter of the weapon. The result was a much more compact and aerodynamic weapon, compared to the egg-shaped casing of the first Soviet A-bomb. When debris from the Soviet test was analyzed, it indicated that the device "probably utilized only plutonium as the fissionable material (although a composite weapon cannot be excluded by the evidence). The efficiency of utilization of the plutonium was greater than that of the first explosion. . . . A study of the radioactive debris suggests that this explosion occurred on or slightly under the surface of the ground."

This was followed by Joe-3 on October 18, 1951. Analysis of its debris indicated that this design had a composite core in which "both plutonium and uranium 235 were used as fissionable materials. The efficiency of utilization of the plutonium in the explosion was determined to be about 35 percent, but that of the other component was not determined. The ratio of uranium 235 to plutonium was probably lower than that employed at present by the United States. If a model employing 7 kg of uranium 235 and 3.5 kg of plutonium is assumed, the yield would have been about 50 kilotons. This explosion did not occur close to the ground and the data are most consistent with an air burst." This was significant, because it showed that it was an operational type of weapon rather than a test device.

As with the first Soviet test, the fallout sampling revealed details about the designs of the two weapons and, from this, the state of Soviet nuclear technology. The 1951 Soviet tests showed that they had mastered more efficient bomb designs. Both of the tests produced yields of forty kilo-

tons (twice that of the first Soviet test). The Joe-3 test had, as the fallout data suggested, been an airburst. The weapon had been dropped from a Tu-4 and proved that the bomber could survive the shock wave from the explosion.

If the Soviets decided to launch an aerial attack on the United States, the Tu-4s would have to use forward bases located on the Chukotski Peninsula in the Soviet Far East, the Kola Peninsula in the northwest USSR, and the Baltic area. These were the closest Soviet-controlled areas to the United States. Even so, due to the limited range of the Tu-4 and the lack of an in-flight refueling capability in the Soviet Air Force, an attack on the United States would require one-way missions.

The CIA estimated that, from the Chukotski Peninsula, Tu-4s could reach targets within an arc between San Diego and Lake Superior. This would cover the atomic facilities at Hanford, Washington, the aircraft plants in Seattle and along the West Coast, and Pacific coast naval bases. Flying from the Kola Peninsula, Tu-4s could strike targets along an arc from Charlotte, North Carolina, to Portland, Oregon. Bombers taking off from the Baltic area could reach an arc from Charleston, South Carolina, to Bismark, North Dakota. From either area, New York, Chicago, Washington, D.C., the industrialized Northeast and Midwest, and the Atlantic seaboard ports would all be within reach.

In the spring of 1952, there was a troubling new development. The SIGINT data indicated that the Soviets had begun flying formations of Tu-4 bombers in and out of the forward bases in Siberia. The airfields were on Dickson Island in the Kara Sea, at Mya Schmidta on the Chukchi Sea, and at Provideniya on the Chukotski Peninsula. It was now clear that the airfields on the Chukotski Peninsula and other areas of Siberia could support Tu-4 operations. It was suspected by U.S. intelligence that the Soviets had upgraded the World War II airfields stretching across Siberia, originally built to support Lend-Lease aircraft shipments, to accommodate Tu-4 bombers. The movements of these Tu-4s into the forward bases could represent preparations for an attack on the United States.

Although the CIA believed that the skill level of the average Tu-4 crew was below that of the average U.S. bomber crew of World War II, they assumed that only the best crews would be used in an atomic attack on the United States. Moreover, the Soviets would have no problem assembling target folders from publicly available information, such as navigation maps, radio frequency lists, and aerial photos of cities and factories. The

targets themselves would be easily spotted using the bombing radar aboard the airplanes.

In the face of a Soviet attack, U.S. air defenses posed only a minimal threat to the bombers. United States radar coverage was spotty against high-altitude aircraft, and it had no radar able to detect low-flying bombers. They would have to be spotted visually, by Ground Observer Corps (GOC) volunteers. The GOC began a twenty-four-hour, year-round alert, called Operation Skywatch, on July 14, 1952. Despite the improved warning, the makeshift collection of piston-engine fighters, jet day fighters, and a limited number of problem-plagued all-weather interceptors would be hard pressed to deal with the obsolescent Tu-4s. The threat of a Soviet attack on the United States had now become an operational reality. To meet the danger, it was necessary to verify the status of Soviet air bases in Siberia. This would require a deep overflight.

Project 52 AFR-18

Following the detection of the Tu-4 movement to the forward bases in the spring of 1952, Defense Department and CIA officials again requested permission from President Truman to make deep overflights of Siberia. The proposal had been in abeyance following the loss of the original modified B-47B in the August 1951 ground accident. In the meantime, however, a more extensive program of shallow overflights had been started. This was a joint navy–air force effort, directed by the JCS, which was targeted against radar sites and airfields in eastern Siberia. The plans were closely held: In Alaska, only the two aircrews, the admiral commanding Fleet Air Alaska, the general in charge of the Alaska Air Command, and their deputies for intelligence knew of the overflights.

These shallow overflights teamed a navy P2V–3W Neptune, which had been fitted with experimental SIGINT equipment in its nose, and an air force RB-50 photoreconnaissance aircraft. The Neptune would identify, locate, and hone in on radar and radio signals across a wide range of frequencies. Once the installations were located, the RB-50 would photograph the radar sites and airfields. The P2V–3W was piloted by Cmdr. James H. Todd; Lt. (jg) Richard A. Koch was the copilot for the overflights. The modifications to the P2V–3W were completed early in 1952, and in March it was flying test missions out of Kodiak Island against the radar of the Alaska Air Command. After these flights were completed successfully, the pair of aircraft was ready to begin overflights.

The first joint overflight was made on April 2, 1952. The two aircraft maintained strict radio silence, even during takeoffs and landings. The Neptune normally took off from Kodiak or Shemya in the Aleutian Islands. The overflights were made during daylight, with the P2V–3W flying at 15,000 feet. Its crew had to wear oxygen masks, because the P2V–3W was not pressurized. The RB-50, which was pressurized, flew behind and above the Neptune. (The two aircraft had to coordinate their actions without radio transmissions.) The routes were fifteen to twenty miles inland from the Soviet coast. The joint overflights continued through the spring of 1952. Twice the Neptune was intercepted by Soviet MiG-15s. One of the interceptions was made over the Bering Straits, close to St. Lawrence Island. The other occurred over Soviet territory. The MiG-15s scrambled from a snow-covered runway, then caught up with the slow-flying navy airplane. Both times, no hostile action was taken; the MiG-15 pilots simply flew alongside the P2V–3W, identified the aircraft, and took photos of the intruder.

The recovery base used at the end of an overflight varied according to the route. For one overflight, the Neptune's final destination was Ladd Air Force Base in Alaska. The P2V–3W came in for its landing late one night without radioing the tower. The Neptune had been detected on radar, and F-94s had taken off to intercept the unidentified airplane. Its arrival was unexpected, and the reception was hostile. As soon as the Neptune stopped, it was surrounded by gun-toting air police. They forced the exhausted navy crewmen to throw their dog tags onto the tarmac. The crew members remained aboard the airplane, under guard, for several hours, until they were cleared by higher authorities.

The final joint overflight was made on June 16, 1952. In all, nine missions were flown; the two airplanes had covered areas from the Kamchatka Peninsula, through the Bering Straits, and north to Wrangel Island, off the northern Siberian coast. Soon after these joint shallow overflights were completed, preparations began for an overflight program to penetrate deep into the heartland of Siberia. It was given the designation Project 52 AFR-18.

In June 1952, air force headquarters sent a directive letter to SAC's Reconnaissance Division, outlining the general mission plan and the rules that were to be followed for the overflights. There were to be two overflights: a "northern run," to cover targets west of the Chukotski Peninsula, and a "southern run," over the Kamchatka Peninsula and eastern Siberia. Air force headquarters also directed that no target could be

overflown twice. Added input came from General Ramey, who recommended that the two B-47Bs making the overflights penetrate the Soviet coastline together, then fan out to fly their individual routes. This was considered to be a directive by General Ramey and would be followed in the flight planning.

As Maj. Gen. Frank A. Armstrong, commander of the Sixth Air Division, based at MacDill Air Force Base in Florida, and a limited number of staff personnel prepared the flight plan, a few changes were made. First, they proposed that Priority Target Number 1, Provideniya on the Chukotski Peninsula, be overflown by both missions rather than only once, as in the air force headquarters directive letter. The other was that the two proposed routes not have a common penetration point. Such a flight plan would result in a lower altitude at the penetration point and a slightly longer mission, and the routes would be less favorable with respect to Soviet air defenses.

By late July the two routes had been finalized. The northern run went from Ambarchik on the East Siberian Sea to Provideniya on the Chukotski Peninsula. The southern run went from Provideniya, then turned southwest past Anadyr to Magadan, then back east over the Kamchatka Peninsula. Due to the poor weather in August over Siberia, the flight planners recommended to General Ramey that the missions be scheduled for September. The available target information was also assembled for study by the crews. A report noted: "These materials are extremely poor since little information concerning the target area is available."

As the overflight routes were being planned, the aircraft were being prepared. On July 5, 1952, air force headquarters ordered SAC to modify two B-47Bs for special reconnaissance missions over "unfriendly areas" should approval be given. The primary modifications required for the overflights were the addition of a tail turret, which mounted a pair of .50-caliber machine guns, and a bomb bay camera pod.

The pilot selected to lead the overflights was Col. Donald E. Hillman, the deputy commander of the 306th Bomb Wing, which was the first and, at the time, the only wing to operate the B-47B. In late July or early August, Colonel Hillman was asked by General Armstrong to accompany him to SAC headquarters at Offutt Air Force Base. General Armstrong did not provide any details as to why. After arriving at Offutt, they were personally briefed by Gen. Curtis E. LeMay, who described the reports of Soviet airfield construction, said that it had been judged necessary to photograph the airfields in order to verify the reports, and told Hillman that he had been chosen to lead the mission over Soviet territory.

Once Hillman returned to MacDill, he began detailed flight planning. This was done in the strictest secrecy, behind Hillman's locked office door. Air force intelligence advised him that once the B-47s were detected, they could expect to meet resistance from a MiG-15 regiment headquartered at Provideniya, which was the target for both overflights, as well as fire from antiaircraft guns. Because this was a photographic mission, the B-47s would have to fly in daylight and clear weather. The men would have to rely on surprise, the airplanes' speed and altitude, evasive routing, the electronic countermeasures aboard the bombers, and, as a last resort, the B-47B's unreliable tail turret.

The two crews selected for the overflights also began flying practice missions on the newly modified B-47Bs. All the men were hand-picked and considered the best available. Flying with Colonel Hillman were Majors Lester E. "Ed" Gunter (copilot) and Edward A. "Shakey" Timmins (navigator). The crew of the other airplane was Col. Patrick D. Fleming (pilot) and Majors Lloyd F. "Shorty" Fields (copilot) and William J. "Red" Reilly (navigator). Theirs were the only missions being flown at MacDill Air Force Base; a series of fatal B-47 accidents had resulted in the aircraft being grounded. The priority of the overflights was such that the training flights continued despite the grounding order.

At 11:00 A.M. on August 12, Secretary of Defense Robert A. Lovett met with President Truman to discuss the overflights. Lovett gave the president memoranda, target justifications, and flight maps from JCS chairman Gen. Omar N. Bradley and DCI Walter Bedell Smith. Truman studied the documents and maps, then gave his approval for the northern run but asked that "special consideration" be given to eliminating Priority Target Number 11. This would reduce the penetration depth of the northern run by some 275 miles and keep the route nearer to the coast.

As for the southern run, President Truman expressed concern over the length of the flight and the depth of its penetration. He was particularly apprehensive over the fact that the egress route was virtually parallel to the ingress route. Truman called it "running the gauntlet" and turned down the mission. He suggested that the JCS might want to consider some alternative that would not have the aircraft over the USSR for such a prolonged period.

The president emphasized that his approval of the northern run was subject to discussion with and concurrence of officials of the State Department. If there was a disagreement, President Truman added, he was prepared to hear both sides. As for the southern run, he said that he was willing to reconsider the matter "if some less provocative and safer pro-

posal can be made." Truman's only other concern was that the loss of a B-47 to the Soviets would compromise the air force's latest equipment. He wanted to make sure that the JCS "had considered this aspect as an added element of risk."

Three days later, General Ramey notified General LeMay by letter that President Truman had approved Project 52 AFR-18 but had authorized only the northern run; Priority Target Number 11 would be deleted from the flight. The letter continued: "Coverage of the Northern Route will be limited to a single flight with only one pass over each prescribed target. An abort after penetration will terminate this approval." Truman's concern about the loss of a B-47 was also mentioned. General Ramey wrote: "In event of crash or forced landing in unfriendly territory the aircraft will be destroyed to the greatest extent practicable."

With Truman's approval, Project 52 AFR-18 moved forward toward a September overflight date. The reality that Colonel Hillman and his crew would soon be flying deep into Siberia, and what might happen to them, weighed on General Armstrong's mind. He would be the one to decide when the mission would be flown based on the weather forecast. A few days before the two crews were to depart on a "training mission" to Alaska, their families attended a MacDill Officers' Club social. General Armstrong took Hillman's wife aside and told her, "I feel like I'm sending Don on a mission equivalent to sending Christ to Calvary." Hillman later noted that however much this might have eased Armstrong's conscience, "they certainly generated wifely concerns on the home front, and there was little I could do or say to allay them."

Finally, on Sunday, September 21, 1952, the two B-47Bs and their KC-97 tankers left MacDill on the first leg of the trip to Siberia. Their initial destination was Rapid City Air Force Base, where they would spend a six-day layover. During this time, the aircraft made several additional local training flights. It was also here that Project 52 AFR-18, like its predecessor the year before, almost came to a fiery end.

The B-47B was brand new and attracted a lot of attention at the base. One of those curious about the aircraft was Brig. Gen. Richard E. Ellsworth, the wing commander at Rapid City. General Ellsworth asked if he could make a flight in the B-47, and Colonel Hillman agreed. With General Ellsworth in the copilot's seat, the crew ran through the preflight checklist, and the B-47B began its takeoff roll. As the airplane's speed increased, Hillman saw to his horror that the flaps were still fully retracted. In the confusion of the mixed crew, this item had been missed.

The airplane was going too fast and was too far down the runway for a ground abort. Without the flaps, however, the B-47 could not reach flying speed, would roll off the end of the runway at two hundred knots, and explode in a fireball.

Colonel Hillman pulled down on the flap handle and watched as the indicator showed the flaps very slowly beginning to lower. It was not until nearly the end of the runway that the B-47 reached flying speed. Hillman later noted: "I was looking at grass" when the airplane finally lifted off. Project 52 AFR-18 had been saved for another day. Hillman never forgot how close a shave it had been.

On Saturday, September 27, one of the KC-97 tankers took off for Eielson Air Force Base in Alaska. The tanker was followed on September 28 by the two B-47Bs, and by the remaining KC-97 on Monday, September 29. All the aircraft arrived at Eielson without incident. It was only then that the other B-47 crew members were finally told that this was most definitely not a routine training flight.

The controlling factor for the overflight was now the weather. Despite the earlier predictions that it would be clear over Siberia during September, for a full two weeks conditions remained too poor for the overflight to be made. The crews continued to study the overflight route and flight plan. Finally, the forecast looked good, and on the evening of October 14, General Armstrong told the crews that they would go the next morning.

The First B-47 Overflight of the USSR

Just after sunrise on October 15, 1952, the two KC-97 tankers took off from Eielson, setting Project 52 AFR-18 in motion. An hour later, Hillman and Fleming also took off in their separate B-47Bs. They rendezvoused with the KC-97s near Point Barrow, Alaska, and took on full loads of fuel. If Hillman's B-47 had suffered a problem at this point, Fleming would have made the overflight. Because both aircraft were flying normally, the mission continued as briefed.

The two B-47s left the tankers behind and flew west until they reached Wrangel Island, about a hundred miles north of the Siberian coast. Fleming's B-47 photographed and mapped the island, then headed east to the communications relay point off the coast of Alaska. Fleming began flying a racetrack pattern, to await any messages from Hillman's B-47.

Hillman continued southwest, toward the Siberian coastline. As he drew closer to the coast, he turned the B-47 south for a point on the coast

between Stanovaya and Ambarchik. The aircraft made landfall at about noon and continued to fly south. The crew turned on the bomb bay cameras; they would be left running throughout the overflight to prevent them from freezing up, which could happen if they were turned on and off. The weather had, to this point, been good. Soon after the aircraft crossed the coastline, however, the B-47's crew saw scattered two-tenths cloud cover and some haze, which partially obscured the ground. The B-47 then turned east, back toward Alaska. The flight planners had hoped that Soviet radar operators would think that the B-47 was a friendly, if unknown, aircraft flying in from the western USSR.

The B-47 covered the first two of its five targets, taking photographs and radarscope images. By this time, the B-47 had burned off much of the fuel aboard, and it was able to fly above 40,000 feet and reach about 480 knots true airspeed, well over the B-47B's normal cruising speed. As the aircraft headed toward the third target, its warning receivers began picking up Soviet radar signals; the B-47 was being tracked. Hillman alerted Gunter, sitting behind him in the copilot's seat, to be ready for the MiG-15s known to be stationed in the area. Gunter turned his seat around and manned the tail turret controls.

A few minutes later, Gunter reported over the intercom that he had Soviet fighters in sight. The MiG-15s were below and behind the B-47, trying to catch up with the fast-flying bomber. With their airplane now identified as hostile, Hillman broke radio silence. He reported to Fleming their location and situation; if they were shot down, the United States would know what had happened to them. Gunter continued to watch the MiG-15s, but they had scrambled too late and were unable to intercept the B-47. Hillman and the rest of the crew were still worried. The speed, altitude, and course of their airplane were now known to Soviet air defenses, and other flights of MiG-15s might already be positioning themselves to attack the B-47.

The B-47 continued on the planned overflight route, making periodic course changes to cover the three remaining targets. Despite their earlier concerns, the crew did not see any additional MiG-15s. Hillman later suspected that this was due to their repeated course changes, or perhaps because the Soviets did not have large numbers of interceptors stationed in that area. The B-47 covered Egvekinot, then flew along the coast and reached Provideniya, the MiG regimental headquarters. This completed the overflight, and the cameras were turned off. The airplane headed out of Soviet airspace toward the Seward Peninsula of Alaska. Hillman

flew directly toward Eielson Air Force Base, landing well after dark. The flight had lasted seven and three-quarter hours and covered 3,500 miles. Of this, some 800 miles had been over the USSR. A few minutes after Hillman's airplane landed, Fleming's backup B-47 touched down.

Ground crews immediately unloaded the camera magazines, each containing about three hundred feet of nine-inch film, and sent them to the base darkroom. The film was developed, then duplicated before it was flown to Washington, D.C., for analysis. General Armstrong was pleased by how the mission had turned out.

The Soviet response to the overflight was also quick in coming. On the morning of October 16, Hillman was told by intelligence officers that intercepted messages indicated the Soviet regional commander had been sacked and a second MiG regiment was to be moved into the area. A few hours later, Hillman and his crew again boarded their B-47B and made a nonstop flight from Eielson Air Force Base back to MacDill.

Six months later, in April 1953, Colonel Hillman was reassigned to SAC headquarters. A few days after his arrival, he was ordered to report to General LeMay's office. When he entered, General LeMay stood up and closed the door. Without saying a word, he pinned a Distinguished Flying Cross (DFC) on Hillman's blouse. When he saw the puzzled look on Hillman's face, LeMay gave him a slight and rare smile. "It's secret," he said. The two other members of Hillman's crew, as well as Colonel Fleming and his crew, also received DFCs. The award citations said only that they were for "extraordinary achievement while participating in aerial flight."

The B-47B overflight had consequences far beyond the intelligence it had returned. The mission had established the precedent for subsequent overflight operations. The president of the United States, acting on the advice of the JCS, the DCI, and the secretaries of defense and state, had authorized a covert deep overflight of a hostile power. The president's decision to approve or disapprove the mission was on a case-by-case basis, as a result of his assessment of the risks versus the importance of the flight to the national security of the United States.

Just as important was the reason for the overflight. The B-47 was sent over Siberia to determine whether the USSR was preparing for an attack on the United States. When the photos from Hillman's overflight were analyzed, they showed that the Soviets were not massing Tu-4 bombers at Siberian air bases. Although the Soviets were making long-range training flights to the forward bases, these were not in preparation for a

nuclear attack on the United States. The B-47B overflight also established the principle, as Colonel Leghorn had foreseen, that aerial reconnaissance in the nuclear age was a means of providing advance warning of possible threats against the United States.

Ju Jitsu

After Crampton completed the overflights, he was given command of No. 101 Squadron, which had recently been reequipped with the RAF's first Canberra light jet bombers. Although Crampton was pleased to be given such a choice assignment, he found that the pilot's seat of the Canberra seemed small after having flown the RB-45C—"not unlike a Ford Escort after a stretched Cadillac," he said.

While Crampton was trying to settle in, a second series of RB-45C overflights was being proposed. Sir John Slessor, chief of the air staff, suggested to General Vandenberg a joint U.S. Air Force–RAF effort codenamed Ju Jitsu. Slessor's September 12, 1952, letter read: "I gathered from Nate [Twining] that the President's reactions were 'Why don't you do more of it'? On that, I suggested to Nate that we might each find three crews and do six sorties simultaneously in November. . . . I think it would be a great help in getting the Old Man's [Churchill] approval to do another Ju Jitsu if we could say that the U.S. as well as British crews would take part."

The SAC London headquarters backed Slessor's proposed joint operation and also warned of the problems that not having U.S. participation might cause. It reported to General Twining: "Firstly, one of the races scheduled will be over a course in which we have a primary interest and second, it is entirely possible that without our participation the Betting Commissioner [Churchill] here may reject Sir John's application." United States participation proved impossible, and on September 18, General Vandenberg replied to Slessor: "I agree with you it would be desirable for participation by aircrews of the USAF in the operation for the reasons you have stated. However, I regret to say that it will not be feasible to do so because of political considerations."

In October 1952, Crampton was again ordered to Bomber Command; he was told that the special-duty flight was being re-formed and was asked if he wanted to again be its commander. He accepted, and within a few days he was back at Sculthorpe, working with "Hak" Mixson and undergoing refresher training. There were a few crew changes;

Sanders was back as his navigator, but Sergeant Lindsay had been badly injured in a crash. His place as copilot was taken by flight lieutenant McAlistair Furze, one of the flight commanders with No. 101 Squadron. "MacFurze," as he was less formally known, quickly mastered the RB-45C systems, which pleased Crampton. He said later that Furze "would have elbowed me out of the captain's seat given half a chance." The other replacement was flight lieutenant Harry Currell, who took over as pilot from Bill Blair.

The special-duty flight trained through November 1952 and by early December was nearly ready for the overflights. The three routes were similar to those of the April overflights and were intended to get radarscope photos of long-range aviation airfields and other Soviet facilities. The missions were scheduled for the night of December 12–13, 1952. Only a few days before the overflights were to be made, however, they were abruptly called off. The special-duty flight was disbanded and its members were sent back to their original units. In a December 16, 1952, letter, air chief marshal Sir Hugh P. Lloyd told Maj. Gen. John P. McConnell: "I am only sorry that the operation ended the way it did—without the answers."

Why Ju Jitsu was so abruptly canceled was the subject of much rumor among the crews. Crampton recalled that among the rumors was the belief that the political risks of the overflight were too great—specifically, that if one of the RB-45Cs had gone down in the USSR, it might have triggered a war. Certainly, events in the fall of 1952 were heading in a dark and dangerous direction.

Chapter 2
Covert Overflights Under Eisenhower

The whole art of war is being transformed into mere prudence, with the primary aim of preventing the uncertain balance from shifting suddenly to our disadvantage and half-war from developing into total war.
—Carl von Clausewitz, On War, 1832

The history of the Cold War reached a turning point in the fall of 1952. For six years, Stalin had slowly, patiently laid the groundwork. During that time, he was deified as "the greatest genius of all times and peoples," while the KGB worked to cleanse Soviet society of Western influences, eliminated Eastern European communist leaders whom Stalin suspected of independent mindedness, and destroyed or silenced the remaining Jewish intellectuals. Stalin was now ready to unleash his new Great Purge.

It was heralded by the opening on October 5, 1952, of the Nineteenth Congress of the Communist Party of the USSR. The meeting took place amid a growing climate of fear. The delegates were warned about warmongers and foreign agents trying "to exploit unstable elements in Soviet society"; they were told that the Soviet people must be vigilant every minute. The purge in Eastern Europe was already under way. In Czechoslovakia, a show trial was held in November 1952 of fourteen senior communist officials, eleven of whom were Jewish. They were described as being part of a vast conspiracy involving American and Israeli spies, "Trotskyists," "valets of the bourgeoisie," and "Jewish Freemasons." Eleven were hanged, and the other three were sentenced to life imprisonment. The *New York Times* said that the Czech trial "may well mark the beginning of a major tragedy." The prediction was about to be fulfilled.

On January 13, 1953, came the announcement of the "Doctors' Plot." A *Pravda* article and editorial, approved by Stalin himself, said that "a terrorist group of doctors" had attempted "to shorten the lives of leading figures in the Soviet Union by means of harmful treatment." The doctors were described as paid agents of the United States, Britain, and the

"Zionist spying organization" and were part of a plot by Western capitalists who were "preparing feverishly for another world war." The following six weeks saw hundreds of articles in the Soviet and Eastern European press as the purge campaign was spread as widely as possible. The Jews of the USSR and Eastern Europe would be the first victims; they would be deported to the camps or killed outright. They, in turn, would be followed by all the others, numbering in the millions, selected by Stalin for death.

Yet the coming purge may have been only a prelude. Some in the Soviet military felt that Stalin was ultimately preparing for a third world war. Among them was Maj. Gen. N. N. Ostroumov, the deputy chief of the operations department of the air force staff. In the spring of 1952, Stalin ordered the creation of a hundred new tactical bomber regiments. General Ostroumov and his colleagues did not see why so many bombers were needed unless Stalin was planning for a new war. General Ostroumov noted: "Public consciousness was gradually being prepared, and the country purposefully made ready, for approaching trials—more precisely, for war."

Then history took a new course.

The Death of Stalin

At 8:30 A.M. on Wednesday, March 4, 1953, all programs on Radio Moscow suddenly stopped. Several minutes later, an announcement was made that Stalin had suffered a cerebral hemorrhage during the night of March 1. This was followed by a medical bulletin indicating that Stalin was dying. On March 5, two more bulletins were issued indicating that Stalin's condition had further deteriorated. At 6:00 A.M. on March 6, Radio Moscow announced that Stalin had died the night before.

Stalin's heirs began a struggle for power and personal survival. They reclaimed their important party and government posts and eliminated Lavrenty P. Beria, who oversaw foreign intelligence, domestic police, forced labor camps, and the Soviet nuclear program. The new "collective leadership" had justly feared that Beria was about to turn on them. It was also becoming clear that the nature of Soviet society, and its relationship with the rest of the world, was changing. Within weeks after Stalin's death, articles against Jews stopped and Stalin's name appeared less often or not at all. In April, the arrested doctors were released and rehabilitated. Within the USSR, people began to speak of a "thaw." Most

of all, the new Soviet leadership needed a temporary reduction of international tension.

The new Soviet premier, Georgi Malenkov, signaled the change in a March 15 speech: "At present, there is no litigious or unsolved question which could not be settled by peaceful means on the basis of mutual agreement with the countries concerned. This concerns our relations with all states, including the United States of America."

Over the following months, many of the issues dating from the earliest days of the Cold War were settled. The USSR dropped its territorial claims against Turkey and "reconsidered" its former position on joint control of the Straits. The USSR began talks with Iran on frontier problems, financial claims, and trade issues.

The most pressing issue dividing East and West was, of course, the Korean War. Since the fall of 1951, Stalin had encouraged the Chinese and North Koreans to take a hard line in the truce negotiations. He believed that as long as the war remained a stalemate, it drained U.S. resources, created divisions between the Western allies, provided the USSR with intelligence on U.S. military technology and tactics, and allowed the USSR to accuse the United States of war crimes, such as the use of bacteriological weapons in Korea. Stalin's heirs moved to end the war. This proved difficult, because the remaining sticking point in the truce talks was the issue of the repatriation of prisoners. The UN would not forcibly return captured North Korean and Chinese soldiers who did not want to go home, as the communist negotiators demanded, and the war continued.

June and July 1953 saw some of the heaviest fighting of the Korean War. American aircraft were hard pressed to provide support to the beleaguered ground forces. The Chinese and North Korean human wave attacks threatened a breakthrough. As a result, U.S. Navy carriers operating off Korea were supplied with A-bombs, and the United States began hinting that they might be used. Eventually, the UN position on repatriations was accepted by the communist side, and the truce agreement was signed on July 27, 1953. Soon after, Malenkov said that, with the end of the Korean War, "There is a certain improvement in the international situation. After a long period of growing tension, some relaxation of the international atmosphere has begun to be felt for the first time in the postwar years."

With the death of Stalin, the Cold War took different shapes and moved in new directions. Yet the USSR remained a totalitarian dicta-

torship with a hostile ideology and the military capability to do grievous damage to the West. The relaxation in tensions of which Malenkov spoke proved short lived. Soviet military power would soon be greatly increased, as would the climate of fear. The struggle between the USSR and the West continued in the back alleys of the world.

And in the clear blue sky.

The RAF Canberra Overflight

Several months after the Ju Jitsu RB-45C overflights were canceled, a RAF Canberra made one of the most obscure missions in the secret air war against the USSR. Due to British security practices and the passage of time, not even the exact date of this overflight can be identified. Unlike the RB-45C missions, this was primarily a British operation, with only limited U.S. Air Force involvement and none by the CIA. Also unlike the RB-45C missions, this one almost ended in disaster.

The overflight had its origins a year or more beforehand. Around 1952, Western intelligence discovered that the Soviets had built a missile test range at Kapustin Yar, a short distance southeast of Stalingrad along the Volga River. According to one account, the first indication came from the detection of what appeared to be missile telemetry signals. The initial data was not conclusive, however. Later intercepts by SIGINT ground stations in Turkey finally confirmed that the signals were from missile telemetry. Additional information was provided by released German ex-POWs and captured engineers who had worked in the emerging Soviet missile program.

Photographing the Kapustin Yar site became a priority. Bob Amory, then the deputy director for intelligence at the CIA, pressed for an overflight of the area, saying: "We just can't ignore it. This is going to be a major new thing, this whole missile development, and we've got to get on top of it in the beginning and judge it." General Nathan Twining told Amory that the air force could not fly the mission. The RAF filled the gap.

The U.S. Air Force had previously supplied the British with a K-30 100-inch focal length camera. The terms were simple: "Do what you want with it. Don't tell us, but give us copies of the pictures." The K-30 camera was fitted into a Canberra jet bomber and used for taking oblique photos of Eastern Europe from friendly airspace. Reportedly, during one test flight the camera provided clear photos of St. Paul's Cathedral in Lon-

don from an aircraft flying off the English coast at Dover. The border missions flown with the K-30 camera were code-named Project Robin and continued through late 1955.

The combination of the Canberra and the K-30 camera was also to be the means for the Kapustin Yar overflight. In the spring of 1953, a plan was developed to modify a Canberra to make a long-range, daylight overflight across the southern USSR. The aircraft selected was a standard Canberra B-2 bomber rather than the PR-3 reconnaissance version then entering service. The K-30 camera was squeezed into the aft fuselage and looked out the airplane's left side. Fuel tanks were added to the bomb bay to give the B-2 the long range needed for the mission. To increase the airplane's maximum altitude, all excess equipment was removed, which put the Canberra above the reach of Soviet MiG-15s. The modified Canberra made two or three short-range penetration flights over Eastern Europe. With these successfully completed, Prime Minister Churchill gave his approval for the Kapustin Yar mission.

The Canberra overflight was made in late August 1953. The airplane took off from Giebelstadt in West Germany, close to the East German border. As soon as it took off, Soviet radar tracked the airplane. The Canberra headed due east as it climbed, reaching an initial altitude of 46,000 feet. It then crossed into Czechoslovakian airspace and passed over Prague. Still flying east, it passed over southern Poland and the city of Krakow, then crossed over the Soviet border and headed toward Kiev. The aircraft continued to follow a cruise-climb profile in which its altitude increased as the fuel was burned.

Although Soviet air defenses had to deal with only a single aircraft flying on a straight-line course, their fighters proved incapable of intercepting the Canberra. Despite the MiG pilots being vectored by ground controllers using radar data, they could not see the Canberra, now flying at 48,000 feet. Worse, a number of units put on a Keystone Kops routine. In one air defense sector, a ground controller sent the MiGs west instead of east. As the Canberra passed Kharkov, the MiG pilots trying to intercept it became confused and started firing at one another.

As the Canberra neared Kapustin Yar, a MiG pilot, his fighter buffeting in a near stall, momentarily lined up his gun sight on the target and fired a burst. At least one of his cannon rounds hit the Canberra. The British aircraft was able to continue flying and maintain its altitude, but the damage caused it to vibrate. The MiG pilots then lost sight of the Canberra. The British pilot was able to take the photos of the Kapustin Yar

missile test range; then he turned his aircraft to the southeast and followed the Volga River until he exited Soviet airspace over the Caspian Sea. The Canberra's epic flight was brought to a successful close with a landing in Iran.

The near loss of the Canberra caused the British to abandon any further thoughts of similar long-range, daylight overflights of the western USSR. Amory recalled the British attitude was "God, never again." The failure of Soviet air defenses to destroy the Canberra, along with the errors by a number of units, caused a major Soviet purge. Several generals and other officers were removed from their posts. One Soviet general was reduced in rank to lieutenant colonel; he committed suicide. Other personnel were sentenced to punishment battalions.

The United States was told about the Kapustin Yar overflight in February 1954, and copies of the photos were later supplied to the air force and CIA. Although Amory recalled that there were "some fair pictures," others have said that they were of poor quality, apparently because of the aircraft's vibrations, and provided little information on the site.

The Return of the Special-Duty Flight

Following the cancellation of the Ju Jitsu missions, John Crampton completed his tour with No. 101 Squadron in July 1953, then spent "ten very indifferent months" as a staff officer. He was then ordered to High Wycombe and was told that the special-duty flight was once more being revived. Crampton was offered command. By this point, he said later, "I had begun to view the entire project as mine and would have been most upset if the job had been offered to anyone else."

Crampton and the other crewmen from the Ju Jitsu missions were reassembled in March 1954. As Crampton remarked later, "It was back to Sculthorpe, 'Hak' Mixson, the four stretched Cadillacs, American flying clothing *and* the American language plus the raised eyebrows." Crampton was worried throughout the month of training they underwent that the operation might be blown, because a considerable number of people knew that something was going on, even if they did not know what. The crew chiefs discussed aircraft problems and ordered spare parts using walkie-talkies. Crampton thought that any Soviet spy or sympathizer in the area could monitor the base activities with ease.

During this training period, the four aircraft were again repainted with RAF markings. This raised another potential security threat. A hobby

popular in the early 1950s among British boys was aeroplane spotting. Although U.S. Air Force B-45s were common in England, ones with RAF markings attracted attention. One young spotter living near Prestwick Airport recalled his excitement at seeing an RAF RB-45C making a refueling stop at the airport. He and several of his friends grabbed their Brownie box cameras, positioned themselves behind the old terminal building, and photographed the airplane as it lined up for takeoff. As it roared into the air, however, the airport police arrived and seized their cameras. The group was taken to the police station, their film was removed, and they were, the spotter recalled, "given one hell of a ticking off."

Crampton and Sanders returned to Bomber Command to collect the flight plans. As before, there were three routes. The two northern routes were much the same as on the April 1952 overflights, but the southern mission stretched about a thousand miles inside Soviet airspace and covered about thirty targets. As before, night radarscope photos would be taken of long-range air force bases, air defense sites, cities, and other targets. Since the first overflights, Bomber Command's chief scientific officer, "Lew" Llewelyn, had worked to improve the quality of the radarscope photos. He even devised a way to use them to produce stereoscopic 3-D images.

Intelligence officers briefed Crampton and Sanders on the air defenses they would face. The Soviets had a radar network that could track the RB-45Cs, but there were no radar-equipped jet night fighters. This meant that the ground controllers would have to position the MiGs within visual range of the reconnaissance aircraft before the Soviet fighters could make an attack. Given the RB-45Cs' speed and altitude, this was not seen as a major risk. Also, due to the RB-45Cs' performance, flak guns were dismissed as a threat. Crampton and Sanders were told that the SIGINT data on Soviet air defenses was as important as the radarscope photos. The RAF ground stations and the U.S. Air Force SIGINT aircraft would be on alert to intercept Soviet radio traffic. Because it took several weeks to organize this effort, the overflights would have to be made on the planned date.

On the evening of April 28–29, 1954, the three RAF RB-45Cs took off from Sculthorpe and headed toward northern Denmark, where they met up with their tankers. After topping off their fuel tanks and giving the boom operator a final salute, the three airplanes turned off their navigation lights and headed into the night. One of the northern routes was flown by Gordon Cremer, Bob Anstee, and Don Greenslade; the other

mission was made by Harry Currell, John Hill, and Joe Acklam. Crampton, who was flying with Rex Sanders and McAlistair Furze, had chosen the longer, southern route for himself.

Crampton's airplane climbed through a thin layer of clouds at 30,000 feet, and he and Furze saw the stars. Sanders reported that the mapping radar and photographic equipment were working perfectly. He would give Crampton new course changes, then ask for straight and level flight for the run-up to each target. These were scattered across much of the southern USSR; the RB-45C was virtually zigzagging. This, Sanders later noted, was effective evasive routing and might have added to their safety, but "it certainly prolonged our time over Russia."

Sanders, in the nose of the airplane, continued to report that he was having no problems with the radarscope photos. Furze, in the copilot's seat behind Crampton, was busy monitoring the airplane's systems. This left Crampton to contemplate an odd sight. Occasionally, he could see flashes from the ground reflecting on the clouds. They were similar to lightning or flashes from an active bombing range at night. They were causing no harm, but Crampton was puzzled by them. The RB-45C was flying at an altitude of 36,000 feet at a speed of Mach 0.7. It had covered most of the targets and was heading south toward Kiev. Crampton noticed that the flashes in the clouds seemed to be more frequent and were always directly below their RB-45C. This, he thought, was unusual for a natural phenomenon, but the intelligence officer's briefing had dismissed the possibility of flak. The flashes certainly looked like the flak he had seen while flying missions over Nazi Germany years before.

Then, in a single heart-stopping moment, a solid line of golden antiaircraft flak exploded about two hundred yards in front of the RB-45C at exactly the same altitude as they were flying. Crampton reacted instinctively; he pushed the throttles wide open and made a hard turn until the aircraft was pointed west. He then began a gentle, hundred-feet-per-minute descent to pick up speed until the RB-45C reached its Mach limit and began to buffet. He eased off the power slightly but continued the descent to throw off the gunners' aim.

At this point, Sanders came on the intercom. "Hey, what about my photos?" he asked. From his position in the nose, Sanders could not see outside the aircraft and did not know about the flak bursts. Crampton "replied succinctly" that they had been tracked, then told him about the flak and requested a course back to Furstenfeldbruck, West Germany, which was their tanker rendezvous point and emergency landing field. Crampton also told Furze to watch for any MiG that might try to inter-

cept them. The RB-45C was unarmed and would have to try to lose any fighters in the darkness. Speed was critical to avoiding any MiGs, and Crampton flew the RB-45C on the right side of the Mach buffet. He said later, "It sort of trembled affectionately."

Such precautions were necessary; the commander of Soviet air defenses in the Kiev region, Gen. Vladimir Abramov, had ordered two fighter pilots to ram the RB-45C. The ground controllers tried to position the MiGs for a collision but were unable to do so. None of the aircraft, British or Soviet, sighted those from the other country. Although the Soviets thought the airplanes were on a reconnaissance flight, they did not exclude the possibility of a nuclear attack. The Soviets also misidentified the airplanes. They thought they were U.S. Air Force B-47s rather than RB-45Cs.

To further increase his airplane's speed, Crampton momentarily thought of jettisoning the two empty, 1,200-gallon wingtip tanks. He decided that although this might add a few knots, once the tanks were found they would identify the intruder as American and create an international incident. "Anyway," he noted later, "the thought of them bouncing down the High Street of Kiev West at two o'clock in the morning disturbing the ladies and frightening the children did not appeal. We were not flying over Russia to do that."

The flight back was about a thousand miles long and seemed to Crampton to take an eternity. During the time, he thought about how close they had come to being hit. The flashes he had seen earlier had been flak bursts. The gun batteries had been tracking them but had misjudged the airplane's altitude; the gunners had set the shells to explode well below the aircraft's true altitude. The Kiev gun batteries had the correct altitude but had overestimated the RB-45C's speed. As a result, the gunners had led the airplane too much, and the bursts had been several hundred yards ahead of it.

Finally, Crampton's aircraft crossed out of Eastern European airspace and reached West Germany. The crew found the waiting tanker, but when they attempted to refuel, the boom would not stay in the RB-45C's receptacle. Crampton thought that the fixture might have been damaged by the flak over Kiev. With the airplane low on fuel, Crampton diverted to a landing at Furstenfeldbruck. The airplane was refueled on the ground, then took off again and landed at RAF Sculthorpe. The other two RB-45Cs completed their missions without incident, although numerous MiGs had been sent to intercept them.

Like the April 1952 overflights, the second set of missions proved successful. There would, however, be no encore by the special-duty flight. A few weeks later, in early May, the unit was disbanded for the last time. The crew members returned to regular assignments, and the use of RB-45Cs by the RAF would be shrouded in legends for the next four decades.

The Air Battle over the Kola Peninsula

The B-47B overflight made by Colonel Hillman and his crew in October 1952 was apparently the only such deep penetration mission flown during the Truman administration. Three weeks later, Dwight D. Eisenhower was elected president of the United States. The first several months of the new administration were spent in a wide-ranging reassessment of U.S. military policy, including the question of overflying the USSR.

On June 23, 1953, the air staff gave a top-secret briefing on aerial reconnaissance to the new secretary of the air force, Harold Talbott. The briefing began by stating: "There are major deficiencies in our knowledge of Soviet strengths and purposes which imperil the security of the United States." After describing the results of the overflight of the Chukotski Peninsula, the briefing argued for an ongoing program of overflights on a much larger scale than considered before. Although short-range overflights could cover some important target areas, atomic production and similar facilities suspected to be located in the Urals and western Siberia would require deep penetration missions.

This overflight program could provide a wide range of data. The briefing noted that, in the western USSR alone, there were eighteen long-range air force bases, two submarine bases, and thirteen industrial and military concentrations on which intelligence was needed. It continued: "A few missions could confirm or deny the readiness status of the Long Range Air Force." The overflights would also provide information on the status of Soviet aircraft, missiles, armament, electronics, and unconventional weapons systems. Such information was critical, the briefing continued, to U.S. research and development, procurement, and advance planning as well as present and future U.S. force levels.

The briefing estimated that "currently available aircraft, flying at 40,000 feet, have a reasonably high probability of penetrating behind the curtain and returning safely." The political results of a U.S. aircraft being shot down over the USSR "represent the calculated risk," but the briefing added, "The military and political worth of pre-hostilities re-

connaissance outweighs the possible negative consequences. This is especially true if initial overflights are undertaken on a highly selective basis to gauge returns and Soviet reactions."

The briefing concluded: "We have the means of acquiring this intelligence now. We lack an overall policy favorable to planning and conducting overflights and a straightforward mechanism for implementing such a policy. We therefore strongly recommend that you announce a policy which will permit the commencement of overflights of Soviet controlled territory with an absolute minimum of delay."

These recommendations were accepted by President Eisenhower. Over the next year, additional deep overflights were made. They were even more tightly held than the B-47B overflight approved by President Truman, with paperwork kept to a minimum. Eisenhower would authorize the individual flight plan, then the JCS would instruct SAC to fly the missions. The primary focus was on Siberia; three additional B-47B overflights were made against targets in this area. Although the 1952 overflight was able to acquire partial photographic coverage, the later three flights provided only radarscope images. The Kola Peninsula area was covered by another B-47B overflight, which was also limited to radarscope photos.

In the spring of 1954, Eisenhower approved a second overflight of the Kola Peninsula. The JCS sent orders to the 91st Strategic Reconnaissance Wing at Lockbourne Air Force Base in Ohio. The wing was to send a detachment of RB-47E aircraft and their KC-97 tankers to RAF Fairford in preparation for the mission. The Kola Peninsula overflight was apparently the first such mission made by an RB-47E.

Unlike the modified B-47B used on the previous deep overflights, the RB-47E was a production reconnaissance version of the B-47E bomber. The first test flight of an RB-47E had been made on July 3, 1953, and the aircraft entered operational service that November. The most visible change was the extension of the airplane's nose, to house a forward-pointing K-38 camera. Three K-17 cameras were mounted in the bomb bay. The RB-47E's systems had been improved over the earlier aircraft, including replacement of the B-47B's machine guns with a pair of 20mm cannons. Despite this, the tail turret remained unreliable.

Early on the morning of May 8, 1954, three RB-47E crews reported for a preflight briefing. Two of the crews were told that they would fly to a point a hundred miles north of the Soviet port city of Murmansk, then turn around and head back to England. The third crew, consisting of Capt. Harold "Hal" Austin (pilot), Capt. Carl Holt (copilot), and Maj.

Vance Heavilin (navigator), was briefed separately by two SAC intelligence officers. The crews were to continue south, cross into Soviet airspace, and take photos of nine airfields where advanced MiG-17 fighters were suspected to be based. Their six-hundred-mile route went from Murmansk south to Arkhangelsk, then southwest to Onega. They would then turn due west and exit Soviet airspace.

The three RB-47Es took off from RAF Fairford at about 7:00 A.M., then refueled from the KC-97 tankers off the coast of Norway. The RB-47Es continued in a loose formation around the North Cape of Norway, then turned south toward Murmansk. At the preassigned point, the first two RB-47Es reversed course and headed back. Their crews watched as Austin's RB-47E continued to fly south.

Austin's plane crossed the Soviet coast at noon, flying at nearly 40,000 feet and an airspeed of 440 knots. He said later that "the weather was clear as a bell across the entire western part of the continent." Vance Heavilin turned on the bomb bay and the radarscope cameras. Then, Carl Holt recalled, the RB-47E started generating contrails "like six white arrows pointing in our direction." The formation of contrails had not been in the preflight weather forecast, and it provided the MiG pilots with a visual guide to the airplane's position. The RB-47E crews' first targets were two large airfields near Murmansk. As they passed over the first airfield, Holt could see MiGs circling to gain altitude; he knew it would be only a matter of time before they reached the RB-47E.

As the RB-47E finished taking photos of the second airfield, it was joined by a flight of three MiGs. They did not engage the U.S. airplane but rather flew about a half mile off its wings. While the MiG pilots made a visual ID of the RB-47E, Austin and his crew continued to fly the mission as briefed. About twenty-five minutes later, another flight of six MiGs arrived. Like the previous trio, they simply observed the intruder aircraft. The RB-47E crew covered two more major airfields near Arkhangelsk, then began turning to the southwest, toward the next set of airfields. They had been over the USSR for about an hour, with a MiG "escort" for much of the time.

Within a few minutes, two flights of three MiG-17 fighters each began to approach the RB-47E from the rear. Any doubt about the intentions of these six MiG-17s was soon removed. The first MiG-17 began a pass from the left rear. The cannons under the fighter's nose fired, and Austin and Holt could see cannon tracers passing above and below their airplane. Because of the high speed and altitude, the handling of the MiG-17 was poor, making it hard for the pilot to aim. The MiG passed below

and in front of the RB-47E without scoring any hits. Austin put the RB-47E into a shallow dive, descending several thousand feet and picking up about twenty knots of indicated airspeed. When Holt tried to shoot back, he found that the tail guns would not fire. In addition, the radar screen did not work, so Holt had to look out the rear canopy and try to aim the guns manually.

Holt was still trying to get the guns to fire when the second MiG-17 began its attack run. This time, the fighter was coming in from almost directly behind the RB-47E. Austin said later, "I don't care who knows, it was scary watching tracers go over and under our aircraft." Austin told Holt that he had better get the guns to fire or the next MiG would come directly up their tailpipes and they would be dead ducks. As the third MiG-17 began its pass, Holt, still aiming manually and feeling "a little like Wyatt Earp," managed to fire off a short burst. He missed the MiG, but its pilot saw the gun flashes and broke off his pass. The other MiG pilots became more cautious, staying at an angle of thirty to forty degrees to the side of the RB-47E, which put them outside the firing cone of the tail guns. They did not realize that the tail guns would not fire at all now, despite Holt's efforts and pleadings.

The fourth MiG-17 began its firing run, coming in at an angle of forty-five degrees or more. This made a much more difficult deflection shot for the MiG pilot. Despite this, one of his cannon rounds hit the top of the left wing, striking about eight feet from the fuselage, in the wing flap. The fragments hit the fuselage near the number 1 main fuel tank. The crew felt a sharp whap. The shell knocked out the airplane's intercom and damaged the UHF radio, causing it to stick on channel 13, the command post common frequency. Despite the damage and fear, the crew continued to fly the mission as briefed, out of habit. Austin believed that this was due to the "hard, LeMay-type SAC training" given to the combat crews.

By this time, the RB-47E had covered its last photo target and had turned west, toward Finland. The six MiG-17s were running low on fuel and broke off their pursuit, but the RB-47E was quickly joined by another flight of three MiG-17s. Two of them made firing passes, but the added speed caused them to miss. The third MiG-17 then pulled up along the right side of the RB-47E, "close enough to shake hands," Austin recalled, and paced the aircraft for two to three minutes. By this point, the RB-47E and its pursuing MiG-17s were well into Finland airspace, but this did not prevent two more MiGs from making firing passes. At one point, a MiG pilot even tried to ram the RB-47E by sideslipping his MiG into

the airplane. He missed, and the MiG stalled out directly below the RB-47E. One of the cameras got a close-up shot of the MiG-17. Finally, the MiGs ran low on fuel or were ordered to break off the attacks. The MiG-17 pilot flying alongside gave the RB-47E crew a smart salute, which Austin returned, and headed back to the Soviet border.

The ordeal of Austin and his crew was not yet over. They were about thirty minutes behind schedule, and they were not sure how the damage to the airplane's wing and fuselage would affect its fuel consumption. At first, it did not look too bad. The RB-47E flew toward the rendezvous point for their standby KC-97 tanker, which was waiting off the coast of Norway. When Austin tried to call the tanker, all he heard was the pilot reporting that he was leaving the area. As the RB-47E cleared the coast of Norway, the fuel situation was getting worse. Austin climbed to 43,000 feet and throttled back to max-range cruise. All that they had endured would be in vain if they ran out of fuel; the film would be lost if the airplane went down.

As the RB-47E approached within a hundred miles of the British coast, Austin radioed for the strip alert KC-97 tanker at RAF Brize Norton to take off. Due to the damaged UHF radio, the tanker pilot, Jim Rigley, heard only a word or two of the transmission, but this was enough for him to recognize Austin's voice. Rigley requested permission to take off, but the RAF was having an emergency, and permission was refused. Rigley announced that he was going anyway and took off. Austin said later that he was never more thrilled to see an airplane as when he spotted the KC-97 tanker. He pulled into position, and the tanker began transferring fuel into the RB-47E. Holt said later that all the fuel gauges were on empty when they made contact.

After they had taken 12,000 pounds of fuel aboard, Austin released from the boom, gave the boom operator a salute, and headed toward RAF Fairford. They made a low pass of the tower and came around. As they did, the tower crew gave them a green light to land. They made a normal landing, turned off the runway, and parked on the ramp. After they stopped, the hatch opened and the crew chief came up the ladder. His first words to the three crewmen were, "What the hell kind of seagull did you hit?"

Aftermath

The air battle over the Kola Peninsula did not go unnoticed. The following day, the Swedish Defense Staff reported that a group of aircraft

of unknown nationality had crossed into Swedish airspace from Finland. On May 15, 1954, a Finnish newspaper reported that residents of northern Finland had heard an air battle between jets on May 8. The newspaper added, "It is possible that American and Russian planes had been involved." The Finnish foreign ministry, however, denied that any such battle had taken place. A spokesman for the U.S. Air Force in Wiesbaden, West Germany, said that no U.S. aircraft had been in the area and the air force had no knowledge of any such incident. The Soviets said nothing.

Austin, Holt, and Heavilin were personally debriefed by General LeMay at SAC headquarters. Due to "need to know," they were not shown the photos, but LeMay told them they were really good. During their meeting, LeMay asked Austin, "Why were you not shot down?" Austin said he was convinced they would have been shot down if the MiG-17 pilots had been willing to attack from directly behind their aircraft, flying straight into the RB-47E's cannons. LeMay agreed, and commented that he was "convinced that most fighter pilots are basically cowards anyway." He added: "There are probably several openings today in command positions there, since you were not shot down."

Holt had believed that the United States was in a Cold War with the USSR, not a "hot one." During the meeting, he innocently said to General LeMay, "Sir, they were trying to shoot us down." LeMay, smoking his trademark cigar, paused, leaned back, and replied, "What did you think they would do, give you an ice cream cone?"

General LeMay awarded the three crewmen a pair of DFCs each in lieu of a Silver Star. During the presentation, LeMay apologized for not getting them the Silver Star, explaining that that medal required the approval of a board, which had no need to know about the mission.

Austin also received a separate award. After the RB-47E's run-in with the "seagull," the airplane required sheet metal work. The ground crew cut out a section of aircraft skin. In its center was a gaping hole from the cannon hit. About three weeks after the overflight, the squadron maintenance officer came to Austin's house with the damaged aircraft skin mounted in a wooden display case. He presented it to Austin and said that he did not want anyone seeing him with it on base.

Although the potential of covert overflights of the USSR was now clear, the damage inflicted on the RAF Canberra and Austin's RB-47E showed the risks. Despite this, there continued to be a pressing need for intelligence, particularly on the Soviet missile program. In May 1954, soon af-

ter the near loss of the RB-47E, Philip G. Strong, of the CIA's Office of Scientific Intelligence, persuaded a reluctant DCI Dulles to ask the air force to take the initiative in seeking approval for an overflight of the Kapustin Yar test range. The air force and CIA had several meetings over the next few months, but the proposed mission was finally turned down by the air force in October 1954. The risks of using conventional aircraft in daylight overflights of heavily defended areas of the USSR were too high to be politically acceptable.

Night missions could still be done with a politically acceptable level of risk, but these would be limited to radarscope photos rather than visual photographs. At least four more such night overflights were made of the western USSR in the year following the near loss of Austin's RB-47E. The first of these, made several months later, was a night overflight of Moscow. During the flight, however, the RB-47E ran into stronger-than-forecast headwinds. This caused the aircraft to burn fuel at a faster rate than planned, and it had to turn back before covering all its radarscope targets. The airplane was able to return safely.

The other three missions, made in March 1955, were a repeat of the RAF overflights. This time there were three U.S. Air Force RB-45Cs, led by Maj. John Anderson. Like the earlier RAF missions, there were three routes, although the overflight of the Ukraine was made farther south than the two tracks flown by Crampton. The three RB-45Cs took off from RAF Sculthorpe and climbed to 35,000 feet as they flew east. The aircraft simultaneously crossed the borders of the Baltic States, Poland, and Czechoslovakia. The crews successfully covered their assigned targets, including military bases and cities. The Soviets sent numerous fighters after them, but the Soviet ground controllers were unable to position the MiGs for interceptions. The RB-45Cs all landed safely in West Germany, and the crews received DFCs.

Continued Short-Range Overflights

After the end of the Korean War, there remained a need for short-range overflights in the Far East to cover targets in the USSR, China, and North Korea. Requests for the overflights were submitted by the FEAF commander to higher headquarters and the JCS. If they approved, the requests were submitted to President Eisenhower. Once he approved, the authority to proceed was sent down the chain of command to the operational unit. The overflights themselves were directed by four com-

manding officers and a single intelligence officer at FEAF headquarters. The date and time of an overflight were based on such factors as sun angle, weather, crew and equipment status, activity in the target area, and the readiness of support units such as SIGINT and air-sea rescue units.

To make the overflights, a special unit was established in late 1953, as part of the 15th Tactical Reconnaissance Squadron, at Komaki Air Base in Japan. The unit commander was Maj. Robert E. "Red" Morrison, and his detachment of some eight pilots flew RF-86Fs, fighters that had been stripped of their machine guns and modified to carry three cameras. (The unit motto was "We killum with fillum.") The two K-22 cameras, fitted with 40-inch focal length lenses, were positioned on either side of the pilot's seat and provided near-panoramic stereo coverage. A K-17 mapping camera with a wide-angle 6-inch lens was located in front of and below the pilot's seat. The only visible changes were a bulge on either side of the fuselage, to house the camera magazine. (Fake gun ports were painted on the nose to make the aircraft look like a standard F-86.) Due to the modifications, the RF-86Fs had a redline speed of Mach 0.9 at sea level. To extend the airplane's range, they each carried two 200-gallon and two 120-gallon drop tanks.

The unit made a total of nine overflights of airfields in the USSR and China between April 1954 and February 1955 and at least another three in July and August 1955. Targets included Vladivostok, Sakhalin Island, Sovetskaya Gavan, Dairen, and Shanghai. Normally, two to four aircraft would make an overflight. They would fly in daylight at an altitude normally between 45,000 and 48,000 feet, and only when there was no possibility of contrails forming from their jet exhaust.

One of the earliest overflights made by the unit was by 2d Lt. Robert J. Depew and 1st Lt. Rudolf Anderson, Jr., on May 1, 1954. The target areas were the Chinese port city of Dairen and the Soviet-controlled military facilities at Port Arthur. Even with the four drop tanks, the distance was too great to fly the mission from Japan. They took off from Komaki Air Base at 4:00 A.M. and flew to K-8 air base outside Kunsan, South Korea. The camera magazines were loaded and the drop tanks refueled. This had to be done quickly, because having the RF-86Fs in South Korea was technically a violation of the cease-fire agreement; no aircraft were to be operated in North or South Korea that were not there when the fighting stopped. Burdened with an added ton of fuel in the two two-hundred-gallon tanks, the aircraft took off and headed toward China.

By the time the tanks were empty and jettisoned, Depew and Ander-

son were flying at about 54,000 feet. Depew later said that he always flew as high as possible to avoid radar and MiGs and to put his airplane above the contrail level. This was a full 12,000 feet above the normal F-86 service ceiling, and the aircraft handling was touchy. The RF-86F flew nose high and felt as though it was at the edge of a stall. To correct this, the crew cranked the wing flaps down an inch to an inch and a half. One benefit of such high altitudes was that the fuel consumption per hour was ridiculously low. Finally Depew and Anderson spotted land ahead. Dairen was clear, and they covered the area. The two airplanes then made a wide 180-degree turn to the left and covered Port Arthur, a short distance to the west. They saw no evidence of being detected. "But," Depew later said, "we didn't linger in the area." They flew back to K-8, where new 120-gallon drop tanks were fitted to the airplanes; they were refueled, then returned to Japan.

The following day, Depew and Anderson went to FEAF headquarters in Tokyo to view their film. This was the only time that Depew saw the results of his missions, and he recalled it as a great experience. At one point in the viewing, a colonel said, "Jesus Christ, look at all the submarines." Depew asked him to point them out, and they counted fourteen or fifteen. The next day, Depew and Anderson flew back to Komaki Air Base. They did not tell the other pilots where they had been.

The longest and most difficult of these overflights was made by Major Morrison on February 19, 1955. The mission was originally planned as a two-airplane flight to photograph an airfield near the Soviet city of Khabarovsk. The city was on the Amur River, which formed the border between the USSR and China.

The mission ran into trouble soon after takeoff. As the two RF-86Fs were climbing over the Sea of Japan, Morrison's wingman signaled that he had a mechanical problem and turned back. Morrison continued on alone. By the time he was approaching Soviet airspace, he had already dropped the first two tanks. When he tried to release the second pair, one of the tanks hung up. Its added weight and drag prevented him from reaching the planned altitude. To further complicate matters, the preflight briefing on the winds aloft did not match their actual speed and direction.

As a result, when the calculated time to reach Khabarovsk arrived, the city was nowhere to be seen. Morrison could see the Amur River, and he flew along it. He tuned the airplane's radio direction finder to the Khabarovsk radio station. When the city finally came into sight, Morri-

son first rolled the RF-86F to the left, then the right. This enabled him to see the ground and correct the airplane's flight line so he would pass directly over the airfield. Morrison then turned on the cameras, and he felt the RF-86F shudder. It was the last drop tank, finally separating from the airplane. The tank, with all markings carefully filed off, fell toward Khabarovsk. Morrison successfully photographed the airfield, but his airplane was now low on fuel. He made his way back to Chitose Air Base, Japan, then flew through a break in the clouds and lined up on the runway. Because the airplane was so light, he had difficulty forcing it onto the runway. He turned off the runway onto the parking apron, and his engine stopped. The RF-86F had run out of fuel.

It was not until March 28, 1955, that Depew made his second overflight. This was a mission out of K-8 to cover North Korea. He and his wingman, George Best, took off, crossed the thirty-eighth parallel, then flew west to east on the North Korean side of the demilitarized zone. A second overflight of North Korea, also with Best as wingman, was made soon afterward. Depew's fourth and final overflight was made in late July or early August 1955. Depew and Henry Parsons flew out of Chitose Air Base on the northern end of Hokkaido. The target area was the Kurile Islands and Sakhalin. As they headed toward the area, the weather started to close in. When it was obvious that they could not photograph the targets, they turned around and landed back at Chitose. After they landed, Parsons said that he had seen a MiG below them during the flight. Depew did not know if it was looking for them, but this was the only time an enemy fighter was spotted. Depew believed that he was the only unit pilot to make four overflights and the only one to overfly mainland China, North Korea, and the USSR.

The watch on coastal areas of mainland China, opposite Taiwan, also continued after the Korean War. In the early spring of 1955, intelligence reports were received indicating a possible Communist Chinese buildup. Lieutenant Colonel Marion E. Carl, commander of Marine Photo Squadron 1 (VMJ-1), was ordered to move the unit's F2H-2P Banshee reconnaissance aircraft to Taiwan in preparation for overflights of the mainland. Carl was the first Marine ace in World War II, a test pilot, and the first Marine to fly a helicopter and a jet; he set a world speed record in the D-558-I Skystreak and a world altitude record in the D-558-II Skyrocket.

On May 11, 1955, only a week after Carl had been told of the assignment, the first flight of two F2H-2Ps completed its mission without inci-

dent. The next day, four flights of two airplanes each were sent over the mainland. Carl led one of the flights, but it was not without incident. Seventh Fleet had directed the mission be flown at 40,000 feet, because details in photographs taken at this altitude would be in the correct scale. But the altitude caused the F2H-2Ps to produce contrails. Carl and his wingman were about thirty to forty miles inland when Carl looked back and saw two MiGs coming in from below and behind their aircraft. He immediately lowered the airplane's nose, turned toward the MiGs, and flew past them. He then made a split-S, opened the speed brakes, and went straight down. The Banshee was shaking from the Mach buffet as he leveled off just above the ground. Carl looked back, believing that he had become separated from his wingman during the high-speed descent. He was surprised to see him tucked tightly into position. They crossed over the Chinese coast and landed back in Taiwan. When Carl mentioned later about how close together the aircraft had been, the wingman replied, "Colonel, I wasn't about to lose you over Red China."

Although they had escaped unharmed, Carl went to see Vice Adm. Mel Pride to ask for several changes in the project. He wanted to pick the altitude for the flights based on the photo scale needed. This was because at 40,000 feet the aircraft would produce contrails, which could be seen a hundred miles away, losing them the element of surprise. In addition, the Banshee's operating envelope was too restricted. Only about thirty knots separated the stall and Mach buffet. Vice Admiral Pride agreed, and from then on the F2H-2Ps flew at 30,000 feet. Carl also got Pride to rescind an order that pilots and aircraft carry no identification. This, Carl argued, would put any captured pilots in the position of being spies rather than military personnel. Finally, Carl asked for fighter escorts. Pride said that he could give VMJ-1 four F2H-2 Banshee fighters, but no pilots were available. Carl gave several of the reconnaissance pilots a quick course in air combat, and the overflights were ready to resume.

The biggest problem was not Chinese air defenses but the weather. Over the next month, Carl flew eleven more missions, always in a F2H-2 fighter. On six consecutive missions, he had to abort the overflight at the coast or deal with a target area obscured by cloud cover for as much as 120 miles inland. Although the Chinese continued to send MiGs after the F2H-2Ps, there were no engagements. A U.S. radar on one of the coastal islands tracked the Banshees and MiGs, and a radio operator gave the Marine pilots the MiGs' positions. The Banshees had no problems evading the Chinese fighters. The weather cleared in early June

1955, and on June 6, Carl flew a highly successful overflight. His last mission, on June 12, was aborted by clouds. The next day the unit was ordered to halt operations. The photos showed no evidence of an impending invasion.

The 15th Tactical Reconnaissance Squadron's special overflight unit was disbanded in late 1955 or early 1956. At this time, the Nationalist Chinese Air Force took over the responsibility for overflight operations against mainland China, although the efforts were made in cooperation with the U.S. Air Force. These Nationalist Chinese overflights were made using RT-33s, RF-84s, RF-86s, and later RB-57s. Because they were flown by Nationalist Chinese pilots, the issue of the loss of an American pilot did not arise. In addition to continuing the watch for any invasion preparations, the overflights monitored the development and deployment of advanced weapons on the mainland.

At the same time that these activities were taking place in the Far East, similar short-range covert overflights were being made over Eastern Europe. The aircraft used for such overflights in the mid-1950s was the RF-100A Slick Chick. In 1954, six brand-new F-100As were pulled off the assembly line, stripped of their guns and ammunition, and fitted with five cameras. These were two split vertical K-38s with a 36-inch lens and two tri-camera K-17s and one prime vertical K-17C, each with a 6-inch lens. It was a tight fit. The two K-38 cameras had to be mounted horizontally in the gun bays; they viewed the ground with mirrors. To accommodate all the cameras, the lower fuselage had to be bulged out. During test flights in mid-1954, the cameras could spot golf balls in Los Angeles from 53,000 feet.

For missions over Eastern Europe, the RF-100As were operated by the 7499th Support Group, a specialized unit operating RB-50Gs and RB-57As for border SIGINT and photographic missions. A typical RF-100A overflight started with a takeoff out of Hahn or another West German air base. The aircraft would then climb to altitude and go to full afterburner until it was supersonic. The pilot began a straight-line supersonic dash across the border, then turned on the cameras. The RF-100A flew a straight-line path to remain supersonic, because any turns meant a loss of speed. At a predetermined point, the pilot would begin a climbing turn to reverse direction, then dive to regain speed. By the time the pilot began the return run, the RF-100A was again supersonic. It would then make a straight run back for the border.

The flight path was horseshoe or keyhole shaped, so the pilots came to call the overflights "keyhole missions." A few times the pilots reported

that MiGs were scrambled after them, but they never came close. Flak guns also fired on the RF-100As, but their crews were not good enough to hit the fast-moving and high-flying aircraft. The RF-100As were used primarily over Eastern Europe, but one or more were operated out of Japan and Taiwan around 1956. Subsequently, in early 1959, four RF-100As were supplied to the Nationalist Chinese Air Force, but they found the aircraft unsuitable and never used it for mainland overflights.

Toward Lands Unknown

The accomplishments of the early missions over the USSR, Eastern Europe, and China were both great and mixed. They were the initial steps in transforming Col. Richard Leghorn's ideas about the Cold War role of reconnaissance into reality. The first B-47B overflight had shown that there was not a buildup of Tu-4 bombers in Siberia, and the ongoing overflights of the Chinese coast eased fears of an invasion of Taiwan.

By the summer of 1955, however, this was no longer enough. Soviet military power had grown considerably in the two years since the death of Stalin, but how much it had grown was not clear. The United States had no hard, reliable intelligence data on the size and capabilities of Soviet military forces. As a result, intelligence estimates were little better than guesswork. In such a vacuum, fears grew. The time had come for Leghorn's vision of a new kind of reconnaissance to become a reality. To make it possible would require the construction of the most extraordinary aircraft built during the 1950s. Leghorn would play a part in this as well.

Chapter 3
The Birth of the U-2

Nobody had really worked out how anything was to be done; nobody knew where it would be developed, where flight-testing could be done, where people could be trained or by whom, who could fly it or anything.

—Richard M. Bissell, Jr.

Among the reservists recalled to active duty following the Chinese intervention in the Korean War was Col. Richard S. Leghorn. In April 1951, he was assigned to Wright-Patterson Air Force Base as head of the Reconnaissance Systems Branch at the Wright Air Development Center (WADC). Leghorn's superior was Col. Bernard A. Schriever, the assistant for Air Force Development Planning. Colonel Schriever was an air force officer willing to support ideas that were unacceptable to his more conventional colleagues. Leghorn now had the opportunity to turn his ideas about pre-D-day reconnaissance into reality.

The Beacon Hill Study

The air force at this time was also seeking advice from engineers and scientists on national defense issues. In July 1951, the air force negotiated a contract with MIT to establish Project Lincoln (later called Lincoln Laboratory) to undertake research on air defense. Project Lincoln's first study, however, was requested by Colonel Schriever and was a review of long-term air force development requirements for intelligence and reconnaissance. The study was called Beacon Hill and drew its members from New England universities and industrial firms.

As the study was being organized in July 1951, Leghorn prepared a five-page paper titled "Comments on Intercontinental Reconnaissance Systems, 1952–1960." It read in part: "Recent analysis has established that certain objectives must be sought in reconnaissance systems. These objectives fall broadly in two groups. . . . Pre-'D'-Day Reconnaissance and Post-'D'-Day Reconnaissance. A short intense campaign as contemplated

by SAC requires the collection of as much planning information as possible prior to 'D'-day. As the SAC striking capability improves with improved development and production of atomic weapons and high performance, invulnerable vehicles, need for Pre-'D'-Day intelligence assumes even greater relative importance.

"Vehicles for Pre-'D'-Day Reconnaissance must meet the following requirements: (1) minimum chances of detection, (2) minimum chance of interception, (3) an unmanned vehicle is greatly preferred, (4) the vehicle configuration must lend itself readily to a 'cover plan' excuse such as a scientific or weather mission gone astray."

Given Leghorn's support for an unmanned system and the need for the vehicle to have a built-in cover story, it is not surprising that he was most enthusiastic about the Project Gopher reconnaissance balloon. In assessing the different options, Leghorn wrote: "Project Gopher has perhaps the greatest potential for Pre-'D'-Day Reconnaissance. Because of its extreme importance, maximum budgetary support is required. The nature of the Gopher vehicle is such that photography is the most promising data collecting technique.

"Next to the Gopher, the Snark Missile, succeeded by the Navaho Missile, offers good possibilities. . . . Photographic techniques offer best promise, with thermal and radar techniques having limited possibilities.

"Drone aircraft might have promise as an interim system to Snark.

"The RB-47 and subsequent manned aircraft operating at high subsonic or supersonic speeds can possibly be developed into Pre-'D'-Day Reconnaissance Systems with operational capabilities in lightly defended areas. . . ."

During January and February 1952, members of the Beacon Hill study group spent every weekend attending briefings on high-flying aircraft and reconnaissance balloon projects. One of the more unusual ideas the members considered was an invisible airship. This huge vehicle was to be nearly flat in shape and covered with a blue-tinted, nonreflective coating. Its mission would be to fly along the border of the USSR at 90,000 feet at very low speeds with a giant camera to photograph areas of interest. When the classified Beacon Hill Report was issued on June 15, 1952, it described radical methods of improving intelligence on the USSR, such as photographic, radio, and radar surveillance, passive infrared, and microwave surveillance.

One of the report's most important conclusions read: "We have now reached a period in history when our peacetime knowledge of the ca-

pabilities, activities, and dispositions of a potentially hostile nation is such as to demand that we supplement it with the maximum amount of information obtainable through aerial reconnaissance. To avoid political involvements, such aerial reconnaissance must be conducted either from vehicles flying in friendly airspace, or—a decision on this point permitting—from vehicles whose performance is such that they can operate in Soviet airspace with greatly reduced chances of detection or interception."

The Quest for an Advanced Reconnaissance Aircraft

During the summer of 1951, Leghorn was also working on a proposal for the highly specialized reconnaissance aircraft needed to carry out the evolving policy. Leghorn realized that the quickest way to produce such an aircraft was to modify an existing design. The highest-flying jet aircraft at the time was the Canberra, which was being adapted by the Glenn L. Martin Aircraft Company for air force use as the B-57. At Leghorn's insistence, representatives of English Electric, the British manufacturer of the Canberra, were invited to WADC. Together with Leghorn, they designed a version for covert, peacetime overflights. The new aircraft would have long, high-lift wings, new Avon 109 engines, a single pilot, and a lighter structure than that of a standard military aircraft. As a result, the new Canberra could reach an altitude of 63,000 feet early in a mission, increasing to 67,000 feet as the fuel burned off, which put it above the reach of Soviet MiG-17 fighters. It could cover up to 85 percent of the intelligence targets in the USSR and China.

The aircraft did not, however, meet the design standards of the Air Research and Development Command (ARDC). The head of ARDC's reconnaissance division, Lt. Col. Joseph J. Pellegrini, did not see the usefulness of Leghorn's specialized covert reconnaissance aircraft, and he ordered modifications that would meet military design specifications for combat aircraft. But the beefed-up airframe, along with other military equipment, reduced the aircraft's peak altitude. Frustrated by the changes being made to his aircraft design, Leghorn transferred to a job in the Pentagon in early 1952, working directly as deputy to Colonel Schriever.

Leghorn's new assignment made him responsible for planning the air force's reconnaissance activities for the coming decade. In the short term, reconnaissance balloons would undertake wide-area searches of the So-

viet bloc, looking for new targets. For close area reconnaissance, a specialized, high-altitude, lightweight aircraft would be used. It would be designed, as with the Canberra rejected by ARDC, specifically for covert missions at altitudes of 70,000 feet. With this task completed, Leghorn was released from active duty in late January 1953, and he returned to Eastman Kodak. He had planted the seeds for the events to follow.

In concert with Leghorn's Canberra proposal, Maj. John Seaberg, at WADC, was also looking at advanced reconnaissance aircraft. Major Seaberg, like Colonel Leghorn, was a reservist recalled to active duty. Seaberg had worked as an aeronautical engineer at the Chance Vought Company. He became convinced, like Leghorn, that the technology existed to build an aircraft able to fly at 70,000 feet. In March 1953, Seaberg issued a request for proposals for a reconnaissance aircraft with an operational radius of 1,500 miles and the ability to conduct "pre- and post-strike reconnaissance missions during daylight, good visibility conditions." The aircraft was to fly at 70,000 feet or more, carry a payload of 100 to 700 pounds of reconnaissance equipment, and be flown by a single pilot.

Wright Air Development Center decided to seek responses only from the smaller aircraft companies, believing that they would give the project more attention. In July 1953, Bell Aircraft Corporation, Fairchild Engine and Airplane Company, and Martin Aircraft Company all received study contracts. The Bell design was for a large, twin-engine aircraft; the Fairchild entry was a single-engine aircraft with an intake above the cockpit. The Martin design was the long-winged version of the B-57 approved by ARDC. Due to the insistence on meeting military standards, and the resulting increase of structure and equipment weight, the maximum altitude of the Martin aircraft was reduced to about 64,000 feet, less than Leghorn's original concept.

There was also now a fourth, unsolicited contender. In the fall of 1953, John H. "Jack" Carter, an assistant director at Lockheed Aircraft, was at the Pentagon. During the visit, he went to see Eugene P. Kiefer, an old friend and colleague from the air force's Office of Development Planning. Kiefer told Carter about the development program for a new reconnaissance aircraft and mentioned that he thought the air force was making a mistake by trying to make the aircraft suitable for both strategic and tactical reconnaissance.

When Carter returned to California, he immediately met with Lockheed vice president L. Eugene Root, who had been the senior civilian at

the Office of Development Planning, and urged that Lockheed submit a design. In contrast to the conventional thinking of the three existing contenders, Carter proposed that the aircraft's "development must be greatly accelerated beyond that considered normal." It would "require very strenuous efforts and extraordinary procedures, as well as non-standard design philosophy." This included deleting the landing gear, disregarding military design specifications, and building the aircraft with a low structural load limit. The resulting aircraft was designed to fly at an altitude of 70,000 feet. Carter believed: "If extreme altitude performance can be realized in a practical airplane at speeds in the vicinity of Mach 0.8, it should be capable of avoiding virtually all Russian defenses until about 1960."

Lockheed had the one aircraft designer innovative enough to turn Carter's ideas into a practical reality: Clarence L. "Kelly" Johnson. In 1943, he had promised the Army Air Forces that he would design, build, and deliver the prototype XP-80 jet fighter in only 180 days. To accomplish this, Johnson assembled a specialized design shop called the Skunk Works. After World War II, the Skunk Works had enjoyed such successes as the T-33 trainer, the F-94 interceptors, and the XF-104, the prototype of the F-104, the first production Mach 2 fighter. There had also been occasional failures, such as the XF-90, an overweight, underpowered fighter that had tried to meet conflicting design requirements.

These experiences, good and bad alike, had refined Johnson's ideas about the experimental aircraft design process. He knew exactly what was needed for the new reconnaissance aircraft, which was designated the CL-282. Johnson took the XF-104 fuselage and added high-aspect-ratio wings. The airframe was stressed to only 2.5 g's rather than the normal military design standard of 5.33 g's. The aircraft was powered by a J-73 engine. Just as the CL-282's wings resembled those of a glider, many of its design features were also adapted from glider technology. Rather than a spar passing through the fuselage, the wings were bolted on, as in a glider. To further save weight, the CL-282 took off from a wheeled dolly and landed on two skis and a reinforced belly. The cockpit was not pressurized, to further save weight; the pilot would have to rely on a pressure suit. The aircraft could carry 600 pounds of camera equipment to a peak altitude of just over 70,000 feet, and it had a range of 2,000 miles.

Johnson submitted the CL-282 design in early March 1954 to now Brigadier General Schriever's Office of Development Planning. Schriever liked the concept; it met all the requirements of Leghorn's

intelligence and reconnaissance planning objectives. Schriever asked Johnson to submit a more complete proposal. This would give a full description of the CL-282, along with a plan for construction and maintenance of thirty aircraft.

Schriever brought Johnson to Washington, D.C., in early April 1954, where Johnson gave a briefing on the CL-282 to a panel of senior Pentagon officials, including Lt. Gen. Donald L. Putt, deputy chief of staff for development, and Trevor N. Gardner, special assistant for research and development to the secretary of the air force. Although Gardner liked the aircraft, the air force members of the panel seemed reluctant about the concept. General Schriever bypassed ARDC, which had rejected Leghorn's original Canberra proposal, by going to Gen. Thomas D. White, the air force vice chief of staff. General White authorized the production of a limited number of CL-282s, providing that General LeMay agreed. This was because SAC would be the ultimate user of the new airplane.

General Schriever was encouraged by White's support, and a briefing was prepared for General LeMay on the CL-282. This stressed the CL-282's unique technical qualities for prehostilities reconnaissance and implied that such a specialized aircraft should be operated by a special unit. What the briefers did not know was that the air staff had proposed in June 1953 that SAC establish a similar unit to fly the JCS-directed overflights of the USSR, which General LeMay had rejected. LeMay saw reconnaissance in the traditional role of assembling target folders and bomb damage assessment. He also apparently saw such an elite unit, with no war fighting function, as damaging to the morale of the regular SAC units.

Consequently, the CL-282 briefing to General LeMay, given in late April or early May 1954, ended in failure. Its emphasis on prehostilities reconnaissance and the airplane's unique nature apparently renewed LeMay's suspicions about the air staff's intentions. If he accepted the CL-282, he would be stuck with the same kind of peacetime "prima donna flying unit" that he had rejected nearly a year before. LeMay quickly made his anger clear. One of those who heard about it later said: "Not long into the briefing, LeMay took a cigar out of his mouth and said, 'This is a bunch of shit. I can do all of that stuff with my B-36.'" He got up and stormed out of the room, saying that the briefing was a waste of his time.

A more temperate assessment of the CL-282 came from Major Seaberg, who received the proposal on May 18, 1954. Seaberg did not

like Johnson's use of the unproven General Electric J-73 engine, preferring the Pratt & Whitney J-57, which was planned for the Martin, Fairchild, and Bell aircraft. The existing XF-104 fuselage was too small to be fitted with the J-57, however. Seaberg also had doubts about the lack of landing gear and about a single-engine aircraft, believing that a twin-engine configuration would be more reliable. By this time, the Martin RB-57D had been selected as an interim aircraft, and the Bell design, the X-16, was to be the long-term project. The contract for twenty-eight X-16s was signed in September 1954. Both aircraft were large and conventional, with two engines and landing gear, and designed to military specifications.

On June 7, 1954, Johnson received a letter from Brig. Gen. Floyd B. Wood, ARDC's assistant deputy chief of staff for development, formally rejecting the CL-282 proposal. The reasons given were the unusual design and the use of a single engine and because the air force was already committed to the RB-57D program. Johnson and the other Skunk Works engineers continued to refine the CL-282 design; there was still support for the aircraft from General Schriever and senior civilian Pentagon officials. Its time would soon be at hand.

Development of Project Gopher

Running parallel with the high-altitude aircraft program was the development of reconnaissance balloon technology. Project Gopher was to establish design criteria for an operational reconnaissance balloon able to carry a 500-pound payload to more than 70,000 feet for a period of fourteen days. The earlier problems between the Wright Air Development Center (WADC) and General Mills became worse, with the air force complaining about General Mills's costs and General Mills objecting to WADC's technical direction.

Despite these ill feelings, General Mills began a series of Project Gopher test flights between April and July 1952, with the launches made from the University of Minnesota Airport. Many of these flights were camera tests using gondolas built by Stanley Aviation Corporation. They carried a K-17 camera with either a 6- or 12-inch focal length lens. The cameras had been modified to reduce their weight and power requirements. The gondolas were slowly rotated to provide panoramic coverage from the horizon down to a point below the balloon. Other Project Gopher flights were made to test balloon technology.

The test flights of the camera gondolas experienced a number of setbacks. The first, made on April 14, 1952, suffered a poor launching. The gondola struck the ground, damaging the battery and resulting in no data from the flight. The next flight, made on April 30, like several of the others to follow, suffered a camera failure. The third flight in the series, launched on June 4, was recovered with more than two hundred exposures. Samples were forwarded to air force intelligence for analysis. The flights continued through the summer, with mixed results. At the same time, the relationship between WADC and General Mills continued to deteriorate. In August 1952, the air force contract with General Mills was terminated, and test flights shifted to the Holloman Air Development Center in New Mexico.

The first Gopher test flight at Holloman, which was made on August 29, suffered a failure of the gondola rotation system after only four exposures had been taken. The next two flights, made on September 4 and 10, each brought back more than two hundred photos. Such success was tempered by the loss of the next two flights, and camera problems on the following pair of launches. The final flight, launched on November 21, brought the year's tests to a close.

The Project Gopher test flights faced unique security problems. Since the initial sightings of "flying saucers" in June and July 1947, including the "Roswell incident," in which strange debris was found in New Mexico, the belief had developed among the general public that they were seeing alien spaceships and that the air force knew about it and was covering it up.

A later report on Holloman balloon operations noted the problems this caused: "A further advantage, or disadvantage, of plastic balloons is that from a distance they look remarkably like flying saucers. When floating at ceiling altitude, their configuration is somewhat saucer-shaped; and they can either hover for a week over much the same spot or cruise at 250 miles an hour in the jet stream. They can be seen with [the] unaided eye glistening at altitudes above 100,000 feet. . . . In addition, metallic masses of more than a ton may be lifted by these vehicles, thus giving radar returns not usually associated with balloons.

"In the early days of plastic ballooning, in fact, it was sometimes possible to track a long-distance flight from Holloman or from some other center of balloon operations such as Minneapolis–St. Paul simply by following flying saucer reports in the daily papers."

One example of a Project Gopher sighting occurred with a balloon

flight on May 21, 1952. There were gusty winds at launch time, and the General Mills handling crew dropped the payload during the preparations. Unlike most of the Project Gopher test flights, this balloon did not carry a camera gondola but rather a 123-pound J-250 code-sonde telemetry beacon. This transmitted data on the temperatures of the outside air and of the helium within the balloon. The balloon was launched from the University of Minnesota Airport at 7:38 A.M, but the signal soon faded out and the balloon was lost as it climbed. The calculated maximum altitude for the balloon was 78,700 feet.

At about 7:00 P.M. that evening, at Sturgeon Bay, Wisconsin, some three hundred miles due east, Coral E. Lorenzen, a young newspaper reporter with the *Green Bay Press-Gazette,* was heading for Kellner's Drugstore. In addition to being a reporter and an amateur astronomer, Coral and her husband, Jim Lorenzen, had established a small flying saucer club, called the Aerial Phenomena Research Organization, several months before. As Coral Lorenzen rounded the corner, she heard someone say, "There's the 'flying-saucer woman'; ask her what it is." Lorenzen looked up and saw a silver, ellipsoid object. As the crowd asked her if it was a flying saucer, Lorenzen decided to triangulate the object's position to determine its altitude and size. She went into the drugstore, called the police, and asked if there were any police cars north of the town. She went back out to the street and asked if anyone had binoculars. The owner of Eames Restaurant said he had a pair and went to get them. As he left, Lorenzen looked up at the object in time to see its underside starting to emit a red glow.

Lorenzen again called the police and learned that two officers were watching the object from Fish Creek, located eighteen miles north of Sturgeon Bay. From their position, the object was an almost perfect circle at an elevation of about sixty degrees. At Sturgeon Bay, the elevation was about forty-five degrees, and the object was elliptical. All the observers thought the object was slowly moving to the northeast. Looking through the low-power binoculars, Lorenzen thought the object looked metallic, and the red belly was apparent. She aligned the object with a television antenna on a building across the street; its pole almost covered the object. By 7:40 P.M., the object had drifted off to the northeast; the two officers at Fish Creek lost sight of it about five minutes later.

The following day, Coral and Jim Lorenzen returned to measure the angle, width, and elevation of the antenna. This, with the distance to Fish Creek, allowed them to triangulate the object. The completed calcula-

tions indicated that the object was about 780 feet in diameter and had been at an approximate height of forty miles. After the sighting was publicized by Coral Lorenzen, General Mills issued a press release saying that the sighting had probably been a balloon launched that morning that might have been over the area at the time. (General Mills did not, of course, mention that it was a test of balloon reconnaissance.)

What Coral Lorenzen measured was not the actual size of the balloon but the reflection from it. Floating thirteen miles up, the eight-story-high balloon was a perfect mirror for the sun's rays. The red belly, which Coral Lorenzen speculated might be "some type of special light used in high-altitude photographic technique," was the result of sunlight passing through the atmosphere. Skyhook balloons seen under such conditions were often described as red or green.

Although the high-altitude balloons brought unwanted attention to Project Gopher from flying saucer believers, a more serious security threat presented itself at the end of the mission, when the gondola parachuted to a landing. If it were found by a member of the public, the camera could give away the mission. A completely separate air force scientific balloon program, called Moby Dick, was used to provide cover. This used plastic balloons, flying at altitudes between 50,000 and 75,000 feet, which carried radio beacons that were tracked by ground stations. By plotting a balloon's position as it drifted, the direction and speed of high-altitude wind could be determined. Moby Dick was also widely publicized, and although its first flights would not be made until February 1953, Project Gopher could use the advance publicity about Moby Dick as the perfect cover for its operations.

All Project Gopher flights that carried the complete camera gondola were marked "Moby Dick" and had no classification markings. They had a label asking for the gondola's return and offering a cash reward, and another label warning of a possible fire hazard. (The internal heater used flammable hydrogen peroxide.) The WADC assessment was that unless "unauthorized finders" tried to disassemble a gondola, which required special tools, "no breach of security was considered likely."

Concurrent with the Project Gopher test flights were efforts at developing a midair recovery system. RAND Corporation studies of balloon reconnaissance indicated that the best way to recover a gondola at the end of its operational mission was to catch it in midair, to avoid the difficulties of a search on land or open ocean. In November 1951, the equipment laboratory at WADC was requested to conduct flight tests at the

navy parachute test facility at El Centro, California, to develop the equipment and techniques needed for midair recovery of payloads of up to five hundred pounds.

A C-119 cargo airplane was fitted with a pickup winch and grappling hook. The pilot would try to snag the descending parachute with the hook. During the tests, twelve out of the fifteen parachutes dropped were successfully contacted, although not all the parachutes contacted were recovered. With improved equipment and techniques, a success rate of nearly 100 percent was thought possible by WADC. Despite such optimism, the mood at WADC about midair recovery in early 1953 was reportedly grim. One recovery attempt almost ended in a crash, and most of the engineers thought the task was hopeless. In the spring of 1953, air force balloon activities were reorganized. Project Gopher was removed from WADC and transferred to the newly established Air Force Atmospheric Devices Laboratory, which also had responsibility for Moby Dick. One result of the transfer was a complete redesign of the midair recovery equipment, which put the program back on track.

At the same time, the air force had to decide whether or not to turn Project Gopher into an operational balloon reconnaissance system. At a meeting of senior air force generals held on July 3, 1953, a decision was reached to "go ahead full blast" with development of what was now called Project Grandson. Based on this approval, over the summer of 1953, the Cambridge Research Center prepared a Project Grandson development plan for ARDC. An operational balloon reconnaissance system would be designed and tested in long-range flights. The production equipment would then be built and the launch and recovery crews trained. Everything was to be ready by July 1955. If President Eisenhower gave his approval, the campaign would begin in November 1955, with the balloons being launched from sites in Western Europe and Turkey. During the campaign, a total of some 3,000 balloons would be launched in a four-month period. The development plan was subsequently approved.

The balloon reconnaissance effort was meant to update the information available from the wartime GX photos and to fill the gaps in coverage, such as the areas east of the Urals. The effort would also identify the changes that had occurred in the previous decade and locate unknown targets. Such data could then be used to produce target folders, plan the routes of SAC bombers to their targets, and prepare synthetic radar predictions for crew training.

The Intelligence Systems Panel and the CL-282

Although the Beacon Hill study had made recommendations about future air force reconnaissance policy, it was not until July 1953 that the air force established a follow-up advisory committee to determine ways to implement these recommendations. The new group was called the Intelligence Systems Panel and had as its chairman Dr. James G. Baker, who had been part of the original Beacon Hill study. Others on the panel who also had been part of Beacon Hill were Edwin H. Land, founder of Polaroid Corporation; Carl F. P. Overhage, a physicist at Kodak; Allen F. Donovan, of the Cornell Aeronautical Laboratory; and Stewart E. Miller, of Bell Telephone Laboratories. At the request of the air force, there were also two representatives from the CIA, Edward L. Allen and Philip G. Strong.

The Intelligence Systems Panel held its first meeting on August 3, 1953, at Boston University. Strong told them that the best intelligence on the interior of the USSR was the GX photos from World War II. As a result, the panel would have to look at ways to provide coverage of the whole Soviet landmass. The members were briefed on various systems, such as the reconnaissance balloons, and modifications to existing or planned aircraft, such as the RB-47, RB-52, and RB-58. More exotic concepts included reconnaissance versions of the Snark and Navaho missiles. With this, the panel adjourned for nine months.

During this prolonged hiatus, the Lockheed CL-282 was proposed by Kelly Johnson, and its backers began looking for support outside the air force. On May 12, 1954, six days before WADC began its evaluation of the CL-282, Trevor Gardner, his special assistant, Frederick Ayer, Jr., and Garrison Norton, an adviser to air force secretary Harold E. Talbott, met with Strong to explain the advantages of the CL-282 over the other proposals. These included a greater maximum altitude and a lower radar cross section, which might make the aircraft impossible for Soviet radar to spot. Strong was impressed with the aircraft and promised to discuss it with the CIA's newly hired special assistant for planning and coordination, Richard M. Bissell, Jr.

Bissell was a graduate of Groton and Yale, earning a Ph.D. from Yale in 1939. He taught economics first at Yale, then at MIT. During World War II, he managed the movements of Allied cargo ships around the world as executive officer of the Combined Shipping Adjustment Board. Bissell returned to MIT after the war, becoming a full professor in 1948.

That same year, he became deputy director of the Marshall Plan, a position he held until joining the Ford Foundation in 1951 as a staff member. Bissell was typical of the generation that dominated U.S. government and business from the 1950s to the 1980s. They were smart and well educated, typically at Ivy League universities. Although their degrees were in the humanities, they were cool and detached, focusing on numbers and logic rather than human factors.

Bissell joined the CIA in January 1954 and was soon deeply involved in planning the overthrow of Guatemalan president Jacobo Arbenz, who was suspected by Washington officials of being a communist. In mid-May, Strong approached Bissell with the CL-282 proposal. Bissell thought the idea had merit; he advised Strong to get several scientists to provide advice but then thought nothing more about the airplane.

At about the same time, the second meeting of the Intelligence Systems Panel was held on May 24 and 25 at Boston University and the Polaroid Corporation. During the meeting, Donovan made an evaluation of Martin's modified B-57. Although Donovan did not have the precise design specifications or drawings, he was able to estimate what could be done by lengthening the B-57's wings and lightening the airframe. He concluded that the resulting aircraft could not meet the requirements put forth in the Beacon Hill Report. He explained to the other panel members that no twin-engine aircraft designed to meet military specifications could fly above 65,000 feet. Unless the aircraft could reach higher than 70,000 feet, it would not be safe from Soviet interception.

Donovan also told the panel members that there was such an aircraft being designed: the CL-282. Donovan related what Strong had told him earlier about Lockheed's efforts. The other panel members were interested, and the group's chairman, Baker, urged Donovan to go to Lockheed to evaluate the design, as well as to gather ideas about high-altitude reconnaissance from other aircraft companies.

The Threat of Surprise Attack

Throughout the early 1950s, the threat of a Soviet surprise attack hung over American society, defining and shaping it. Today, it is hard to appreciate how pervasive this fear of another Pearl Harbor was, but at the time it was a fact of everyday life. "Duck and cover" films, showing what to do during a nuclear attack, were normal parts of elementary school

curriculum. In many towns, an air raid siren would sound at noon. Given the climate of fear, it is not surprising that a poll in the summer of 1955 found that more than half of American adults thought that it was more likely that they would die in a Soviet attack than from old age.

Such concerns were shared by government advisers and intelligence officials. In 1952 and 1953, the RAND Corporation undertook a series of studies addressing the threat. These underlined how vulnerable the United States and its military forces were to such a sudden attack. In one of the 1953 studies, the scenarios included a low-level attack by fifty Tu-4s, each carrying a single A-bomb with a yield of between forty and a hundred kilotons. The RAND staff concluded that this attack profile, which was well within Soviet capabilities, could result in the destruction of two-thirds or more of the SAC bomber force on the ground.

The RAND study also dealt with the need for better intelligence for early warning of an attack. One section noted: "A substantial reduction in vulnerability would result from advanced indications of enemy activities *provided these could be translated into sufficiently unambiguous states of alert* [emphasis in original]; but from the limited data now available at RAND, the probability of such action appears to be small." The study also warned: "The circumstances attending Pearl Harbor and the initiation of the Korean War show that the mere existence of indicators of enemy activity does not necessarily guarantee that these will be translated into adequate states of national alert."

The CIA also came to a grim estimate about its ability to provide advance warning of a Soviet attack on the United States. By the late summer of 1954, the CIA said it was improbable that it could give warning of a clear Soviet intent to attack or an attack that was going to take place at a particular time, "except in the event of high level penetration of the Soviet command, which today seems unlikely, or in case of some exceptional intelligence bonus or breakthrough." The best that U.S. intelligence could do was to say that the USSR would be fully prepared to attack by a given date, but it was unable to say whether an actual attack were planned, whether the moves were a show of force or whether they were only preparations against a U.S. attack.

The CIA thought that preparation for a full-scale Soviet air attack on the United States, involving 850 Tu-4 bombers, could be detected fifteen to thirty days before a possible attack. However, a more limited attack, carried out by between 50 and 100 Tu-4s, could be made with minimal advance warning. In this case, the first indication that an attack was un-

der way could be the detection on radar of the incoming bombers, as with Pearl Harbor.

This was the situation facing President Dwight D. Eisenhower during the first eighteen months of his administration. He was among the most intelligent men ever to hold the office of president, but in an age when the term *egghead* was a pejorative, he was smart enough to publicly conceal his intelligence behind tangled syntax and western novels. As the former Supreme Allied Commander in Europe during World War II, Eisenhower was familiar with all aspects of intelligence—human spies, aerial photos, and SIGINT—as well as their limitations. He understood that even with the best intelligence, the picture would always be incomplete and surprise was still possible. As president, Eisenhower understood that the Cold War would be a prolonged struggle, and the United States would have to organize its efforts for the long haul. As a fiscal conservative, Eisenhower believed that excessive military spending would damage the U.S. economy and the fabric of society itself. The United States could not be a democracy and a "garrison state."

To avoid these pitfalls, Eisenhower wanted to base the size of U.S. military forces on meeting real Soviet threats rather than suppositions and possibilities. To do this, however, would require solid intelligence on all aspects of Soviet activities. Such intelligence was in short supply, and Eisenhower was quick to express his dissatisfaction with the quality of intelligence and estimates he received after becoming president in January 1953. To give an example, a CIA estimate issued on August 3, 1953, said, regarding a Soviet thermonuclear weapons program: "Research which may be relevant has been noted, but there is no evidence of development activity at the present time. There is no direct evidence on which to base an estimate of the lead the U.S. may have in this field; nevertheless, there is a growing Soviet capability for quantity production of thermonuclear materials, and therefore more advanced research and development, and even field testing by mid-1954, are possible. It would be unsafe to assume that the USSR will not have a workable thermonuclear weapon by mid-1955."

Nine days later, the USSR exploded Joe-4, the first Soviet H-bomb test. Its yield was 400 kilotons. It had been made only nine months after the first full-scale U.S. H-bomb test, the Mike shot of November 1, 1952. Although the Soviet H-bomb produced a much lower yield than the U.S. bomb, it was far lighter and would be a more practical weapon than the device tested in the Mike shot.

There was also intelligence that the Soviet long-range air force was about to begin an upgrading. By 1953, the jet-powered B-47 was in U.S.

Air Force service, and the larger, longer-range B-52 was beginning flight tests. The Soviets, however, still relied on the short-range, piston-engine Tu-4 as their only strategic bomber. In mid-1953, a ground observer at a Soviet test base was able to get a glimpse of part of a new, large aircraft with a swept-back vertical fin. From the brief sighting, the new aircraft appeared to be larger than the B-47 and was considered to be a heavy or near-heavy jet bomber.

A year later, in the spring of 1954, the aircraft was seen in flight for the first time. It was the prototype Mya-4 (NATO code name Bison), a large, four-engine jet bomber with swept-back wings. An early CIA estimate of the Mya-4 gave it the ability to fly from the Chukotski Peninsula and strike targets within an arc from Los Angeles, Denver, and Minneapolis with a 10,000-pound bomb load, then return to Soviet territory without refueling. On a one-way mission, the Mya-4 was estimated to have the capability to cover the whole United States. Eisenhower decided that the situation was unacceptable. The action he took would make Leghorn's ideas a reality and forever change the nature of intelligence and foreign relations.

The Technological Capabilities Panel

On March 27, 1954, Eisenhower attended a session of the Office of Defense Mobilization's Science Advisory Committee, where he told them about the Mya-4 and described the threat it represented to the United States if used in a surprise attack. The Mya-4 had better speed, range, and altitude than a Tu-4 and could be armed with the Soviet H-bomb. In contrast, the U.S. radar network and interceptor force were still inadequate against even the Tu-4 threat, and SAC was not prepared to escape a surprise attack. Eisenhower challenged the scientists on the committee to advise him about any new technologies that could improve U.S. offensive and defensive capabilities as well as the effectiveness of intelligence-gathering methods. James R. Killian, Jr., the president of MIT, offered to form a panel to undertake the study.

On July 26, Eisenhower gave his approval for Killian to recruit and lead the group. Its members would have carte blanche access to all the nation's most closely guarded secrets. The group was originally called the Surprise Attack Panel but was later given a more neutral title, the Technological Capabilities Panel, or TCP.

As organized by Killian, TCP had a total of forty-one scientists, engineers, and military communications experts divided into three sections.

Project One dealt with continental defense, Project Two covered striking power, and Project Three looked at intelligence capabilities. Given Project Three's subject matter, it was logical for Killian to recruit members of the air force's Intelligence Systems Panel for the group. When Killian asked Edwin Land to lead Project Three, the request forced Land to make a major decision about his life. He was forty-five years old, a millionaire from his invention of the instant camera, and on a leave of absence from Polaroid. He had been living in Hollywood, providing technical advice to Alfred Hitchcock on 3-D films. Land left Hollywood, rejoined Polaroid, and took the appointment.

Land's attitudes toward innovation and bureaucracy were similar to those of Kelly Johnson. Land preferred "taxicab committees," groups small enough to fit in one cab. Project Three was the smallest of the three groups, with only six members. In addition to Land, there was Baker, also from the Intelligence Systems Panel; Edward M. Purcell, from Harvard, who had been on the Beacon Hill study; Joseph W. Kennedy, a chemist at Washington University; John W. Tukey, a mathematician at Princeton University and Bell Telephone Laboratories; and Allen Latham, Jr., an engineer with Arthur D. Little, Inc.

Just as their membership overlapped, the Intelligence Systems Panel and Project Three now had intertwining histories. On August 2, 1954, Donovan met with L. Eugene Root at Lockheed. For the first time, he learned of the air force reconnaissance competition. Kelly Johnson then described to Donovan his CL-282 design. Donovan, a lifelong sailplane enthusiast, realized that the design was exactly what was needed. Donovan returned to the East Coast on August 8 and asked Baker to hold a meeting of the Intelligence Systems Panel in order to discuss the CL-282. Baker and other panel members had prior commitments, and it would be nearly two months before the meeting could be held.

The reason for this delay was that Land and Baker went to Washington in mid-August to arrange intelligence briefings for the TCP members. While in Washington, Strong showed Land a drawing of the CL-282 and told him that it had been rejected by the air force. Although Land had heard Donovan's brief mention of the Lockheed concept at the May 24–25 meeting of the Intelligence Systems Panel, it had not registered. Upon seeing the drawing, Land became a backer of the airplane. He telephoned Baker and said, "Jim, I think I have the plane you are after." A few days later, Land showed the CL-282 drawing to Baker and the other Project Three members. Baker had also heard Donovan mention the airplane but, like Land, had not seen the drawing or heard any spe-

cific details. Baker began designing a camera and lens system that could fit in the cramped confines of the modified XF-104 fuselage.

At the end of August, Land met with Bissell to discuss the CL-282. Bissell later recalled not knowing what Land wanted to use the airplane for or even why he had been contacted. Despite this, the discussion attracted Bissell's interest, and in early September he asked a young air force officer on his staff to put together a general report on aerial reconnaissance. Bissell forwarded this to the Deputy Director of Central Intelligence (DDCI), Lt. Gen. Charles Pearre Cabell, on September 24. Bissell's covering memorandum called attention to the section dealing with the CL-282.

That same day, Donovan gave his report on the CL-282 to the Intelligence Systems Panel. Land and Strong could not attend. The panel members on hand were initially upset to learn that the air force had begun a design competition for a new reconnaissance aircraft without telling them, but they quickly came to share Donovan's enthusiasm for the CL-282. It had the three attributes necessary, in Donovan's view, to reach 70,000 feet. These were a single engine, for lightness and reliability; large, gliderlike wings, to take maximum advantage of the low thrust of a jet engine at high altitudes; and a low load factor, again for lightness. Donovan argued that such a specialized aircraft did not need to meet standard military specifications, because it would fly far above the reach of Soviet interceptors.

When Baker told the other members of the Project Three panel about Donovan's report, their interest in the CL-282 grew. The TCP panels formally started work on September 13 and spent the next twenty weeks attending briefings and meeting with every element of the U.S. military and intelligence community. Land recalled that the members of Project Three were becoming more and more distressed at the poor capabilities of U.S. intelligence. He said later, "We would go in and interview generals and admirals in charge of intelligence and come away worried. Here we were, five or six young men, asking questions that these high-ranking officers couldn't answer." Their worry was not limited to military intelligence; Land recalled that the members were also not impressed with the CIA. In such a situation, the CL-282 became an increasingly attractive means of collecting intelligence.

Throughout September and October 1954, the Project Three members held meetings to discuss aspects of the CL-282. By the end of October, the members had dealt with all the outstanding issues, with one exception: the basic question of who would conduct the overflights. Land

felt strongly that it should not be the air force. He believed that military overflights in armed aircraft, such as the B-47 missions, could provoke a war. As a result, Land recommended that the overflights be made in a civilian aircraft with no markings. The best organization to handle the operations was, in Land's view, the Central Intelligence Agency.

In late October, the Project Three members met with DCI Allen W. Dulles to discuss the CL-282. Dulles was reluctant to undertake the mission. He did not want to become involved in what he saw as a military project, even one that had been rejected by the air force. Dulles had given his backing to the earlier air force overflights, including the proposed 1954 Kapustin Yar mission, but he did not see this as a role for the CIA. Land recalled later that he had the impression after the meeting that Dulles somehow thought that overflights were not fair play.

Although DCI Dulles was reluctant, the air force was still committed to the X-16 and wanted nothing to do with the CL-282. The interest shown in the Lockheed aircraft caused WADC to ask Lt. Gen. Donald L. Putt, the air force deputy chief of staff for development, to oppose further work on the CL-282. The WADC argued that the X-16 was the better design because it had two engines, wheels, a pressurized cockpit, and armor. It also warned that if J-57 jet engines were used in the CL-282s, there would not be enough for use in the B-52s, F-100s, F-101s, and F-102s that the air force had ordered. Donovan learned of the WADC objections, and on October 19, 1954, he met with General Putt to argue in favor of the CL-282.

This resulted in a further meeting on November 18 with fifteen scientists from TCP to discuss the different reconnaissance aircraft designs. Also attending the meeting was Major Seaberg. He recalled later that none of the scientists were introduced, but from their questions he could tell that there were aerodynamic, propulsion, and optical experts in the group. Seaberg presented his analysis of each of the four competing designs. He found that the Lockheed, Bell, and Fairchild designs were close aerodynamically. The Martin RB-57D, a modification of an existing aircraft, was less refined. He maintained his opinion that the J-73 jet engine was not adequate for very-high-altitude flight. But Seaberg had also calculated what the CL-282 could do with a J-57 engine. His data indicated that the CL-282 would be competitive with both the Bell and Fairchild aircraft.

Despite the opposition of WADC, and DCI Dulles's doubts, they were now irrelevant. The TCP reported to the president. Land had gone over

the heads of the CIA and the air force. The importance of the backing that TCP gave to the CL-282 also went far beyond which airplane would be built. Leghorn's ideas had now been endorsed by a panel of scientists advising the president. This panel had concluded that pre-D-day reconnaissance was essential to the safety of the United States in order to prevent a surprise attack.

President Eisenhower Gives His Approval

Although the final TCP report was not due until February 1955, Land and the other Project Three members moved to gain Eisenhower's backing. In the first half of November 1954, Land and Killian met with Eisenhower to discuss the CL-282. Killian recalled later: "After listening to our proposal and asking many hard questions, Eisenhower approved the development of the [CL-282] system, but he stipulated that it should be handled in an unconventional way so that it would not become entangled in the bureaucracy of the Defense Department or troubled by rivalries among the services."

At the same time, Land and the other TCP members were also trying to convince DCI Dulles that the CIA should be in charge of the overflights. On November 5, Land wrote a report to Dulles outlining the group's reasons for this conclusion. The cover letter said: "I am not sure that we have made it clear that we feel there are many reasons why this activity is appropriate for CIA, always with Air Force assistance. We told you that this seems to us the kind of action and technique that is right for the contemporary version of CIA. . . . Quite strongly, we feel that you must always assert your first right to pioneer in scientific techniques for collecting intelligence—and choosing such partners to assist you as may be needed. This present opportunity for aerial reconnaissance seems to us a fine place to start."

Land's report also included a summary of how the project was to be organized. It would be run by the CIA with air force staff assistance, with the first intelligence within twenty months of approval. The cost was estimated to be $22 million, which included development, testing, and construction of the first six CL-282s, training and operation of the task force, and initial logistical support. The summary stressed that time was limited; within a few years the Soviets would develop the ability to intercept the aircraft. Thus, "very prompt action" was needed.

The report itself began by saying that it had been clear for a number

of years that photographic reconnaissance of the USSR would "provide direct knowledge of her growth, of new centers of activity in obscure regions, and of military targets. . . . During a period in which Russia has free access to the geography of all our bases and major nuclear facilities, as well as to our entire military and civilian economy, we have been blocked from the corresponding knowledge about Russia. We have been forced to imagine what her program is, and it could well be argued that peace is always in danger when one great power is essentially ignorant of the major economic, military, and political activities within the interior zone of another great power. This ignorance leads to somewhat frantic preparations for both offensive and defensive action, and may lead to a state of unbearable national tension. . . . We cannot fulfill our responsibility for maintaining the peace if we are left in ignorance of Russian activity."

Much of the memorandum was aimed at addressing DCI Dulles's concerns over the CIA becoming involved with the overflights. At one point Land noted, "For the present it seems rather dangerous for one of our military arms to engage directly in extensive overflights. . . . we recommend that CIA, as a civilian organization, undertake . . . a covert program of selected flights." Land also stressed how superior the CL-282 would be compared to the traditional agents that Dulles preferred: "No proposal or program that we have seen in intelligence planning can so quickly bring so much vital information at so little risk and at so little cost. We believe that these planes can go where we need to have them go efficiently and safely, and no amount of fragmentary and indirect intelligence can be pieced together to be equivalent to such positive information as can thus be provided."

Land's arguments, along with the knowledge that he had President Eisenhower's backing, finally won over DCI Dulles. Similarly, Major Seaberg's data on a J-57-powered CL-282, presented at the November 18, 1954, meeting with the TCP members, along with Eisenhower's backing, silenced air force doubts about the design. The following day, November 19, the final decision was made at a luncheon held by air force secretary Talbott. The participants—Dulles and Cabell from the CIA; Gardner, Ayer, and General Putt from the air force; Kelly Johnson from Lockheed; and Land from TCP—all agreed "that the special item of material described by Lockheed was practical and desirable and would be sought. . . . It was agreed that the Project should be a joint Air Force-CIA one. . . ."

Ironically, the last remaining group of doubters was Lockheed's senior management. When Kelly Johnson had gone to the meeting, his instructions from Lockheed management were "to not commit to any program during the visit, but to get the information and return." Although Lockheed had expended considerable effort during the spring and summer to find backers for the CL-282, by November 1954 the company was heavily committed to several military and civilian projects. During the luncheon, Gardner had told Johnson that he was essentially being drafted for the project and, if necessary, Johnson might have to take a leave of absence from Lockheed to work on the project. Johnson arrived back in California on the evening of November 19 and immediately met with Lockheed management. Johnson used Gardner's comments to convince them to approve the project.

On November 23, the Intelligence Advisory Committee, which included the directors of intelligence for the air force, army, navy, Atomic Energy Commission (AEC), State Department, and Joint Chiefs of Staff, and an assistant to the director of the Federal Bureau of Investigation, approved DCI Dulles's request to undertake the CL-282 project. The following day, Dulles signed a three-page memorandum requesting Eisenhower's approval.

On the afternoon of November 24, a meeting was held at the White House to discuss the project. On hand were DCI Dulles, DDCI Cabell, Secretary of State John Foster Dulles (the DCI's brother), Secretary of Defense Charles E. Wilson, air force secretary Talbott, and General Putt. President Eisenhower approved their proposal to build thirty CL-282 aircraft at a cost of about $35 million. Afterward, DCI Dulles said that the CIA could not fund the entire project without drawing attention to it. The group agreed that the air force would have to carry a substantial part of the financing. Eisenhower also asked Secretary of State Dulles about the foreign policy problems that might occur due to the overflights. John Foster Dulles said that difficulties might arise but "we could live through them." President Eisenhower concluded by saying that those present were to go ahead with building the equipment, but before operations were initiated, there would be a final review.

Building the Aquatone

On November 26, 1954, the day after Thanksgiving, DCI Dulles told Bissell that he was to direct the overflight program. Although Bissell had

known general details about the CL-282 for several months, only now was he made aware of the specific plans for what was code-named Project Aquatone. On December 2, Dulles told Bissell that he was to attend a meeting at the Pentagon the following day to discuss organization. The guidance he was given was minimal. When Bissell asked Dulles which agency was to run the project, he was told that nothing had been clearly decided. Bissell then asked who was going to pay for the project. The DCI answered, "That wasn't even mentioned. You'll have to work it out."

Representing the CIA at the December 3 meeting was Bissell and Herbert I. Miller, who soon became the executive officer for Aquatone. On the air force side were Gardner, General Putt, and several other senior officials. Much of the discussion was centered on how to divert the J-57 engines for use in Aquatone. They agreed that a separate contract for the added engines might endanger project security. The air force officials promised to turn over a number of engines to avoid this possibility. Then, as Bissell later recalled, "the ugly subject of money came up." Bissell asked who would pay for the CL-282 airframes. He recalled later: "I looked down the table to the right and everyone was looking in my direction . . . and everyone from the left was also looking in my direction." It was clear that they all expected the CIA to fund that part of the project. Bissell explained that the DCI had access to the Contingency Reserve Fund. The money could be spent by the DCI with the approval of the president and the budget director.

When Bissell returned, he told Dulles that the contingency fund would have to be used to pay for the airframes and cameras. The DCI told Bissell to prepare a memo for President Eisenhower and begin putting together his project staff for Aquatone. Eisenhower approved the use of the fund in mid-December 1954. Initially, the project staff consisted of Miller and the small existing staff of Bissell's Office of the Special Assistant to the DCI. As the administrative workload grew, a finance officer and a contract officer were added; in May 1955, an administrative officer, James A. Cunningham, Jr., a former Marine pilot, also joined.

Colonel Osmond J. "Ozzie" Ritland was named the air force liaison officer to the project staff in December 1954. Colonel Ritland had joined the Army Air Corps in 1932 and served as a fighter pilot and flew Army Air Mail. In 1935, he left the service and became a pilot with United Airlines. He returned to the Army Air Forces (AAF) in 1939 and was assigned as a test pilot. He conducted engineering, performance, and functionality tests of virtually all fighters, bombers, and cargo aircraft used

by the AAF. After the war, he continued working on development of new aircraft and systems. In February 1950, he was named commander of the 4925th Test Group (Atomic), which was responsible for making drops of live weapons at the Nevada Proving Grounds for atmospheric nuclear tests.

Once Kelly Johnson was notified of the presidential approval, he began putting together the team that would build the Aquatone. This originally consisted of twenty-five engineers and production personnel. The demands of the project forced Johnson to start pulling personnel from the main Lockheed plant, and soon the group numbered eighty-one people. Among those who were summoned was Ben R. Rich, an engineer who worked on engine inlet designs. He had heard rumors that Johnson was building an atomic-powered bomber, or a fighter with rocket engines, and so was surprised when he was shown a drawing of a gliderlike aircraft. He was then told, "You've just had a look at the most secret project in the free world."

A little over a week after getting the go-ahead, Johnson had worked out the details of the Aquatone. The design had evolved from that of the original CL-282 concept, with the changes not limited to replacement of the J-73 by a J-57 engine. The most obvious difference was the replacement of the CL-282's "T"-tail, inherited from the XF-104, with a low-mounted stabilizer. The wingspan had also been increased from seventy to eighty feet. The cockpit was now to be pressurized, because a ten-hour mission in a pressure suit was impractical. The original CL-282 belly skids were also not practical and were replaced by bicycle landing gear, which consisted of a main landing gear and a small tail wheel. The wings were supported by pogos, which the pilot would release after takeoff. On landing, the aircraft would balance on its bicycle gear until it slowed, then tip over onto one wing. To prevent damage, skids were added to each wingtip. The result was lighter than conventional landing gear that could still support the full weight of the aircraft.

Johnson promised that the prototype aircraft would be ready for its first test flight on August 2, 1955, with four aircraft delivered by December 1, 1955. To meet this schedule, the small team at the Skunk Works immediately began working forty-five hours a week. Soon after, another eight hours were added on Saturdays. Sometimes engineering would work staggered shifts to have engineering coverage in the shop. They divided up and worked the day shift, then the swing shift, and finally the graveyard shift over three weeks. The conditions they worked

under were "slum-like." Building 82, the home of the Skunk Works, was an old wartime bomber production hangar; the engineers were crammed into two floors of overcrowded offices. They never wore suits or ties and often behaved like college sophomores. One example of this was their cover names. Due to the extreme security of the project, each engineer was to use a cover name if he had to deal with outsiders while working on the project. The engineers scoffed at this, and Ben Rich picked the name Ben Dover (as in "bend over") after a British music hall star.

Kelly Johnson oversaw every aspect of the Aquatone project. Each area had only one to four engineers working on it. The wing group had four members, although others would pitch in as needed. One of the group, William "Bill" Bissell (no relation to Richard Bissell, whom the engineers knew only as "Mr. B."), started out drawing the leading edge assembly, then progressed to the wing ribs, then the aft structure between the rear beam and wing flaps and aileron. Each of the groups had full responsibility for its area; there was no one else to accept credit or blame. If a problem was discovered, it was dealt with in hours, not in days or weeks. If an error was made, it was admitted; nothing got past Johnson. Due to the speed of the schedule and the uncertainties of high-altitude flight, much of the design data was estimated, and work began from there. Once data did become available, the engineers looked at the design to see if it was adequate.

The Aquatone was built with a philosophy that one specific mission would be primary, that only a small number of aircraft would be built, that the aircraft and equipment would have special care, that the system life expectancy would be short, that flights would be infrequent, and that comfort or convenience would be secondary. Subsystems were simple, and the flight controls were manual and unboosted. The pilot had to use his own skill and strength to fly the airplane. The camera systems were simply turned on and off as required. Because the aircraft would operate only in clear weather, the pilot's skill, a modified sextant, and a homing compass were the only navigation equipment required. The aircraft would be flown by a small number of carefully selected pilots, so it could have flight characteristics far more demanding than those of a normal service aircraft. Similarly, because it would be serviced by a limited number of selected specialists, it did not have to fit within the standard air force organizational structure.

Central to the aircraft's philosophy was extreme lightness; every pound of weight removed from the aircraft meant another foot of altitude

gained. Johnson bluntly said that he would trade his grandmother for a lighter airplane. As a result, the aircraft's features were more like those of a glider than a conventional jet fighter. The wings were bolted on, as with a glider. The tail assembly was held in place with three small bolts. The aircraft's skin was the thinnest aluminum that could meet the strength requirements. To keep weight down, Johnson and the Skunk Works engineers were forced to come up with innovative solutions. Below an altitude of 35,000 feet, the aircraft would be subjected to turbulence that could tear apart its fragile structure, but rather than beefing up the structure, Johnson devised a system, similar to that used on gliders, called "gust control." The ailerons and tail surfaces were positioned so the aircraft would fly slightly nose high, which lessened the stress from wind gusts.

The result was an aircraft that was designed to be just strong enough. It had everything it needed to perform its mission of taking a camera to more than 70,000 feet and nothing that it did not need. The aircraft was a combination of sleek lines and the most severe functionality. Although the CIA code name for the project was Aquatone, the Skunk Works engineers had their own name for the aircraft. They called it the Angel.

The design and fabrication of the two prototypes and a static test article were done under extreme secrecy, which was not limited to the engineers' cover names. "Sterile" drawings and purchase orders were used, and the parts from outside contractors were sent to non-Lockheed addresses. Henry Combs, an engineer with the project, recalled later: "In the interest of secrecy, nothing was marked 'Secret.'" The reasoning was that if a drawing fell into uncleared hands, its importance would not be recognized. This applied not only to Lockheed. At the same time that James Baker was working on the cameras for Aquatone, he was also doing unclassified lens work for the Smithsonian Institution. Herbert Miller advised him not to take any special security precautions with the CIA lenses. By working on the lenses in the open, they would be completed faster and not be compromised. This approach of "hidden in plain sight" proved highly successful.

Even with such care, there were still security problems. When Johnson ordered several altimeters from the Kollman Instrument Company, he specified that they be calibrated to 80,000 feet. This immediately attracted unwanted attention, because the instruments went only to 45,000 feet. Central Intelligence Agency security personnel quickly briefed sev-

eral company officials and produced a cover story that the altimeters were to be used in experimental rocket planes.

All this work was done in spite of the fact that the contract with Lockheed was not yet finalized, nor was the CIA–Air Force relationship settled. Lockheed worked for nearly three months under a letter contract with the CIA, signed on December 22, 1954. The original Lockheed proposal, made in May 1954, had been for twenty CL-282 aircraft fitted with J-73 engines. During the negotiations with CIA general counsel Lawrence R. Houston, Lockheed revised this to twenty single-seat aircraft, a two-seat trainer, and spare parts. The air force was to supply the J-57 engines. The price that Lockheed was asking, Houston told them, was too high, because the CIA would also have to pay for the cameras and life-support equipment out of the available Contingency Reserve Fund money. In the meantime, Lockheed had begun design and fabrication work and had submitted its first payment vouchers. To keep the effort going, Bissell wrote a check to Lockheed for $1,256,000 on February 21, 1955. Rather than sending the check to the corporate headquarters, Bissell mailed it to Johnson's home in Encino. Although the check arrived safely at his mailbox, it was thought more prudent to set up a special account.

The CIA contract with Lockheed, No. SP-1913, was finally signed on March 2, 1955. It was a $22 million fixed-price contract for twenty aircraft, all single seat. The first was to be delivered in August 1955 and the final one in November 1956. In contrast to the standard air force contract, the CIA proposed using "performance specifications" rather than the more rigid technical specifications. This, Johnson believed, would save money. There would be a review at the three-fourths point if costs exceeded the fixed price. This proved unnecessary; the aircraft were all delivered on time and under budget.

Since the original meeting in December 1954, talks had continued between CIA and air force representatives. Although the original agreement was that the CIA would pay for the airframes and cameras and the air force would supply the J-57 engines, there remained many details yet to be decided. Foremost of these was who would run the operation. Meetings were held starting in March 1955 between Dulles and air force chief of staff Nathan Twining. General Twining was determined that SAC was to have full control once the airplanes and pilots were operational. Dulles, overcoming his earlier reluctance, could not agree to this, and the talks dragged out for several months. It was President Eisenhower who finally settled the issue. He stated bluntly, "I want this whole thing

to be a civilian operation. If uniformed personnel of the armed services of the United States fly over Russia, it is an act of war—legally—and I don't want any part of it."

With this settled, the remaining issues were quickly decided. The formal CIA–air force agreement was signed on August 3, 1955, by Dulles and Twining at SAC headquarters. The air force would have responsibility for pilot selection and training, weather information, mission planning, and operational support. The CIA was responsible for cameras, security, contracting, film processing, and arranging the use of foreign bases. Lockheed would handle construction and testing of the aircraft.

With the first prototype aircraft nearing completion, there was still one position that Johnson needed to fill. One day he called Tony W. LeVier, Lockheed's chief test pilot, into his office. Johnson asked, "Tony, you want to fly my new airplane?" LeVier replied, "What's it like? What is it?" Johnson answered, "I can't tell you unless you agree to fly it." LeVier, of course, agreed. He had done the early test flights on the XF-104, an airplane with almost no wings. LeVier now found himself test pilot of an airplane with wings longer than its fuselage. The first flight of the Aquatone was still several months off. For now, Johnson had another task in mind for LeVier, or rather for "Anthony Evans."

The Ranch

The extraordinary security precautions taken to hide the existence of the Aquatone meant that the aircraft could not be test-flown at Edwards Air Force Base or at the Lockheed facility at Palmdale. After LeVier agreed to be the project pilot, Johnson told him that his first job was to find a test site. He should look for a place that was, Johnson said, "remote, but one not too remote." LeVier and Dorsey Kammerer, the Skunk Works chief shop foreman, set off on a two-week search in Lockheed's Beechcraft Bonanza. Their cover was a hunting trip to Mexico. In reality, they scouted some fifty airports and dry lakes throughout California, Arizona, and Nevada.

Based on their survey, Johnson selected a lakebed he referred to only as "Site I." His initial plan was for an extremely bare-bones facility. The base would be used only for the test flights and pilot training, then abandoned. Because it was to be a temporary facility, Johnson wanted to keep the costs low. His initial estimate for construction was between \$200,000 and \$225,000. The base requirements were subsequently increased by the

CIA. These envisioned a roughly 300 percent expansion and a somewhat more permanent base, which Johnson estimated would cost about $450,000.

Although Johnson was happy with Site I, Bissell and Ritland were not. None of the fifty sites that LeVier had looked at met the project's security requirements. Ritland claimed to know a suitable site and offered to take them to it. During the bomb runs he made while commander of the 4925th Test Group (Atomic), he had flown many times over a little, X-shaped airfield just east of the Nevada Proving Grounds called Nellis Auxiliary Field No. 1. The old World War II training field and gunnery range had long been abandoned. It was located next to a dry lakebed named Groom Lake.

On April 12, 1955, LeVier, Johnson, Bissell, and Ritland flew out to Nevada on a two-day survey of the most promising sites. To get to the old Nellis Auxiliary Field No. 1, they had to illegally penetrate AEC airspace over the Nevada Proving Grounds. They came in low and without clearance. Ritland recalled later: "We flew over it and within thirty seconds, you knew that was the place. . . . Man alive, we looked at that lake, and we all looked at each other. It was another Edwards, so we wheeled around, landed on the lake, taxied up to one end of it, and Kelly Johnson said, 'We'll put it right here, that's the hangar.'"

Bissell was equally impressed and recalled later that it was "a perfect natural landing field . . . as smooth as a billiard table without anything being done to it." Johnson was initially reluctant, because Groom Lake was farther from Burbank than Site I. More important, it was downwind of the Nevada Proving Grounds and would be subject to radioactive fallout from the nuclear tests. Johnson's initial doubts were overcome, however, and all four finally agreed that the Groom Lake site was ideal for the Angel test flights.

Ritland returned from the survey trip and boarded a flight from Los Angeles to Washington to see Maj. Gen. Vincent G. Huston, head of the AEC's Division of Military Application. "Look, this is what we want to do," Ritland told him. He also wrote three memos for Trevor Gardner: one for the air force, a second from the AEC, and a third to the Air Training Command, which ran the gunnery ranges at Nellis Air Force Base. This was to prevent the training flights from interfering with the CIA's activities.

During the last week in April 1955, Johnson was in Washington for discussions with CIA officials about the status of the Aquatone program and

the base. The more distant location, as well as the expansion of Johnson's initial layout, increased the cost estimate of "Site II" to $832,000. The CIA officials accepted his suggestion that Site II should be named Paradise Ranch. Johnson later said: "It was kind of a dirty trick since Paradise Ranch was a dry lake where quarter-inch rocks blew around every afternoon." The name was later shortened to "the ranch." On May 4, 1955, LeVier, Johnson, and Kammerer returned to Groom Lake in the Bonanza. Using a compass and surveying equipment, they laid out a 5,000-foot, north-south runway near the southwest corner of the lakebed. They also marked out a general area for the hangars and other buildings, then returned to Burbank. As before, they overflew the nuclear test site, passing over a steel tower that contained a twenty-nine-kiloton nuclear device code-named Apple-2. The device was detonated the next morning.

Lockheed could not build the base itself, because it lacked the license to work on the Nevada Proving Grounds, so it had to subcontract the work to a company that had such a license. To hide Lockheed's connection with the base, the fictional CLJ Company (for Clarence L. Johnson) put the work out for bids. This almost backfired, because CLJ did not have a Dunn & Bradstreet credit rating, which raised suspicions. The contract was awarded to the Silas Mason Construction Company.

Work at the ranch was undertaken at a hurried pace during June and July. In Burbank, the first aircraft was now completed and was undergoing final tests. The ranch had to be ready for the airplane's arrival. Primary efforts were construction of a 5,000-foot runway for all-weather operations, construction of a road to the site, hangars, living quarters, offices, and support facilities. A well was drilled to supply limited fresh water. LeVier and fellow Lockheed test pilot Bob Matye spent a month preparing the lakebed for test flights. Groom Lake's use as a gunnery range during World War II had left its surface littered with .50-caliber shell casings as well as debris from the targets. The latter included half a steamroller. LeVeir suggested to Johnson that markings for four runways be painted on the lakebed. Johnson refused, because this would cost $450 and they were short of funds.

As the ranch was being readied, the flight test team was also assembled. In June, Ernest Joiner was told by his boss to report to Lockheed's Building 82 and see Kelly Johnson. No one at Lockheed knew what Johnson was doing in that building, but after Joiner was shown the project, he knew he was in for a "wild ride." Working on Aquatone had its do-

mestic aspects as well. Joiner told his wife that he had a new assignment at Lockheed. "What is it?" she asked. "I can't tell you," Joiner replied. "Where will you be working?" she asked. "I don't know," he replied. It was, Joiner said more than four decades later, nearly the end of a beautiful relationship.

Open Skies

In the two years following the death of Stalin in 1953, the new Soviet leadership took a series of policy steps to ease tensions, and there was considerable pressure for a Four-Power summit. Agreement was quickly reached on a meeting between July 18 and 23, 1955, in Geneva, Switzerland. On hand would be President Eisenhower, Prime Minister Anthony Eden of Great Britain, Premier Edgar Faure of France, and, leading the new collective Soviet leadership, Premier Nikolai Bulganin.

In preparation for the Geneva Summit, Nelson A. Rockefeller, special assistant to the president for psychological warfare, assembled a small group of advisers in early June and held a series of meetings at the Marine Corps base at Quantico, Virginia. The "Quantico Panel," as it later became known, was to come up with proposals that the president might make. As with others in the government, they were worried about a possible Soviet surprise attack. Based on what intelligence was then available, Rockefeller and the other panel members believed that the United States had a significant military lead as of mid-1955. They also believed that this lead was narrowing and by 1960 the Soviets might be in a position to launch an attack or use their nuclear forces to blackmail the United States and its allies.

The panel also concluded that arms control would not be possible unless each side could be sure of the size of the others' forces. Reliable methods of inspection would have to be developed before any arms control agreements could be reached. What the Quantico Panel proposed was a two-step approach. First would be mutual inspections of military facilities in order to test the feasibility of such procedures. The second step would be an international agreement allowing legal overflights of any country for reconnaissance.

Although the Quantico Panel's recommendations did not gain the approval of Secretary of State John Foster Dulles, Eisenhower remained interested in their ideas. He knew that the price would be high for covert overflights, even with the Aquatone, because the missions would enrage

the Soviet leadership. If the Soviets accepted the idea of legal overflights, however, he would have the information the United States needed, without the risk of provoking the USSR.

The session on July 21, the third day of the Geneva Summit meeting, was scheduled to deal with disarmament. Eisenhower began by reading the prepared text of his statement, then, about two-thirds of the way through, he interjected: "I should address myself for a moment principally to the delegates from the Soviet Union, because our two great countries admittedly possess new and terrible weapons in quantities which do give rise in other parts of the world, or reciprocally, to the fears and dangers of surprise attack. I propose, therefore, that we take a practical step, that we begin an arrangement, very quickly, between ourselves—immediately.

"These steps would include: To give each other a complete blueprint of our military establishments, from beginning to end, from one end of our countries to the other; lay out the establishments and provide the blueprints to each other.

"Next, to provide within our countries facilities for aerial photography to the other country—we to provide you the facilities within our country, ample facilities for aerial reconnaissance, where you can make all the pictures you choose and take them to your own country to study; you to provide exactly the same facilities for us and we to make these examinations, and by this step to convince the world that we are providing as between ourselves against the possibility of great surprise attack, thus lessening and relaxing tensions.

"Likewise we will make more easily attainable a comprehensive and effective system of inspection and disarmament, because what I propose, I assure you, would be but a beginning."

Although Premier Bulganin's initial response to what the press dubbed "Open Skies" was positive, Eisenhower's hope proved fleeting. At the reception, Communist Party first secretary Nikita Khrushchev dismissed it as an espionage plot against the USSR, at one point saying that the United States wanted "to look into our bedroom windows." (The actual quote was "bluer.") Khrushchev gave a more complete account of why he rejected Open Skies in a subsequent conversation with his son, Sergei Khrushchev, soon after he returned from the summit meeting. Sergei asked his father if he could accept Open Skies. The elder Khrushchev explained that he thought the Americans were really looking for targets for a war against the USSR. With the climate of mutual

fear, if the Americans were to understand that the USSR was militarily weak and defenseless against an aerial attack, there would be great pressure for a preemptive first strike. For Nikita Khrushchev, security could be maintained only if the United States was kept in the dark about Soviet weaknesses.

Following the Geneva Summit, Richard S. Leghorn wrote an article on Open Skies for *U.S. News & World Report;* it was published in the issue of August 5, 1955. The article argued that even if the Soviets said no to the proposal, the United States could still take action. He wrote: "We could make clear that aerial inspection and the information it would provide is so important to world peace that we probably will go ahead on our own. . . . we would carry out the inspection covertly, even in the face of Soviet military opposition." Such covert reconnaissance, Leghorn believed, "can be carried out with a very, very small probability of loss." The means would be "a few hand-tooled reconnaissance aircraft," which would have performance "substantially superior to any air-defense system around an area as vast as the Soviet Union."

When the magazine hit the streets, Leghorn got a quick call from Killian, whom he had known while a student at MIT. Leghorn was told to come to the White House, where he was admonished not to publish any further articles on the possibilities of aerial reconnaissance. At the meeting, Leghorn met Bissell and was told about Aquatone. Leghorn now learned that his ideas on reconnaissance as a means of peacekeeping had become national policy.

The Angel Takes Wing

In the early-morning hours of July 24, 1955, the day after the Geneva Summit ended, the disassembled Aquatone prototype, designated Article 341, was loaded on an air force C-124 cargo airplane at the Burbank airport. To hide Article 341 from prying eyes, it was covered with sheets. The cargo airplane took off for the ranch. Later that morning, Lockheed personnel took off in a DC-3. They lacked a "need to know," so they were not told where the ranch was located. During the flight, the window curtains were drawn so they could not see any landmarks.

When they arrived, they found that the ranch was, as Joiner later described, "a work in progress." One of the hangars had been completed, but it still needed electrical wiring. The most important building, the mess hall, had been finished. Initially, the telephone was in the bushes,

but the Lockheed personnel quickly had a working office. The work was done without regard to rank or status. The workbenches were built by Johnson himself. The ranch was a Wild West outpost in the middle of the desert. Joiner recalled a bobcat that "camped out" under the office floor, and a rattlesnake found a home in an aircraft wheel well.

As the final work was being done on the base, Article 341 was reassembled, then towed out of the hangar by a Jeep pickup. With LeVier in the cockpit, the engine was started and successfully run up. The first taxi test was made on July 27, with LeVier taking the aircraft to fifty knots on the lakebed. A second pair of runs was made on August 1, also on the lakebed. The first run proved successful, except that the aircraft rolled two miles before stopping. When LeVier complained that the brakes were no good, Johnson said that they just needed to be burned in. After Joiner inspected the brakes, Johnson said, "Take it back to the barn."

LeVier made the second run to the south, back toward the base. He quickly accelerated to seventy knots and cut the throttle. As he later reported, "It was at this point that I became aware of being airborne, which left me in utter amazement, as I had no intentions whatsoever of flying." LeVier tried to land the airplane, but he could not judge his height above the featureless lakebed. He made a hard touchdown in a slight left bank, then bounced back into the air. The second touchdown was much smoother. LeVier applied the brakes, with little effect, and the right tire blew. The aircraft rolled nearly another mile before stopping.

Johnson, Bissell, and Cunningham were watching as the aircraft touched down in a cloud of dust. They jumped into a Jeep and went roaring after the airplane. Reaching the now-stopped aircraft, they signaled LeVier to climb out while a ground crew used a fire extinguisher on the hot brakes. Damage to Article 341 was minor: a blown right tire, a leaking oleo strut on the landing gear, and damaged brakes. A taxi test the following day, which was done on the base runway, took the airplane up to eighty-five knots. Johnson and LeVier agreed that it was ready to fly. Runway markings were painted on the lakebed to give a visual reference to the airplane's height.

The first flight was scheduled for August 4, but a disagreement arose between Johnson and LeVier. Johnson wanted the touchdown to be made on the nose gear first. LeVier, on the other hand, had talked with B-47 pilots, who told him to make a two-point landing, the nose and tail wheel touching simultaneously, or the airplane would start to porpoise. The flight was delayed due to a series of problems in addition to a rain-

storm approaching from the west. Article 341 took off at 3:57 P.M. LeVier climbed to 8,000 feet, cycled the landing gear and flaps, and checked the aircraft's stability and control.

LeVier was now ready to make the landing. As Johnson had requested, LeVier attempted to land nose gear first. The airplane began to porpoise, and LeVier added power and went around again. The second landing attempt was unsuccessful, as were the next three tries. By this time, light rain was falling and the drops were sticking to Article 341's windshield. All this time, Johnson, in the DC-3 chase plane, had been offering advice. Finally, LeVier decided to land his way. He made a two-point landing, then used the gust control to reduce lift. Even as he rolled out, LeVier could feel the aircraft porpoise slightly. Landing time was 4:36 P.M. Ten minutes later, the storm hit, dumping two inches of rain and flooding Groom Lake.

LeVier made a second flight on August 6 to test the landing procedure. When this was successfully accomplished, Johnson scheduled the "official" first flight for August 8. On hand were Bissell, Colonel Ritland, and other CIA officials. The aircraft took off and climbed to an altitude of 32,000 feet.

Johnson had delivered the aircraft in the eight months he had promised. With this milestone out of the way, the Lockheed test team began a hard-driving flight program. LeVier made another nineteen flights by early September. The initial flights tested the aircraft's stall envelope, maximum load, and speed. LeVier then took the aircraft to higher altitudes. He reached 52,000 feet on August 16, then raised this to the initial design altitude of 65,600 feet on September 8. LeVier then returned to normal test duties and was replaced by Bob Matye, Ray Goudey, Robert Schumacher, and Bob Sieker.

These early flights were made without an autopilot. As a result, the pilot's workload was high. Goudey made a six-hour flight without an autopilot and was tired afterward from the stress of keeping within the six-knot difference between the stall speed and the Mach limit of the aircraft. Subsequent flights were made to qualify the autopilot, which proved reliable.

The flight test programs showed that only a few changes were needed. Double brakes were added to improve the airplane's stopping ability, and one of the aircraft's oil coolers was removed. When problems appeared, they were dealt with immediately rather than causing the program to be grounded for study and analysis. One flight indicated that there was a

problem with the airflow around the aft fuselage interacting with the exhaust plume of the engine, resulting in a loss of thrust. Johnson looked at the data and had a one-inch strip trimmed off the rim of the aft fuselage. "Okay," he said, "let's take off and try again."

The aircraft quickly proved its high-altitude capabilities. On three separate flights, Matye broke the world altitude record of 65,880 feet set by a Canberra on August 29, 1955. On his third such altitude flight, on September 22, Matye suffered the first flameout while flying at an altitude of 64,000 feet. After a brief relight at 60,000 feet, the engine flamed out again, forcing him to make a slow descent to 35,000 feet before he could attempt another restart. Although the incident validated the partial-pressure suit, emergency oxygen system, regulator, and emergency descent procedures, it was the first indication of engine problems.

The Aquatone was equipped with an interim Pratt & Whitney J-57–P-37 engine, which was taken off the shelf, then modified for high-altitude flight. The engine was heavier and produced less thrust than planned. More serious, the P-37 version proved to be touchy; flaming out at any mishandling by the pilot. The problems were most serious in the final climb between 57,000 and 65,000 feet, an altitude later known as the "badlands." The P-37 engine also showed excessive oil use; almost the entire sixty-four-quart capacity was lost in the course of a flight. Some of the oil ended up as fumes in the cockpit, which smeared the windshield and obscured the pilot's vision. The engine also suffered from turbine blade wear.

While Lockheed and Pratt & Whitney engineers worked on these problems, the airplane had been given a name. Lieutenant Colonel Leo Geary and Col. Allman T. Culbertson looked through the aircraft designator handbook to see what was available. They decided they could not call it a fighter or a bomber or a transport, and they did not want anyone to suspect that it might be for reconnaissance. The X-16 had been given an experimental designation as cover, but they decided that the "utility" category was best. At the time, there were two utility-type aircraft, the U-1 and the U-3. So Geary told Culbertson that the CL-282 would be officially known as the U-2.

"Sheep-Dipping"

When President Eisenhower approved Project Aquatone, he told DCI Dulles that its pilots should not be U.S. citizens. The assumption was that

the United States could disavow a captured pilot if he was not an American. The CIA recruited one Polish and four Greek pilots, but then it ran into problems. The Polish pilot had experience only in light aircraft and was never allowed to fly the U-2. For the Greeks, language proved to be a barrier, although several were good pilots. An air force officer was attached to the group to help them during preliminary training. Despite this, only two of the Greeks passed the ground school and reported to the ranch. The pair made a few flights but washed out by the autumn of 1955. The four pilots could not be sent back to Greece, so they flew support and chase missions at the ranch for a year or more afterward.

With the attempt to train foreign pilots a failure, Bissell worked with Lt. Gen. Emmett "Rosy" O'Donnell, the air force deputy chief of staff for personnel, to find possible SAC fighter pilots. The requirements were 1,000 hours of jet flight time, single-seat experience in overwater flight using a sextant, air defense experience, and being a reserve officer. Beyond these requirements, they were looking for pilots who were intelligent, focused on flying, and completely fearless in the air. The search was narrowed to pilots from four units: the 31st and 508th Strategic Fighter Wings at Turner Air Force Base in Georgia and the 12th and 27th Strategic Fighter Wings at Bergstrom Air Force Base in Texas. These F-84 units were being phased out, and in the confusion the disappearance of a few pilots would not be noticed.

The first two pilots approached were Marty Knutson and Carmine Vito. Knutson was a lead F-84 pilot, which meant he was assigned a nuclear weapon and target. He knew firsthand that U.S. intelligence on the USSR was poor. The target folder he was given to study contained a map of the USSR dated 1939 and a picture postcard of the town from the same era. Knutson and Vito were hurriedly summoned back from a weekend leave in New York. They appeared the worse for wear at 8:00 A.M. on Monday morning at the commander's office. Rather than a chewing out, they were offered a mysterious special assignment. It was top secret, they were told; if they were interested, appointments would be set up at the Albany Hotel.

When they both agreed, they were told to go to a nighttime meeting at a specific room at the hotel, which had the reputation of being a bordello. There they were interviewed separately by several mysterious civilians from "the government." These strangers offered them what every young fighter pilot wanted: excitement, cheap thrills, some money, and the chance to do something important for the country. They could not resist.

All the pilots who agreed to the assignment began a series of trips and meetings around the country. They were subjected to lie detector tests and medical exams, including a week's stay at the Lovelace Clinic in Albuquerque, New Mexico. This was also their introduction to covert activities. During each meeting, a radio was playing and the water faucets were left running to foil any concealed listening devices. The men were also fitted for partial-pressure suits. According to Knutson's later recollection, they were not told exactly what they would be doing. Finally, six pilots were selected: Marty Knutson, Carmine Vito, Wilburn S. Rose, Glenn Dunnaway, Carl Overstreet, and Hervey Stockman. The six resigned their Air Force Reserve commissions, then, as civilians, signed CIA contracts. This process, called "sheep dipping," was meant to hide their military backgrounds. Once they had completed their CIA duties, however, they could rejoin the air force, with the time in the U-2 program counted toward promotion.

Finally, in early 1956 they were loaded on a C-54 and flown from Burbank to the ranch. Even at this point, the pilots had not been told what they would be doing, and they had visions of flying rocket ships and high-Mach fighters. The C-54 landed, the door was opened, and the six pilots saw what looked like a glider. Knutson recalled later, "Four guys got off the airplane, me and another guy said thanks, but no thanks." With a little encouragement, they joined the others, who then took their first look into the cockpit. They saw a control yoke adapted from the P-38. Knutson recalled, "All of the pilots had come from a fighter background, and fighter pilots flew with sticks and bomber pilots flew with wheels or yokes. Fighter pilots did not like bomber pilots and thought they were beneath them, so when we looked in the cockpit and saw a yoke all six of us got back on the airplane and said thanks but no thanks." It was not until their second day at the ranch that the six pilots were told that they would be making overflights of the USSR.

Their training was conducted by six SAC pilots under the command of Col. William F. Yancey. The SAC pilots, who had been checked out in the U-2 by the Lockheed test pilots in September 1955, taught the sheep-dipped CIA pilots the difficult task of flying the aircraft. The initial flights were landing training in a T-33 trainer. The transition to flying the U-2 was made all the more difficult by the fact that, despite the earlier Lockheed proposal, there was no two-seat trainer. All instruction had to be given on the ground or by radio. Their initial flights in the U-2 were touch-and-go landing practice missions. These were followed

by high-altitude and cross-country missions to the Allegheny Mountains and back.

The CIA pilots found that the U-2 demanded their complete attention at all times. They had to monitor the aircraft's speed to stay within the limits, making fine adjustments to the fuel flow. The pilot checked the airplane's fuel usage with a totalizer rather than a fuel gauge. The counter was preset by the ground crew to the total gallons loaded in the wing tanks. A flow meter subtracted each gallon of fuel as it was burned. The pilot kept a log of the fuel consumption, which was compared to the preflight estimate. As a backup, the pilot also kept track of fuel usage by monitoring speed and time in the air. All the while, the pilot had to adjust the autopilot, navigate the aircraft, and operate the reconnaissance equipment. The pilot's already difficult task was further complicated by the engine problems. Knutson recalled later that the aircraft averaged seven flameouts per mission.

The beginning of CIA pilot training also marked a step-up in activities at the ranch. The population of 75 at the time of the initial test flights had grown to 250 Lockheed, CIA, air force, and contractor personnel. In early 1956, there were four U-2s at the site; by March the number had grown to nine, which were used to support flight test activities, camera testing, and pilot training. Individuals working at the ranch were typically flown out to the site on Monday morning. They would spend the week there, then return to Burbank on Friday afternoon.

Life at the ranch was rugged, with summer heat of more than a hundred degrees, along with dust and wind, followed by snow and bitter cold in winter. The ranch was small and meant to be temporary, with only enough people to do the job correctly and on time. Among the rudimentary facilities were three T-shaped hangars, a control tower, a runway, storage tanks for the special LF-1A fuel, several water wells, and a mess hall. The base commander was Richard Newton, from the CIA. Although the site was called "the ranch," it had now acquired the official name of "Watertown Strip." This was reportedly for Watertown, New York, the birthplace of DCI Dulles.

The week's activities, Lockheed engineer William Bissell later recalled, were "work, work, and excitement." Hours were long, the pace was intense, and amenities were few. Housing was "all right"; if a person was spending the week or most of a week at the site, he was usually assigned to a bunk in a four-man house trailer. These were later described as being "very nice." They were cleaned every day and were warm in winter. Persons staying overnight usually bunked in old army or air force bar-

racks. They were recalled by Bissell as being one story and not as nice as the trailers but "okay." The barracks were also cleaned every day. Without question, the high point of life at the ranch was the mess hall. Bissell said later, "The food was par excellence. All you could eat and very well prepared. I don't remember ever having a bad meal."

Given the accelerated schedule of the U-2 program, there were few opportunities and little time for recreation. Bissell did recall going to movies at night in an old, unheated barn. It was about a quarter mile from the building area, "off in the boondocks," and predated the construction of the base. Power for the projector and a light or two was supplied by a long drop line. It was, Bissell observed, "quaint."

Radar Tracking and Flying Saucer Sightings

The high-altitude training flights made by the CIA pilots permitted an assessment of radar's ability to detect the U-2. Edwin Land's support of the CL-282 design, as well as Eisenhower's approval of the program, was based on the belief that Soviet radar could not detect an airplane flying at more than 70,000 feet. The logic was that Soviet radar was based on U.S. technology supplied during World War II. Because U.S. radar had difficulty spotting targets at more than 40,000 feet, it was assumed that Soviet radar would have similar shortcomings.

This belief seemed to be confirmed by a 1952 study of Soviet World War II radar, as well as tests in 1955 that used U.S. radar. As a result, it was believed within the CIA that the best the Soviets could hope to do was pick up the aircraft sporadically. They would not be able to track the aircraft, direct fighters against it, or even be sure what was going on. The training flights over the United States also supported the theory that the U-2 was hard to detect on radar. On each flight, the aircraft was spotted only one or two times.

Based on this, the CIA estimated that it would take the Soviets a year or two before they could develop a radar network able to track the U-2 with sufficient precision to allow them to lodge a diplomatic protest. It was assumed that with detailed supporting evidence, any Soviet protest would generate sufficient political pressure to force the United States to halt the overflights. As a result, it was expected that the U-2's operational lifetime would be limited. Until the Soviets did have such a radar network, however, the U-2 would have free run.

Although the radar data from the training overflights indicated that the U-2 was nearly "invisible" to radar, there were visual sightings of the

aircraft at altitude. Most of these came from airliner pilots and usually occurred in the early evening on flights going east to west. One of the most heavily traveled air routes, Chicago to Los Angeles, passes close to Las Vegas and the ranch. The piston-engine airliners of the mid-1950s, such as the DC-3, DC-6, and Constellation, flew at 20,000 feet. At twilight, a low-flying airliner would be in darkness whereas a U-2 at 70,000 feet would still be illuminated by the sun. Its bare metal wings reflected the sunlight, and it appeared as a fast-moving, fiery object far higher than the airliner and many miles distant.

Most airliner pilots were ex-military pilots, and they knew of no aircraft that flew higher than 45,000 feet. Because the object was obviously much higher than that, they assumed that it could only be a flying saucer. The pilots would report the sighting to air-traffic controllers. Under ideal conditions, it was also possible to spot a U-2 in full daylight from the air and even from the ground. The aircraft would appear as a flash or glint. Ground observers and airline pilots wrote letters reporting the sightings to Project Blue Book, the air force investigation unit.

Blue Book staff members who had been briefed on the U-2 established procedures to handle such reports. If a sighting report came in that might have been caused by a U-2, the project staff would be contacted with the time, date, and location of the sighting. The staff would then have to check the flight logs. This was a laborious process, because an individual route flown by a U-2 would have to be matched with the location and other details of the sighting. With the training and test operations under way, there were numerous flight logs to go through, which involved considerable work for the project staff.

Once a match was found, Blue Book had a problem. They knew what had caused the sighting, but it was a closely guarded secret. Rather then tell a witness that he had seen a secret ultra-high-flying airplane, the sighting was explained away as some natural phenomenon, such as ice crystals or temperature inversions. The exact number of flying saucer sightings caused by U-2s is unknown. Many years later, Cunningham made an off-the-cuff comment: "Hell, they were half of them." This referred to the reports that Blue Book sent to the project staff as possible U-2 sightings rather than the more than 13,000 total sightings reported.

Practice Overflights of the United States

By early 1956, the final political and technical preparation for overseas deployment of the U-2 were under way. On February 24, DCI Dulles met

with Senators Leverett Saltonstall and Richard B. Russell, who were the ranking members of the Senate Armed Services Committee and its subcommittee on the CIA. Dulles briefed them on Project Aquatone and asked if some members of the House of Representatives should also be told about the U-2. Based on their advice, Dulles talked with two ranking members of the House Appropriations Committee, Representatives John Taber and Clarence Cannon. For the next four years, they remained the only congressmen with knowledge of the U-2 effort.

Also in February, Bissell and his staff were developing the cover story for the overseas U-2 operations. He decided that the aircraft should be described as a high-altitude weather research aircraft being operated by the National Advisory Committee on Aeronautics (NACA), a civilian group involved in high-altitude and high-speed flight. The odd-looking U-2 would fit right in. The NACA cover story was approved by the end of March 1956. The U-2s at Watertown Strip were subsequently painted with NACA markings; the base itself was later described as a site being used by NACA for weather research with air force support.

With the NACA cover story prepared, the staff turned its attention to the contingency plans to be used if a U-2 were lost over hostile territory. Bissell told the cover officer to "produce a document which sets forth all actions to be taken . . . not only press releases and the public line to be taken, but also the suspension of operations and at least an indication of the diplomatic action. . . . We should at least make the attempt in this case to be prepared for the worst in a really orderly fashion." The cover officer developed a plan based on the weather plane story, which Bissell approved. Subsequently, the project staff prepared a series of statements to be used in different scenarios, including one in which the U-2 pilot was captured alive. Even in this case, the policy was that the United States would continue to use the weather research cover story.

Flight tests of the U-2 had shown that it met all the original performance specifications. It had a maximum altitude of 72,000 feet, placing it far above the reach of Soviet fighters, and a range of 2,950 miles, making it able to cover most of the Soviet landmass. Its camera systems showed higher resolution than any operated before. Even the flameout problem had finally been solved. Starting in March 1956, the first J-57–P-31 engines began to be delivered. These hand-built engines proved to be impossible to flame out. They had no oil use and better blade wear. A P-31 engine was also 276 pounds lighter than the P-37, as well as producing 13,000 pounds of thrust versus the 10,200 pounds of the P-37 version.

The final action before deployment could begin was an air force operational readiness inspection. This is the series of tests used to determine whether a new unit is ready to become operational. The exercise lasted for a week, with Colonel Yancey and his detachment serving as observers. The group went through each aspect, from flight crews to camera technicians and the mission planners, to check out the unit as a complete system.

The final test was a series of eight simulated overflights of the United States, conducted from April 10 through 14, 1956. The U-2s were to take off from the ranch and overfly targets throughout the country. The aircraft were fitted with the A-2 camera package: three K-38 cameras fitted with 9.5-inch film magazines. One camera was pointed to the right, another looked straight down, and the third was pointed to the left. The cameras were lightened to meet the 450-pound payload limit of the U-2. The camera bodies were fitted with new 24-inch focal length f/8.0 lenses designed by Jim Baker. These lenses were able to resolve sixty lines per millimeter, a 240 percent increase over previous lenses. Baker personally ground each lens and made the final optical tests before delivering the lenses to the CIA. The A-2 package also included a 3-inch tracking camera, for a continuous photographic record of the U-2's flight path.

The only incident during the readiness tests occurred on April 14. Cunningham was in his office in Washington when the project officer called to inform him that a westbound U-2 flying over the Mississippi River, at the border of Tennessee, had suffered a flameout. The pilot was able to restart his engine, but it flamed out again and then began to vibrate so severely that he could not attempt another restart. This possibility had been foreseen, and sealed orders had been sent to air bases around the country with instructions about what to do in the event of a forced U-2 landing. Cunningham told the project officer to ask the pilot how far he thought the U-2 could glide. Based on the pilot's estimate, Cunningham would alert the nearest SAC base. The pilot, who was by now over Arkansas, radioed that he thought the U-2 could reach Kirtland Air Force Base, outside Albuquerque, New Mexico, some three hundred miles away.

Within minutes, Cunningham called Colonel Geary to tell him about the emergency. Geary, in turn, called Brig. Gen. Ralph E. Koon, the air force assistant director of operations. General Koon then called the base commander at Kirtland, told him about the sealed orders, and ex-

plained that an unusual aircraft would make a dead stick landing at his base in the next half hour. The base commander was told to have the air police keep onlookers away from the airplane and to get it into a hangar as soon as possible.

The base commander got everything in readiness for the arrival of the mysterious airplane, but the half hour passed with no sign of the aircraft. He called the Pentagon to ask where it was. As he was on the phone, the base commander saw the U-2 glide to a landing on the runway. As it did, he remarked, "It's not a plane, it's a glider." The air police received a bigger shock as they surrounded the airplane. After the U-2 had come to a stop, the pilot, dressed in a close-fitting green partial-pressure suit and white helmet, climbed out of the cockpit. As he did, one of the air policemen was heard to say that the pilot looked like a man from Mars.

When the exercise was completed, Colonel Yancey's group went over all the results. Yancey concluded that the U-2 was ready for deployment. He briefed a Pentagon panel, which included the secretary of the air force and the chief of air staff. After listening to his presentation, they agreed that the detachment was ready. Just over two weeks later, the deployment to England began.

Chapter 4
Genetrix and Homerun

Navigation difficulties in the Arctic region may have caused unintentional violations of Soviet air space, which, if they in fact had occurred, the Department regretted.

—U.S. State Department note on the Project Homerun overflights

In the early months of 1956, the United States had, in effect, two parallel overflight programs. Both were in a state of flux. The air force had years of overflight experience, but the near loss of the RB-47E showed that daylight overflights of heavily defended areas of the USSR, using conventional aircraft, were becoming too risky. Additionally, President Eisenhower, in approving the U-2, had decided that future missions would be made by the CIA rather than the air force. As yet, however, the CIA's U-2 was still unproven, with the test flights still under way, the deployment still to be made, and Eisenhower's final approval yet to be given.

But before the air force overflight program was taken over by that of the CIA, it would make the largest-scale efforts yet seen. The first of these would be the culmination of the years of work developing a balloon reconnaissance capability. The second was a program of mass RB-47 overflights, conducted under the most difficult of operating conditions.

The WS-119L Reconnaissance Balloon

Senior air force generals meeting on July 3, 1953, had approved development of the operational WS-119L balloon reconnaissance system under the code name Grandson. There remained the daunting task of transforming the technology tested with the Moby Dick and Gopher projects into an operational system, then produce the necessary equipment and train the launch and recovery crews.

Problems were soon to appear. The air force had to show that the WS-119L balloons could successfully drift across the Soviet landmass with-

out going astray. This seemed simple, because a number of Moby Dick and Skyhook balloons had been caught by the jet stream and crossed the Atlantic at high speeds. In December 1954, air force personnel launched eight Moby Dick balloons from Scotland as long-range test flights. They expected that the balloons would be carried by the jet stream across the USSR. In reality, all eight of the balloons went south and ended up making lazy circles over Yugoslavia and North Africa. A second series of launches were made in January 1955, but none of these balloons remained aloft.

The WS-119L was in serious trouble. With the start of the operational flights only ten months away, it had not yet been shown that the WS-119L could successfully cross the Soviet landmass. As a result, the CIA became unofficially involved in the program. Philip G. Strong, in addition to his duties with the CIA, was also a member of several air force scientific advisory boards. Through these, Strong became aware of the problems with WS-119L.

The CIA had long experience with the use of balloons in covert activities. A major effort was the launching of balloons from West Germany to drop propaganda leaflets. The campaign began on August 13, 1951, against Czechoslovakia under the slogan "Winds of Freedom Blow from West to East." Over the years, some 300 million leaflets were sent by balloons to Eastern Europe and the western USSR. These leaflet efforts were not the only CIA project involving large balloons. Strong learned that the CIA had previously launched a large balloon from Scotland. The balloon drifted across the USSR and was recovered near South Korea. Strong provided the data on the CIA balloon flight to the air force, which used it as evidence that the WS-119L balloons could successfully make the long journey.

In the spring of 1955, the organizational framework for the operational reconnaissance balloon flights against the USSR was put together. On April 22, the 1st Air Division (Meteorological Survey) was established at SAC. This was composed of the 1110th Air Support Group, which would launch the balloons from bases in Scotland, West Germany, Norway, and Turkey; the 6926th Radio Squadron (Mobile), which would track the balloons' homing beacons once they cleared communist airspace; and the 456th Troop Carrier Wing (TCW), which had responsibility for recovering the gondolas. With the training effort about to begin, the code name Grandson was dropped and replaced with Grayback.

Training was scheduled to begin on May 1, 1955, and be completed

on September 1. The most difficult challenge was faced by the aircrews of the 456th TCW, based at Charleston Air Force Base in South Carolina. They would have to master, in a short time, the task of midair recovery, which had previously been done only by test crews, and often not successfully. Each recovery crew consisted of the aircraft commander, two copilots, a navigator, radio operator, flight engineer, winch operator, and four pole handlers. The crewmen had mixed backgrounds. Most were ex-B-50 gunners who wanted to stay on flight status; others were airmen right out of basic training. Airman Third Class Paul M. Lovrencic recalled later that he and the other new crewmen were subjected to pranks. Lovrencic was once sent all over Charleston Air Force Base looking for a bucket of prop wash.

The 456th TCW was equipped with specially modified C-119F cargo aircraft. The only visible change was the rear fuselage. Rather than the normal rear doors, the unit's aircraft were fitted with a special "beavertail" door, which could be opened in flight. This allowed two poles to be extended from the aircraft. Several loops of rope with hooks attached were strung between the poles to catch the gondola's drogue chute. To allow the C-119Fs to conduct patrols along the balloons' estimated flight paths, the aircraft were fitted with two Benson tanks, each holding 500 gallons of fuel. The aircraft could remain aloft for up to thirteen hours, but the gross weight was increased to 72,800 pounds from the maximum 68,000-pound, single-engine takeoff weight.

Initial midair recovery training was done using concrete blocks or sand-filled fifty-five-gallon oil drums. The base parachute shop rigged four old twenty-eight-foot personnel chutes to the top of the practice gondola. The fifteen-foot drogue chute was attached to the end of a hundred-foot line. A half dozen of the practice gondolas were carried on a training flight. The C-119F climbed to 15,000 to 20,000 feet, and the recovery gear was rigged. A gondola was then pushed out of the airplane. The C-119 pilot flew a figure-eight pattern and could make three or four attempts to catch the drogue chute before the gondola hit the water.

The recovery training soon ran into problems. Much of the early training was trial and error, and deliveries of the modified C-119Fs were slow. There were also shortages of supplies and equipment, a limited number of recovery gear sets, and a shortage of qualified instructors.

Problems also beset the 1110th Air Support Group launch crews at Lowry Air Force Base, outside Denver. Originally, "Moby Dick Hi" was to be an operational suitability test to train the crews, test the equipment, and determine the vulnerability of the reconnaissance balloons to air de-

fenses. The first WS-119L launch was made on May 11, but it ended in failure. This became the pattern. Of the nine WS-119L launches made during May 1955, none was successful. Twenty-six launch attempts were made in June, but only six were judged fully successful. During July, due to shortages of hydrogen gas, homing beacons, and supplies, only twelve launches were made, resulting in four successes. To solve the problems would require as much trial and error as careful analysis. As a result of the recovery training delays and the balloon problems, the planned date for the start of overflight missions was pushed back by the air force to December 1, 1955.

The problems with the balloon launches and midair recovery training continued in August. Despite improved launch equipment, about half of the balloon launches ended in failure. The most spectacular of these occurred on August 17. At 10:15 A.M., Mrs. Charles Argo saw a balloon descending toward her home on South Glencoe Street in a town near Denver. Her three children and a neighbor's child were playing in the front bedroom, and she called for them to get out. The balloon hit the corner of the house where they had just been, shattering a window. The balloon then broke a power pole across the street, knocking out electricity to several homes. Within minutes, a crowd of some two thousand people had gathered; the local children tore up the plastic balloon and kept the pieces as souvenirs.

At Charleston Air Force Base, the recovery training continued, with the personnel organized into combat crews that trained as a single unit. The difficulty of midair recovery was becoming apparent. The C-119F pilots had to fly just above the drogue chute in order to snag it with the loops. If the pass was miscalculated, the drogue chute could be drawn into an engine. This occurred three times during training missions. Twice, the nylon melted from the heat of the propeller, preventing the propeller from being feathered. During the other incident, the propeller blades cut through the parachute, damaging the blades.

A more serious problem occurred during a training flight commanded by Noel Wien, son of the founder of Wien Alaska Airlines. Rather than being caught by the loops, the drogue chute passed over them and trailed behind the C-119F like a drag chute. The drogue chute's hundred-foot line struck the airplane's elevator, jamming it into the full up position. The C-119F went into an uncontrolled climb, stalled, then fell through into a dive. As it did, the drogue chute collapsed, freeing the elevator and allowing Wien to recover. As the airplane pulled out, however, the drogue chute reinflated, and the line again forced the elevator into the full up

position. This cycle was repeated several times before a crewman was finally able to cut the line, freeing the practice gondola. After the C-119 landed, the copilot walked into squadron operations and announced that he was through with the mission.

Despite the risks, only one fatal accident occurred. Early on the morning of August 23, a C-119F was taking off on a training flight when its left engine failed and the aircraft, heavy with fuel, crashed into a residential district. The C-119F skidded along the ground and broke up. Five of the crew were killed in the crash; five others were able to escape from the wreckage with major injuries and another received only minor injuries. An accident review board found that the airplane's left engine had a history of problems, but it was unable to identify a specific cause for the failure.

As the summer of 1955 drew to a close, there was a change in the fortunes of Grayback. The training efforts were nearing an end, the early problems were being cleared up, and the time for overseas deployment was drawing nearer. In addition to the recovery training, a combat crew had to fly a series of simulated patrol and intercept missions. Their final task would be the midair recovery of an actual gondola from a Moby Dick Hi flight.

One of these recoveries was made by a crew commanded by Capt. Harold E. Mitchell. After taking off from Charleston Air Force Base, the aircraft flew across the United States to Hamilton Air Force Base in California, then out over the Pacific. It was guided to the balloon by its homing beacon, which transmitted an individual three-letter Morse code signal. The C-119F's direction finder gave a left-right indication. The aircraft flew toward the balloon's position, finally spotting it visually. George Mathews, the airplane's navigator, recalled that it "appeared as a very bright light high in the sky." The aircraft climbed to 20,000 feet, and the crew rigged the recovery equipment.

The C-119F's radio operator cut the gondola free using a device that looked like a rotary telephone dial. When the airplane was in position, a specific series of numbers was dialed into the device and transmitted to the balloon. The balloon received the signal, decoded it, then released the gondola. The parachutes deployed and the C-119F snagged the payload.

Bringing the gondola aboard proved difficult, Mathews later recalled. The gondola was dangling a few feet behind the aircraft, but before it could be swung in and set on the floor of the airplane, the line had to be transferred to an upper pulley. Mathews said later, "We had all kinds

of trouble doing this. We were all in the rear leaving the poor copilot flying the plane. He kept sending messages back that the engines were overheating, we were running low on fuel and various other kinds of problems all of which we ignored being determined not to lose the package. We got it on board and I remember it as a cream colored plastic box . . . with several glass covered apertures on it."

The Moby Dick Hi flights were also used to test the vulnerability of the balloons to jet fighters. The Air Defense Command was told the balloons' launch times, estimated flight paths, and locations. The balloons proved to be hard to spot visually and on radar. Once the balloons were located, interceptors were sent aloft to shoot down the balloons. The pilots scored several kills, but the risk was estimated, based on about twenty balloons, to be acceptable.

These activities attracted unwanted public attention. As with earlier balloon flights, they sparked a number of flying saucer sightings in the Colorado Springs area and at Durango, Colorado. The most serious problem occurred on September 11, when a C-119 "weather plane" (as later newspaper reports called it) cut down a balloon that had been launched from Lowry Air Force Base five days before. The midair recovery attempt failed, and the gondola and control box landed near Fowler, Indiana. Several of the enlisted crew members parachuted from the airplane to secure the equipment. While they were guarding the equipment, a crowd began to gather. One of the crewmen told the onlookers that the balloon had been brought down by "electrical impulse guns" and that one of the boxes contained "small animals" that were being flown to test the effects of high-altitude flight. Finally, two trucks from Chanute Air Force Base arrived and removed the equipment.

The crewman's comments were published, and inquires began to be made that threatened the project's security. To counter this, the air force invited the press to watch a WS-119L launch from Lowry Air Force Base on September 14. The *Denver Post* carried a photo of Maj. Joe Collins, the 1110th Air Support Group's operations officer, and Maj. Thomas McBroom, the Detachment 1 commander, standing in front of a WS-119L payload. It showed the two ballast boxes, camera gondola, and control box. By hiding the balloon in plain sight, the air force was able to keep its mission a secret.

During Moby Dick Hi, 141 balloons were launched. Of these, thirty-three were successfully cut down by the C-119Fs, resulting in eleven successful midair recoveries. The operational suitability test, which formally

ended on October 16, 1955, had sorted out many of the technical, equipment, and training problems, and WS-119L was judged to be ready.

The overseas deployment of the 456th TCW began in early October 1955. The forty-nine C-119Fs were flown with minimum crews to their air bases at Adak and Kodiak in Alaska; Itazuke, Johnson, and Misawa in Japan; and at Kadena on Okinawa. The ground personnel, winch operators, and pole handlers traveled to the West Coast by troop trains, then crossed the Pacific in troopships. The 1110th Air Support Group launch crews and other personnel also went by troopships to Western Europe, then on to the five launch sites: Gardermoen, Norway; Evanton, Scotland; Giebelstadt and Oberpfaffenhofen, West Germany; and Incirlik, Turkey.

Political arrangements had been reached between the United States and the host countries. In the case of Norway, the presence of U.S. military personnel represented a significant policy change, because Norway had not previously allowed foreign troops to be permanently based on its soil. The arrangements made with the British were particularly extensive, which was not surprising given the joint U.S. Air Force–RAF RB-45C overflights. The United States would share the intelligence with the British, although the British indicated an interest in developing their own balloon reconnaissance project.

The RAF liaison officer for WS-119L, squadron leader F. H. Martin, wrote in a paper for the chiefs of the air staff: "The USAF have calculated that some 68 percent photographic coverage of Soviet territory might be achieved through use of the balloons. . . . If the expected success rate is achieved, then a highly effective method of peacetime aerial reconnaissance of a potential enemy's territory will have evolved." While U.S. Air Force personnel were setting up in England for the launches, RAF officers were being sent to America to learn about "balloonology."

Arrangements were also made for the "weather balloon defense" cover story. Major General Roscoe Wilson wrote to RAF marshal Sir William Dickson: "It is believed that this cover story will be acceptable in view of past publicity given balloon launches by the USAF. It is recognized that stray balloons may fall in Soviet areas. In this eventuality, the balloons will be identified as USAF meteorological research balloons."

President Eisenhower and other government and military officials also discussed the project. Eisenhower had ambivalent feelings about the reconnaissance balloons, being deeply concerned about the Soviet reaction to them. In a later conversation with the Joint Chiefs of Staff, Eisenhower said that if the Soviets were sending balloons over the United States, the country would be discussing mobilization. For this reason,

Eisenhower and Secretary of State Dulles were "rather allergic" to the balloons. The military, on the other hand, felt that the photographs would be worth any difficulties.

President Eisenhower gave his approval on December 27, 1955. With the go-ahead to begin flights, the code name was changed for the final time. The reconnaissance balloons were now called Genetrix. According to one account, Eisenhower's approval was influenced by photos taken during the final Moby Dick Hi flights, which had carried actual camera gondolas to take intelligence-quality photos for evaluation. One of the balloons had passed high over Fitzsimonds General Hospital outside Denver, where Eisenhower was recovering from his September 24, 1955, heart attack. This balloon's photos were among those shown to Eisenhower when his approval was being sought. He was impressed with their resolution and the amount of information that could be gleaned from them.

Eisenhower did insist on a limitation. The maximum altitude of the balloons was not to exceed 55,000 feet. This gave only a narrow altitude margin against the MiGs, but it was done with an eye toward the future U-2 missions. Eisenhower did not want the Soviets to develop an interceptor able to reach the altitudes that the U-2 could fly. The altitude restriction affected the amount of hydrogen the balloons were filled with, the amount of ballast they could carry, and their mission lifetimes.

Genetrix: Reconnaissance Balloons over the USSR

It took several days before operations could begin. The first action was to establish the cover. On January 9, 1956, the day before the launches were to begin, air force headquarters issued a press release that Moby Dick flights were being extended to other areas in the Northern Hemisphere. The press release noted that the program had been under way for the previous two years to obtain weather data above 30,000 feet. It continued: "Large plastic balloons, which have often been mistaken for 'flying saucers,' will carry meteorological instruments, including cameras to photograph clouds and radio equipment to record and telemeter atmospheric information." It concluded by noting that "small research stations for the purpose of launching balloons have been activated in Japan, Okinawa, Alaska, Hawaii, and Europe."

Also on January 9, a balloon launch was made from Okinawa to further bolster the cover story. Despite bad weather and damaged equipment, the launch was successful and, more important, received press at-

tention. These cover missions, which were called White Cloud, involved the launching of ten balloons each from Okinawa, Hawaii, and Alaska between January 9 and July 1956. The State Department requested that this first cover launch be made the day before the Genetrix reconnaissance flights were to begin.

The next day, January 10, 1956, nine Genetrix balloons were launched—eight from Incirlik, Turkey, and one from Giebelstadt, West Germany. The original plan was for a maximum effort, launching as many balloons as possible in order to saturate Soviet air defenses. Instead, air force headquarters directed that only ten "effective" balloons were to be launched a day. This was defined as a balloon that was successfully launched and was believed to have entered Soviet airspace. Over the next several days, the other launch sites also began operations. Oberpfaffenhofen, West Germany, launched its first five balloons on January 11; Evanton, Scotland, launched a single balloon on January 12; and Gardermoen, Norway, sent up three balloons on January 13. By now, the daily quota of ten effective balloons was being met, and operations were in full swing.

Each balloon carried a gondola with a duel framing camera with two 6-inch focal length trimetrogon lenses, which were located on opposite sides of the gondola. The setup was designed by Duncan Macdonald at BUORL. The twin cameras had two separate supplies of 9- by 9-inch film. There was enough film to take five hundred photographs, each of which could cover an area fifty miles on either side of the balloon. The gondola also carried a small tracking camera, which recorded the balloon's flight path. This allowed the positions of features in the high-resolution photos to be located using landmarks. The cameras were turned on each morning by a photoelectric cell and operated throughout the day, until the light level became too low and the photoelectric cell turned them off. The complete camera gondola was thirty-six by thirty by fifty-seven inches, about the size of a home refrigerator, and weighed 380 pounds.

As the first balloons ran the gauntlet of Soviet air defenses, their arrival was eagerly awaited by the recovery crews stationed in the Pacific. Each crew wanted to make the first midair recovery. Starting on January 11, the 456th TCW's Weather Section began making forecasts of the balloons' positions and trajectories. On January 13, three of the balloons turned on their high-frequency (HF) radio beacons. The ground stations picked up the signals and triangulated their positions. The C-119F recovery aircraft, flying in two-plane formations, were sent after the bal-

loons. One of the aircraft, call sign Center 39, was commanded by Capt. Slaughter Mimms. During training, Mimms's crew had been named the unit's lead crew and participated in the training of the other crews. They had been given the nickname El Tigre, the tiger crew.

As Mimms's aircraft flew toward the balloons' location, the radio operator, A1c. Don Shannon, picked up the homing signal. The C-119F began to climb toward the recovery altitude of 20,000 feet. The beaver-tail door was opened, and the four pole handlers, Lovrencic and A1c. Paul A. Ellis, Jim Murphy, and William B. Cullpepper, began rigging the poles. The cargo compartment was cold, and Lovrencic said later that they were ill equipped to work in those conditions. The crew had to use oxygen due to the high altitude, but the walk-around bottles were heavy and cumbersome and their oxygen was quickly exhausted. Sometimes the crewmen would take a few breaths, quickly do some work, take a few more breaths, and repeat the cycle. (Without oxygen, a person remains conscious for only a few minutes at 20,000 feet.)

The recovery gear was rigged and the balloon was spotted visually as it floated at about 50,000 feet. Shannon transmitted the cut-down signal, and the gondola released from the balloon. The parachutes opened, and the gondola began the slow descent toward the waiting recovery airplane. Mimms made several figure-eight passes at the drogue chute, finally catching it at 9,000 feet. The winch operator, SSgt. Jim Muehlberger, began to reel in the gondola, which was now trailing behind the C-119F. The crew went through the complicated recovery sequence until the gondola was hanging just behind the aircraft. The crew then reached out, grabbed the gondola, and pulled it aboard the C-119F, then the beavertail door was closed. When Mimms and his crew landed, they were met by the wing commander, Col. James L. Daniels, who presented them with a case of whiskey for making the first midair recovery. The other two balloons were caught by other crews later that day.

On January 17, a week after operations began, the quota for Genetrix launches was raised to twenty per day by air force headquarters. This was increased on February 25 to thirty balloons, then to forty balloons per day on February 28. As had occurred many times before, the balloons attracted attention. They created a wave of flying saucer sightings in England, Germany, and Norway. The Norwegian newspaper *Aftenposten* reported that a *flyvende tallerken* (flying saucer) was seen on February 3. It was a Genetrix balloon that had been launched from Gardermoen at 10:30 A.M. The sky was clear, and the balloon was seen above the Nor-

wegian towns of Grorud, Oslo, Holmestrand, Larvik, and Porsgrunn during the following three and a half hours.

As a safety feature, the Genetrix balloons were programmed to dump their ballast and separate the gondola if they were still below 15,000 feet thirty to forty minutes after launch. This was to prevent a balloon from endangering civil aircraft. As a result, however, a number of balloons landed near the launch sites. Three balloons landed in Kent, England, and were reported to the local police. Several of the balloons launched from Gardermoen landed near Vormsund, Norway, and another at Skarnes. Sweden, to the east of Norway, was also the site of several balloon landings. One balloon was found near Hedemora, Sweden. The balloon's envelope covered several large pine trees; the gondola and ballast boxes were recovered.

Once the remaining Genetrix balloons had crossed into communist airspace, the responses of Eastern European and Soviet air defenses were monitored. Radio transmissions made during the attempted interceptions provided extensive data on Warsaw Pact radar networks, radar sets, the ground-controlled interception techniques that were used, the altitude capabilities and tracking accuracies of the radar, and the methods used by the different Warsaw Pact nations to "hand off" the balloons as they crossed from one country's airspace to another. United States and NATO radar operators at facilities around the borders of the USSR were also able to locate a number of previously unknown radar sites.

While western ground stations monitored their actions, Soviet and Warsaw Pact air defenses began taking a toll on the Genetrix balloons. According to an intelligence report that later reached the CIA, a balloon was shot down by Bulgarian antiaircraft fire over the former Royal Palace of Vranya, located some thirty kilometers southeast of Sofia. The report said that a fire started at the palace, which was being used as a convalescent home for scientists. A special commission estimated the damage at 12,000 leva. (The report added that experience with balloons to date indicated it was unlikely that they could cause a fire.) Three other balloons were reported to have been brought down in the Plovdiv area in central Bulgaria.

The balloons proved to be difficult targets. The MiG fighters sent after them were operating at their altitude limits, making the aircraft unstable and hard to handle. As they closed on the balloons, the MiG pilots had only a few seconds to take aim and fire. The increased tempo of operations also took a toll in the form of operational accidents. Ac-

cording to one published account, two Genetrix balloons were spotted over Hungary on January 21, 1956. Two MiGs were ordered to attack them. During the hurried takeoff, the two fighters collided, killing one of the pilots.

Despite the losses inflicted on the balloons, they still continued to reach the Pacific recovery zones in acceptable numbers. Captain Mimms's crew continued to be the most successful. Following the first midair recovery on January 13, 1956, the crew made a second recovery several days later. Their third midair recovery followed on January 23. The crew also received credit for two assists. In the first case, the gondola came down in Japan and was picked up by a helicopter and flown to Johnson Air Base. The other gondola landed in the ocean, and the crew dropped smoke and dye markers to pinpoint its location. As they circled overhead, awaiting the arrival of an amphibian to make the pickup, the crew spotted a Japanese fishing boat heading toward the floating gondola. The C-119F made several low passes to scare it off. Lovrencic recalled later, "I believe the passes were so low you could see the whites of the eyes as some of the crewmen jumped overboard." An SA-16 amphibian eventually landed on the water and took the gondola aboard.

Most of the crews, however, had no such success. The Alaska-based recovery units were repeatedly frustrated. George Mathews, the navigator in Capt. Harold E. Mitchell's crew flying out of Kodiak, Alaska, later recalled: "It soon became apparent that something was wrong. We would launch for a recovery with the transmitting frequency and the cut down code, track the thing, find it (sometimes) and dial in the code which was supposed to cut it down. Nothing would happen. The balloon would go sailing on to the east. We would confirm we had the right balloon, had the proper code and were doing everything right but we could never cut the things down.

"This went on for some time with the same results. We never knew what went wrong. There was much speculation that the folks who didn't want us to catch the things figured out a way to render the balloon receivers inoperative or that the receivers were failing due to poor design or power failure but it was hard to believe that that many would have failed."

Genetrix Defeated

In the first two weeks, 219 balloons were launched, of which 52 reached the recovery zones. This was an acceptable recovery rate. Then the bal-

loons stopped arriving. Between January 26 and January 30, 1956, a total of 112 balloons were launched, but none made it through to the recovery zones. Initially, the 1st Air Division thought that the sudden increase in the loss rate was due to the HF transmitters. They were turned on by a timer, which was set according to the estimate of when the balloons would be clear of communist airspace. These predictions were proving inaccurate, and the HF transmitters were being turned on too early. In one case, signals from a group of eighteen balloons were detected over northern China. The signals were also detected by communist ground stations, and the balloons' locations and courses were plotted. Only three of the balloons ever reached Japan.

The impact of the sudden drop-off in recoveries was being felt in Washington. At 9:53 A.M. on January 31, Secretary of State Dulles called air force secretary Quarles to say that with the recoveries down, he was not sure it was worth continuing with Genetrix. Quarles tried to reassure him, saying that the recoveries were expected to lag behind the launches. Dulles replied that the subject might come up at the White House, and he felt that the Soviets "are on to the game now."

Dulles remained concerned, and on February 3 he made a telephone call to W. Park Armstrong, Jr., special assistant for research and intelligence, to say that he was anxious to keep a close watch on the recovery situation, specifically on whether there was any evidence of "diminishing returns." If this was the case, Dulles said, he wanted the balloon flights stopped. Armstrong told him that a few of the balloons had begun to transmit but had not yet reached the recovery zones. Dulles told Armstrong that both he and President Eisenhower were nervous about the balloons, and he reiterated that if they were failing to produce "substantial results," he wanted the launches stopped. The telephone call ended with Dulles and Armstrong agreeing that a Soviet protest over the reconnaissance balloons was near.

The following day, February 4, 1956, Soviet deputy foreign minister Andrei A. Gromyko handed a note protesting balloon operations to U.S. ambassador Charles E. Bohlen. Similar notes were also sent to Turkey and West Germany. The Soviet note protested "the launching by United States military organs from the territory of Western Germany, and also from United States Air Force bases situated on the territories of several nations bordering on the Soviet Union, of balloons into the airspace of the USSR. The apparatus suspended from the aerial spheres includes au-

tomatic photographic cameras for aerial photography, radio transmitters, radio receivers and other things. . . . Investigation shows these spheres and their suspended apparatus are manufactured in the United States."

The note continued that the balloon flights constituted a "gross violation of Soviet airspace . . . contrary to obligations assumed by the U.S. government in accordance with the U.N. Charter and incompatible with normal relations between states. . . . The Soviet Union presents a decisive protest and demands that the government of the United States take measures for the prompt cessation of the impermissible activities of the American military organs."

Ending the Genetrix flights was not the only goal of the Soviet's protest note. For the previous several weeks, communist bloc newspapers and news agencies had been undertaking a campaign against the propaganda balloons being launched under secret CIA sponsorship. A few days before, a Tass dispatch from Berlin said that "launching such balloons represents a serious danger to planes flying in the airspace of the German Democratic Republic, including aerial communications of West Germany with Berlin," and that they represented a violation of international law. The protest note continued that the Soviet government had asked the United States in September 1955 to halt the propaganda balloon launches. It complained that the United States had taken no such action, then added, "According to data at the disposal of Soviet organs, the flights of these aerial spheres over territory of the Soviet Union have not only not ceased but have increased of late."

At 10:15 A.M. on February 6, two days after the delivery of the Soviet note, Eisenhower and Secretary of State Dulles met. The president said that he thought it was time to suspend the balloon operations. Dulles agreed but added that it should be done "so it would not look as though we had been caught with jam on our fingers." He continued that a suitable reply to the Soviet note would be prepared. At 12:12 P.M., Dulles called Quarles and informed him of the president's decision to halt operations. Dulles asked if the telephone call was sufficient authority for Quarles to proceed; Quarles said it was and that the balloon launches would be halted until further notice. By the time the stand-down order reached the European launch sites, another fifteen balloons had been launched. This brought the final total to 448 Genetrix balloons.

Two days later, on February 8, the State Department reply to the Soviet note was delivered to the foreign ministry in Moscow. The U.S. note

began by saying: "In the Soviet government note there is an apparent confusion between a publicized meteorological operation and previous Soviet allegations concerning the launching of propaganda balloons directed towards the Soviet Union. In this latter connection, the U.S. Government recalls certain oral observations were made by the Soviet Foreign Minister on September 28 to the American Charge d'Affaires in Moscow who denied any U.S. Government responsibility for activities of which the Soviet Government complained. The U.S. Government wishes to reaffirm that it is not directly or indirectly participating in any project to dispatch propaganda balloons over the Soviet Union."

The U.S. reply continued that regarding the "meteorological balloons," the United States "is happy to supply information complementary to what is already public knowledge." After mentioning the air force press release, the U.S. note continued, "The Soviet Government is presumably aware of this announcement, but for convenient reference a copy is attached." The U.S. note added: "In the interest of scientific research, it would be much appreciated if the Soviet Government would return the instruments which have come into its possession."

After noting that the balloons posed no threat to civil aircraft, the U.S. reply concluded: "The U.S. Government would be happy to explain further to the Soviet Government the safety measures incorporated in the project. Provisionally, however, in order to avoid misunderstandings, and in view of the Soviet Government's objections, the U.S. Government will seek to avoid the launching of additional balloons which, on the basis of known data, might transit the USSR."

On the evening of February 9, the Soviet foreign ministry put some fifty of the recovered Genetrix balloons on display for the world's press. The press conference was held at the Spiridonovka Palace, official residence of Foreign Minister Molotov. The palace's driveway and courtyard were lined with dozens of recovered balloons and gondolas. Soviet army meteorological specialist Col. A. V. Tarantsev said that the balloons "carried no meteorological equipment—only cameras and automatic radio equipment designed to trace the balloon's flight." Colonel Tarantsev also showed several photographic negatives from a balloon and said that they "incontrovertibly prove the espionage character of American balloons." He added that the photos showed not only cloud formations but also terrain, "which is in no way necessary for photographing clouds for meteorological purposes."

Soviet foreign ministry press chief Leonid Ilyichev declared that the balloons represented a menace to air navigation and persons on the ground, then added, "All such attempts by American military organs are an attempt to conduct a policy 'to brink of war' which has been condemned by peoples." Ilyichev continued that during January 1956, the USSR captured "a great number of balloons launched by the United States," and press accounts said that five hundred balloons had been launched by the U.S. military. He continued: "The United States military have also launched balloons carrying leaflets and propaganda literature against the Soviet Union."

The diplomatic flap created by the Soviet protest and display of the captured Genetrix balloons worried senior CIA officials. They were afraid that Eisenhower might ban future overflight operations just when the U-2 was ready for deployment. Deputy director of Central Intelligence Cabell wrote to air force chief of staff Twining in February to warn of the "additional political pressures being generated against all balloon operations and overflights, thus increasing the difficulties of policy decisions which would permit such operations in the future." General Cabell's concerns included the U-2 and the propaganda balloons that the Soviets found so objectionable. He apparently feared that as a result of the controversy over the Genetrix overflights, Eisenhower might also curtail the leaflet balloon operations.

Despite Cabell's request, in mid-March 1956 Twining asked President Eisenhower to approve development of a new reconnaissance balloon system. It would fly much higher than either the U-2 or Genetrix and could be ready for operations in eighteen months. The president told General Twining that he was "not interested in any more balloons."

Ironically, despite CIA fears and President Eisenhower's dislike of balloon overflights, the controversy over the Genetrix overflights proved to be brief. While the Soviets were protesting the reconnaissance balloons, the U.S. Army announced that a Soviet weather balloon had been found the previous weekend in northern Japan. The five- by three-and-a-half-foot balloon carried meteorological equipment with Russian markings, including a label saying "Instrument to measure air current." Subsequently, the air force announced that five Soviet weather balloons had been found in Alaska during the previous three years. The United States sent a diplomatic note to the Soviets on March 1 pointing this out and adding, "It is illogical that the Soviet government should demand one

rule for itself and another for the rest of the world." The Soviets were placed on the defensive by the balloons and denied that their balloons had entered Western airspace.

The Results of Genetrix

As Eisenhower was ordering a halt to Genetrix launches, and the diplomatic exchanges were beginning, the C-119F crews were busy recovering the last of the balloons. On February 6, 1956, a Genetrix balloon entered the recovery zone. This was the first in a week and was the sole survivor of the eighteen balloons launched on January 31. The gondola was successfully recovered in midair.

On February 8, four balloons out of the eighteen launched on February 3 also reached the recovery zone. Of these four, one gondola was cut free, but the midair recovery failed and the gondola was lost at sea. A second balloon self-terminated; the gondola landed in the ocean and was found by Japanese fishermen on February 15. The third balloon entered the recovery zone at night and was cut down over Japan by a C-119F. The gondola landed in trees; but due to the rough terrain, deep snow, and snow slides, recovery was put off to await better conditions. The fourth Genetrix balloon did not respond to the cut-down signal, so a U.S. fighter was sent after it. The balloon was shot down and the gondola was recovered by a boat. These were the last balloons to reach the recovery zones.

The 1st Air Division estimated that about 379 Genetrix balloons actually entered Soviet bloc airspace. Of these, 235 were lost to fighters or ground fire. Of the 144 that transmitted radio signals, more than half also fell victim to Soviet air defenses or other causes, such as using ballast at a higher rate than expected due to the 55,000-foot altitude ceiling imposed by Eisenhower. Only 66 balloons made it to the recovery zones; of these, 44 were successfully recovered.

The C-119F crews made sixteen successful midair recoveries. Of these, eight gondolas were recovered in midair by aircraft from Detachment 1 of the 744th Troop Carrier Squadron (TCS) at Itazuke Air Base, Japan. Three of these were caught by Captain Mimms and his crew. Another five were successfully recovered by crews from Detachment 1 of the 746th TCS at Johnson Air Base. The units at Kadena (on Okinawa), Misawa (in Japan), and Kodiak (in Alaska) each caught one gondola. The crews at Adak (in Alaska) were unsuccessful. Of the remainder, twenty-one gondolas were returned by Japanese nationals and agencies, two each were

recovered by the army and navy, and three were picked up by air force amphibians and helicopters.

There was a total of 13,813 usable exposures in forty gondolas (the cameras in four gondolas had malfunctioned). The coverage amounted to 1,116,449 square miles of the USSR and China, or 8 percent of their total landmass. This coverage was spotty, however. Of the forty-four gondolas recovered, thirty had been launched from Turkey, seven from Giebelstadt (in West Germany), six from Oberpfaffenhofen (in West Germany), one from Evanton (in Scotland), and none from Gardermoen (in Norway). (In 1957 and 1958, two more gondolas were found.)

The reason for the spotty coverage was that the prevailing winds caused many of the balloons to drift across southern Europe, the Black Sea, and the deserts of China. Between this and the disproportionately large number of balloons from Turkey, the coverage was concentrated in the southern USSR, northern China, and Korea. The primary target areas, however, were in higher latitudes. Despite this, the Genetrix photos provided some of the best and most complete coverage of the USSR taken since World War II. The areas covered were outside those of the GX photos. The Genetrix photos were to serve as the baseline for all future overhead coverage and could be used to spot any later changes, such as new facilities.

This photographic baseline was not the only Genetrix result of importance to the upcoming U-2 program. The SIGINT data from the Eastern European and Soviet attempts to intercept the balloons provided intelligence on the locations and capabilities of their radar as well as the interception procedures used. Western radar sites also tracked the balloons as they drifted over Eastern Europe. This provided the most accurate data on high-altitude wind currents over the Soviet bloc to date. Both the SIGINT and wind data was later used in planning the U-2 flights.

Despite these accomplishments, the initial results of Genetrix appeared disappointing. It had operated for only twenty-seven days rather than the several months originally planned. The 448 balloons launched were a small fraction of the 2,500 envisioned. The coverage also fell far short of that planned. Genetrix's true importance awaited the future.

Project Homerun: The Mass RB-47 Overflights

Since the late 1940s, independent of the overflights, the United States had conducted intelligence-gathering flights along the borders of the So-

viet bloc. Most of these were SIGINT missions to pick up radar signals and radio transmissions. Other flights carried long-range cameras that photographed coastal and border areas while flying outside Soviet airspace. Although the areas that could be covered by such border flights were limited, the flights were an early source of information about the Soviet military.

The border photographic flights were determined by the sun. During the winter months, days in the northern USSR are short. The sun is low on the horizon, and the ground is hidden in shadows. In the far northern regions of the USSR, above the Arctic Circle, the nights last twenty-four hours and the land is shrouded in darkness. With the approach of spring, the sun appears to climb higher in the sky, the days grow longer, and objects on the ground are better illuminated. In the spring of 1955, a series of border photographic missions was conducted under the designation Project Seashore. Four RB-47Es, modified to carry K-30 cameras, operated out of Eielson Air Force Base in Alaska. Their missions covered the eastern and northern coastline of the USSR. On April 18, one of the RB-47Es was intercepted by a Soviet MiG and shot down. The crew members were unable to make a distress call before they were lost, and the Soviets did not make a protest. All the United States knew was that the aircraft had disappeared. This was the ninth U.S. aircraft lost while on a border flight since a navy Privateer was shot down by the Soviets over the Baltic in April 1950.

When the photos from the Seashore missions were analyzed, they indicated a buildup in Soviet forces on the northern coast of the USSR. Interest grew in an ambitious program of overflights to locate and identify air defenses throughout the entire region, both photographically and electronically. In early February 1956, soon after he had terminated the Genetrix balloon launches, President Eisenhower approved Project Homerun. This was to be on a much larger scale than Project Seashore and be conducted under far more difficult operational and weather conditions.

A special SAC detachment was formed to conduct the overflights. It consisted of sixteen RB-47Es from the 10th Strategic Reconnaissance Squadron, based at Lockbourne Air Force Base in Ohio, five RB-47H SIGINT aircraft of the 343d Strategic Reconnaissance Squadron at Forbes Air Force Base in Kansas, and two squadrons totaling twenty-eight KC-97 tankers. One of the tanker squadrons came from Lockbourne and

the other was based at Thule, Greenland, which was the site used for the operation.

The RB-47s and KC-97s arrived at Thule on March 21, 1956. The air base was located 690 miles north of the Arctic Circle, on Greenland's North Star Bay. The base had a single 10,000-foot, ice- and snow-covered (and sometimes fog-shrouded) runway. All maintenance work had to be done in the open, in temperatures of minus thirty-five degrees Fahrenheit. The air- and ground crews were housed in special barracks that resembled railroad refrigerator cars. These were designed like cold-storage lockers, with foot-thick insulated walls and standing on pillars three feet above the snow. Each unit was self-sufficient, with its own food and water supply, for use when the base was hit by a "phase"—a sudden high wind that dropped temperatures and reduced visibility to zero. These could last for a few hours or up to four days.

Despite the snow-covered surroundings, fresh water was in short supply at Thule. Each barracks had a water storage tank that was refilled by a truck. The water was used for showers, sinks, and washing machines. It had to be used sparingly; a person taking a shower wet down for ten seconds, soaped up, then rinsed for fifteen seconds. The water was then recycled for the toilets, which used the "armstrong" flush system. The toilets were hand-pumped; they used a complex series of valves, which caught many an unaware newcomer. The sewage was transferred to a storage tank, then emptied by another truck. Both the water and waste couplings leaked badly, and a six-foot-long icicle a foot in diameter would form on each. The one on the waste coupling was referred to as a "fudge sickle." The two forms of recreation at Thule were drinking in the barracks and drinking in the club.

The crews spent their first week at Thule in arctic survival training and practicing arctic flight operations—takeoffs and landings on the ice-covered runway, learning to use the grid navigator, and midair refueling, all under total radio silence. Initially there were problems: The RB-47E crews were below standard in aerial refueling. By the end of March, however, everything was in readiness for the operational missions.

The mission planners had divided the 3,500-mile-long northern coastline of the USSR into three segments. The first went from the Kola Peninsula eastward to Dikson on the Kara Sea. The second went from Dikson to Tiksi on the Laptev Sea, and the final segment was from Tiksi east to the Bering Strait. The individual missions were planned by the unit, us-

ing information and guidelines from air force headquarters. The mission planners were headed by Lt. Col. Glenn E. "Buck" Rogers and Maj. George A. Brown, who spent almost two weeks working out the majority of the mission routes and hardly seeing the outside of the secure operations room for that entire period. Major Brown had been the operations officer for Project Seashore and had flown one of the missions.

A normal overflight mission involved an RB-47E photographic aircraft paired with an RB-47H SIGINT aircraft. The latter were production SIGINT aircraft that had had their bomb bays converted into a pressurized compartment for three electronic warfare officers, commonly called "Crows." The photo airplane led and the SIGINT aircraft followed in normal wing formation. Because of the long distances to the target areas, each reconnaissance aircraft was supported by a KC-97 tanker. The KC-97s took off first, to reach the refueling point over the North Pole ahead of the RB-47s. Usually four or five missions were flown each day. Each crew was briefed only on its own assignment; no one knew what the other crews were doing. All the missions were flown under total radio silence, from the takeoff to the landing back at Thule. If a single word was said over a radio, all the missions for the day were canceled.

As the reconnaissance aircraft neared the Soviet coastline, the RB-47s separated. The RB-47E photographed bases and installations and the RB-47H crew monitored the radar signals generated by the intrusions. Most of the Thule missions, as the crews called them, penetrated only a few miles inside Soviet airspace. The island of Novaya Zemlya, or, as the crews called it, "Banana Island," was also photo-mapped. This included the nuclear test site that had been built on the island the previous year. Some of the RB-47s, however, flew deep inland behind the Ural Mountains, mapping the timber, mining, and nickel smelting industries scattered throughout the region. All of the missions were flown in daylight.

The crews and aircraft were rotated among the assigned missions. Because of the scope and secrecy of the Homerun missions, none of the senior commanders or operational officers were allowed by air force headquarters to fly a mission. Most accepted the directive, but Col. William J. Ming, commander of the 26th Strategic Reconnaissance Wing, which had supplied the RB-47Es, kept asking. Finally, Brig. Gen. Hewitt T. Wheless, the 801st Air Division commander who was overseeing the operation from Thule, told him to "forget it."

The Thule missions began to wind down, beginning with the departure of the RB-47Hs back to Forbes Air Force Base on May 4. Before the

RB-47Es returned to Lockbourne Air Force Base, however, they made Project Homerun's grand finale. This was a mass RB-47E overflight of the Soviet Far East on May 6, 1956. Six RB-47Es took off from Thule, headed over the North Pole, then turned south toward the USSR. They entered Soviet airspace at Ambarchik and, flying abreast, continued south at 40,000 feet in broad daylight. After penetrating deep into the USSR, the RB-47Es turned due east, continuing to photo-map the entire region, and finally exited over Anadyr on the Bering Strait. The six RB-47Es landed at Eielson Air Force Base in Alaska. The following day, the airplanes returned to Thule. The RB-47Es departed Thule for Lockbourne on May 10, 1956, bringing Project Homerun to a close.

A total of 156 missions were flown during the seven-week effort, without the loss of a single aircraft or person due to Soviet action or accident. This was all the more remarkable given the extreme weather conditions and the long distances flown over the Arctic wastes. No mission was ever recalled or canceled due to violation of radio silence.

The results were similarly remarkable; when the photographic and SIGINT intelligence from Project Homerun was analyzed, it indicated that the northern coastline of the USSR was virtually undefended. Siberia was largely an empty wilderness. The RB-47 crews found little in the way of roads, towns, or other signs of human habitation. There were only a few radar sites and air bases scattered across the vast distances. Despite the large number of overflights, carried out over a prolonged period, there were only three or four attempts by Soviet MiGs to intercept the RB-47s, and all had ended in failure.

The discovery that the northern flank of the USSR was largely undefended was of great significance. It meant that U.S. and RAF bombers coming in from the North Pole ran little risk of detection. The vast spaces that had provided both Czarist Russia and the Soviet Union with defense in depth against ground invasion had now been turned against them. The U.S. and RAF aircraft would not have to run a gauntlet of air defenses all the way to their targets. Rather, they would not be detected until they approached the heavily defended areas. This limited the risks to the bombers, and it limited the time that Soviet air defenses would have to destroy them.

It was not until several days after the final RB-47Es had returned home that the Soviets finally protested the Project Homerun overflights. On May 14, 1956, a protest note was delivered to the U.S. embassy in Moscow. Two weeks later, President Eisenhower met with his senior ad-

visers to discuss a number of matters, including the protest note. On hand were DCI Allen Dulles; Adm. Arthur W. Radford, chairman of the JCS; Gen. Nathan F. Twining, air force chief of staff; Undersecretary of State Herbert Hoover, Jr.; and Col. Andrew Goodpaster, Eisenhower's military assistant. Eisenhower said that he wanted to give the Soviets every chance to move in peaceful directions and to put U.S.-Soviet relations on a better basis and see how far they would go. For this reason, he said, it was desirable to be wise and careful in what the United States did.

Undersecretary Hoover then read a draft reply to the Soviet note. Eisenhower thought a passage might be added to the effect that the U.S. government had instructed its aviation services to be especially careful regarding the possibility of navigation error in the Arctic regions. This was added to the draft text. The following day, May 29, the State Department presented a note to the Soviet embassy explaining that navigation difficulties may have caused unintentional violations of Soviet airspace and, if so, the State Department regretted them.

Independence Day 1956

The Genetrix balloon flights and the Homerun RB-47 overflights were the high point of the first decade of the secret air war against the USSR. Never before had overflight operations been conducted on such a scale. They also brought this first era to a close; never again was this level of activity attempted. As with the RAF RB-45C overflights, Genetrix and Homerun became the subject of myth and speculation. Various fragmentary accounts of the reconnaissance balloons were published in later years, but much of what was written was in error. Several times, General LeMay talked about a mass RB-47 overflight of the USSR, but, again, the details he provided were erroneous.

By the summer of 1956, the launch crews of the 1110th Air Support Group had returned to Lowry Air Force Base, where they were to resume scientific and military balloon launches. Whereas they still had a role, the same was not true of the 456th TCW. With the end of Genetrix launches, there seemed to be no need for a specialized midair recovery wing. For this reason, the unit was deactivated over the Fourth of July holiday. Its personnel went on leave after the seven-month deployment before reporting to their new duty assignments.

The United States celebrated the 180th anniversary of the Declaration of Independence in the traditional manner, with fireworks, county fairs,

picnics, and political speeches. Only a handful of people knew just how historical this day was. Yet even those few could not realize how the world would be changed by what had taken place. On this Independence Day, Leghorn's vision and Eisenhower's Open Skies proposal had become a covert reality. A window had opened on Soviet military and industrial power. The nature of intelligence and foreign relations had been fundamentally changed. The U-2 Mission 2013 had been flown.

Chapter 5
Early U-2 Overflights

There was no drama, no drumbeats or fanfare. There's none of this taxiing out like World War II, with your Spitfire canopy back and white scarf. You're buttoned into this baby . . .

—Hervey Stockman, on the start of Mission 2013

By early 1956, the U-2 had met all of its altitude and range design goals, the cameras had been proven, and the aircraft had been shown to be nearly impossible to track by U.S. radar systems. With Genetrix and Homerun under way, the final preparations were being made for the overseas deployment of the CIA's first U-2 detachment. Work was also being carried out on selecting the targets that would be covered, planning the overflight routes, and preparing to analyze the resulting photos.

Final Preparations

In February 1956, the British foreign secretary met with DCI Allen Dulles to discuss basing the U-2 detachment in England. A memorandum was sent to British prime minister Anthony Eden asking for his approval. Eden was not that interested, due to the controversy over the Genetrix balloons. Secretary of State John Foster Dulles had to approach Eden in order to gain his approval. The deal that was struck reflected the "special relationship" between the United States and England that had been developed during World War II. The United States would share the photos taken during the overflights with British intelligence. As a result, Britain would enjoy the results of the missions without the risks of flying them. Eden gave his approval.

The base selected by Bissell for the U-2 operations was Lakenheath in Suffolk, England. Deployment began on April 29, 1956. The first two U-2s were delivered to the base by air force C-124 transports and reassembled in an isolated hangar. By May 4, all of the aircraft, personnel, and equipment had arrived. The CIA U-2 detachment was given two

names. For public consumption, it was designated the 1st Weather Reconnaissance Squadron, Provisional (WRSP-1). The "provisional" designation gave the unit increased security; provisional air force units did not have to report to higher headquarters. Within the CIA, it was known as Detachment A.

The pilots and ground crews began the uneasy adjustment to life in England. First off, the spring of 1956 was a cold one. In addition, several of the Detachment A personnel were housed off base at a local pub, called Bird in the Hand, at Mildenhall. They found it difficult to adapt to the rigid mealtimes, cold bedrooms, and rationed bath times. Events intervened, however, to make Detachment A's time in England brief.

During April, Khrushchev and Bulganin made a state visit to Britain; they arrived at Portsmouth harbor aboard the Soviet navy cruiser *Sverdlov*. Despite British government orders to the contrary, the Secret Intelligence Service (SIS) sent a diver, Lionel "Buster" Crabbe, to inspect the ship's sonar and other equipment below its waterline. Crabbe, overage and out of shape, was never seen alive again, and the Soviets publicized the incident. As a result of the ensuing controversy, Eden fired the head of SIS, Sir John Sinclair, and had to tell Parliament that the operation had been conducted "without the authority or knowledge of ministers."

In the meantime, the U-2s were reassembled and made check flights. British aircraft spotters were quick to notice them. The June 1, 1956, issue of *Flight* magazine carried a brief report entitled "The Mysterious Stranger" on the sightings. It read: "The testimony of a *Flight* reader that he has seen a strange aircraft over the Lakenheath, Suffolk, district should not be ignored. 'In the sky,' he says, 'it looks like the wartime Horsa glider.' He believes it to have one jet engine and reports a high tailplane and unswept wings of high-aspect ratio."

With the aircraft attracting unwanted attention, and fearing another incident, Prime Minister Eden withdrew permission for the U-2s to operate from Britain. The CIA was given twenty-four hours to get the airplanes out of the country. On June 11, Bissell ordered the U-2s moved to Wiesbaden, West Germany. This was done without West German officials being informed. The Detachment A commander, Col. Frederick McCoy, had hoped that the move could be made without drawing attention to the aircraft. This proved impossible; the U-2s were quickly noticed.

Two more U-2s were soon delivered, bringing the total to four aircraft. They were also fitted with the improved J-57–P-13 engines to reduce the risk of a flameout on an operational mission. With the new engines, the

aircraft designation was changed from U-2A to U-2B. Wiesbaden was to be only a temporary U-2 base. The air force was preparing an old World War II air base at Giebelstadt, West Germany, close to the East German border, as the permanent site. Earlier that year, the air base had been used as a Genetrix balloon launch site.

While the U-2s were being deployed, the Ad Hoc Requirements Committee (ARC) was developing the initial target list for planning the overflights. Edwin Land had recommended such a permanent task force in the Project Three report. The ARC was formally established on December 1, 1955. Bissell named James Q. Reber to be the intelligence requirements officer for the U-2 and chairman of ARC. The first meeting of ARC was held on February 1, 1956. Military representatives came from the army, navy, and air force. The original CIA members were from the Office of Research and Reports and the Office of Scientific Intelligence. Subsequently, the CIA membership was expanded to include the Office of Current Intelligence as well as the Directorate of Plans, which was responsible for covert action.

The ARC began drawing up a list of collection requirements for the initial overflights. The priority of the targets was determined by their ability to meet the three overriding U.S. intelligence objectives of the mid-1950s regarding the USSR. These were long-range bombers, guided missiles, and nuclear energy. In doing this, ARC had to take into account the differing needs and interests of its members. The CIA was primarily interested in strategic intelligence targets, such as aircraft and weapons factories, power plants, and nuclear facilities, as well as roads, bridges, and inland waterways. The military representatives, in contrast, put greater importance on Order of Battle intelligence. The air force, for example, wanted data on the location of Soviet and Eastern European airfields and radar sites.

The ARC list of priority targets was sent to the project staff for use in planning the overflight routes. Each proposed flight plan was given an individual mission number (Mission 2013, Mission 4016, Mission 6011, or Mission 8009). As a result, not all missions were flown, nor were the missions always flown in numerical order. Although ARC was not responsible for flight planning, it did assist the project staff with detailed target information. The ARC also wrote a detailed justification for the selection of each mission's targets. When the U-2 was finally ready for overflights, ARC's justification, along with the flight plan, would be submitted to President Eisenhower for his approval.

As the target selection and mission planning were under way in the spring of 1956, the CIA's Photo-Intelligence Division (PID) was completing its long-standing preparations to analyze the flood of images that the overflights would bring. The head of PID, Arthur C. Lundahl, had been initially briefed on Aquatone by DCI Dulles and Bissell on December 13, 1954. Lundahl was directed by Dulles to begin a compartmentalized effort within PID, called Project Equine, to plan for exploiting the U-2 images. At that point, PID consisted of only thirteen staff members, far too small a group to handle the task.

For Lundahl, as with Leghorn, the U-2 was the realization of a longstanding vision. Lundahl's studies for a Ph.D. in geology had been interrupted by the outbreak of World War II, and he joined the navy. He served as a photointerpreter in the Pacific, then remained with the navy after the war. Lundahl was a civilian with the Naval Photographic Interpretation Center in Washington, D.C., from 1946 until 1953. The U.S. Navy, like the air force, saw photoreconnaissance in the limited role of assembling target folders and damage assessment. In contrast, Lundahl argued that aerial reconnaissance could be used to determine every aspect of a society—where people were born, where they lived, what they ate, where they worked, and how long they lived.

Early in his photointerpretation career, Lundahl had written a paper entitled "Consider the Mata Hari with Glass Eyes." As with Leghorn's speech, Lundahl's paper articulated a vision of the role that photointerpretation could and should play in the Cold War. Partly due to this paper, in May 1953 the CIA established the PID. Lundahl was the obvious choice for the head of the division, but his civil service grade was too low. Director of Central Intelligence Dulles corrected this with the stroke of a pen, raising Lundahl two civil service grades and making him the head of PID.

Although Lundahl continued to have ambitious goals for PID, it was as yet a tiny segment of the CIA. The PID consisted of only thirteen officers and was located in a room in M Building, a decaying World War II WAVE barracks. The PID officers also had different backgrounds than most CIA officers. They came from midwestern and immigrant families, were World War II veterans with experience in photoreconnaissance or -interpretation, and had gone to college on the GI Bill. They were eager to show the potential of photoreconnaissance in an agency focused on agents and covert action.

The start of Aquatone gave them the chance. The initial growth of PID was slow. Not until May 1955 did the CIA's Directorate of Support au-

thorize an increase in personnel. Soon after, PID moved to larger quarters in Que Building. In January 1956, Lundahl's vision of PID finally began to be transformed into a reality. Under the code name HTAutomat, after the New York City restaurant, PID was to be doubled in size; it prepared to move to new quarters. The facility was to be a national-level center in support of all the military services, combining photointerpretation, photogrammetry, data processing, graphic arts, and collateral and analytical research. Automat could provide any level of photoanalysis services at any time of the day or night. Its total staff was increased to around a hundred personnel.

Their initial work was with the photos taken during the April practice overflights. The targets on these missions were U.S. installations analogous to the Soviet targets that the U-2 was to photograph. Just as these missions were the unit's operational readiness inspection before going overseas, the analysis by the Automat personnel was to ensure that PID's preparations were also complete. When the analysis of the photos was completed, it was clear that the Automat was ready for overflights to begin.

By the summer of 1956, PID was moving into its new home. This was the Steuart Building, at 5th Street and New York Avenue in northwest Washington, D.C. The building was a rundown Ford dealership in the midst of a ghetto. The Automat occupied the fourth through the seventh floors of the building; on the ground floor, cars continued to be sold. The new offices had no parking, no cafeteria, and no air-conditioning. During the summer, the floor tiles curled up from the humidity. In winter, the building lacked adequate heat. The ceiling tiles, produced from compressed seaweed during the materiel shortages of World War II, flaked off constantly.

Like ARC, the PID personnel did not have a direct role in planning the overflight routes. However, once the basic flight plan was completed by the project staff, PID personnel produced lists of bonus targets along the planned routes that could be covered with slight changes in course. This would significantly increase the amount of intelligence from each mission.

All was now in readiness. The ARC had selected the targets, the U-2s were in place, and Automat was ready to analyze the photos. All that was needed before the U-2 could enter Soviet skies was President Eisenhower's decision.

Threats and Risks: Eisenhower Decides

In making his decision to send the U-2 over the Soviet Union, President Eisenhower had to balance the threats facing the United States with the risks of an incident. The threats—military, economical, and political—that the United States faced in 1956 were clear. Soviet nuclear forces had continued to expand during the year and a half since Eisenhower had approved development of the U-2. Less clear were the risks that the U-2 would face in Soviet skies.

The pace of Soviet nuclear tests had increased greatly. Between 1949 and 1951, there were only three tests. From August 1953, when the Soviets tested their first H-bomb, until the end of 1955, there were sixteen detonations. More significant, the final two tests involved refined H-bomb designs. The first test was made on November 6, 1955, at Semipalatinsk, in Soviet Central Asia. Based on the sonic data and the fallout collected, a U.S. intelligence report concluded that this H-bomb test was "an air burst of a boosted fission weapon using a U-235 core which obtained an energy yield of approximately 215 kt [kilotons]. It was probably a weaponized version of the 1953 boosted configuration reduced to a more easily deliverable size."

This test was followed by a second one on November 22, also at Semipalatinsk. It was an airdrop of a more advanced weapon design. The H-bomb was designed to have a yield of 3 megatons, but for the test this was reduced by half. The test was successful, producing a detonation of 1.6 megatons. It was clear by early 1956 that the Soviets were able to not only produce increased numbers of A-bombs but design high-yield H-bombs.

The Soviet ability to deliver these weapons to U.S. targets was also increasing. The Mya-4 jet bomber made its public debut at the 1954 May Day air parade. The bomber, which was given the NATO code name Bison, initially did not spark much concern. The single aircraft shown was considered a prototype, and air force intelligence did not believe that production would begin before 1956 or that the Soviet strategic bomber force would be ready before 1960. The U.S. lead in manned bombers seemed secure.

The Soviets traditionally exhibited new aircraft designs at May Day and Aviation Day air parades. Although the 1955 May Day air parade was canceled, practice flights seen by Western air attachés during April brought

disquieting news. As many as thirteen Mya-4s were spotted during the rehearsals, which seemed to indicate a significant increase in heavy bomber production over that previously estimated. During the practice flights, yet another new Soviet bomber was spotted. This was the Tu-95, NATO code name Bear. The Tu-95 used four turboprop engines and did not attract the attention that the Mya-4 did.

A CIA estimate, dated June 23, 1955, had originally stated that there were twenty Mya-4 and twenty Tu-95 heavy bombers operational with the long-range air force. Based on the April 1955 Mya-4 sightings, this estimate was increased. It was thought that as many as forty Mya-4s had actually been produced by July 1955. The initial production rate at the Fili Airframe Plant outside Moscow was estimated to be eight to ten Mya-4s per month, increasing to fifteen per month by January 1957. If additional plants were used, the total could reach twenty to thirty per month. Based on this, the CIA estimated the total Soviet heavy bomber force could reach 350 Mya-4s and 250 Tu-95s by mid-1958.

The increased projections of Soviet bomber production instilled fears of a Soviet surprise attack. Another National Intelligence Estimate, approved on July 1, 1955, dealt with the warning that the United States could expect to receive of a Soviet attack. It noted that the higher speed of the Soviet bombers would reduce the time needed to move them into position. Expansion of facilities at the forward bases would, by 1958, also reduce the time needed to service the aircraft. The CIA concluded: "The specific advance warning of unusual and possibly threatening air activity which could be given, assuming that movement to the staging bases was discovered and correctly interpreted, would probably be on the order of 12-18 hours."

The director of intelligence of the air force had a less optimistic view. In a footnote, he argued that movements into and out of the forward bases would be routine by 1958. He also believed that it was "unlikely that such movement would be discovered and correctly interpreted before its value as warning had passed."

Soon after these two estimates were issued, a further indication of large numbers of Soviet bombers came at the July 13, 1955, Aviation Day air parade outside Moscow (only a few days before the Geneva Summit was to begin). An initial group of ten Mya-4s flew over the reviewing stand, followed by two more groups of nine aircraft. This again seemed to indicate a high production rate of Soviet heavy bombers.

The issue of Soviet bomber strength, which was known as the "bomber

gap," became a public issue in early February 1956 when air force chief of staff General Twining testified before the House Armed Services Committee. General Twining told the congressmen that the Soviets already had more Mya-4s than the United States had B-52s and that the Soviets would be able to "maintain this advantage for some time if they keep on the production curve we are now predicting." In May 1956, *U.S. News & World Report* carried articles entitled "Can Soviets Take the Air Lead?" and "Is U.S. Really Losing in the Air?"

Although President Eisenhower understood that the U-2 could provide information on the actual rather than the estimated size of the Soviet bomber force, he was fearful that its missions would poison relations with the USSR and could even trigger a war. For this reason, he found it difficult to authorize the U-2 overflights. He was concerned that a malfunction might cause a U-2 to crash in the Soviet Union, and he asked DCI Dulles what the consequences of that might be. According to Colonel Goodpaster's later recollections, Dulles said that it was unlikely that a U-2 would be lost. If one were to go down, however, the assumption was that the fragile aircraft would disintegrate and the pilot would not survive. The Soviets would know that the airplane had come from the United States but would not be able to prove it in any convincing way. As a further safeguard, the U-2 carried a self-destruct package on all missions over "denied areas." The pilot was to throw two switches before baling out: the first to arm the system and the second to start a seventy-second timer. The explosive charge was designed to destroy the camera package rather than the entire airplane.

Fears that a U-2 might be lost in an accident over the USSR were not academic. There had been many close calls during the test and training flights. Although the new engines had corrected the flameout problems, the U-2 was still a demanding aircraft to fly. As if to underline Eisenhower's concerns, the first fatal U-2 crash occurred while the president was considering whether to authorize the overflights.

On May 15, 1956, CIA pilot Wilburn S. Rose took off in a training flight from the ranch in Article 345. After takeoff, he discovered that neither pogo had released. This was not unusual; on earlier flights, one or both of the pogos had sometimes hung up. If this occurred, there was an unwritten rule that the pilot should not fly over the mess hall. Rose made a low-level pass over the runway and was able to shake loose the left-hand pogo. He then attempted to make a right turn to come back over the runway to shake loose the right-hand pogo. In the process, he allowed

the U-2's speed to drop. The aircraft, which was heavy with fuel, stalled and was too low to recover. The U-2 hit the ground at the end of the runway and disintegrated over a wide area. Rose was killed on impact. To replace him, another CIA pilot, Howard Carey, was brought in late to the first class to begin training at the ranch.

The CIA reassured Eisenhower that it was possible that the Soviets might not be able to detect the U-2. But with the start of overflights only a few weeks away, others began to have doubts. On May 28, the CIA's Office of Scientific Intelligence issued a vulnerability study of the U-2. The report's conclusion read: "Maximum Soviet radar detection ranges against the Project aircraft at elevation in excess of 55,000 feet would vary from 20 to 150 miles. . . . In our opinion, detection can therefore be assumed." Although the U-2 could be detected by Soviet radar, the report added that Soviet radar still had major limitations. The report continued: "It is doubtful that the Soviets can achieve consistent tracking of the Project vehicle."

The same day as the vulnerability study was issued, May 28, DCI Dulles met with President Eisenhower to discuss the U-2's readiness for operations. Bissell was eager to start the overflights, because the SAC weather experts assigned to the project predicted that the best weather over the western USSR would be between June 20 and July 10. Eisenhower still had not reached a final decision on the overflights. Three days later, on May 31, Dulles and air force chief of staff General Twining prepared a paper, the Aquatone Operational Plan. President Eisenhower had previously granted permission to the air force to conduct overflights of Eastern Europe. In the operational plan, Bissell informed Eisenhower that he would use this existing permission to begin U-2 overflights of Eastern Europe. With the overflights about to begin, the code name for the U-2 program was changed from Aquatone to Chalice.

Eastern European Overflights

Bissell consulted with the commander of U.S. Air Forces Europe, then began planning for an overflight of East Germany, Poland, and Czechoslovakia. This was given the designation Mission 2003 and was scheduled for June 20. The pilot selected to be the first to take the U-2 over a denied area was Carl Overstreet. He was, however, the last to know. Overstreet was on leave, making a short trip back home. Hervey Stockman was elected by the other five pilots to tell him when he got back.

On the morning of June 20, Overstreet went through the suiting up process, then began prebreathing pure oxygen to remove the nitrogen from his bloodstream. This was to prevent the bends in case the cockpit lost pressure. Overstreet was then taken to the waiting U-2 and strapped in. Finally, the clearance was given. Overstreet advanced the throttle, and the U-2 roared down the runway and into the sky.

The Mission 2003 route went across Czechoslovakia, then as far east as Warsaw, Poland. The U-2 was carrying an A-2 camera package, which was operating normally. Overstreet turned the U-2 back west, overflying Berlin and Potsdam, East Germany. Down below, antigovernment rioting had broken out four days before, and Soviet troops had been called in to suppress them. This was a foreshadower of later turmoil throughout Eastern Europe. Meanwhile, Eastern European air defenses were trying to intercept the intruder, but without success. Overstreet landed back at Wiesbaden, West Germany, after a successful flight.

Immediately after his return, the Detachment A personnel removed the film magazines from the three cameras, and they were flown to the United States for processing. The film arrived at PID on June 22 for analysis. The PID interpreters judged the photographs from Mission 2003 to be of good quality.

On June 21, the day after Overstreet's U-2 mission, Colonel Goodpaster met James Killian, Edwin Land, and Bissell to discuss extending operations to the USSR. They presented photographs and data to Goodpaster on the reconnaissance operation. There was also discussion of the yield to be expected, altitudes and other operational conditions, control, and direction of the overflights. They also discussed what to do in the event of a malfunction and the loss of an aircraft. Killian and Land objected to the "weather plane" cover story and made a bold proposal: In the event that a U-2 was lost, they argued, the United States should not attempt to deny responsibility but rather state that the overflights were being made "to guard against surprise attack." Their idea was set aside for further study, which it never received. In 1956, it was not possible for the United States to admit that it was spying in peacetime.

Goodpaster told them that President Eisenhower, who was recovering from abdominal surgery, had indicated his approval for the mode of operation proposed in the Aquatone Operational Plan of May 31. Eisenhower desired that the entire pattern of overflights be designed to cover all the vital targets quickly. As a result, Goodpaster said, "close in operations" (the Eastern European overflights) might be limited "prior to ini-

tiating deeper operations." Goodpaster also reported to them that Eisenhower had stressed that West German chancellor Konrad Adenauer should be notified "before deep operations are initiated." Both the CIA and the State Department had recommended that Adenauer be told before Soviet overflights were made. (Existing policy dictated that he not be informed about Eastern European overflights.) Bissell said that he would get in touch with Goodpaster once Adenauer was contacted.

This was not the only reason for a delay in the start of overflights. The Soviet authorities were angry over the Homerun overflights and wanted to demonstrate that they had the means to stop such intrusions. To do this, foreign air force delegations from some twenty-eight countries were invited to the Moscow Air Show, which was to open on June 24, 1956. The U.S. delegation was led by air force chief of staff Twining. (He and Eisenhower had discussed the Soviet invitation during the same meeting that dealt with the Soviet protest of Project Homerun.) Twining requested that no overflights of the USSR be made until after he and the U.S. delegation left.

The air show was held at Tushino airfield outside Moscow. The foreign delegations were treated to mass flybys of Soviet fighters. More than a hundred MiG-19s and Yak-25s flew over the reviewing stands. There was also a flyby of new Soviet fighter prototypes. These included a new version of the Yak-25, three Sukhoi Deltas, and two new MiG designs, one of which later entered service as the MiG-21. The bomber display was low key compared to earlier years. There were only four Tu-95s and three Mya-4s.

The air show was followed by a reception for the delegations hosted by the Soviet defense minister, Marshal Georgi Zhukov, and attended by Nikita Khrushchev and other party and government officials. Once this had been completed, Khrushchev took the leaders of the U.S., British, and French delegations to a park, sat them down at a picnic table, and launched into a long toast "in defense of peace." Midway through the toast, Khrushchev turned to General Twining and asked, "Today we showed you our aircraft. But would you like to have a look at our missiles?" Twining replied, "Yes." The unpredictable Khrushchev then turned aggressive. "Well, we will not show them to you. First show us your aircraft and stop sending intruders into our airspace. We will shoot down uninvited guests. We will get all of your Canberras. They are flying coffins."

As he was speaking, Khrushchev noticed one of the U.S. military attachés pouring out his glass under a bush. Khrushchev turned to U.S.

ambassador Charles E. Bohlen and said, "Here I am speaking about peace and friendship, but what does your military attaché do?" The attaché was pressured into drinking an enormous "penalty" toast to Soviet-American friendship, after which he soon left.

Bohlen and Twining were upset about Khrushchev's abrupt change in tone, but the mood soon changed back again. Khrushchev's bluster and threats were followed by a friendly trip through the countryside. When General Twining and his group left the USSR on July 1, they received a warm send-off by the commander in chief of the Soviet Air Force, chief marshal of aviation P. F. Zhigarev, and other senior Soviet military officials.

With Twining's visit over and Chancellor Adenauer notified about the U-2 missions, the political restrictions on the start of U-2 overflights of the USSR had been removed. The weather over the western Soviet Union, however, prevented the start of operations. While the project staff waited for the clouds to pass out of the area, two more Eastern European overflights were made, both on July 2. Mission 2009 covered targets in Czechoslovakia, Hungary, Romania, Bulgaria, Yugoslavia, and East Germany; Mission 2010 overflew East Germany, Czechoslovakia, Hungary, Romania, and Poland. Both pilots completed their missions and returned successfully.

That same afternoon, Bissell and DDCI Cabell gave President Eisenhower a detailed briefing on the first U-2 overflight of Eastern Europe, Mission 2003 on June 20. Although Eisenhower found the information that the flight had provided to be "very interesting, very positive," his main interest was in knowing whether the U-2 had been tracked. Bissell told him that although Eastern European radar had picked up the U-2, they had incorrectly estimated its altitude as being only 42,000 feet. He added that the CIA was still awaiting information on that morning's twin overflights to determine whether or not they had been detected. Bissell added that Detachment A had four aircraft operational and could average two overflights per day. He said that the crews were "ready and eager to go beyond the satellites."

On July 3, Colonel Goodpaster met with Eisenhower to discuss the start of Soviet U-2 overflights. Goodpaster suggested to Eisenhower that the best procedure would be to conduct the overflight operations for a ten-day period, followed by a report. This would meet Eisenhower's wishes that the operations concentrate on the highest-priority items. After a discussion, the president agreed. Eisenhower added

that there should also be a report on how much time was needed for each major area.

Goodpaster notified Bissell later that day of Eisenhower's approval and that operations were to run through July 14 and interim reports were to be provided. A final report was to be made at the end of the ten-day period. Late that evening, Bissell went to the project headquarters at the Matomic Building for a final review. His final go/no go decision depended on many factors, but the most critical was the weather forecast over the target areas and at the takeoff and landing airfields. Just before midnight Washington time, Bissell made the decision to begin the flights. At Wiesbaden, West Germany, it was just before 6:00 A.M. on the morning of Wednesday, July 4, 1956.

Mission 2013

The go signal was sent to Wiesbaden via secure communications lines. Such last-minute approvals were to continue throughout the U-2 overflight program. Article 347 was the U-2 selected to make Mission 2013, the first overflight of the Soviet Union. The U-2 had been fitted with an A-2 camera package, and Hervey Stockman had been selected as the pilot. After taking off and climbing to the proper altitude, Stockman and Article 347 crossed into East German airspace. The flight path passed over East Berlin, then northern Poland. Stockman flew over Poznan, where rioting had broken out on June 28.

Leaving Poznan behind, Stockman continued east and crossed into Soviet airspace over Belorussia. Above him the sky was a deep blue-black; far below the curvature of the Earth was visible. Years later, Stockman would recall: "I knew what I was there for. I knew that we had good reason to be there, but there is enough Christian spirit in me that I would be a liar if I didn't say I did feel for just a moment there, 'this is another guy's air.'" All seemed serene as Stockman continued toward Minsk. He had been assured by Kelly Johnson that it would take several years for the Soviets to develop a defense against the U-2.

Reaching Minsk, Stockman made a left turn to put his airplane onto a heading that would take him toward Leningrad. When he looked at the drift sight, which was like an inverted periscope that allowed him to see ground landmarks, he noticed something disturbing. Below him were MiG fighters trying to reach his U-2. He recalled that they were very small in the viewer, and initially he did not believe what he was seeing. The

MiGs were making snap-up attacks, trying to trade speed for altitude and get a lucky shot at the U-2.

The Soviet MiGs made more than twenty attacks against Stockman and Article 347. The cameras photographed the airplanes as they struggled for altitude, only to flame out and fall back toward Earth. The U-2 had proven untouchable but not invisible.

While the MiGs made their futile attacks, Stockman continued north. His course took him over a number of Soviet long-range air force bomber bases, to count the number of Mya-4s that were operational. Finally, he reached Leningrad, which was the main target of Mission 2013. The city's naval shipyards were the center of Soviet submarine production.

While Stockman was overflying the USSR, Khrushchev and the rest of the Soviet leadership were attending the Fourth of July reception at the U.S. ambassador's residence in Moscow. This was only the second time that the Soviet leadership had attended the reception in the postwar years. Khrushchev had been told about the overflight before leaving for the reception. He said nothing at the reception, but he thought that, after the Moscow Air Show, the United States was demonstrating that it could do anything it wanted. He and other members of the Soviet leadership believed that the overflight was in response to the display of fighters and threats.

Finally, Stockman turned west and covered targets in Estonia and Latvia, along the Baltic coast. He landed back at Wiesbaden after eight hours and forty-five minutes in the air. The film was removed from the cameras for shipment to the United States while Stockman was debriefed on the flight. Mission 2013 was over, and nothing would be the same again.

The U-2 over Moscow: Mission 2014

The primary target for the second U-2 overflight, Mission 2014, was the Soviet capital itself. Not only was Moscow the political and administrative center, but many important Soviet research and development facilities were located near the city. To cover these targets, the U-2 would face for the first time what would become its nemesis: surface-to-air missiles (SAMs). The threat had been developing in tandem with the U-2 itself.

The first indication appeared as early as July 1953, when an unusual road network was spotted outside Moscow by Western observers. It con-

sisted of three roughly parallel roads, each a mile long, that were intersected by eleven crossroads about half a mile wide, forming a herringbone pattern. This did not match the expected configuration of a SAM site, but its location was where one might be expected. Soon after, a long, grass-covered bunker was spotted near a herringbone site. The bunker had what appeared to be a pair of spinning disks at one end. These were dubbed "yo-yo," after their appearance. Subsequent information showed that these were actually antennas used to track the target aircraft and to guide the SAMs.

By December 1955, when a National Intelligence Estimate on Soviet guided missile programs was issued, about forty herringbone sites had been identified around Moscow; the location of about twelve had been pinpointed. This indicated that the sites were eight to nine miles apart and arranged in two circles about twenty-five and forty-five nautical miles from Moscow. About twenty-five of the sites were considered operational, with the rest in various stages of construction. A few sightings of similar sites in the initial stages of construction had also been reported from the Leningrad area. Sightings were also made of "missile-like objects" at some of the Moscow sites. They were described as being about three feet in diameter and twenty to thirty feet long. At one herringbone site, sixty of the missiles were seen, each parked at one of the recesses along the transverse road network. The new SAM was given the NATO code name SA-1 Guild. The SA-1 was mounted on the back of a trailer and was raised vertically before being fired. The estimate concluded that the SA-1 was in at least limited operational use. Mission 2014 would have to fly twice through the twin rings of SA-1 sites around Moscow.

Mission 2014 was scheduled to take off at 5:00 A.M. on July 5. The procedure was that Bissell would send a single code word twenty-four, twelve, and two hours before the scheduled takeoff time. This was to confirm that the weather prediction was still good and the overflight was still on.

The twelve-hour signal was due at Wiesbaden at 5:00 P.M. on July 4, but it did not arrive. This indicated that the mission was off and the Detachment A personnel could relax. Most of them headed for the Independence Day parties at the base. Then, at 7:00 P.M., two hours late, the signal came through; Mission 2014 was back on. The only pilot still available was Carmine A. Vito, who was selected by default to fly the mission to Moscow.

The next morning, Vito was suited up, underwent the prebreathing, and was briefed on the mission by the unit navigator, weather forecaster,

and Detachment A commander. The two-hour signal had arrived, and the mission was on. Vito climbed into Article 347, which had been checked and refueled after landing from the first overflight. The mission was to be flown under strict radio silence. The clearance for takeoff was a light signal from the tower. At exactly 5:00 A.M., the light flashed and Vito took off.

The route of Mission 2014 was farther south than that of the first overflight, and it traveled farther east. Vito crossed East Germany, then flew over Krakow in Poland, and finally headed due east toward Kiev. As with the first overflight, Soviet radar was quick to pick up the intruding U-2, and MiGs were sent after it. James Killian, who was at a SIGINT ground station during Vito's overflight, watched as the U.S. operators picked up Soviet HF radio transmissions from Soviet ground controllers. The Americans were puzzled by what they were hearing. The Soviet controllers seemed to be attempting to direct fighters against an aircraft flying at 20,000 meters and at a speed of 800 kilometers per hour. The SIGINT operators thought that such a thing was impossible, because they knew of no aircraft that could fly at altitudes of 66,000 feet or higher. The operators were not cleared to know of the U-2 overflights, and Killian did not enlighten them.

The MiG pilots proved as unsuccessful at intercepting Article 347 as they had been the day before. All other air traffic was grounded, and the MiGs tried to make snap-up attacks. These apparently resulted in the loss of several of the fighters when they could not recover. After covering Kiev, Vito turned northwest toward Minsk. The weather was disappointing, with considerable cloud cover. Reaching Minsk, and having completed the targets in the southwestern USSR, Vito turned toward Moscow, virtually following the Minsk-Moscow rail line. The cloud cover started to clear, and Vito saw below the mosaic pattern of collective farm fields.

Ahead was Moscow, nearly covered by clouds. Vito was flying in from southeast of the city, along the Moscow River. His first target was the Ramenskoye bomber arsenal, which was the Soviet counterpart of Edwards Air Force Base. Farther along the river was the Fili Airframe Plant, where the Mya-4 bombers were built. Vito continued toward the city, but the clouds were becoming thicker. He was able to photograph part of Moscow, including the Kremlin in one corner of a frame, before the clouds closed in below him. As he covered the targets, Vito could also see the herringbone patterns of SA-1 sites. He spotted three of the distinctive patterns, but his airplane was not fired on or even detected. Later,

Vito was asked what his reaction was when he saw that Mission 2014 took him twice through the SA-1 defensive ring. He replied, "Hell, it was my job and I just flew the mission to the best of my abilities." Despite his success, Vito was the only U-2 pilot ever to overfly Moscow; no other mission was ever sent over the Soviet capital.

Vito continued over the city and past the clouds. He was able to photograph the Kaliningrad missile plant and the Khimki rocket-engine plant, both located to the north of Moscow. Clearing the Moscow defenses, Vito continued farther east for some two hundred kilometers. Finally, he turned back west, covering targets in the Baltic States of Estonia, Latvia, and Lithuania, before the cloud cover closed in below him all the way back to Wiesbaden. He had to make a ground-controlled approach (GCA) through the clouds. The landing was successful, and after touchdown the film magazines were removed for shipment to the Automat.

Due to the 5:00 A.M. takeoff time of Mission 2014 as well as the six-hour time difference, it was still early morning on July 5 in Washington, D.C., when Vito landed back at Wiesbaden. When DCI Dulles arrived at work later that morning, he asked Bissell if any overflights had been made over the Independence Day holiday. Bissell replied that one had been made on July 4, another had been completed that morning, and both Leningrad and Moscow had been covered. "Oh my Lord," said a shocked Dulles. "Do you think that was wise the first time?" Bissell replied, "Allen, the first is the safest."

Eisenhower was also interested in knowing how the overflights went, specifically if they had been tracked. He told Colonel Goodpaster "to advise Mr. Allen Dulles that if we obtain any information or warning that any of the flights had been discovered or tracked, the operation should be suspended." Eisenhower's primary concern was whether the Soviets could track the overflights along most of their routes. This would allow them numerous tries at interceptions. The president already knew from the briefing on the June 20 Eastern European overflight that, despite earlier expectations, the U-2 could indeed be detected.

Colonel Goodpaster called both DCI Dulles and Bissell and was told that it would be another thirty-six hours before the reports on Soviet tracking and intercept attempts would be available. Later that day, Dulles and Bissell met with Goodpaster to ask if the U-2 overflights could continue. Goodpaster replied that his understanding of the president's directive was that the flights should continue "at the maximum rate until the first evidence of tracking was received."

The reports on Soviet radar tracking of the first two overflights were available on July 6. They showed that the Soviets could track the U-2 but not consistently. They were able to detect it, however, and make several "very unsuccessful attempts at interception." Counter to what might have been expected, the Soviet's radar coverage was weakest around the two primary targets of Moscow and Leningrad. The Soviets were not aware that the two cities had been overflown.

Overflights Continue

Detachment A stood down for four days after Mission 2014, apparently due to weather conditions. As a result, Eisenhower's ten-day authorization was more than half over before overflights resumed. Possibly to make up for lost time, a more ambitious effort was made once flights resumed. Bissell gave his approval to make a pair of overflights on July 9. These were Missions 2020 and 2021.

The two missions flew different paths. Mission 2020 was primarily focused on covering Eastern Europe. The flight path went across East Germany, passing just north of Berlin, then across northern Poland. The U-2 entered Soviet airspace and flew a zigzag pattern over Lithuania and the southern edge of Latvia, then headed south toward Minsk but turned to the southwest well before reaching the city. The U-2 flew across central Poland, including Warsaw, then back over East Germany before landing at Wiesbaden.

The distance flown by Mission 2020 over the USSR was relatively limited. In contrast, Mission 2021 was a long-range one over the central USSR. After takeoff, the U-2 entered Czechoslovakian airspace, flew south of Prague, then turned southeast, crossed over Austria, entered Hungarian airspace, and continued southeast. Well south of Budapest, it turned to the northeast, entered Soviet airspace, and covered a series of targets, including L'vov, Kiev, and Minsk. It followed a meandering path back across Belorussia and Poland, then again crossed over Czechoslovakia before landing back at Wiesbaden. Unfortunately, a broken camera shutter on one of the day's missions ruined many of the photos.

What was to be the final overflight during the initial series—deep into the southern USSR—was made on July 10. Mission 2023 was targeted against the Crimean peninsula. The U-2 flew across East Germany, Poland, part of the USSR, the northern tip of Romania, then back over

the southern USSR. The initial target was Kishlnev, followed by the Crimean peninsula and the city of Kerch, on the Sea of Azov. These were followed by the Black Sea port of Sevastopol, the inland city of Simferopol, and the port of Odessa. The return route was nearly a straight line across Romania and Hungary to Czechoslovakia. The U-2 turned northwest, covering Prague and a final set of targets in East Germany, then flew west and landed back at Wiesbaden.

The same day that Mission 2023 was flown, the Soviets handed a note protesting the July 4 and 5 overflights to the U.S. embassy in Moscow. The note was quite specific as to routes and times. It stated that the July 4 overflight route covered Minsk, Vilngas, Kaunas, and Kaliningrad; the depth was 320 kilometers; and the duration was one hour and thirty-two minutes. The July 5 overflight was given as Brest, Pinsk, Baranovichi, Kaunas, and Kaliningrad; the depth was 150 kilometers; and the flight had a duration of one hour and twenty minutes. The note said that the overflights had been made by a "twin-engine medium bomber of the United States Air Force" and concluded that the "violation of the air frontiers of the Soviet Union cannot be interpreted as other than intentional and conducted for the purposes of reconnaissance."

As soon as the Soviet protest note arrived at the White House on the evening of July 10, Goodpaster called Bissell and told him to stop all U-2 overflights. The next morning, Goodpaster met with Bissell to review U-2 activities. Bissell told him that three additional overflights had taken place since those mentioned in the protest note but added that no more flights were planned. On July 16, the Polish ambassador to the United States made an oral protest about the June 20 and July 2 overflights of Poland. The first was described as entering Polish airspace at Zgorzelec and the second as entering from the direction of Gubin. A similar protest by the Czechoslovakian government followed on July 21.

It was not until July 19 that the State Department responded to the Soviet note. It said: "A thorough inquiry has been conducted and it has been determined that no United States military planes based, or flying in or adjacent to the European area at the time of the alleged overflights could possibly have strayed, as alleged, so far from their known flight plans, which carefully exclude such overflights as the Soviet Note alleges. Therefore the statement of the Soviet Union is in error." The U.S. statement was narrowly correct; the U-2 was not a "military" aircraft. There were no U.S. replies to the Polish and Czechoslovakian protests.

The End of the Bomber Gap

Between June 20 and July 10, a total of eight overflights of the Soviet bloc, five over the USSR and three over Eastern Europe, had been made. The result was a mass of film that had to be carefully analyzed at the Automat. The film from the first overflight was flown directly to the United States after Stockman landed. Several PID members were on hand as it was processed to check the images. Also on hand was James Baker, who had been invited by the project staff to get a firsthand look at how his A-2 lenses had performed. The films from the July overflights were generally good, marred only by some clouds and the shutter failure on one of the July 9 missions.

The U-2 overflights covered nine Soviet long-range air force bomber bases in the western USSR. As the photointerpreters examined the images, they saw that all the airfields had nuclear weapon loading pits. The weapon was placed in the pit, the bomber was rolled over it, and the weapon was lifted into the airplane's bomb bay. But what the photointerpreters did not see was far more important. At none of the nine airfields were there any Mya-4 Bisons. At the time, the air force was claiming that there were almost a hundred Bisons operational.

The U-2 photos proved that this estimate was likely wrong. Vito's photos of the Fili Airframe Plant allowed the Mya-4 production rate to be determined. The bomber's fuselages were built at the Fili Airframe Plant, then shipped by barge down the Moscow River to the Ramenskoye bomber arsenal, where the wings were attached. Although it was not yet possible to determine how many Bisons the Soviets had, it was clear, thanks to the U-2, that they did not have a large force and that they could not out-produce the United States. It was finally realized that the aerial parades of Mya-4s, which had set in motion the whole bomber gap controversy, had been deliberate deceptions. The Soviets had simply flown the same formations of Bisons around in circles, which made it appear that the Soviets had far greater numbers of bombers than in reality.

Following the missions, large briefing boards were shown to President Eisenhower. In addition to the bomber bases, there were boards showing the major Soviet cities. In the Leningrad photos, the shipyards building Soviet submarines were clearly visible. One surprise was that the Soviets had made no attempt to conceal or camouflage their military facilities. The whole of the USSR was wide open to the U-2's cameras.

For the PID photointerpreters, it was a time of discovery. They now had the ability to produce exact data on Soviet facilities, using information that was only days or weeks old rather than the years-old and incomplete information from German POWs or émigrés. The photointerpreters took a vicarious pleasure in being able to disprove existing intelligence estimates and in showing the value of aerial photography compared to intelligence from other sources. Due to the volume of photographs, it was late August 1956 before PID completed its initial analysis of the overflight missions. (One complication was the delays caused by PID's move from the Que Building to the Automat in the Steuart Building on July 9.) As a result, the bomber gap controversy lingered for several months.

It was not until November 1956 that the CIA issued its revised estimates of Soviet bomber production. Although these were based on U-2 photos, Eisenhower insisted that knowledge of the program's existence be kept from Congress. As a result, the new bomber estimates became a political football. Some congressmen claimed that the earlier high estimates were inflated to support expanded air force appropriations; others claimed that the new, lower estimates were at the direction of the White House to keep defense spending down. Eisenhower did nothing to clear up the questions. In the years to come, both the congressional posturing and Eisenhower's silence would have an increasing impact on American politics.

The Soviets were also analyzing the first series of U-2 overflights. Khrushchev was angry about the overflights, but for political rather than military reasons. He was not nervous about the photos the U-2 had taken; he believed that the Americans had made the overflights to show their superiority over the USSR. He wanted to shoot down one of the U-2s and decided to avoid protests until then. He told his son Sergei: "I can see the Americans laughing there when they are reading our protests, knowing that we can do nothing more except this." During one overflight of Kiev, a U-2 was fired on by antiaircraft artillery, which had no chance of hitting the high-flying U-2. Khrushchev ordered that stopped, saying: "We are only showing our people that we can do nothing firing artillery around cities."

Afterward, a meeting was held between military officials and aircraft designers to discuss what the U-2 was and how to deal with it. The National Air Defense (PVO) leadership, a separate branch of the Soviet armed forces, believed that the overflights had been made by RB-57Ds.

Noted Soviet aircraft designer Andrei Tupolev disagreed with their assessment; he believed it could not have been a twin-engine aircraft such as the RB-57D. He, like the Project Three members, realized that such an aircraft could not reach very high altitudes. Tupolev believed that the overflights were instead made by an aircraft similar to his prewar ANT-25, a very lightweight, single-engine aircraft with high-aspect-ratio wings designed for ultra-long-range flights from the USSR to the United States. As a result, he believed that the aircraft could not have carried any weapons; rather it was a reconnaissance aircraft with a very light payload and was no threat as a bomber.

The next question was how to deal with the U-2. The obvious solution was advanced SAMs. The SA-1s had proved totally ineffective; although the system around Moscow became operational with some 3,200 missiles, the sites being built around Leningrad were subsequently abandoned. A new, higher-altitude, mobile SAM, the S-75 (NATO code name SA-2 Guideline), was under development; it could reach the altitudes flown by the U-2. Advanced supersonic fighters, the MiG-21 and Su-7, would also be put into production.

The U-2 and the Suez Crisis

Due to the Soviet protest, President Eisenhower ordered a halt to all U-2 operations over the USSR and Eastern Europe. Many in the CIA saw the U-2 program as being in danger. Ironically, at the same time, the U-2 effort was expanding, with a new group of pilots completing the training and deploying to Turkey. International events also saw the U-2 assuming a new role, one not envisioned by Project Three. Rather than strategic reconnaissance, the airplane would be used to gather up-to-the-minute tactical intelligence. Its targets would not be enemy nations, such as the Soviet Union, but America's closest allies.

The recruitment of a second group of CIA U-2 pilots began in January 1956 as the first group was training at the ranch. One of the second group was Francis Gary Powers, who, like the others, was from an F-84 squadron at Turner Air Force Base. Powers later recalled that when he went to the Radium Spring Inn, he was initially told only that he and the other pilots had been picked to be part of a special mission. It would be risky but important and would involve the pilots being overseas for eighteen months without their families. Powers could discuss the mission with his wife but no one else. If he was interested, he should come back to

the hotel the following night. Powers thought it was an operation similar to the Flying Tigers.

The next evening, Powers returned seeking answers. He was told that he would be flying for the CIA and that he would be flying over the USSR. He was told to think about it overnight. After a sleepless night, Powers agreed to the mission. As with the first group, Powers and the others went through a series of briefing and medical checks along with a lie detector test. Finally, on May 13, 1956, Powers became a civilian. A few days later, he signed a contract with the CIA, and he and the others were sent to the ranch. They arrived in late May, about a week after the U-2 crash that killed Wilburn S. Rose. The second group was more fortunate; they would have no fatalities or washouts.

One incident did occur during Powers's initial high-altitude flight, however. He was rather nervous, and he forgot to raise the landing gear after takeoff. Once he reached altitude, he was disappointed in the U-2; he had been told that it could reach far higher altitudes. He did not discover the problem until it was time to descend. Due to the tight speed limits on the U-2 at altitude, a descent was made by easing the engine back to idle and extending the landing gear and speed brakes. When Powers reached for the landing gear handle, he discovered that it had been down the whole time. Yet, even with the added drag of the extended landing gear, the U-2 still broke the altitude record of 65,890 feet set the year before by a specially modified RAF Canberra. Powers's impression of the aircraft improved greatly.

The pilots completed their training in early August 1956, and deployment of Detachment B began to Incirlik, Turkey. Arrangements for the use of Incirlik had been made by Foy D. Kohler, the U.S. chargé d'affaires, who met on May 1, 1956, with the Turkish prime minister, Adnan Menderes. Kohler told him that the effort was a continuation of the Genetrix program, which had used Incirlik as a launch site. The U-2, Kohler continued, would fly 10,000 feet higher than any Soviet fighter. Menderes immediately gave his approval. It would be late August before Detachment B was ready for redeployment and early September before the unit was ready for operations. Events in the Middle East were moving much faster.

On July 26, Egyptian president Gamal Abdel Nasser nationalized the Suez Canal Company in retaliation for the U.S. and British decision to withdraw support for his Aswan Dam project. As tensions began to build, President Eisenhower ordered use of the U-2 over the Middle East. This

was conducted by Detachment A aircraft and pilots, because the U-2s were not yet in Turkey. On August 29, Missions 1104 and 1105 took off from Wiesbaden to cover targets in the eastern Mediterranean. Because of the long distances covered, the U-2s could not land back at Wiesbaden but rather recovered at Incirlik. The two aircraft were serviced, and the next day different CIA pilots again flew over the Middle East. The overflights covered Egypt, Israel, Jordan, Lebanon, and Syria. Their photos also showed a buildup of British troops at their bases on Malta and Cyprus.

With the Suez Crisis growing, President Eisenhower told a meeting of congressmen about the British and French actions, then said, "I don't like to do this to my friends, but I will G-2 [spy on] them if I have to." To coordinate intelligence from the U-2 as well as from decoded cables, SIGINT, and agents, the "Paramount Committee" was established on September 12. It had representatives from the CIA, State Department, National Security Agency (NSA), army, navy, and air force; it met, often several times a day, at the Automat. To speed up the processing and analysis of the U-2 photos, a forward center was established at Wiesbaden.

During September 1956, Detachment A pilots flew another eight missions over the Middle East. However, flying out of West Germany, they were poorly located to cover targets in and around the eastern Mediterranean. By early September 1956, the Incirlik-based Detachment B was operational. The first special mission flown by the unit was made on September 11. It was not until more than two weeks later that another was made. On September 27, Powers was briefed to fly over the Mediterranean to look for any concentration of two or more ships. If Powers spotted any, he was to photograph the vessels. His route took him as far west as Malta, then back to Turkey. During the flight, Powers spotted several ships and photographed them. The mission was considered a success.

As the overflights of the Middle East increased, there were also reminders of how dangerous flying the U-2 was. In the space of just over two weeks, there were two fatal U-2 accidents. The first occurred at the ranch on the night of August 31, 1956. Soon after the second group of CIA pilots completed its training, a third group arrived. One of this group, Frank G. Grace, Jr., was making a night training flight. After takeoff, he pulled up too abruptly and stalled Article 354 about fifty feet above the ground. The U-2 fell, cartwheeled on its left wing, then struck a telephone pole near the runway. Grace was killed in the crash. The climbout of a U-2 was very steep; on the first several flights the pilots felt as

though they were going over on their backs. To avoid stalling the airplane, more experienced pilots always cut back on the throttle abruptly after the pogos fell out.

Whereas Grace's death could be hidden behind the security of the ranch, the second fatality, on September 17, could not, and it brought unwanted publicity for the U-2. Howard Carey had taken off from Wiesbaden when Article 346 broke up in flight, killing him. Initially, there was confusion over the cause, and speculation ranged all the way to sabotage. According to Powers's later recollections, the crash was determined to have been caused by two Royal Canadian Air Force interceptor pilots who buzzed Carey's U-2 while he was climbing. The U-2 was caught in their wake turbulence and simply disintegrated. Ironically, Carey had not been an original member of the first group of CIA pilots. Rather, he had been brought in as a replacement for Wilburn Rose after he was killed.

Detachment B soon took over the special missions, making nine of the ten flown in October. Powers recalled making several such flights, which first covered Cyprus, looking for any fleet being assembled, then overflew Egypt and Israel. These special missions also covered Valletta, Malta; the port of Toulon, France; and the island of Cyprus. All this was done without the British or French knowing about the operations. The British closed a number of areas and bases on Cyprus in order to conceal their military buildup. This made no difference to the U-2s, because the Automat simply counted the growing number of tents and multiplied by the number of men in each. From such "tentology," the interpreters reported that increasing numbers of troops were arriving in Cyprus.

The buildup of forces was also apparent in Israel. Photographs of Israeli Air Force bases showed large numbers of French-built Mystere fighters and Vautour fighter-bombers. President Eisenhower noted on October 15: "Our high-flying reconnaissance planes have shown that Israel has obtained some 60 of the French Mystere pursuit planes, when there had been reported the transfer of only 24." By mid-October, Britain, France, and Israel had finalized their plans to invade Egypt, overthrow Nasser, and regain control of the canal. Before the plans could be carried out, however, the Hungarian Revolution began.

On October 23, a student protest brought a quarter of a million people into the streets of Budapest, demanding free elections and the removal of Soviet troops. Street fighting soon began, with steelworkers tearing down a statue of Stalin and mobs attacking secret-police headquarters.

Soviet troops fought back but were unable to deal with what had become a full-scale revolution. By October 25, there were reports of five thousand dead in Budapest and news that a reform-minded communist, Imre Nagy, was now the Hungarian prime minister. The following day, October 26, Eisenhower was speculating that with Soviet control in Eastern Europe deteriorating, they might be in a desperate mood and resort to extreme measures, even World War III. Despite such fears, on October 28 a cease-fire was declared in Hungary.

The same day, U-2 missions were bringing grim news from the Middle East. French Nord Atlas transport aircraft were photographed at Tymbou airfield, and RAF Hunter fighters and Canberra bombers were arriving at Akrotiri airfield. President Eisenhower was notified by the CIA that an attack was imminent. That same afternoon, Israeli paratroopers were dropped into the Sinai Peninsula, followed by mechanized columns striking deep into Egypt. On October 30, Powers was overflying the Sinai when he saw, through the drift sight, puffs of black smoke from the first daylight battle in the war.

During October 30 and 31, there were developments in both the Suez Crisis and the Hungarian Revolution. Acting according to their plan with Israel, the British and French presented an ultimatum on October 30 to the Egyptians and Israelis demanding that both sides withdraw ten miles from the canal and allow Anglo-French forces to occupy key points along it. The Israelis, as planned, agreed. The same afternoon, Nagy announced that Hungary would no longer be a one-party state and that he was bringing noncommunists into the government. He also said that Hungary was withdrawing from the Warsaw Pact and would be a neutral nation.

The following day, October 31, the USSR professed to accept the changes and promised "to withdraw Soviet Army units from Budapest as soon as this is recognized as necessary by the Hungarian government." In a meeting with Eisenhower, Secretary of State John Foster Dulles said that it was "the beginning of the collapse of the Soviet Empire." Eisenhower was more cautious. That same evening, the Egyptians rejected the ultimatum, and the British and French had their excuse to intervene and take the Suez Canal. British and French aircraft began bombing airfields in Egypt.

During the morning of November 1, an Incirlik-based U-2 overflew Egypt. It first photographed Cyprus, then flew on to the Sinai, where it made several passes to provide complete coverage of the fighting be-

tween the Egyptian and Israeli armies. The aircraft then turned west to Cairo, where the pilot photographed the main Egyptian airfield at Almaza. The U-2 continued on to another airfield, then turned first southeast, then north along the Nile River and again passed directly over Almaza airfield. The U-2 successfully completed its mission, and the film was sent to Wiesbaden for processing and analysis. When the interpreters looked at the photographs of the first pass over Almaza airfield, they saw Egyptian military aircraft lined up in neat rows. When they looked at the second pass, they saw burning wreckage. In the short time between the two passes, a joint Anglo-French strike force had bombed the airfield. The before-and-after photos of Almaza were shown to President Eisenhower, who commented to PID chief Lundahl, "Ten-minute reconnaissance, now that is a goal to shoot for."

As the bombing campaign continued, the situation changed radically. On November 2, Nagy complained that Soviet troops were moving into Hungary. Two days later, on November 4, the Soviets attacked Budapest with 200,000 troops and 4,000 tanks, in order, so they said, "to help the Hungarian people crush the black forces of reaction and counter-revolution." The rebels and units of the Hungarian armed forces resisted the Soviet attack, but they were crushed within days. The CIA requested permission to airdrop weapons and supplies to the rebels, but Eisenhower refused. He also banned all overflights of Hungary, even by U-2s. The same day that the Soviets attacked, Eisenhower was told by the CIA that the British and French were about to land troops in Egypt. Drops of British and French paratroopers near Port Said, at the north end of the canal, began at dawn on November 5.

In response to the airdrops, Soviet prime minister Nikolai Bulganin sent a threatening message to the British, French, and Israelis. It bluntly warned the British and French that they were now second-rate powers and the USSR could deal with them as they were dealing with Egypt. Bulganin also warned them that the USSR now had ballistic missiles that could carry nuclear weapons. Eisenhower continued to believe that the Soviets were still "ready to take any wild adventure" and that if the Soviets did strike at the British and French forces, the United States would have to retaliate.

The following day, November 6, was Election Day. As Americans went to the polls, Eisenhower continued to worry about World War III. He was particularly concerned that the Soviets might move aircraft to Syrian air bases as a prelude to a strike on the British and French forces, which had

now finally begun amphibious landings at Port Said. President Eisenhower ordered DCI Dulles to have an Incirlik-based U-2 make an overflight of Syria. He and his wife then were driven from the White House to their home at Gettysburg to vote.

As events turned out, the intelligence on possible Soviet aircraft movements into Syria came as Eisenhower was on the road to Gettysburg. The previous day, a U-2 had overflown Syria before covering targets in northern Egypt. The film from the mission had arrived at Wiesbaden that evening for processing and analysis. The results were relayed to the Paramount Committee by midmorning on November 6. When President Eisenhower returned to the White House at noon, he was told by Colonel Goodpaster that there were no Soviet aircraft in Syria.

By this time, deep internal divisions had appeared within the British cabinet over continuing the operation. The final blow, however, was U.S. economic pressure. The Suez Crisis had caused a heavy run on the English pound and a sharp drop in British gold reserves. By Election Day, the British were looking to the United States for economic aid. When the British asked for a loan to support the pound, they were told bluntly that the U.S. price would be British acceptance of a cease-fire by midnight on November 6. Prime Minster Eden was forced to accept a humiliating retreat. The British were unable to overthrow Nasser or reclaim the Suez Canal, whereas Eisenhower had been reelected president in a landslide victory. Eisenhower was relieved that the Suez Crisis ended before the Soviets could become involved, but he remained concerned over possible Soviet moves into Syria. Between November 7 and December 18, Eisenhower approved fourteen additional U-2 flights over the area.

The Resumption of U-2 Overflights of the Soviet Bloc

The U-2 operations during the Suez Crisis showed the capability of the aircraft to provide intelligence on fast-breaking situations. This was not, however, the purpose for which the U-2 had been built. In the wake of the July 10, 1956, Soviet protest, and the realization that the U-2 could not overfly Eastern Europe and the USSR without being detected, Eisenhower was greatly disturbed. In a meeting with DCI Dulles on July 19, the president recalled that he had been told that "not over a very minor percentage of these [flights] would be picked up." He asked, "How far should this now be pushed, knowing that detection is not likely to be avoided?" Eisenhower and Dulles discussed the possibility of establish-

ing a third U-2 detachment in the Far East, but Eisenhower noted that he had "lost enthusiasm" for U-2 operations.

This reaction was based on both international and domestic considerations. Eisenhower noted that if the Soviets were to overfly the United States, "the reaction would be drastic." He was also aware of the need to maintain the trust of the American people. Eisenhower was worried that if the American public found out about the overflights, they would be shocked by the realization that the United States had violated international law, which banned unauthorized overflights. He noted: "Soviet protests were one thing, any loss of confidence by our own people would be quite another."

Eisenhower continued to express such concerns two months later, at a September 17 meeting with DDCI Cabell, Bissell, and Adm. Arthur W. Radford, the chairman of the Joint Chiefs of Staff. As they reviewed the results of the July 1956 overflights, Bissell noted that there were still many more intelligence targets yet to be covered. To meet the need, a total of fifteen separate areas would have to be photographed. Bissell then pleaded for authorization to resume overflights, arguing that as the days got shorter, conditions were increasingly unfavorable. At both this meeting and a follow-up meeting on October 3, Eisenhower remained unconvinced. At the October 3 meeting, he again noted that the U-2 had been detected and that the arguments in favor of the overflights did not take into account world opinion. He said that for many years the United States had been working "to create an opinion in the world that we are not truculent and did not want war." If the U-2 overflights were to become known, world opinion would view them as "provocative and unjustified."

The halt in operations took a toll on Detachment A. In the three months since the stand-down order following the Soviet protest, the unit made only eleven overflights, all in the Mediterranean area. The lack of missions over the USSR, the slow pace of activities, and the change in mission all resulted in a decline in pilot morale. This problem was made worse by Carey's crash on September 17, the same day as the first White House meeting. Conditions improved for the unit in early October 1956, when it moved to the renovated facilities at Giebelstadt, West Germany. A security problem was soon discovered at the new base, however. A long black limousine belonging to a Soviet bloc embassy was spotted parked near the runway whenever the U-2s were taking off.

Although the USSR and Eastern Europe were still out of bounds for

the U-2, two of the Mediterranean missions covered Soviet bloc targets. On September 6 and October 12, U-2s covered targets in Yugoslavia and Albania. These were on the fringes of the Soviet bloc, however, and were not the kind of mission that the CIA pilots had been selected to fly.

What finally changed Eisenhower's mind about resuming U-2 overflights was the Soviet's brutal crushing of the Hungarian Revolution. His decision was made easier with his own reelection. On November 15, 1956, Eisenhower met with Admiral Radford, DCI Dulles, Bissell, and the acting secretary of state, Herbert Hoover, Jr. Eisenhower explained to them his reluctance toward authorizing Soviet overflights: "Everyone in the world says that, in the last six weeks, the United States has gained a place it hasn't held since World War II. To make trips now would cost more than we would gain in the form of solid information." Hoover agreed, saying, "If we lost a plane at this stage, it would be almost catastrophic."

And yet, despite Eisenhower's concerns about international and domestic public opinion, his desire to maintain a "correct and moral" position, as well as fears that the U-2 overflights might trigger a war, as president he had the responsibility of defending the United States. As a result, Eisenhower approved the CIA request to make overflights of the USSR and Eastern Europe. This was not the open-ended authorization of deep penetration as during the July 1956 missions. Instead, the overflights would be of border areas; Eisenhower said that the aircraft should "stay as close to the border as possible." He specifically rejected a more ambitious mission, saying, "but not the deep one."

The first of these overflights, Mission 4016, was to be over the southern USSR and was to be the first Soviet overflight made by Detachment B. Word of the approval was sent to Incirlik via a coded message. Powers was walking through the Detachment B compound when he was stopped by the unit's commander, Col. Ed Perry, and told, "You're it, Powers." He asked, "When?" and Perry replied, "If the weather holds, a couple of days." That's how Powers learned he was to overfly the USSR.

Mission 4016 was scheduled for November 20, 1956. Powers went to bed early the night before but found he could not sleep, due to the early hour, the warm temperature, and the tension. He recalled later telling himself that the only difference would be that the next day's flight would be a little longer and over a different country. But he was not fooling himself, and sleep came hard even with sleeping pills. Powers was awakened at 5:00 A.M., went to breakfast, and began the prebreathing. During this two-hour period, Powers studied the color-coded flight map. Red de-

noted target areas to be flown as precisely as possible. Alongside were notations regarding when the camera and electronic equipment were to be switched on and off. Blue indicated the general route to be followed; some deviations were allowed if required, such as by fuel use. Brown lines showed routes back to alternate airfields should he not be able to return to Incirlik.

After a last-minute briefing on the weather, the unit's intelligence officer asked Powers if he wanted to carry a cyanide capsule. Called an L-pill, it was a thin glass capsule containing liquid potassium cyanide. If a pilot was facing capture, all he had to do was bite down on the pill to break the thin glass, and death would follow within ten to fifteen seconds. Six of the L-pills were produced, apparently under the designation "MK-Naomi." Powers shook his head. He, like most of the other U-2 pilots, did not carry the L-pill. His refusal, he later recalled, was not for any profound reasons. He was simply worried that the glass might break in the flight suit pocket and he would be exposed to the cyanide fumes. Powers dismissed his reasons as "a trifle silly."

Powers was taken out to the waiting U-2 and helped up the ladder and into the cockpit. He started up the engine, checked the instrument readings, then closed the canopy and activated the pressurization system. At the light signal, he advanced the throttle, and the U-2 took off.

After leveling out at the assigned altitude, Powers continued to monitor the instrument readings. Exactly thirty minutes after takeoff, he reached for the radio call button and gave two clicks. This was the signal that everything was operating normally and he was continuing with the flight. Incirlik replied with a single click, indicating that he was to proceed as planned.

Powers's flight route first headed east over Iraq, where he photographed targets in and around Baghdad. He continued east, photographing a rail and repair shop at Andemeshk, Iran. He then headed back west, along the Soviet-Iranian border to Soviet Armenia, and finally crossed into Soviet airspace between the Black and Caspian Seas.

Mission 4016 then followed a zigzag path over an area farther east than that covered by Mission 2023 on July 10, 1956. At Sangachaly, Powers photographed an airfield that was base to more than forty-five MiGs. A single eight-gun antiaircraft site guarded the base. The next target was the Baku-Nagdal area, the USSR's primary oil production and refining region. He continued on to a military depot near Kafan, which contained forty-six vehicles and sixty-nine towed artillery pieces, then to a military

camp near Nakhichevan. This was followed by Yerevan, which was the capital of Soviet Armenia, and its suburbs.

Up to this point, the overflight had been successful. As Powers neared the Kara area, an inverter light-out problem appeared. This meant that either the U-2's electrical generator had failed and the aircraft was limited to battery power, or simply that the instrument light had failed. Powers aborted the rest of the mission as a precaution and returned to Incirlik after six hours and five minutes in the air. The flight had been detected, and a number of unsuccessful intercept attempts had been made by Soviet fighters. Despite Khrushchev's earlier comment to his son, the Soviets made a secret diplomatic protest of the flight.

The other two overflights authorized by Eisenhower were conducted on December 10, 1956, and covered targets in Bulgaria, Yugoslavia, and Albania. The first, Mission 4018, was to be made from Detachment B in Incirlik; the second, Mission 2029, would be flown by Carmine Vito from Detachment A at Giebelstadt, West Germany. Mission 4018, like the previous overflights, was detected on radar. Bulgarian fighters made ten different intercept attempts against the U-2, but the first overflight proved uneventful.

The second, Mission 2029, nearly ended in a bizarre disaster. Vito was known to the other pilots as the Lemon-Drop Kid, because he always carried a supply in the knee pocket of his flight suit. Vito and several of the other pilots were known to have such snacks in flight. Vito was also one of the few pilots to carry the L-pill. During Vito's prebreathing on the morning of December 10, an air force sergeant placed the L-pill into the right knee pocket of Vito's flight suit. The sergeant did not realize that this pocket also contained Vito's supply of lemon drop candies.

After Vito took off, he started pulling the lemon drops from his knee pocket. About halfway into Mission 2029, with the U-2 over Bulgaria, Vito reached for a lemon drop, opened his faceplate, and, without looking, popped it into his mouth. Closing the faceplate, Vito began sucking on the object but thought it strange that it was smoother than the other lemon drops and had no flavor. Vito reopened the faceplate, spat the object onto his gloved flight suit, and saw that he was holding the L-pill. Had he bitten down, he would have died. The loss of the aircraft would have also meant the end of the overflight program.

Vito told the other pilots about the L-pill incident several days later. The conversation was overheard by the Detachment A security officer, who reported it to headquarters. When Cunningham learned of the in-

cident, he immediately ordered that each L-pill be placed in a small box, so it could not be mistaken for anything else. The L-pills remained available in this form for the next three years.

The Last U.S. Air Force Overflights: RB-57Ds over Vladivostok

The two overflights of December 10 brought the total of U-2 missions over the USSR to six, covering the western and far southern regions, and seven over the whole of Eastern Europe. Three other missions made the following day brought the end of air force overflights. While the U-2 had undergone its accelerated development and begun operations, the air force had been working on the RB-57D. In September 1956, five RB-57Ds were deployed to Yokota Air Base in Japan. In December, two more were added. These were "Group A" aircraft, which were designed to undertake photoreconnaissance missions and collect fallout samples from Soviet nuclear tests. They had extended wings, new J-57 engines, and a single pilot.

During the fall of 1956, the air force chief of staff, Gen. Nathan Twining, began urging President Eisenhower to approve overflights of the Soviet Far East using the new RB-57Ds. The aircraft had a maximum speed of 430 knots and could reach an altitude of 64,000 feet. General Twining argued that because the RB-57Ds flew faster than the U-2s and nearly as high, they could probably escape detection. President Eisenhower was eventually persuaded and gave permission for three RB-57Ds to make overflights of targets around Vladivostok.

The missions were based out of Yokota and were flown on December 11, the day after the Bulgarian U-2 overflights. The weather conditions were ideal—bright and clear. The three RB-57Ds entered Soviet airspace simultaneously just after 1:00 P.M. local time at three different points around Vladivostok; they overflew three different targets. But despite General Twining's expectations, the U.S. aircraft were picked up by Soviet radar, and MiG-17s were sent after them. The RB-57Ds' speed and altitude placed them out of reach, however. When the film was analyzed, the MiG-17s were visible below the converted bombers.

A Soviet protest note followed on December 15 and left no doubt as to the Soviet's ability to track and identify intruding aircraft: "On December 11, 1956, between 1307 and 1321 o'clock, Vladivostok time, three American jet planes, type B-57, coming from . . . the Sea of Japan, south of Vladivostok, violated the . . . air space of the Soviet Union. . . . Good

weather prevailed in the area violated, with good visibility, which precluded any possibility of the loss of orientation by the fliers during their flight. . . . The Government of the Soviet Union . . . insists that the Government of the USA take measures to punish the guilty parties and to prevent any further violations of the national boundaries of the USSR by American planes."

Eisenhower was furious that the RB-57Ds had been spotted. On December 18, 1956, he met with John Foster Dulles to discuss the Soviet protest and decide what action to take. Dulles said: "I think we will have to admit this was done and say we are sorry. We cannot deny it." He also noted: "Our relations with Russia are pretty tense at the moment." Eisenhower agreed, saying this was no time to be provocative. He instructed Colonel Goodpaster to call Secretary of Defense Charles Wilson, Joint Chiefs of Staff chairman Admiral Radford, and DCI Dulles and inform them that "effective immediately, there are to be no flights by U.S. reconnaissance aircraft over Iron Curtain countries."

The United States did not reply to the Soviet protest note until January 11, 1957. Despite Dulles's initial suggestion that the United States apologize for the RB-57D overflights, Eisenhower would not agree to such an admission. Instead, the U.S. note said that the "only authorized United States Air Force flights in the general area of the Sea of Japan were normal training flights."

The RB-57D missions over Vladivostok were the last time U.S. military aircraft made overflights of the USSR. The U.S. Air Force and U.S. Navy overflight program, which had been under way for the previous eight years, was shut down. United States military aircraft would be restricted to the border photographic and SIGINT missions.

Chapter 6
Soft Touch

In late August 1957 the missions were flown—rapidly to minimize possible counteraction, and many of them to cover as much useful area as possible.
—Henry S. Lowenhaupt on the Soft Touch U-2 overflights

Just over a year after the U-2 made its debut in Soviet skies, it made its most ambitious series of overflights, code-named Soft Touch. These ranged throughout Soviet Central Asia and Siberia and were targeted against Soviet nuclear production and test sites, aircraft production plants and industrial facilities, and the USSR's ballistic missile program. Such targets were critical to understanding Soviet military capabilities. But before the U-2 could undertake the Soft Touch missions, it first had to become invisible.

Project Rainbow and the "Dirty Birds"

At the end of 1956, the CIA U-2 program was in limbo. President Eisenhower was reluctant to authorize overflights but was also unwilling to close down the CIA effort. He did let the U-2s cover targets in the Middle East and fly SIGINT missions along the Soviet border. The first CIA U-2 SIGINT flight was Mission 4019, flown by a Detachment B aircraft on December 22, 1956. The flight carried a SIGINT package, known as the System-V unit, in the aircraft's camera bay in place of the A-2 package. The Mission 4019 route took the aircraft from the Black Sea along the Soviet border to the Caspian Sea, then to Afghanistan.

The System-V package worked well. Such border SIGINT missions became a mainstay of the CIA's U-2 activities in the coming years. They were not without risks, however. On March 18, 1957, Mission 4020 accidentally strayed into Soviet airspace while on a border flight, due to a compass problem and a slight error in the pilot's dead reckoning. Due to cloud cover, the pilot did not realize that he was over the USSR until he saw Soviet fighters trying to intercept his U-2.

As valuable as these border SIGINT missions were, if the U-2 was to again overfly Soviet targets, modifications would have to be made to reduce the aircraft's susceptibility to being detected by radar. On August 16, 1956, Kelly Johnson flew to the East Coast for an urgent meeting with Bissell, Land, and Dr. Edward Purcell to discuss ways of developing "radar camouflage" for the U-2. Although Purcell was a Nobel laureate and had worked on radar development at MIT, Johnson was not keen on his theories. They involved adding various radar-absorbing material to the U-2's airframe, and the extra weight would reduce the aircraft's altitude. For this reason, Johnson disparaged the modified U-2s as "Dirty Birds."

The first Dirty Bird modification, called the "trapeze," involved attaching poles to the wings and tail surfaces of the U-2. At the ends of each pole was a small-gauge wire with tiny ferrite beads attached at exact intervals to completely encircle the U-2. Any radar signals in the 70-MHz range striking the aircraft would either become trapped in the loop or be so weakened that the echoes would not be picked up by radar. The trapeze was flight-tested in the fall of 1956 at the ranch, but it was never used operationally. In addition to the loss of some 1,500 feet of altitude due to the weight and drag, the wires would vibrate and "sing." The trapeze also made the U-2 harder to fly, because it made it difficult for the pilot to maintain the slightly nose-high attitude required while flying at maximum altitude.

In early 1957, another modification, called "wallpaper," began to be tested, also at the ranch. Wallpaper consisted of flexible sheets of a fiberglass honeycomb sandwich. The inner surface was glued onto the metal exterior of the nose, fuselage, and tail of U-2 Article 341, which was the prototype aircraft. The outer surface was covered with a grid of solid squares (dark in color, each twenty-one millimeters square). The squares were separated by four millimeters of light-colored (or, perhaps originally, clear) material. The inner and outer sheets were separated by a seven-millimeter-deep layer of honeycomb.

The wallpaper contained a printed circuit that was designed to absorb radar signals in the 65- to 85-MHz range. The modified U-2, flown by Lockheed test pilots, then began making a series of radar measurement missions during the early months of 1957. A test range, consisting of several radar sets and a trailer to house instrumentation, was operated by EG&G (which stands for Edgerton, Germeshausen & Grier) at a site near the ranch. Article 341 flew a specific course over the range while the EG&G technicians measured its radar return at different frequencies.

One disadvantage of the wallpaper was that it trapped heat within the U-2, which led to the fourth fatal U-2 accident. On April 2, 1957, Lockheed test pilot Bob Sieker was flying above the EG&G range at about 72,000 feet when the heat buildup caused a hydraulic pump to fail, which led to an engine flameout. When the engine shut down, cockpit pressurization was lost and Sieker's suit inflated. Tragically, the clasp at the bottom of his faceplate failed under the sudden pressurization, and it popped open. Sieker was unable to close it, and he lost consciousness in about ten seconds. Article 341 went into a flat spin as it fell toward the ground. When the airplane reached a lower altitude, Sieker apparently revived and attempted to bail out, but he was struck by the U-2's horizontal stabilizer and killed.

The U-2 crashed in a long valley near Sunnyside, Nevada. The site was so remote that it took the search party four days to find the wreckage. Sieker's body was found about fifty feet from the airplane; his faceplate was found in the cockpit. Article 341 had come down in one piece and was still recognizable as a U-2. The debris was concentrated within a short distance of the wreckage, because the flat spin had slowed the impact speed. Parts of Article 341, along with spare parts and parts salvaged from other crashed U-2s, were later reassembled to produce a flyable airframe. This was counter to the expectations that a crashed U-2 would be totally destroyed.

Article 341's condition indicated that the "weather plane" cover story was no longer tenable, because the camera and SIGINT equipment could be recovered. In addition, the long recovery effort attracted press attention. An April 12 article in the *Chicago Daily Tribune* carried the headline, "Secrecy Veils High-Altitude Research Jet; Lockheed U-2 Called *Super Snooper.*"

Detachment C and the Resumption of Soviet Overflights

Despite the loss of Sieker and Article 341, the flight tests, along with tests of a U-2 airframe on a fifty-foot boom, seemed to indicate that the wallpaper was successful, and it was accepted as a modification to the CIA U-2s. The results of the wallpaper tests, along with a number of other issues, were discussed at a May 6, 1957, meeting with President Eisenhower. On hand were Deputy Secretary of Defense Donald Quarles, General Twining, Acting Secretary of State Christian Herter, DCI Dulles, DDCI Cabell, and Bissell. In describing the Project Rainbow radar camouflage

work, Bissell said that once the wallpaper was added to the operational U-2s, the "majority of incidents would be undetected."

Despite such assurances, Eisenhower continued to express concerns about the effects of the U-2 overflights on U.S.-Soviet relations. He worried that the USSR might, for example, close off access to Berlin in retaliation. There had been no U-2 overflights of the USSR since Powers's November 1956 mission, and the only Eastern European overflight since the twin overflights of Bulgaria in December 1956 was a mission over Albania on April 25, 1957.

Despite these fears, President Eisenhower gave approval for a series of overflights. The initial missions would be made against the Soviet Far East from Alaska. These would be followed, once the Dirty Birds were ready, by the Soft Touch series of overflights against Soviet Central Asia.

Unlike the July 1956 series of missions, Eisenhower kept close control of these overflights. Bissell brought the flight map for each mission to the White House for Eisenhower's personal approval. The president would spread out the map on his desk and look over the route, with his son John (an army officer then serving as a White House aide) and Colonel Goodpaster watching over his shoulder. When Eisenhower was satisfied, he would initial the map with "DDE." Only then could the mission go forward.

Although Bissell's assurances about the Project Rainbow tests were one reason that Eisenhower gave his approval for renewed overflights, a more pressing concern was the Soviet ballistic missile program. The data came from radar tracking of Soviet launches from the Kapustin Yar missile test range. In October 1954, a contract had been issued to General Electric to construct a very-high-power radar based in Turkey. With a fixed antenna 175 feet tall and 110 feet wide, the AN/FPS-17 radar was the largest and most powerful radar then in existence. The contract with the air force specified that the radar was to be operational in eight months, on June 1, 1955. To speed up development, the radar used standard GE high-power television transmitters to create the six horizontal beams. Construction work began at Site IX outside Diyarbakir in eastern Turkey in February 1955, but the radar just missed its scheduled completion, going into operations fifteen minutes late.

The new Turkish radar detected its first Soviet missile launch on June 15, 1955. Subsequent tracking data indicated an ongoing series of missile launches, to ranges of 75, 150, 300, and 650 nautical miles. The pace of the Soviet ballistic missile effort was far greater than that of the United

States. Beginning in mid-1953, at least three hundred missiles were launched from Kapustin Yar over a four-year period. However, these were battlefield support rockets for use by the Soviet Army rather than long-range strategic missiles.

On May 15, 1957, this situation changed radically when the Soviets made the first launch of their R-7 intercontinental ballistic missile (ICBM). The lift-off was successful, but ninety-eight seconds into the flight, one of its five booster engines failed. The missile went off course and the debris landed some four hundred kilometers downrange. Subsequently given the NATO code name SS-6 Sapwood, the ICBM could deliver a nuclear warhead from the northwest USSR to the eastern United States.

The Soviet ballistic missile program was a reflection of changes in military policy brought about by Khrushchev. Upon becoming first secretary, he had been deeply shocked when he was briefed on the power of nuclear weapons. He recalled later, "I couldn't sleep for several days." Khrushchev believed that large conventional forces, such as armies or navies, had been made obsolete by nuclear weapons. He reduced the 5.7-million-man Soviet military by more than a million men during 1955–56, scrapped ambitious plans for a large surface navy, and limited production of Mya-4 and Tu-95 bombers to a total of only about a hundred aircraft.

In contrast, he saw the SS-6 as a means of countering the massive U.S. bomber force. An ICBM could strike its target in a half hour and was unstoppable by any defensive measures. Such a weapon would, in Khrushchev's view, make the U.S. B-47s and B-52s obsolete. He also saw missiles as a military panacea for the Soviet Union. This extended not only to ICBMs but also to ground forces and air defense. Missiles were cheap to operate, because they required fewer personnel than bombers, fighters, ground artillery, or antiaircraft guns. This would allow him to release manpower and funding to be used to raise the Soviet standard of living while still protecting the USSR from "capitalist aggression." Finally, the futuristic nature of missiles, and their advanced technology, projected an image of a dynamic, forward-looking USSR that Khrushchev found politically useful.

The United States had only limited information on the first SS-6 test. The launch site was believed to be in Central Asia, to the east of the Aral Sea. The intended impact point was identified as being near Klyuchi, on the Kamchatka Peninsula. This was to be the target of the next U-2 overflight of the Soviet Union, and the first by Detachment C.

The third group of CIA pilots completed training in late 1956. In addition to the death of Frank G. Grace, Jr., another crash, although not a fatal one, plagued the group. On December 19, 1956, Bob Ericson was flying over Arizona at 35,000 feet in Article 357 when a small leak depleted his oxygen supply. Ericson was soon suffering from hypoxia and could not act quickly enough to control the U-2's speed. It quickly exceeded the 190-knot limit and broke up at a speed of 270 knots. He was able to jettison the canopy and was sucked out of the airplane at 28,000 feet. His parachute opened automatically at 15,000 feet, and he landed safely. Article 357 crashed on the Navajo Indian Reservation and was a total loss.

Detachment C's deployment to Naval Air Station (NAS) Atsugi, Japan, began in early 1957. The Japanese government was not informed of the unit's planned activities, because it had no control over U.S. military activities. The deployment did run into a snag, due to a decision that the pilots' families could now go overseas with them. It was difficult to find housing on the base or in surrounding communities. As a result, the unit's first overflights were not made from Japan but from Alaska.

In June 1957, several Detachment C aircraft and pilots were flown to Eielson Air Force Base in preparation for the overflights. Although the Dirty Bird U-2s had not yet been delivered to the operational units, this was not seen as a serious problem. Air force radar Order of Battle reports and National Security Agency SIGINT data indicated that the Soviet Far East's radar network was equipped with older radar sets, and its personnel were considered to be of a lower quality than those in the western USSR. As a result, the area's defenses were judged to be ineffective.

The first Detachment C overflight, Mission 6002, was made on June 7–8, 1957 (due to the crossing of the international date line), with the Klyuchi ICBM impact area as the target. The U-2 took off from Eielson Air Force Base, but as the aircraft neared the Kamchatka Peninsula, the pilot observed that the target area was covered with clouds and he would not be able to photograph the impact site. As a result, he aborted the mission without crossing into Soviet airspace and returned successfully to Alaska.

The second attempt to overfly the Klyuchi ICBM impact area was made on June 19–20. This time the weather was good, and the U-2 entered Soviet airspace. The aircraft was tracked by Soviet radar as it covered the Kamchatka Peninsula, but no intercept attempts were made. When the film from Mission 6005 was processed, however, it was found that a cam-

era malfunction had ruined every third frame of film. It would be another three months before Detachment C would try again.

Planning for Soft Touch

Planning for the Soft Touch overflights began with selection of the targets by the Ad Hoc Requirements Committee (ARC). On May 27, 1957, ARC selected the Soviet atomic facilities near Tomsk and farther east at Krasnoyarsk, as well as the Semipalatinsk nuclear test site, as prime objectives for Soft Touch. Other major objectives for the overflights were the Soviet ICBM launch site in Central Asia, aircraft factories in Omsk and Novosibirsk, the industrial plants in the Kuznetsk Basin, uranium mining sites near the Chinese border, and a uranium metal plant northeast of Novosibirsk. These targets were scattered across a huge area and required takeoff and landing airfields in Pakistan and Iran. It was July 1957 before these could be arranged and flight planning could begin in earnest.

Henry S. Lowenhaupt, an analyst with the CIA's Office of Scientific Intelligence, was assigned to work up target briefs for each of the atomic targets to be covered by the U-2. He had been part of the Manhattan Engineering District, working at Oak Ridge. After the war, he participated in gathering intelligence on Soviet atomic activities. Following the first Soviet A-bomb test in 1949, he proposed a B-25 overflight of the Urals to photograph Soviet production facilities. The aircraft would take off from Iran, cover the targets in the Urals, then ditch beside a U.S. aircraft carrier in the Barents Sea off Novaya Zemlya. His plan went to Secretary of State Dean Acheson, who turned it down.

Lowenhaupt did his targeting work in the "Blue Room," a small, centrally located, secure facility that was, despite its name, actually painted light green. Each U-2 mission was to be planned around one or two of ARC's highest-priority targets but would cover as many lower-priority targets as possible along the way. The vertical camera in the A-2 package covered only a five-mile-wide band, so for an oblong target area, the flight path had to be oriented lengthwise across it. The flight path also had to be adjusted to allow for any errors in either the pilot's navigation or the target's actual location.

The Soft Touch planners were caught in a dilemma. The United States needed U-2 coverage of these targets because so little was known about them; but to plan the flights, exact information was needed as to the fa-

cilities' precise locations and purposes. Without such information, the U-2 pilots would have difficulty finding and photographing the targets. As a result, for each of the target areas the planners had to assemble bits of data—travelers' tales, old maps, attaché reports, interrogations of defectors and ex-POWs, data on prewar Soviet industrial facilities—as well as what little technical intelligence was available, such as sonic data, environmental samples, and Genetrix balloon photos.

The situation was particularly bad regarding the Semipalatinsk nuclear test site, because there was no intelligence on the area except for the sonic data from the nuclear tests. The town of Semipalatinsk, which means "seven tents," was on the old caravan route between China and the cities of Samarkand and Bukhara. The general area had been identified from sonic data after the first Soviet A-bomb test. Over the next eight years, some twenty nuclear tests had been conducted at the site, but the location of any one test could be determined only to within thirty miles. As a result, the size and exact location of the Soviet test area was not known.

Lowenhaupt finally asked Dr. Donald Rock to average the sonic data from the five largest nuclear tests made at Semipalatinsk. The resulting "centroid" was some seventy miles due east of Semipalatinsk. There were no landmarks on the open desert that could be identified visually by the pilot. Lowenhaupt wrote later: "This was an arbitrary pin-point for a highest priority target whose location was so poorly known that it ought to be represented as a hand-sized blur on a standard aeronautical chart—hardly a realistic target in operational terms."

The situation regarding the atomic facilities at Tomsk was better, although still "woefully sparse." Although there were early rumors of atomic activity in the Tomsk area, the evidence was limited to three marginal reports and a fur hat. The most recent report came from an ethnic German who claimed to have worked as a blacksmith in the Tomsk area during 1955. He told an army interrogator that the locals had suggested that "Atomsk" would be a better name for the town. He did not know of any specific atomic facilities but had heard of an underground plant called Kolonne 5 (Labor Brigade 5) located northeast of the Tomsk II railroad station.

Another ethnic German told a British interrogator that he had heard of a facility that was involved "in manufacturing fillings for atomic weapons locally known as the Post Box." In Tomsk II, he reported seeing a large building with barred windows and a large sign reading "In-

formation Office, Personnel Department, Post Box." When he was reinterrogated, the ethnic German mentioned a prohibited area north of Tomsk II and reported seeing trains carrying coal, wood, and building supplies going into the area. He added that he had seen three large chimneys belching black smoke six to eight kilometers north of Tomsk II.

The interrogator was not impressed, saying that the source had a poor memory and seemed to have some kind of mental disorder. The ethnic German was also preoccupied with his plans to emigrate to Canada. Lowenhaupt noted that "neither of these two reports tended to inspire confidence in the existence of a major atomic installation in the Tomsk area, let alone its precise location."

More concrete information came from another German ex-POW who had worked as a tailor in a small factory some twenty kilometers north of Tomsk city. He told an air force interrogator that during April or May 1949 some 12,000 prisoners had been put to work in a secure area located several kilometers north and west down the Tom River. The tailor said that many military officers on the construction staff had come to his shop to have their uniforms fitted properly. He said that the unit arrived with their families from Tallin, where they had just finished another large project. In charge was a Soviet general who arrived with his staff in late April. The tailor also reported that the guard unit at the site belonged to a different organization and did not live or mingle with the construction personnel. The tailor's Russian supervisor told him that the fenced-off area was to become an atomic energy plant.

Although the tailor's story was judged credible, it was a fur hat that provided the conclusive evidence. In the summer of 1956, John R. Craig, a CIA science officer, obtained the fur hat from an ethnic German who had lived in Tomsk. Tests showed that the hat was contaminated by fifty parts per billion of uranium that had been slightly enriched with the U-235 isotope. This was evidence that a uranium separation plant existed in the Tomsk area. Lowenhaupt indicated that this was the target for the U-2 overflight, and he gave as its position the site where the tailor had reported the 12,000 prisoners.

Information about atomic facilities at Krasnoyarsk was even more scarce, because the city had been off limits to foreigners by 1948. A Soviet defector code-named Icarus reported in early 1951 that many trainloads of mining equipment had been sent to Krasnoyarsk the year before from Wismut, A.G., the Soviet-controlled uranium mining firm in East Germany. As a result, Icarus believed that the activity at Krasnoyarsk

was uranium mining. It was not until a returning German ex-POW had been interrogated that additional details were available. Despite the Soviet rules and regulations to prevent such an occurrence, he had spent several years as a construction worker at the Krasnoyarsk atomic facilities. He reported secondhand information about many kilometers of concrete-lined tunnels.

Then in early 1957 came a surprise. A Genetrix gondola washed ashore at Adak in the Aleutian Islands. The base commander was Col. Richard Philbrick, who also happened to be one of the few individuals who knew what the strange object was. Colonel Philbrick ordered an airman to keep the gondola in water so the film would not stick to itself. He also notified the CIA's Arthur Lundahl of the gondola's discovery. The film was intact when it was finally processed, after a year floating in the cold waters of the northern Pacific. The results were called "one of the most valuable sets of coverage."

This was an understatement. The Genetrix balloon had floated directly over the Krasnoyarsk area and returned photos showing an enormous construction effort—a new city of apartment buildings, laboratories, warehouses, and machine shops and a vast mining effort. One photo showed an electric railroad leading into a mountain; nearby were a nuclear storage area and a probable ore crushing plant. The site was named Dodonovo, after an old village, and was identified as a nuclear refining facility. Lowenhaupt expected that the higher-resolution U-2 photos would clarify the function of the underground installation.

The other, lower-priority, nuclear targets were located from similar evidence. Icarus identified a uranium metal plant northeast of Novosibirsk (New Siberia), and it had been photographed by western attachés from the Trans-Siberian Railroad in 1952 and 1954. Their photos were compared to data in the Industrial Register, and the facility was identified as the Stalin Auto Works. In 1956, Dr. Nikolaus Riehl and other German scientists who had worked on uranium metal research for the Soviets expanded on the data that Icarus provided. The facility could be located within a half mile of permanent map landmarks.

The location of several uranium concentration plants operated by Combine 6 in the Fergana Valley area was indicated by a 1947 Jewish refugee who had driven a bread truck to each of the plants. The refugee was interrogated extensively, then resettled with appreciation in Brazil. During these interrogations, the refugee drew a series of maps. In his maps of the area east of the point where the Syr Darya River turned north

toward the Aral Sea, he reversed north and south. In areas west of this point, his maps were right side up. In several cases, his reports were confirmed by returning German ex-POWs. Other uranium concentration plants operated by Combine 8 were believed to be located farther east, near Pamir Knot and south of Alma Ata, but their location was, at best, poorly known, and targeting seemed doubtful.

As the Soft Touch routes were being planned, the Lockheed Skunk Works completed the radar camouflage modifications to a handful of U-2s. By July 1957, the Dirty Bird U-2s were delivered to Detachment B in Turkey. A Dirty Bird U-2 was first used on Mission 4030, flown on July 21. This was apparently a special mission over the Middle East. Ten days later, on July 31, the same U-2 was flown by James Cherbonneaux on a SIGINT mission over the Black Sea. The airplane carried various receivers to monitor the reaction of Soviet air defenses to the Dirty Bird modifications. The aircraft flew within the Soviet-claimed twelve-mile limit and was aloft for eight hours. Cherbonneaux recalled later that Soviet radar was able to detect the U-2 even with its wallpaper.

At the same time, the first B camera was delivered. Whereas the A-2 camera package was based on existing camera bodies with new lens designs, the B camera was a completely new concept. Designed by James Baker and engineered by Hycon's William McFadden, it used a 36-inch focal length f/10 lens assembly on a swivel mounting to provide horizon-to-horizon coverage. There were development problems; the moving lens caused blurred photos. Some wanted to cancel the B camera and stay with the A-2 package. Supporting the B camera were the CIA's photointerpreters, including Dino Brugioni, an assistant to PID chief Arthur Lundahl. Their solid support was due to the B camera's wider coverage and its resolution of a hundred lines per millimeter compared to sixty lines per millimeter on the A-2. Their efforts proved successful.

The B camera used an 18- by 18-inch photo format. Rather than a single roll of film, two 9.5-inch-wide strips of ultrathin Eastman Kodak film were used. The twin rolls, each a mile long, weighed a total of about three hundred pounds. Baker designed the B camera's film supply to be counter rotating. The film on the rear reel rotated forward as it was exposed, and the forward film reel rotated onto a reel at the back of the camera. As a result, the weight remained balanced and the U-2's center of gravity was not changed. However, the two halves of a photo could be as much as a mile apart, at opposite ends of each roll of film.

The B camera had two preprogrammed photographic sequences. In Mode I, the camera took a series of seven photos—one vertically and the

others at angles of 24.5 degrees, 49 degrees, and 73.5 degrees to both the left and right of the airplane's flight path. The vertical and the left and right 24.5-degree images were in pairs, which made objects appear three dimensional when seen through a stereo viewer. The best resolution in the vertical photograph was 2.5 feet from an altitude of more than 70,000 feet; the seven images covered a total width of about a hundred nautical miles. Resolution dropped off in the oblique photos, due to the increased distance from the U-2 to the object on the ground. In Mode II, the camera took only the vertical and 24.5-degree photos, which increased the number of exposures and nearly doubled the camera's operation, although at the cost of a narrower band of coverage.

Soft Touch over the USSR

The Soft Touch overflights began with the landing of a C-124 cargo airplane in Pakistan carrying eight pilots and ground crews from Detachment B. It was to be an intensive twenty-three-day-long series of nine missions covering the USSR and China. The series began on August 4, 1957, with a mission that covered China, Mongolia, and the USSR.

The second mission was to locate the Soviet ICBM launch site somewhere in Central Asia. The Soviet missile program had been active since the first SS-6 launch on May 15 but had yet to show much success. On June 10 and 11, three attempts to launch a second SS-6 were made. All three tries had to be canceled before launch due to system problems, and the ICBM was removed from the pad. Then on July 12, another SS-6 was launched. This time, the guidance system failed thirty-eight seconds after lift-off, and the missile began to spin so rapidly that it broke up.

On August 5, 1957, Eugene "Buster" Edens took off in a Dirty Bird U-2 in search of the launch site. Despite the additional launch attempts, the mission planners were still not certain of the ICBM's test site location. As a result, the Mission 4035 route followed the main railroad lines in the area east of the Aral Sea on the assumption that the launch site would have to be supplied by train. One part of Edens's flight path was along the main Moscow-Tashkent rail line southeast from Aralsk, which ran along the bank of the Syr Darya River. As Edens followed the rail line, he could hear the whine from the B camera's motor and feel a thump as the lens locked into position as it took each photo.

Edens landed safely, and the two large film rolls were removed from the U-2 for processing. The PID photointerpreters pored over the film, looking for any indication of the launch site. Finally, they spotted an odd-

looking structure in the B camera's oblique photographs. It was an ICBM launch pad some fifteen miles north of the railroad line. Because Edens had followed the rail line, the U-2 had not passed directly over the pad, and only oblique, low-resolution images of the area were available. A follow-up mission to provide vertical photos of the pad and related facilities was soon being planned. Although this was approved, the flight was not made until after the end of the Soft Touch series.

With the pad's location finally determined, it was time for the site to be given a name. The standard practice was to name any newly discovered Soviet facility after a nearby town. For several decades, however, Soviet maps had been systematically altered to hide the exact locations of cities. For this reason, the CIA used maps of Siberia and Central Asia prepared during World War II by Mil-Geo, the geographic component of the German Wehrmacht. The location of the launch site was on a 1939 Mil-Geo map. The pad was located at the end of a spur line extending into the desert. This apparently led to a prewar quarry, which was later used as the pad's flame pit. At the point where this spur line joined the main rail line was a railroad station named Tyuratam.

Dino Brugioni, who was responsible for assembling all collateral information on new facilities (such as the Mil-Geo maps), selected Tyuratam as the name of the launch site. In the local language, this meant "arrow burial ground." Others argued that the site should be named after Novokazalinsk or Dzhusaly. Brugioni countered that these towns were too far away (fifty-seven miles and forty-two miles, respectively) and that, given the open nature of the U.S. space program, the Soviets were sure to eventually give the exact location of the site. His argument was accepted, and the site became officially known within the CIA as the Tyuratam Missile Test Center.

The next of the Soft Touch missions was not flown until August 11, six days after Edens's highly successful mission. This overflight was a failure, however, because the B camera malfunctioned after taking only 125 exposures. This failure was followed by a halt in operations for nine days. It resumed with a maximum effort against Soviet nuclear facilities.

On August 20, 1957, two U-2s took off for targets in the USSR. During one of these flights, Mission 4045 made by Sammy Snyder, the U-2 passed over part of the Semipalatinsk nuclear test site, flew on to Novokuznetsk, then went farther north to the primary target of Tomsk. There, guided by a German tailor and a fur hat, at the maximum range of the U-2, Snyder found a huge Soviet nuclear complex. It included not

only a gaseous diffusion plant for uranium 235 enrichment, as the fur hat had indicated, but a reactor area, a plutonium chemical separation facility, and housing and administrative areas. The site was exactly where the tailor had said it would be. Snyder began the return leg, photographing the new city of Berezovsky, where another large uranium processing facility was located.

The following day, August 21, three U-2s took off on overflights. Two of these covered targets in the USSR and the other headed east for China and Tibet. One of the Soviet overflights was Mission 4050, flown by James Cherbonneaux. The primary target areas were industrial facilities around Stalinsk in the Kuznetsk Basin and uranium concentration plants around Alma Ata. The Mission 4050 flight route passed over a number of other targets, one of which gave Cherbonneaux more of a thrill than he had counted on.

After crossing into Soviet airspace, Cherbonneaux flew a search pattern over the western end of Lake Balkhash, looking for a suspected Soviet missile-related installation. He found and photographed the Soviet SAM and radar test site at Sary Shagan. In addition to the test of new SAM missiles, the radar at Sary Shagan was being used to track the incoming warheads of missiles launched from Kapustin Yar, some 1,400 miles to the west. Nearby was a new city of 20,000 people, which served as the headquarters for the test range. Sary Shagan was to later be the basis for the emerging Soviet antiballistic missile (ABM) program.

Cherbonneaux then turned north, heading, as Snyder did the day before, toward Semipalatinsk. The test area was a primary target, but the confidence that Lowenhaupt and the other analysts had in its location was so slight that Semipalatinsk and Karaganda were made the way points, with the route adjusted so as to pass through the centroid. For security reasons, there was no mention of the test site in the flight documents. The thinking was, why give away knowledge if you don't have to, as Lowenhaupt later recalled. There was apparently no thought given by any of the planners to the dangers of flying the fragile U-2 into a nuclear test.

Cherbonneaux flew over the Semipalatinsk airfield and its nuclear weapon assembly facility. Parked on the ramp was a bomber. He continued toward the calculated centroid. Over the empty desert, Cherbonneaux glanced at the drift sight and received a shock. He had flown many times over the U.S. nuclear test area at Frenchman's Flats, near the ranch, and recognized what he saw. Down below, Cherbonneaux

later recalled, he saw circular graded contours, like those he had seen before in Nevada.

Cherbonneaux brought the drift sight up to its maximum four-power magnification and spotted a large tower with a nuclear device "shot cab" at its top. His flight path would take him directly over it. He realized that not only was this a nuclear test site, but a test was imminent. Cherbonneaux began to sweat and hyperventilate at the thought that the weapon might be detonated as he passed over the tower. He recalled years later shouting into his faceplate, "Wait, goddamnit. Wait, will you? Let me pass and then light your fire."

Cherbonneaux's U-2 was fitted with an A-2 camera package, and as he passed over the tower he turned it on. He recalled that it seemed to take an eternity for the U-2 to pass over the tower, and his heart was pounding in his throat. He was sure he and his airplane were about to be evaporated by a nuclear blast. Five minutes later, Cherbonneaux had cleared the test site and was laughing at himself for being so "chicken." The overflight went on to cover the aircraft factories at Omsk; the uranium mill at Kadzhi-Say, near Lake Issyk Kul, to the south of Alma Ata; and the uranium mines of Bystrovka.

Cherbonneaux recalled later being impressed with the vastness of Soviet Central Asia, describing it as "almost unimaginable" and making him feel "achingly lost and alone." Through the drift sight he could see no contrails from Soviet MiGs, so he concluded that the wallpaper was working to keep him hidden from Soviet radar. This heightened Cherbonneaux's sense of being alone. It could mean that no one knew where he was, because his U-2 was also out of range of U.S. border listening posts.

Suddenly the engine on Cherbonneaux's U-2 began making rough noises. This made him fully alert, although he knew from long experience that the perceived roughness of an engine was in direct proportion to the distance the pilot had to fly to reach a friendly border.

Soon after, Cherbonneaux caught sight of the snow-covered peak of K2, the mountain that was his guide back to Pakistan. He had been in the air for about eight hours and was still about an hour away from crossing the border. At this point, he became aware of a new concern, which quickly eclipsed his earlier worries about a nuclear test or a rough-running engine. He had to urinate. Although the pressure suit had a fitting that allowed the pilot to urinate in flight, Cherbonneaux had never been able to use it. Already exhausted by the long overflight, he was in in-

creasing pain. By the time he entered the landing pattern, he later recalled, the pain was so bad that he almost touched down short of the runway. After the U-2 stopped, a ground crewman opened the canopy. Cherbonneaux pushed him aside, "vaulted" down the ladder, and relieved himself on the runway.

As he began the postflight debriefing, Cherbonneaux expected that his discovery of a Soviet nuclear test site would make him a hero. But because his debriefers had not been told that this was one of Mission 4050's targets, they disbelieved him. He was told by one debriefer, "There is no atomic test facility in that part of central Russia." The information was passed on to CIA headquarters, and their reply was a rebuke.

Four hours after Cherbonneaux overflew Semipalatinsk, the Joe-36 nuclear test was made, with a yield of half a megaton. This was an airdrop rather than a tower test. In the photographs of the Semipalatinsk airfield, both the drop aircraft and the bomb itself were visible. The tower and shot cab that Cherbonneaux had spotted were actually being prepared for a low-yield nuclear test, which was not made until September 13. Cherbonneaux was told about the nuclear test at lunch the next day. John Parangosky, a CIA official with the unit, took him aside and sheepishly said "Apologies, Jim" and told him that "collateral intelligence sources" indicated that a test had been made.

Soft Touch Results

On August 23, 1957, DDCI Cabell, Bissell, and air force chief of staff General Twining met with President Eisenhower to discuss the results from Soft Touch. They showed Eisenhower some of the photos from the early flights and talked about the effectiveness of the radar camouflage. Bissell explained that the Soft Touch operation was about to conclude with the transfer of the U-2s back to Incirlik in Turkey. Bissell asked for permission for one of the U-2s to make an additional overflight of the USSR on its return trip. Eisenhower turned down the request, not wishing to make any more overflights for the moment.

Even without this additional mission, the Soft Touch overflights had opened a huge window into Soviet nuclear, missile, and industrial efforts. They had covered many of the research and development facilities located in Soviet Central Asia. They also highlighted the fundamental change brought about by overhead reconnaissance. When told that the Tomsk atomic site had been photographed, DCI Dulles was said to have

exclaimed jubilantly, "You mean you really did know that something atomic is going on way out there in the wilds of Siberia?"

The Mission 4045 report said that the Tomsk complex "covers an irregular shaped area of about 40 square miles on the right bank of the Tom River. No single atomic energy complex in the western world includes the range of processes taking place here. The villages of Iglakovo and Beloborodovo are encompassed in the housing and administrative area along the river. On the west edge of the area, a large thermal power plant with an estimated capability of 400 megawatts is undergoing further expansion. Further power is provided by Gres II in Tomsk and by tie-ins to the Kuzbas Grid. East of this plant is located the feed and processing section and gaseous diffusion plants. One gaseous diffusion building is uncompleted. On the east edge is located the reactor area. One of the two reactors appears to be in the final stage of construction. A maintenance and construction area is just north of these areas. On the northeastern edge, a plutonium chemical separation area is uncompleted. A mud lake dump area is on the northern edge of the complex outside of the fence which encompasses the whole installation. It is rail served by a spur line from Tomsk."

Subsequent analysis indicated that one of the reactors was operational and two more were under construction. The gaseous diffusion U-235 enrichment facility at Tomsk had four operating buildings and a fifth under construction. This was about one-sixth the size of the U.S. gaseous diffusion plant at Oak Ridge. From a later Soviet defector, the CIA learned that the site was code-named Post Box 5, Tomsk and was called Berezki (Birch Woods).

Analysis of the photos, DDCI Cabell told the Joint Chiefs of Staff on August 28, 1957, would provide information "on electric power consumption, cooling water consumption, plant arrangement and size, new construction and the physical details which, when analyzed, should enable us to make a much better estimate of the Soviet critical materials production." It took several months for the Tomsk facilities to be fully understood. The problem arose because the Soviet second-generation atomic facilities were not copies of U.S. counterparts but rather had been designed from scratch. The photointerpreters had to reconstruct the totally foreign engineering shown in the U-2 photos.

The Soft Touch overflights provided intelligence not only on Tomsk but also on the whole production cycle of Soviet nuclear weapons, from the mining and processing of the raw uranium ore to the production of

nuclear materials and finally to the testing of the finished weapons at Semipalatinsk. Despite the poorly known location, the uranium mines at Bystrovka were eventually located on the film. The uranium mill at Kadzhi-Say proved to be large and modern. The U-2 mission to Novosibirsk showed that the uranium metal plant was a large installation. Also at the site was a possible lithium isotope separation plant under construction.

One disappointment was the mission to Krasnoyarsk; no photos could be taken of the site due to cloud cover. It was not until many years later that the "Dodonovo mining site" was finally understood. "Krasnoyarsk 26," as the Soviets called it, was actually an underground city with three plutonium production reactors. They had been built inside a mountain to protect them against U.S. attack.

Although the existence of the U-2 overflights was carefully hidden from all but a few, Congress was briefed on the initial results of the Soft Touch missions without being told the source. Such sanitized intelligence on the limitations of the Soviet nuclear program was given in a CIA briefing on November 26–27, 1957. It noted: "The availability of fissionable material will impose some limitations on the extent of Soviet nuclear warhead production between now and 1966."

Soft Touch was the high point of the U-2 program. The huge amounts of intelligence brought back by the flights were the fulfillment of the hopes expressed by Dr. Land and the other members of Project Three in 1954. Yet despite these accomplishments, the U-2 would never again conduct overflights on such a massive scale. The number of overflights would decline, then be halted altogether for more than a year. This would occur, ironically, at a time when the United States faced a new political and military threat from the USSR.

Additional U-2 Overflights

Despite the repeated SS-6 launch failures, both the Soviet efforts and CIA interest continued. Within a matter of a week, both would meet success. On August 21, 1957, a fourth SS-6 lifted off the Tyuratam launch pad. This time, the ICBM's systems operated successfully, and the missile followed the planned trajectory toward the Klyuchi impact area. The dummy warhead separated from the second stage, although it broke up when it reentered the atmosphere. Despite this, the launch was judged a success. The launch was announced by the Soviets on August 26. The

official Tass announcement stated: "A super-long-distance intercontinental multi-stage ballistic rocket was launched a few days ago. The tests of the rocket were successful. They fully confirmed the correctness of the calculations and the selected design." The statement continued that ICBMs would "make it possible to reach remote areas without resorting to a strategic air force, which at the present time is vulnerable to up-to-date means of anti-aircraft defense." Tass also said that "a series of explosions of nuclear and thermonuclear [hydrogen] weapons has been staged in the USSR in recent days. . . . The tests were successful."

Publically, administration officials downplayed the Soviet ICBM test, saying that it would not cause a speedup of the Atlas program. The Soviet test itself was dismissed by some as an experiment and not even as a prototype of an ICBM. Secretly, however, the CIA wanted better photos of the Tyuratam complex than the oblique images that Edens's overflight provided. Planning had been under way since the site was discovered, and Eisenhower gave his approval.

Mission 4058 was flown on August 28, 1957, one week after the SS-6 ICBM test and only two days after the Soviet announcement. The overflight, which used an A-2 camera package, obtained excellent vertical photos of the main launch complex. The pad was a huge, tablelike structure hanging over a large flame pit. A railroad track brought the missile up to the pad. This was the only launch pad at the Tyuratam site. About five days after the Mission 4058 photos were processed and analyzed, the Automat model shop built a cardboard miniature of the site showing the facilities and surrounding railroad sidings and access roads.

Lundahl later described the impact of the U-2: "Some cases where we had literally pieced together bits of folklore, mapping information, traveler's reports . . . we would have stuck all these little bits of information on a map and made a great melange of things." When the U-2 photos of Tyuratam arrived, he noted, "One look at the aerial photos of that place literally wiped out most of that folklore and gave us hard, crisp information that was measurable and reaffirmable by anyone who wanted to look at the pictures. It was really like seeing the dawn after a long dark night of ignorance." It would be nearly two more years, however, before a U-2 would again visit Tyuratam.

On September 7, ten days after the Tyuratam overflight was made, the Soviets conducted their second successful SS-6 test flight in a row. The missile lifted off the pad and headed for the Klyuchi ICBM impact area on the Kamchatka Peninsula, some 3,500 miles away. But, as with the first

launch, its large, cone-shaped dummy warhead broke up as it reentered the atmosphere. Khrushchev was on hand for the launch.

Although the warhead needed to be redesigned, the SS-6 missile itself seemingly had been proven. Preparations began for the next SS-6 launch, to take place in about a month's time. It would provide a demonstration of the Soviet's newfound missile and scientific prowess. And it would change the world.

Soviet missile activities were also the subject of the next two overflights of the USSR. On June 22, 1957, the first launching from Kapustin Yar of a ballistic missile with a range of 950 nautical miles was made. By August 29, seven such flights had been detected by Turkish radar. The new Soviet missile, subsequently give the NATO code name SS-4 Sandal, was not a battlefield support rocket but rather a strategic medium-range ballistic missile, able to strike U.S. air bases surrounding the USSR. This posed a major threat, because U.S. bombers relied on these forward bases, which could be destroyed without warning in a missile attack.

The first of these overflights was to assess the status of the SS-4 program. The U-2 took off from Incirlik, Turkey, on September 10, and covered the Kapustin Yar missile test range. As it passed above the site, the U-2's A-2 cameras photographed a Soviet missile on its launch pad. Despite the growing importance of monitoring Soviet missile activities, it would be more than two years before Kapustin Yar would again be photographed.

A second missile-related overflight followed six days later. In the three months since its June 19–20, 1957, overflight, Detachment C had received a Dirty Bird U-2. On September 15–16, this aircraft finally covered the Klyuchi impact area. The results from Mission 6008 were excellent, but the effectiveness of the wallpaper was less so. The Dirty Bird U-2 was tracked by Soviet radar while five Soviet MiGs trailed the aircraft.

While the U-2s had been photographing Soviet missile facilities, a consensus had been building within ARC on the need for intelligence on the Soviet naval maneuvers that were scheduled to take place in the Barents Sea area during October 1957. Some of the ARC members wanted a SIGINT mission over the ships; others wanted an overflight of the Murmansk and Severomorsk shipyards in the northwest USSR. This would require two separate missions, because the U-2 could not carry both the SIGINT and camera packages. In late September, Eisenhower gave his approval for the two missions.

The first to be flown, Mission 2037, was the SIGINT flight. The U-2

would not penetrate Soviet airspace but would remain over international waters to pick up the radar and radio emissions from ships of the Soviet Northern Fleet. The U-2 selected for both this SIGINT mission and the later overflight was Article 351, which had just been delivered to Detachment A from Lockheed after modifications. To extend the aircraft's range to more than 4,000 nautical miles, it had been fitted with "slipper tanks." These were on the wings' leading edges, ten feet from the fuselage, and each held a hundred gallons of fuel.

The flight would carry a System-IV SIGINT package consisting of eleven receivers to pick up signals in a range from 150 to 4,000 MHz. It was built by Ramo-Wooldridge, later to become TRW. Although much smaller than the equipment carried by the RB-47Hs, the receivers filled the camera bay. There was only enough room for the small, 70mm tracking camera, which recorded the U-2's flight path.

Mission 2037 took off from Giebelstadt on October 11, 1957, at 5:25 A.M. local time. The weather conditions were poor: total darkness, a 200-foot ceiling, and only 660-foot visibility. The pilot was Jacob Kratt, who faced a daunting task. In addition to the usual demands of flying the U-2, the high northern latitudes added strong headwinds and cloud cover. As the sun rose, Kratt could see below his U-2 a solid cloud deck, completely obscuring the ground and ocean. He would have to navigate by dead reckoning for nearly 4,000 nautical miles, using only his radio compass and clock.

When Kratt reached Tromso, in the extreme northeastern end of Norway, after more than three hours in the air, he turned on the System-IV and began collecting electronic emissions. Over the next three and a half hours, Kratt flew a triangular pattern over the cloud-covered Barents Sea. During the third leg, as Article 351 headed back toward Tromso, Kratt spotted contrails below him, which might have been from Soviet fighters. When the airplane arrived back at Tromso, the cloud cover had thinned enough for Kratt to see the Norwegian coast. He found that the U-2 was fifty-four nautical miles south of the planned course, apparently due to winds aloft. Kratt turned south and landed back at Giebelstadt at 3:18 P.M. local time; he had been in the air for nine hours and fifty-three minutes and covered more than 3,900 nautical miles.

The next day, Article 351 was serviced, and the System-IV package was removed and replaced with an A-2 camera package. On the morning of October 13, 1957, Article 351 was again on the runway at Giebelstadt undergoing final preparations for Mission 2040, the overflight of the north-

west USSR. During the preflight, 1,535 gallons of fuel were pumped into the U-2's tanks by air force personnel. The crewman who oversaw this was to set the fuel counter on the U-2's instrument panel with the same number of gallons. As each gallon was burned, the counter would be reduced by one digit, allowing the pilot to compare the fuel being used to that predicted in the flight plan. During the preflight, however, the crewman made an error. He set the counter to 1,500 gallons, which was 35 gallons less than the true amount aboard.

As with the previous mission, the weather at Giebelstadt was terrible. The fog was so low that the tip of Article 351's vertical fin could not be seen, and the white center strip on the runway was barely visible. The pilot selected for Mission 2040 was Hervey Stockman, who had made the first overflight of the USSR the year before. This was to be his second Soviet overflight. Stockman boarded the airplane just after 6:00 A.M. local time. He was preoccupied by the poor weather conditions and did not notice the incorrect setting on the fuel counter.

The U-2 began its takeoff roll at 6:35 A.M. and climbed into the fog. Stockman passed through an altitude of 4,500 feet and broke out of the clouds into the morning sunlight. As he continued the long climb to altitude, he encountered the first of a series of problems that would dog the flight. The cockpit was getting hot, and he saw a thin film of oil starting to cover a windshield quarter panel from a forward vent. He moved the air temperature control back and forth several times, but without effect.

The cockpit soon become so hot that Stockman broke radio silence to ask Giebelstadt for advice. The base replied that he should pull the air-conditioning circuit breaker. The task was easier said than done; the panel was located on the right side of the cockpit, below the level of the seat. To reach it, Stockman released his shoulder harness, then used his hands to turn his heavy helmet so he could see the panel. He finally found the correct breaker and disabled the air conditioner. The cockpit began to cool, and the flow of oil stopped. Because the temperature dropped when the U-2 reached higher altitude, he repeated the process a half hour later to plug the breaker back in. The air conditioner then began to operate normally.

No sooner had this problem been solved, however, than a more serious one appeared. The U-2 began to run rough and lose altitude. The instruments showed that Stockman was at 62,000 feet and dropping, and the exhaust-gas temperature (EGT) gauge was fluctuating around 600

degrees Fahrenheit. This was close to the point where the engine might be damaged. Stockman noticed that the speed brake switch, located on the throttle, was in the open position. During his struggles with the air-conditioning circuit breaker, a pocket on the upper left arm of his overalls had snagged the switch. Stockman quickly closed the switch, and the shuddering stopped.

Article 351 flew north over West Germany and Denmark, then over Norway. All that Stockman could see was a solid cloud base except for a break at Oslo. Before the flight, Detachment A's navigation unit had prepared a flight plan on an 8½- by 11-inch green card, which listed each turn point, the calculated time of arrival, and the estimated fuel usage. At each turn point, Stockman was to write the actual time of arrival and the fuel counter reading. By the time he reached the fourth turn point, designated Echo, Stockman thought that something was wrong with the fuel consumption estimate. Only a third of the way into the mission, he was ninety-two gallons behind the fuel curve. This indicated strong headwinds, but the handling problems this normally caused were not apparent. Stockman did not realize that due to the ground crewman's error in setting the fuel counter, he was actually only fifty-seven gallons behind the fuel curve.

This potential shortage of fuel continued to worry Stockman. Halfway to turn point Fox, he saw that the clouds extended all the way to turn point George. He decided to head directly for turn point How, where he could see a break in the clouds. This cut half an hour off the flight, which Stockman hoped would save enough fuel to enable him to complete the mission. Four hours and fifteen minutes into the flight, Stockman rounded the North Cape of Norway and began to be "painted" by Soviet radar. He continued east over the Barents Sea to a point 125 nautical miles north of the Soviet city of Gavrilovo. Stockman then turned south, following a curving flight path that brought him to a point ten nautical miles off the Soviet coast. Here he turned on the A-2 cameras. The U-2 continued along the coast to a point twenty nautical miles north of Kildin Island, where he turned southwest and crossed over the Soviet coastline.

The first target was the naval facility at Severomorsk. After covering the area from an altitude of 70,200 feet, Stockman headed toward Olenegorsk, fifty nautical miles to the south. This course took the U-2 five miles to the east of Murmansk. Stockman saw through the drift sight three large ships, which he thought were cruisers, anchored off the port of Grosnyy. He also spotted fifteen to twenty destroyers and numerous

new airfields scattered through the area. After reaching Olenegorsk, Stockman began a wide, right-hand turn to the west, heading toward Monechegorsk. As he started the turn, he saw that he was not alone.

The contrails of two Soviet MiGs were climbing toward him from the ten o'clock position. He swung the drift sight around until he was able to spot one of the MiGs. He was not able to visually identify it, but the fighter's rate of climb was such that he thought (correctly) that it was a MiG-19. The airplane was coming from the Soviet city of Afrikanda, and Stockman knew that a MiG-19 squadron was based near the city. The MiG-19 passed below the U-2 at an altitude of 55,000 feet, then turned and began flying a parallel course. The 70mm tracking camera photographed the Soviet fighter as it flew three miles below Stockman's U-2.

While the MiG-19 dogged the U-2, Stockman also had to contend with more problems in the cockpit. During much of the flight, the EGT gauge had periodically fluctuated by forty to fifty degrees Fahrenheit. If the engine overheated, it could cause hydraulic problems. (This had caused the loss of Article 341.) Stockman kept a close watch on the EGT gauge, recorded each fluctuation on the green card, and monitored the engine tachometer, which recorded the engine's revolutions per minute and acted as a less reliable measure of engine performance.

After passing Monechegorsk, Stockman turned north-northwest to a point between Salmiyarvi and Perchenga, then crossed out of Soviet airspace. He had spent a total of one hour over the USSR. He flew west above Norway's Veranger Fjord, just north of the Finnish border. The flight back to Giebelstadt took four hours and followed a flight path similar to that taken on the trip north.

The weather at Giebelstadt was still marginal. Stockman entered heavy clouds at an altitude of 2,500 feet and broke out of the clouds only 400 feet above the ground. The Giebelstadt runway was three-quarters of a mile ahead. The fuel discrepancy had been reduced to only forty-five gallons (thirty-five of which was actually due to the ground crewman's error). Article 351 landed at 3:52 P.M. local time, nine hours and seventeen minutes after takeoff.

The U-2 in Eclipse

Stockman's landing brought an end not only to Mission 2040 but to the operations of Detachment A. The project headquarters decided that Western Europe was no longer needed as a U-2 base. After the initial se-

ries of flights over the western USSR, intelligence interest had shifted to Soviet Central Asia, Siberia, and the Far East. These were the locations for the USSR's missile and nuclear facilities and were out of range of Detachment A. As a result, on September 20, 1957, the unit was notified that its operations would cease in November.

By November 15, all of the unit's personnel and aircraft were back in the United States. The pilots went on to new assignments. Hervey Stockman returned to the air force and later spent nearly six years as a POW in North Vietnam. (The North Vietnamese never realized that he was an ex-CIA U-2 pilot.) Marty Knutson and two other pilots transferred to Detachment B in Turkey. The unit had made a total of six overflights of the USSR (five in July 1956 and Stockman's October 1957 mission), five missions over Eastern Europe, and most of the remaining twelve over the Mediterranean.

Another reason for Detachment A's disbandment was the higher risk it faced. Soviet fighter and radar networks were strongest on the western borders of the USSR. This meant that any flights in this area were likely to be detected and result in diplomatic protests. This was in contrast to the situation along the Soviet's southern border. By staging the Detachment B overflights from bases in Pakistan and Iran, the U-2s might slip through the early-warning radar network undetected. Once inside Soviet airspace, they might not be spotted by ground-controlled intercept radar. During the Soft Touch and subsequent missions in August and September 1957, only four of the ten overflights were detected by the Soviets. This was due to failings in Soviet air defenses, however, rather than Dirty Bird modifications. These had proven ineffective even against the limited defenses of the Soviet Far East.

The ranch was also in eclipse, due to a series of events that had begun early the previous year. Despite the earlier rejection of the CL-282, the test results were so good that in mid-January 1956, SAC officials wanted their own fleet of U-2s. On January 30, 1956, DCI Dulles agreed to have the CIA handle the purchase of the air force U-2s in order to maintain security. The air force transferred the money for the airplanes to the CIA, which then placed an order with Lockheed for twenty-nine more U-2s. (This total was later raised to thirty-one.)

After the pilots of Detachment C completed their training in late 1956, the initial group of air force U-2 pilots arrived at the ranch. They were drawn from SAC fighter wings being disbanded. In selecting its U-2 pilots, the air force did not use the same stringent physical and psycho-

logical standards that the CIA had used. Colonel Jack Nole was selected as the commander of the air force U-2 unit, the 4028th Strategic Reconnaissance Squadron (SRS). On November 13, 1956, he became the first air force pilot to be checked out in the U-2A. In the months to follow, another twenty air force pilots were checked out in the aircraft.

At the same time that the air force pilots were being trained, the ranch faced major problems from its neighbor, the Nevada Proving Grounds. The years 1955 and 1956 had been quiet, with no nuclear tests in Nevada. In the spring of 1957, however, a new test series, called Operation Plumbob, was starting. As Kelly Johnson had feared when Groom Lake was proposed, the site would have to be evacuated due to fallout from the tests. The disruption that this would cause was detailed in a memo by Brig. Gen. Alfred D. Starbird of the Atomic Energy Commission (AEC). It noted: "Expected fallout on Watertown from a given shot should be limited so as to permit re-entry of personnel within three or four weeks without danger of exposure exceeding the established off-site rad-safe criteria, and with the understanding that evacuation for a later shot may be required." The neighbors were about to get rowdy.

On May 14, 1957, AEC radiological safety officers Charles Weaver, Oliver R. Placak, and Melvin W. Carter held two meetings with the ranch personnel to discuss the nuclear testing activities, radiation safety, and the possibility of radiation hazards from Operation Plumbob. They also met with Colonel Nole and a Colonel Schilling, as well as the CIA base commander, Richard Newton, to discuss arrangements for radiation monitors to visit the ranch whenever fallout was anticipated in the area. After several delays, Operation Plumbob began on May 28 with Boltzmann, a twelve-kiloton test shot made from a 500-foot-tall tower on northern Yucca Flat. After additional delays, two smaller tests, Franklin and Lassen, were made on June 2 and 5. Soon after, the exodus from the ranch began.

On June 11, 1957, Colonel Nole led a formation of three U-2s from the ranch to the 4028th SRS's new home at Laughlin Air Force Base, outside the Texas border town of Del Rio. This brought to a close the U-2 training operations at the ranch. Subsequent training for air force U-2 pilots (and some non-American pilots) would be conducted at Laughlin. The Lockheed U-2 flight test operation, which had operated from the ranch for the previous two years, also moved in June 1957. Their new home would be North Base at Edwards Air Force Base. All that remained at the ranch was a small caretaker unit that served as the CIA's headquarters squadron.

Starting in June 1957 and continuing through the summer, even this small group had to be repeatedly evacuated due to fallout at the ranch. The first shot to scatter fallout there was the Wilson test on June 18. This was a ten-kiloton shot carried aloft by a balloon and detonated five hundred feet above Area 9 at northern Yucca Flat, about fourteen miles from the ranch. Radiation from the test was detected inside the facility's buildings. The next shot, the Hood test, was made on July 5, 1957, and had a yield of seventy-four kilotons. This was the largest nuclear test conducted in Nevada. Its shock wave battered the ranch; windows were shattered in Building 2 and the mess hall and broke a ventilator panel in Dormitory Building 102. The most severe blast damage was to a supply warehouse west of the three hangars; the shock wave also buckled doors on a maintenance building on the west side of the base. Soon after, the radioactive cloud drifted across Groom Pass and the Papoose Range, scattering fallout over the damaged buildings.

On July 15, Diablo, a seventeen-kiloton tower shot, was detonated. As with the other two tests, Diablo contaminated the site several hours later. Radiation measurements were taken inside Dormitory Building 103, Trailer 10, a warehouse, the base theater, and the control tower; at the volleyball court; and in several vehicles parked on the Groom Lake Road. Although security guards were periodically deployed to the ranch, for most of the Plumbob test series the site was abandoned. Although limited activities resumed at the ranch in the fall of 1957, air sampling continued to be made on a daily basis throughout 1958 and 1959.

Ironically, with activities at the ranch now reduced to a shadow of past levels, the paperwork for the site's transfer to AEC control was finally completed. On June 20, 1958, Public Land Order 1662 was approved by Assistant Secretary of the Interior Roger Ernst. A total of 38,400 acres surrounding Groom Lake was withdrawn from public use and turned over to the AEC, which gave it the designation "Area 51."

While the ranch was suffering the effects of fallout, the air force U-2 efforts were getting off to a bad start. On June 28, 1957, the 4028th SRS suffered two fatal U-2 crashes within the span of about three hours. In the first, Lt. Ford E. Lowcock, who was the first U-2 pilot to be checked out at Laughlin Air Force Base and had made his first flight in a U-2 only three days before, decided to buzz his house in Del Rio. He failed to pull out and crashed on a brush-covered hill. This was followed by the loss of 1st Lt. Leo E. Smith during a high-altitude training flight. About forty-five minutes after he took off from Laughlin Air Force Base, he crashed

about thirty miles north of Abilene, Texas. The crash turned out to be due to a fuel imbalance between the two wing tanks.

Two more accidents followed before the year was over. Squadron commander Colonel Nole suffered the next, on September 26, when his U-2 broke up at high altitude after the flaps extended. He was able to bail out, in what was then the highest parachute escape in history. Less lucky was Capt. Bennidect A. Lacombe, who was killed on November 28 after he lost control during a night training flight. He bailed out but was too low for the parachute to open. In all, the air force had lost four U-2s and three pilots in six months.

This series of accidents set a pattern for early air force U-2 operations. The air force suffered an accident rate some three to four times higher than that of the CIA's pilots. In part, this was due to the air force's lower standards for pilot selection. Another reason was the different operating philosophy used by the air force. The CIA's U-2 philosophy was that the aircraft would receive special care and that flights would be infrequent. The air force changed this to a typical war plan operation. As a result, in addition to the losses, parts utilization was high because components were not designed for these high flight rates, and the training of crews was extremely difficult because no manuals were available.

While the air force struggled with these problems, their first six operational U-2s were delivered. They were equipped for fallout sampling. This included filter papers, to collect fallout samples, and gas bottles, to collect atmospheric samples. The fallout samples were used to reconstruct the design of Soviet nuclear weapons. The atmospheric gas was tested for krypton 85, an artificial, chemically inert isotope released when uranium from an atomic reactor is dissolved to recover the plutonium. (There was no krypton 85 in the earth's atmosphere before 1944.) This was the most secret aspect of the U.S. nuclear detection program, because measurements of krypton 85 levels allowed estimates to be made of total Soviet plutonium production.

Training flights for the sampling missions began on August 22, 1957, and the first operational sampling flights were made in late October 1957. Three U-2s were deployed to Ramey Air Force Base in Puerto Rico, and the other three aircraft were sent to Plattsburgh Air Force Base in New York. These were followed in February 1958 by the unit's first deployment to Eielson Air Force Base in Alaska, to collect fallout from Soviet nuclear tests at Novaya Zemlya. This was the start of a seven-year program of such missions from more than a dozen locations and involving

some 45,000 flight hours. (Fallout and krypton 85 sampling at altitudes higher than the U-2 could reach were also done using Skyhook balloons.)

Although air force officials were unsuccessful in their attempts to have Eisenhower lift his ban on military overflights, the air force U-2s were being used in border flights. By mid-1960, the 4028th SRS operated twenty-four U-2s. Of these, twelve were configured for long-range oblique photography of coastal areas from outside Soviet airspace. Of the others, four air force U-2s were configured for SIGINT border flights and two were equipped for high-resolution radar photography. These six aircraft also had a standby "Emergency War Order" capability, meaning that they could be used for wartime reconnaissance missions. The other six U-2s were the atmospheric sampling aircraft.

The Launch of Sputnik I

The year 1957 was the start of the International Geophysical Year (IGY), an eighteen-month international scientific study of the Earth, Sun, and outer space. As part of this effort, the United States planned to launch a series of small satellites, called Project Vanguard. President Eisenhower had announced its start soon after returning from the Geneva Summit meeting in 1955. Soon after, Soviet spokesmen said that the USSR was planning to launch satellites during the IGY. This attracted little attention from the American public or political leaders.

During the late spring of 1957, however, these Soviet statements became more numerous and detailed. On June 2, the *New York Times* reported that Professor Alexander Nesmsyanov, president of the Soviet Academy of Sciences, said that work on rockets and instruments for the Soviet satellite had been completed. A few days later, the Soviet publication *Literary Gazette* said that dogs would be used in satellites. The June 23 *New York Times* reported Soviet statements that the first Soviet satellite would be launched in a few months. As with the initial Soviet statements, these attracted little attention.

On July 5, DCI Dulles stated there were indications that the USSR was probably capable of launching a satellite in 1957. He also noted: "The U.S. community estimates that for prestige and psychological factors, the USSR would endeavor to be first in launching an Earth satellite." Despite this assessment and the successful Soviet ICBM tests, the Eisenhower administration remained unconcerned about a possible Soviet satellite. The only contingency planning done was to prepare a congratulatory

statement to be delivered by Detlev Bronk, president of the National Academy of Sciences, should the Soviets succeed in actually launching a satellite.

The Eisenhower administration had more concrete problems in the late summer and early fall of 1957 than the possibility of a Soviet satellite. The nation's economic boom, which had started in mid-1954, was ending. The public was less confident about the future than it had been in many years. The slowdown also forced cutbacks in defense activities. The U.S. ICBM program was stretched out, and fewer missiles than originally planned were scheduled for deployment. The most pressing issue that fall, however, was the integration of Central High School in Little Rock, Arkansas. Orval Faubus, the Arkansas governor, called out the state National Guard to block the court-ordered admission of nine black students to the school. The result was mob violence and a direct challenge to federal authority. After failing to get Faubus to allow the students' enrollment, President Eisenhower sent in troops from the 101st Airborne Division to enforce the court order.

As the summer ended and the crisis at Little Rock developed, Soviet statements on satellites continued. The *New York Times* carried a report on September 1 about the Soviet announcement that two different types of satellites would be launched. This was followed on September 18 by a report from Radio Moscow that the first Soviet satellite would be launched "soon."

On Monday, September 30, a six-day meeting on the IGY's rocket and satellite activities opened in Washington, D.C. One of the first day's speakers was Sergei M. Poloskov, who gave details on the radio frequencies that the Soviet satellite would use. He also made the comment that "now on the eve of the first artificial Earth satellite," which sparked questions about the Soviet's planned launch date. Poloskov sidestepped the questions, which produced roars of laughter. By the following Friday, October 4, 1957, the number of such statements convinced the *New York Times* science correspondent, Walter Sullivan, that the Soviet launch was imminent. Sullivan wrote a story on his suspicions and submitted it to the newspaper.

A special bulletin was issued by Tass at 5:58 P.M. eastern daylight time (EDT). It read in part: "For several years research and experimental designing work has been under way in the Soviet Union to create artificial satellites of the Earth. . . . As a result of the intensive work by research institutes and designing bureaus the first artificial Earth satellite in the

world has now been created. This first satellite was successfully launched in the USSR on October 4." The report continued that the satellite, called "Sputnik I," was in an elliptical orbit with a high point of about nine hundred kilometers, inclined sixty-five degrees to the equator, and with a period of an hour and thirty-five minutes. It would be visible to ground observers using binoculars at dawn and dusk. The Tass statement also said that Sputnik's signals could be picked up by amateur ham operators.

The signals from Sputnik I were first picked up in the United States at 8:07 P.M. EDT by an RCA receiving station at Riverhead, New York. Soon after, the news began to spread by word of mouth and radio and television reports. In one of these reports, an NBC announcer said in an excited voice, "Listen now for the sound which forevermore separates the old from the new." Thousands of listeners heard "beep . . . beep . . . beep."

The launch of Sputnik I was a watershed event. For the first time, humanity had reached beyond its home world. But this was also the tenth year of the Cold War, and Sputnik I was part of that struggle. For Eisenhower and the U-2, the launch of Sputnik I meant new problems. The bomber gap had been quickly closed by the U-2. The "missile gap" would prove far more difficult to bridge, both politically and militarily.

An RB-29 taxies out for a predawn take off. In 1948, an RB-29 became the first Air Force aircraft converted for Cold War ELINT missions. In 1952, an RB-29 was shot down by Soviet MiGs. In 1954, another was damaged and made a crash landing in Japan. U.S. Air Force photo

An early RF-80A in flight. This was a photo reconnaissance version of the first operational U.S. jet fighter. After the start of the Berlin Blockade, RF-80As the made the first covert overflights of the Soviet Far East. Because of the distances covered, the aircraft had to carry large wing tip tanks, which made them vulnerable to interception by Soviet fighters. U.S. Air Force photo

An F-84 Thunderjet taking off on a bombing mission during the Korean War. Due to speed and range shortcomings of the RF-80A, a single F-84 was modified with a camera to make overflights of the Soviet Far East during 1951.
U.S. Air Force photo

One of the RF-86Fs attached to the 15th Tactical Reconnaissance Squadron (TRS) and used for covert overflights of the USSR, mainland China, and North Korea. The blisters on the side and lower fuselage mount two K-22 cameras, while a K-17 camera was located under the pilot's seat. The gun ports were painted on, as the aircraft was unarmed. courtesy of David Menard

Group photo of 15th TRS pilots at Komaki Air Base Japan on March 21, 1954. From left to right: 1st Lt. Samuel T. Dickens, 1st Lt. Charles P. Garrison, Capt. Laverne H. Griffin, Maj. George H. Saylor, 1st Lt. William F. Bissett, Jr., and 1st Lt. Lawrence D. Garrison. The pilots are wearing immersion suits to protect them against cold water should they have to bail out. In the foreground are Maj. Robert E. Morrison (left) and an Air Force intelligence officer. courtesy of Samuel Dickens

A formation of 15th TRS RF-86Fs over Japan in 1954. The camera blisters are visible on the aircraft. The aircraft at the left rear of the formation, with "U.S. Air Force" painted on its side is a standard F-86. courtesy of Jerry Depew

An RF-100A following its delivery from North American Aviation. This was a standard fighter which had been stripped of its guns and fitted with cameras. The bulge under the lower fuselage is visible. The RF-100As were primarily used for short-range overflights of Eastern Europe. Although one or two were operational in the Far East, they apparently did not see much use. U.S. Air Force photo

Early model B-47B refueling from a KB-29 tanker. A B-47B was modified for covert overflights of the Soviet Far East in 1951, but was lost on the ground when it caught fire while being fueled. Subsequently, five long-range, daytime Soviet overflights were made by B-47Bs between 1952 and 1954. U.S. Air Force photo

A head-on shot of a B-47B taken at the time of the Soviet overflights. These were interim reconnaissance aircraft, with a camera package added to the bomb bay. U.S. Air Force photo

An RB-47E flying high above snow-covered fields. Unlike the converted B-47Bs, this was a specially designed reconnaissance aircraft, with an extended nose housing a forward-looking camera. RB-47Es made the sixth daytime overflight of the USSR, a night radarscope mission targeted against Moscow, the Sea Shore border photographic flights and the Project Homerun mass overflights in early 1956. U.S. Air Force photo

The other mainstay of the early overflight program was the RB-45C. This unique black-painted RB-45C was used for nighttime radarscope missions over North Korea, the USSR, and mainland China in 1952. The aircraft was flown by Capt. Howard S. Myers, Jr. The gloss black finish was intended to make it difficult for searchlights to spot the aircraft. courtesy of Capt. Howard S. Myers, Jr. (Ret.)

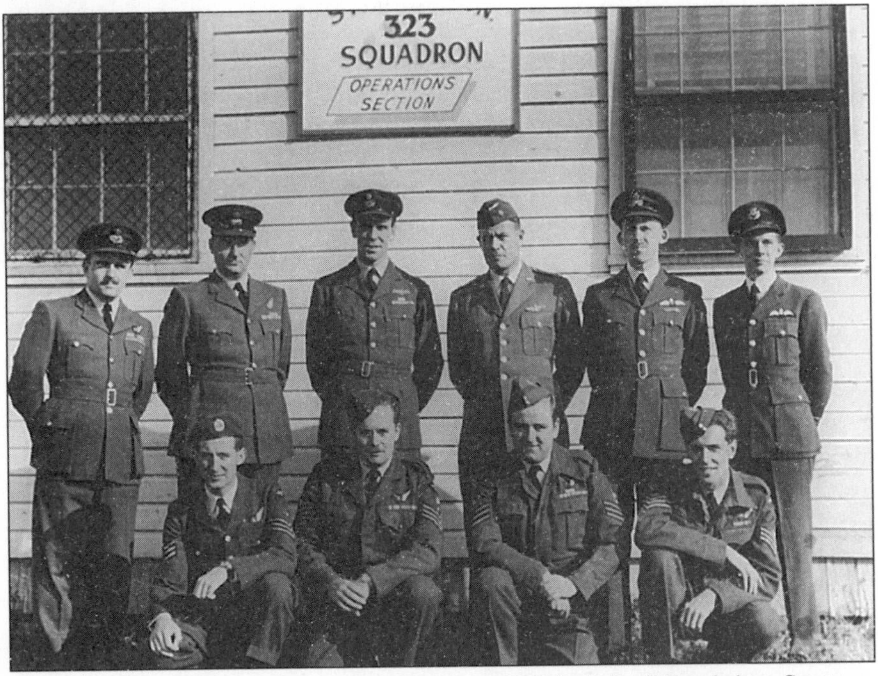

The RAF Special Duty Flight at Lockbourne AFB for RB-45C training, September-October 1951. Back row, left to right: Flight Lt. Rex Sanders; Flight Lt. John Hill; Special Duty Flight commander John Crampton; 323rd Strategic Reconnaissance Squadron commander Marion Mixson; two unknown RAF officers. Front row, left to right: Sgt. L. A. Lindsey; Flight Sgt. G. Acklam; Flight Sgt. R. E. Anstee; and Sgt. D. W. Greenslade. courtesy of Marion Mixson

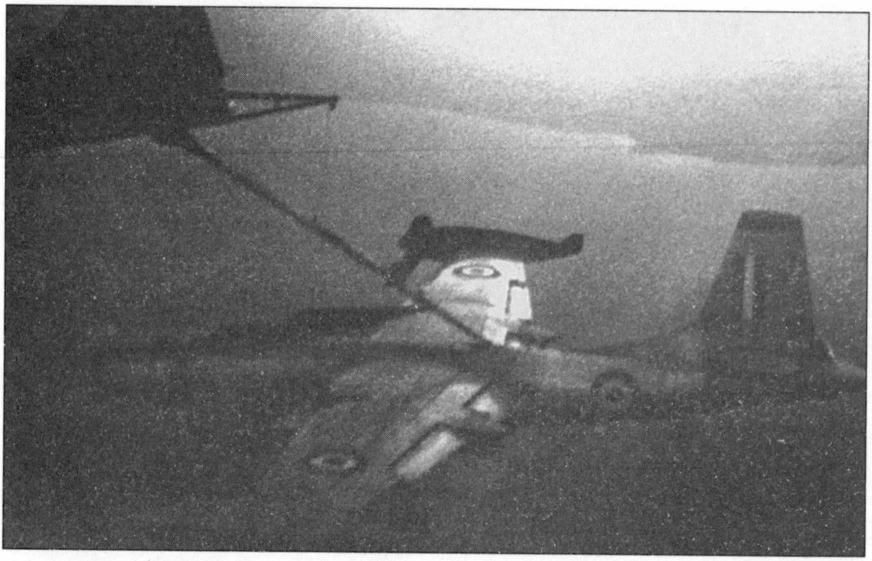

As twilight fades on the evening of April 17, 1952, an RAF Special Duty Flight RB-45C is refueled by a KB-29 tanker over the North Sea, before the aircraft entered Soviet airspace. This is the only known photograph taken during the RAF RB-45C overflights. courtesy of Maury Seitz

An RB-45C at RAF Sculthorpe in May 1952, after the first overflights. courtesy of Maury Seitz

Lt. Col. Marion Mixson and Squadron Leader John Crampton at RAF Sculthorpe in November-December 1952, shortly before the second series of overflights was canceled. The two worked together throughout the history of the RAF Special Duty Flight, from its formation in 1951 through the final overflights in 1954. courtesy of Marion Mixson

A famous photograph of the four RAF RB-45Cs (three primary aircraft and one spare) at Sculthorpe in December 1952. In the foreground are the RAF and U.S. Air Force personnel connected with the missions. For some two decades, this photo was the only indication of a joint RAF/U.S. Air Force overflight program. courtesy of Marion Mixson

A group photo taken with one of the RAF RB-45Cs in December 1952. In the back row, starting fourth from the left are Sanders, Hill, Cremer, Mixson, and Crampton. courtesy of Marion Mixson

Genetrix reconnaissance balloon being prepared for launch. The balloon has been partially filled with hydrogen gas. In the background can be seen the gas bottles. courtesy of Robert Burch

The "Fisher Launcher" is in the center, while at the right is a fire truck. Behind the fire truck is a crane holding the gondola and ballast boxes. courtesy of Robert Burch

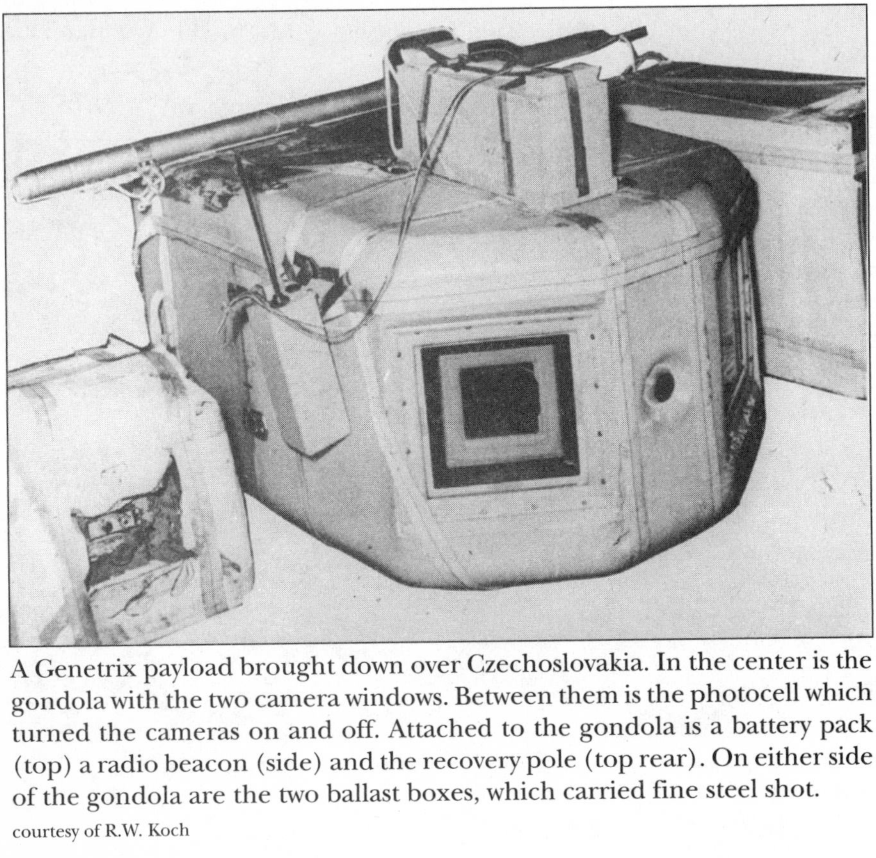

A Genetrix payload brought down over Czechoslovakia. In the center is the gondola with the two camera windows. Between them is the photocell which turned the cameras on and off. Attached to the gondola is a battery pack (top) a radio beacon (side) and the recovery pole (top rear). On either side of the gondola are the two ballast boxes, which carried fine steel shot. courtesy of R.W. Koch

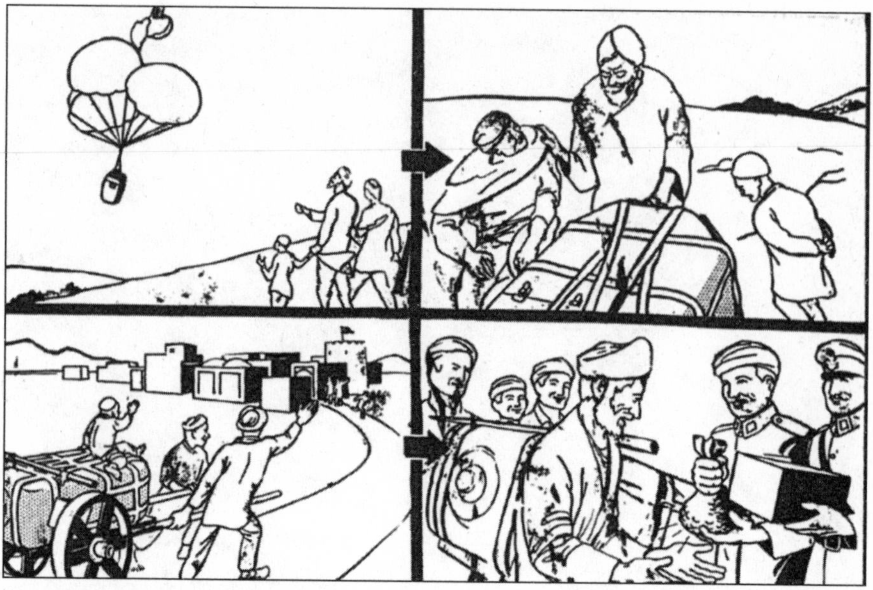

A poster attached to the Genetrix gondola giving recovery directions to a finder. Because there was no telling who might find a gondola, every effort was made to insure they were turned in. A $200 reward was offered for each gondola found. courtesy of Paul Lovrencic

A C-119F transport which had been modified with the beavertail rear door. The new door could be opened in flight, allowing the Genetrix recovery gear to be rigged. U.S. Air Force photo

A group photo taken in flight during the third midair recovery of a Genetrix gondola by Capt. Slaughter Mimms' crew on January 23, 1956. They were the most successful C-119F crew, with a total of three midair recoveries, and a ground and ocean assist. courtesy of Paul Lovrencic

A Genetrix gondola is returned to Johnson Air Base, Japan, following its pickup by a helicopter. courtesy of Paul Lovrencic

Helicopter recovery of a Genetrix gondola in Japan. courtesy of Paul Lovrencic

The launch of a WS-461L balloon from the deck of the U.S.S. Windham Bay in July 1958. The balloon was designed to fly at an altitude of 100,000 feet or more, placing it above the reach of Soviet air defenses. Due to a weakening jet stream and launch crew error, all three reconnaissance balloons came down inside the Soviet bloc. courtesy of Leroy C. Stables

An RB-57A and an RB-57D in flight. The RB-57A was an American built version of the British Canberra, which made the epic August 1953 overflight of Kapustin Yar. The RB-57A was used for border flights of Eastern Europe, then was briefly used by the Nationalist Chinese Air Force for overflights of the mainland. Three RB-57Ds made the last U.S. Air Force overflight of the USSR in December 1956. U.S. Air Force photo

U-2 Article 341 at the ranch. This was the prototype U-2, which was later used for tests of the wallpaper radar camouflage. The NACA markings were part of the cover story that the U-2 was a weather plane used for high-altitude scientific research. Article 341 was lost during the wallpaper tests, causing the death of its pilot. provided by the Edwards AFB History Office

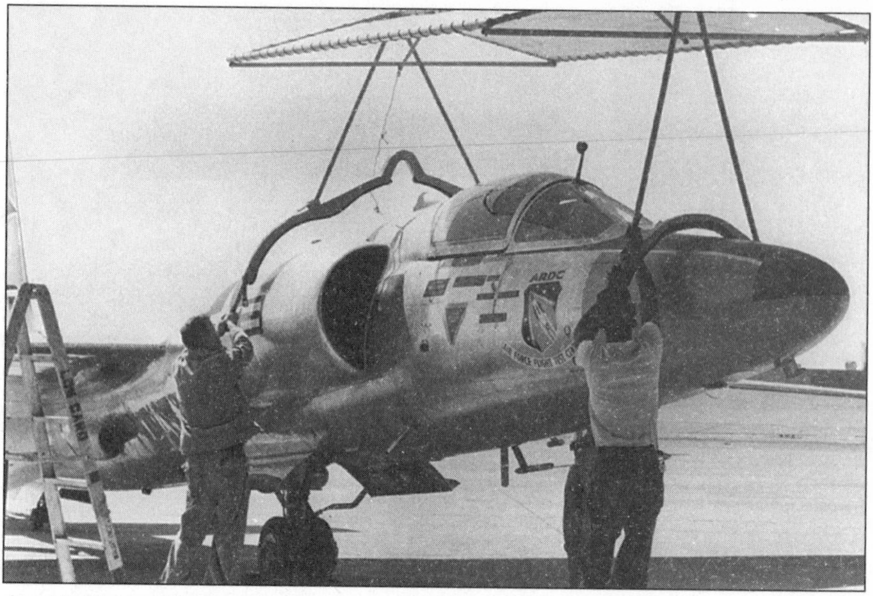

An Air Force U-2 on the ramp at Edwards AFB on August 24, 1960. In addition to the U-2s conducting atmospheric sampling and the border photographic, SIGINT, and radar missions, a small detachment was based at Edwards for various test activities. U.S. Air Force photo

Photo of a NASA U-2C cockpit taken in flight. In the center is the drift sight, which could spot landmarks and pursuing MiGs. Below the drift sight are two knobs that allow it to be used as a sextant for navigation. provided by Lockheed Aircraft

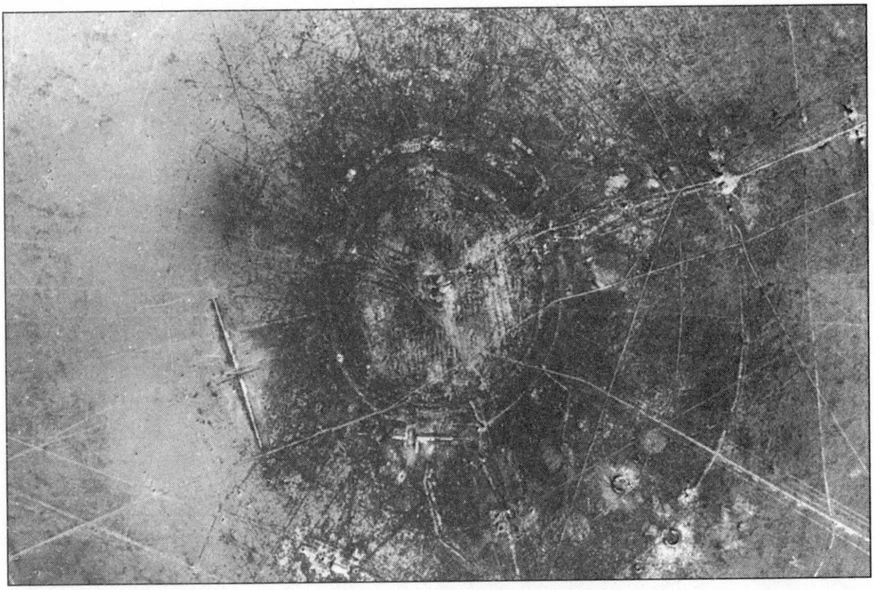

The scorched area of a low-yield nuclear test at Semipalatinsk, photographed by James Cherbonneaux on August 21, 1957 during Mission 4050. It was on this overflight that Cherbonneaux thought that he and his U-2 were about to be destroyed by another Soviet nuclear test. CIA photograph

The SS-6 test pad at Tyuratam. First discovered during the Soft Touch overflights, the ICBM and space activities at Tyuratam became a regular target for U-2 overflights. This pad was used for both the Soviet ICBM tests, and the early satellite and Moon launches. CIA photograph

A U-2D flying near Edwards AFB. The U-2D was a Air Force version that had its camera bay modified to carry either experiments or a second crewman. Edwards AFB History Office photo

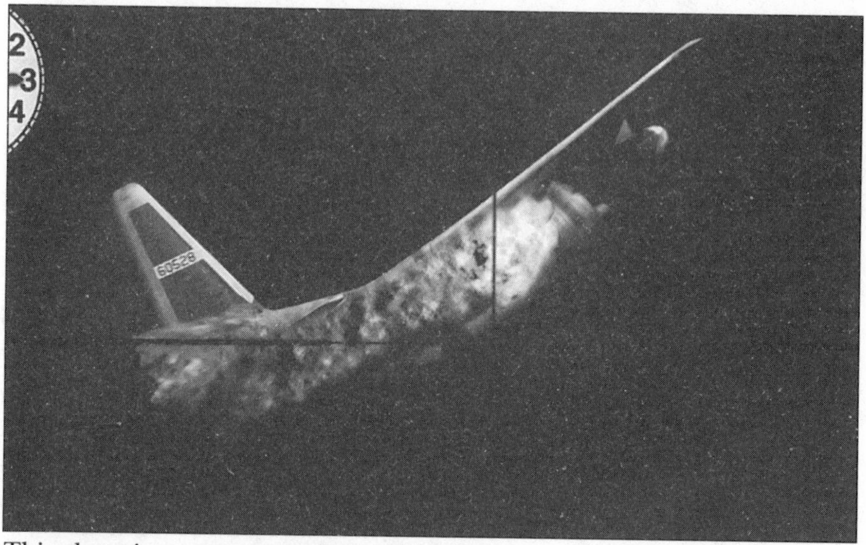

This photo is a computer enhanced image taken from one of the MiG's gun camera film. The C-130A's right outboard engine had been hit and is burning. All 17 crewmen aboard the C-130A were killed when the aircraft was shot down. This was only one of a series of such incidents that occurred involving the loss of SIGINT aircraft during the 1950s and 1960s. courtesy of the National Security Agency

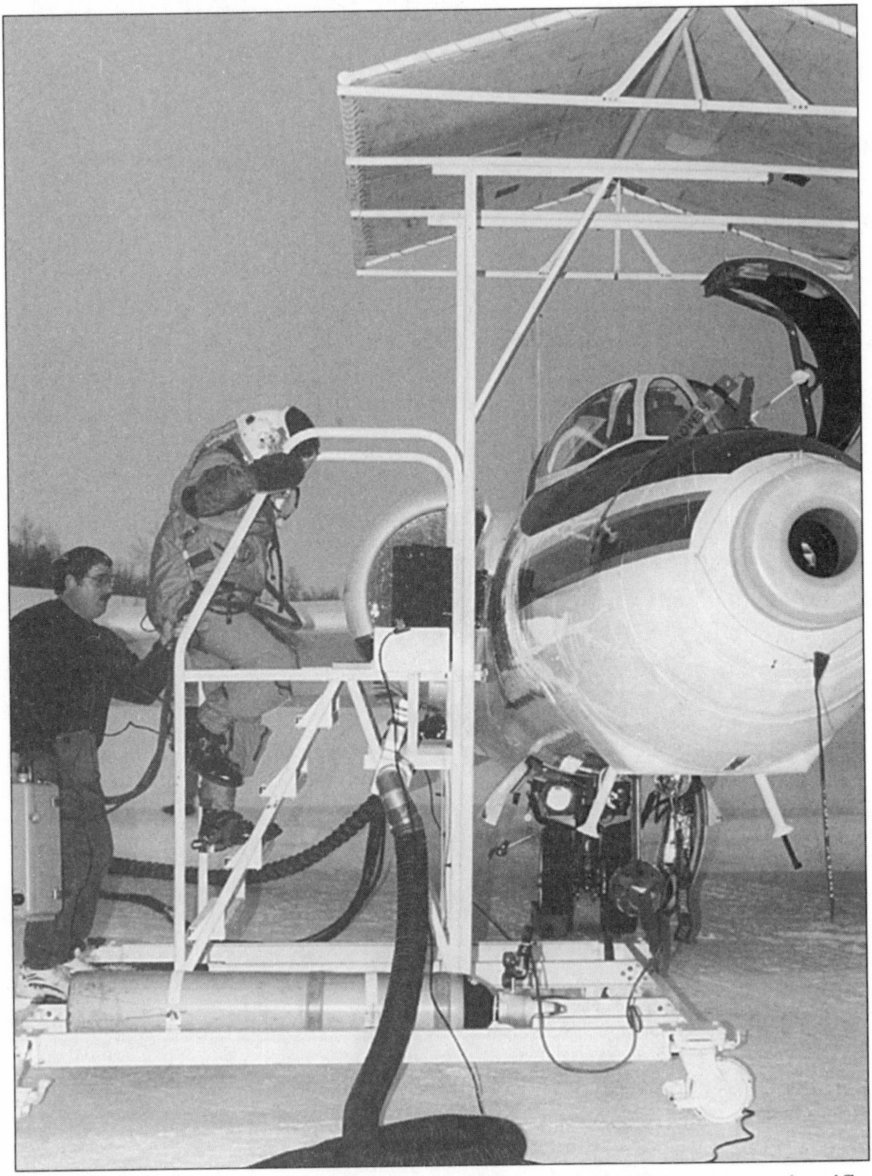

Lockheed-Martin pilot DeLewis Porter boards a NASA ER-2 for a scientific flight over Russia on January 27, 2000. NASA photograph

Chapter 7
The Missile Gap

What principally distressed critics was the administration's failure to respond to Soviet gains with a sense of urgency. . . . Eisenhower refused to introduce crash programs . . . his frequent recreation on the golf course signaled to his opponents first a failure of comprehension, then a failure of energy.

—Charles S. Maier

Initial statements by U.S. government officials attempted to minimize the importance of Sputnik I. On October 8, 1957, Defense Secretary Charles Wilson, at his last press conference, said: "Nobody is going to drop anything down on you while you are sleeping from a satellite so don't start to worry." He dismissed the launch itself as "a neat scientific trick that all scientists in the world are intrigued over."

The following day, President Eisenhower held a press conference and said that the United States had never been in a race with the Soviets to launch the first satellite, and the U.S. Vanguard satellite program had been kept separate from ICBM development. "Now, so far as the satellite itself is concerned, that does not raise my apprehension one iota."

Others in the administration were more strident in their comments. Clarence Randall, a special assistant for foreign economic matters, called Sputnik "a silly bauble in the sky." He said he was gratified that the United States was not the first to put a satellite into orbit, and that far more significant than Sputnik was the U.S. supermarket exhibit in Zagreb, Yugoslavia. At a Washington dinner party several weeks after the launch, Percival Brundage, director of the budget, also dismissed Sputnik, saying it would be forgotten in six months. Perle Mesta, his dinner companion, replied, "Yes, dear, and in six months we may all be dead."

The American public's mood was one of fear; they were looking to Eisenhower, and they were looking for action. But Eisenhower and the administration seemed unwilling or unable to take action. What was done seemed to be done reluctantly. The first impression, of passivity in the face of a stunning Soviet triumph, remained. Beyond the domestic political consequences, the launching of Sputnik also marked the begin-

ning of an aggressive Soviet policy, based in part on the Western perception of Soviet missile strength.

The Perils of Khrushchev

The successful SS-6 test launches and the launch of Sputnik I coincided with the rise of Nikita S. Khrushchev as Soviet ruler. He had a very different temperament than the others who formed the top level of the Soviet government and party. Khrushchev cared nothing for abstract theory; he believed in communism with the simple faith of a peasant as a system better able to provide for the people. He was always active: one moment sentimental, quick with an old proverb and a dirty joke, the next moment in a towering rage. Unlike Stalin, he was not calculating, laying his plans far in advance. Rather, Khrushchev would improvise, creating grandiose plans in the spur of the moment, based on sudden enthusiasms, without having thought out the consequences.

But if Khrushchev's vision was not always clear, he was one of the few in the USSR who could see that changes were necessary. Molotov, Bulganin, and others in the now-tattered "collective leadership" were increasingly opposed to Khrushchev's de-Stalinization activities, "peaceful coexistence" with the West, and ideas for reorganizing economic activities. On June 18, 1957, the hard-liners attempted to oust Khrushchev as first secretary. He called on his supporters and was able to defeat the effort. Over the weeks and months to follow, the hard-liners who had sided against Khrushchev were replaced on the Presidium by his supporters. The former remained in the party but were given undemanding positions. Molotov, for example, was named ambassador to Mongolia.

When Sputnik I was launched, the Soviet press dealt with it almost in passing. *Pravda* simply carried the Tass report, which was printed in a right-hand column partway down the front page. In contrast, the *New York Times* reported the launch in a headline that stretched across the whole front page. When Khrushchev realized the impact that Sputnik had in the West, the Soviets began exploiting it for propaganda. The *Pravda* for Sunday, October 6, 1957, and for days afterward, highlighted the launch, carrying stories about foreign reactions, poetry, and congratulations from allies and foes alike.

Following the initial reaction, Khrushchev wanted a second satellite to be launched in time for the celebration of the Russian Revolution. This was only a month away; to meet the deadline, existing equipment was

quickly assembled. The Sputnik II launch was made on November 3, 1957, in time for the celebration. Aboard was a dog named Laika, the first animal to orbit the earth. The pressurized compartment housing the dog remained attached to the SS-6's final stage.

Khrushchev was quick to underline the political importance of the launch. In a November 6 speech, he said, "It appears that the name Vanguard reflected the confidence of the Americans that their satellite would be the first in the world. But . . . it was the Soviet satellites which proved to be ahead, to be in the vanguard. . . . In orbiting our Earth, the Soviet sputniks proclaim the heights of the development of science and technology and of the entire economy of the Soviet Union, whose people are building a new life under the banner of Marxism-Leninism."

This speech set the pattern for Soviet space activities under Khrushchev. Space spectaculars were timed for political reasons and were then exploited as examples of Soviet scientific, economic, and military capabilities, all due to Khrushchev's leadership. It would prove to be a tactic that Eisenhower and his scientific advisers were unable to cope with.

Eisenhower's bewilderment at the public's reaction continued in the days following the press conference. During an October 15 meeting, Eisenhower said: "I can't understand why the American people have got so worked up over this thing." He did not see Sputnik I as a national emergency that required fundamental changes in U.S. military, scientific, or educational policy. The president believed that it required only limited, short-term responses rather than panicky actions that would increase government spending and create deficits.

The U-2 was largely responsible for shaping Eisenhower's policy. From the U-2 photos, particularly those from the Soft Touch overflights, Eisenhower knew that Soviet nuclear forces and capabilities were only a shadow of those of the United States. The Soviet Union had neither the bombers nor the production capability to challenge the United States. In terms of the SS-6 ICBM, the Soviets had only the one pad at Tyuratam and had flown only two partially successful launches; deployment was still years off. Any lead in missile technology that the Soviets might have over the United States was limited. Sputnik I had no defense implications in Eisenhower's view, and any loss of U.S. prestige was unimportant to him.

The intelligence data from the U-2 missions was the most closely held material in the United States. Only about four hundred people in the country knew about the overflights. This total included the U-2 pilots and ground crews, the photointerpreters, and the president himself. As a re-

sult, not only the public but military and government personnel were completely unaware of the true state of affairs. Eisenhower was unwilling and unable to enlighten them. The U-2 was too dangerous to use freely and too valuable a source to make public.

The possibility of revealing the U-2 had been raised in the wake of Sputnik, however. On November 7, 1957, a few days after the launch of Sputnik II, Eisenhower was to give a wide-ranging television and radio address on the state of U.S. defenses. As the speech was undergoing final revisions a few hours before it was scheduled to be delivered, Secretary of State John Foster Dulles asked the president if it would not be wise to "disclose tonight that the United States has the capability of photographing the Soviet Union from very high altitudes without interference." Eisenhower refused; having denied that the overflights had taken place, he could not now acknowledge them, even though it would have silenced the critics of his policies.

Because of his unwillingness to even allude to the U-2 data, Eisenhower spoke only in generalities about the military relationship between the United States and the USSR. He admitted that the launch of the two Soviet satellites was "an achievement of the first importance" and that the Soviets "are quite likely ahead in some missile and special areas." He continued, however, that "as of today, the over-all military strength of the free world is distinctly greater than that of the communist countries." Despite the Soviet ICBM tests, Eisenhower said, "Long-range ballistic missiles, as they exist today, do not cancel the destructive and deterrent power of our Strategic Air Force." He added that the air force missile effort was making progress, the army had successfully recovered a subscale missile warhead, and more than a billion dollars was being spent per year on U.S. missile development.

Eisenhower closed by stressing the need for economy in defense planning, warning about heading off "in all directions at once," and stressing the need to "clearly identify the exact and critical needs that have to be met." The United States would have to be selective, deciding "what we must have and what we would like to have." Only in this way could the United States have "both a sound defense and a sound economy." What the world needs, he concluded, "even more than a giant leap into outer space" is "a giant step toward peace."

The press response to Eisenhower's speech was, at best, lukewarm. The *New Republic* accused Eisenhower of continued complacency and said that he was "treating Sputnik like a common cold, instead of a dangerous disease." A columnist referred to the speech as "another tranquillity pill."

As necessary as continuing the secrecy about the U-2 was, the press response made it clear that without specific information about Soviet military capabilities, bland reassurances about U.S. power were not enough to calm the public's mood. The closest Eisenhower came to revealing his feelings was in a November 18, 1957, letter to an old friend, Swede Hazlett. Eisenhower wrote, "You can understand there are many things that I don't dare to allude to publicly, yet some of them would do much to allay the fears of our own people."

One aspect of the November 7 speech was the announcement that a President's Science Advisory Committee (PSAC) would be established to provide assessments of space and defense activities. James R. Killian, Jr., was named chairman. Although he was best known as the president of MIT, Killian had also been secretly involved in shaping U.S. defense and intelligence policy for years. It was Killian who organized the 1954 Technological Capability Panel, which led to the development of the U-2.

The month of December 1957 brought major setbacks for administration policy. The first was the scheduled launch of the Vanguard TV-3 booster, which had originally been a full-up test of the Vanguard booster's three stages. Following Sputnik I, a tiny, six-inch-diameter test satellite was added as payload. As the launch neared, public interest began building, and there were hourly press briefings. The American people needed the launch to be successful in order to have their confidence in U.S. science and technology restored.

Finally, at 11:44 A.M. EST on Friday, December 6, 1957, the Vanguard's first-stage engine ignited. The thrust built up, the ice on the sides of the booster shook loose, and the rocket began to lift off. Three feet above the pad, flames erupted from the side of the rocket. Vanguard TV-3 fell back onto the pad, disintegrating in a huge fireball. The satellite was thrown clear, landing amid the palmetto brush, its transmitter still beeping away. The press response to the failure was one of universal ridicule. The front page of the London *Daily Herald* showed a prelaunch photograph of the Vanguard booster next to one of the explosion. The huge headline read "OH, WHAT A FLOPNIK!"

The Gaither Report and the Birth of the Missile Gap

As the finger pointing grew following the Vanguard launch failure, a new controversy was developing. This was a direct challenge to Eisenhower administration policies, and it gave a name to the deep concerns created by the launch of the Sputniks. The events had begun in April 1957, when

H. Rowan Gaither was asked to serve as the chairman of a study of passive and active defenses against a Soviet nuclear attack. Gaither was a San Francisco lawyer, a former president of the Ford Foundation, and one of the founders of the RAND Corporation.

Originally, the Gaither Committee, as it became known, was to examine the usefulness of civil defense measures, such as blast and fallout shelters. Eisenhower was reluctant to spend large amounts on shelters, and the president told Gaither at a July 16 meeting that he wanted the scope of the study limited. Eisenhower specifically said that he did not want the study to be a "detailed examination of national security policies and programs" with the intent of suggesting changes. Events within the committee and in the world at large intervened.

During the summer of 1957, Gaither became ill, and the chairmanship of the study was taken over by Robert C. Sprague and William C. Foster. Many of the committee's members were dissatisfied with Eisenhower's defense policy, and Sprague became determined to expand the study's mandate despite the president's instructions. The committee reconvened in September 1957, following the Soviet's first successful ICBM test.

At the same time, Albert Wohlstetter of RAND completed a study highlighting the vulnerability of SAC's B-52s to a Soviet surprise attack with ICBMs. Wohlstetter estimated that it would take only 150 ICBMs to destroy SAC's bomber force. The major problem, as Wohlstetter saw it, was the cut in warning time of an attack. A Soviet bomber attack could be detected several hours before the aircraft reached their targets. If an ICBM attack were launched, however, the warning time would be cut to less than half an hour. More important, the United States lacked radar able to detect incoming ICBMs. Until such a system was deployed, there would be no warning at all before the warheads hit. Despite having a total of more than two thousand aircraft, SAC was concentrated at only twenty-nine air bases within the United States, an average of about seventy aircraft per base. As a result, the SAC bomber force could be caught on the ground, just like at Pearl Harbor.

Wohlstetter spoke before the Gaither Committee, arguing forcefully for the conclusions reached in his RAND report. His comments convinced Sprague to shift the focus of the committee's efforts. As a result, nearly all of its time was spent examining the problems of how to protect U.S. nuclear forces against a surprise missile attack. The experience was a frightening one for the members. Foster later said that his

time on the committee was like "spending ten hours a day staring straight into hell."

The finished committee report, formally titled "Deterrence & Survival in the Nuclear Age" but commonly referred to as the Gaither Report, stressed a number of points. First was that the Soviet economy was growing faster than that of the United States, although it still lagged well behind the U.S. total. This growing economic strength was concentrated in the Soviet armed forces and heavy industry. The Gaither Report stated that if the Soviets were to continue to expand their military expenditures at the same rate they had during the 1950s, while U.S. military activities remained constant, the Soviets would soon surpass the United States.

The Gaither Report noted that the Soviet military threat was represented not only by its present size "but also in the dynamic development and exploitation of their military technology." In 1946, the USSR was still a backward country, with most of its industry and productive areas ravaged by war and occupation. The Soviets had no counter to SAC, no A-bombs or production facilities, no jet engine production, no navy, and a limited electronics industry. A decade later, they had nuclear weapons, jet bombers, an ongoing ballistic missile program, jet fighters, SAMs, and a large submarine force.

The Gaither Report said that neither active defenses, such as interceptors, nor passive defenses, such as shelters, could provide significant protection for the U.S. civilian population against a Soviet attack. The safety of the United States rested upon the deterrence provided by SAC; however, this was threatened by the slow response time of SAC and "the prospects of an early Russian ICBM capability."

The report concluded: "By 1959, the USSR may be able to launch an attack with ICBMs carrying megaton warheads, against which SAC will be almost completely vulnerable under present programs. By 1961–1962, at our present pace, or considerably earlier if we accelerate, the United States could have a reliable early-warning capability against a missile attack, and SAC forces should be on a 7 to 22 minute operational 'alert.' The next two years seem to us critical. If we fail to act at once, the risk, in our opinion, will be unacceptable."

The conclusions of the Gaither Report were initially presented to President Eisenhower by Sprague, Foster, and several other committee members on November 4 (the day following the Sputnik II launch). The president asked them to check the report's data before it was formally presented to the National Security Council (NSC). He seemed uncon-

cerned by their fears about the threat posed to SAC from Soviet ICBMs, telling them that for the next five years, bombers rather than missiles would still be the main nuclear delivery system.

The Gaither Report proposed an increase in military spending totaling $18 billion over five years to protect SAC and increase U.S. striking power. This included speeded-up construction of ballistic missile radar to detect incoming Soviet missiles; placing SAC on a heightened state of alert, so the bombers would be able to escape before the missiles hit; dispersing SAC bombers to the widest extent possible; and providing SAC bases with hardened shelters and missile defenses. The report also recommended an expansion of initial Atlas and Titan ICBM deployment from eighty to six hundred missiles, along with similar large increases in deployment of Thor and Jupiter missiles in Western Europe and in the number of Polaris missile submarines built. Although this would require a level of military spending below that of the Korean War period, Eisenhower expressed doubts that the American people would accept it.

The formal NSC meeting on the Gaither Report was held at 9:00 A.M. on November 7 (the day of the presidential speech). On hand were twenty members of the Gaither Committee; Eisenhower; the secretaries of state, defense, and the treasury; the Joint Chiefs of Staff; the three service secretaries; DCI Dulles; and other NSC, White House, and defense officials. At the end of the presentation, Eisenhower simply directed that the various government agencies study the report and indicate what measures should be implemented. He did not see it as a blueprint for action, however. Eisenhower also felt that "the panel had failed to take into account certain vital information and other considerations" (a veiled reference to the U-2 data, to which the Gaither Committee did not have access).

After the formal NSC meeting, Sprague met with Eisenhower and described how vulnerable the U.S. deterrent had become. Eisenhower was not impressed, saying that wars rarely come as a "bolt from the blue" but rather after a period of increasing tension. Sprague came away from the meeting feeling dejected, convinced that Eisenhower did not realize the danger facing the United States due to Soviet missile developments.

The scale of the Soviet ICBM program and an estimate of deployment levels were given a month later. On December 17, 1957, a Special National Intelligence Estimate was issued. It stated: "ICBM development has an extremely high priority in the USSR, if indeed it is not presently on a 'crash' basis. We believe that the USSR will seek to acquire a substan-

tial ICBM capability as rapidly as possible." Based on this assessment, the initial deployment of ten prototype ICBMs would be made sometime in mid-1958 to mid-1959. The Soviets were thought to be capable of producing ICBMs at a rate that would enable them to have a hundred missiles operational about a year after the initial deployment. A total of five hundred production SS-6s would be operational two to three years after the initial ten prototype missiles were deployed.

As this estimate of Soviet ICBM deployment was being prepared, details about the Gaither Report also began to leak. A summary of the report was published in the December 20 issue of the *Washington Post* in an article written by Chalmers M. Roberts. The article described the report as portraying the United States as being "in the gravest danger in its history" and slipping toward the "status of a second-rate power." Roberts added that the long-term prospects of the United States were that of "cataclysmic peril" in the face of a missile-armed USSR. The tone of the Roberts article was far different than the reassurances that had been issued by the White House for the previous months.

The emerging threat posed by Soviet ICBMs had earlier been given a name by Stewart Alsop in an article in the December 14, 1957, issue of the *Saturday Evening Post.* Alsop wrote: "There is no doubt at all that strategic missiles will surely replace the manned bombers, as the longbow replaced the knights' swords. The prospect which immediately confronts us is that the Soviets will achieve this replacement before we do. There will then be a gap—in the Pentagon it is known simply and ominously as The Gap—during which we will be in somewhat the position of the mounted French knights at Crecy, sword in hand, facing the skilled British bowmen killing them at will." Thus the difference between the planned number of U.S. missiles and the number of Soviet ICBMs projected in intelligence estimates became known as the "missile gap."

The Halt in U-2 Overflights

As the missile gap controversy began to develop, Eisenhower remained concerned over the possible Soviet reaction to the U-2 missions. During a January 22, 1958, meeting with John Foster Dulles and General Twining, he said that the overflights might lead to a reaction over Berlin, which, to the world at large, might seem justified. Secretary of State Dulles commented that he had gone along with the U-2 because it would probably be the last chance, and valuable intelligence could be pro-

duced. Twining countered that overflights had been a rather regular practice for the past ten years, and he doubted that there would be any serious reaction by the Soviets.

Despite his fears, Eisenhower authorized a resumption of U-2 operations over the Soviet bloc. An overflight was made five days after the meeting, on January 28, 1958. The target was Albania; it would be the sixth overflight of that country. The purpose was to check for reported Soviet missile installations. The flight was successful, but it would be another month before an overflight of the USSR was made.

This was done on March 1, 1958, by Detachment C. The target area for Mission 6011 was the Soviet Far East, and the pilot selected for the flight was Tom Crull. He took off from Japan in a Dirty Bird U-2 and headed out over Siberia. The mission photographed the Trans-Siberian Railroad, Sovetskaya Gavan, the Tatar Strait, and a strange-looking installation at Malaya Sazanka, which was eventually identified as a facility for installing detonators on nuclear weapons. Despite the poor reputation of radar operators in the Soviet Far East and the wallpaper covering the U-2, the overflight was detected and tracked. Crull saw numerous contrails from Soviet interceptors trying to reach his aircraft. The problem with heat being trapped by the wallpaper also appeared. Crull suffered a flameout, fortunately after his U-2 cleared the coastline and the Soviet fighters were left behind.

On March 6, the Soviets delivered a protest note about the Far East overflight. After reading the note at a meeting with Secretary of State Dulles the next day, Eisenhower said that he had a strong view that such "infractions" should be discontinued. He felt that the response to the Soviet note should say that the United States was not aware of the matter mentioned in the Soviet note but that strong measures would be taken to prevent any recurrence. Eisenhower continued that, in his view, such operations carried a danger of starting a nuclear war by miscalculation. He felt that the Soviets might see a U-2 overflight as the preliminary to a U.S. attack, causing them to strike first. Brigadier General Goodpaster was instructed to call DCI Dulles and tell him that further "special reconnaissance activities" were to be discontinued at once. This halt in U-2 overflights of the USSR would remain in effect for more than sixteen months.

The U.S. response to the March 1, 1958, overflight did not satisfy the Soviets, and they made a second protest on April 21. This note gave detailed information on the mission's flight path. It was clear that the wall-

paper radar camouflage was not effective and that Soviet air defenses had no problem tracking the U-2s. A total of nine Dirty Bird overflights were made of the USSR. In May 1958, however, following the Far East overflight, use of the wallpaper was discontinued.

At the same time that the U-2 operations over the USSR were being halted, the SS-6 ICBM was running into trouble. Following the orbiting of Sputnik II, there were no further ICBM tests or satellite launches for the rest of 1957. Soviet launch activities did not resume until January 30, 1958, with the test launch of an SS-6. The results were not encouraging; as the strap-on boosters separated, they damaged the core stage. The core stage was no longer under control but continued toward the Klyuchi impact area. Due to the damage, the missile's dummy warhead also did not separate. The core stage and dummy warhead reentered the atmosphere with an overshoot of more than eighty kilometers.

The following day, January 31, the United States successfully launched its first satellite, Explorer 1. The booster was a modified U.S. Army Redstone rocket. Its use as a satellite launch vehicle had been originally proposed in 1955 but was rejected due to Eisenhower's desire that the U.S. satellite effort not interfere with the ballistic missile program. A second attempt was made on March 5, but Explorer 2 did not reach orbit. The Vanguard program redeemed itself on March 17, 1958, when Vanguard 1 was successfully placed into orbit. Explorer 3 was launched successfully on March 26; there was another failed Vanguard attempt on April 28.

Whereas U.S. space efforts met with mixed success during this period, the Soviet missile program had continuing difficulties. It was not until March 12 that the next Soviet try to launch an SS-6 ICBM was made. This test used the same SS-6, serial number M1-6, that had remained on the pad during three launch attempts in June 1957. True to M1-6's past behavior, the engines ignited but the main oxygen valve opened prematurely, and the launch was aborted. The reluctant SS-6 was yet again removed from the pad and returned to the factory.

The next two SS-6 attempts, on March 29 and April 4, also ended in disappointment. In both launches, systems problems caused the dummy warheads to overshoot the target area. In the case of the second launch, the dummy warhead missed by a full sixty-eight kilometers. The United States made three successful satellite launches between January and March 1958, but the Soviets had made no attempts since November 1957. The next SS-6 launch, on April 27, was to carry a cone-shaped scientific satellite weighing nearly a ton and a half. This attempt proved to be an

even bigger failure: Eighty-eight seconds after lift-off, the booster broke up and the debris landed in the Central Asian desert.

Success finally came on May 15, 1958, with the launch of Sputnik III. This was the backup payload to what had failed on April 27. Whereas U.S. successes and failures had been covered by the press, Soviet missile and space activities had been carried out under the strictest secrecy. When Sputnik III reached orbit, Khrushchev again exploited the accomplishment. He proclaimed that the United States would require "very many satellites the size of oranges in order to catch up with the Soviet Union." Critics of Eisenhower's defense and space policy were quick to echo Khrushchev's comments. The *New Republic* said that the president seemed to "lack the interest to meet this critical challenge." Eisenhower responded that the United States had started late but would soon have "all the engines of all the strength we shall need."

The Sputnik III launch was followed on May 24 by another SS-6 test launch. According to one account, this time the core stage lost pressurization, which caused its engine's turbo pump to explode. The core stage, with the dummy warhead still attached, landed forty-five kilometers short of the target area. Thus, the Soviets had made a total of four SS-6 test launches (not counting the ever-reluctant M1-6) during 1958, and all had shown major problems. As a result, following the May 24 failure, SS-6 launches were halted, and the missile underwent a redesign effort to correct the defects. Ninety-seven changes were made to the missile's structure, engines, guidance system, warhead, and launch pad equipment. The halt in SS-6 tests lasted about nine months.

Meanwhile, the missile gap controversy had taken on a political life of its own. In June 1958, the CIA produced an even larger estimate of future Soviet missile deployment. This estimate reflected the pessimistic views of White House science adviser Killian and George Kistiakowsky, who chaired the PSAC's missile panel. It stated that the Soviets would have ten ICBMs by early 1959 and as many as a hundred by the end of the year. This would grow to five hundred in 1960 and a thousand by 1961. Because the United States was planning to deploy a total of only 130 Atlas and Titan ICBMs by 1962, the scale of the gap projected by the estimate was apparent to all.

This estimate was soon part of the political debate over the missile gap. In a series of three articles published in July and August 1958, columnists Stewart and Joseph Alsop launched a bitter attack on Eisenhower's defense policy. They accused the president of either "consciously mis-

leading the nation" or "being misinformed about the facts." They wrote: "At the Pentagon they shudder when they speak of the 'gap,' which means the years 1960, 1961, 1962, and 1963. They shudder because in those years, the American government will flaccidly permit the Kremlin to gain an almost unchallenged superiority in the nuclear striking power that was once our speciality."

More important than the rhetoric of the articles was that they made public for the first time the June 1958 CIA estimates of Soviet missile forces. The Alsops wrote that whereas the United States would have only 130 ICBMs in 1962 and 1963, the Soviets were projected to have 1,500 ICBMs in 1962 and 2,000 ICBMs in 1963. It would not be until after 1963 that the Polaris and Minuteman missiles would start to become operational. The Alsops concluded that, as a result of the missile gap, massive nuclear retaliation would no longer be a credible deterrent. "Any man who is not intoxicated by official self-delusion," they wrote, "must at least expect the Kremlin to threaten to strike the first blow." The American public would have to act quickly to "save ourselves."

The WS-461L Reconnaissance Balloons

Beginning in the early summer of 1958, while the domestic controversy over the missile gap was growing, Eisenhower and the U.S. government faced an ongoing series of crises. These would take place in Poland and the Middle East, off the coast of China, and over the status of Berlin. In each case, these crises would involve the secret air war. In some cases, they would provide critical information or be put on hold. In others, operations gone wrong would be the trigger for the crisis.

The first of these crises was the result of a second series of balloon reconnaissance overflights of the USSR. In the spring of 1955, the air force's Air Weather Service discovered that in a six-week period during May and June, the normal west-to-east flow of the jet stream at 55,000 feet underwent a direction change. The jet stream turned upward over the Bering Sea off the coast of Alaska, reaching an altitude of 110,000 feet, and began flowing east to west. This anomaly would allow a balloon to drift across the USSR at an altitude far above the reach of any interceptor or SAM. To exploit this weather phenomenon, the Cambridge Research Center's Atmospheric Devices Laboratory proposed a new reconnaissance balloon project, which was given the designation WS-461L.

Because the altitude that the WS-461L balloon was to reach was twice that of the Genetrix, a new camera would be required. On February 19, 1957, a meeting was held at BUORL to discuss various ideas for new camera designs. Out of this meeting and subsequent discussions, Walter Levison developed the concept of what became known as the HYAC camera (for "high acuity"). This camera combined two incompatible requirements: high resolution and a wide field of coverage. The HYAC used a 12-inch focal length f/5 lens, which was pivoted so it swung back and forth like a pendulum. During each cycle, it "painted" the image across a curved strip of 70mm film about 25 inches long, covering an angle of 120 degrees. As the lens swung back, the film advanced and the next photo could be taken. The exposures were timed so there would be a 10 percent overlap. This was to prevent any gaps from appearing between each frame. The lens had a resolution of a hundred lines per millimeter, comparable to the U-2's B camera.

Levison served as project manager for the HYAC, although the camera itself was designed by Frank Madden, BUORL's chief engineer. Many ideas were also suggested by Dow Smith. Initial tests of the HYAC proved highly successful. On June 20, 1957, the air force's Air Research and Development Command transferred $750,000 for the development of WS-461L. Before the balloon could be used operationally, test flights would have to be approved by President Eisenhower, but because of the Genetrix program, the president became irritated at the mere mention of balloons.

On June 26, 1957, Secretary of State Dulles met with Eisenhower. During the meeting, Dulles told the president that he had been asked to approve a series of WS-461L test flights by the air force. The balloons would go around the world in a westerly direction, be limited in number, and not carry the HYAC camera. Dulles noted that if the flights were successful, they would presumably be followed in 1958, when weather conditions were right, by reconnaissance missions over the USSR. Eisenhower replied that he "strongly disapproved" of the project, especially at this time, and asked Dulles to so inform the air force. The president also said he thought that "projects of this kind" should be approved at a political level before they were far advanced. But Eisenhower was soon to have a change of mind.

On July 3, only seven days after he had disapproved of WS-461L test flights, Eisenhower met with Secretary of Defense Wilson, Deputy Secretary of Defense Donald Quarles, and Secretary of State Dulles to again

discuss WS-461L. The president was told that the test balloons would fly at 100,000 feet, stay aloft for nearly a month, and circumnavigate the world without overflying the USSR. The test balloons would carry meteorological payloads rather than cameras. Eisenhower replied that he "would be delighted to have one tried." He added that the United States should invite scientists to participate in the observations.

A year later, the test flights had been completed and WS-461L was judged ready to overfly the USSR. Again, Eisenhower was approached for permission, and again this proved difficult to gain. At 6:00 P.M. on May 16, 1958, Eisenhower met with Secretary of State Dulles, General Twining, General LeMay, DCI Dulles, Dr. Killian, and a Colonel Gremmer to discuss WS-461L. They were operating under a time limit; approval had to be given and action taken by June 1 at the latest. If this was not done, the project would have to be delayed a year, until the jet stream again reversed direction.

After studying the plan, Eisenhower said that he would defer his decision until after Secretary of State Dulles provided him with the reaction of several experts to the project. The following day, the president called John Foster Dulles and told him that the more he thought about WS-461L, the more negative his judgment was. He was disposed, unless Dulles disagreed, to give a negative response on Monday, May 19. Dulles said that he did not disagree with the president's decision. On May 19, Secretary of State Dulles called General Goodpaster and informed him that the president had refused permission to go ahead with WS-461L. Goodpaster said he would inform the others who had attended the meeting.

Eisenhower's reluctance to approve both WS-461L and additional U-2 overflights was a reflection of his attempts to get the Soviets to undertake serious negotiations on the issues of surprise attack, arms control, and a comprehensive nuclear test ban treaty. In Eisenhower's view, these efforts would be hindered by the balloon and U-2 overflights. The Soviets had put on a show of the captured Genetrix balloons, and nearly every U-2 mission had resulted in a Soviet protest note, sometimes followed up with a detailed account of the aircraft's flight path.

The May 19 decision was not to be the end of WS-461L, however. As with the test flights the previous year, Eisenhower reconsidered. On June 25, more than a month after turning down the air force's first approach, a second meeting was held. Attending were Secretary of State Dulles, Deputy Defense Secretary Quarles, DCI Dulles, and Dr. Killian. The WS-

461L operations were to be "of a highly restricted nature." Although Eisenhower was reluctant to authorize overflight operations, he was interested in any technological advance that promised "invisibility." This was the approach taken in convincing him to approve the WS-461L launches. Quarles told the president that the chances of the balloons being detected were very small and that the odds of their being identified or shot down was practically nil. Although DCI Dulles thought the balloons might be seen, Killian believed that even this probability was small.

Eisenhower gave a reluctant go-ahead for the launches, with the understanding that the group would consider the operational plans, public statements, and cover and diversionary operations. Political considerations were to be given top priority. Eisenhower said that he did not deny the value of the "special information" that was obtained, except when it cost embarrassment and increased international tensions.

The air force would have to move quickly in order to take advantage of the jet stream shift. One novel feature of the WS-461L was that the balloons were not to be launched from a base on land but rather from a ship at sea, beneath the area where the jet stream changed direction. The USS *Windham Bay* (TCVU-92) was selected for the mission. This was a converted escort carrier that transported aircraft from the West Coast of the United States to Japan in support of fast attack carriers assigned to the western Pacific. The *Windham Bay,* operated by Military Sea Transportation Service, had been making routine trans-Pacific voyages since being recommissioned following the outbreak of the Korean War. Its routine was about to change.

The *Windham Bay* was moored at Pier 3 South at NAS Alameda when the first notification came—on June 23, 1958, two days before the meeting with Eisenhower—for it to be ready to take aboard four air force officers, sixteen airmen, eight civilian technicians, and a cargo of special equipment as part of Operation Melting Pot. The air force personnel began to arrive on June 29. At 10:54 A.M. on June 30, after the last of the personnel reported aboard, the ship left its berth and headed out to sea. For the next two days, the *Windham Bay* sailed west toward the initial launch position. With Eisenhower's approval still tentative, the initial launches carried scientific payloads in order to establish cover.

On July 2, the ship reached the launch point and began maneuvering to sail at the same speed and direction of the surface winds. As a result, the flight deck was in dead calm. Balloon S-423 was successfully

launched at 11:52 A.M., then the ship turned due north and launched a second balloon, S-424, at 4:47 P.M. The ship continued on a northerly course toward the next launch point. The following day, July 3, balloon S-425 was launched.

That same day, Secretary of State Dulles, Deputy Defense Secretary Quarles, Dr. Killian, and DCI Dulles jointly agreed on the operational plan for WS-461L. Three balloons with cameras would be launched from the *Windham Bay* on or about July 7. The launch point would be about 50 degrees north latitude and 150 degrees west longitude. The reconnaissance balloons would be programmed to fly at 110,000 feet in daylight on the westerly air currents. In addition, about eight other balloons, without camera equipment, would be launched. These would be programmed to fly at a lower altitude. As a result, they would drift to the east, crossing the United States. It was expected that some of these balloons would be sighted. The cover plan, which had been approved by the State Department and the CIA, was already in place and operating. Eisenhower wrote "OK" on their memo and initialed it.

Although the president had given his approval, several more scientific-cover balloons still had to be launched at lower latitudes. The next of these was S-426, launched on the Fourth of July. The *Windham Bay* then began a five-knot cruise toward the next launch area. To conserve fuel, two of the ship's boilers were shut down. The ship ran into fog, and added lookouts were posted. An attempt to launch S-427 was made on July 7 but had to be canceled due to excessive winds. The launch point was shifted to the southwest, and S-427 was launched on July 8. The ship remained in the same general area for another launch. On July 9, an attempt was made to launch S-428, but unfavorable weather conditions kept it on the flight deck.

A second attempt the next day was successful. Balloon S-428 lifted off, and the ship headed toward the next launch area. It was soon apparent, however, that the balloon was malfunctioning. The payload was cut free by a radio signal, and it parachuted to an ocean landing. The radio beacon was used to pinpoint the payload's location, and a whaleboat crew brought the equipment back to the ship. Despite this failure, S-429 was successfully launched on July 11.

The time had now come for the reconnaissance balloons to be launched. With a total of six of the eight required scientific-cover balloons successfully launched, the *Windham Bay* set course for a launch position in "operating area Bravo."

In planning the WS-461L operations, the State Department had insisted that the payload be equipped with a timer that would cut it free after four hundred hours. The State Department wanted to prevent the balloons from crossing the Atlantic and entering Canadian airspace. President Eisenhower, in giving his approval, ordered that the timers not be used. Despite his order, an air force crewmen aboard the *Windham Bay* activated the timer aboard the reconnaissance balloon and set it for a four-hundred-hour flight time.

During the early-morning hours of July 12, the plastic balloon and camera payload for S-430 were laid out on the flight deck, and launch preparations began. At 6:29 A.M., the ship began maneuvering to prepare for the inflating and launch of the balloon. The S-430 was released at 7:58 A.M. and climbed into the Pacific sky. The *Windham Bay* began sailing to the next launch point, which took the rest of July 12 and most of the following day. Finally, at 4:16 P.M. on July 13, the S-431 was launched. The ship remained in the area pending a decision on the need for another launch at that location. As with the first launch, S-431 had its timer activated.

The third and final launch area was reached at 1:35 P.M. on July 14. Launch preparations began, then the ship started maneuvering for S-432's launch. Lift-off came at 3:03 P.M. The ship remained in the vicinity of operating area Bravo pending a decision to launch another balloon. As with the other two balloons, S-432's payload timer had been activated.

At 7:00 A.M. on the morning of July 16, a decision was made that no further balloon launches would be required in operating area Bravo. As a result, the *Windham Bay* proceeded south to conduct the final set of scientific-cover launches. The ship arrived at the next launch point after two days and began the prelaunch maneuvering at 9:00 A.M. on July 18. The S-433 lifted off at 10:11 A.M. After confirming that the launch was successful, the ship headed toward the next planned point.

The ship arrived at the designated location on July 19 without incident, and launch preparations began for S-434. At 12:55 P.M., only two minutes after the *Windham Bay* began its launch maneuvers, an unknown ship was sighted. It was tracked on a heading of ninety degrees, with a speed of 3.5 knots. It passed the *Windham Bay* at 1:38 P.M. at a distance of 16.2 nautical miles. After another twenty minutes had elapsed, S-343 was launched successfully. The *Windham Bay* then set course for the final launch position. Later that afternoon, the unknown ship reappeared. At 5:28 P.M. it was tracked and was determined to have changed

course to a heading of eighty-eight degrees. The unknown ship again passed the *Windham Bay,* this time at a distance of 15.6 miles.

The following morning, July 20, the final balloon, S-435, was launched at 9:06 A.M. At 9:13 A.M., the launching phase of Operation Melting Pot was declared completed, and the *Windham Bay* set course toward San Francisco. At 12:19 P.M. on July 21, the ship passed under the Golden Gate Bridge, and less than an hour later it was again moored at Pier 3 South at NAS Alameda. The air force and civilian personnel left the ship.

It seemed that all had gone well, and the three WS-461L reconnaissance balloons would complete their missions over the USSR and Eastern Europe. But, as Levison later wrote, "The launch was delayed to the tail end of the operational window, which resulted in the balloons not getting through the area of interest. They almost made it, but not quite."

The Loss of the Balloons

The first indication that something had gone wrong with the balloons came at 11:00 P.M. on July 28, 1958, when DCI Dulles was notified that one of the balloons had come down in Poland. Eisenhower did not learn of the impending incident until the next morning, July 29. The president was in a meeting with John Foster Dulles when General Goodpaster came in with the news. Dulles said later that Eisenhower was "as angry about that as he had ever seen him." Eisenhower said they had all let him down in a most terrible way. He was also angry at Dulles, because he had agreed to the project believing that it was properly safeguarded. The president added that he would never again permit measures of this sort to be taken. A furious Eisenhower directed Goodpaster to tell the air force that "the project is to be discontinued at once and every cent that has been made available as part of any project involving crossing the Iron Curtain is to be impounded and no further expenditures are to be made."

Eisenhower's anger was also directed at Deputy Defense Secretary Quarles. In a subsequent telephone call, Eisenhower "complained, in salty language, about the laxity in the defense forces—he said he would have, if he had done some of the things that have been done in the last few days—shot himself. . . . The president suggested firing a few people—and said that people in the service either ought to obey orders or get the hell out of the service."

The WS-461L balloons were not the only aerial incident to raise Eisenhower's anger. On July 26, three days before, the Soviets had

protested that an RB-47 had violated the border of the Caspian Sea and strayed fifteen miles inside Soviet airspace until it was driven off by MiGs. (The United States subsequently denied that the airplane had deliberately flown over Soviet territory.)

Dulles returned to the State Department and began to make a series of telephone calls for more information about the balloons. At 12:25 P.M. he called Hugh S. Cumming, Jr., the special assistant for intelligence. In the telephone log, Cumming said that "the AF officer was stupid and without authority set it at 400 hours instead of by command to bring it down and it dropped at 400 hours—the airspeed was miscalculated." In answer to a question by Dulles, Cumming said that the locations of the balloons were known by signals, presumably the payload's recovery beacon. Cumming continued that he did not know what action had been taken on the air force officer, but they would have to pick up the pieces.

Dulles then talked with Deputy Defense Secretary Quarles, who said that he should also be criticized, and felt critical of himself, over the incident. Quarles said that this was one of the risks they took with this type of operation. Dulles replied that "the chances were not estimated very accurately" and recalled someone saying that if the balloons remained aloft for the first day or two, there was no chance that they would come down until the radio command brought them down. Quarles countered that the balloons should have been programmed that way. Turning to the question of how to handle the incident, Dulles said that the first thing to do was to get out an innocuous statement as quickly as possible.

Several hours later, Quarles called Dulles back and said that he had looked over the proposed draft statement and was left with a strong impression that no useful purpose would be served by adding to what had been said in the original cover story. Dulles said that he was not aware that this action had been taken, and that if the United States were to make a second statement, "it will look like a guilty conscience." Quarles told Dulles that the balloon carried camera equipment and the Soviets would probably recover the photos, depending on the camera's condition after landing. The camera was explained, as with Genetrix, as taking weather data. Both Quarles and Dulles agreed that it was best to "sit tight."

The second balloon was believed to have dropped its payload on July 30, also inside the Soviet bloc. The third was expected to suffer the same fate during the afternoon of July 31. Despite the passage of several days, there was still no information available from any sources on the reaction to the loss of the first balloon.

Also on July 31, Eisenhower wrote a memo to Secretary of Defense Neal H. McElroy. It began, "There is disturbing evidence of a deterioration in the processes of discipline and responsibility within the Armed Forces. . . . They include, in particular, unauthorized decisions which have apparently resulted in certain balloons falling within the territory of the communist bloc, [and] a reported violation of the Soviet border in the Caspian Sea area by one of our reconnaissance aircraft following a route that contravened my standing orders. . . ." The memo concluded, "I believe it is essential that action be taken at once, with provision for the appropriate degree of security, to fix responsibility in these instances through formal investigation and report, and to institute a general tightening of discipline and command and executive responsibility within the defense establishment."

As angry as Eisenhower was over the loss of the WS-461L balloons and the RB-47 incident, he had much more serious issues to deal with in the summer and fall of 1958. A pair of interlinked crises in different parts of the world would command his attention, as well as that of the CIA's U-2s.

China, Lebanon, and the U-2

The Nationalist Chinese Air Force had assumed responsibility for the photographic reconnaissance overflights of the mainland by the latter half of 1955. These missions used RF-84Fs and RF-86Fs to cover coastal and inland target areas. Because these aircraft were flown by Nationalist Chinese Air Force pilots, the issue of captured Americans was avoided. The converted fighters, however, lacked the range and altitude to cover targets deep inside the mainland. To allow the Nationalists to cover interior areas, a group of pilots began training in the RB-57A during late November 1956. This was completed in October 1957, and two RB-57A-1s were transferred to the Nationalist Chinese Air Force. The aircraft were painted with Nationalist markings but retained their overall black finish. The aircraft were equipped with two K-38 cameras and a T-11 mapping camera.

The initial overflight plans came from the U.S. Air Force and were evaluated by the Nationalist Chinese Air Force's project office, which, under the agreement, could approve, modify, or reject the plan. Once this had been completed, the primary and backup pilot would independently work out the detailed flight plan, to serve as a cross-check.

The first RB-57A-1 overflight was made on December 6, 1957. The pilot selected was Maj. Si-Liang Lu. Although the maximum altitude of the RB-57A was 55,000 feet, well below that of the U-2, its pilot had to wear the MC-2 partial-pressure suit and undergo the prebreathing procedure. Lu recalled later that the Nationalist RB-57 pilots were not given L-pills. They did carry peasant clothing and mainland money as survival gear. However, China had many local dialects, and a downed pilot would be recognized as soon as he spoke.

The first RB-57A-1 overflight was successful and was followed on December 15 by a second mission. The third was made on January 7, 1958. The aircraft took off and landed in complete radio silence. An overflight could last five to six hours. Once the aircraft landed, the film was developed and copied, and the Nationalist and U.S. Air Forces made separate evaluations. Once completed, the reports were exchanged. The first three overflights evaded Chinese air defenses. Although the peak altitude of the RB-57A was only 55,000 feet, it was thought that this would still put it above the reach of MiG-15s and MiG-17s.

The Nationalist Chinese Air Force's operations sparked a strong reaction by the mainland authorities. These included not only the overflights but also drops of propaganda from B-26s, B-17s, and RB-69 Neptunes, which the mainland authorities seemed to regard as the major threat. On December 9, 1957 (three days after the first RB-57A overflight), Chen Geng, the deputy chief of staff of the Chinese People's Liberation Army (PLA), reported: "This year, planes from Taiwan have frequently invaded [the air space] of important coastal cities and the inner land of the Mainland, dropping large numbers of reactionary leaflets and 'condolence gifts,' creating a very bad impression on the masses. Because some leading members of our Army failed to take anti-aircraft operations seriously and their superiors failed to supervise them closely, [we have been] unable to shoot down any of the invading planes [dispatched by] Chiang [Kai-shek]. In order to improve quickly this situation, we have arranged for the Air Force and all military regions to take every positive and effective step necessary to attack the Chiang planes that are invading the Mainland, trying our best to shoot them down."

The efforts by the mainland Chinese were soon to have results. The fourth RB-57A overflight was made on February 18, 1958, with Capt. Kwan-Hua Chao as the pilot. The airplane took off from Tao Yuan Air Base on a mission to cover targets on the Shan Tung peninsula. Captain Chao first flew due east, to gain altitude, then turned north and flew un-

til he was over the East China Sea, where he turned to the northwest and paralleled the Chinese coast.

As he flew toward the Shan Tung peninsula, Chinese radar sites detected the inbound airplane. A pair of MiG-17s of the PLA Navy were scrambled from Ching Tao Air Base. The two MiGs were guided to the RB-57A by ground controllers and the fighters' own radar. Despite the earlier estimate, the two MiG-17s were able to reach the RB-57A as it cruised at about 55,000 feet. They lined up on it and opened fire with their cannons. Their shells hit the RB-57A's left wing and engine, and the reconnaissance aircraft went down. It crashed into the Yellow Sea, near the town of Chingtao. Captain Chao was killed.

As tensions increased between mainland China and Taiwan during the spring of 1958, Eisenhower approved a U-2 overflight. This was only the second overflight of mainland China, the first having been made during the Soft Touch series the previous summer. The mission, which was flown on June 18, 1958, by Detachment C, covered Chinese coastal areas and the adjoining islands looking for any troop buildup. The photos showed no indications that an invasion was planned. Ironically, the day before the U-2 overflight, the Nationalist Chinese Air Force lost a second reconnaissance aircraft over mainland China. On June 17, 1st Lt. Muo-Chong King was flying an RF-84F on a tactical reconnaissance mission over Fu Kin Province, on the Taiwan Strait. He was intercepted by PLA Air Force MiGs, and during the chase his airplane crashed into a mountain and he was killed.

While attention was focused on China, problems were developing in the Middle East. In early May, rioting broke out in Lebanon between Arabs and Christians. By the time Lebanese president Camille Chamoun requested U.S. aid, the disturbances had died down. Then, on July 14, the same day that S-432 was launched, a coup overthrew the pro-Western government of Iraq. The king, crown prince, and premier were all killed by street mobs and the pro-Nasser army. The following day, Eisenhower agreed to a renewed request for U.S. help by Chamoun and ordered U.S. troops into Lebanon. The pro-Western government of Jordan was also seen as threatened by the unrest, and on July 17 British paratroopers were sent in to assist King Hussein against any coup attempts.

Because the U.S. Marine and Army troops positioned in Beirut and at the airport were vulnerable to outside attack, U.S. military commanders asked that tactical reconnaissance missions be flown to determine

whether any Middle Eastern countries or the USSR were about to intervene. Detachment B's U-2s covered the areas surrounding the U.S. deployment as well as Egyptian and Syrian military camps, airfields, and ports. A close watch was also kept on the activities of Soviet submarines based in Egypt, which posed a threat to the U.S. Sixth Fleet. Although Eisenhower's ban on U-2 overflights of the USSR remained in effect, the Turkish-based U-2s also flew SIGINT missions along the USSR's border and over the Black Sea, always staying outside Soviet airspace. Later Eisenhower said: "The troops will never know that they had a guardian angel watching over them."

United States and British actions in the Middle East did spark intervention, although in indirect form, half a world away. On July 17, two days after the United States intervened in Lebanon, Mao decided to shell the Nationalist-controlled islands of Quemoy and Matsu. During the evening of July 18, Mao held a meeting with the Central Military Commission and senior air force and navy officers; he said that the "Arab people's anti-imperialist struggle" needed more than moral support and China should take real action in order to restrain the United States in the Middle East. He believed that the shelling would shock the United States as well as Europeans and Asians, delight the Arab world, and cause African and Asian peoples to take the Chinese side. Mao also saw the shelling as a means of testing U.S. intentions and resolve toward China and to ensnare it in the Far East. Orders were issued to move PLA Air Force units to bases on the Taiwan Straits, then begin the shelling. By July 27, forty-eight MiG-17s were at Liancheng and Shantou.

Mao, however, began to have second thoughts. He decided to hold off on starting the shelling for several days, noting: "The solution of the problem in the Middle East takes time. Since we have time, why should we be in a big hurry? We will hold our attack plans now, but one day we will put it into implementation." This period of "wait and see" continued for three weeks. Between July 31 and August 3, soon after the attack was postponed, Khrushchev visited China for extensive discussions with Mao and other Chinese officials. They did not, however, tell Khrushchev of their plans to shell the offshore islands.

On August 20, Mao finally made up his mind and ordered the artillery units to begin a sudden and heavy shelling of the Nationalist troops on Quemoy, but not Matsu, in order to isolate them from resupply. If the Nationalist forces withdrew from the islands, the Chinese would make a decision about whether to follow up the shelling with a landing. On that

same day, Detachment C made another U-2 overflight of mainland China. On August 21, the Central Military Commission issued orders to start the shelling of Quemoy on August 23. The targets were to be headquarters, artillery emplacements, radar sites, and ships in the harbor. The initial plan was to continue the shelling for three days, then stop, so the next actions could be taken according to the responses of Taiwan.

The massive artillery bombardment began on schedule, with about 400 guns firing 20,000 shells against Quemoy. The shelling continued around the clock and extended longer than originally planned. By the end of the first week, some 120,000 shells had hit Quemoy. The island was effectively blockaded, and the Nationalist government was seeking U.S. aid, including navy escorts for the supply ships.

The choices facing Eisenhower were grim. He believed that if the United States did not become involved, the Chinese would see their way clear to invade the island and put Taiwan at risk. Its loss, in turn, would put the whole of the Far East in danger, including Japan, Thailand, the Philippines, and Vietnam. Both Eisenhower and Secretary of State Dulles believed that U.S. assistance to the Nationalists would limit the Chinese actions to shelling and blockade. If this failed and the Chinese did invade, the United States would have to use tactical nuclear weapons to strike their airfields.

At a meeting on September 4, 1958, Eisenhower and Secretary of State Dulles discussed the political and psychological risks of using nuclear weapons and the plans for withdrawing U.S. troops from the Middle East. The minutes of the meeting also recorded: "Evidence that a highly secret U.S. Air Force aircraft had been downed in the Soviet Union was noted." Dulles also told the president that a note had been received from the USSR about the balloons.

Now Eisenhower had two more crises to deal with.

The Downing of a Project Sun Valley C-130A-II

The aircraft shot down inside Soviet airspace was a C-130A, which had been specially modified to collect radio transmissions. A total of ten aircraft had been modified under the designation Project Sun Valley. When completed, the aircraft were redesignated "C-130A-IIs" and assigned to the 7406th Support Squadron flying out of Rhine-Main Air Base in West Germany. The C-130A-IIs were soon undertaking missions along the Soviet border from Norway to Turkey.

At 10:21 A.M. on September 2, 1958, a C-130A-II, serial number 56-0528, took off from Incirlik, Turkey. The planned route went to the northeast, to the Turkish Black Sea port of Trabzon, then southeast to the Turkish city of Van, and back again. The airplane was to remain a hundred miles away from the Soviet border. Its mission was later described as "a routine check of the behavior of radio beams and frequencies by which aircraft navigate over Turkey." Aboard the C-130A-II were seventeen crewmen.

The aircraft was due over Trabzon at 11:42 A.M. The plane was flying at 25,500 feet, but its crew could not see the ground due to heavy clouds. Navigation was done using radio beacons. At the appropriate time, the crew reported in, and the Trabzon radio operators gave them an updated weather report. This was acknowledged with a "Roger." Nothing more was heard from the aircraft. What the crew did not realize was that their radio compass was actually locked on to Soviet beacons, which were transmitting on nearly the same frequencies as those in Turkey.

The crew's families were notified the following day that the C-130 was missing. They were told that a search was under way but the weather was poor. The families were not told that a SIGINT ground station in Turkey had picked up the final minutes of the C-130A-II's flight. It had crossed the border and was flying above Soviet Armenia. Four MiG-17s, flown by Senior Lieutenants Lopatkov (aircraft #582, the flight leader), Govrilov (#583), Kacheyaev (#201), and Ivanov (#218), were sent after the C-130A-II. The MiG pilots' radio transmissions were as follows:

> 582. I see the target to the right.
>
> Its altitude is 100 [10,000 meters] as you said.
>
> I am 201. I see the target. Attack! I am 201. I am attacking the target!
>
> Attack, attack 218, attack!
>
> The target is a transport, four engined. I am attacking the target.
>
> Target speed is 300 [kilometers per hour]. I am going along with it. It is turning towards the fence [border].
>
> The target is burning.
>
> There's a hit!
>
> The target is banking.
>
> Open fire!
>
> 218, are you attacking?

Yes, yes, I . . .

The target is burning . . . the tail assembly is falling off the target. 582, can you see me? I am in front of the target.

Look, look at him, he will not get away, he is already going down.

Yes, he is going down. I will finish him off, boys. I will finish him off on this run.

The target has lost control. It is going down.

The target has turned over . . . aha, you see, it is falling!

All right, form up, head for home.

The target started burning after my third pass. . . .

The day following the C-130A-II shoot down, September 3, 1958, Soviet deputy foreign minister Georgi N. Zaroubin handed Richard H. Davis, the U.S. chargé d'affaires, a protest note over the WS-461L balloons. The note said: "Several balloons carrying equipment which included automatic cameras for aerial photography, a receiver and transmitting radio set, etc., have been brought down in the air space of the Soviet Union lately. An examination of the equipment showed that it had been manufactured in the U.S.A. and that the balloons are being launched by the U.S. Air Force." The Soviet government had protested earlier balloon flights, which "represented a gross violation of the air space of the Soviet Union" as well as of international law. The note concluded by saying that the USSR "hopes that the U.S. government will take immediate measures to stop such actions by American authorities."

The United States quickly responded to the protest, saying on September 5 that an investigation had been made, which confirmed that the air force had launched a number of high-altitude weather research balloons. These had been sent aloft from the U.S. West Coast and had carried cameras to photograph cloud formations and other weather phenomena. The note asked for the return of the recovered balloons.

Despite the protest over the WS-461L balloons, the Soviets did not yet make any mention of the C-130A-II. From the SIGINT data, it was clear that the airplane had been shot down, but the United States did not know the fate of the crew. The SIGINT information was also highly classified and could not be made public. On September 6, 1958, the U.S. embassy sent a note to the Soviet foreign ministry saying that a U.S. Air Force transport had disappeared over Turkey and requesting any information the Soviet government might have on the airplane.

The Soviet reply to the U.S. note was made on September 12. It said,

"The Soviet organizations which were charged with conducting an investigation . . . have reported that they found the wreckage of a burned plane 55 km. northwest of the city of Yerevan. They also found the remains of bodies there, from which it can be assumed that the six members of the crew were killed." The noted continued that "the plane had deliberately violated the state border of the Soviet Union" and that "the Soviet government lodges a decisive protest . . . against this new gross violation of the USSR state border by a U.S. military aircraft." The note also complained that despite reassurances that the United States would take "strict measures" to prevent violations, it had not done so. "Such a policy of the U.S. government can only be considered designed to increase the tension between the Soviet Union and the U.S.A."

The coffins containing the six crewmen's partial remains were turned over to the United States on September 24. The bodies were so badly shattered in the crash that only three could be identified. The Soviets did not give any information about the fate of the other eleven crewmen. *Time* magazine suggested that they might have been captured alive or were still hiding out in the Armenian hills.

On October 11, 1958, the Soviets displayed a recovered WS-461L payload at a foreign ministry press conference. A. Ya. Popov, the foreign ministry press department's acting director, told the assembled reporters that, despite earlier promises, the United States had not stopped the launching of balloons into Soviet airspace but had continued "this intolerable action against the USSR." Popov said: "The containers suspended from the balloons house an aerial camera with a large supply of film and a control unit; a narrow-gauge camera which records the readings of the instruments and is designed to determine the coordinates of the aerial photos; a transmitting and receiving radio set, and an automatically jettisoned ballast."

Popov then introduced Col. A. V. Tarantsev, who had been at the display of the captured Genetrix balloons more than two years before. He said that the new balloons had technical improvements that much increased their photographic capabilities. Among these improvements was the HYAC, which Colonel Tarantsev described as being "a camera and film of great sensitivity assuring photographs from altitudes of 30 to 35 km. which clearly show up individual objects, such as planes on an airfield. . . . It is claimed that this equipment is used for photographing clouds. However, it is a well-known fact that such high-quality photography is not required for studying the cloud cover."

From the Taiwan Straits to the Berlin Ultimatum

All these events took place against the background of the easing of the Taiwan Straits crisis and the issuing of a Soviet ultimatum over the status of Allied forces in West Berlin. On September 4, Mao met with the Politburo Standing Committee to assess the situation. Mao concluded that the shelling succeeded in making the United States very nervous and "mobilized the people of the world to join our struggle." He decided not to invade Quemoy and Matsu but to coordinate the shelling with diplomatic efforts to put pressure on the United States.

The United States was not the only nation worried by the Chinese actions. The Soviets were not informed in advance of the Chinese plans and now were concerned that they might be drawn into a war with the United States. The Soviet foreign minister, Andrei Gromyko, made a secret trip to China on September 6 and 7, 1958. The Chinese leadership reassured Gromyko that they did not intend to involve the Soviets. In fact, they made a startling proposal: If the United States were to use tactical nuclear weapons against China, the USSR should stand aside. Only if the United States were to use high-yield H-bombs should the Soviets retaliate. Gromyko sent an urgent cable to Khrushchev on the Chinese proposal.

To Khrushchev, the proposal indicated that the Chinese were placing their own national interests above those of the "Socialist camp." It was also a challenge to Moscow's leadership, because the proposal that the USSR should do nothing if China were attacked was unacceptable both politically and ideologically. Khrushchev immediately sent a letter to Eisenhower, stating: "An attack on the Chinese People's Republic, which is a great friend, ally, and neighbor of our country, is an attack on the Soviet Union." Khrushchev's nuclear guarantee to the Chinese was not a blank check, however. He added: "We have not the least doubt that the Chinese people will strike back at the aggressor in a fitting manner."

Also on September 7, the United States began providing naval escorts for the Nationalist transport ships. The first convoy reached Quemoy without being fired on, but a second convoy was badly shelled, with one Nationalist ship set on fire and the rest driven off. The U.S. escort ships were not fired on by the Chinese while the U.S. ships stayed three miles off the Chinese coast and did not fire on the Chinese shore batteries. For the next week, attempts to run Nationalist convoys to Quemoy were unsuccessful.

On September 9, as the convoy efforts continued, Detachment C made its third overflight of mainland China. As before, this covered both the coastal areas and interior and again showed that no preparations were being made for an invasion. Besides the shelling, starting on August 19, there had also been an ongoing series of dogfights between Nationalist Chinese Air Force F-86s and Chinese MiG-17s. As Eisenhower looked at the U-2 photos during one briefing, he stroked his chin and pondered a decision. Finally he said, "We'll see what we can do about it [the dogfights]." In September, the president authorized the supply of Sidewinder air-to-air missiles to the Nationalist Chinese Air Force. By mid-September, the missiles were in use and were taking a heavy toll on the Chinese MiGs.

The reports of the losses suffered by Chinese MiGs concerned Khrushchev, and on October 4 he sent a telegram to Mao asking about this and offering to supply the Chinese with SA-2 SAMs. Mao denied that the Chinese had suffered heavy MiG losses but accepted the SA-2 offer. He said that the Soviets should sell them the SAMs and let the Chinese operate them. The Soviets should send a few people to train the Chinese in their use. It would take the better part of a year before this could be accomplished, however. In the short term, the Chinese would have to decide on their next set of actions.

Starting in early October, the Chinese held almost daily meetings. Mao decided that although the shelling would continue, it would no longer be daily and would be limited to 30,000 to 50,000 shells per day. Later, this would become variable: Sometimes the shelling would be heavy; other times only a few hundred shells were fired at random during the day. Mao justified this by saying: "Whenever we need tension, we could pull the noose tighter. Whenever we want a relaxation, we can give the noose more slack."

To exploit what Mao saw as disagreements between the United States and the Nationalists, he drafted the "Message to the Compatriots in Taiwan." It was broadcast under the name of Chinese defense minister Peng Dehuai on the morning of October 6, 1958. It announced that the shelling was being halted at 1:00 P.M. for seven days to allow the Nationalist troops and civilian residents on Quemoy to be resupplied. It also called on Taiwan to abandon its Mutual Defense Treaty with the United States and begin negotiations to peacefully end the thirty-year-long Chinese civil war, saying that "the U.S. imperialists" were their common enemy.

The Message to the Compatriots in Taiwan marked the effective end of the crisis. The suspension was with the precondition that U.S. ships stop providing escorts to the transports. On October 8, Secretary of State Dulles said that the U.S. escorts were ending, and the Chinese extended the shelling halt for another two weeks. On October 22, during this period, Detachment C made a fourth overflight of China, and the Chinese were considering what to do next. Mao suggested that the Chinese announce that they would shell only on odd-numbered days. Although it sounded like a joke, Mao said that the Chinese were in a political battle, and this was the way it was supposed to be fought. Mao also made an oblique reference to U.S. threats to use nuclear weapons. He said that China had only hand grenades right now, not A-bombs, and although hand grenades could be useful against Chiang Kai-shek's forces on Quemoy and Matsu, it would not be a good idea to use them in fighting the United States, which had nuclear weapons.

The policy was announced on October 25. On even-numbered days there would be no shelling; on odd-numbered days the firing would be directed at Quemoy's airport, ships, and beaches. Fire might be withheld on odd days if no ships or airplanes were coming into Quemoy.

When Eisenhower heard of the Chinese announcement, he recalled later, "I wondered if we were in a Gilbert and Sullivan war." The odd-day shelling allowed mainland China to increase or reduce tensions as needed, such as when Mao ordered heavy shelling of Quemoy on November 3, 1958, in hopes of affecting the U.S. congressional elections. Mao wanted to promote the Democrats' victory and give the Nationalist troops an excuse for not withdrawing. Despite this, the Taiwan Straits crisis faded away, although another was soon to take its place.

In the late summer and early fall of 1958, despite the repeated crises, it seemed that Eisenhower's efforts to bring the Soviets to the negotiating table were paying off. On August 22, the United States offered to suspend nuclear tests for one year with the condition that the USSR also halt its testing. On August 30, Khrushchev agreed to the proposal, and the talks were scheduled to begin on October 31. On September 8, the United States sent a note to the USSR requesting their answer to a U.S. proposal for a "study of the technical aspects of safeguards against the possibility of surprise attack." A week later (and a few days following the protest over the C-130A-II), the Soviets indicated that they were willing to participate and suggested that the talks should start on November 10 in Geneva. The nuclear test ban talks soon hit a snag, however. The So-

viets conducted two final low-yield nuclear tests at Semipalatinsk on November 1 and 3 before finally agreeing to a test moratorium.

The question that increasingly dominated East-West relations was that of the future of Germany. The West German "economical miracle" had revived Soviet fears over their control of Eastern Europe. This included East Germany becoming dependent on imports from West Germany, and Poland and Czechoslovakia aligning their economies with that of West Germany. In this "domino theory," Soviet troops would be forced out of Eastern Europe, and East Germany would become isolated and vulnerable "to subversive activities and sabotage from within."

The Soviets also feared West Germany's growing military power. Just as U.S. leaders were scarred by Pearl Harbor, the Soviet leadership was similarly obsessed with the attack by Nazi Germany on the USSR in 1941. During an interview on October 24, 1958, newspaper columnist Walter Lippmann found Khrushchev beset by fears of an aggressive West Germany. Khrushchev described the situation in West Germany as similar to that on the eve of World War II, and he blamed the United States for German rearmament and for pushing Germany toward the east.

The future of East Germany also weighed heavily on Khrushchev's mind. Because of the hard-line policies of East German party leader Walter Ulbricht, the country's economy was in shambles, and large numbers of the population were fleeing to West Berlin. As a result, East Germany was dependent militarily and economically on Soviet aid. Yet the USSR was even more dependent ideologically on East Germany. Khrushchev believed that if communism failed in East Germany, it would be seen as discrediting the Soviet system itself.

Finally, the attempt to oust Khrushchev as first secretary in 1957 also had an impact on his foreign policy. Molotov had attacked Khrushchev's concessions with the West as having accomplished nothing. For this reason, Khrushchev believed that he had to show he could be forceful and successful in dealing with the West. Faced with these threats, Khrushchev took what he considered to be defensive measures. To the Western nations, these were seen as an ultimatum carrying the potential of nuclear war.

The Berlin Crisis of 1958–62 began with a speech by Khrushchev at a Soviet-Polish friendship meeting in the Moscow Sports Palace on November 10, 1958. He accused the Western powers of using West Berlin as a base from which to undermine East Germany and the other countries of Eastern Europe. The Western powers had violated all of the

wartime four-power agreements on the demilitarization of occupied Germany, Khrushchev declared, and the only part of the Potsdam Agreement they still honored was that of the four-power occupation of Berlin. This situation could not go on any longer, and the status of Berlin had to be normalized.

Khrushchev elaborated on these statements in lengthy notes to the United States, Britain, and France. He declared that the previous agreements on Berlin were now null and void. He further declared that if the Western powers did not enter into negotiations on a German peace treaty and turning West Berlin into a demilitarized "free city" within six months, the USSR would sign a unilateral peace treaty with East Germany. This would transfer all Soviet rights in Berlin to the East Germans, including control of air and ground access to the city. Preliminary talks had already been held with the East Germans; once the free city of West Berlin was established, they would sign an agreement allowing free passage into and out of the city. This was conditional, however, on no hostile activity being undertaken from West Berlin. Khrushchev's notes also threatened that if the Western powers refused to recognize the transfer of Soviet controls on Berlin to the East Germans, or attempted to interfere, this would "result immediately in appropriate retaliation" by the Warsaw Pact.

With the six-month deadline and threatening tone, the notes were seen by the United States and other Western powers as an ultimatum over Berlin. Khrushchev's action was a combination of crude brinksmanship and boasts of Soviet power, sweeping in scope, marked by improvisation, and fundamentally ill conceived. The improvisation was shown by the fact that it was not until Christmas Eve 1958 (a month after the notes) that Gromyko prepared two drafts of the German peace treaty, one with both West and East Germany and the other with East Germany alone. The first text included a partial withdrawal of foreign troops from German soil, which Gromyko noted "would be effectively tantamount to a collapse of NATO." As unacceptable as this would be to the Western powers, Khrushchev believed that they would still find this preferable to the unilateral peace treaty, which would leave them at the mercy of the East Germans regarding access to West Berlin.

Khrushchev probably believed that his Berlin ultimatum would be a panacea for his foreign policy and political problems. It would restrain the United States in Europe and the Far East, prevent West Germany from threatening Soviet control in Eastern Europe, and force the Western powers to recognize East Germany as a sovereign state. Giving East

Germany control of movements out of West Berlin would halt the flood of refugees and prevent Khrushchev from being blamed for "losing" East Germany. Forcing the West to accept a solution of the German question on Soviet terms would silence Khrushchev's domestic and Chinese critics who were pressing for a harder line with the West and give Khrushchev flexibility for talks with the United States. Finally, all this was in the form of a "peace agreement" designed to appeal to Western public opinion.

In his dealings with the United States over the Berlin ultimatum, Khrushchev, like Stalin before him (and, for that matter, Lenin), used a "good cop–bad cop" approach, combining threats and conciliatory gestures aimed at reassuring and dividing the West. In February 1958, long before the Berlin ultimatum was conceived, the Soviets were suggesting that Vice President Richard M. Nixon make a trip to the USSR and Khrushchev visit the United States. The middle man was Yuri Gvozdev, a KGB officer at the Washington, D.C., embassy. Gvozdev continued to play this role after Khrushchev issued his Berlin ultimatum. He passed a note to Nixon saying, "Don't worry about Berlin. There is not going to be any war over Berlin." He later told U.S. officials that Khrushchev was "very interested" in a Nixon visit and would "bid very high for it in terms of constructive proposals on Berlin."

In January 1959, Soviet deputy prime minister Anastas I. Mikoyan visited the United States to meet with Eisenhower. Mikoyan said that he had been instructed by Khrushchev to propose to the president "to end the Cold War." He said: "It is necessary to make a start and while the first agreement might not be important, it is possible for it to snowball and lead to a great improvement." Mikoyan reassured Eisenhower that Khrushchev's ultimatum was not intended to "undermine the prestige of the Western powers or to make them 'lose face.'" He continued, "We do not want to fight over Berlin, and we hope you don't want to, either." What Khrushchev proposed, Mikoyan said, was that the United States and the USSR hold talks on a German peace treaty, keeping West German chancellor Konrad Adenauer out of the picture. Mikoyan described him as an opponent of the treaty who would exploit U.S.-Soviet differences, try to delay an agreement, and base his position upon force.

The visit of Mikoyan also marked the final attempt to gain a Soviet accounting for the eleven missing C-130A-II crewmen. By early November 1958, the United States had received what was apparently an eyewitness account of the shoot-down. The C-130A-II was seen flying through thin clouds; two Soviet fighters shot off its right wing and the transport

crashed. The report continued: "A group of villagers ran to the scene and tried to rescue any survivors. However, when they approached the aircraft, an explosion occurred and they were forced to remain in the background and let it burn. When the flames had died down, probing revealed a total of 18 bodies, 12 of these burned beyond recognition." About an hour later, after the flames had subsided, a convoy of ten government vehicles arrived at the crash site, and a number of officials made a search of the wreckage.

On November 13, 1958, Deputy Undersecretary of State Robert Murphy invited Soviet ambassador Mikhail Menshikov and Soviet air attaché Maj. Gen. Mikhail N. Kostiouk to his office. Murphy again asked for information on the eleven missing airmen. When the Soviets did not provide any, Murphy told them that it appeared that the transport had strayed across the border accidentally, due to Soviet radio beacons, and was then shot down. When Menshikov expressed doubts about this, Murphy offered to play them a tape recording. Menshikov refused to listen, claiming not to be able to assess it from a technical viewpoint. Murphy said that was why General Kostiouk had been asked to accompany the ambassador. Menshikov refused a second time.

When Mikoyan visited Washington in early January 1959, he was asked by both Vice President Nixon and Secretary of State Dulles about the C-130A-II. Again he denied any knowledge beyond that already given by the Soviets, then asked, "Why are Americans so suspicious about this?" After Mikoyan refused to tell what had happened to the missing crewmen, Eisenhower approved the public release of the recording in February 1959. The Soviets dismissed it as a "fake" and a "gross forgery" but offered no new information and continued to deny that their MiGs had shot down the C-130A-II. This remained the Soviet position for the next forty years. The families of the crewmen were told nothing about their fate.

SS-6 Diplomacy

Behind Khrushchev's Berlin ultimatum lurked the long shadow of the Soviet SS-6 ICBM. Soviet missile developments, and their early successes in space, had emboldened Khrushchev to undertake a more aggressive foreign policy. Whereas earlier generations spoke of "saber rattling," Khrushchev and other Soviet officials missed no opportunity to boast of Soviet missiles. On December 4, 1958, a Soviet delegate at the Geneva

Conference on Surprise Attack said: "Soviet ICBMs are at present in mass production." Five days later, Khrushchev claimed that the USSR had an ICBM able to carry a five-megaton nuclear warhead a range of eight thousand miles.

The new year of 1959 brought additional statements. At the opening of the Soviet Communist Party Congress in February 1959, Khrushchev said: "Serial production of intercontinental ballistic rockets has been organized." Several months later, Soviet defense minister Rodion Malinovsky said that Soviet missiles could hit "precisely any point" and "our army is equipped with a whole series of intercontinental, continental and other rockets of long, medium and short range." When Eisenhower was asked about Malinovsky's statement at a press conference, he replied, "They also said that they invented the flying machine and the automobile and the telephone and other things. . . . Why should you be so respectful of this statement this morning, if you are not so respectful of the other three?"

Unlike the crises over Lebanon and the Taiwan Straits, which both saw extensive use of U-2 overflights, the Berlin ultimatum resulted in a continued ban on U-2 overflights of the USSR. Eisenhower's fear of the political consequences of the loss of an aircraft remained strong, as did his assessment that the Soviets were much weaker than the United States and his belief that the value of the intelligence did not equal the political price that would have to be paid. In time, however, Khrushchev's continued exploiting of the missile gap, and the domestic political consequences that resulted, would force Eisenhower's reluctant approval to let the U-2s return to Soviet skies.

Chapter 8
From Touchdown to Grand Slam: The Final U-2 Overflights

The pilot reported over the emergency frequency that he was experiencing oxygen difficulties.

—NASA cover statement, May 3, 1960

We have parts of the plane, and we also have the pilot, who is quite alive and kicking. The pilot is in Moscow, and so are the parts of the plane.

—Nikita S. Khrushchev, May 7, 1960

Although crises came and went during 1958, the issue of the missile gap continued to simmer. The situation did not become clearer but rather more contentious and confused. After the SS-6 test on May 24, 1958, the Soviet ICBM program made no more launches for nearly nine months. Even adding the Sputnik launches, the Soviets made far less than the twenty to fifty ICBM launches that the CIA estimated would be needed before the SS-6 was operational. This was subject to two interpretations. The CIA believed (correctly) that the SS-6 was in trouble and flights had been halted pending modifications. The air force concluded that testing had been completed and deployment was soon to begin. At the same time, the missile gap and the space race between the United States and the USSR was taking on a whole new dimension.

The Missile Gap and the Moon Race

With the first successful U.S. satellite launches, both public and political attention began turning toward the Moon. It was an enthusiasm that Eisenhower did not share, but on March 24, he gave reluctant approval to proposals by the air force and army to launch moon probes. The public interest in space, as well as the psychological damage that would result from the Soviets reaching the Moon first, had forced Eisenhower's hand.

On July 10, 1958, as the U.S. effort was under way, a missile stood on the pad at Tyuratam. The launch attempt, which the CIA believed was an SS-6 ICBM test, was a failure. In reality, it was a test of an SS-6 that had been fitted with a dummy third stage that was to send a small, unmanned probe to impact on the Moon or make a flyby to photograph its surface.

In mid-August, the United States and the USSR were poised to launch missions to the Moon. On August 17, the United States was the first to try, launching a Thor-Able rocket. The initial lift-off was successful, but the booster exploded seventy-seven seconds later. At Tyuratam, a three-stage SS-6 was also being prepared, but its countdown was plagued with prelaunch malfunctions. When word was received of the U.S. failure, the Soviets decided to delay the launch for a month.

The first Soviet moon launch was made on September 23, but it ended after only ninety-three seconds. The strap-on boosters separated prematurely from the core stage, and they exploded on impact with the ground. The second Soviet try was made on October 12, in what had been literally a race to the Moon. The day before, the Pioneer 1 probe had been successfully launched from Florida. Despite Pioneer 1's head start, the Soviet probe could still reach the Moon first, because its flight duration was only a day and a half. But again the Soviet attempt failed; the booster exploded 104 seconds after lift-off. Pioneer 1 fared little better; its final velocity was short of that needed to reach the Moon. As a result, it soared 70,700 miles into space, then fell back to Earth and burned up over the Pacific on October 13, 1958.

Following the twin launch failures, the Soviets halted their launch attempts pending an investigation of the failures. The next Soviet moon launch was not made until December 4, 1958. The attempt seemed headed for success until 245 seconds into the flight, when the core stage engine's turbo pump failed. The core stage and moon probe reentered the atmosphere and burned up.

The United States was having little more success; on November 7, the air force launched Pioneer 2, but the second stage failed to fire and it burned up in the atmosphere. Two days after the Soviet failure, the U.S. Army made its first moon launch, using a Juno II booster. Pioneer 3's velocity was too low; it reached an altitude of 66,654 miles before falling back to Earth.

Throughout this period, Sen. Stuart Symington, a former secretary of the air force under President Truman and a likely Democratic presidential candidate in the 1960 election, continued to stress the missile gap issue. Symington argued that the CIA was in error in its count of six successful SS-6 tests, saying that the total number of tests made in 1957 and 1958 was between fifty-five and eighty launches. He also disagreed with a new National Intelligence Estimate on Soviet guided missiles and space capabilities, issued on August 19, 1958. It stated that the Soviets

"could achieve an operational capability with ten or more, but less than 100 ICBMs by the end of 1959 . . ." The number was estimated to reach a hundred ICBMs one year after the initial deployment, with five hundred missiles expected to be deployed sometime in 1961 or at the latest in 1962. The senator argued that the CIA was underestimating both the current Soviet missile program and their future capability.

Director of Central Intelligence Dulles asked the CIA's Guided Missile Intelligence Committee to conduct a review of the estimates of Soviet missile forces and the status of their efforts. The key question was how to reconcile the handful of SS-6 tests with the estimates of large, short-term deployment. Based on this review, an attachment to the earlier estimate was issued on November 25, 1958. Although the estimate continued to project a large Soviet ICBM force, it pushed back the deployment dates. The CIA now estimated that the Soviets would not have any ICBMs deployed during 1958, and a force of five hundred missiles was not projected until sometime in 1962. The attachment noted that the projected time scale "would require an extremely high order of planning . . . and . . . an increase in the average rate of ICBM firings for test and training purposes."

Symington was briefed on the amended estimate on December 16, 1958. He was told that intelligence coverage of the Soviet missile tests rested "on a sophisticated, integrated collection system" and "that no significant number of test firings to 3,500 nautical miles have passed unnoticed." Director of Central Intelligence Dulles summarized the record of known Soviet ICBM and space launches for Symington. There had been six successful SS-6 tests between August 1957 and May 1958; two unsuccessful ICBM tests, with the most recent in July 1958 (actually the dummy third-stage test); three successful Sputnik launches; and four attempts to launch space missions of an unknown nature, the most recent in December 1958 (the failed Sputnik and the three failed moon launches).

Despite Dulles's reassurances that fifty-five to eighty ICBM tests would not have been missed, Symington remained convinced that the CIA was in error about the number of SS-6 launches and the total number of Soviet missiles that the United States would face. He added that a slowdown in the Soviet ICBM program "was a wonderful thing to believe if it was more important for the U.S. to balance the budget than to have national defense."

In February 1959, Defense Secretary Neil H. McElroy told the Senate

Preparedness Investigating Committee that in the early 1960s the Soviets might enjoy a three-to-one advantage over the United States in operational ICBMs. McElroy stressed that this gap would be only temporary and that the United States would emerge with a technological advantage due to its development of the advanced solid-fueled Minuteman and Polaris missiles rather than deploying large numbers of first-generation, liquid-fueled Atlas and Titan ICBMs.

McElroy's admission of a possible three-to-one Soviet advantage, along with the earlier propaganda statements by Soviet officials, gave ammunition to administration critics. Symington accused McElroy of deliberately "downgrading" the estimates of Soviet missiles in order to balance the budget. He accused the administration of trying to lull the American people into a "state of complacency not justified by the facts," and he predicted that rather than 500 Soviet ICBMs in 1962, as the CIA estimated, "they will have 3,000."

More important was a change in the status of the Soviet ICBM and space programs. On January 2, 1959, the Soviets successfully launched Luna 1. Although Luna 1 was intended to impact the Moon, a guidance error caused it to miss. The probe flew past the Moon and entered an orbit around the Sun. The Soviets depicted the flight as a complete success and exploited it for propaganda purposes. The Luna 1 launch was the last Soviet moon probe attempt for the next six months. Soviet efforts now shifted back to SS-6 flight testing.

By the end of 1958, the modification work to the SS-6 was completed, and the first test version of the production ICBM was ready to begin launches. The first attempt was made on December 24, 1958, but ended in failure. The same fate befell the next try on February 17, 1959. These two failures were followed by six launches between March 23 and June 18. Of these, three were successful. The resumption of SS-6 flights after a halt of several months indicated that deployment was soon to begin. With the military and political consequences of the missile gap continuing, pressure increased on Eisenhower to resume U-2 overflights.

Eisenhower and the Question of Overflights

The question of resuming overflights was raised on February 12, 1959, in a meeting between Eisenhower and Defense Secretary McElroy, Deputy Defense Secretary Quarles, and Joint Chiefs of Staff chairman General Twining. McElroy pointed out that no matter how often Dulles

briefed Symington and other Democratic congressmen, they would never believe him without photographic proof. McElroy therefore asked the president to consider the question of additional overflights of the USSR.

Eisenhower was not convinced of the need for additional overflights, saying that the effort to build a photoreconnaissance satellite, code-named Corona, was "coming along nicely" and that U-2 overflights should be "held to a minimum pending the availability of this new equipment." Quarles disagreed, saying that the reconnaissance satellite would not be ready for eighteen months to two years. This argument did not seem to sway the president, because he discounted the possibility that the Soviets could build a force of ICBMs large enough for a first strike in the near future. Eisenhower's primary concern, as he had said many times before, was that overflights were unduly provocative. He stated that although one or two overflights might possibly be permissible, he was opposed to an extensive program (that is, another Soft Touch).

There was an open issue regarding the U-2 overflights, however. In the fall of 1958, Eisenhower had considered and approved a reconnaissance mission "in the north" (of the USSR). This was not flown at the time and could not now be flown until March 1959. Due to the long delay, a new authorization was required. The mission was discussed at the February 12 meeting. The flight was rated a number-one priority, and General Twining agreed that the area to be covered was extremely important. Eisenhower considered the northern mission. Although it was a single mission rather than an extensive series, he finally decided against it. On March 4, 1959, General Twining was notified that the president had disapproved any additional "special flights" by the U-2 unit due to "the present abnormally tense circumstances."

This was a reference to the ongoing Berlin Crisis. The Soviets had submitted their draft peace treaty on January 10, 1959, and continued their efforts to pressure the Western powers. This continued into March, when Khrushchev relaxed the six-month deadline for a German peace treaty and proposed a four-power conference of foreign ministers in either Geneva or Vienna to begin negotiations on Germany and Berlin.

Despite the apparent easing of the crisis, Eisenhower remained ambivalent about continued U-2 overflights. On April 6, 1959, he gave tentative approval for overflights "in the north and south" (of the USSR). He had a lengthy discussion with General Goodpaster regarding the flights, asking for his advice. Goodpaster analyzed the proposals as to the

importance of possible costs and possible gains and told Eisenhower that he was disposed to favor the two missions. Goodpaster added that although he was confident in his assessment of the costs and gains, he was less sure about their relative importance and would defer to the president's assessment in this regard. Eisenhower continued to contemplate the overflights. He called Secretary of State Dulles, who was now suffering from terminal cancer. Dulles said that if the proposed flights were "in the east" (of the USSR), he would have no objections, but he would not approve missions over the north and south. Dulles added that if the current negotiations failed, the United States would need the most accurate information possible.

The following day, April 7, Eisenhower met with McElroy and Bissell and told them that he had changed his mind and decided not to go ahead with the overflights. The president explained that as the world was going now, there seemed to be no hope for the future unless there was some progress in negotiations. He added that it seemed that the Soviets really did want a summit meeting and it was important that some kind of progress be made, even though he was not sure this was possible. There were, however, "straws in the wind" that indicated this was not totally hopeless. In the current situation, the United States could not afford "the terrible propaganda impact that would be occasioned if a reconnaissance plane was to fail."

Eisenhower did agree on the need for information, which was highlighted "by the distortions several senators are making of our military position relative to that of the Soviets." He continued that their "demagoguery" was helped by the uncertainties regarding Soviet missile programs. Despite this, the president believed that the missions would not be worth the political costs. He told McElroy and Bissell that if they thought the situation had changed, or in the event that an emergency or a crisis occurred, they could raise the matter again.

SIGINT Missions Against the SS-6

Although Eisenhower still opposed overflights of the USSR, he was willing to authorize U-2 SIGINT border flights. These missions would pick up the telemetry signals radioed from the SS-6 ICBMs in flight, which indicated how the systems aboard the missile performed and provided measurements of the amount of fuel burned and the missile's speed. In June 1959, Eisenhower authorized Missions 4120 and 4121 along the So-

viet-Iranian border, code-named Hot Shop. The first Hot Shop mission was flown on June 9 and involved a CIA U-2 and an air force RB-57D. As the airplanes cruised high above Iran, their receivers were able to make the first telemetry intercepts from an SS-6 during first-stage flight, some eighty seconds after launch. The second Hot Shop mission was flown against the SS-6 launch on June 18 and was also successful.

The U-2 SIGINT missions against Soviet missile launches became a regular activity. United States intelligence knew several days in advance when a launch would take place. Francis Gary Powers, who flew a number of these missions, recalled later that the Soviets often scheduled their launches at night. He noted, "They were often spectacular, lighting up the sky for hundreds of miles." The SIGINT package aboard a U-2 flying at 70,000 feet could pick up telemetry signals earlier in the missile's flight than a ground station could.

The U-2s sometimes worked as a team with other, lower-flying aircraft. Although an RB-57D was used for the first Hot Shop mission, the standard aircraft was the EB-47E (TT, for "Tell Two"). These were three B-47Es modified with a capsule in their bomb bay for two Crows and their receiving equipment. A T-shaped antenna was mounted on either side of the airplane's nose. These modifications were made by Boeing starting in March 1958.

The Tell Two aircraft were normally based at Incirlik, due to its proximity to the Tyuratam and Kapustin Yar missile ranges. The five-man EB-47E (TT) crews (pilot, copilot, navigator, and two Crows) were kept on alert status, awaiting a Soviet missile launch, rather than flying prescheduled missions. The primary and backup Tell Two crews were ready to take off within fifteen minutes of the klaxon going off. A third crew acted as a reserve, and a fourth crew was off-duty or on leave. This led to particular demands on the three alert Tell Two crews. Because the Soviets usually launched in the early-morning hours, the crew would try to rest in the barracks, called the "Holiday Inn." Meanwhile, the one or two RB-47H crews also at Incirlik and the fourth Tell Two crew would be pulling pranks, having fun, and generally making as much noise as possible. The Tell Two crews could count on the klaxon going off at the worst possible time—during a thunderstorm, right after the crews went to bed, when a primary crewman got sick, when dinner was about to be served, and always when the crew decided to stay up. But when it sounded, the crew would always dash out of the Holiday Inn, man their aircraft, and take off into the night.

To cover Tyuratam launches, the Tell Two took up a racetrack pattern over Iran, sometimes with a U-2 above them, and awaited the launch. The operation was tightly held within the Iranian government, with only the Shah, the minister of defense, and a senior general knowing about the flights. If the launch was canceled or the missile blew up just after liftoff, the Tell Two crew would leave empty handed. If the missile climbed above the airplane's horizon, the two Crows would begin recording its telemetry signals. The Tell Two's SIGINT equipment consisted of several fixed-frequency receivers and recorders. The Crows had only a limited ability to evaluate frequencies other than those programmed into the receivers. The Crows would monitor the equipment and change the reels of tape.

The NSA now had to translate the large volume of telemetry data, collected by ground stations and the U-2 and Tell Two missions, into a coherent picture of the SS-6's design. The telemetry format proved to be relatively simple, and soon several of the channels were identified as being for missile velocity and acceleration data. Before this could be used to derive performance data, however, two other problems had to be worked out. The data was for only the portion of the SS-6's flight that was above the horizon. The U-2s could pick up signals from just before the burnout of the first-stage, strap-on boosters, and ground stations could monitor only the last 20 percent of the powered flight. These would not indicate the absolute values of the measurements—that is, what the "zero" value was.

The solution to this problem came through a lucky break. During the summer of 1959, abnormal radio propagation conditions allowed a weak intercept to be made. After extraordinary efforts, this yielded telemetry records running from before launch to well after the core stage burnout. With this record, the total number of digital clicks on the missile's "speedometer" could be calibrated with the burnout velocity needed to reach the impact zone on the Kamchatka Peninsula. As a result, this established the velocity meter calibration for subsequent launches. There still remained a second problem, however. The United States did not know the weight of the missile or any of its payloads. This data was provided by covert action.

Following the launch of Luna 1, the Soviets sought to impress the world with their achievement. To do this, they included in a touring exhibition what U.S. intelligence assumed was only a mock-up of the Luna 1 and its third stage. Others were not so sure it was only a mock-up, and

a covert examination was arranged. When the exhibit closed at one stop, a group of intelligence officers had unrestricted access to the exhibit for twenty-four hours. They discovered that it was an actual third stage, although the rocket engine and most of the electronic and electrical components had been removed. The group examined the third stage to estimate its performance, structural characteristics, wiring format, and engine size.

As the third stage continued its tour, a second examination by a four-man team from the CIA's Joint Factory Markings Center was planned at its next stop; the team was to identify what organizations had produced the third stage and its components. The only way to accomplish this was to "borrow" the third stage after it left the fairgrounds. A week was spent planning the operation with the local CIA station personnel, working out access and escape procedures, acquiring tools and local clothing, and spotting weaknesses in Soviet security.

When the exhibit closed, the displays were crated up and loaded on trucks for the trip to the rail yard. There, a Soviet checker noted each item as it arrived and was loaded aboard the train. He did not have communications with the fairgrounds, however. Taking advantage of this, arrangements were made that the crate containing the third stage was the last truckload to leave the fairgrounds. As the truck drove toward the rail yard, it was preceded and followed by station cars, to spot any Soviet surveillance. The truck was stopped at the last possible turnoff, where a canvas cover was thrown over the crate and a new driver took over. The original driver was taken to a hotel for the night, and the truck was driven to a salvage yard that had been rented for the operation. The Soviet checker at the rail yard waited a short while, then went to dinner and then to his hotel, where he was kept under surveillance.

Finally, the all clear was given, and the markings team arrived at the salvage yard at about 7:30 P.M. Two members of the team set to work prying open the wooden top of the crate to gain access to the third stage. The effort left them panting and sweating in the humid air. As they worked, the dark salvage yard was suddenly flooded with light. After an anxious few moments, the group realized that it was not an ambush, just the streetlights coming on.

Two of the markings team worked at the nose, removing one of the clear plastic windows in the nose cone that allowed viewing of the Luna 1. They removed their shoes to prevent leaving marks inside the nose cone, and crawled inside. They photographed the factory markings on

the Luna, then removed it from the basket mounting to make a closer examination of the area. The other team members worked at the rear of the third stage, first removing the base plate to gain access to the interior. Once inside, they found that the engine mounting brackets were still in place, as were the fuel and oxidizer tanks. They spent several hours working inside the third stage, photographing or writing down all the factory markings.

Finally, they began putting the third stage back together. This ran into a snag when the Luna would not fit back on its mounting. It took almost an hour, numerous tries, and many anxious moments before it was finally back in place. Before the team sealed up the third stage, they carefully checked that no matches, pencils, or scraps of paper had been left inside. The window and base plate were reattached, and the crate was checked for anything left behind before being closed up. The markings teams packed up their equipment and left the salvage yard at 4:00 A.M. An hour later, a driver came and moved the truck from the salvage yard to a prearranged spot, and the original driver took over and drove to the rail yard. The Soviet checker arrived at 7:00 A.M. and found that the truck and crate had already arrived. He checked the crate in and watched it being loaded aboard a flatcar. The Soviets never suspected that it had been gone.

These covert examinations of the third stage were critical to the interpretation of the SIGINT data. The third stage was determined to weigh 2,600 pounds empty and 18,000 pounds fueled. This was the missing piece to the puzzle, and it soon fell into place. On July 18, 1959, the Soviets resumed launches to the Moon. Their first attempt failed at 153 seconds into the flight, when the inertial guidance system failed and the booster had to be blown up by ground controllers. Despite this failure, the Soviet efforts, as well as those by the NSA, the U-2 pilots, the Tell Two crewmen, and the covert operatives, were all about to be rewarded.

The next Soviet moon attempt, on September 12, 1959, was successfully launched and sent Luna 2 to an impact on the Moon. This was followed on October 4, 1959, the second anniversary of Sputnik I, by the launch of Luna 3. It looped around the Moon and photographed the far side, which was never visible from Earth. The film was processed and the photographs were scanned, then transmitted back to Earth. This was the first time that this part of the Moon was seen by human eyes. It was a stunning breakthrough in space science and planetary astronomy. The twin Luna successes also illuminated the remaining mysteries of the SS-6.

The third-stage telemetry from the Luna 2 and 3 launches was monitored, and velocity measurements were found that were identical to that of the SS-6 telemetry, indicating that the same device was being used in both. Because this device had already been calibrated from the lucky intercept of the prelaunch telemetry, the performance of the third stage could be calculated using the empty and fueled weights determined from the covert inspections. This, in turn, exactly matched the velocity change needed to reach lunar escape speed after the SS-6 core stage burned out. The calculations also showed that the payloads announced by the Soviets for the three Luna flights were accurate.

The reentry of the SS-6 core stages used to launch Luna 2 and 3 were observed by newly established radar sites on Shemya Island in the Aleutians. The core stages traveled 3,800 miles downrange, landing in the Pacific not far from the radar sites. This, along with the weight of the third stage, was the key to determining the performance of the SS-6 ICBM. If the third-stage engine had not ignited, the third stage would have also landed 3,800 miles downrange. Thus, the SS-6 ICBM could deliver an 18,000-pound warhead 3,800 miles. With this data point established, a series of range-to-warhead weight curves could be calculated for the basic ICBM. These also indicated that the SS-6 could put 3,000 pounds into orbit, which matched the announced weight of Sputnik III.

As a result of these efforts, the United States had an understanding of the capabilities of the SS-6 ICBM, even though the Soviets had never released a photo of it. In addition, the U.S. reconstruction of its configuration was based on U.S. design concepts that proved to be erroneous. By the summer of 1959, however, the most pressing question about the SS-6 was not its performance but its numbers. To answer this, Eisenhower again authorized U-2 flights over the USSR.

Touchdown

The first U-2 overflight of the Soviet Union in more than sixteen months was Mission 4125, code-named Touchdown. It was flown against a confused international situation. The conference of foreign ministers had held meetings on Germany and Berlin starting on May 11, 1959. Although the Western powers made several concessions, including discussing an interim agreement on Berlin, the Soviets held firm, even renewing their six-month deadline for a German peace treaty on June 10. The Soviets came away from the meetings with the belief that they were

making progress in their efforts to push the West out of Berlin. Despite the renewed threat of a unilateral peace treaty, arrangements were also made for a trip to the USSR by Vice President Nixon in July.

Despite Eisenhower's change of mind in April, efforts continued to gain approval for overflights. The president indicated that a flight path across the target area, entering from one direction and leaving in another, would raise fewer problems. Several days later, on July 7, Eisenhower met with DCI Dulles and Bissell about the possibility of one or more overflights. They suggested a flight path entering and leaving Soviet airspace from the south. Eisenhower asked that a meeting be arranged with them and Secretary of State Christian Herter for the following day. When the July 8 meeting began, Eisenhower said that he wanted to hear Herter's views on the proposed overflight. Herter replied that the intelligence objectives outweighed "the danger of getting trapped." He noted that only a single mission was being proposed and that although there was always the risk of losing an aircraft, the experience so far had been good. Herter also said that he had been interested in the idea of a flight "straight through" but understood that this was not practical.

Eisenhower then expressed his own concerns about the flight. He said that Khrushchev seemed to be almost looking for an excuse to be belligerent. He could readily say that "such an event" (that is, the overflight or the loss of an aircraft) marked the end of serious negotiations. Eisenhower further said that there was a question in his mind of whether the United States was getting to the point where it must decide if it was trying to prepare to fight a war or prevent one. But Eisenhower said that, in view of their unanimous recommendation, he would approve the overflight.

The primary targets for the Touchdown overflight were Soviet nuclear facilities in the Urals and ballistic missile activities at Tyuratam. The second-generation facilities at Tomsk and other sites in Siberia had been photographed during Soft Touch, but the original Soviet nuclear plants built in the Urals during the late 1940s had not yet been covered. Fragmentary details were known about three facilities. The Soviet's major plutonium-production site was at Kyshtym, located between Sverdlovsk and Chelyabinsk. To the north of Sverdlovsk, at Verkh Neyvinsk, was a gaseous diffusion plant producing enriched uranium. Farther to the north, at Nizhnyaya Tura, was an unidentified nuclear facility. Until the United States better understood these facilities, it lacked a complete picture of the USSR's ability to produce fissionable materials.

With the ban on U-2 overflights in effect, the only way to determine the production capabilities of these sites was to measure their electrical consumption. The output of fissionable material from a plant was directly proportional to the amount of power it consumed. The Soviets understood this as well as the CIA, and as a result electrical power generation, transmission, and usage in the Urals was a classified subject.

Just as the unlikely keys to the Tomsk facilities were a fur hat and a story of a tailor, the initial clue to the Urals nuclear facilities came from a photo in a Soviet magazine. In August 1958, several months into the overflight ban, Charles V. Reeves showed Henry S. Lowenhaupt a photograph of the Sverdlovsk Central Dispatching Office of the Urals Electrical Power System in the July issue of *Ogonek,* which was the Soviet equivalent of *Look.* On the wall was a schematic diagram of major power stations, electrical lines, and substations. The photo had been subjected to thorough Soviet censorship measures. Names and gauges had been taped over, and the published photo was cropped, so the complete diagram was not visible. And it was not clear whether the photo was of the local Sverdlovsk area or of the whole Urals grid.

Reeves had previously worked at the Boston Edison Company and had controlled power generation and distribution in the Boston area using a similar dispatching station. His job at the CIA was to assemble data on the electrical power production and consumption in the area of Soviet nuclear plants. He suggested to Lowenhaupt that the photograph would indicate the power flow to the nuclear facilities in the Urals. Decrypting the picture took until April 1959 and required the use of 103 Soviet press reports, 11 POW reports, 4 delegation visits, and some 25 photographs of power lines in the Sverdlovsk area. A lucky break came from the Genetrix balloons. The gondola recovered from Adak, Alaska, in 1957 showed power lines in the area to the west and south of Sverdlovsk; a second gondola, recovered in early 1958 "from a watery resting place" in Iceland, showed transmission lines south of the Verkh Neyvinsk area.

Finally, after painstaking work by Reeves, all the pieces finally fell into place. The gaseous diffusion plant at Verkh Neyvinsk had a power supply of 1,000 megawatts plus or minus 15 percent, or about half that of the Oak Ridge facility. The Kyshtym plutonium reactor was estimated to have a power consumption of 150 megawatts, plus or minus 20 percent; about 100 megawatts was apparently consumed by the unknown nuclear complex near Nizhnyaya Tura. His estimate was the basis for planning the Touchdown overflight.

Following Eisenhower's approval, a message was quickly sent to Detachment B that Touchdown was to be flown the following day—July 9, 1959. The pilot selected for Mission 4125 was Marty Knutson, who had originally been with Detachment A and had flown one of the twin Soviet overflights on July 9, 1956. As a diversion for the overflight, a second U-2 took off and flew along the Soviet-Iranian border. The hope was that the Soviets' attention would be focused on this aircraft, allowing Knutson's U-2 to slip across the border undetected.

Knutson successfully took off, crossed into Soviet airspace, and headed north toward the Urals. He approached the Sverdlovsk area from the south, covering the unidentified facility at Nizhnyaya Tura and the Verkh Neyvinsk gaseous diffusion plant. The plutonium reactor at Kyshtym could not be photographed due to cloud cover. Knutson then turned south, covered his targets in Soviet Central Asia, including Tyuratam, then successfully landed at the recovery base.

The photographs from the B camera were judged to be excellent, and they confirmed Reeves's estimates of power consumption from the *Ogonek* photograph. Examination of the U-2 photos showed that he was correct about the substation array at Nizhnyaya Tura, which proved to be a nuclear weapons fabrication and storage site. They also showed that his power estimate of the Verkh Neyvinsk gaseous diffusion plant, based on lines and generation stations, was only 10 percent high, which was remarkable accuracy given the complexity of the analysis. The photographs of Tyuratam also showed interesting developments. The 1957 U-2 missions had shown only a single launch pad at the site. Launch Complex A had been used for all the Sputnik, Luna, and ICBM launches. The Touchdown photos showed that a second, large, rail-serviced launch complex was under construction about ten nautical miles to the east. Launch Complex B was later determined to be the prototype for the operational SS-6 launch pads.

Although Mission 4125 was successful, Eisenhower was unwilling to authorize any further overflights during 1959, due to the still-troubled international situation. Vice President Nixon's July 1959 visit to the USSR was marked by the verbal brawl of the "kitchen debate," and the conference of foreign ministers talks broke down on August 5. Despite these events, Khrushchev was invited to the United States, with the visit scheduled for September 15 to 27. He suspended the peace treaty deadline and hinted that it might be dropped altogether.

As on other occasions, Soviet missile and space activities were used for political ends. Khrushchev, who arrived in the United States three days after the launch of Luna 2, stressed this accomplishment. During private conversations with President Eisenhower, Khrushchev also boasted of Soviet missile capabilities. Eisenhower told Khrushchev that the Berlin situation was "abnormal" and that negotiations over Berlin "should not be prolonged indefinitely." They agreed to a European summit meeting in the spring of 1960 to discuss Germany, followed by a visit to the USSR by Eisenhower later in the year.

Just as important was an issue that was not raised: Khrushchev never mentioned the U-2 overflights. Eisenhower and his advisers concluded that Khrushchev had tacitly accepted the overflights as a peacekeeping tool. They were mistaken; Khrushchev told his son Sergei that he did not bring up the U-2 because it would have been a sign of Soviet weakness. Khrushchev believed that Eisenhower would, yet again, deny that the United States had made the flights. The Soviets would wait until they could finally bring down a U-2.

Although the Luna 2 and 3 flights were what grabbed public attention, the SS-6 ICBM tests had been continuing. The first true production SS-6 was launched on July 31, 1959. The first launch of a fully loaded operational SS-6 followed on October 22. Khrushchev told a press conference in November 1959: "Now we have such a stock of missiles, such an amount of atomic and hydrogen weapons, that if they attack us, we could wipe our potential enemies off the face of the Earth." He continued: "In one year, 250 rockets with hydrogen warheads came off the assembly line in the factory we visited." United States officials placed great weight on his remarks, because the Soviets had been launching an average of one missile per week since the early fall of 1959. To keep track of these missile activities, Eisenhower authorized fourteen U-2 SIGINT border flights during this period.

U-2s over Tibet and RB-57Ds over China

Although the Touchdown mission marked the tentative resumption of Soviet overflights, the bulk of U.S. overflight activities now shifted to China and the surrounding countries of Southeast Asia. This also marked a shift in the nature of the missions the U-2 was undertaking. Rather than the original role of strategic and tactical intelligence, a large part of the

aircraft's activities was now being devoted to support of CIA covert actions in Tibet. Beginning in 1957, the CIA dropped radio operators and arms into Tibet to support a resistance movement.

On January 1, 1959, Bissell replaced Frank Wisner as CIA's deputy director for plans (DDP). As head of the U-2 project, Bissell had opposed the idea of bringing control of all CIA air activities under a single office. As DDP, however, Bissell's opinion soon changed. On February 16, the Development Projects Staff was renamed the Development Projects Division and made part of the Directorate of Plans. Thus, Bissell had personal control of the U-2, the development of the Corona reconnaissance satellite and the A-12 Oxcart Mach 3 reconnaissance aircraft, and added control of aircraft used for support of covert activities, including the Tibetan resistance efforts. Although Bissell's reorganization of CIA air activities was logical in terms of increasing its efficiency, use of the U-2s to support covert action rather than for strategic or tactical reconnaissance disturbed several of Eisenhower's advisers, especially James Killian and Edwin Land. They were worried that Bissell was spending too much time on covert action, to the detriment of the overhead reconnaissance programs.

The U-2 overflights in support of the Tibetan operation began in May 1959. A mission on May 12 covered Tibet and China as well as Laos and North Vietnam. This was followed two days later by another U-2 mission over Tibet and China. The U-2 photos were used to produce the first accurate maps of Tibet. Starting in the spring of 1959, the aircrews and mission planners no longer had to rely on the incomplete charts they had been using during the first two years of the airdrops. A second series of U-2 overflights covering Tibet and China was flown on September 3, 4, and 9. These were followed by another overflight on November 4.

While U-2s were being used to support the covert actions in Tibet, other U-2 missions were being flown against targets in North Vietnam and Laos. The situation in the area was rapidly deteriorating in early 1959, with growing communist guerrilla activities in Laos that were being supported by communist North Vietnam. In July, communist guerrillas began attacking Laotian army posts. The Laotian government declared a state of emergency and on August 25 asked for U.S. military assistance. President Eisenhower replied that the request "was under study as a matter of urgency," and he sent in the U-2s. The first of the 1959 overflights of Tibet, made on May 12, also covered North Vietnam and Laos. After receiving the Laotian government's request, Eisenhower authorized overflights of the area. The first of these was made on August

29, only four days later. The overflight of Tibet made on September 4 also covered targets in Laos. Two more overflights of North Vietnam and Laos were made on September 7 and 12; the November 4 Tibet mission also photographed targets in Burma.

The North Vietnamese Order of Battle was determined from the U-2 photographs, but the interpreters were less successful with activities in Laos. A number of trails were spotted going from North Vietnam into Laos, but it could not be determined if they were being used by the local population, by animals, or by North Vietnamese infiltrators. The heavy jungle hid most activities, and caves in the area could be used by infiltrates and for supplies. For a long time Eisenhower pondered the briefing boards he was shown after the U-2 missions. He specifically referred to the difficulties that the U.S. Army had faced dealing with the Moros in the Philippines early in the century, and the success of Tito's forces in Yugoslavia during World War II. He observed: "In such terrain the advantage clearly lies with the enemy." Although the United States provided aid and advisers to the Laotian and South Vietnamese governments, as well as covert support, Eisenhower did not approve large-scale U.S. involvement.

While the CIA's U-2s were being used over Tibet and North Vietnam, the Nationalist Chinese Air Force was undertaking an extensive overflight program against eastern China, using RB-57Ds. Following the loss of the RB-57A, the deep overflights were halted. The need remained apparent, however, and the United States soon agreed to supply higher-flying RB-57Ds. In early July 1958, the three remaining Nationalist RB-57A pilots were sent to Laughlin Air Force Base for conversion training. The schedule was tight, with only about ninety days of training, but the pilots had few problems. Two more Nationalist pilots were sent to Laughlin for RB-57D training in late 1958.

In early October 1958, soon after the first three Nationalist pilots had completed their training and returned to Taiwan, two RB-57Ds were delivered to Tao Yuan Air Base and repainted with Nationalist Chinese markings. The aircraft had an unusual paint scheme. The underside of the fuselage and wings, as well as the vertical tail, were painted black, and the top of the aircraft was painted white. The normal payload for the RB-57Ds was two split vertical K-38 cameras with a 36-inch lens and a pair of KC-1 oblique cameras in a bay behind the cockpit. One of the airplanes also had provisions to replace the two K-38s with a pair of KA-21 cameras fitted with a 48-inch lens.

With the pilots trained and the RB-57Ds delivered, there remained only the granting of U.S. approval to begin the overflights. The Navy Commander in Chief, Pacific (CINCPAC) requested authority from the Joint Chiefs of Staff to resume overflights of the mainland using the RB-57D. He gave as justification the need for confirmation that no Chinese buildup had taken place opposite Taiwan before U.S. forces in the area were further phased down, and that no high-performance fighters were being based on the mainland. There was also a need for photographic coverage of Chinese installations in order to be prepared should shelling resume.

The CINCPAC noted that such overflights had been made for several years, and if the stand-down in the wake of the RB-57A-1 loss was continued for a prolonged time, "it will become more of an issue than if it is done now as a matter of business as usual." Because the RB-57D had an altitude capability of 66,000 feet, the chances of a loss were virtually nil until the interceptor capability of the PLA Air Force was markedly improved. He noted that although the mainland Chinese were unable to destroy the RB-57Ds, the aircraft would "undoubtedly be detected and tracked." As a result, there could be protests of various types. The CINCPAC's request was subsequently approved.

The first RB-57D overflight of the mainland was made on January 6, 1959, with now Lt. Col. Si-Liang Lu as the pilot. In contrast to the tentative U-2 overflights, the Nationalist RB-57D missions were much more extensive. It was not unusual for two missions to be flown on a single day. Chinese fighters were active but ineffective against the RB-57Ds. During the eleven overflights made between January and March, a total of 202 MiGs were sent after the aircraft. Of these, 106 of the Chinese pilots were able to spot the RB-57Ds. As many as four or five waves of MiGs would be scrambled during an overflight. A Tu-4 bomber was reportedly modified as a flying command post to guide the MiGs, but all the Chinese efforts proved in vain. As the CINCPAC had predicted, the Chinese protested the missions in the *People's Daily* newspaper.

A total of five more RB-57D overflights were made during April, but none were flown during May 1959. The missions resumed on June 14 with the first Nationalist overflight of the area around Peking. The photos taken by Lieutenant Colonel Lu brought back disquieting news. At an airfield about a hundred miles south of Peking, ten MiG-19s were spotted. There were also indications that at least one MiG-19 might have tried to intercept Lu's RB-57D. The MiG-19s had better high-altitude perfor-

mance than the MiG-17 and were, in fact, capable of Mach 1 in level flight. They posed a more credible threat to the RB-57D overflights than had existed before. Despite this possibility, two more overflights were made in June, without mishap.

It was not until October 2, 1959, that the next RB-57D overflight was made. It, along with another mission four days later, was successful. On the morning of October 7, 1959, another overflight began. The RB-57D took off from Tao Yuan, Taiwan, with 1st Lt. Ying-Chin Wang at the controls. This was the twenty-second RB-57D overflight of the mainland, and Wang's sixth. The route was a near-straight flight toward Peking. As the RB-57D flew onward, it was tracked by the radar of a U.S. Navy ship in international waters. As the aircraft neared Peking, the radar showed it beginning to lose speed and altitude. This continued for a lengthy period before the aircraft disappeared. The RB-57D did not return to Taiwan, and Wang was presumed to have been shot down.

The following day, the CIA's Office of Current Intelligence issued a memorandum on the incident. Most of the report dealt with the possibility that the RB-57D had been shot down by a MiG-19. It was noted that "strenuous intercept efforts" had been made against the RB-57D overflight in the past, that high-altitude test flights by the PLA Air Force had been frequent during the previous three weeks, and that there had been two recent attempts at high-altitude interceptions against similar flights. There were, however, no indications of Chinese fighter activities in the area. The CIA report concluded that the loss was unexplained.

But what neither the CIA nor the air force realized was that Wang's RB-57D was the SA-2's first combat kill. Chinese radar picked up his airplane before it crossed the coast. The airplane continued to be tracked as it covered Hangchou, Nanking, and Tsinan and continued toward Peking. Following the Taiwan Straits crisis, five SA-2 SAM battalions were supplied to the Chinese. They were ready for the RB-57D as it neared the city at about noon.

A volley of three SAMs was fired at the aircraft, and one or more exploded nearby, damaging it. The RB-57D began to gradually descend, then crashed. The wreckage was found about eighteen kilometers from the small town of Tung Yuan, located southeast of Peking. The nose of the aircraft was embedded in the ground and the tail was sticking up. The wings had been ripped off and were four hundred to five hundred meters away from the fuselage. The body of First Lieutenant Wang was found about a hundred meters away.

The loss of the aircraft marked the end of the RB-57D overflight program. The surviving aircraft was used for two more border flights rather than deep overflights and was then returned to the United States. Although it may not have been known that the aircraft was shot down by an SA-2, it was clear that the RB-57D could no longer safely make mainland overflights. In late 1959, the first group of Nationalist Chinese Air Force pilots was selected to begin training in the U-2. They were not, however, the first foreign pilots to take the U-2 over a denied area.

The RAF U-2 Overflights: Missions 8005 and 8009

In early 1958, a new participant entered the U-2 program. Bissell had earlier proposed that the U-2 be made a joint program between the United States and Britain. Royal Air Force pilots would be added to the program, and the British prime minister, like the U.S. president, could authorize an overflight. Eisenhower gave his consent, and Bissell approached the RAF, which was eager to become involved in the program. Also eager was the new British prime minster, Harold Macmillan, who wanted to rebuild the special relationship following the debacle of the Suez Crisis. He agreed to Bissell's proposal.

The four RAF U-2 pilots selected were squadron leader Christopher H. Walker and flight lieutenants Michael G. Bradley, David E. Dowling, and John W. MacArthur. All were instructor pilots, single, and in their late twenties. Walker was the unit commander. Unlike the CIA pilots, they were not "sheep dipped" but were RAF pilots temporally "assigned" to the meteorological office. They came to the United States in early 1958 for a series of medical tests and briefings, then reported to Laughlin Air Force Base for U-2 training. MacArthur made his first U-2 training flight on June 3, with Dowling following on June 4. Bradley and Walker made their initial U-2 flights on June 10 and June 12.

The training seemed to be going well, until July 8. On this day, Walker was scheduled for a high-altitude flight. During the afternoon, word was received at Laughlin that the U-2 had crashed near Wayside, Texas, and Walker was dead. By midnight, an investigation team was sent to the crash site, lead by Col. Howard Shidal, the wing's operations officer. They had been at the crash site only a few hours when more bad news was received. During the early-morning hours of July 9, Capt. Alfred B. Chapin, Jr., an air force U-2 pilot also making a high-altitude flight, had been killed in a crash. His aircraft had gone down outside Tucumcari, New Mexico, less

than a hundred miles away from the Walker crash site. Although Walker had made his first U-2 flight only a month before, he had been doing well. Chapin had been flying U-2s for a year and was considered the wing's best pilot. The pattern of the wreckage indicated that both aircraft had broken up at high altitude due to a loss of control. With little to go on, an autopilot failure was suspected, although another possible cause was a failure in the oxygen system.

A new RAF pilot, flight lieutenant Robert T. Robinson, was selected to be Walker's replacement as unit commander. In contrast to the covert recruitment of the CIA U-2 pilots, Robinson's was distressingly public. He was flying a Canberra back to England when he received a radio transmission: "Flight Lieutenant Robinson. Upon landing you are to report immediately to the Vice-Chief of the Air Staff at the Air Ministry." Robinson was alarmed by the message, because pilots were never called by name over the radio. His initial reaction was, my God, what have I done?

The vice chief of the air staff was not very forthcoming. Robinson was told only that he was to go immediately to the United States, that he would be flying a very-high-altitude aircraft, and that he would be operating it in Europe. He was also being promoted to squadron leader. Not until Robinson met with CIA officials in Washington, D.C., did he learn about the U-2 program. He spent the next two weeks traveling to the Lovelace Clinic in New Mexico to undergo medical tests, to the David Clark Company in Massachusetts to be fitted with the partial-pressure suit, and finally to a CIA facility in Virginia for escape and evasion training.

Then Robinson reported to Laughlin Air Force Base. After completing the lengthy ground school, he made his first U-2 flight on September 29, 1958. He later recalled: "I must admit that on the first flight, I wouldn't exactly say I got a fright, but it was much harder than I expected." The three other RAF pilots, Bradley, Dowling, and MacArthur, had by now completed their training and been sent to Detachment B in Turkey. Robinson followed in January 1959. Although no Soviet overflights were being made, the RAF pilots took their turns flying missions over the Middle East and making the SIGINT border flights.

As the RAF pilots were becoming involved in the U-2 program, the aircraft were undergoing a series of modifications. The most obvious was the new paint scheme. To hide the U-2 from MiGs performing the zoom-climb maneuver, it was suggested that camouflage paint be applied to the aircraft. In late 1957, Lockheed ran a series of tests at Edwards Air Force Base and began using a two-tone finish of blue-black on top and light

blue on the underside. Additional tests indicated that an overall matte blue-black finish was more effective for hiding the U-2 against the black sky at high altitude. Another addition was a lightweight ejection seat. This was deemed necessary due to the fatal high-altitude accidents.

As a result of these changes, the U-2 altitude capability was reduced; the weight and drag of the sinister-looking black paint alone cost 250 feet. Studies were done in 1958 of equipping one U-2 with the larger Pratt & Whitney J-75 engine. These were in short supply, and the initial engines came from the canceled Martin Seamaster flying boat program. A total of nine J-75–P-2 engines were obtained and converted to the J-75–P-13 configuration. After a three-month test flight program, the first J-75-powered U-2 was declared operational. The engine produced an added 4,200 pounds of thrust and added only 2,050 pounds to the aircraft. Even with the added weight of the engine and equipment, the U-2 could now fly at 74,600 feet, a 2,500-foot increase over the original J-57-powered aircraft. The new version was designated the U-2C. The new aircraft had much different handling characteristics. Under some flight conditions, as little as four knots separated the Mach limit and stall buffet.

The first of the reengined aircraft, Article 360, was delivered to Detachment C in Japan during July 1959. Detachment B at Incirlik received two U-2Cs in August 1959. On September 24, 1959, Detachment C pilot Tom Crull took Article 360 up for a test flight. The U-2C was carrying a camera but no film and had a lighter than normal fuel load. Crull decided to attempt to set a new altitude record. He succeeded; but in the process, more fuel was used than the flight plan had allowed for. The airplane flamed out ten miles short of NAS Atsugi, and Crull was forced to make a wheels-up, dead stick landing on a glider club's airstrip outside Fijisawa. The U-2 skidded along the runway, then slid into the grass. Crull was not injured, nor was Article 360 seriously damaged, but the problems were only beginning.

Within a minute, the U-2 was surrounded by a crowd of Japanese civilians. Crull stayed in the cockpit until Detachment C security personnel, wearing Hawaiian shirts and carrying large pistols, arrived from Atsugi. Their heavy-handed efforts to protect the airplane drew the attention of Japanese reporters, and photos of the U-2 appeared in newspapers and magazines. Article 360 was dismantled and returned to Lockheed for repairs.

The RAF pilots had been in Turkey for a year before Prime Minster Harold Macmillan finally authorized an overflight of the USSR. It was

to cover targets in the Ukraine, and the pilot selected to fly it was Robert Robinson. Mission 8005 was flown on December 6, 1959, using Article 351, the same U-2 flown by Stockman on his October 13, 1957, mission. One of the primary targets was the Kapustin Yar missile test range; another was the Soviet long-range air force bomber arsenal at Saratov Engels airfield. The base was located north of Kapustin Yar, along the Volga River. The city of Kuybyshev, farther to the northeast, was also covered. The photo that Robinson was most proud of was of an aircraft factory. The flight plan required that he fly exactly down a specific road in a town. This was necessary because the airframe plant was on one side of the road and the engine factory was on the other side. Robinson was able to film both targets. He landed safely, and the mission was considered a success.

Mission 8005 also settled whatever doubt remained about the bomber gap. When the photos from the B camera were examined, they showed some thirty Bisons lined up wingtip to wingtip at the Saratov Engels airfield. This represented nearly the entire force of Mya-4s. The airfield also had nuclear weapon loading pits. There was a single runway; the Bisons were lined up along a taxi strip. The photo was subsequently shown to DCI Dulles by Lundahl and Bissell. Despite the accomplishments of the U-2 program, Dulles still saw its results with the eyes of a case officer, in terms of human spies. As Dulles looked at the photo, he lit his pipe, took several deeps puffs, then turned to Frank Wisner, who had previously directed the CIA's covert operations. "How much would you have paid for the information in this photograph?" Dulles asked. Wisner thought for a few moments, then said, "About a million dollars." Dulles subsequently called it the "million-dollar photo."

It was not bombers, however, but Soviet ICBMs that were the focus of U.S. concern. In November 1959, a new National Intelligence Estimate was issued on the Soviet missile program. The United States estimated that about eighteen SS-6 tests had been conducted and that a high percentage had reached the impact zone on the Kamchatka Peninsula. The estimate concluded that, based on the recent firing activities, the Soviets were proceeding in an orderly fashion rather than on a "crash" basis. United States intelligence did not know when serial production of SS-6s began and had not identified operational launch sites. Given the status of the test program, the United States assumed that deployment had begun. For planning proposes, it was assumed that the first ten SS-6s would be operational on January 1, 1960.

Although the estimate indicated a less threatening situation, the missile gap controversy flared anew in January 1960. In their testimony before the Senate, DCI Dulles, Secretary of Defense Thomas Gates, and air force chief of staff Nathan Twining all gave differing figures for the number of deployed Soviet ICBMs. This led to sharp questioning of Dulles, who could not disclose that the information was based on U-2 overflights. Many congressmen believed that the new estimate was an effort to downplay the missile gap and justify an inadequate defense policy. Senator Stuart Symington was predictably critical, saying on January 26 that "the intelligence books have been juggled so that the budget books can be balanced."

The rough handling that Dulles received from Congress left him determined to obtain permission from Eisenhower for more overflights in order to settle the missile gap question. To do this required flying U-2 missions over areas where ICBM deployment was suspected. Although several possible areas had been identified, the information was general, such as reports that certain areas had been placed off-limits to civilians. The SS-6 was so large that analysts believed it would be deployed close to rail lines. Dulles suggested that the easiest way to find any deployed missiles was to have the U-2s cover Soviet rail lines.

Dulles received the backing of the President's Board of Consultants on Foreign Intelligence Activities. In a February 2, 1960, meeting with Eisenhower, Gen. James Doolittle proposed that overflights be used to the maximum extent possible. Eisenhower replied that this was one of the most "soul-searching" decisions a president had to make. He was also thinking of the upcoming Paris Summit meeting. General Goodpaster's notes of the meeting stated, "The president said that he has one tremendous asset in a summit meeting, as regards effect in the free world. That is his reputation for honesty. If one of these airplanes were lost when we are engaged in apparently sincere deliberations, it could be put on display in Moscow and ruin the president's effectiveness."

Although Eisenhower was not willing to send the U-2 hunting for ICBM sites, Harold Macmillan was. On February 10, 1960, Mission 8009 took off to cover suspected missile sites in the southern USSR. The pilot was John MacArthur. When the photos were analyzed, they failed to show a single missile. In the coverage of Kazan, a new Soviet supersonic jet light bomber, the Tu-98 Backfin was spotted. The aircraft did not enter production, however. Mission 8009 was the second, and last, British U-2 overflight.

Operation Topper

Although Mission 8009 found no missiles, the missile gap question itself remained open. The controversy, and the deep divisions within U.S. intelligence that it generated, continued. The air force believed that the Soviets could have as many as a hundred ICBMs; the army and navy argued that the Soviets had few or no ICBMs deployed. The CIA split the difference. Soviet ICBM tests were also continuing. Between early November 1959 and the spring of 1960, an additional seven generally successful SS-6 tests were made, including two into the Pacific over a distance of 6,500 nautical miles. This brought the total number to twenty-five launches.

It was clear that additional U-2 overflights were required, both to resolve the missile gap controversy and to support the Tibetan resistance efforts. In mid-February 1960, Eisenhower approved a package of four overflights. Three were to cover China and Tibet and be flown by Detachment C under the designation Operation Topper. The fourth, flown by Detachment B and planned for March, was to be over the Soviet Union. Despite the approval of a single Soviet overflight, Dulles was still unhappy with the restrictions that Eisenhower placed on U-2 operations. On March 1, 1960, he sent a memorandum to the National Security Council arguing that the objective of gaining more intelligence on Soviet missile deployment could best be achieved by freer use of the U-2.

The first two Operation Topper missions were flown on March 30, 1960. One covered Tibet and the other covered Tibet and western China. Both were successful. The third mission, made on April 4, also produced good photographs but fell victim to a minor technical problem that almost destroyed the aircraft. When Article 349 took off, the landing-gear doors failed to close completely. This caused drag and increased fuel consumption. The pilot completed the mission, but the aircraft ran out of fuel well short of the recovery field. The pilot was forced to make a belly landing in a rice paddy in Thailand. The site was inaccessible to large vehicles, and the U-2 had to be disassembled with the help of local villagers. It was taken to an air base and loaded aboard a C-124 under the cover of darkness. In appreciation for the help with the recovery, the village was given money to build a new school.

As the Tibetan overflights were being prepared, the Soviet overflight was being planned. It had now been more than eight months since the last American overflight, the Touchdown mission in July 1959. The long

intervals between Soviet overflights were beginning to have an effect on morale. For some of the U-2 pilots, there was a sense that time was running out. Bob Ericson later recalled: “I thought that, hey, they are going to push this thing to the bitter end, they lose one, and that would end the whole program. And that was the way I kind of accepted that. That hopefully, it would not be me.” Francis Gary Powers also later recalled: “The longer the layoff, the greater the tension. The fewer the overflights, the more apprehensive we became about the next one.”

The Soviets were now firing SA-2s at the U-2s. Powers recalled that some of the SAMs were coming close to the U-2’s altitude but could not be accurately controlled due to the thin air at high altitude. For this reason, he was not overly concerned. Efforts were made to route the U-2 overflights around known SAM sites. The CIA also asked in early 1960 for an assessment by the air force’s Air Technical Intelligence Center (ATIC) of Soviet air defense capabilities against the U-2.

On March 14, this was sent to Bissell. It stated: “The greatest threat posed to the U-2 is the Soviet SAM. Although the ATIC analysis concedes a remote possibility that the SAM may be less effective than estimated, their present evaluation is that the SAM (Guideline) has a high probability of successful interception at 70,000 feet providing that detection is made in sufficient time to alert the site.”

Square Deal

When Eisenhower approved the Soviet overflight in mid-February, he had placed a March 30 cutoff date for the mission. Arranging the use of the airfield at Peshawar, Pakistan, ran into complications, and Mission 4155, code-named Square Deal, could not be flown by the March deadline. The president agreed to an extension of the cutoff date to April 10, 1960.

On April 9, one day before the deadline, Bob Ericson took off from Peshawar. As had been done with recent overflights, a second U-2 made a diversionary mission along the Soviet-Iranian border. After crossing into Soviet airspace, Ericson’s first target was the SAM and antiballistic missile (ABM) test site at Sary Shagan. The U-2 then headed toward the Semipalatinsk nuclear test site and the nearby bomber base and nuclear storage area at Dolon.

Despite earlier expectations, Ericson’s U-2 was picked up; by the time he was nearing the Semipalatinsk area, Soviet air defenses were at full

alert. A pair of Su-9 fighters equipped with air-to-air missiles was ready to intercept the U-2, but the Soviet bureaucracy foiled the attempt. The Su-9 pilots calculated that their fighters would be too low on fuel to land back at their base. Instead, they would be forced to land at the Semipalatinsk airfield. This was a closed area, and special permission was needed for the landing. By the time that permission was given, Ericson had flown several legs over the test site and was out of range.

Having covered Semipalatinsk and Dolon, the U-2 headed back toward Sary Shagan, where it crisscrossed the area to photograph railroad lines. Sary Shagan was protected by SA-2 sites, but again Soviet errors permitted the U-2 to escape. The SAM missiles had been removed from their launchers during a training stand-down. By the time they were reloaded, Ericson had come and gone.

Ericson then flew west and photographed Tyuratam. Yet again, Soviet Su-9 fighters had a chance at the U-2. They were at a nearby airbase, although they were not fully operational. Hurriedly, two Su-9s were armed, one with missiles taken from a MiG-19, and scrambled. Due to the inexperience of the pilots and their ground controllers, they were unable to make an interception. Soviet radar continued to track the U-2 at an altitude estimated to be 68,000 feet as it covered the city of Mary, then finally left Soviet airspace over Iran. Ericson landed at the Zahedan airfield in Iran after more than six hours in the air.

Khrushchev ordered that a commission be established to investigate why the Soviet Air Force and the PVO failed to bring down Ericson's U-2. Their investigation showed serious shortcomings in air combat training, in the command and control of air force and PVO personnel and weapons, and in the use of radio equipment. Perhaps the most serious failure was in Soviet SIGINT. A Soviet ground station in the Transcaucasus had intercepted radio communications regarding the overflight several days before it occurred. Due to various chance events, the information was not reported to higher authorities before the flight. Khrushchev was furious at what the commission uncovered, and a number of generals and other senior officers were severely reprimanded.

To avoid another failure, the PVO main staff charted the anticipated routes that future U-2 overflights might take. The previous four overflights had covered targets in the southern USSR, Soviet Central Asia, and Siberia. Since the Soft Touch missions in 1957, research and development facilities in these areas had become the focus of U-2 activities. The missions had all been flown into or out of Pakistan and Iran. With an idea

of where the U-2s would be coming from, what targets they would be covering, and where they would be headed, their flight paths could be predicted.

The CIA was also assessing the results of Square Deal. The intelligence results from the B camera photos were superb. Although ABM activities at Sary Shagan had been suspected for some time, few of those who saw the photos from Square Deal were prepared for the scale of what they showed. There were dozens of separate facilities scattered across an area about the size of the state of New Jersey.

Ericson had taken the first photographs of two new Soviet ABM radar sites, the Hen House and the Hen Roost. The sites were on the western shore of Lake Balkhash and looked out across the Sary Shagan complex toward the Kapustin Yar launch site. Both sites had fixed antennas of staggering size. The Hen House antenna building was more than nine hundred feet long and fifty feet high. The Hen Roost was actually two antennas that were each more than five hundred feet long. The northern Hen Roost antenna, which acted as the receiver, was about sixty-five feet tall; the southern transmitting antenna was only fifteen feet tall. The two antennas were separated by more than half a mile. In subsequent years, the Hen House was deployed around the USSR, and the Hen Roost served as the prototype of the Dog House ABM radar built later around Moscow.

Although the Hen House and Hen Roost radar sites showed the level of defensive activities that the Soviets were undertaking, the Square Deal photos of Tyuratam showed that an expansion of the Soviet ICBM program was under way. In addition to the SS-6 pads at Launch Complexes A and B, construction was under way on a new two-pad, road-serviced facility. Launch Complex C was thought to be for a new, second-generation ICBM. It was later used for test launches of the SS-7 ICBM, which was given the NATO code name Saddler. It was a much lighter weight ICBM that used storable propellants and could be kept ready for launch for a prolonged period.

Although the Square Deal photos showed the value of the U-2, the data from the System-V SIGINT package also indicated its growing vulnerability. One of the reasons that the Mission 4155 flight route was selected for the March overflight was because the mission planners believed that entering Soviet airspace from Pakistan offered the best chance to avoid detection. Despite this, the U-2 had been picked up and tracked by Soviet radar from an early stage of the flight. Bissell was told

on April 26, 1960, that the Square Deal mission indicated that penetrating Soviet airspace without detection from Pakistan would not be as easy in the future as it had been in the past. Despite this, the need for intelligence, the political pressure of the missile gap, and Dulles's support for more overflights meant that the program would be pushed to the bitter end.

The Last Overflight

On March 28, 1960, even before the Square Deal mission was flown, Eisenhower gave his approval for another Soviet overflight to be made. Any doubts he may have had were eased when the Soviets did not protest the April 9 mission. The impression from the Camp David meeting, that the Soviets accepted the U-2 overflights, was reenforced. Presidential science adviser George Kistiakowsky later said, "This was virtually inviting us to repeat the sortie."

Although Eisenhower had given his authorization to make the overflight, he left the specific flight plan up to the CIA. Three possibilities emerged, all of which were to look for operational ICBM sites. The first was designated Operation Sun Spot and would cover targets in the southern USSR, such as Tyuratam and Vladimirovka. There seems to have been little interest in this mission, perhaps because the area had already been well covered. The CIA's attention was on the northern USSR. In late 1959, evidence began to mount that the Soviets were building an operational SS-6 facility in this area. The CIA was eager to obtain photographs of an operational SS-6 site to allow the interpreters to spot similar facilities in later overhead imagery.

Two different plans were proposed to cover the northern and central railroads. The first was Operation Time Step. This involved the U-2 taking off from the air force base at Thule, Greenland, overflying the nuclear test site at Novaya Zemlya, then continuing on to cover the rail lines between the Polyarnyy Ural Mountains and Kotlas. The aircraft would exit Soviet airspace in the Murmansk area before landing at Andoya, Norway.

Problems with the Time Step plan were soon apparent. The overflight was likely to run into bad weather, affecting both navigation and photography, because the entire route was above sixty degrees north latitude. A more serious problem was the risk of the flight itself. Whereas the Homerun RB-47 overflights of the USSR in early 1956 had shown that

the whole northern coast of the USSR was virtually undefended, this was not true four years later.

The new Soviet radar network in the Arctic was detected using the most unique SIGINT systems ever devised. Rather than picking up the signals from an aircraft, the signals were received on Earth after being reflected from the Moon. Passive moon relay (PAMOR), or, more commonly, Moonbounce, was the idea of Jim Trexler of the Naval Research Laboratory. Picking up radar signals bounced off the Moon was a demanding task. Due to the half-million-mile round-trip, the radar signals were a million billion times weaker than if they had been picked up by an airplane ten miles away.

The Moonbounce system went into operation in 1957. The 150-foot dish-antenna was built at the Chesapeake Bay Annex of the Naval Research Laboratory. Soon after, it began picking up strong signals in the 160-MHz band from a powerful, new Soviet long-range, early-warning radar, later given the code name Tall King. The radar used a hundred-foot-wide rotating antenna that could pick up a high-flying aircraft at a distance of up to six hundred kilometers. The Moonbounce system was able to pinpoint the location and deployment of the Tall King radar sites in the Arctic.

By early 1960, it was clear from the Moonbounce SIGINT data that the Soviet Arctic was well covered by Tall King. An assessment sent to Bissell on March 14 stated: "Operation 'Time Step' is our last choice because we can assume, with a 90 percent probability of being correct, that we will be detected on entry, tracked accurately throughout the period in denied territory (approximately four hours), and will evoke a strong PVO reaction. This flight plan would permit alerting of SAM sites, and prepositioning of missile equipped fighters in the Murmansk area (point of exit) thus enhancing the possibility of successful intercept. In addition, we must assume that even were the Soviets unable to physically interfere with such an incursion, sufficient evidence will be available to permit them to document a diplomatic protest should they desire to do so."

The third possibility, Mission 4154, was the most ambitious U-2 overflight ever. The idea had been developing ever since the initial overflights showed the U-2's capabilities. Rather than a limited penetration, the U-2 would fly across the whole width of the USSR. Secretary of State Herter had mentioned his interest in such a flight during the discussions about the Touchdown overflight. There were still doubts about the possibility at that time. By early 1960, however, these doubts had faded. The flight,

which was given the code name Grand Slam, now seemed the best possibility for finally photographing operational Soviet ICBM sites.

The takeoff was from Peshawar, Pakistan, with the first targets being Tyuratam and portions of the rail lines north of Aralsk. The next objectives were the industrial and nuclear facilities in the Urals. These included Chelyabinsk, the Soviet plutonium-production facilities at Kyshtym, which had not been photographed during the Touchdown mission due to clouds, then Sverdlovsk. The U-2 would turn northwest to photograph the railroads west of Perm, then Kirov. The next targets were two suspected ICBM sites at Yurya and Plesetsk, in the central and northeastern USSR. The final part of the flight would cover the shipyards at Severodvinsk, where Soviet nuclear submarines were built, then cross the White Sea to follow the railroad lines to the naval bases of Murmansk and Polyarnyy. The U-2 would leave Soviet airspace, fly around the tip of Norway's North Cape, and land at Bodo, Norway.

The Grand Slam flight was 3,800 miles long, with 2,900 miles over the USSR, and would take some nine hours to complete. The flight was theoretically within the capabilities of the U-2, but its pilot would have to follow the planned fuel and altitude schedule exactly. There were also the risks from Soviet air defenses. The Square Deal overflight had been tracked, and there was little reason to believe that Grand Slam would escape detection. More important, once the U-2 left the Tyuratam area and started north, it would be easy for the Soviets to predict that the industrial and nuclear facilities in the Urals would be the next targets. As with Time Step, this would allow the Soviets to alert SAM sites so they would be ready for the U-2's arrival. Due to Grand Slam's long flight path, it was not possible to add evasive maneuvers, such as the zigzag flight path of Square Deal. Many of the same objections to Time Step could be made about Mission 4154 but were not, and Grand Slam was selected.

Grand Slam

Francis Gary Powers was selected as the pilot for Grand Slam. Since 1956, he had made a total of twenty-seven operational flights: one overflight of the USSR, an overflight of China, six SIGINT missions along the Soviet border, and nineteen special missions over the Middle East. He had also served as backup pilot for Ericson on the Square Deal overflight. He was considered the most skilled pilot at long-range navigation; something the Grand Slam mission required.

As with the previous overflight, Grand Slam ran into delays. The first was due to Norwegian military maneuvers. Bissell informed the White House that the overflight could not be made until April 19, 1960. The maneuvers ended, but several weeks of bad weather over the northern USSR delayed the mission further, and Bissell asked President Eisenhower for a time extension. On April 25, General Goodpaster called Bissell and told him that "one additional operation may be undertaken, providing it is carried out prior to May 1. No operation is to be carried out after May 1." Eisenhower did not want the U-2 to fly after May Day, because this was too close to the Paris Summit meeting, which was scheduled to open on May 16.

Finally, the weather appeared to clear over the northern USSR, and on April 27, the day before the Grand Slam overflight was to be made, a C-130 took off from Incirlik. Aboard were Powers and his backup pilot, as well as the detachment commander, navigator, intelligence officer, doctor, crew chief, mechanics, camera and electronics technicians, and the radio operators who would receive the final approval for the flight. The transport landed at the airfield at Peshawar, Pakistan, and the ground crew set up in a remote hangar. Accommodations were primitive; the crew slept on cots and cooked their own rations.

For this overflight, a new procedure was used. Rather than bringing the U-2 to the base and leaving it there until the overflight was made, it would be flown to Peshawar the night before. The aircraft would then be refueled and the B camera loaded in preparation for an early-morning takeoff. The U-2 would be on the ground only six hours. Due to darkness and the short stay, there would be little chance that any Pakistanis would see the aircraft and possibly report its presence. If the overflight were delayed for some reason, the U-2 would fly back to Incirlik before sunrise. The U-2C selected for Grand Slam was the best aircraft assigned to Detachment B, and Powers had complete trust in it.

Powers went to bed at 4:00 P.M., but the hangar was hot and noisy and he got little sleep. While he tossed and turned that evening, the U-2 was flown in and serviced. Powers was awakened at 2:00 A.M. on April 28 and was dressing when a message arrived that the flight would be delayed twenty-four hours. Weather over the northern USSR was poor. The U-2 took off for the flight back to Incirlik before dawn. That afternoon, Powers again went to bed early, then was awakened at 2:00 A.M. on April 29. He had already started the prebreathing when the mission was again delayed twenty-four hours. The U-2 was again flown back to Incirlik. The

bad weather continued, and there was no attempt to make the overflight on April 30. By that afternoon, conditions over the northern USSR had improved, and another attempt was planned.

Grand Slam was almost out of time. The next day, May 1, 1960, was the last chance that Mission 4154 could be flown under Eisenhower's deadline. The plan to hide the U-2's presence at Peshawar had also backfired. The two round-trips on April 27 and 28 meant that the original U-2 scheduled for the overflight now had to be grounded for its periodic maintenance inspection. On the night of April 30, Bob Ericson flew a replacement airplane to Peshawar. The aircraft was U-2C Article 360, and it did not have Powers's complete trust.

After Article 360's belly landing on the Japanese glider strip, it had been sent back to Lockheed's Burbank plant for repairs. At the same time, one of Detachment B's U-2s was sent to Lockheed for maintenance. Once work on Article 360 was finished, it was sent to Detachment B as a replacement. Powers later called the aircraft a "dog," recalling that there always seemed to be some problem with it. Article 360's current idiosyncrasy was in one of the fuel tanks, which occasionally did not feed all its fuel.

Powers was again awakened at 2:00 A.M., ate breakfast, and began the prebreathing. He and the backup pilot had no need for additional briefing, because they had both studied the map and knew the route. The U-2C had been fueled to capacity, but the long distance of the flight and the possible fuel tank problem were in the back of everyone's minds. The unit commander, Col. William M. Shelton, suggested that if the airplane ran low on fuel, Powers should cut across Finland and Sweden to reduce the flight time of the final legs of the mission.

As Powers was suiting up, Colonel Shelton asked, "Do you want the silver dollar?" This was the replacement for the L-pill. In January 1960, the previous Detachment B commander wondered what would happen if the L-pill broke inside the U-2's cockpit. (The same question had occurred to Powers several years before.) The program manager, James Cunningham, realized that the volatile potassium cyanide would kill the pilot. Cunningham ordered the L-pills destroyed and a replacement developed. It looked like a standard straight pin. The body of the pin was actually a sheath, which covered a finer needle smeared with algal, an extremely powerful shellfish toxin. The pin was hidden inside a small hole drilled into a silver dollar, which Cunningham had supplied. The silver dollar had a loop attached at one end, which was unscrewed to re-

trieve the pin. The pilot had only to stick himself with the pin to cause death. Powers and the other pilots were fascinated by the device, which looked like a good luck charm.

Powers had not carried the L-pill on his two overflights, and before Colonel Shelton had asked, he had not wanted the silver dollar. But this flight was different, because he did not have full confidence that Article 360 could get him across the USSR. Powers replied, "Okay," and Colonel Shelton tossed him the silver dollar. Powers slipped it into his outer flight suit pocket. At about 5:20 A.M., Powers climbed into Article 360 with Ericson's help and was strapped in. The morning was blazing hot as Powers completed the preflight checklist. Takeoff was scheduled for 6:00 A.M., but when the time came, there was no signal.

The delay was due to problems relaying the authorization message from Incirlik to Peshawar. The Incirlik radio operator found that neither the prearranged daytime nor nighttime frequencies were working. This was a common problem at sunrise during the spring and fall, when the ionosphere does not support radio transmissions reliably. As the delay dragged on, Colonel Shelton went out to the airplane and told Powers about the problem. By this time, Powers was sure that the overflight would again be canceled. All the sextant measurements had been computed on the basis of a 6:00 A.M. takeoff time. With the delay, they were now useless. Powers was also extremely uncomfortable; he had been in the U-2 for nearly an hour, and the morning heat was causing him to sweat profusely. If the delay continued much longer, Powers would have to be replaced by the backup pilot, John Shinn.

Finally, the radio operator at Incirlik began sending the message in the clear on one of the guard frequencies, between the daytime and nighttime frequencies. The Peshawar radio operators had been hearing Morse transmissions as they tuned from one of the assigned frequencies to the other, but they were unreadable. Finally, one of them decided to try the guard frequencies where the signals were strongest. He was finally able to detect a break in the letters and realized that it was the authorization message. Colonel Shelton, who had been waiting for the go/no go message, leaped from the radio van and ran across the field to give Powers the signal to take off.

As Ericson closed the canopy, Powers yelled his thanks and locked it from the inside; the ladder was pulled away and the engine was started. At 6:26 A.M. local time, Powers and Article 360 roared down the Peshawar runway and made the steep ascent into the sky. Once airborne, Powers

turned toward the Afghanistan border. Once the U-2 reached the penetration altitude of 66,000 feet, Powers clicked the radio switch once, to indicate that the flight was going well and he would proceed as planned. A single click from Ericson came as acknowledgment. Grand Slam, the twenty-fourth U-2 overflight of the USSR, was under way.

As had been done on the previous overflights, another U-2 made a diversionary mission along the Soviet-Iranian border. This was to draw off Soviet attention, to allow Powers's U-2 to slip into Soviet airspace undetected. But this time the attempt did not work; Powers's U-2 was spotted by Soviet radar while it was still fifteen miles south of the Soviet-Afghan border. An alert was called, and PVO staff officers were summoned to their command post at the Defense Ministry in Moscow. May Day proved to be a poor choice for the overflight. Due to the national holiday, there was less military air traffic than normal, and it was easier to pick up and track the U-2. In addition, the Soviet authorities had ordered the grounding of airliners over much of the USSR.

For the first hour and a half of the overflight, Powers flew above a solid bank of clouds. The atmosphere at the Defense Ministry, airfields, command posts, SAM sites, and radar stations was extremely tense. Marshal S. S. Biryuzov, commander in chief of the PVO, received several irate telephone calls from Khrushchev and other senior leaders. They were furious that the PVO was unable to cope with a single subsonic aircraft. Marshal Biryuzov replied emotionally, "If I could become a missile, I myself would fly and down this damned intruder."

The initial attempts to down Powers's U-2 proved ineffective. As it flew over the Tashkent area, as many as thirteen Soviet fighters scrambled in unsuccessful attempts to intercept the U-2. A SA-2 battalion along the flight path was not on alert duty, so it could not fire. The U-2's route was such that it initially did not seem that a successful SA-2 launch would be possible, and the fighters were unable to get into position for zoom-climb attacks. The U-2 was periodically lost on radar, then reacquired. This made tracking difficult and raised the tension level.

The first break in the clouds did not appear until the U-2 was southeast of the Aral Sea. Powers found that he had drifted slightly to the right of the planned route, and he corrected his course. Far below, he saw the contrail of a supersonic fighter going in the opposite direction. A few minutes later, he saw another contrail but this time on the same heading as the U-2. Powers now knew that he was being tracked, because the Soviet fighter was being vectored by ground radar. Ahead was Tyuratam,

but there were large thunderheads over the launch complexes. Powers turned on the B camera and photographed the surrounding area. After he left the Tyuratam area, the clouds closed in again. It was not until three hours into the flight that they began to thin. Powers was able to see a small town, and he tuned the radio compass to the local radio station. He was slightly off course, and he corrected again.

By this time, the Moscow command post was predicting that the U-2 was heading toward the Sverdlovsk area. Khrushchev was notified at 8:00 A.M. Moscow time, as he was preparing to leave for the May Day parade. He demanded that the U-2 be brought down, regardless of the cost. He viewed the overflight on a Soviet holiday, and two weeks before the Paris Summit, as a political provocation.

The clouds finally cleared as the U-2 was about fifty miles south of Chelyabinsk. To the west were the Ural Mountains. They were still snow covered, whereas the surrounding areas were green with spring growth. With the clouds behind him and the U-2 on course, Powers began to relax a little. It was then that Article 360 began to have problems. The autopilot malfunctioned, causing the aircraft to pitch nose up. Powers disengaged the autopilot, retrimmed the airplane, and hand-flew it for several minutes. He then reengaged the autopilot. The plane flew normally for ten to fifteen minutes, but the problem recurred. Powers went through the same process but this time left the autopilot disengaged.

Powers now faced an abort situation; if he continued, he would have to hand-fly the aircraft the rest of the way across the USSR. Even with the autopilot functioning, the airplane required his full attention. Hand-flying the U-2 would make a difficult mission even harder. But the aircraft was close to the midway point in the overflight, and visibility ahead looked excellent. Powers decided to keep going.

He covered Chelyabinsk, then turned due north to photograph the Kyshtym plutonium production facilities. The next part of the flight route was to the northeast. During this time, the U-2 was the subject of an extraordinary attack. A brand-new Su-9 fighter was at Kaitsova airfield, near Sverdlovsk, on a delivery flight to its assigned regiment. The fighter had no missiles, and its pilot, a Captain Mitjajin, did not have the pressure suit needed at high altitudes. Despite this, he was ordered to take off and ram the U-2 with his fighter. The chances of actually hitting the U-2 were slight, and Captain Mitjajin's odds of surviving the collision were nil. Nevertheless, the captain made a zoom climb, although he was unable to spot the black-painted U-2.

Powers, unaware of the planned attack, was now about thirty to forty miles southeast of Sverdlovsk. He made a ninety-degree left turn, then rolled out on a new heading that would take him across the southwestern edge of the city. He began recording the various instrument readings in his flight log. His U-2 was flying at 70,500 feet and had entered the engagement zone of an SA-2 battalion outside Sverdlovsk. The unit commander, Maj. M. R. Voronov, gave the order "Destroy target," and one SA-2 SAM roared off its launch rail.

As Powers was writing in the log, he heard a dull "thump" and felt the U-2 being jerked forward. A brilliant orange flash illuminated the sky and the inside of the cockpit. This was from the explosion of the SAM below and behind the U-2. Powers began checking the instruments; all the readings appeared normal. The right wing then began to droop. Powers turned the control wheel, and it leveled out. Then, very slowly, the aircraft began to nose down. Powers pulled back on the control yoke, but the airplane's nose continued to drop. The nearby blast from the SAM's warhead had damaged the airplane's right stabilizer, which then broke off. The U-2 flipped over on its back, which broke off both wings.

The fuselage began to spin, with its nose pointed upward. Powers was thrown forward in the cockpit by the g forces, making it impossible to use the ejection seat. The cockpit had also depressurized, and Powers's suit inflated. He finally released the canopy, then his seat belt, and was immediately thrown halfway out of the cockpit. His faceplate frosted over, and he could see nothing. The g forces were too strong for him to climb back into the cockpit, and he could not reach around the windshield to activate the switches on the destruct package. Realizing that the effort was useless, Powers tried to kick free of the aircraft. He finally broke the oxygen hoses that held him to the airplane and was thrown clear.

Powers's parachute opened automatically at 15,000 feet, and he removed his faceplate. In the distance, he could see part of the U-2, possibly a wing, falling like a fluttering leaf. Below was a small village; he was coming down in a populated area. Powers tore up a map that showed routes back to Turkey and Pakistan, then took out the silver dollar, removed the pin and hid it in the pocket of his outer flight suit, and threw away the silver dollar. As Powers descended, he thought seriously for a moment of using the pin, but he still hoped to escape.

Powers landed in a plowed field about twenty-five feet from two men and a tractor. As they helped Powers to his feet, two more men arrived from a car driving nearby. The village was less than a hundred yards away,

and suddenly Powers saw twenty to thirty schoolchildren running toward them, followed by a like number of adults. Powers never had a chance to escape.

At first, no one in either Moscow or Sverdlovsk realized that the U-2 had been destroyed. The initial reports to the Moscow command post said that a missile had been fired, and then that the target "began to blink," as if it was jamming the radar. The radar screens at Sverdlovsk were filled with returns from falling debris from the U-2. The radar operators though they were caused by chaff being dropped by the U-2 and assumed that the airplane was undamaged. Sharing their confusion were two MiG-19 pilots from Kaitsova. They had seen the first SAM explode but thought it was self-destructing after missing the target. Finally, a target blip appeared on radar, which was immediately engaged by another SA-2 battalion. A SAM volley was fired, and a direct hit was scored on one of the MiG-19s. Its pilot, Senior Lt. Yuri Safronov, was killed. In all, eight SA-2s were reportedly fired during the engagement. Soon after the MiG-19 was destroyed, the radar screens cleared and it was realized that the U-2 had been shot down. Marshal Biryuzov telephoned Khrushchev with the news.

Cover Stories

Even before Powers was overdue at Bodo, Norway, there were indications that something had gone wrong. The CIA Operations Center in Washington, D.C., learned at 3:30 A.M. on May 1 that the Soviets had discontinued tracking the U-2 at a point southwest of Sverdlovsk two hours before. The CIA officials who began to gather could only assume that the airplane had been lost, and they started collecting all the available information. Unfortunately, one major piece of information was erroneous. The NSA had intercepted a Soviet radio message that seemed to indicate that Powers's U-2 had descended to a lower altitude and made a broad turn back toward Sverdlovsk before being shot down. From this, many, including President Eisenhower and DCI Dulles, concluded that the U-2 had suffered a flameout and been at a lower altitude than 70,500 feet when it was shot down.

Bissell and the other CIA officials assumed that Powers had been killed, and they decided to stick with the cover story that the U-2 was a weather plane operated by NASA. The National Aeronautics and Space Administration had been established in October 1958 as the U.S. civil-

ian space agency. In the process, it had inherited the U-2 cover story. A statement was prepared based on the cover story but modified with what was known about Powers's flight. The takeoff site was given as Incirlik, in order to hide Pakistan's involvement.

At the same time, the PVO was also launching its own investigation. When Marshal Biryuzov told Khrushchev that the U-2 had been shot down, Khrushchev expressed doubts. Biryuzov immediately ordered that an investigation team be sent to Sverdlovsk. The team, which included representatives from the Central Committee, military counter-intelligence, the KGB, the General Staff, and the PVO, arrived several hours later and began a search for aircraft parts and other material. They found U-2 debris scattered over several square kilometers of farm fields and forests. This included the cockpit, wings, fuselage, and engine. Most significant, the team also recovered long, nine-inch-wide rolls of exposed film. Much of this could later be developed with little damage, allowing the Soviets to discover what had been photographed. At the same time, Powers was being flown to Moscow for interrogation at KGB headquarters. The poison pin had been found after repeated searches.

A revised cover story was issued by the public information officer at Incirlik late on May 2. He said that an unarmed Lockheed U-2 weather plane had vanished during a routine flight over the Lake Van area of Turkey. The pilot, a civilian employee of Lockheed on loan to NASA, had reported trouble with his oxygen system. This story was followed the next day, May 3, by a NASA statement repeating that a U-2 was missing and that the pilot had reported oxygen system problems. The intention was that if the Soviets protested over the crash, NASA and the U.S. government could say that the pilot had lost consciousness and the airplane had strayed across the Soviet border under the control of its autopilot.

On May 5, Khrushchev set a trap for the United States. At a meeting of the Supreme Soviet, he announced that on May Day a U.S. "spyplane," in "an aggressive provocation aimed at wrecking the Summit Conference," had violated Soviet airspace and been shot down by a missile on his personal orders. Khrushchev said nothing about the fate of the pilot.

The same day as Khrushchev's speech, NASA issued another press release, which again referred to the oxygen system problem. There were subsequent press reports that all U-2s had been grounded for inspections of their oxygen systems. On May 6, a State Department spokesman flatly stated: "There was no—N-O—no deliberate attempt to violate Soviet air space, and there has never been." He dismissed as "monstrous" any sug-

gestions that the United States would try to deceive the world about the purpose of the flight. At the same time, however, there was the first indication that Powers had survived. At a diplomatic reception on the evening of May 5, U.S. ambassador Llewellyn Thompson overheard Soviet deputy foreign minister Yakov Malik tell the Swedish ambassador that "we are still questioning the pilot." Thompson cabled the news to the State Department, but the U.S. government stuck with the weather plane cover story.

Khrushchev sprang the trap on May 7. In a second speech before the Supreme Soviet, he announced that Powers was alive and had confessed to working for the CIA. Acting on the orders of the detachment commander, an air force colonel, Powers had taken off from Peshawar, Pakistan, on a spy mission over the USSR. Intending to land at Bodo, Norway, he had instead been shot down over Sverdlovsk by a missile. Parts of the U-2 had been recovered and brought to Moscow. This information had been deliberately withheld from his May 5 statement, Khrushchev explained, "because had we told everything at once, the Americans would have invented another version."

Khrushchev took glee in demolishing the U.S. cover story. He said, "If one believes the version that the pilot lost consciousness owing to oxygen trouble and that the aircraft was subsequently controlled by the automatic pilot, one must also believe that the aircraft controlled by the automatic pilot flew from Turkey to Pakistan, touched down at Peshawar Airport, stayed there three days, took off early in the morning of May 1, flew more than two thousand kilometers over our territory for a total of some four hours."

Khrushchev then set another trap, attempting to further humiliate President Eisenhower. He noted that perhaps Eisenhower was unaware of the flight. But if this were true, then it was the "militarists" in the United States who were actually "bossing the show."

In an attempt to distance President Eisenhower from the flights, the State Department fell into the second trap. A statement was issued that the U-2 had probably been on an intelligence-gathering mission but "there was no authorization for any such flight" from Washington. On May 9, Secretary of State Herter stated that specific U-2 overflights were not subject to presidential approval. Dulles offered to resign and take responsibility for the failed overflight, but President Eisenhower was not willing to have the world believe that he was not in charge of his own government.

On May 11, 1960, President Eisenhower made an opening statement at a press conference. It was the first time a president had ever admitted approving peacetime intelligence operations. Eisenhower stated: "No one wants another Pearl Harbor. This means that we must have knowledge of military forces and preparations around the world, especially those capable of massive surprise attack.

"Secrecy in the Soviet Union makes this essential. In most of the world no large-scale attack could be prepared in secret, but in the Soviet Union there is a fetish of secrecy and concealment. This is a major cause of international tension and uneasiness today. Our deterrent must never be placed in jeopardy. The safety of the whole free world demands this. . . . Ever since the beginning of my Administration I have issued directives to gather, in every feasible way, the information required to protect the United States and the free world against surprise attack and to enable them to make effective preparations for defense."

Eisenhower concluded by calling intelligence activities "distasteful but vital" and saying he would again bring up the Open Skies proposal at the Paris Summit in order to reduce tensions and ensure against possible surprise attack. He ended his statement with, "I will have nothing further to say about this matter."

As Eisenhower had predicted the previous February, that same day the U-2 debris was put on display in Moscow's Gorky Park. Khrushchev and other Soviet leaders toured the exhibit as the press photographed the proceedings.

When the Paris Summit opened on May 16, 1960, Khrushchev insisted on speaking first, then launched into a long denunciation of the overflights and demanded that President Eisenhower apologize and the flights be stopped. Eisenhower replied by saying that the missions had ended and would not resume, but he refused to make a formal apology. Khrushchev lost his temper, and the summit was over.

As soon as it was known that Powers had survived, the RAF pilots immediately left Turkey, to hide British involvement. The RAF pilots were called to a meeting at the Air Ministry with Sir George Ward, secretary of state for Air. He wanted their opinion on whether Powers would tell the Soviets anything about their part in the U-2 program. Rumors had already begun to appear in the British press and in Parliament that there had been close cooperation. Finally Ward decided not to make any comment. The RAF pilots were told to "vanish" for a while. Robinson spent the next several months in Spain.

The overseas detachments were closed down soon afterward. On the night of May 27, 1960, a coup overthrew the government of Turkish premier Adnan Menderes. The new government had not been briefed on the U-2, and project headquarters ordered a halt to all U-2 flights, both the border SIGINT missions and routine maintenance flights. Three of the four U-2s of Detachment B were eventually dismantled and flown back to the United States in C-124 transports. The fourth aircraft was kept in a hangar for several years, in case U-2 operations from Turkey were resumed, before it was finally returned to the United States. The U-2 incident also sparked Leftist protests in Japan. As these anti-American demonstrations grew, the Japanese government asked the United States on July 8, 1960, to close down Detachment C. The following day, the U-2s were disassembled, loaded on C-124s, and returned to the United States.

To continue U-2 operations against Cuba and North Vietnam, the CIA consolidated the aircraft and pilots at North Base at Edwards Air Force Base. Detachment G, as it was known, comprised eight pilots from Detachment B and another three from Detachment C. The code name Chalice was dropped following Powers's loss and replaced with Idealist.

The RB-47H Incident

When the U-2 was shot down, President Eisenhower ordered a halt to all overflight activities, both of the U-2 and the resupply missions for the Tibetan resistance. The border SIGINT and photographic missions were allowed to continue, because they were flown over international waters and in friendly airspace. These efforts were quite extensive, with the air force making more than a hundred SIGINT and photographic missions per month in Western Europe. Additional missions were flown by the navy and RAF.

One part of this effort was a single RB-47H and its support KC-135 tanker from the 55th Strategic Reconnaissance Wing, which was based at RAF Brize Norton, England. This aircraft flew about six sorties per month in the Barents Sea, the Baltic Sea, and along the border between East and West Germany. The crew for the RB-47H border mission flown on July 1, 1960, consisted of Capt. William G. Palm (pilot), Lt. Freeman B. Olmstead (copilot), Lt. John R. McKone (navigator), and Capt. Eugene E. Posa, Lt. Oscar L. Goforth, and Lt. Dean B. Philips (Crows). Before Palm went to England, his eleven-year-old daughter, Michelle, gave him a plastic Snoopy toy as a good luck charm. Palm carried it in his flight

suit pocket. This was Lieutenant Goforth's first operational mission. The crew was briefed that this was a quiet area and nothing was going to happen. The mission would last about twelve hours, and they were not to come any closer than fifty nautical miles to the Soviet coastline.

Their RB-47H took off from Brize Norton, then flew north and refueled from a KC-135 tanker off the coast of Norway. After rounding the North Cape of Norway, the RB-47H flew a course paralleling the Kola Peninsula. McKone took periodic radar navigation fixes on the Soviet coast. It was not unusual for the RB-47Hs to have "escorts," and as the airplane flew along its course, Olmstead spotted the contrail from a jet fighter pacing them. He told Palm, then swiveled his seat backward to watch it. The MiG turned toward them, then headed back toward its base without coming closer than two to three miles. McKone took another radar fix, which showed that the RB-47H would reach its turn point two minutes early.

Olmstead glanced toward the right wing and was surprised to see a MiG flying only forty feet away. He could even see the pilot, Capt. Vasily A. Polyakov. Olmstead called out, "Check, check, check, right wing." Palm looked back. "Where in hell did that guy come from?" he said. The RB-47H had reached its turn point, fifty miles from the USSR and well outside its claimed territorial waters. McKone told the pilot, "Bill, turn left now." Palm began the slow turn that would put them on course toward Novaya Zemlya. Captain Polyakov saw the maneuver and, believing that the RB-47H was on a photographic reconnaissance mission and was flying directly toward a new Soviet nuclear submarine base, decided to take action. He came up behind the RB-47H, which was still making its course change, and opened fire.

Olmstead saw the gun flashes from the MiG's cannons and tried to return fire with the tail turret by aiming visually. He fired about two-thirds of his ammunition, but without effect. The cannon shells from the MiG did have an effect, striking the number 2 and 3 engines under the left wing. The engines caught fire, and the RB-47H went into a spin. The aircraft recovered, but a second burst of cannon fire, lasting some twenty seconds, struck it. Palm said, "Stand by, stand by," which was the initial step in a bailout order. For the next ten seconds, Palm and Olmstead fought to regain control of the fatally damaged aircraft, then Palm said, "Bail out, bail out."

Palm, Olmstead, and McKone all successfully ejected and landed in the cold water of the Barents Sea. Olmstead, who suffered a crushed vertebra in the ejection, and McKone climbed into their life rafts. Palm be-

came entangled in his parachute and drowned. Olmstead and McKone floated for about six hours before they were picked up by a Soviet trawler. They, like Powers, were taken to KGB headquarters for interrogation. Palm's body was returned to the United States. The three Crows were never found.

It was not until July 11, 1960, that the Soviets announced that they had shot down the RB-47H and were holding Olmstead and McKone. Khrushchev lashed out, saying at a press conference that U.S. policy was aimed at "provoking a serious military conflict" and this "new act of perfidy" showed that Eisenhower's assurances that overflights had been halted was "not worth a bad penny." Olmstead and McKone would be prosecuted with the "full severity of Soviet law." Soviet foreign minister Andrei Gromyko requested an urgent UN Security Council meeting to discuss "the new aggressive activities of the U.S. Air Force," which he said were "a threat to the peace of the world."

In their attempts to humiliate the United States and undercut Eisenhower, the Soviets overreached themselves. They falsely claimed that the RB-47H crew had entered Soviet airspace and that Olmstead and McKone had confessed to being on an espionage mission. When the UN meeting was held, the Soviets paid the price for their misstatements. The U.S. ambassador to the UN, Henry Cabot Lodge, revealed that the RB-47 had been tracked on radar; he presented a map showing that it had never entered Soviet airspace. Lodge referred to the Soviet attack as a "criminal and reckless act of piracy" and said that recent Soviet actions had made people wonder "whether the Soviet leaders are actually seeking a pretext for war."

The Soviets fared badly in the debate. Even the weakest U.S. allies accused the Soviet Union of piracy. In the subsequent vote, a number of neutralist nations backed the U.S. position. It was clear that the Soviets had shot down the RB-47H over international airspace, then lied about the location. The idea of a trial was dropped, and Olmstead and McKone were released after seven months as a "goodwill" gesture.

August 19, 1960

Powers was subjected to prolonged interrogation following his capture. The instructions he had been given by the CIA in the event of capture were, as the CIA's official history later noted, "meager." With the debris from Article 360 in Soviet hands, it was not possible for him to deny that

he had been on a reconnaissance mission. Given these circumstances, Powers did attempt to conceal as much classified information as possible while giving the appearance of cooperating.

The most important operational information Powers sought to conceal was the altitude of the U-2. He told the interrogators that he had been flying at 68,000 feet, which he described as the maximum the aircraft could reach. (Neither statement was true.) He also said that this had been his first overflight, rather than his third, and he depicted himself as not knowledgeable about the aircraft's equipment or the intelligence results of the program. This was to close off lines of questioning. He also hid the existence of the special missions. The fact that the United States had spied on its allies was the most damaging information Powers possessed.

He also refused to give the Soviets the names of the other U-2 pilots or denounce the United States. He resisted Soviet claims that he had been ordered to use the poison needle, that he thought the U-2 self-destruct charge had been rigged to kill him, that he was to have acted as a saboteur, and that the flight was intended to wreck the Paris Summit. Despite British fears, Powers was never asked about the RAF U-2 pilots, nor was he questioned about overflights of China or Eastern Europe. A subsequent CIA damage assessment indicated that Powers gave the Soviets far less information that had originally been feared, and that they were quite satisfied with his conduct.

The final act in the secret air war against the USSR took place on August 19, 1960. At the end of a three-day show trial, Powers was convicted of espionage. The headline in the next day's *New York Times* read, "Powers Gets A 10-Year Sentence; Soviet Asserts Penalty Is Mild, But Eisenhower Finds It Severe." The show trial was an attack on Eisenhower, the CIA, and America, to score propaganda points and inflict the maximum amount of humiliation. Powers himself was almost incidental, and he was exchanged for a captured Soviet spy two years later. But August 19, 1960, was also the day that the Soviet victory became meaningless.

On the left side of the same *New York Times* front page that carried the story of Powers's sentencing was another headline: "Space Capsule Is Caught In Mid-Air By U.S. Plane On Re-Entry From Orbit." The article said that a C-119, flown by Capt. Harold E. Mitchell, had successfully recovered the capsule from the Discoverer 14 satellite. This was described by the air force as a scientific satellite designed to fly military experiments.

Discoverer 14 was, in fact, Corona Mission 9009, a covert photoreconnaissance satellite directed by the CIA. During its one-day mission, Discoverer 14 made a total of seven passes over the USSR and one over Eastern Europe. This single mission photographed more than 1.3 million square miles of the USSR. This was a larger area than that covered by all twenty-three successful U-2 overflights or by the forty Genetrix gondolas. Most of the Mission 9009 photographs were of areas that had not previously been covered by overflights. The United States now had the means to photograph vast areas of the USSR in a single mission, with zero political risk.

Over the next year, additional Corona satellites were launched. By September 1961, their photos showed that instead of a missile gap, there was a missile bluff. As Eisenhower had suspected but the U-2 was unable to prove, the Soviets had not deployed a large ICBM force. Plesetsk was the only site where SS-6 ICBMs were deployed; the SS-7 facilities at Yurya were still under construction. Khrushchev had exploited Soviet missile and space achievements to create the illusion of great missile strength. The reality behind the bluff was that the U.S. ICBMs and Polaris missile submarines far outnumbered the handful of Soviet missiles. Not until the late 1960s would the Soviets finally overtake the U.S. missile force.

Although the Corona satellite represented a whole new method of photoreconnaissance, it built upon the decade of experience provided by the border missions and overflights. Its mode of operation was that first proposed by Leghorn and carried out by the U-2. The reconnaissance was to assess the total strengths and weaknesses of the USSR, measure its military power, and provide warning of a possible Soviet surprise attack. Corona was managed by Richard Bissell and Ozzie Ritland, who had worked together on the U-2 development, under the same kind of partnership between the CIA, the air force, and industry that had proven so successful with the U-2. Corona also had the total backing of President Eisenhower. This was critical, because Corona went through twelve straight failures. Boosters exploded, the satellites malfunctioned in orbit, the film broke, and the capsules failed to reenter. It was not until Discoverer 13, a test mission without a camera, that all the steps worked. Eisenhower never wavered. He had decided that Corona was vital to the survival of the United States, so the project would go forward.

The technology used by Corona had its origins in the balloon reconnaissance programs. The payload aboard Discoverer 14 was a modified version of the HYAC camera originally developed for the WS-461L re-

connaissance balloon. Captain Mitchell, like the other pilots in the recovery unit, was a veteran of the Genetrix program. The C-119Fs they flew were the beaver-tail version modified for Genetrix; the recovery gear was based on that used to catch the gondolas in midair.

With the successful recovery of Corona Mission 9009, the organizational structure needed for operational satellite reconnaissance was established by Eisenhower. Again, this was based on the overflight experience. Before Eisenhower left office in January 1961, the National Reconnaissance Office was established to manage the development and operation of satellite systems. It was based on the same team concept that had been used by the U-2 and Corona. The Automat was also transformed into the National Photographic Interpretation Center. This brought together photointerpreters from both the CIA and military services. In the wake of the loss of Powers's U-2, the targeting procedures of the satellites and aircraft were formalized in the Committee on Overhead Reconnaissance. It, like the original Ad Hoc Requirements Committee, was run by James Q. Reber.

For the next three decades, the organization and structure originally created by Eisenhower for the U-2 overflights would provide the basis for Cold War satellite reconnaissance. It would then continue on, after the Union of Soviet Socialist Republics was no more.

Chapter 9
Reflections on a Secret War

. . . this was an extraordinary moment. When I saw the Grenzpolize [East German border guards] helping the demonstrators on the Wall, I thought that the long war that had gone on all my adult life since World War II was now coming to an end.

—Vernon Walters, U.S. ambassador to Germany

In August 1960, as Powers was convicted and Discoverer 14 was returning its photographs, the Cold War entered its thirteenth year. This was three times longer than either the Civil War or World War II had lasted. Yet the Cold War was to continue for another thirty-one years, and its most dangerous times were yet to come. In 1960, the continuation of Khrushchev's Berlin ultimatum, the building of the Berlin Wall, and the Cuban missile crisis were still in the future. It was an epic struggle between two incompatible ideologies with fundamentally different views of the rights of the individual and the power of the state, with the fate and future of humanity at stake.

The Secret Air War After the U-2

The loss of the U-2 and the success of the Discoverer 14 mission marked a fundamental change in the secret air war against the USSR. Never again would a reconnaissance aircraft make an overflight of the USSR. No subsequent U.S. president or British prime minister was willing to authorize a Soviet overflight, because it was no longer necessary. Corona and later satellites could survey broad expanses of the USSR far more completely than any aircraft ever could.

Another shift was a diminishing role for the CIA in aerial operations. Starting in late 1960, Detachment G's U-2s made covert overflights of Cuba and North Vietnam. On the eve of the 1962 Cuban missile crisis, however, responsibility for the Cuban overflights was transferred from the CIA to the air force. The CIA also lost responsibility for U-2 opera-

tions over North Vietnam following the August 1964 Tonkin Gulf incident. Even before the loss of Powers's U-2, the air force had taken over most of the border U-2 SIGINT flights.

In 1967 and 1968, the CIA made a number of A-12 Oxcart overflights of North Vietnam and North Korea. This Mach 3 aircraft, originally designed as the U-2's replacement, had made its first test flight in April 1962 from Area 51. Development proved difficult and expensive, and there was political reluctance within the U.S. government to its use. When the A-12 finally did go into operation, it was in the tactical reconnaissance role rather than the strategic missions for which it had originally been designed.

The CIA's use of the A-12 proved brief. By the spring of 1968, the air force's SR-71s were operational. This was a later version of the A-12, with a two-man crew and a heavier equipment load. The SR-71s took over the missions over North Vietnam, and the A-12s were retired and put into storage. The SR-71s also replaced the air force U-2s making the Cuban overflights. In later years, SR-71s would make overflights of the Middle East and Central America. No SR-71 overflight was ever made of the USSR or China, despite popular belief.

The primary activities of the CIA's U-2s during the 1960s were overflights of mainland China flown by Nationalist Chinese Air Force pilots. These began in January 1962 and continued into early 1968. The Nationalist Chinese U-2 operations proved costly. Chinese air defenses brought down five U-2s, and others were lost in training accidents. Twenty U-2s had originally been ordered by the CIA, and another four had been built by Lockheed from spare parts and usable portions of crashed aircraft. By the summer of 1966, the CIA had only six U-2s left. Two were on Taiwan, one was at North Base, and three were undergoing maintenance at Lockheed. Due to the added weight of equipment and modifications, these U-2Cs had lost almost half their range and several thousand feet of altitude capability.

Kelly Johnson had been considering ways to improve the U-2's performance, and on August 1, 1966, DCI Richard M. Helms and Secretary of Defense Robert S. McNamara agreed to the construction of a completely new aircraft, the U-2R. This aircraft had a wingspan of 103 feet (compared to the 80 feet of the U-2C), a longer fuselage, an increased peak altitude of 74,000 feet, and better flying characteristics. The first U-2R test flight was made on August 28, 1967, and deliveries of twelve

aircraft were completed in December 1968. They were split evenly: six to the CIA and six to the air force. The CIA's six older U-2Cs were placed in flyable storage.

By the time the Nationalist Chinese pilots began flying the new U-2Rs, however, mainland overflights had been halted. Chinese air defenses posed too great a threat, and on April 10, 1968, the United States decided that only border flights would be made by the Nationalist Chinese. The CIA U-2Rs saw only limited activity in the years to follow. They flew missions over the Middle East in 1970 and 1974 in order to police cease-fire agreements between Israel and the Arab countries, and they were again making border flights against North Vietnam in 1973 and 1974.

On August 1, 1974, the CIA U-2 operations ended. Its U-2Rs and four of the U-2Cs were turned over to the air force, which also now assumed the CIA's previous overflight missions in the Middle East. During the 1970s and 1980s, air force U-2Rs made overflights of the Middle East and Central America, along with the SR-71s.

The other two ex-CIA U-2Cs had already been permanently loaned to NASA in 1971. These were modified to undertake earth resources studies and astronomical observations. To fly the aircraft, CIA pilots Jim Barnes, Bob Ericson, and Marty Knutson, as well as ex-RAF U-2 pilot Ivor "Chunky" Webster, joined NASA. Webster had been assigned to the U-2 program between 1961 and 1964. These pilots were later joined by another former CIA U-2 pilot, James Cherbonneaux.

The End of the Cold War

To a person growing up in the early 1960s, who practiced duck and cover drills in school and who heard the air raid siren go off at noon every Monday, it seemed that the Cold War had always existed and always would. There seemed no exit from the struggle; this would require the end of the world as we knew it. Either the United States or the Soviet Union would have to cease to exist in their current form, or both would be destroyed in a nuclear war. Neither possibility was imaginable. But every war ends.

When that end came, it would be with unbelievable suddenness. The long-standing Soviet fears about their control over Eastern Europe proved fully justified. Within the USSR as well, even after seven decades of totalitarian police state rule, propaganda, and bloody purges that had claimed tens of millions of victims, the spark of freedom still burned. By

the late 1980s, their populations were no longer willing to believe the official lies, nor were they afraid. The USSR, its economy overstretched by the inefficiencies of central planning, corruption, and the burden of its huge military machine, could no longer hold its empire together.

During 1989, one by one, like falling dominos, the communist governments of Eastern Europe were replaced by multiparty democracies. At the same time, East German vacationers in Hungary were crossing the border into Austria in a mass exodus. At home, huge demonstrations developed in major cities as the people demanded freedom. By early November, the communist East German government was powerless to stem the tide. In an effort to retain some control, the authorities decided to ease travel restrictions. On the evening of November 9, 1989, an East German party official named Guenter Schabowski was holding a press conference when an assistant walked in and handed him the announcement. The cryptic statement said that visas would be easier to get and more travel to the West would be permitted. A reporter asked when the new rules would take effect. Schabowski looked at the paper and finally said, "Now, I suppose."

East Berliners took his offhand comment as a decision that the Wall was now open, and they rushed to the checkpoints. The East German border guards had orders to shoot anyone trying to cross the Wall, and many had died in escape attempts over nearly thirty years. The chief guard at the Bornholmer Bridge on this night was Harald Jaeger. As the crowd gathered, he called his commander for orders. He was told not to let anyone through without proper papers. The crowd continued to build, and Jaeger became increasingly concerned. He finally told his superiors, "I'm letting the people out." The barricade was opened, and the crowd surged through. The scene was soon being repeated at the other crossing points.

As the whole world watched on CNN, a party began in the streets of West Berlin. People danced atop the Berlin Wall, the symbol of the division of Europe and the Cold War for nearly three decades. The Wall's concrete slabs and barbed wire seemed as eternal and immovable as the struggle itself. But now, from this night on, its existence was irrelevant. People began taking sledgehammers to the Wall, punching holes through it. As the Wall began to disappear, it was clear to all that the end of the world as we knew it was at hand.

World War II finally ended at midnight on October 2, 1990. After the perils of Khrushchev over a German peace treaty, the final agreement

posed only limited difficulties. The USSR accepted a united Germany within NATO, and the West Germans renounced all past territorial claims, limited the size of its army, renounced nuclear, chemical, and biological weapons, paid for the removal of Soviet troops, and agreed to permanently ban the Nazi Party and preserve the grave sites and monuments to those who had fought against Nazi Germany. The United States, the USSR, Britain, and France gave up all their occupation powers. As midnight struck, the city that had played such a central role in the struggle between East and West was, for the first time in more than forty-five years, again "Berlin, Germany."

Inside the USSR, Soviet leader Mikhail Gorbachev faced the difficult task of both changing and preserving the Soviet Union. The USSR had been evolving into a multiparty state ever since Gorbachev renounced the Communist Party's monopoly on power. His efforts faced opposition from those who wanted faster reforms and the old-line communists who dreamed of a return to the old ways. Meanwhile, the Baltic States, the Ukraine, Armenia, and the other republics wanted independence. In revealing the truth about such once hidden events as Stalin's purges, Gorbachev undercut his hard-line opponents, but he also proved beyond doubt that the whole history of the USSR was a blood-stained lie.

By August 1991, events were no longer under his control. Hard-liners staged a coup intended to halt reform, reinstitute communist control, and prevent the breakup of the USSR. As the world again watched on CNN, the people of the USSR took to the streets to announce that they would not return to the old ways. The tank crews sent out to restore order refused to fire on their own people, and they joined those opposing the coup. Within three days, the attempt to turn back the clock failed. The hard-liners had brought about the very thing they had tried to prevent: the breakup of the USSR and the loss of Communist Party control. Gorbachev resigned his Communist Party posts, including that of general secretary, and ordered that party control over all aspects of Soviet life be ended. Four months later, the USSR was no more. And then, after so very, very, long, the Cold War was finally over.

Casualties of the Secret Air War

Despite the risks of the covert overflights and the near losses of the RAF Canberra and the RB-47E, all the overflights were successful until the loss of Powers's U-2. The border flights were another story, however. The overflights relied for survival on surprise, their irregular schedules, and weak-

ness in Soviet bloc air defenses. The border flights were far more numerous, and they were made on regular schedules and along predictable flight paths. Their crews faced the danger of unpredictable MiG pilots, with international airspace proving to be scant protection. Most of the time, the Soviet fighters simply flew alongside. Other times, they tried to harass or chase off the SIGINT aircraft. But for more than two hundred U.S. aircrewmen, these encounters ended in death.

For the families of those lost in the secret air war against the USSR, there was the pain of not knowing what happened to their fathers, sons, and brothers. From time to time, claims appeared that some of the crewmen shot down had survived, had been taken prisoner by the Soviets, and were still being held. The Soviets maintained their silence, refusing in several cases, including that of the C-130A-II, to admit that they were responsible for the loss of the men. So it remained for decade after decade. But with the fall of the Soviet Union, some of the families received answers. A joint U.S.-Russian team began investigating the incidents, interviewing retired ex-Soviet pilots and unearthing the after-action reports. In the case of the Project Sea Shore RB-47E, the team was able to confirm that the aircraft had actually been shot down. All that had been known in the West before this was that the aircraft had disappeared.

One of the cases the team looked at was the loss of the C-130A-II. On August 28, 1993, at the invitation of the now-independent Armenian government, a recovery team from the U.S. Army Central Identification Laboratory Hawaii began an archaeological excavation of the crash site, near the village of Sasnashen. There was ample evidence of the crash, thirty-five years before, in the village. Part of the C-130's wing was being used as a fence, and other parts of the airplane were also in the village. The local villagers were interviewed about the incident, and none recalled seeing any parachutes.

The crash site was on a barren, rock-strewn hillside. The area was marked with a grid, and the recovery team dug down and sifted the dirt. In the process, some 2,000 bone and tooth fragments as well as pieces of life-support equipment, personal effects, and aircraft wreckage were found. The team also learned that those who died on this hillside had not been forgotten. After the crash, a memorial of stones appeared, secretly built by the local villagers. The local KGB would knock down the memorial, but it was rebuilt again and again.

Examination began of the remains and items recovered from the crash site, as well as of the three sets of remains returned by the Soviets in 1958

that were still unidentified. In 1996 and 1997, the three sets of remains were finally identified. In 1998, a group identification was made of the fragments found at the crash site. All seventeen crewmen were determined to have died in the crash. The Russian government also provided documents and gun camera footage from the incident. This confirmed the forensic evidence that no one had bailed out of the C-130A. On September 2, 1998, the fortieth anniversary of the shoot-down, the recovered remains were buried at Arlington National Cemetery. Interred as a group, they would forever be a crew.

Although the shooting down of the C-130A-II was believed by many at the time to have been a deliberate ambush, the aircraft was not, in fact, intentionally led off course. The root cause was the Soviet use of powerful radio beacons on frequencies close to those in Turkey, in violation of international agreements on navigational aids. Although warnings about radio beacons along the Soviet border had been issued, weather conditions at the time of the incident prevented the crew from realizing that they had accidentally crossed the border. The MiGs were not lying in wait but were scrambled when the aircraft was detected and had difficulty locating it.

On the grounds of the National Security Agency headquarters, a memorial now stands to all those who died in the secret air war. In 1996, a C-130A in storage at Davis-Monthan Air Force Base in Arizona was flown to the Raytheon/E-Systems facility at Greenville, Texas, where the original Sun Valley C-130As had been modified nearly forty years before. The C-130A's Vietnam-era camouflage was stripped off, and the airplane was repainted with markings identical to those of the aircraft lost over Soviet Armenia. The work was done by active-duty and retired military personnel, some of whom had flown on C-130A-II missions. The memorial was dedicated on September 2, 1997, by NSA director Lt. Gen. Kenneth A. Minihan. A plaque lists the names of those lost. Behind the aircraft are eighteen trees symbolizing each type of aircraft lost during the Cold War and in Vietnam.

The Meaning of the Struggle

Just as it was only with the end of the Cold War that the aircrews' sacrifices could be recognized, so too only with the secret air war's end could the meaning of that struggle be fully understood. Rivalries and wars are as old as organized human society, but with the development of nuclear weapons, the need to know one's enemies took on a new dimension. Hu-

mans now had the power to destroy whole nations, and the logical method was a surprise attack.

The secret air war was an expression of the policy established to meet this new threat. Both Truman and Eisenhower decided that the supreme national interest of the United States—indeed, its very survival—required that covert flights be made over the USSR and its allies. This policy carried great risks. Shooting down an aircraft making an overflight carried the potential of starting the very war that the overflight was intended to prevent. Yet, as Dr. Land had argued in his letter to DCI Dulles, it was not possible for the U.S. government to meet its responsibilities when it lacked even a basic understanding of Soviet activities.

What this policy also required was a new kind of reconnaissance aircraft. Although converted fighters and bombers were acceptable for wartime reconnaissance, the risks and political sensitivities of covert missions required something more. Just as Leghorn's idea of pre-D-day reconnaissance was counter to the existing view of reconnaissance as simply assembling target folders, his ideas about this new kind of aircraft were also counter to existing design concepts. The RB-57D and the X-16 were traditional aircraft designs that were expected to undertake an extraordinary mission. What Kelly Johnson did was to reverse the process. He did not design an airplane to fly a mission. Rather, he let the mission design the airplane. The result was the U-2, an aircraft that was the mirror image of its competitors.

There are parallels between the U-2's design philosophy and that of the *Spirit of St. Louis*. Most of the contenders trying to fly from New York to Paris in 1927 used conventional trimotor and multiman airliners, because it was assumed that three engines gave a margin of safety. What Charles A. Lindbergh realized was that aircraft engines were reliable enough to operate for thirty-plus hours, and several engines only multiplied the risk of engine failure. They did not provide a safety margin, because for most of the flight the trimotor aircraft were too heavy with fuel to fly on two engines.

In the same way, the twin engines of the RB-57D gained nothing, because the aircraft could not maintain altitude with only one engine, and over denied areas, altitude was the airplane's only protection from MiGs. A single-engine, single-seat aircraft would be simpler, lighter, higher flying, and more reliable. As with the *Spirit of St. Louis,* the U-2 was built to be the lightest possible single-engine airframe that could still hold the fuel load. The original Ryan M-2 aircraft was modified with added fuel tanks as well as an extended wing to provide the increased lift to com-

pensate for the increased weight. Similarly, the U-2 had its start as a much-modified version of the XF-104, a lightweight jet fighter.

Although it was the air force, navy, and CIA pilots and aircrews who carried out the national policy of making covert reconnaissance missions, it was the president who was ultimately responsible for the direction of this policy and its success or failure. Although the initial overflights were made at the direction of President Truman, it was Eisenhower who was the architect of the policy that the crews carried out and that has continued to the present day. It was Eisenhower who authorized both the U-2 and Corona, who made Leghorn's ideas national policy, and who established the National Reconnaissance Office.

Eisenhower ran the U-2 program as commander in chief rather than as a political figure. He kept the program tightly held, restricting the number of people who knew of the program or its results. He refused to reveal the U-2 after Sputnik or during the missile gap controversy, even though doing so would have effectively countered Democratic charges that he was weakening U.S. defenses. As a result, Eisenhower was never able to convince the American public that his policies were justified. The capability that the U-2 represented, despite Eisenhower's reluctance to use it, was too important to exploit for short-term political gain. Eisenhower took the political heat.

The political impact of the loss of Powers's U-2 continues to echo to the present day in subtle and unrecognized ways. On the negative side, the clumsy cover stories issued following the loss were the first step in creating the conspiratorial mentality that beset the United States at the end of the twentieth century. The U-2 incident was followed by the Bay of Pigs, the Kennedy assassination, Vietnam, Watergate, and subsequent scandals. Each event increased public cynicism and destroyed public faith in government, until belief in conspiracies became automatic.

It is now common to find intellectuals expressing the belief that the Grand Slam overflight was not authorized by Eisenhower, and that it was a CIA plot to derail the easing of tensions between the United States and the USSR and efforts to reach arms control agreements. Similar conspiracy theories exist regarding the RB-47 overflights. It has been claimed that these were made without authorization by Gen. Curtis E. LeMay in an attempt to provoke the USSR into starting World War III. Despite the academic respectability given the claims by the stature of those spreading them, they are unsupported by evidence.

At the same time, President Eisenhower's admission that he had authorized the U-2 overflights marked the start of legitimizing overhead

reconnaissance. Within a few years, both the United States and the USSR were operating photoreconnaissance satellites. In 1972, the Strategic Arms Limitation Treaty tacitly acknowledged the acceptability of satellite reconnaissance by saying that its provisions would be verified by "national technical means." Neither the United States nor the USSR was yet willing to admit that this was a polite euphemism for reconnaissance satellites. That changed in 1978 when President Jimmy Carter publicly acknowledged that the United States operated reconnaissance satellites. By this time, the disclosure did not cause a ripple.

Reconnaissance After the Cold War

Following the end of the Cold War, satellites remained central to U.S. strategic reconnaissance. A satellite can cover Iraq or North Korea in two or three passes. However, satellites are limited for tactical reconnaissance. A satellite can photograph a specific target only when it passes over the target. The result is a series of snapshots rather than continuous coverage. Due to this limitation, there has been an increasing interest in unmanned aerial vehicles (UAVs) for tactical reconnaissance overflights.

The use of unmanned aircraft for reconnaissance has a long history. In the early 1960s, modified Firebee target drones were fitted with cameras to conduct reconnaissance. These Model 147 drones became a mainstay of U.S. Air Force reconnaissance overflights of Vietnam and China. With the end of the war, the drones were retired and interest waned in the concept. Following the Gulf War, which showed shortcomings in U.S. tactical reconnaissance, interest revived. The advantage of UAVs over satellites is their ability to stay aloft for several days, keeping a constant watch on a target area.

A wide range of UAVs has appeared in the past several years, ranging from designs as simple as radio-controlled model airplanes to more complex designs such as the Predator and Global Hawk. These are equipped with real-time data links that allow ground controllers to see activities as they are taking place. Because the UAVs are flown from the ground rather than being preprogrammed, as the Model 147 drones were, the flight plan can be modified in real time to cover fast-breaking situations.

Another change in post–Cold War reconnaissance is the realization of Eisenhower's Open Skies proposal. On March 20, 1992, the United States, Russia, the Ukraine, and twenty-one other countries reached agreements allowing overflights of one another's territory using transport aircraft equipped with photographic and SIGINT equipment. For

both the United States and Russia, a quota of forty-two such overflights per year was established. The goal, as it had been nearly forty years before when Eisenhower first proposed the idea, was mutual inspection.

Despite all the changes in aerial reconnaissance in the post–Cold War era, from the debut of new systems, such as the UAVs, to the retirement of the SR-71 in 1990 due to cost and internal air force politics, one aircraft has remained constant. Ever since that August afternoon in 1955 when the long-winged Article 341 was first tested in the sky above the ranch, U-2s have been the mainstay of U.S. aerial reconnaissance. In 1979, the Carter administration decided to restart U-2R production, some eleven years after the final aircraft of the original batch had been delivered.

The first aircraft of the new production run made its initial test flight on May 11, 1981. It was not a U-2R, however, but rather an ER-2 for NASA. This was a demilitarized variant for use in earth resources studies, thus the ER designation. With the deliveries under way, the air force retired the remaining U-2Cs. Among these aircraft was Article 347, the U-2 that made the first two overflights of the USSR. It was placed on display at the National Air and Space Museum in Washington, D.C. Deployment of the new air force U-2Rs to England began in 1983, and the first of two ER-2s went into operation with NASA the previous year.

The U-2Rs made their biggest deployment ever during the Gulf War. The U-2s were some of the first aircraft sent to the Persian Gulf area, and they flew some eight hundred missions. These monitored the Iraqi buildup; then, once the air war began, they provided bomb damage assessments and warnings of Scud missile launches. When the Gulf War ended, they continued to enforce the terms of the cease-fire agreement, monitoring the deployment of Iraqi forces and watching for any reconstruction of the country's capability to build nuclear, chemical, or biological weapons. Despite the ongoing development of the UAVs, the U-2Rs will remain a mainstay of U.S. aerial reconnaissance efforts for several decades to come.

Flight 00-040

The Cold War was the longest conflict in American military history. Yet once it ended, it faded quickly from public consciousness. A generation has grown up since the fall of the Berlin Wall. They learn of those events, read accounts, and meet people who were part of that time, but they can-

not truly know what it was like to face doomsday. As time rushes onward into the unknown wonders and terrors of the twenty-first century, events that a decade ago would have been unimaginable, even as fantasy, pass nearly unnoticed. One such event occurred as this book was being completed. Just as the U-2 overflights defined many of the events of the Cold War, a scientific flight by a NASA ER-2, the civilian version of the U-2R, showed how different the world is today.

One of the studies undertaken by the ER-2s was of lowered ozone levels in the Arctic. By the end of the 1990s, concerns were being expressed that levels could drop to those of the Antarctic ozone hole. To collect data on Arctic ozone levels, the SAGE III Ozone Loss and Validation Experiment (SOLVE) was organized. The experiment, run by NASA's Office of Earth Science in coordination with the European Commission, involved scientists from NASA, Europe, Russia, Japan, and Canada. The SOLVE missions were flown out of an airfield at Kiruna, Sweden, north of the Arctic Circle.

On January 27, 2000, Lockheed-Martin contract pilot DeLewis "Dee" Porter went through the prebreathing procedure, then boarded the ER-2. He was assisted by Jim Sokolik, a Lockheed-Martin life-support technician. Flight 00-040 was a routine scientific mission with a flight plan filed and permissions granted. The ER-2 took off from the snowy runway and set a course to the southeast. Working in conjunction with the ER-2 was a NASA DC-8. The converted airliner took measurements at lower altitudes.

Porter and the ER-2 flew over Sweden, crossed over Finland, then entered Russian airspace. Flight 00-040 passed over St. Petersburg, once known as Leningrad, then passed west of Moscow, which had once been the capital of a nation known as the Union of Soviet Socialist Republics. The flight path was a straight-line course. When Porter reached Kursk, in southwestern Russia, he made a 180-degree turn, then flew back along the earlier path. The landing back at Kiruna, Sweden, was uneventful. After the mission was over, NASA issued a press release, but it attracted little interest.

The flight of a U-2 over Russia was apparently not considered newsworthy.

Sources

Books

Andrew, Christopher. *For the President's Eyes Only*. New York: Harper Collins, 1995.

———. *Her Majesty's Secret Service*. New York: Penguin Books, 1985.

Andrew, Christopher, and Oleg Gordievsky. *KGB: The Inside Story*. New York: Harper Perennial, 1991.

Bailey, Bruce M. *We See All: A History of the 55th Strategic Reconnaissance Wing*. 55th ELINT Association Historian.

Bering, Henrik. *Outpost Berlin*. Chicago: edition q, inc., 1995.

Bortoli, Georges. *The Death of Stalin*. London: Phaidon Press Limited, 1975.

Brugioni, Dino A. *Eyeball to Eyeball: The Inside Story of the Cuban Missile Crisis*. New York: Random House, 1991.

Brugioni, Dino A., and Frederick J. Doyle. "Arthur C. Lundahl: Founder of the Image Exploitation Discipline," in Robert A. McDonald, *Corona Between the Sun & the Sky*. Bethesda, Md.: The American Society for Photogrammetry and Remote Sensing, 1997.

Carl, Maj. Gen. Marion E., and Barrett Tillman. *Pushing the Envelope: The Career of Fighter Ace and Test Pilot Marion Carl*. Annapolis, Md.: Naval Institute Press, 1994.

Davies, Merton E., and William R. Harris. *RAND's Role in the Evolution of Balloon and Satellite Observation Systems and Related U.S. Space Technology*. Santa Monica: The RAND Corporation, September 1988.

Divine, Robert A. *The Sputnik Challenge*. New York: The Oxford University Press, 1993.

Eisenhower, Dwight D. *Waging Peace 1956–1961*. Garden City, N.Y.: Doubleday & Co., 1965.

Freedman, Lawrence. *U.S. Intelligence and the Soviet Strategic Threat*. Princeton, N.J.: Princeton University Press, 1986.

Gatland, Kenneth. *Robot Explorers*. London: The Macmillan Company, 1972.

Glennon, John P. *Foreign Relations of the United States, 1955–1957. Volume XXIV, Soviet Union, Eastern Mediterranean*. Washington, D.C.: U.S. Government Printing Office, 1989.

Halloway, David. *Stalin & the Bomb*. New Haven, Conn.: Yale University Press, 1994.

Harford, James. *Korolev*. New York: John Wiley & Sons, Inc., 1997.

Johnson, Clarence L. "Kelly," and Maggie Smith. *Kelly: More Than My Share of It All*. Washington, D.C.: Smithsonian Institution Press, 1985.

Killian, James R. Jr. *Sputnik, Scientists, and Eisenhower*. Cambridge, Mass.: The MIT Press, 1982.

Knaack, Marcelle Size. *Post-World War II Bombers 1945–1973*. Washington, D.C.: Office of Air Force History, 1988.

Lewis, Richard S. *Appointment on the Moon*. New York: Ballantine Books, 1969.

Lorenzen, Coral E. *Flying Saucers: The Startling Evidence of the Invasion From Outer Space*. New York: Signet Books, 1966.

McLaughlin Green, Constance, and Milton Lomask. *Vanguard: A History*. Washington, D.C.: NASA, 1970.

Medvedev, Roy. *Khrushchev*. Garden City, N.Y.: Doubleday, 1983.

Miller, Jay. *Lockheed U-2*. Austin, Tex.: Aerofax, Inc, 1983.

Moodey, James L., ed. *Dictionary of American Naval Fighting Ships. Volume VIII: Historical Sketches, Letters W through Z*. Washington, D.C.: Naval Historical Center, 1981.

Nelson, Michael. *War of the Black Heavens*. Syracuse, N.Y.: Syracuse University Press, 1997.

Pedlow, Gregory W., and Donald E. Welzenbach. *The CIA and the U-2 Program, 1954–1974*. Washington, D.C.: Central Intelligence Agency, 1998.

Peebles, Curtis. *Watch the Skies!* Washington, D.C.: Smithsonian Institution Press, 1994.

———. *The Corona Project*. Annapolis, Md.: Naval Institute Press, 1997.

Pocock, Chris. *Dragon Lady: The History of the U-2 Spyplane*. Shrewsbury, England: Airlife Publishing Ltd., 1989.

Powers, Francis Gary, and Curt Gentry. *Operation Overflight*. New York: Holt, Rinehart and Winston, 1970.

Prados, John. *The Soviet Estimate*. New York: The Dial Press, 1982.

Price, Alfred. *The History of U.S. Electronic Warfare, Volume II*. Port City Press, 1989.

Rich, Ben. R., and Leo Janos. *Skunk Works*. Boston: Little, Brown, 1994.

Richelson, Jeffrey. *American Espionage and the Soviet Target*. New York: William Morrow and Company, 1987.

Rostow, W. W. *Open Skies.* Austin, Tex.: University of Texas Press, 1982.

Schaffel, Kenneth. *The Emerging Shield: The Air Force and the Evolution of Continental Air Defense 1945–1960.* Washington, D.C.: Office of Air Force History, 1991.

Ulam, Adam B. *Expansion and Coexistence: Soviet Foreign Policy 1917–73.* New York: Holt, Rinehart and Winston, Inc., 1974.

Welzenbach, Donald E. "The Anglo-American Origins of Overflying the Soviet Union: The Case of the 'Invisible Aircraft,'" in Roger G. Miller, ed., *Seeing Off the Bear: Anglo-American Air Power Cooperation During the Cold War.* Washington, D.C.: Air Force History and Museum Program, 1995.

White, William L. *The Little Toy Dog,* New York: E. P. Dutton & Co., 1962.

Wynn, Humphrey. *RAF Nuclear Deterrent Forces.* London: HMSO, 1994.

Zaloga, Steven J. *Target America.* Novato, Calif.: Presidio Press, 1993.

Ziegler, Charles A., and David Jacobson. *Spying Without Spies: Origins of America's Secret Nuclear Surveillance System.* Westport, Conn.: Praeger Publishers, 1995.

Articles and Papers

Ahern, Charles R. "The Yo-Yo Story: An Electronic Analysis Case History." *Studies In Intelligence* (Winter 1961).

Asker, James R. "Washington Outlook." *Aviation Week & Space Technology* (January 31, 2000).

Austin, Harold. "A Cold War: Overflight of the USSR." Carl Holt, "Comments from the Back Seat!" *Daedalus Flyer* (Spring 1995).

Beck, Joan. "Communists, R.I.P.—obituary for a party." *San Diego Union* (September 3, 1991), B-section.

Brown, Donald C. "On the Trail of Hen House and Hen Roost." *Studies In Intelligence* (Spring 1969).

Brown, George A. "In the National Interest" and "Project 'Sea Shore.'" Manuscripts.

Brugioni, Dino A. "The Million-Dollar Photograph." *Studies In Intelligence* (Summer 1979).

———. "The Tyuratam Enigma." *Air Force Magazine* (March 1984).

Caruthers, Osgood. "Powers Gets a 10-Year Sentence; Soviet Asserts Penalty Is Mild, But Eisenhower Finds It Severe." *New York Times* (August 20, 1960).

Cassai, Nello. "Sorry—AF Balloon Carry No Imps, Mice." *Denver Post* (September 14, 1955).

Crampton, John. "Russian photo-shoot." *Air Pictorial* (August 1997).

Eliot, Frank. "Moon Bounce ELINT." *Studies In Intelligence* (Spring 1967).

Elliott, Simon. "Back To the Future." *Flight International* (December 22, 1993/January 4, 1994).

Fenton, Ben. "US spying balloons were based in Britain." *The Daily Telegraph* (August 10, 1998).

Finer, Sydney Wesley. "The Kidnaping of the Lunik." *Studies In Intelligence* (Winter 1967).

Geissinger, Steven. "Venerable U-2s proved to be adept at spying in Persian Gulf War." *San Diego Union-Tribune* (February 15, 1992), A-section.

Greer, Kenneth E. "Corona." *Studies In Intelligence* (Spring 1973).

Gup, Ted. "The Doomsday Blueprints." *Time* (August 10, 1992).

Haines, Gerald K. "CIA's Role in the Study of UFOs, 1947–90." *Studies In Intelligence,* Vol. 01, No. 1 (1997).

Hall, R. Cargill. "The Eisenhower Administration and the Cold War: Framing American Astronautics to Serve National Security." *Prologue* (Spring 1995).

———. "Strategic Reconnaissance in the Cold War." *Prologue* (Summer 1996).

———. "The Truth About Overflights." *MHQ* (Spring 1997).

Harrison, Hope. "Ulbricht and the Concrete 'Rose': New Archive Evidence on the Dynamics of Soviet East German Relations and the Berlin Crisis, 1958–61." Cold War International History Project Web Page.

———. "New Evidence on Khrushchev's 1958 Berlin Ultimatum." Cold War International History Project Web Page.

Hillman, Donald E., and R. Cargill Hall. "Overflight Strategic Reconnaissance of the USSR." *Air Power History* (Spring 1996).

Hillman, Donald E., with R. Cargill Hall. "And . . ." *Air Power History* (Spring 1996).

Holm, Skip. "Article Aloft." *Air Progress Aviation Review,* Vol. 3 (1986).

Hopkins, Robert III. "The Tell Two Stratojets." *Air Enthusiast* (Midsummer 1990).

Jolidon, Laurence. "Soviet Interrogation of U.S. POWs in the Korean War." Cold War International History Project Web Page.

Lashmar, Paul. "Shootdowns." *Aeroplane Monthly* (August 1994).

———. "Skulduggery at Sculthorpe." *Aeroplane Monthly* (October 1994).

———. "Canberras Over the USSR." *Aeroplane Monthly* (February 1995).

———. "The UK and the U-2." Part 1. *Aeroplane Monthly* (August 1995).

———. "The UK and the U-2." Part 2. *Aeroplane Monthly* (September 1995).

Leghorn, Col. Richard S. "U.S. Can Photograph Russia From the Air Now." *U.S. News & World Report* (August 5, 1955).

Lowenhaupt, Henry E. "The Decryption of a Picture." *Studies In Intelligence* (Summer 1967).

———. "Mission to Birch Woods Via Seven Tents and New Siberia." *Studies In Intelligence* (Fall 1968).

Macy, Robert. "Pilots recount chilling chapters in American history." *Antelope Valley Press* (October 8, 1999), A-section.

Merlin, Peter W. "Dreamland: The Secret History of Area 51." Manuscript.

Miller, Roger G. "Freedom's Eagles: The Berlin Airlift, 1948–1949." *Air Power History* (Fall 1998).

Narinsky, Mikhail M. "The Soviet Union and the Marshall Plan." Cold War International History Project Web Page.

Northrup, Doyle L., and Donald H. Rock. "The Detection of Joe 1." *Studies In Intelligence* (Fall 1966).

Orlov, Col. Alexander, PVO (Ret.). "The U-2 Program: A Russian Officer Remembers." *Studies In Intelligence* (Winter 1998–99).

Parrish, Scott D. "The Turn Toward Confrontation: The Soviet Reaction to the Marshall Plan, 1947." Cold War International History Project Web Page.

Peebles, Curtis. "A Traveller in the Night." *Journal of the British Interplanetary Society* (August 1980).

Pocock, Chris. "From Peshawar to Bodo—Mission Impossible? Cold War Forum Web Page.

Poe, Gen. Bryce II, USAF (Ret.). "The Korean War: An Airman's Perception, O-2 to O-10." Manuscript.

Powles, Edward. "Spy Spitfires Over China. Part 1." *Aeroplane Monthly* (November 1998).

———. "Spy Spitfires Over China. Part 2." *Aeroplane Monthly* (December 1998).

Rankin, Allen. "One of Our Airplanes Is Missing Again." *Reader's Digest* (June 1959).

Ross, Jim C. "Marty Knutson." *Aeronautical Pioneers* (July/August 1998).

Schmemann, Serge. "New Germany emerges at heart of new Europe." *San Diego Union* (September 13, 1990), A-section.

———. "Soviet rule ends with Gorbachev." *San Diego Union* (December 28, 1991), A-section.

Shaw, Brackley. "Origins of the U-2: Interview with Richard M. Bissell, Jr." *Air Power History* (Winter 1989).

Varfolomeyev, Timothy. "Soviet Rocketry That Conquered Space. Part 2." *Spaceflight* (February 1996).

———. "Soviet Rocketry That Conquered Space. Part 3." *Spaceflight* (June 1996).

———. "Sputnik Era Launches." *Spaceflight* (October 1997).

Weathersby, Dr. Kathryn. "Deceiving the Deceivers: Moscow, Beijing, Pyongyang, and the Allegations of Bacteriological Weapons Use in Korea." Cold War International History Project Web Page.

Weir, Kenneth W. "The U-2 Story." Society of Experimental Test Pilots 1978 Report to the Aerospace Profession.

Welzenbach, Donald E. "Observation Balloons and Reconnaissance Satellites." *Studies In Intelligence* (Spring 1986).

Welzenbach, Donald E., and Nancy Galyean. "Those Daring Young Men and Their Ultra-High-Flying Machines." *Studies In Intelligence* (Fall 1987).

Wheelon, Albert D., and Sidney N. Graybeal. "Intelligence for the Space Race." *Studies In Intelligence* (Fall 1961).

Wonus, M. C. "The Case of the SS-6." *Studies In Intelligence* (Winter 1969).

Xiapbing, Li; Chen Jain; and David L. Wilson. "Mao Zedong's Handling of the Taiwan Straits Crisis of 1958: Chinese Recollections and Documents." Cold War International History Project Web Page.

Yip, Wai. "RB-57A and RB-57D in Republic of China Air Force Service." *AAHS Journal* (Winter 1999).

Zabetakis, Stanley G., and John F. Peterson. "The Diyarbakir Radar." *Studies In Intelligence* (Fall 1964).

Zubok, Vladislav M. "Khrushchev and the Berlin Crisis (1958–62)." Cold War International History Project Web Page.

———. "Khrushchev's Nuclear Promise to Beijing During the Crisis." Cold War International History Project Web Page.

Television Programs, Videotapes, and CD-ROMs

Kelly's Way. Edwards Air Force Base: Flight Test Historical Foundation, 1993.

NOVA. "Spy Machines." Public Broadcasting System, 1987.

"Spy in the Sky." *The American Experience.* Public Broadcasting System, 1996.

"Top Secret: Spy Planes of the Cold War." The Discovery Channel, 1999.

CD-ROM. *The U-2: A Revolution in Intelligence.* Washington, D.C.: National Defense University, September 17, 1998.

Documents

"Soviet Capabilities for the Development and Production of Certain Types of Weapons and Equipment." Central Intelligence Group, October 31, 1946.

"Briefing for the Secretary of the Air Force," June 23, 1953. Directorate of Intelligence, Headquarters, U.S. Air Force.

Soviet After Action Report, November 13, 1955, No. P2009 OP, Tsk 4626, TFR 185-92.

"Joint Chiefs of Staff Decision on JCS 2150/2: A Memorandum by the Chief of Naval Operations on Photo Reconnaissance of the China Coast From Swatow North to Latitude 26° 30' N," July 28, 1950.

"Comments on the Recommendation of the Joint Chiefs of Staff on Photo Reconnaissance of Certain Portions of the China Coast." Department of State, Office of the Secretary.

"Taiwan—Philippine Islands—Southeast Asia," August 25, 1950.

Letter. Maj. Gen. C. P. Cabell, Director of Intelligence, to Col. William A. Adams, Director of Intelligence, HQ. SAC, October 5, 1950, with attachments.

Memorandum for the Record. Problem: To establish requirements for development of a reconnaissance capability by use of recoverable free-balloons, October 3, 1950.

Moore, C. B. "Data Report on Four Stratosphere Balloon Flights Made for Photographic Laboratory," September 8, 1950.

Subject: (Top Secret) Photographic Reconnaissance Balloons, November 6, 1950.

Letter. Lt. Gen. Curtis E. LeMay to Gen. N. F. Twining, April 26, 1951.

Interdepartmental Memorandum. To: G. O. Hagland. From: C. B. Moore. Subject: Progress Report for January 1952. Part XI—Project Gopher. Rough Draft, February 7, 1952.

Memorandum for the Record. Problem: To reply to R&R from Director of Research and Development. Subject: Status Report on Project Gopher dated 29 Nov 1951. Written December 12, 1951.

"Soviet Capabilities for a Military Attack on the United States Before July 1952." Central Intelligence Agency, October 23, 1951.

"Estimate of the Effects of the Soviet Possession of the Atomic Bomb Upon the Security of the United States and Upon the Probabilities of Direct Soviet Military Action." Central Intelligence Agency, April 6, 1950.

"Soviet Capabilities for Attack on the US Through Mid-1955." Central Intelligence Agency, March 5, 1953.

"Soviet Capability for a Military Attack on the United States Before July 1952." Central Intelligence Agency, October 23, 1951.

Memorandum to: General Montgomery. Subject: Project 52 AFR-18.

Memorandum for: Chairman, Joint Chiefs of Staff. Subject: Reconnaissance Requirements, August 12, 1952.

Letter. Maj. Gen. R. M. Ramey to Commanding General, Strategic Air Command. Subject: Special Aerial Photographic Operations, August 15, 1952.

"RAF Tornado Witness." *Aeroplane Monthly* (February 1983), 106.

Letter. From: Director of Naval Intelligence. To: Director of Intelligence, U.S. Air Force. Subject: Photography; request for, May 25, 1954.

Depew, Robert J. "Overflight." Manuscript, NRO History Office.

Hall, R. Cargill. "Interview with Robert John ("Jerry") Depew." National Reconnaissance Office Oral History Program, May 7, 1998.

Report. "Status of Air Force Project Gopher," March 6, 1953.

"The Sturgeon Bay Saucer: An early sighting by an important ufologist." ufx.org Web page.

Report. "Status of Air Force Project Gopher," March 6, 1953.

Letter. To: Brig. Gen. G. E. Price and Maj. Gen. R. G. Ramey. Subject: Future Development Action—Gopher Project, April 14, 1953.

Letter. To: Director of Research and Development, Through Director of Intelligence. Future Development Action—Gopher Project, June 9, 1953.

Memorandum for the Record. Problem: To take action on a Memorandum to Gen. Samford from Mr. Ayer, dated 22 December 1953, regarding political acceptability of Project Grandson, December 1953.

Memorandum for: Mr. Ayer. Subject: Status of Grandson, September 24, 1953.

"Probable Warning of Soviet Attack on the U.S. Through Mid-1957." Central Intelligence Agency, September 14, 1954.

"Soviet Capabilities for Attack on the U.S. Through Mid-1955." Central Intelligence Agency, August 3, 1953.

"Soviet Capabilities for Attack on the U.S. Through 1957." Central Intelligence Agency, February 24, 1954.

Soviet Gross Capabilities for Attacks on the U.S. and Key Overseas Installations and Forces Through 1 July 1958." Central Intelligence Agency, June 23, 1955.

Letter. Edwin H. Land to Allen W. Dulles, November 5, 1954.

Report: "A Unique Opportunity for Comprehensive Intelligence—A Summary."

Attachment 1. Memorandum for: Director of Central Intelligence. Subject: A Unique Opportunity for Comprehensive Intelligence.

Memorandum of Conference with the President, November 24, 1954.

"Maj. Gen. Osmond J. Ritland," Air Force Space Command History Web Page.

Jack Gordon, U-2 seminar.

Letters. William S. Bissell to Curtis Peebles, January 11, 1999, and February 25, 2000.

Henry Combs, U-2 seminar.

Letter. Maj. Gen. O. J. Ritland to Lt. Gen. B. A. Schriever, January 10, 1961, and copy of Colonel Harrington's remarks. Edwards Air Force Base History Office.

U.S. Air Force Oral History interviews, Maj. Gen. Osmond J. Ritland, March 19–24, 1974, Vol. 1, 142–44. Edwards Air Force Base History Office.

Ernest Joiner, U-2 seminar.

Gen. Andrew J. Goodpaster, USA (Ret.), U-2 seminar.

Hall, R. Cargill, and Richard S. Leghorn. "Interview With Sergei Khrushchev," July 5, 1995, at Brown University.

Benedict Koziol, U-2 seminar.

Marty Knutson, U-2 seminar.

Voyager Newsletter, Issue No. 7.

"History of the 456th Troop Carrier Wing and Project 119-L, 1 January 1955 through 9 July 1956." Tactical Air Command.

"History of the 1st Air Division, Historical Study No. 62." Headquarters, Strategic Air Command, November 1956.

Letter. George Mathews to Curtis Peebles, September 29, 1986.

Tapes. Paul M. Lovrencic to Curtis Peebles, September 5, 1987, and April 8, 1988.

"Big Lowry Balloon Does $4,000 Damage." *Denver Post* (August 17, 1955).

C-119F Accident Report, Headquarters, Air Force Inspection and Safety Center, Norton Air Force Base.

"1st Air Division (Meteorological Survey), Final Report Project 119L." Strategic Air Command, n.d..

"Lowry Balloon Starts Secret Weapon Talk." *Denver Post* (September 12, 1955), no page.

Letters. Robert L. Burch to Curtis Peebles, September 21, 1986, and March 23, 1988.

Memorandum of Conversation with the President, February 6, 1956, 10:15 A.M.

Memorandum for the Record. Conference of Joint Chiefs of Staff with the President, February 10, 1956.

Letter. James A. Winker to Curtis Peebles, May 31, 1988.

"Press Release by Headquarters, U.S. Air Force Simultaneous With Start of Operation, 9 January 1956."

"The flying disc's riddle are solved: Weather Balloon." *Aftenposten* (February 4, 1956), translation by Svein Tonning.

"Big balloons moving through the district." *Akershus Arbeiderblad/Romerikes Blad* (January 18, 1956), translation by Svein Tonning.

Photo captions. *Dagens Nyheter* (March 8, 1956).

"Balloons over Bulgaria." CIA intelligence report, April 17, 1956.

"Arguments that the balloons caused accidents are rejected." *Aftenposten* (February 11, 1956), translation by Svein Tonning.

John Foster Dulles Phone Log, January 31, 1956, and February 3, 1958. Dwight D. Eisenhower Library.

"Photographing Soviet Territory From Air, Reds Say in Protest." *Los Angeles Times* (February 6, 1956).

Dulles Phone Log, February 6, 1956, and "Memorandum for the Files," February 6, 1956, W. B. Macomber, Jr. Dwight D. Eisenhower Library.

Text of U.S. reply to Soviet note on balloons, February 8, 1956. Dwight D. Eisenhower Library.

"50 Captured Balloons Displayed by Russians." *Los Angeles Times* (February 10, 1956).

"How Far Up Is Home?" *Newsweek* (February 20, 1956).

"'It's Brink of War Act,' Say Russ Over Balloons." February 10, 1956, newspaper clipping. San Diego Aerospace Museum.

"Russian Balloon Found in Japan." *South Bay Daily Breeze* (February 8, 1956).

"Russian Balloons Fly Over Alaska, U.S. Replies to Kremlin's Protest." *Los Angeles Times* (March 2, 1956).

"5 Russ Balloons Found in Alaska, Air Force Says." *Los Angeles Times* (March 3, 1956).

"Russ Challenge U.S. on Alaska Balloons." *Los Angeles Times* (March 25, 1956).

Smith, Maj. Gen. Foster Lee, USAF (Ret.). "Military Reconnaissance Missions Mid-1950s," July 1998.

Letter. Brig. Gen. William J. Ming, August 30, 1996.

Chris Pocock, U-2 seminar.

Interviews with Dino A. Brugioni, August 5, 1995, and March 9, 1996.

"Soviet Gross Capabilities for Attacks on the US and Key Overseas Installations and Forces Through 1 July 1958." Central Intelligence Agency, June 23, 1955.

"Probable Intelligence Warning of Soviet Attack on the US Through Mid-1958." Central Intelligence Agency, July 1, 1955.

Memorandum for the Record, June 21, 1956.

Memorandum for the Record, July 3, 1956.

Memorandum for: Brig. Gen. Andrew J. Goodpaster. Subject: U-2 Overflights of Soviet Bloc, August 18, 1960.

"Air Defense of the Sino-Soviet Bloc, 1955–1960." Central Intelligence Agency, July 12, 1955.

"Soviet Guided Missile Capabilities and Probable Programs." Central Intelligence Agency, December 20, 1955.

"Intrusions, Overflights, & Shootdowns." *Air Power History* (Summer 1989), 14.

The David Frost Show, April 28, 1970. Transcript. Francis Gary Powers File, Central Intelligence Agency.

E-mail. "Re: Wallpaper." Peter W. Merlin to Curtis Peebles, December 12, 1999.

Tass announcement of ICBM test, August 26, 1957.

Merlin, Peter W. "Area 51 Suffered Effects of Nearby Nuclear Testing."

Brown, Buddy L. "The Dragon Lady." Edwards Air Force Base History Office files.

Memorandum for: Mr. Robert LeBaron, Deputy. To: The Secretary of Defense for Atomic Energy. Subject: Notes on Technical Cooperation With British and Canadians in the Field of Atomic Energy Intelligence, March 21, 1951.

Memorandum of Conference with the President, September 6, 1960.

Tass announcement of the launch of Sputnik I, October 4, 1957.

"International Affairs." *Time* (October 14, 1957).

"Deterrence & Survival in the Nuclear Age," November 7, 1957.

"The Soviet ICBM Program." Central Intelligence Agency, December 17, 1957.

Memorandum of Conversation with the President, January 22, 1958.

Memorandum of Conversation with the President, March 7, 1958, and Memorandum for the Record, March 7, 1958.

Interview with Walter Levison, April 17, 1996.

McNickle, Col. Melvin F. "Amendment to ARDC System Directive." June 20, 1957.

Memorandum of Conversation with the President, June 26, 1957.

Memorandum for the Record, July 3, 1957.

Memorandum for the Record, May 17, 1958.

Memorandum of Telephone Conversation with the President, May 17, 1958.

Memorandum for the Record, May 19, 1958.

Memorandum for the Record, June 25, 1958.

Deck Log, USS *Windham Bay,* June 29 to July 21, 1958.

Memorandum Subject: (TS) High Altitude Balloon Reconnaissance Program, July 3, 1958.

John Foster Dulles, telephone call to Mr. Cumming, July 29, 1958, 12:25 P.M.

John Foster Dulles, telephone call to Secretary Quarles, July 29, 1958, 12:29 P.M.

John Foster Dulles, telephone call from Secretary Quarles, July 29, 1958, 2:57 P.M.

Note. Message from Mr. Ayer, July 30, 1958.

Memorandum for Secretary of Defense, July 31, 1958.

"Mixing the Potion of War?" *Newsweek* (September 8, 1958), 34.

Memorandum of Conversation with the President, Newport, Rhode Island, September 4, 1958.

"U.S. Air Force Cold Warriors to be Buried at Arlington." Release No. 457-98, September 1, 1998.

"Soviet Government Note to U.S. Government." *The Current Digest of the Soviet Press,* Vol. X, No. 36 (1958), 16.

"U.S. Bids Moscow Return Balloons." *New York Times* (September 7, 1958).

"In USSR Ministry of Foreign Affairs." *The Current Digest of the Soviet Press,* Vol. X, No. 37 (1958), 24.

"Aerial Piracy." *Time* (September 29, 1958), 12.

"Intolerable Acts of U.S. Military Agencies." *The Current Digest of the Soviet Press,* Vol. X, No. 41 (1958), 20, 21.

Information Report. Subject: Crash of U.S. Military Aircraft in Armenia, September 1958; November 7, 1958.

"The Soviet ICBM Program." Central Intelligence Agency, December 17, 1957.

Memorandum for the President. Subject: Evaluation of Information on Soviet Ballistic Missile Capabilities, contained in a letter to the President from Sen. Stuart Symington dated 29 August 1958. Written October 10, 1958.

"Soviet Capabilities in Guided Missiles and Space Vehicles." Central Intelligence Agency, August 19, 1958.

Memorandum for: Chairman, Guided Missile Intelligence Committee. Subject: Soviet ICBM Development Program, October 9, 1958.

Memorandum to Holders of NIE 11-5-58. Central Intelligence Agency, November 25, 1958.

Memorandum for the Record, February 12, 1959.

Memorandum for the Record, March 4, 1959.

Memorandum of Conference with the President, April 7, 1959, written April 11, 1959.

Memorandum for the Record, July 7, 1959.

Memorandum of Conference with the President, July 8, 1959.

Chronological Development of the Kapustin Yar/Vladimirovka and Tyuratam Missile Test Centers, USSR, 1957 Through 1963. National Photographic Interpretation Center, November 1963.

"Soviet Capabilities in Guided Missiles and Space Vehicles." Central Intelligence Agency, November 3, 1959.

Memorandum for the Record, February 8, 1960.

"Soviet Capabilities in Guided Missiles and Space Vehicles." Central Intelligence Agency, May 3, 1960.

Presidential Statement on U-2 Incident at News Conference, 11 May 1960.

Memorandum of Conference with the President, August 9, 1960, 11:00 A.M., written August 10, 1960.

"Space Capsule Is Caught in Mid-Air by U.S. Plane on Re-Entry From Orbit." *New York Times* (August 20, 1960).

"Key figures in events leading to the fall of Berlin Wall on Nov. 9, 1989." *San Diego Union-Tribune* (November 7, 1999), G-section.

"Excerpts from the treaty to reunify Germany." *San Diego Union* (September 13, 1990), A-section.

"Military Affairs—Armenia." *Air International* (October 1993).

"Former foes reach an Open Skies accord." *San Diego Union-Tribune* (March 21, 1992), A-section.

"NASA ER-2 completes first science flight over Russia," January 29, 2000.

Flight 00-040 map, January 27, 2000.

Index

T

W

X Y Z